July 10–13, 2016
Halifax, Nova Scotia, Canada

Association for Computing Machinery

Advancing Computing as a Science & Profession

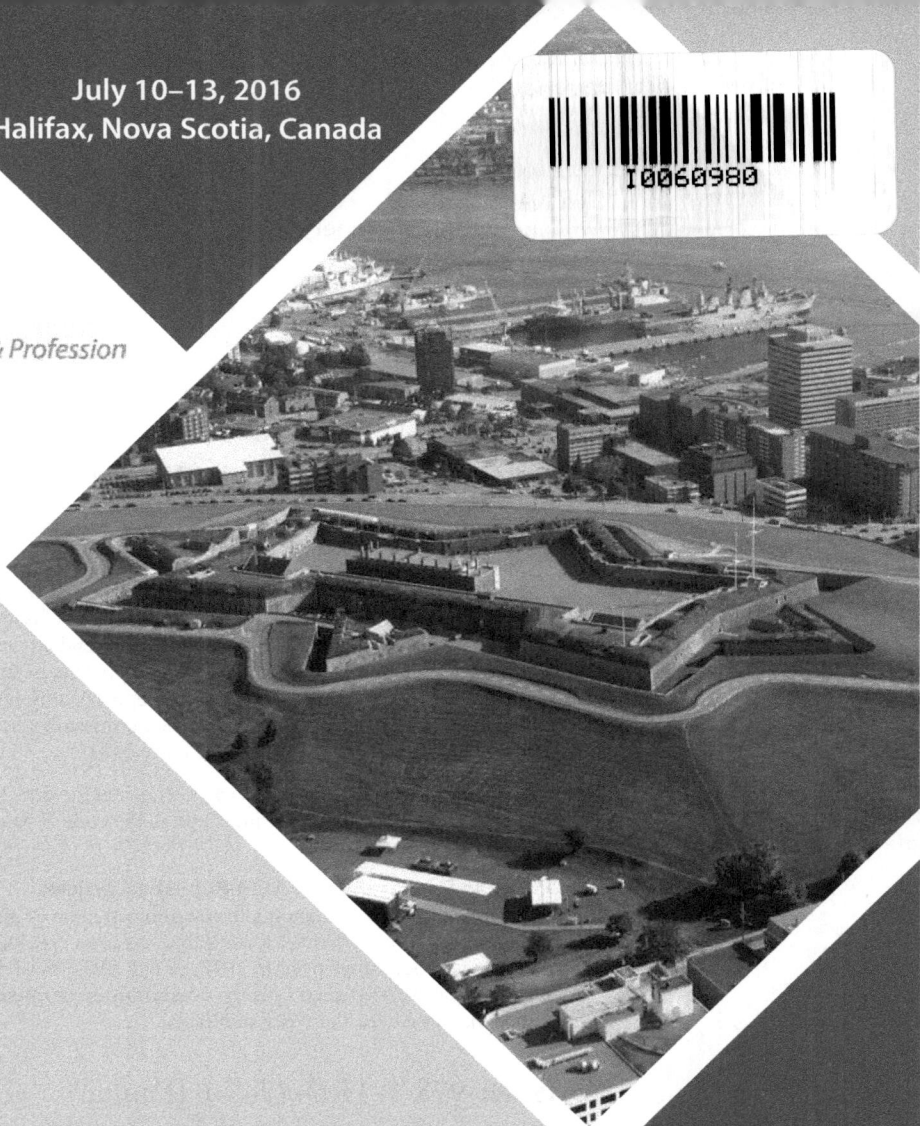

I0060980

HT'16

Proceedings of the 27th ACM Conference on
Hypertext and Social Media

Sponsored by:
ACM SIGWEB

In-cooperation with:
ACM SIGCHI

Supported by:
Dalhousie University and Nova Scotia College of Art & Design

Association for Computing Machinery

Advancing Computing as a Science & Profession

The Association for Computing Machinery
2 Penn Plaza, Suite 701
New York, New York 10121-0701

Notice to Past Authors of ACM-Published Articles
ACM intends to create a complete electronic archive of all articles and/or other material previously published by ACM. If you have written a work that has been previously published by ACM in any journal or conference proceedings prior to 1978, or any SIG Newsletter at any time, and you do NOT want this work to appear in the ACM Digital Library, please inform permissions@acm.org, stating the title of the work, the author(s), and where and when published.

ISBN: 978-1-4503-4247-6 (Digital)

ISBN: 978-1-4503-4611-5 (Print)

Additional copies may be ordered prepaid from:

ACM Order Department
PO Box 30777
New York, NY 10087-0777, USA

Phone: 1-800-342-6626 (USA and Canada)
+1-212-626-0500 (Global)
Fax: +1-212-944-1318
E-mail: acmhelp@acm.org
Hours of Operation: 8:30 am – 4:30 pm ET

Printed in the USA

Preface

Welcome to the 27th ACM Conference on Hypertext and Social Media, Hypertext 2016, in Halifax, Nova Scotia, Canada. The Hypertext conference series is concerned with all aspects of modern hypertext research, including social media, the user experience, the semantic web, adaptive hypertext and hypermedia, as well as narrative systems and applications.

The ACM Hypertext 2016 conference invited submissions in three main tracks: Collaboration in the Social Web; Narrative, Adaptation and Multimedia Storytelling; and User Experience and the Web. We also welcomed submissions in additional categories including the new Creative track, as well as to the well-established categories of late-breaking results and demonstrations, plus papers submitted to the satellite events, the workshops and the doctoral consortium.

Collaboration in the Social Web focuses on the analysis and exploration of links between topics, people and activities in social media and beyond, including social groupware, which integrates social media interaction into a structured collaboration process and adds various structure and computational support to social media. Such collaboration could be with the use of existing social media systems as a communication or collaboration platform, or with new systems, applications, methods, practices and tools that support communication and collaboration in the Social Web.

Through *Narrative, Adaptation and Multimedia Storytelling*, we acknowledge that hypertext and Web systems are fundamentally about communication between people, and that people are storytellers. The track covers a broad range of topics in New Media and digital storytelling, from both technological and human points of view. This area includes technologies to support content curation and creation, dynamic linking and navigation, as well as data analysis, interactive visualization and presentation, and novel forms of digital narratives. It also includes exploration of existing practices of online storytelling, plus new media artistry and writing, online reportage and journalism, applications of digital storytelling, and critical theory around online expression.

The track *User Experience and the Web* is a recognition that navigating through the abundance of information on the Web is a complex cognitive and interactive process involving several factors, many of which are not well-understood. The track focuses on interdisciplinary efforts from several disciplines, such as cognitive psychology, cognitive science, Web design, human-computer interaction, information science, artificial intelligence, machine learning and recognises that other aspects of computer science as well as hypertext are needed to make interaction with the Web as easy and effortless as possible.

We received 76 submissions, comprising 54 full papers, 18 short papers and 4 posters. Each submission was reviewed by at least three programme committee members, followed by a metareview by the track chairs, who recommended acceptance or rejection of the papers. In some cases, full paper submissions were accepted as short papers, and promising submissions that were not sufficiently mature have been accepted as posters. The final decisions were taken by the programme chairs, with the exception of submissions with one of the organizing team's members involved, which were handled separately by the remaining programme/general chairs. We accepted 16 regular papers, 23 short papers and 7 posters, which are included in the main proceedings. The Extended Proceedings contain a selection of submissions to the Creative track, late-breaking results, demonstrations, doctoral consortium papers and workshop papers. The conference will make two awards, these being the Douglas Engelbart Best Paper Award and the Ted Nelson Newcomer Award. Three candidates for each award have been selected by the chairs and the winners will be selected during the conference by an awards committee.

We are pleased to host two keynote speakers who beautifully complement our technical programme, with blogger Hossein Derakhshan providing a unique perspective on the changes in how people use social media, and Katy Börner from the Indiana University Bloomington with her remarkable scientific visualisation ideas.

In closing, we wish to thank our fellow chairs for shaping this conference, the programme committee and the sub-reviewers for their insightful reviews, and to the ACM staff for its support of organizational issues. The Hypertext 2016 conference, and its workshops, tutorials, keynotes, social activities and student grants, have been made possible through the sponsorship of ACM SIGWEB. Finally, we wish to thank the authors of all submitted works as your participation is what makes this conference a success!

James Blustein
HT'16 General Chair
Dalhousie University, Canada

Eelco Herder
HT'16 General Chair
L3S Research Center, Germany

Jessica Rubart
HT'16 Programme Chair
Ostwestfalen-Lippe University of Applied Sciences, Germany

Helen Ashman
HT'16 Programme Chair
University of South Australia

Table of Contents

Hypertext 2016 Conference Organization

General Chairs: Jamie Blustein *(Dalhousie University, Canada)*
Eelco Herder *(L3S Research Center, Germany)*

Program Chairs: Jessica Rubart *(OWL University of Applied Sciences, Germany)*
Helen Ashman *(University of South Australia)*

Track Chairs: **Track 1: Collaboration in the Social Web**
Weigang Wang *(University of Manchester, United Kingdom)*

Track 2: Narrative, Adaptation and Multimedia Storytelling
David Millard *(University of Southampton, United Kingdom)*

Track 3: User Experience and the Web
Herre van Oostendorp *(Utrecht University, the Netherlands)*

Creative Track: Stacey Mason *(University of California, Santa Cruz, USA)*

Workshop Chair: Dongwon Lee *(Penn State University, USA)*

Poster and Demo Chairs: Kevin Koidl *(Trinity College Dublin, Ireland)*
Ben Steichen *(Santa Clara University, USA)*

Doctoral Consortium Chair: Johan Bollen *(Indiana University, USA)*

Publicity Chairs: Denis Parra *(Catholic University of Chile)*
Christoph Trattner *(Know-Center, Austria)*

Program Committee: Luca Maria Aiello *(Yahoo Labs, Spain)*
Franck Amadieu *(University of Toulouse, France)*
Kenneth Anderson *(University of Colorado at Boulder, USA)*
Claus Atzenbeck *(Hof University, Germany)*
Martin Atzmueller *(University of Kassel, Germany)*
Sören Auer *(University of Bonn & Fraunhofer IAIS, Germany)*
Shlomo Berkovsky *(CSIRO, Australia)*
Mark Bernstein *(Eastgate Systems, Inc., USA)*
Maria Bielikova *(Slovak University of Technology, Slovakia)*
Tom Blount *(University of Southampton, UK)*
Niels Olof Bouvin *(Aarhus University, Denmark)*
Peter Brusilovsky *(University of Pittsburgh, USA)*
Iván Cantador *(Autonomous University of Madrid, Spain)*
Ilknur Celik *(Middle East Technical University, Northern Cyprus)*
Federica Cena *(University of Torino, Italy)*
Aline Chevalier *(Université Toulouse, France)*
Alvin Chin *(BMW Group, USA)*
Jessie Chin *(University of Illinois at Urbana Champaign, USA)*

Hypertext 2016 Sponsor & Supporters

Sponsor: sig web

In-cooperation with: SIGCHI

Supporters: DALHOUSIE UNIVERSITY   Dalhousie University, Halifax, Canada

N·S·C·A·D UNIVERSITY   Nova Scotia College of Art & Design, Halifax, Canada

Data Visualization Literacy

Katy Börner

Cyberinfrastructure for Network Science Center, SOIC and Indiana University Network Science Institute
Indiana University, Bloomington, IN, USA
Visiting Professor, Department of Computer Science and Applied Cognitive Science, University of
Duisburg-Essen, Duisburg, Germany
Visiting Professor, Royal Netherlands Academy of Arts and Sciences (KNAW), Amsterdam, The
Netherlands
katy@indiana.edu

1. ABSTRACT

In an age of information overload, the ability to make sense of vast amounts of data and to render insightful visualizations is as important as the ability to read and write. This talk explains and exemplifies the power of data visualizations not only to help locate us in physical space but also to help us understand the extent and structure of our collective knowledge, to identify bursts of activity, pathways of ideas, and borders that beg to be crossed. It introduces a theoretical visualization framework meant to empower anyone to systematically render data into insights together with tools that support temporal, geospatial, topical, and network analyses and visualizations [2, 3, 4]. Materials from the Information Visualization MOOC (http://ivmooc.cns.iu.edu) and maps from the Places & Spaces: Mapping Science exhibit (http://scimaps.org) [1] will be used to illustrate key concepts and to inspire participants to visualize their very own data.

2. REFERENCES

[1] K. Börner. *Atlas of science: Visualizing what we know.* The MIT Press, 2010.

[2] K. Börner. *Atlas of knowledge: Anyone can map.* MIT Press, 2015.

[3] K. Börner, A. Maltese, R. N. Balliet, and J. Heimlich. Investigating aspects of data visualization literacy using 20 information visualizations and 273 science museum visitors. *Information Visualization*, page 1473871615594652, 2015.

[4] K. Börner and D. E. Polley. *Visual insights: A practical guide to making sense of data.* MIT Press, 2014.

HT '16 July 10-13, 2016, Halifax, NS, Canada

© 2016 Copyright held by the owner/author(s).

ACM ISBN 978-1-4503-4247-6/16/07.

DOI: http://dx.doi.org/10.1145/2914586.2914604

Killing the Hyperlink, Killing the Web:
The Shift from Library-Internet to Television-Internet

Hossein Derakhshan
New Media Society
Tehran, Iran
hodertemp@gmail.com

ABSTRACT

The Web, as envisaged by its inventors, was founded on the idea of *hyperlinks*. Derived from the notion of hypertext in literary theory, a hyperlink is a relation rather than an object. It is a system of connections that connects distant pieces of text, resulting in a non-linear, open, active, decentralized, and diverse space we called the World Wide Web.

But in the past few years, and with the rise of closed social networks, as well as mobile apps, the hyperlink — and thereby the Web — are in serious trouble. Most social networks have created a closed, linear, centralized, sequential, passive, and homogeneous space, where users are encouraged to stay in all the time — a space that is more like television. The Web was imagined as an intellectual project that promoted knowledge, debate, and tolerance; as something I call *library-internet*. Now it has become more about entertainment and commerce; I call this *tv-internet*.

This topic is extensively articulated in "The Web We Have to Save," published in July 2015 by Matter magazine[1].

---

[1] https://medium.com/matter/
the-web-we-have-to-save-2eb1fe15a426#.nh8n86sqw

HT'16, July 10–13, 2016, Halifax, Nova Scotia, Canada
ACM ISBN 978-1-4503-4247-6/16/07.
DOI: http://dx.doi.org/10.1145/2914586.2914605

Extracting Social Structures from Conversations in Twitter

A Case Study on Health-Related Posts

Abduljaleel Al-Rubaye
BioComplex Laboratory, School of Computing
Florida Institute of Technology
Melbourne, Florida, USA
aalrubaye2013@my.fit.edu

Ronaldo Menezes
BioComplex Laboratory, School of Computing
Florida Institute of Technology
Melbourne, Florida, USA
rmenezes@cs.fit.edu

ABSTRACT

Online Social Networks (e.g., Twitter, Facebook) have dramatically grown in usage and popularity in recent years. In addition to keeping track of friends and acquaintances, these networks provide powerful means of exchanging and sharing information on many different topics of interest (e.g., sports, religion, politics, health concerns, etc.). Moreover, the use of these networks has introduced a completely new way of collaboration among people, virtually creating spheres of friends who generally feel comfortable discussing a variety of subjects and even helping each other to grow in knowledge about certain subjects. In this work, we built and analyzed networks of social groups on Twitter related to the top leading causes of death in the United States. Due to space limitations, we present results for the state of Florida and only for the top four leading causes of death. We show that using a concept of time window in the creation of relations between users, we can reconstruct social networks for these conversations and these networks have characteristics that are similar to typical social networks. The argument is that social network information can be extracted even in cases where users are not directly talking to each other (as it is the case in most of Twitter).

CCS Concepts

•Networks → Online social networks; *Social media networks;* •Applied computing → *Health care information systems;*

Keywords

Social Network Structures; Conversational Data; Twitter

1. INTRODUCTION

Modern life has made humans live longer but also more aware of their health—the quality of one's health mostly defines his/her general well-being. In order to be healthy, most of us try to be informed about the latest developments

HT '16, July 10 - 13, 2016, Halifax, NS, Canada

© 2016 Copyright held by the owner/author(s). Publication rights licensed to ACM.
ISBN 978-1-4503-4247-6/16/07...$15.00

DOI: http://dx.doi.org/10.1145/2914586.2914599

in medical research, medical practices, treatments, drugs, etc. The acquisition of knowledge is more prominent with individuals who are already suffering from serious health conditions, particularly the ones that may lead to death [14].

In many cases, people who have been diagnosed with serious health conditions may suffer the symptoms of their condition for a considerable period of time, which naturally makes people form support groups to share their feelings as well as share their daily experiences with their social peers. In fact, peer-to-peer and virtual support groups are nowadays easy to be formed and exist for any malice one may be afflicted by. Another issue worth considering relates to side effects that are associated with a major diseases such as behavioral risks which could be improved by communicating with other individuals with the same condition [3, 10].

The use of online social networks is a popular way to communicate and find other people who have the same interests. Nowadays, communication through online social networks have become a significant part of our lives. Interacting with people using online social networks can work for patients with serious diseases by providing an environment that improves health education as well the increase of their knowledge by exchanging and sharing experiences [16].

Twitter is one of the most popular online social networks, connecting millions of people worldwide [15]. Recent numbers show that Twitter has about 320 million monthly active users, and they post around 500 million tweets a day [21]. Users can be connected to each other and are able to post short text messages with a maximum 140 characters long. When they tweet (write new messages), their followers are able to see the messages but can also reply or retweet the messages (repeat the same message content to one's followers). The concept of retweet is the prime reason information spread among the users. In this way, Twitter is an excellent platform for sharing information (e.g., thoughts, ideas, feelings and daily experiences). A tweet contains some properties such as the tweet's creation date and time, location of author, possibly a geo-tag, and some other parameters [15] that may be used when doing data analysis as well as help on the contextualization of the information in each tweet.

In this paper, we present an analytical work on Twitter in order to create networks of users according to the conversational history of their tweets. We focus in this study on conversations that have mentioned at least one of the health conditions among the top leading causes of death in the United States. The overall goal is to demonstrate that the creation of networks from co-mentions of terms leads to networks that may have non-trivial structural properties

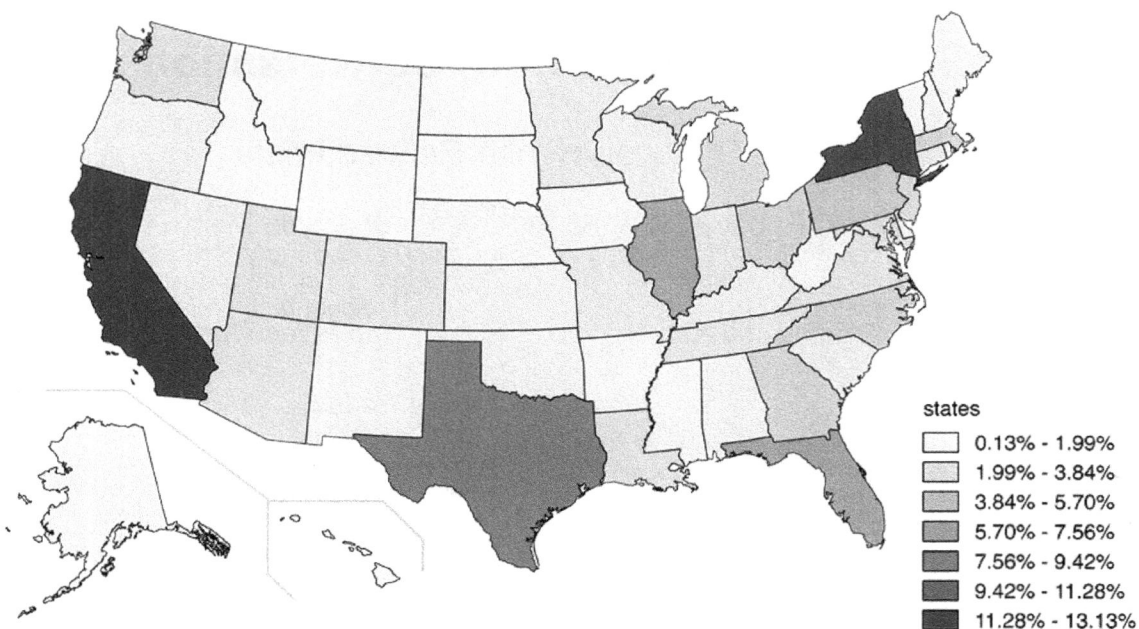

Figure 1: A choropleth map showing the total number of tweets collected per state in the USA normalized by state's census population [4]. According to [5] since the number of Twitter users per state is correlated to the state's population, we normalized the total collected tweets by each state's census population.

common to social networks which, in turn, could lead to the assertion that social structures may be embedded in the actual conversational nature of Twitter.

In order to reconstruct the structure of the networks formed from various diseases, we apply the concept of *time window* to the relation between nodes in the network as introduced by Ferreira et al. [12]—a time window is a predefined period of time used to limit network relations to a specific duration. By selecting different sizes for the time window, we basically create different networks related to the same topic. We then analyzed the networks that were generated for four health conditions in order to understand the effect of a time window to the representativity of the network. Networks are analyzed using two properties of social networks: *clustering coefficient* and *degree distribution*. The *clustering coefficient* is a measurement that determines how tightly the nodes are connected to each other in a network, while the *degree distribution* of a network is the probability distribution of degrees over the entire network [1]; it is the distribution of node connectivity.

This paper is divided as follows. In Section 2 we discuss works related to our research. We follow in Section 3 with a description of how we used collected data from Twitter and used the concept of time-window to create network structures. In Section 4, we take a look at the analysis of the social structures extracted from the conversational data and how typical they are compared to standard social network structures. We conclude this work in Section 5 with a summary of our contributions and discussion about possible future work.

2. RELATED WORKS

The large amounts of data circulating on Twitter facilitates the analytical process that is needed to conduct various social studies. Many works on health-related topics have been performed using Twitter data. Salathé et al. [20] collected data from Twitter in order to measure the effectiveness of a new vaccine by measuring the sentiments that were expressed on Twitter towards that vaccine. The results showed that users who have similar sentiments exchange information more than those who shared different sentiments. Moreover, the authors found that, in the created network, a cluster of negative sentiments could increase the disease outbreak. Paul and Dredze [19] have shown that there are strong correlations between public health data and what people post on Twitter confirming that Twitter has a broad applicability to studies in public health. Ghosh et al. [13] collected Twitter data to identify the public health awareness regarding obesity in the United States. Using geocoded attributes, they introduced a text mining method to present the density map and the spatial pattern of obesity in the population and hence where it might be beneficial to launch obesity-related awareness programs.

The concept of time window that is used in our work has also been successfully involved in other works. Ferreira et al. [11, 12] employed the time-window concept for evaluating the long-range correlations among seismic events; they showed that it is possible to experimentally find the best size for the time window by looking at expected values for some of the network metrics. Meng et al. [17] provided data analysis of social networks. In their work, they performed a comparison among networks of a given dataset that were constructed over different time intervals. By analyzing the networks structures, they showed that varying the size of the time interval has an impact on network properties.

3. HEALTH-RELATED CONVERSATIONS

Our data collection was done focused on the issue of diseases. Recall that we want to understand whether conversations in social media contain any social structure that could be reconstructed and studied. Our first step is to determine the list of diseases that we will use to collect data on Twitter and eventually attempt to unveil social structures. After the definition of the scope, we run programs based on the Twitter API to collect the necessary data. Last, we define how to transform the data into networks that can be analyzed by standard network metrics.

3.1 Determining Health Conditions to Study

The Centers for Disease Control and Prevention (CDC) is one of centers of the Department of Health and Human Services that provided reliable, standard, and detailed annual reports about various health issues in the United States. Among other things, it issues a list with the top leading causes of death in the United States [6]. This list also contains statistics and metadata about the United States mortality rate and information about race, sex, and age of the deceased.

The report identifies 113 causes of death in the United States but it focuses more on the 13 top leading causes which are (in order: *Heart diseases, Malignant neoplasms, Chronic lower respiratory diseases, Cerebrovascular diseases, Alzheimer's disease, Diabetes mellitus, Influenza and pneumonia, Nephritis and Nephrotic syndrome, Septicemia, Chronic liver disease and cirrhosis, Hypertension, Parkinson's disease*, and *Pneumonitis due to solids and liquids*.

subsectionCollecting Data

The data used in this paper was collected using Python and the Twitter streaming API. We have specified words related to the leading causes of death and used the parameter *track* in the streaming API to select tweets containing the specified words. The collected data was stored in MongoDB and the interfacing between MongoDB and Python was handled with the use of PyMongo.

We collected 60 days of data (12,518,372 tweets), specifically from February 17 to April 17 of 2015. We tracked all the tweets (from anywhere in the world) that were mentioning any of the aforementioned health conditions. Furthermore, to have the best possible results, we took into consideration the fact that some of these conditions include multiple diseases, and many of them are known as different names. Table 1 shows the keywords used for each of the health conditions tracked.

In order to extract those tweets that were posted from the USA, we applied a filter using either the geographic coordinates of the tweet or the users' location—the location of the user who posted the tweet as defined in his profile. Since the number of geocoded tweets were only around 7% of all collected tweets, the location of a user was used to supplement the number of tweets with locations. A Twitter user is free to use any string to indicate his location (e.g. Mars, My House, Dark Side of the Moon, are all accepted "locations" on this field). So we had to use a geocoding API to remove locations that are not useful. After that, we had locations for around 76% of all tweets collected where they were used to filter out the data and keep 2,351,991 tweets

originated from the USA (see Figure 1). California had the highest number of tweets (278,771 total) while North Dakota had the lowest (with only 2,703 tweets) during the collected period. The number of times that a particular health condition has been mentioned in tweets for the entire country is shown in Table 2.

3.2 Network Creation

In the networks we constructed, Twitter users are considered to be the nodes and two users are connected to each other if both have mentioned the same health condition in their tweets *within a time window of each other*. If we do not consider a temporal restriction, all tweets that mentioned the same health conditions would be related to each other which consequently leads to a structure that has trivial characteristics (a clique). According to [9, 12] the relationship between events (Tweets in our case) can be more understandable if they were occurred in a closer time period. An useful analogy to the real-world is that if two people talk about the same subject in a social gathering within a short period from each other, there is a reasonable probability that they are talking to each other or are part of the same group conversation. Hence, we decided to use a concept of time proximity of tweets, where users are connected to each other if they have mentioned the same health condition within what we call a *time window* as used by Ferreira et al. [12] and depicted in Figure 2.

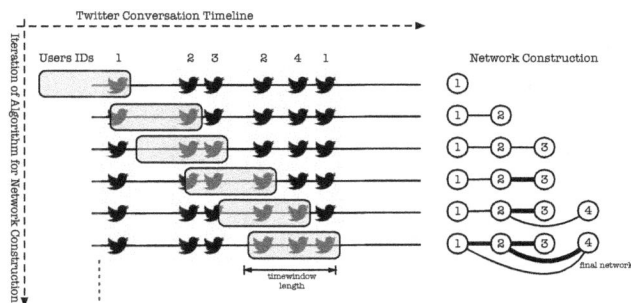

Figure 2: Illustration of the time-window concept (left) used to create networks (right). "Birds" represent tweets by users that take place from left to right representing the temporal sequence of events. The window shown in shaded color has a predefined length of time. The end of the window is aligned with each tweet and those events that mentioned the same health condition within the window trigger the connection of the users who tweeted. When the window moves to another event (y axis), some connections between users may get reinforced because the two tweets continue to be within the time window leading to a weighted graph. The network is updated at each step of the moving of the time window.

Clearly one of the issues to overcome is the choice for the length of the time window. If the length is too large or too small the network generated might not contain useful information. In order to avoid direct bias, we worked in this paper with twelve different sizes: one hour, two hours, three hours, ..., and twelve hours. This means that we

Table 1: The keywords that have been used to track each health condition.

Health Conditions	Keywords
Heart diseases	*heart diseases, diseases of heart, artery disease, heart attack, heart failure*
Malignant neoplasms	*malignant neoplasms, cancer, malignant tumoral disease*
Chronic lower respiratory diseases	*chronic lower respiratory diseases, copd, asthma, bronchitis, emphysema*
Cerebrovascular diseases	*cerebrovascular diseases, stroke, brain attack*
Alzheimer's disease	*alzheimer*
Diabetes mellitus	*diabetes*
Influenza or Pneumonia	*influenza, flu, pneumonia*
Nephritis, Nephrotic syndrome	*nephritis, nephrotic, kidney diseases, kidney failure, kidney disorder*
Septicemia	*septicemia, blood poisoning, bacteremia, sepsis*
Chronic liver disease and cirrhosis	*chronic liver disease and cirrhosis, liver disease, liver cirrhosis*
Hypertension	*hypertension, hypertensive, high blood pressure*
Parkinson's disease	*parkinson*
Pneumonitis due to solids and liquids	*pneumonitis due to solids and liquids*

Table 2: The number of times that a health condition was mentioned in tweets within the USA.

Health Conditions	Count
Heart diseases	121,728
Malignant neoplasms	1,395,590
Chronic lower respiratory diseases	76,934
Cerebrovascular diseases	135,447
Alzheimer's disease	97,022
Diabetes mellitus	291,309
Influenza or Pneumonia	190,962
Nephritis, Nephrotic syndrome	39,465
Septicemia	3,203
Chronic liver disease and cirrhosis	2,910
Hypertension	31,868
Parkinson's disease	23,714
Pneumonitis due to solids and liquids	44

have twelve different for each of the health conditions. The idea is to find which of these time windows yield structural information. The use of a time window naturally leads to weighted networks. If two users are within the time window for more than one iteration of the slide of the window (as in Figure 2) their connection gets reinforced; when two tweets are near to each other on the timeline, their users tend have a strong connection.

4. EXPERIMENTAL RESULTS

Recall that we aimed to generate networks of Twitter users who tweeted about the same health condition; also we considered the users of each US state separately. It means that each network represents Twitter users of one US state. Since we assigned twelve different sizes for the time window to generate networks related to each one of the health conditions, we generated the total number of 7,344 networks. Because of the small amount of collected data (only 44 tweets) related to *Pneumonitis due to solids and liquids*, we excluded this disease in the process of generating networks; thus, we generated 144 networks (12 time windows × 12 health conditions) for each US state plus Puerto Rico.

Obviously, assigning different lengths for the time window results in different structures with different properties. Figure 3 shows different structures related to the same disease that were generated using twelve different time windows where table 3 describes the general size of these networks. By increasing the size of the time window, we basically consider a larger period of time and more users get connected. It means that selecting a larger time window increases the density of communities within the network. On the other hand, smaller time windows result in networks that consist of smaller clusters and the density of such networks is lower.

To understand the characteristics of our generated networks, we evaluated and analyzed the structures based on the standard measurements: *Degree Distribution*, *Average Path Length*, and *Clustering Coefficient*.

4.1 Degree Distribution Evaluation

Social networks have expected characteristics for many of their strutural characteristics such as clustering levels, degree distributions, and average path lengths between nodes. The degree distribution is the probability $P(k)$ that a vertex i has degree k [8]. According to Clauset et al. [7], the degree distribution of a network tends to follow a power-law model expressed as

$$P(k) = ck^{-\alpha},$$

where k is the degree, and the exponent value α, in most cases, falls in the range $(2 < \alpha < 3)$. Since we generated weighted networks, it is the weighted degree distribution that is used, meaning that k represents the sum of the weights of the edges incident to a particular node. Figure 4 shows the distribution of the exponent α of the weighted degree distribution. The distribution is displayed as a box plot that shows minimum, maximum, median, first quartile, and third quartile values of the exponents for the networks analysed. It also shows the outliers, which represent the values that are above or below the quartiles. We can notice that the median value of the distributions tend to increase as the size of the time window increases.

According to Barabási et al. [2], most social networks have scale-free characteristics. Scale-free networks have a few highly connected nodes *hubs*. In scale-free networks, the nodes' weighted degree distribution exhibits a power-law distribution, where exponent α falls in the interval $(2 < \alpha < 3)$, as is was mentioned before.

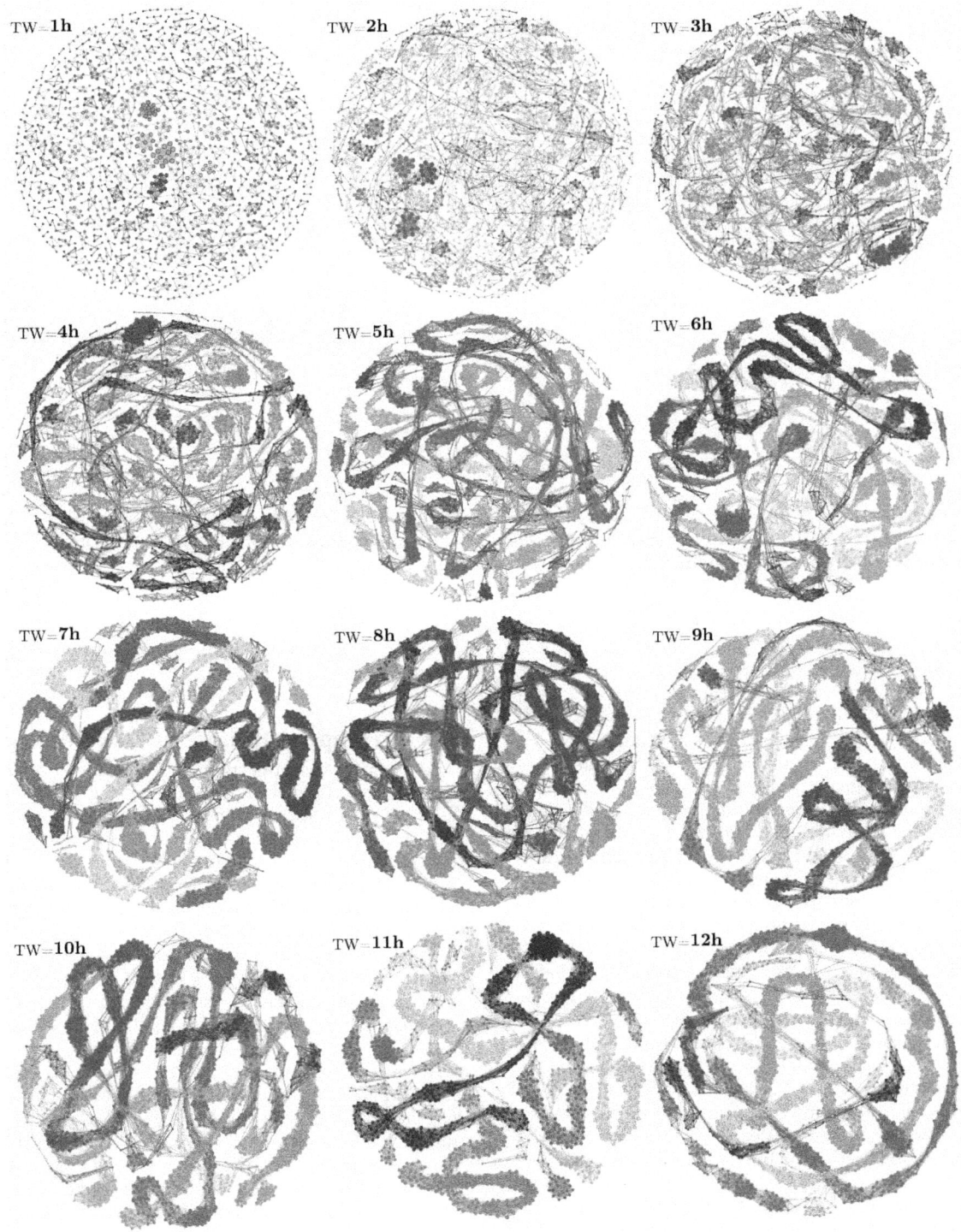

Figure 3: The networks of Twitter users from Alabama who tweeted about heart diseases.

Table 3: The number of nodes n and edges m of the generated networks represented in figure 3.

	1h	2h	3h	4h	5h	6h	7h	8h	9h	10h	11h	12h
n	1,514	1,729	1,756	1,759	1,760	1,760	1,760	1,761	1,761	1,761	1,761	1,761
m	2,387	5,199	7,980	10,680	13,306	15,901	18,397	20,895	23,447	25,904	28,384	30,879

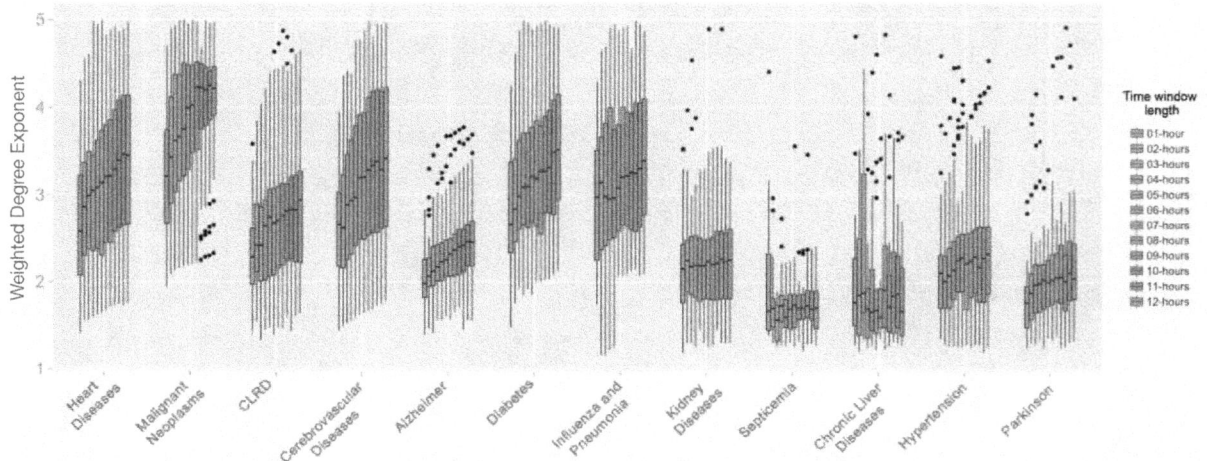

Figure 4: Each health condition is represented in a column in which there are twelve box plots. Each box plot shows the distributions of the weighted degree distribution's exponent of all the networks related to one health condition and generated using the same time window size.

According to Clauset et al. [7], due to fluctuations in the degree distributions, the power-law behavior is not easy to understand. In this paper, we followed the approach that was introduced by Clauset et al. to test the behavior of a weighted degree distribution and see whether it obeys a power-law or not. Using this approach, we compared the a power-law fitting against three other types of distributions, namely, *exponential*, *lognormal*, and *truncated power-law*. The results of the comparison process are two values, R and p. The retrieved value R represents the likelihood ratio between the distributions we compared while the p-value indicates whether the result is significant or not (values lower than 0.05% are considered significant). In the comparison process between two distributions, if R was positive and p was significant, we can say that the distribution behaves more as a power-law. However, if we get a negative value of R and a significant p-value, then the second distribution is favored. Moreover, after comparing the two distributions, if the p-value was insignificant, the behavior of the degree distribution remains unclear. Figure 5 illustrates power law, exponential, log normal, and truncated power-law fittings of six sample networks' weighted degree distribution and the results of comparing these distributions are detailed in Table 4.

After the comparison was performed, we found that only 117 out of 7,344 networks follow a power-law distribution, which indicates that the time window approach we utilized did not retrieve the scale-free characteristics. The results also show that among 117 networks that follow a power-law, the number of networks that was generated using the time window of one hour was larger than the other networks (see Figure 6). However, power-law distribution is not a necessary condition in social networks and many real-world networks have distributions that are not a direct power law [7].

4.2 Average Path Length Evaluation

Another metric important in social networks is the average path length between pairs of nodes, which calculates the shortest path between each pair of nodes in a network. In other words, it measures how much two nodes in a network are separated from each other. Figure 7 shows the distribution of the average path length values for all networks related to the health conditions. Based on the figure we notice that for all health conditions the median of the time window of one hour is the lowest compared to the median values related to other time windows. Except for *Malignant neoplasms*, by increasing the length of the time windows, the median value increases while the variance tends to be higher.

According to Watts et al. [22] social networks tend to have a smaller average path length. A smaller value of path length leads to the likelihood of having a higher connection among a network's nodes. In the networks generated using the time window of one hour, we observed that the average path lengths are lower. This reveals that these networks have closer properties to social network characteristics.

4.3 Clustering Coefficient Evaluation

Another characteristic we aimed to analyze is the global clustering coefficient of a network. The clustering coefficient is defined as the measurement of the tendency of a network's nodes to cluster together; the more clustered a network is, the more likely it is that two adjacent nodes of a given node

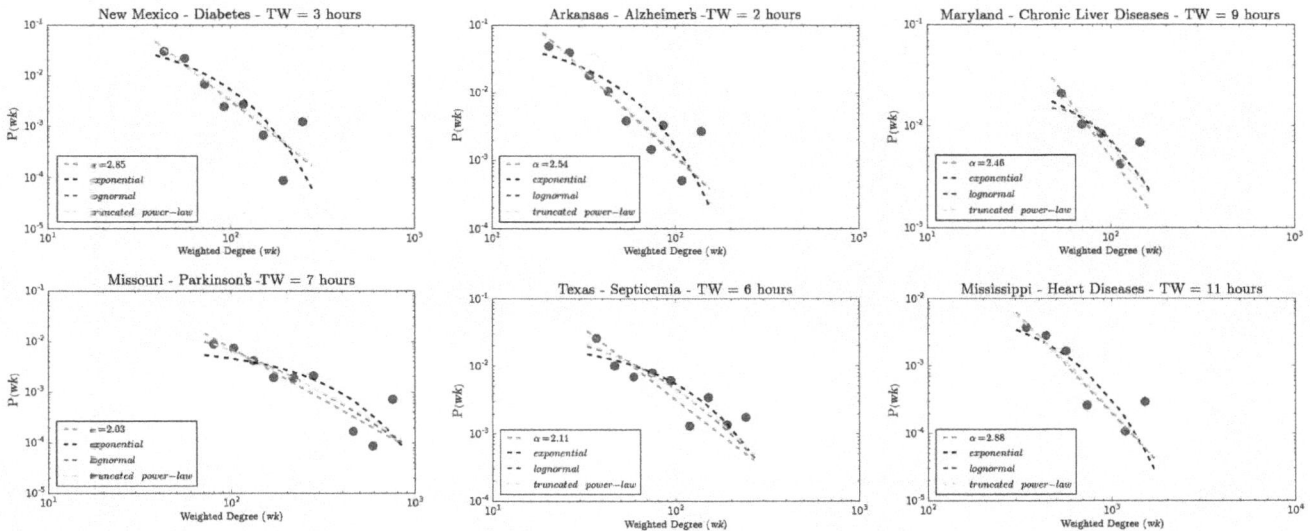

Figure 5: Fittings of six sample networks' weighted degree distributions.

Table 4: Testing the power-law distribution behavior of the networks mentioned in Figure 5. For each network, we give the likelihood ratios R and the p-value. We also show the exponent of distribution α. Significant p-values are shown in bold. Negative R values mean that alternative distribution is favored while positive R values indicate that the distribution follows a power-law. After performing all the comparisons, we list the behavior of the corespondent distribution on the last column.

Network	TW	α	Exponential		Log normal		Truncated power-law		Behavior
			R	p	R	p	R	p	
Mississippi-Heart Diseases	11 Hours	2.883	3.792	**0.0001**	-1.146	0.251	-1.767	0.105	power-law
New Mexico-Diabetes	3 Hours	2.849	3.827	**0.0001**	-0.749	0.453	-1.362	0.176	power-law
Arkansas-Alzheimer	2 Hours	2.537	3.710	**0.0002**	-0.683	0.494	-1.384	0.153	power-law
Maryland-CLD	9 Hours	2.457	-1.550	0.121	-1.070	0.284	-2.059	**0.037**	not a power-law
Missouri-Parkinson	7 Hours	2.028	1.109	0.267	-2.423	**0.015**	-3.126	**0.0001**	not a power-law
Texas-Septicemia	6 Hours	2.113	-1.320	0.186	-1.937	0.052	-2.790	**0.0002**	not a power-law

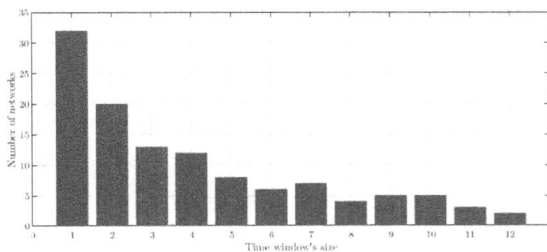

Figure 6: Number of the networks related to each one of the time windows in which the networks' weighted degree distribution follows a power-law.

k are also connected directly. Figure 8 illustrates the distribution of the clustering coefficient values for all networks related to each one of the health conditions.

Recall that social networks have characteristics of small-world networks; they tend to be clustered. According to Newman [18], social networks have a high clustering coef-

ficient. Based on the retrieved results, we notice that despite the lengths of the time windows, almost all the generated networks have a high value of clustering coefficient. Although expected, the time window approach used here appears to recover a high clustering coefficient, which is one of the properties of the social network of the groups interested in the health conditions studied. Moreover, the twelve causes of death have very similar clustering levels, which indicates that the clustering of users (perhaps forming support groups) is similarly strong in all cases. Initially, we hypothesized that certain conditions would be more clustered if people's awareness about a certain condition was higher. The results negate this hypothesis.

5. CONCLUSION AND FUTURE WORK

In this paper, we aimed to extract social structures from health related tweets. The main goal was to find if the generated networks created from conversations between Twitter users behave like social networks (even when users are not talking directly to each other). To construct the networks, we collected tweets related to the leading causes of death from Twitter. The collection process was carried out in a

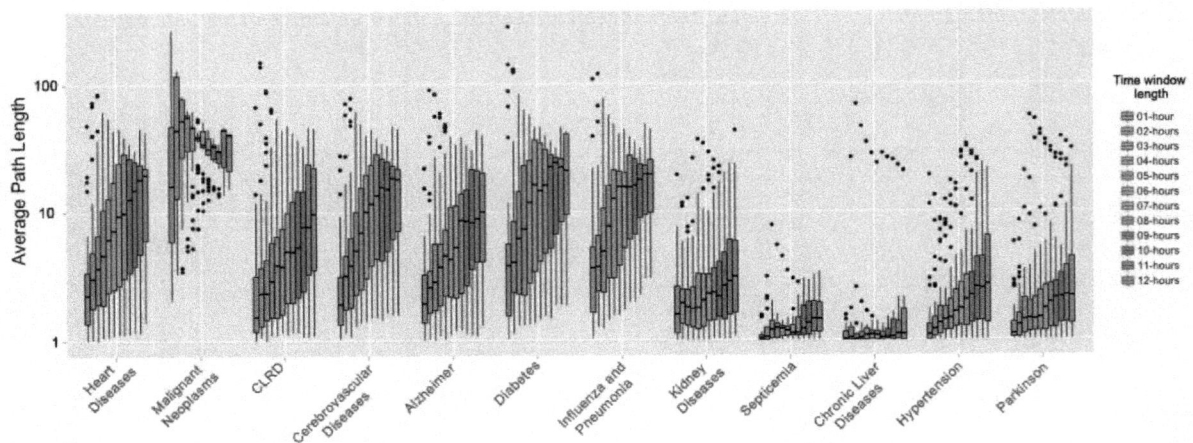

Figure 7: Each health condition is represented in a column in which there are twelve box plots. Each box plot shows the distributions of the average path length value of all the networks related to one health condition and generated using the same time window size.

period of 60 days (February 17 – April 17, 2015). We generated the networks of Twitter users of the same US state that mentioned the same health condition and described their characteristics. The concept of a time window was used to generate these networks. By selecting twelve sizes for the time window (one hour, two hours, ..., twelve hours) we generated twelve different networks for each one of the health conditions. We then analyzed those networks' characteristics: *weighted degree distribution, average path length,* and *clustering coefficients.*

By analyzing the weighted degree distribution of the networks and comparing different fits for a distribution, we noticed that the only 1% of the networks' distribution follows a power-law. In addition, the results show that the networks that were generated using the time window of one hour have a lower value of average path length compared to other networks. Furthermore, the results revealed that, despite the time-window size, the majority of the networks have a high clustering coefficient. Moreover, we found that the level of awareness about the diseases does not lead to having more clustered networks.

This leads that most of the networks do not have characteristics of scale-free networks in which the degree distribution follows a power-law. However, the time window approach retrieved the properties of small-world networks in which the average path length is low and the clustering coefficient is high. In order to get more accurate results, we may need to consider collecting a larger data set for a longer period of time. Moreover, to test whether or not the time window approach is a good tool to extract online social structures from Twitter, we may need to collect a different kind of data (e.g., data related to politics, sports, or the economy) and then compare those findings to this work's results.

In this work, we implemented the simplest way of moving the time window over the data line, where it was moved tweet by tweet. Based on that, in future work, we would try to define a different way of shifting the time window. This work can also be extended to different levels, where tempo-

ral and spatial aspects may be considered in constructing networks.

In summary, this work is the first showing that conversations in online social networks contain social structures, that is, that there seem to have structure information embedded in unstructured conversational data and that temporal regularities in the conversation affects the formation of such structure. Our approach demonstrate that even when social structures are not explicitly defined, they may be extracted from social conversations (unstructured data).

6. REFERENCES

[1] R. Albert and A.-L. Barabási. Statistical mechanics of complex networks. *Reviews of modern physics,* 74(1):47, 2002.

[2] A.-L. Barabási and E. Bonabeau. Scale-free networks. *Scientific American,* 288(5):50–59, 2003.

[3] A. Barak, M. Boniel-Nissim, and J. Suler. Fostering empowerment in online support groups. *Computers in Human Behavior,* 24(5):1867–1883, 2008.

[4] U. C. Bureau. Annual estimates of the resident population by sex, race, and hispanic origin for the united states: States, and counties: April 1, 2010 to july 1, 2014. Technical report, 2014.

[5] S. H. Burton, K. W. Tanner, C. G. Giraud-Carrier, J. H. West, and M. D. Barnes. " right time, right place" health communication on twitter: value and accuracy of location information. *Journal of medical Internet research,* 14(6), 2012.

[6] Centers for Disease Control and Prevention. Deaths: Final data for 2013. National vital statistics reports: National Center for Health Statistics, National Vital Statistics System.

[7] A. Clauset, C. R. Shalizi, and M. E. Newman. Power-law distributions in empirical data. *SIAM review,* 51(4):661–703, 2009.

[8] L. d. F. Costa, F. A. Rodrigues, G. Travieso, and P. R. Villas Boas. Characterization of complex

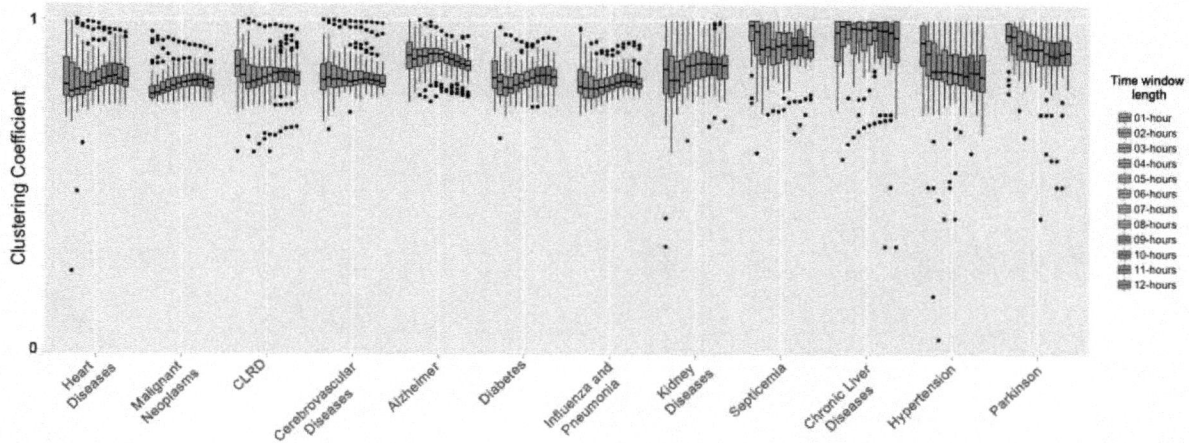

Figure 8: Each health condition is represented in a column in which there are twelve box plots. Each box plot shows the distributions of the clustering coefficient value of all the networks related to one health condition and generated using the same time window size.

networks: A survey of measurements. *Advances in Physics*, 56(1):167–242, 2007.

[9] A. Das Sarma, A. Jain, and C. Yu. Dynamic relationship and event discovery. In *Proceedings of the fourth ACM international conference on Web search and data mining*, pages 207–216. ACM, 2011.

[10] eHealth Initiative. A report on the use of social media to prevent behavioral risks factors associated with chronic diseases, 2013.

[11] D. S. Ferreira, A. R. Papa, and R. Menezes. The small world of seismic events. In *Complex Networks V*, pages 97–105. Springer, 2014.

[12] D. S. Ferreira, A. R. Papa, and R. Menezes. Towards evidences of long-range correlations in seismic activity. *arXiv preprint arXiv:1405.0307*, 2014.

[13] D. Ghosh and R. Guha. What are we 'tweeting'about obesity? mapping tweets with topic modeling and geographic information system. *Cartography and geographic information science*, 40(2):90–102, 2013.

[14] J. Guidry, L. Aday, D. Zhang, and R. Winn. The role of informal and formal social support networks for patients with cancer. *Cancer practice*, 5(4):241–246, 1996.

[15] B. A. Huberman, D. M. Romero, and F. Wu. Social networks that matter: Twitter under the microscope. *Available at SSRN 1313405*, 2008.

[16] C. H. Kroenke, L. D. Kubzansky, E. S. Schernhammer, M. D Holmes, and I. Kawachi. Social networks, social support, and survival after breast cancer diagnosis. *Journal of Clinical Oncology*, 24(7):1105–1111, 2006.

[17] L. Meng, T. Milenković, and A. Striegel. Systematic dynamic and heterogeneous analysis of rich social network data. In *Complex Networks V*, pages 25–37. Springer, 2014.

[18] M. E. Newman. The structure and function of complex networks. *SIAM review*, 45(2):167–256, 2003.

[19] M. J. Paul and M. Dredze. You are what you tweet: Analyzing twitter for public health. In *ICWSM*, pages 265–272, 2011.

[20] M. Salathé and S. Khandelwal. Assessing vaccination sentiments with online social media: implications for infectious disease dynamics and control. *PLoS computational biology*, 7(10):e1002199, 2011.

[21] Twitter.com. Twitter usage / company facts., 2015.

[22] D. J. Watts and S. H. Strogatz. Collective dynamics of small-world networks. *nature*, 393(6684):440–442, 1998.

Trends in Eye Tracking Scanpaths: Segmentation Effect?

Sukru Eraslan[1,2]
[1]School of Computer Science
University of Manchester
Manchester, UK
seraslan@metu.edu.tr

Yeliz Yesilada
[2]Middle East Technical
University Northern Cyprus
Campus, Kalkanli, Guzelyurt
Mersin 10 Turkey
yyeliz@metu.edu.tr

Simon Harper
[1]School of Computer Science
University of Manchester
Manchester, UK
simon.harper@manchester.ac.uk

ABSTRACT

Eye tracking has been widely used to investigate user interactions with the Web to improve user experience. In our previous work, we developed an algorithm called *Scanpath Trend Analysis (STA)* that analyses eye movement sequences (i.e., scanpaths) of multiple users on a web page and identifies their most commonly followed path in terms of the visual elements of the page. These visual elements are mainly the segments of a page generated by automated segmentation approaches. In our previous work, we also showed that the STA algorithm performs better than other existing algorithms in terms of providing the most representative scanpath of users. However, we did not know whether the validity of the algorithm is limited to a particular segmentation approach. In this paper, we investigate the effect of two different segmentation approaches on the STA algorithm. The results suggest that the validity of the algorithm is not affected by the segmentation approach used. Specifically, the resulting scanpath of the STA algorithm is the most representative scanpath of users in comparison with the resulting scanpaths of other existing algorithms regardless of the segmentation approach used.

CCS Concepts

•**Human-centered computing** → **Human computer interaction (HCI)**; *User models; Usability testing;* Laboratory experiments; Empirical studies in HCI;

Keywords

eye tracking; scanpath; trend analysis; web pages; visual elements; segmentation

1. INTRODUCTION

Eye tracking has been widely used to understand how users traverse the Web with the goal of improving user experience [6]. In particular, [3] conducted an eye tracking study

HT '16, July 10-13, 2016, Halifax, NS, Canada

© 2016 ACM. ISBN 978-1-4503-4247-6/16/07. . . $15.00

DOI: http://dx.doi.org/10.1145/2914586.2914591

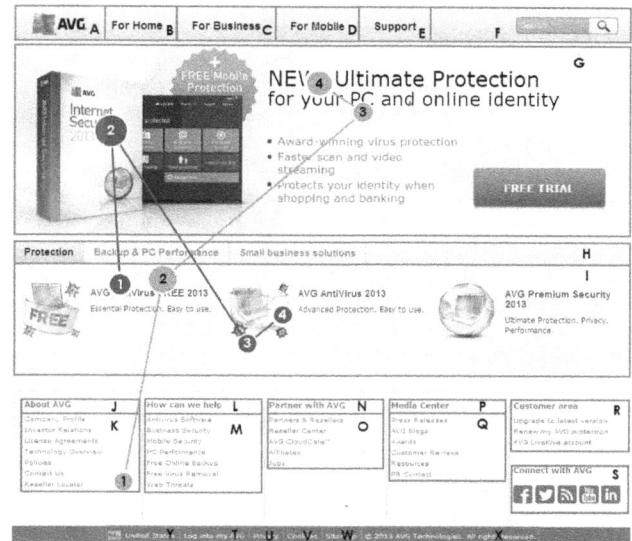

Figure 1: A gaze plot that represents a particular scanpath on the AVG web page

to understand how sighted users interact with tabular calendars to enter dates and then developed an audio interface for these calendars based on their findings. According to their evaluation, the audio interface improved the experience of visually impaired users. Eye tracking studies can also be a guide to evaluate the usability of web pages. For instance, transition probabilities between elements of a web page can be a guide to assess the efficiency of the arrangements of the elements on the page [6].

While a user is traversing a web page, his/her eyes become relatively stable at certain points called *fixations*. A quick eye movement made from one fixation to another is referred to as a *saccade*. A sequence of fixations and saccades represents a *scanpath*. Figure 1 shows two user scanpaths on the AVG web page which is segmented into its visual elements, such as logo and menu items. [2]. As illustrated in the figure, fixations are illustrated by circles where the radius is directly proportional to the fixation duration. Additionally, straight lines are used to illustrate saccades.

Scanpath analysis allows to investigate user interactions with visual elements of web pages which can be used for various goals. For example, web pages can be transcoded (i.e., re-engineered) to improve user experience in constrained environments, such as on small screen devices [1] and in audio access by screen readers [27]. Specifically, the firstly and mostly fixated visual elements can be moved to the earlier positions of web pages, such that the users can directly access these elements without a lot of scrolling/zooming or listening clutter. This is referred to as *Experiential Transcoding* in the literature [27]. Scanpath analysis can also be a guide for web designers to make their design more usable and/or investigate whether their expected path for a specific goal is followed by users [6].

Individual scanpaths are mainly related to specific users, and therefore they are not useful for providing generalisable results. Hence, they have a limited benefit for evaluating and improving the usability of web pages. For example, if a web page is transcoded for a particular user, it may not be suitable for another user as their interests may not be the same. In our previous work, we developed an algorithm called *Scanpath Trend Analysis (STA)* that analyses multiple scanpaths on a particular web page and identifies the most commonly followed path in terms of the visual elements of the page (Section 3) [10]. The resulting scanpath is called a *trending scanpath*. It differs from an absolute path which is followed by all users. Existing algorithms tend to identify an absolute path, however they typically fail in providing a representative path due to the variations caused by individual differences (Section 2). In the STA, if a particular visual element is not shared by all users but it gets at least the same attention as the shared elements, it deserves to be in the trending scanpath.

In our previous work, we also evaluated the STA algorithm by using an eye tracking study and our evaluation showed that the STA algorithm performs better than other existing algorithms in terms of providing the most representative scanpath of users (Section 3) [10]. The degree of representativeness was measured by the sequential similarities between the individual scanpaths and the resulting scanpath. However, in the evaluation, we only used the improved and extended version of the Vision-based Page Segmentation (VIPS) approach to discover the visual elements of the web pages [2]. Therefore, we did not know whether the validity of the algorithm is limited to the VIPS approach. In this paper, we investigate the effect of two different segmentation approaches on the STA algorithm (Section 4). Our experimental results show that the validity of the algorithm is not affected by the segmentation approach used (Sections 6-8). Specifically, the STA algorithm provides the most representative scanpath in comparison with other existing algorithms regardless of the segmentation approach used.

2. RELATED WORK

In order to investigate how users interact with visual elements of a web page, user scanpaths are firstly represented in terms of the visual elements. These scanpaths can then be analysed for different goals by using various algorithms. Existing algorithms are mainly designed for comparing a pair of scanpaths, computing transition probabilities between visual elements, detecting patterns in given scanpaths and identifying a representative scanpath of users [9]. The comprehensive review of all of these algorithms can be found in [9].

The Levenshtein algorithm, commonly known as the String-edit algorithm, has been widely used to compare two scanpaths to find a distance between them [16]. The distance is

the minimum number of editing operations (addition, deletion and substitution) needed to transform one scanpath to another. It can then be used to calculate the similarity between the two scanpaths as a percentage with Equation 1 below where S is the similarity, d is the distance and n is the length of the longer scanpath [23, 9].

$$S = 100 \cdot (1 - \frac{d}{n}) \qquad (1)$$

By default, the costs of the editing operations are the same and they are equal to one. Due to the differences in the sizes of visual elements and/or the geometrical distances between visual elements on a page, the substitution cost for a particular pair of visual elements may differ from the substitution cost for another pair of visual elements [16]. It has been suggested to generate a substitution cost matrix to keep the substitution costs between all pairs of visual elements and then integrate this matrix into the String-edit algorithm [22]. Albeit this algorithm is useful to compare two scanpaths, it is not applicable for identifying the most commonly followed path of mutliple users.

To compute transition probabilities between visual elements of a web page, a transition matrix can be generated by analysing all available scanpaths on the page [25]. This matrix, however, does not tell the most commonly followed path of users [15]. Specifically, it does not directly tell which visual element should be positioned at the end of the common scanpath.

There are various options for User Experience (UX) researchers who want to detect patterns in multiple scanpaths. One of these options is *eyePatterns* tool[1] which allows to discover patterns in given scanpaths. However, its algorithm to discover patterns is mainly designed for detecting exact patterns which consist of minimum three visual elements [25]. Particularly, it is not able to detect ABC in the scanpaths ABCY and ABXC because of the extra element X. Another option is the Sequential Pattern Mining (SPAM) algorithm[2] [14, 12]. In contrast to *eyePatterns* tool, the SPAM algorithm is more tolerant to extra elements in scanpaths. Next option is the T-Pattern Detection which is a commercial product[3]. It has been used to recognise repetitive patterns in user scanpaths on web pages by [4, 17]. It consists of many parameters, such as the critical interval type, and the adjustments of these parameters can easily affect the detection process.

In order to identify an absolute path which is followed by all users, the Dotplots algorithm was suggested for hierarchical clustering of individual scanpaths [13]. In addition to the Dotplots based hierarchical clustering, *eMINE* scanpath algorithm[4] was proposed which also uses a hierarchical clustering but with the String-edit and the Longest Common Subsequence (LCS) algorithms [8, 7]. In this clustering, the String-edit algorithm is used to find the two most similar scanpaths from the list and then the LCS algorithm is used to find the common scanpath of the two similar scanpaths.

Due to the variations in individual scanpaths, existing algorithms are likely to provide no result or an unacceptably short result that may not be representative for understand-

---

[1] http://sourceforge.net/projects/eyepatterns/
[2] http://www.philippe-fournier-viger.com/spmf/
[3] http://www.noldus.com/theme/t-pattern-analysis
[4] http://emine.ncc.metu.edu.tr/software.html

ing users' behaviors on web pages. To address this limitation, in our previous work, we developed an algorithm called *STA (Scanpath Trend Analysis)* to analyse multiple scanpaths on a particular page and identify the most commonly followed path in terms of the visual elements of the page. The STA algorithm is briefly introduced in the following section and detailed description can be found in [10].

3. STA: SCANPATH TREND ANALYSIS

The STA algorithm consists of three stages which are as follows: (1) Preliminary Stage, (2) First Pass, and (3) Second Pass. These stages are briefly introduced below.

Preliminary Stage: The STA algorithm firstly takes eye tracking data (a series of fixations for each user) on a specific web page and the visual elements of the page. In the preliminary stage, the fixations are correlated with the visual elements. As a result, the individual scanpaths are represented in terms of the visual elements. For instance, according to the scanpaths illustrated in Figure 1, one of the users fixated the elements I, G, I and I respectively, and therefore his/her scanpath is represented as IGII.

First Pass: The first pass is responsible for analysing the individual scanpaths to identify the trending elements by considering the total number of fixations and the total duration of fixations (i.e., dwell time) on the elements. The same element can be fixated more than once by a user and this can be consecutive (e.g. K**IGG**) and/or non-consecutive (e.g. **G**KI**G**). In the STA, each non-consecutive visit is called a visual element instance. For instance, the scanpath **IG**II includes two instances of the element I. The algorithm differentiates these instances by assigning them different numbers based on their total durations as the durations are correlated with information processing [24, 11]. Specifically, the first number is assigned to the longest instance of a particular element in an individual scanpath (e.g. **I1** G1 **I2 I2**). Once the instances are differentiated, the trending instances are identified. The instance becomes trending when it satisfies the following two criteria: (1) The total number of fixations on the instance is greater than or equal to the minimum total number of fixations on the instances shared by all of the individual scanpaths (2) The total duration on the instance is greater than or equal to the minimum total duration on the instances shared by all of the individual scanpaths. When the trending instances are identified, other instances are removed from the individual scanpaths as they will not be included in the trending scanpath.

Second Pass: The trending scanpath is constructed in the second pass. The STA algorithm firstly abstracts the individual scanpaths (e.g. G1 [100 ms] G1 [200 ms] I1 [200 ms] → G1 [300 ms] I1 [200 ms]) and then calculates the priority value (ψ) for each instance in each individual scanpath with Equation 2 below where P is the instance position in the individual scanpath (the first position is zero) and L is the length of the individual scanpath. We take the max and min values as 1 and 0.1 respectively to give 1 point the first instance and 0.1 points to the last instance.

$$\psi = 1 - P \cdot \frac{max - min}{L - 1} \quad (2) \qquad \Psi = \sum_{i=1}^{n} \psi_i \quad (3)$$

When all of the priority values are calculated, the total priority value (Ψ) for each instance is calculated with Equation 3 above where n is the number of individual scanpaths. The algorithm then positions the instances into the trending scanpath based on their total priority values in descending order. If multiple instances have the same total priority value, their total duration and the total number of fixations on the instances are also considered.

Once the trending instances are positioned in the trending scanpath, their numbers are eliminated (e.g. G1 → G) and then the consecutive repetitions are removed (e.g. IGII → IGI). Thus, the trending scanpath is represented in terms of the visual elements.

4. EYE TRACKING STUDY

We have already evaluated the STA algorithm by using an eye tracking study [10]. In the evaluation, we used the extended and improved version of the VIPS approach to segment the web pages into their visual elements [2]. According to our evaluation, the STA algorithm is able to provide the most representative scanpath of users in comparison with other existing algorithms. However, we did not know whether the validity of the STA algorithm is limited to the VIPS approach. Therefore, our research question here is:

> *"Is the STA algorithm able to provide the most representative scanpath of users regardless of the segmentation approach used?".*

In order to investigate whether or not the validity of the STA algorithm is restricted to a particular segmentation approach, we conducted a new eye tracking study with 41 users at Middle East Technical University Northern Cyprus Campus. The methodology used in this study was previously used in our another eye tracking study [8, 7, 10]. The details of the complete methodology can be found in [8, 7, 10].

4.1 Participants

Twenty-one male and 20 female users participated in the study. The majority of these users were students, along with some academic staff at the university. There were also some other users from outside of the university. All the users were daily web users, apart from one male user who claimed that he used the web a few times in a week. Thirty-six users were between the ages of 18-24 and five users were between the ages of 25-34. Moreover, all the users had a high school diploma, except from one user who also held a master's degree.

4.2 Equipment and Materials

The eye movements of the users were recorded by using Tobii T60 eye tracker that was built-in a 17" monitor. The screen resolution was 1280 x 1024. These users were requested to perform specific tasks on the stored versions of the Apple, Babylon, AVG, Yahoo, Godaddy and BBC web pages (See Open Data Section). As an example, Figures 2-5 show the Apple and BBC web pages with their segments discovered by two different approaches [2, 21].

4.3 User Tasks

The tasks performed were classified into two categories which are the browsing and searching tasks. For the browsing tasks, the users were requested to browse on the web

Figure 2: The Apple web page segmented with the VIPS approach

Figure 4: The Apple web page segmented with the BOM approach

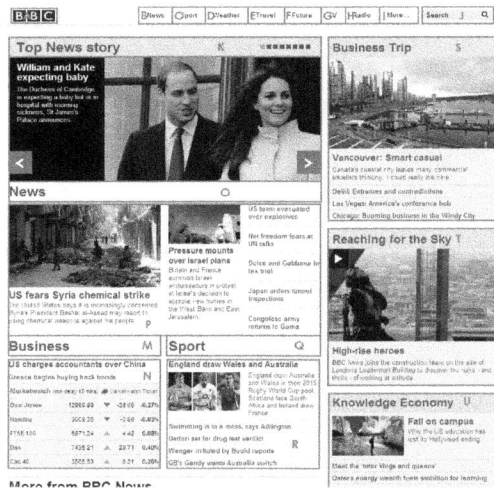

Figure 3: The BBC web page segmented with the VIPS approach

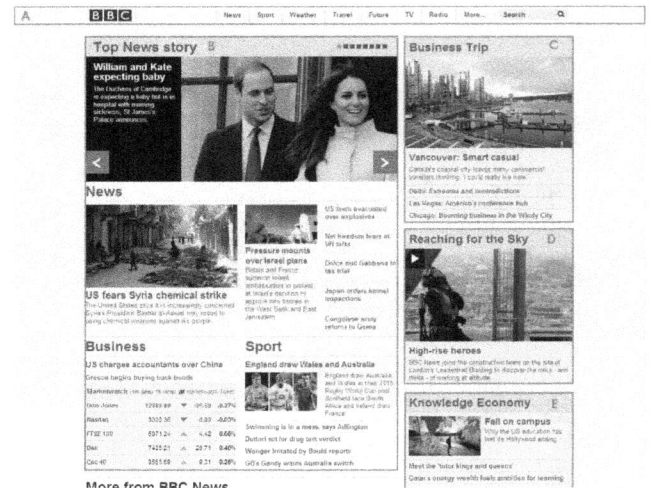

Figure 5: The BBC web page segmented with the BOM approach

pages without a particular goal. However, for the searching tasks, they were asked to find specific information or items on the web pages. The searching tasks are listed below.

- **Apple** *a*) Can you locate a link which allows watching the TV ads relating to iPad mini? *b*) Can you locate a link labelled iPad on the main menu?

- **Babylon** *a*) Can you locate a link that you can download the free version of Babylon? *b*) Can you find and read the names of other products of Babylon?

- **AVG** *a*) Can you locate a link which you can download a free trial of AVG Internet Security 2013? *b*) Can you locate a link which allows you to download AVG Anti-virus Free 2013?

- **Yahoo** *a*) Can you read the titles of the main headlines which have smaller images? *b*) Can you read the first item under the News title?

- **Godaddy** *a*) Can you find a telephone number for technical support and read it? *b*) Can you locate a text box where you can search for a new domain?

- **BBC** *a*) Can you read the first item of the Sport News? *b*) Can you locate the table that shows market data under the Business title?

4.4 Procedure

The users were firstly requested to read an information sheet about the study. After that, they were requested to sign a consent form to accept that they were informed about their rights and they were volunteer to participate in the study. Following this, their gender, age-group and education level were noted. The eye tracking sessions were then started. During the sessions, they visited the web pages two times in a random order where one of views was for the browsing tasks (30 seconds) and another view was for the searching tasks (maximum 120 seconds).

5. METHODOLOGY

The objective of this paper is to investigate whether or not the STA algorithm provides the most representative scanpath of users in comparison with other existing algorithms regardless of the segmentation approach used. Therefore, the result of the STA algorithm should have the highest similarities to the individual scanpaths in comparison with the results of other algorithms. In order to achieve our objective, we firstly segmented the six web pages by using both the VIPS [2] and the Block-o-Matic (BOM) [21] segmentation approaches. Both of these segmentation approaches use the DOM structure and the visual representation of the web pages, but uses different algorithms for segmentation. In particular, the BOM segmentation also applies a logical approach to group the segments based on the four Gestalt laws (Proximity, Similarity, Closure and Simplicity) [21]. As a result of segmentation process, both of these approaches provide a tree of segments. Thus, they have a granularity parameter which affects the number of segments and the size of segments. The VIPS provides more and smaller segments at higher granularity levels whereas the BOM provides fewer and bigger segments at higher granularity levels. A study conducted by [2] suggests that the fifth granularity level is mostly preferred by users, and therefore we used the fifth level to segment the web pages with the VIPS approach. In contrast, there is no suggestion for the BOM's granularity level, so we used the default one (0.3).

Unfortunately, the current publicly available implementation of the BOM segmentation approach[5] failed to properly segment some of the web pages. Hence, we applied a systematic approach to fix these problems by following the algorithm given their paper [21, 20]: (1) If there is an empty block (i.e., segment) which covers only white space, the block is excluded. (2) If there is a larger block which covers other smaller blocks, the larger block will be used. (3) If there is a number of blocks which have overlaps, the borders of these blocks are adjusted such that they do not have overlaps. (4) If there is a group of items which are not covered by any block, they are included in the closest block. Figure 6 shows the segmentation of the AVG page with the implementation of the BOM approach. There was a group of menu items (For Home, For Business, For Mobile and Support) between the block L4 and the block L5 and they were not covered by any block. Because of the rule 4, these items were included in the closest block which is the AVG logo (the block L4).

Once the web pages were segmented properly and the visual elements were discovered, the individual scanpaths were represented in terms of the visual elements. We then applied the STA and other existing algorithms (the *eyePatterns* Discover Patterns algorithm [25], the Dotplots based algorithm [13], the SPAM algorithm [14, 12], and *eMine* algorithm [8, 27]) to all of the individual scanpaths on the six web pages for the browsing and searching tasks. With the SPAM algorithm, multiple scanpaths were detected for some of the pages. To be fair, we selected the one with the highest similarities to the individual scanpaths. This means that we chose its best result from this aspect.

We then compared the resulting scanpaths with the individual scanpaths. For this purpose, we used the standard String-edit algorithm to calculate the similarities to the individual scanpaths as it has been widely used in the literature

---

[5]http://www-poleia.lip6.fr/~sanojaa/BOM/

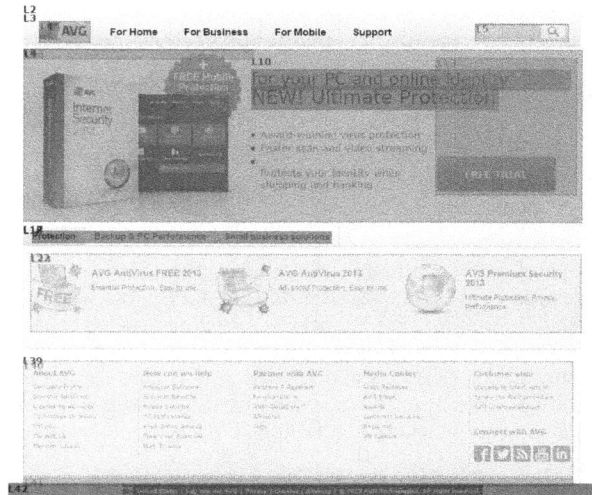

Figure 6: The AVG web page segmented with the BOM approach

(see Section 2). To investigate whether the differences between the results of the STA and other existing algorithms are statistically significant and not caused by chance, we conducted a statistical analysis [19]. Since the algorithms were applied to the same scanpaths, the repeated measures design was used here. Hence, when the differences between the results of two algorithms (i.e., the similarities to the individual scanpaths) were normally distributed, the dependent T-Test was applied which provides t value. Otherwise, the Wilcoxon Signed Rank test was applied which provides Z value. We assessed the normality of the results by using the Shapiro-Wilk test.

The statistical analysis was conducted with 95% confidence interval [19]. In this confidence interval, when the p value is less than 0.05, we can mention a significant difference between the results of two algorithms. However, the probability of identifying a significant difference due to chance raises when the number of pairwise comparisons raises [18]. In our statistical analysis, the STA algorithm was compared with other four algorithms in a pairwise manner on each web page for both the browsing and searching tasks. Therefore, the p value was adjusted by using the Bonferroni correction method [18]. In other words, the p value was divided by the number of pairwise comparisons ($0.05/4 = 0.0125$) [18]. As a result, the p value should be less than 0.0125 in our analysis to show a significant difference between the results of two algorithms.

In order to illustrate the strength of the differences between the results of the STA and other algorithms, we also calculated the effect sizes. The Cohen's d value was calculated as the effect size when the T-test was appropriate (0.2: Small Effect, 0.5 : Medium Effect, 0.8: Large Effect). Otherwise, the r value was calculated as the effect size (0.1: Small Effect, 0.3: Medium Effect, 0.5: Large Effect) [5, 19]. The following section presents our statistical analysis for both the VIPS and the BOM segmentation approaches [2, 21].

6. RESULTS

This section presents the statistical comparison of the results of the STA and other existing algorithms for both the

Table 1: The trending scanpaths generated by the STA algorithm (See Open Data Section for the pages with their visual elements)

Segmentation Approach	Task	Apple	Babylon	AVG	Yahoo	Godaddy	BBC
VIPS	Browsing	FCGHIFHBGEJF	MHIRQP	IGI	IJH	ONO	LP
	Searching	CFEFCHIEDBEGB	MNPQRS	GI	IGIJI	OMNFM	LPRSN
BOM	Browsing	DBADCED	K	ECEC	IJLH	HGIHKI	B
	Searching	BDCECA	GK	CE	IGI	HGIHKDGBG	B

VIPS and BOM segmentation approaches. Table 1 shows the results of the STA algorithm. The individual scanpaths and the results of other existing algorithms can be found in our external data repository (see Open Data Section). The repository also includes the computed similarities between the individual scanpaths and the resulting scanpaths of the STA and other existing algorithms.

6.1 Results for the VIPS Approach

Table 2 and Table 3 present the mean (M), median (MD), standard deviation (SD), minimum (MIN) and maximum (MAX) similarities between the individual scanpaths and the results of the STA and other algorithms on the six web pages for the browsing and searching tasks when the VIPS approach was used to segment the web pages [2]. As presented, the *eyePatterns* Discover Patterns algorithm could not provide any results in none of the cases. Moreover, *eMINE* algorithm and the Dotplots based algorithm could not provide any result in some cases. For example, no result could be provided by *eMINE* algorithm on the Babylon page for the browsing task when the VIPS was used [2].

Table 2: The similarities between the individual scanpaths and the results of the STA and other existing algorithms for the browsing tasks when the VIPS is used [^{a}: No result is provided]

Page	Algorithm	M	MD	SD	MIN	MAX
Apple	STA	25.64	25.36	4.85	14.29	38.89
	eMINE	2.82	2.78	0.72	1.75	5.56
	eyePatterns	a	a	a	a	a
	Dotplots	a	a	a	a	a
	SPAM	11.26	11.11	2.88	7.02	22.22
Babylon	STA	13.14	11.90	4.31	6.35	27.27
	eMINE	a	a	a	a	a
	eyePatterns	a	a	a	a	a
	Dotplots	a	a	a	a	a
	SPAM	2.66	2.27	1.01	1.47	6.25
AVG	STA	13.14	11.54	7.50	5.26	37.50
	eMINE	4.38	3.85	2.50	1.75	12.50
	eyePatterns	a	a	a	a	a
	Dotplots	a	a	a	a	a
	SPAM	17.52	15.38	10.00	7.02	50.00
Yahoo	STA	14.26	13.04	4.64	8.57	27.27
	eMINE	4.75	4.35	1.55	2.86	9.09
	eyePatterns	a	a	a	a	a
	Dotplots	a	a	a	a	a
	SPAM	19.01	17.39	6.19	11.43	36.36
Godaddy	STA	12.66	11.11	4.94	5.36	30.00
	eMINE	4.22	3.70	1.65	1.79	10.00
	eyePatterns	a	a	a	a	a
	Dotplots	4.22	3.70	1.65	1.79	10.00
	SPAM	12.66	11.11	4.94	5.36	30.00
BBC	STA	7.49	6.78	2.86	3.45	16.67
	eMINE	3.81	3.51	1.45	1.72	8.33
	eyePatterns	a	a	a	a	a
	Dotplots	a	a	a	a	a
	SPAM	3.81	3.51	1.45	1.72	8.33

As illustrated in Table 2 and Table 3, in the majority of the cases, the results of the STA algorithm were more sim-

Table 3: The similarities between the individual scanpaths and the results of the STA and other existing algorithms for the searching tasks when the VIPS is used [^{a}: No result is provided]

Page	Algorithm	M	MD	SD	MIN	MAX
Apple	STA	28.93	29.41	7.88	13.79	45.00
	eMINE	5.98	5.88	2.08	2.30	10.00
	eyePatterns	a	a	a	a	a
	Dotplots	a	a	a	a	a
	SPAM	14.95	14.71	5.20	5.75	25.00
Babylon	STA	19.77	18.75	8.57	5.56	50.00
	eMINE	13.28	12.50	5.67	3.70	33.33
	eyePatterns	a	a	a	a	a
	Dotplots	a	a	a	a	a
	SPAM	16.60	15.63	7.08	4.63	41.67
AVG	STA	10.01	9.11	4.10	2.78	22.22
	eMINE	10.01	9.11	4.10	2.78	22.22
	eyePatterns	a	a	a	a	a
	Dotplots	10.01	9.11	4.10	2.78	22.22
	SPAM	20.02	18.22	8.20	5.56	44.44
Yahoo	STA	24.07	25.66	11.38	6.67	62.50
	eMINE	4.85	5.13	2.30	1.33	12.50
	eyePatterns	a	a	a	a	a
	Dotplots	4.85	5.13	2.30	1.33	12.50
	SPAM	14.56	15.39	6.89	4.00	37.50
Godaddy	STA	15.60	14.81	4.47	7.14	29.41
	eMINE	6.75	6.67	1.84	2.86	11.76
	eyePatterns	a	a	a	a	a
	Dotplots	3.37	3.33	0.92	1.43	5.88
	SPAM	10.12	10.00	2.75	4.29	17.65
BBC	STA	15.75	15.63	5.61	5.81	26.32
	eMINE	6.96	6.90	2.69	2.33	12.50
	eyePatterns	a	a	a	a	a
	Dotplots	a	a	a	a	a
	SPAM	10.44	10.34	4.03	3.49	18.75

ilar to the individual scanpaths in comparison with other algorithms. For example, on the Apple page for the browsing task, the mean similarity between the result of the STA and the individual scanpaths are equal to 25.64% whereas the mean similarities between the results of *eMINE* algorithm and the SPAM algorithm to the individual scanpaths were equal to 2.82% and 11.26% respectively. Moreover, no result was provided by the *eyePatterns* Discover Patterns algorithm and the Dotplots based algorithm on the Apple page for the browsing task.

According to our statistical analysis (see Table 4 and Table 5), the STA algorithm performed significantly better than all other algorithms in eight out of 12 cases with a large effect in terms of providing the most representative scanpath and this not an occurrence by chance ($p < 0.0005$). In some cases, the results of the STA and some algorithms had the same similarities to the individual scanpaths. For example, the result of the STA algorithm and the SPAM algorithm have the same similarities to the individual scanpaths on the Godaddy page for the browsing task. In three cases, the SPAM algorithm performed better than the STA algorithm (the browsing and searching tasks on the AVG page and the browsing task on the Yahoo page). However, apart from the

Table 4: The statistical comparisons of the STA and other existing algorithms for the browsing tasks by using the VIPS [[a]: No result, [b]: The same similarities to the individual scanpaths, [c]: Not relevant to the Wilcoxon test, N: The sample size, *p<0.05, **p<0.01, ***p<0.0005]

Page	Algorithm Compared	Test	N	df	t or Z	d or r
Apple	eMINE	T-Test	40	39	33.952***	6.6
	eyePatterns	a	a	a	a	a
	Dotplots	a	a	a	a	a
	SPAM	T-Test	40	39	32.230***	7.5
Babylon	eMINE	a	a	a	a	a
	eyePatterns	a	a	a	a	a
	Dotplots	a	a	a	a	a
	SPAM	Wilcoxon	39	c	-5.446***	0.6
AVG	eMINE	Wilcoxon	40	c	-5.512***	0.6
	eyePatterns	a	a	a	a	a
	Dotplots	a	a	a	a	a
	SPAM	Wilcoxon	40	c	-5.512***	0.6
Yahoo	eMINE	Wilcoxon	40	c	-5.513***	0.6
	eyePatterns	a	a	a	a	a
	Dotplots	a	a	a	a	a
	SPAM	Wilcoxon	40	c	-5.513***	0.6
Godaddy	eMINE	Wilcoxon	40	c	-5.513***	0.6
	eyePatterns	a	a	a	a	a
	Dotplots	Wilcoxon	40	c	-5.513***	0.6
	SPAM	b	b	b	b	b
BBC	eMINE	Wilcoxon	40	c	-5.445***	0.6
	eyePatterns	a	a	a	a	a
	Dotplots	a	a	a	a	a
	SPAM	Wilcoxon	40	c	-5.445***	0.6

Table 5: The statistical comparisons of the STA and other existing algorithms for the searching tasks by using the VIPS [[a]: No result, [b]: The same similarities to the individual scanpaths, [c]: Not relevant to the Wilcoxon test, N: The sample size, *p<0.05, **p<0.01, ***p<0.0005]

Page	Algorithm Compared	Test	N	df	t or Z	d or r
Apple	eMINE	T-Test	33	32	21.743***	4.0
	eyePatterns	a	a	a	a	a
	Dotplots	a	a	a	a	a
	SPAM	T-Test	33	32	20.694***	2.1
Babylon	eMINE	Wilcoxon	39	c	-5.444***	0.6
	eyePatterns	a	a	a	a	a
	Dotplots	a	a	a	a	a
	SPAM	Wilcoxon	39	c	-5.305***	0.6
AVG	eMINE	b	b	b	b	b
	eyePatterns	a	a	a	a	a
	Dotplots	b	38	b	b	b
	SPAM	T-Test	38	37	-15.056***	-1.5
Yahoo	eMINE	Wilcoxon	34	c	-5.089***	0.6
	eyePatterns	a	a	a	a	a
	Dotplots	Wilcoxon	34	c	-5.089***	0.6
	SPAM	Wilcoxon	34	c	-5.089***	0.6
Godaddy	eMINE	T-Test	35	34	17.701***	2.6
	eyePatterns	a	a	a	a	a
	Dotplots	T-Test	35	34	19.665***	3.8
	SPAM	T-Test	35	34	13.632***	1.5
BBC	eMINE	T-Test	39	38	16.686***	2.0
	eyePatterns	a	a	a	a	a
	Dotplots	a	a	a	a	a
	SPAM	T-Test	39	38	13.622***	1.1

SPAM algorithm, none of the algorithms performed better than the STA in our tests.

6.2 Results for the BOM Approach

Table 6 and Table 7 show the mean (M), median (MD),

Table 6: The similarities between the individual scanpaths and the results of the STA and other existing algorithms for the browsing tasks when the BOM is used [[a]: No result is provided]

Page	Algorithm	M	MD	SD	MIN	MAX
Apple	STA	26.85	26.20	5.39	15.91	40.00
	eMINE	4.43	4.17	1.47	2.27	10.00
	eyePatterns	a	a	a	a	a
	Dotplots	4.43	4.17	1.47	2.27	10.00
	SPAM	13.30	12.50	4.42	6.82	30.00
Babylon	STA	4.16	3.13	2.89	1.92	14.29
	eMINE	4.16	3.13	2.89	1.92	14.29
	eyePatterns	a	a	a	a	a
	Dotplots	4.16	3.13	2.89	1.92	14.29
	SPAM	4.16	3.13	2.89	1.92	14.29
AVG	STA	22.60	18.18	11.85	8.33	66.67
	eMINE	5.71	4.55	3.01	2.08	16.67
	eyePatterns	a	a	a	a	a
	Dotplots	5.71	4.55	3.01	2.08	16.67
	SPAM	22.82	18.18	12.03	8.33	66.67
Yahoo	STA	15.95	15.38	4.36	9.30	30.77
	eMINE	4.25	4.01	1.26	2.33	7.69
	eyePatterns	a	a	a	a	a
	Dotplots	a	a	a	a	a
	SPAM	12.75	12.02	3.77	6.98	23.08
Godaddy	STA	21.84	20.71	5.95	10.91	35.29
	eMINE	3.93	3.45	1.31	1.82	8.33
	eyePatterns	a	a	a	a	a
	Dotplots	a	a	a	a	a
	SPAM	15.72	13.81	5.23	7.27	33.33
BBC	STA	9.52	6.07	15.03	3.33	100.00
	eMINE	9.52	6.07	15.03	3.33	100.00
	eyePatterns	a	a	a	a	a
	Dotplots	9.52	6.07	15.03	3.33	100.00
	SPAM	9.52	6.07	15.03	3.33	100.00

Table 7: The similarities between the individual scanpaths and the results of the STA and other existing algorithms for the searching tasks when the BOM is used [[a]: No result is provided]

Page	Algorithm	M	MD	SD	MIN	MAX
Apple	STA	27.30	25.00	10.24	10.00	54.55
	eMINE	9.42	8.70	3.66	3.33	18.18
	eyePatterns	a	a	a	a	a
	Dotplots	a	a	a	a	a
	SPAM	23.55	21.74	9.14	8.33	45.45
Babylon	STA	10.94	9.09	5.46	2.70	28.57
	eMINE	10.94	9.09	5.46	2.70	28.57
	eyePatterns	a	a	a	a	a
	Dotplots	5.47	4.55	2.73	1.35	14.29
	SPAM	10.94	9.09	5.46	2.70	28.57
AVG	STA	11.14	10.53	4.29	3.57	22.22
	eMINE	11.14	10.53	4.29	3.57	22.22
	eyePatterns	a	a	a	a	a
	Dotplots	11.14	10.53	4.29	3.57	22.22
	SPAM	22.29	21.05	8.59	7.14	44.44
Yahoo	STA	13.87	14.29	6.47	3.95	33.33
	eMINE	4.62	4.76	2.16	1.32	11.11
	eyePatterns	a	a	a	a	a
	Dotplots	4.62	4.76	2.16	1.32	11.11
	SPAM	13.87	14.29	6.47	3.95	33.33
Godaddy	STA	25.30	24.00	7.22	16.67	44.44
	eMINE	7.04	6.90	2.05	3.85	12.50
	eyePatterns	a	a	a	a	a
	Dotplots	3.52	3.45	1.02	1.92	6.25
	SPAM	14.08	13.79	4.10	7.69	25.00
BBC	STA	9.33	7.69	4.98	2.08	25.00
	eMINE	9.33	7.69	4.98	2.08	25.00
	eyePatterns	a	a	a	a	a
	Dotplots	9.33	7.69	4.98	2.08	25.00
	SPAM	9.33	7.69	4.98	2.08	25.00

standard deviation (SD), minimum (MIN) and maximum (MAX) similarities between the individual scanpaths and

Table 8: The statistical comparisons of the STA and other existing algorithms for the browsing tasks by using the BOM [^{a}: No result, ^{b}: The same similarities to the individual scanpaths, ^{c}: Not relevant to the Wilcoxon test, N: The sample size, *p<0.05, **p<0.01, ***p<0.0005]

Page	Algorithm Compared	Test	N	df	t or Z	d or r
Apple	eMINE	T-Test	40	39	34.303***	5.68
	eyePatterns	a	a	a	a	a
	Dotplots	T-Test	40	39	34.303***	5.68
	SPAM	T-Test	40	39	32.244***	2.75
Babylon	eMINE	b	b	b	b	b
	eyePatterns	a	a	a	a	a
	Dotplots	b	b	b	b	b
	SPAM	b	b	b	b	b
AVG	eMINE	Wilcoxon	40	c	-5.513***	0.62
	eyePatterns	a	a	a	a	a
	Dotplots	Wilcoxon	40	c	-5.513***	0.62
	SPAM	Wilcoxon	40	c	-1.000	0.11
Yahoo	eMINE	Wilcoxon	40	c	-5.513***	0.62
	eyePatterns	a	a	a	a	a
	Dotplots	a	a	a	a	a
	SPAM	Wilcoxon	40	c	-4.939***	0.55
Godaddy	eMINE	T-Test	40	39	23.654***	4.16
	eyePatterns	a	a	a	a	a
	Dotplots	a	a	a	a	a
	SPAM	Wilcoxon	40	c	-5.376***	0.60
BBC	eMINE	b	b	b	b	b
	eyePatterns	a	a	a	a	a
	Dotplots	b	b	b	b	b
	SPAM	b	b	b	b	b

Table 9: The statistical comparisons of the STA and other existing algorithms for the searching tasks by using the BOM [^{a}: No result, ^{b}: The same similarities to the individual scanpaths, ^{c}: Not relevant to the Wilcoxon test, N: The sample size, *p<0.05, **p<0.01, ***p<0.0005]

Page	Algorithm Compared	Test	N	df	t or Z	d or r
Apple	eMINE	T-Test	33	32	15.323***	2.33
	eyePatterns	a	a	a	a	a
	Dotplots	a	a	a	a	a
	SPAM	T-Test	33	32	9.358***	0.39
Babylon	eMINE	b	b	b	b	b
	eyePatterns	a	a	a	a	a
	Dotplots	Wilcoxon	39	c	-5.444***	0.62
	SPAM	b	b	b	b	b
AVG	eMINE	b	b	b	b	b
	eyePatterns	a	a	a	a	a
	Dotplots	b	b	b	b	b
	SPAM	T-Test	38	37	-16.001***	-1.64
Yahoo	eMINE	T-Test	34	33	12.492***	1.92
	eyePatterns	a	a	a	a	a
	Dotplots	T-Test	34	33	12.492***	1.92
	SPAM	b	b	b	b	b
Godaddy	eMINE	Wilcoxon	35	c	-5.160***	0.62
	eyePatterns	a	a	a	a	a
	Dotplots	Wilcoxon	35	c	-5.161***	0.62
	SPAM	Wilcoxon	35	c	-5.160***	0.62
BBC	eMINE	b	b	b	b	b
	eyePatterns	a	a	a	a	a
	Dotplots	b	b	b	b	b
	SPAM	b	b	b	b	b

the results of the STA and other existing algorithms on the six pages for the browsing and searching tasks when the BOM approach was used to discover the visual elements of the web pages [21]. As illustrated in these tables, no result

could be provided by the *eyePatterns* Discover Pattern algorithm again. The Dotplots based algorithm also could not provide any result on the Apple page for the searching task and on the Godaddy and Yahoo pages for the browsing task.

According to Table 6 and Table 7, the results of the STA algorithm were more similar to the individual scanpaths in comparison with other algorithms in five out of 12 cases. For example, on the Apple page for the browsing task, the mean similarity between the result of the STA and the individual scanpaths are equal to 26.85% whereas the mean similarities between the results of *eMINE* algorithm, the Dotplots based algorithm and the SPAM algorithm to the individual scanpaths were equal to 4.43%, 4.43% and 13.30% respectively. Moreover, as mentioned above, no result was provided by the eyePatterns Discover Patterns algorithm on the Apple page for the browsing task.

As illustrated in Table 8 and Table 9, the STA algorithm performed significantly better than all other algorithms in five out of 12 cases with a large effect in terms of providing the most representative scanpath with a large effect, except on the Apple page for the searching task where the effect size was small between the STA algorithm and the SPAM algorithm. In three cases, apart from the *eyePatterns* Discover Pattern algorithm, all of the algorithms provided the results which have the same similarities to the individual scanpaths (the browsing task on the Babylon and BBC pages and the searching task on the BBC page). In addition, the SPAM algorithm performed better on the AVG page for the searching task in comparison with the STA and other algorithms. In the rest of the cases, none of other algorithms provided better results than the STA algorithm, even though they provided the same results as the STA algorithm in some cases.

To sum up, the STA algorithm provided the most representative scanpath in the majority of the cases. In the rest of the cases, it still provided more representative scanpath in comparison with some of other existing algorithms. As the SPAM algorithm performed better than the STA algorithm in only four out of 24 cases, we can suggest that the STA algorithm is able to provide the most representative scanpath of users regardless of the segmentation approach used.

7. DISCUSSION

The validity of the STA algorithm was tested with the VIPS and BOM segmentation approaches [2, 21]. The results mainly show that the validity of the STA algorithm is not affected by the segmentation approach used. Even though there were some cases where the STA could not provide the most representative scanpath, the STA algorithm performed significantly better than other existing algorithms in the most of the cases regardless of the segmentation approach used (see Section 6).

Our experimental results show that the STA algorithm may not perform better than other existing algorithms when visual elements cover large areas on web pages. In particular, when the BOM segmentation approach was used to segment the web pages [21], the visual elements of the BBC page were quite large, especially the element B which is almost half of the page (see Figure 5). Although none of the existing algorithms performed better than the STA algorithm on the BBC page, the STA algorithm could not provide the most representative scanpath on that page. It is an expected situation because when there are very large visual elements, the variations between the individual scanpaths will be lower as the number of visual elements is limited.

In our previous work, we also showed that when there are more and smaller segments, the STA algorithm provides more representative scanpath [10]. We can also see this conclusion from this paper. As illustrated in Figures 2-5, more and smaller segments were generated by the VIPS segmentation approach in comparison with the BOM segmentation approach. For example, the elements G, H, I and J of the Apple page generated by the VIPS approach are covered by the element E generated by the BOM approach. Thus, the STA algorithm performed better with the VIPS segmentation approach (eight out of 12 cases) in comparison with the BOM segmentation approach (five out of 12 cases). Therefore, we can suggest that the granularity level is an important factor in scanpath analysis with the STA algorithm as it affects the sizes of segments and the number of segments on web pages. If there are very large segments on a web page, the difference between the results of the STA algorithm and other existing algorithms may not be significantly different. However, according to a study conducted by [2], users prefer more and smaller segments in comparison with fewer and larger segments.

As the STA algorithm identifies the trending scanpath by analysing the individual scanpaths, the trending scanpath should be similar to the individual scanpaths as much as possible. Unless all the users follow exactly the same path, a 100% similarity to the individual scanpaths cannot be achieved. Furthermore, when the individual scanpaths are entirely different from each other, such as ABC, DEF and GHI no trending scanpath can be identified. Hence, the similarities between the trending scanpath and the individual scanpaths are strongly associated with the similarities between the individual scanpaths. Table 10 shows the minimum similarities between the individual scanpaths in the test cases. Based on Tables 2, 3, 6 and 7, we can suggest that the median similarity of the trending scanpaths to the individual scanpaths are greater than the minimum similarity between the individual scanpaths in the most of the cases (VIPS: 9 out of 12 cases, BOM: 8 out of 12 cases).

Table 10: The minimum similarities between the individual scanpaths

Segmentation Approach	Page	Browsing Task	Searching Task
VIPS	Apple	10.20	19.54
	Babylon	3.33	11.11
	AVG	10.00	12.50
	Yahoo	17.65	9.33
	Godaddy	8.70	13.89
	BBC	10.00	14.89
BOM	Apple	21.74	18.33
	Babylon	9.62	9.46
	AVG	12.50	16.07
	Yahoo	15.38	10.61
	Godaddy	18.18	20.00
	BBC	3.33	8.33

Since there is a limited number of segmentation approaches with a publicly available implementation, we could only investigate the effect of two different segmentation approaches on the STA algorithm in this paper [26]. When there is another segmentation approach available with its public imple-

mentation, the same methodology can be applied to investigate its effect on the STA algorithm. However, based on the results presented in this paper, we can suggest that the STA algorithm is likely to provide the most representative scanpath in comparison with other segmentation approaches as it also considers the visual elements which are not shared by all users but get at least the same attention as the shared elements.

A new eye tracking study was conducted to investigate the effects of two segmentation approaches on the STA algorithm. This allowed us to re-evaluate the STA algorithm with the VIPS approach by using different users as we had already evaluated the algorithm with the VIPS approach in our previous work [10]. Although the age distribution of our participants was concentrated in the range of 18 and 34 (See Section 4), all of the participants were daily web users (apart from one participant) and they had different educational backgrounds (such as, computer engineering, civil engineering, psychology and business administration). Therefore, we believe that they are an indicator for other web users. Based on the results, we can suggest that the STA algorithm is able to provide the most representative scanpath regardless of the users included. The validity of the STA algorithm could also be tested with a completely different eye tracking dataset with different user groups (such as, older users). In particular, we could test whether the validity of the STA algorithm is limited to specific web pages. For example, a search engine can be included in the evaluation process. However, since the focus of the algorithm is not the contents of the web pages, we believe that the validity of the STA algorithm is not significantly affected by the selection of the web pages. By testing the STA algorithm with a different dataset, however, would allow to generalise the validity of the algorithm.

The STA algorithm is designed to cluster multiple scanpaths into a single representative scanpath. However, there may be some users who use different strategies while they are interacting with web pages. In such cases, the user scanpaths can firstly be categorised into multiple groups where the similar scanpaths are located in the same group, and then the trending scanpath for each group can be computed by using the STA algorithm.

The STA algorithm can be used to improve user experience in constrained environments by guiding web page transcoding (see Section 1). Since the algorithm highlights the most commonly fixated elements in order, the firstly and mostly fixated elements can be accessed earlier in the transcoded version. This allows to avoid spending unnecessary time to find targets. The algorithm also contributes to usability studies, for example, it can used for identifying whether or not users use an expected path for a specific goal. The STA algorithm can also be used in different fields. For example, it can be used in Information Retrieval (IR) research to identify which parts of web pages have higher priority to be shown to users. It can also contribute to Web advertising by guiding to position advertisements on web pages to attract attention of users when they visit the pages.

8. CONCLUSIONS

Eye tracking provides insights into how users interact with web pages. Hence, it helps to identify problems and improve user experience on the Web. In our previous work, we developed the STA algorithm which analyses multiple scanpaths on a web page and identifies the most commonly followed path in terms of the visual elements of the web page [10]. Although we validated the STA algorithm by using an eye tracking study, we did not know whether the validity of the algorithm could be affected by the segmentation approach used. This paper presents the investigation of the effect of two segmentation approaches on the STA algorithm and illustrates that the validity of the algorithm is not limited to a particular segmentation approach.

UX researchers may prefer to analyse user scanpaths by using different types of segmentations for their studies, and therefore a scanpath analysis algorithm should not be restricted to a particular segmentation approach. Based on our experimental results, we can suggest them to use the STA algorithm if they want to identify a trending scanpath on a particular page.

Open Data

The eye tracking study materials (the information sheet, consent form, questionnaire and web pages with their visual elements) are provided in our external repository (http://iam-data.cs.manchester.ac.uk/data_files/24). The repository also involves the individual scanpaths in terms of the visual elements of the web pages. The resulting scanpaths of the STA algorithm and other existing algorithms are also provided with their similarities to the individual scanpaths.

9. REFERENCES

[1] E. Akpınar and Y. Yeşilada. "Old Habits Die Hard!": Eyetracking Based Experiential Transcoding: A Study with Mobile Users. In *Proceedings of the 12th Web for All Conference*, W4A '15, pages 12:1–12:5, New York, NY, USA, 2015. ACM.

[2] M. E. Akpınar and Y. Yeşilada. Vision Based Page Segmentation Algorithm: Extended and Perceived Success. In Q. Z. Sheng and J. Kjeldskov, editors, *Current Trends in Web Engineering - ICWE 2013 Workshops and PhD Symposium.*, volume 8295 of *Lecture Notes in Computer Science*, pages 238–252. Springer, 2013.

[3] A. Brown, C. Jay, and S. Harper. Audio access to calendars. In *W4A '10: Proceedings of the 2010 International Cross Disciplinary Conference on Web Accessibility (W4A)*, pages 1–10, New York, NY, USA, 2010. ACM.

[4] M. Burmester and M. Mast. Repeated Web Page Visits and the Scanpath Theory: A Recurrent Pattern Detection Approach. *Journal of Eye Movement Research*, 3(4):1–20, 2010.

[5] J. Cohen. *Statistical power analysis for the behavioral sciences*. Hillsdale, NJ: Erlbaum, 1988.

[6] C. Ehmke and S. Wilson. Identifying Web Usability Problems from Eye-tracking Data. In *Proceedings of the 21st British HCI Group Annual Conference on People and Computers: HCI... but not as we know it*, volume 1 of *BCS-HCI '07*, pages 119–128, Swinton, UK, 2007. British Computer Society.

[7] S. Eraslan and Y. Yesilada. Patterns in Eyetracking Scanpaths and the Affecting Factors. *Journal of Web Engineering - Special Issue on "Engineering the Web for users, developers and the crowd"*, 14(4&5):363–385, 2015.

[8] S. Eraslan, Y. Yesilada, and S. Harper. Identifying Patterns in Eyetracking Scanpaths in Terms of Visual Elements of Web Pages. In S. Casteleyn, G. Rossi, and M. Winckler, editors, *Web Engineering*, volume 8541 of *Lecture Notes in Computer Science*, pages 163–180. Springer International Publishing, 2014.

[9] S. Eraslan, Y. Yesilada, and S. Harper. Eye Tracking Scanpath Analysis Techniques on Web Pages: A Survey, Evaluation and Comparison. *Journal of Eye Movement Research*, 9(1:2):1–19, 2016.

[10] S. Eraslan, Y. Yesilada, and S. Harper. Scanpath Trend Analysis on Web Pages: Clustering Eye Tracking Scanpaths. *ACM Transactions on the Web (Accept subject to minor revisions)*, -:-, 2016.

[11] B. Follet, O. L. Meur, and T. Baccino. New insights into ambient and focal visual fixations using an automatic classification algorithm. *iPerception: Open-access journal of human, animal, and machine perception*, 2(6):592–610, 2011.

[12] P. Fournier-Viger, A. Gomariz, T. Gueniche, A. Soltani, C.-W. Wu, and V. S. Tseng. SPMF: a Java Open-Source Pattern Mining Library. *Journal of Machine Learning Research (JMLR)*, 15:3389–3393, 2014.

[13] J. H. Goldberg and J. I. Helfman. Scanpath Clustering and Aggregation. In *Proceedings of the 2010 Symposium on Eye Tracking Research & Applications*, ETRA '10, pages 227–234, New York, NY, USA, 2010. ACM.

[14] P. Hejmady and N. H. Narayanan. Visual attention patterns during program debugging with an ide. In *Proceedings of the 2012 Symposium on Eye Tracking Research & Applications*, ETRA '12, pages 197–200, New York, NY, USA, 2012. ACM.

[15] S. Josephson. Using Eye Tracking to See How Viewers Process Visual Information in Cyberspace. In S. Josephson, S. B. Barnes, and M. Lipton, editors, *Visualizing the Web: Evaluating Online Design from a Visual Communication Perspective*, volume 1, chapter 5, pages 99–122. Peter Lang Publishing Inc., New York, 2010.

[16] S. Josephson and M. E. Holmes. Visual Attention to Repeated Internet Images: Testing the Scanpath Theory on the World Wide Web. In *Proceedings of the 2002 Symposium on Eye Tracking Research & Applications*, ETRA '02, pages 43–49, New York, NY, USA, 2002. ACM.

[17] M. Mast and M. Burmester. Exposing Repetitive Scanning in Eye Movement Sequences with T-pattern Detection. In *Proceedings IADIS International conference interfaces and human computer interaction (IHCI)*, pages 137–145, Rome, Italy, 2011.

[18] M. A. Napierala. What is the bonferroni correction? *AAOS Now - American Academy of Orthopaedic Surgeons*, April:1–3, 2012.

[19] J. Pallant. *SPSS Survival Manual: A Step By Step Guide to Data Analysis Using SPSS version 15*. Maidenhead: Open University Press/McGraw-Hill, 4th edition edition, 2007.

[20] A. Sanoja and S. Gançarski. Block-o-Matic: a Web

Page Segmentation Tool and its Evaluation. In *29ème journées "Base de données avancées", BDA'13, Oct 2013*, Nantes, France, 2013. <hal-00881693>.

[21] A. Sanoja and S. Gançarski. Block-o-Matic: A web page segmentation framework. In *Multimedia Computing and Systems (ICMCS), 2014 International Conference on*, pages 595–600, April 2014.

[22] H. Takeuchi and Y. Habuchi. A Quantitative Method for Analyzing Scan Path Data Obtained by Eye Tracker. In *Computational Intelligence and Data Mining, 2007. CIDM 2007. IEEE Symposium on*, pages 283 –286, 1 2007-april 5 2007.

[23] G. Underwood, K. Humphrey, and T. Foulsham. Knowledge-Based Patterns of Remembering: Eye Movement Scanpaths Reflect Domain Experience. In A. Holzinger, editor, *HCI and Usability for Education and Work*, volume 5298 of *Lecture Notes in Computer Science*, pages 125–144. Springer Berlin Heidelberg, 2008.

[24] B. M. Velichkovsky, A. Rothert, M. Kopf, S. M. Dornhöfer, and M. Joos. Towards an express-diagnostics for level of processing and hazard perception. *Transportation Research Part F: Traffic Psychology and Behaviour*, 5(2):145 – 156, 2002.

[25] J. M. West, A. R. Haake, E. P. Rozanski, and K. S. Karn. eyePatterns: Software for Identifying Patterns and Similarities Across Fixation Sequences. In *Proceedings of the 2006 Symposium on Eye Tracking Research & Applications*, ETRA '06, pages 149–154, New York, NY, USA, 2006. ACM.

[26] Y. Yesilada. Web Page Segmentation: A Review. Technical report, Middle East Technical University, March 2011.

[27] Y. Yesilada, S. Harper, and S. Eraslan. Experiential transcoding: An EyeTracking approach. In *Proceedings of the 10th International Cross-Disciplinary Conference on Web Accessibility*, page 30. ACM, 2013.

Seven Words You Can't Say on Answerbag: Contested Terms and Conflict in a Social Q&A Community

Rich Gazan
University of Hawaii
2550 McCarthy Mall, HL 2A
Honolulu, HI 96822
gazan@hawaii.edu

ABSTRACT

On a social Q&A site with thousands of transactions per day, what constitutes inappropriate content is not always obvious. In virtual communities such as this, users largely define and continuously renegotiate what constitutes appropriate participation, and moderators must allow healthy debate while curbing conflict. This paper presents an empirical analysis of Answerbag, a social Q&A site where moderators combined content analysis and transaction log analysis with information retrieval principles to identify non-obvious words associated with reported and unreported instances of conflict on the site. Content and transaction log analysis revealed the processes by which Answerbag users negotiated the meaning of contested terms, and suggested instances when conflict was a positive force for the community.

Keywords
Online communities; Community Q&A; Community management; Boundary objects.

1. INTRODUCTION

This paper's title is adapted from George Carlin's monologue "Seven Words You Can Never Say on Television," [1] in which he questioned why seven widely used profanities were essentially unspeakable in certain public situations. After a performance of the monologue in Milwaukee, Carlin was arrested for disturbing the peace, and an unedited radio broadcast of the routine by station W3AI-FM in New York City led to a listener complaint and a series of legal actions, culminating in the 1978 US Supreme Court ruling that government can censor "indecent" material on public broadcasts. The goal of this paper is to unpack how members of an online community negotiated and renegotiated the meaning of words and their appropriateness in changing contexts, and how moderators of a high-traffic social Q&A site attempted to identify these areas of conflict in parallel with user reports.

Social Q&A sites such as Yahoo Answers [2] and Quora [3] offer some of the same affordances as social networking sites, such as the ability to friend or follow certain topics or users, to "like" or "favorite" content, and to curate profile pages of their past contributions. Through these affordances, individuals and groups can support and promote what they feel is appropriate behavior

and contributions, and publicly question, downrate or disparage content and actions they feel are inappropriate. Areas of the site where these negotiations occur are critical to identify, both for moderators to intervene if discussion degenerates into personal attack, but more importantly to identify points where diverse ideas converge, and the community evolves.

Relying solely on user reports of inappropriate content in a high-traffic environment presents several problems. Wrongly reported content consumes scarce moderator resources. Unreported conflict can fester on the site, and following the "broken window" theory [4], can yield the impression of an undermoderated site where personal attacks go unpunished, or worse, are selectively punished based on moderator whim, increasing the likelihood of more misbehavior. Guiding the few site moderators to areas of the site where conflict or other inappropriate behavior is brewing requires a quick, near-real-time organization of user-generated content into appropriate and possibly inappropriate content, the latter with a fairly high level of confidence to warrant moderator attention.

This participant observation describes how moderation staff at the Answerbag social Q&A site attempted to design an algorithm to detect unreported conflict instances following a site redesign that led to large-scale user conflict [5]. The author supervised paid and volunteer moderators, and had access to their reports and site transaction logs. Content analysis reveals some of the processes by which users debated the meaning of contested words, reshaped community norms, and helped moderators rethink their definition of conflict.

2. BACKGROUND

Online communities are as diverse as the theories and methods used to study them [6]. Lampe et al. [7] studied user motivation for online community participation through the lens of both uses and gratifications theory [8] and organizational commitment theory [9], and found that social and cognitive factors such as a sense of belonging, connection and importance to the community are more important than site usability in predicting long-term participation and continued contribution. Similarly, Jin et al. [10] employed theories of social capital, social exchange and social cognition, and found that user self-presentation and peer recognition were associated with continued participation and contribution.

2.1 Social Q&A

Describing a social Q&A site, where people, ask, answer and rate content while interacting around it [11], as an online community is not accidental. While some Q&A sites are designed around anonymous, fact-based interactions, social Q&A sites allow or require users to create an online identity and user profile, where their past contributions can be browsed by others as a means to identify the trustworthiness of the individual contributor.

The importance of social factors found in online community research more generally has also been observed in social Q&A sites. Raban and Harper [12] found evidence that extrinsic factors such as ratings and social recognition motivated user participation, and intrinsic motivations such as pride in content ownership—distinct from the quality of that content—and altruism were important as well. Designing in affordances to support and encourage these kinds of social interactions yielded social Q&A sites where conversations around content became arguably more important to users than the content itself, even in topic areas where accuracy is paramount, such as health information [13, 14].

2.2 Theoretical framework

The literature of online communities mapped prior research on social processes into the online environment to understand why people would be motivated to contribute and participate. In response to decades of literature in library and information science conceptualizing information seeking in terms of one-to-one, patron-to-librarian reference transactions, Shachaf [15] proposes an input-process-output theoretical framework for information seeking via social Q&A and related services. Her framework for understanding, analyzing, and evaluating social reference includes (a) answer quality, (b) user satisfaction, (c) service viability, and (d) a digital repository. While the majority of social Q&A research has focused on answer quality, and to a lesser extent user satisfaction [11], the viability of the social Q&A service and the community surrounding it have been studied far less often. According to Shachaf, viability is measured primarily through continued participation, but an impediment has been the scarcity of researcher access to backend user data, which tends to be proprietary [16]. This study utilizes backend data from Answerbag, the first social Q&A site in the US, and is conducted as a participant observation, with access to both user and moderator transaction data, to investigate user behavior surrounding potential instances of conflict.

Just as in physical communities, members of online communities are invested in their identities, support their friends, and take ownership of the community by legitimate participation as they define it, all of which can result in conflict. Savolainen [17] adapted the theoretical model of argumentation developed by Toulmin [18] to the Yahoo! Answers social Q&A site, and found that 24% of Q&A contained oppositional or mixed argument patterns, and only 2% of the grounds used in argumentation were emotive appeals such as ad hominem attacks, the level of conflict where moderator review would be appropriate.

2.3 Q&A retrieval and classification

The goal of any information retrieval system is to match query representations with document representations. How documents and queries should be best represented for optimal retrieval has been the subject of decades of research, but at its core, the problem is little changed from the days of the earliest information retrieval experiments [19, 20]. The relevance of a document to a query has been operationalized along two major dimensions: the query term must be common within a document (term frequency), but rare across the collection (inverse document frequency). While the relevance of a given document to a given query is highly contextual [21, 22, 23], and information retrieval is best understood as a probabilistic endeavor, the core challenge is to identify which words across all documents in a collection, or pages on a Website, best represent the content.

Initial information retrieval models reflected the technological realities of their day, assuming a relatively static database, updated in occasional batches, and searched only by professionals as intermediaries for user requests. The rise of networked computing made it possible for users to search collections directly, and was quickly followed by Web 2.0 models of user generated content, then social computing models where users could rate, comment and interact around that content. These new affordances necessitated the creation of new models of social information seeking and retrieval.

Harper, Moy and Konstan [24] developed algorithms to distinguish informational and conversational questions on three social Q&A sites: Yahoo Answers, Answerbag and Ask Metafilter, positing that conversational questions were likely to be more ephemeral, and less relevant for future retrieval. Liu and Jansen [25] implemented and evaluated several classification algorithms for social Q&A along similar lines, based on question subjectivity vs. objectivity, and found fundamental differences in response time and respondent characteristics between the two question types. Similarly, Mendes Rodrigues and Milic-Frayling [26] integrated content analysis and network analysis in their study of the MSN QnA community, and proposed a typology of Q&A user intent, first suggesting a broad typology of social vs. non-social question types, and develop measures of engagement to quantify user participation. They developed a metric of user behavior summarized by a "social score" (p. 1136) designed to be used in parallel with social network analysis metrics, and suggest that future research focus on more fine-grained sense of user intent within the broader categories of social and non-social questions.

However, with the volume and diversity of users and interactions in social Q&A communities, more fine-grained analyses of content types and features have not yet demonstrated reliable predictive power. Burel et al. [27] investigated question selection behavior in the Stack Exchange community, and identified 17 user features (e.g. overall reputation, reputation within a topic, number of answers, etc.), 23 question features (e.g. question age, number of words) and 22 thread features (aggregate of question features with response age normalized) and gauged their relative ability to predict the questions a given user would choose to select based on their history. While they found weak predictive power in question age (newer questions tended to be selected more often), their best results were achieved by combining all the features, indicating that online question answering and the communities around them tend to defy easy distillation into a few relevant features.

Various forms of term analysis have been used to identify undiscovered content in Q&A sites. Yamamoto et al. [28] analyzed a sample word corpus from the Yahoo! Answers and Baidu Zhihao Q&A sites, to present users with adjective facets of noun keywords, allowing them to more easily recognize content of interest, without having to depend on a fortunate choice of query terms.

2.4 Boundary objects

Star and Griesemer conceptualize a boundary object as one that is part of multiple social worlds and facilitates communication between them; it has a different identity in each social world that it inhabits [29].

While boundary objects were initially conceived as tangible items, they are embedded in the context of their social worlds, and in subsequent research the concept has been expanded to include boundary infrastructures [30, 31], and boundary clusters [32], among many others. In a virtual community, where participants share no tangible objects, contested terms may fit the definition of a boundary object as an abstract concept or "ideal type" [29]. Star and Griesemer envisioned boundary objects as the means by which otherwise untenable conflicts between diverse groups might be negotiated; if so, moderators who misinterpret intergroup communication and negotiation around these terms as conflict detrimental to the site, and intervene by removing content, may cause unintentional harm to the community. On the other hand, visibly moderated online communities have been associated with higher information quality [33], and are more self-sustaining [34].

This brief literature review demonstrates that social Q&A sites share some of the same user dynamics that have been observed within online communities more generally, that social factors tend to outweigh content factors when attempting to explain continued user participation, and that analysis of transaction logs and words associated with negotiation and conflict can be productive avenues for research.

3. SETTING
Answerbag was the first social Q&A site in the US. Launched in July 2003, it was initially conceived as a site exclusively for factual Q&A. Its one question—multiple answers architecture acted as a user-generated recommender system, where the answers previous users had rated most helpful were listed first, but all answers were available by scrolling down the page. For its first few years of existence, Answerbag was 100% moderated—every piece of content submitted to the site would go to a moderator for approval, and even errors of spelling and grammar would be corrected. However, as the site grew and social submissions were accepted and quickly overwhelmed factual content, that level of review became impossible, and moderation became crowdsourced.

Registered users could report content they felt was inappropriate via several channels, most commonly via the flag feature. Alongside every Answerbag question, answer or comment was a link labeled "Report," which routed the content for moderator review. Users indicated whether they felt the content was spam, offensive, miscategorized, nonsense or otherwise inappropriate, though all flagged content appended to the same review queue. Users could also email the 2-3 site moderators, part-time contractors who review flagged content, or send private messages to community leaders, a group of 5-7 volunteer members with limited moderation powers. These few individuals constituted the entire moderation staff during November 2009-February 2010, the period under study.

This particular period was selected because it surrounded a December 2009 major site redesign that led to large-scale conflict and the migration of longtime users to other Q&A sites [5], which directly affected Answerbag's viability. After roughly three years of increasing traffic and a relatively stable interface, Answerbag was redesigned by Demand Media, its new owners. The goals were to update the look and feel of the site, create more monetizable ad space, and to add new forms of interaction such as polls and debates. The relaunched site was immediately plagued by malfunctions that limited user interactions, but even when the site functions stabilized, there were far more reports of conflict on the site than the few moderators could investigate.

At this time, the Answerbag database contained approximately 3 million questions, 11 million answers, and drew in excess of 9 million unique visitors per month. The total number of registered users exceeded 200,000, with roughly 5,000 actively posting a combination of factual, conversational and sometimes unclassifiable content each day. The daily volume of flags ranged from approximately 50-150 per day, not including reports via e-mail, IM and other channels. With roughly 15,000 content transactions per day, less than 1% of the content submitted to Answerbag was flagged for review.

Prior to the redesign, roughly a third of user-reported flags were for obvious spam content posted by humans or bots, and quickly acted upon. Another third were submitted by users reporting miscategorized questions and suggesting a more appropriate category, which Answerbag encouraged by awarding points for each accepted flag, and was another low-effort review task for moderators. However, the remaining third focused on reports of conflict between users. These flags required significant moderator time to investigate, since they often occurred across multiple questions and threads. When accusations of coordinated user attacks were lodged, activity histories and IP logs had to be consulted. Since the value and long-term viability of the site relies on preserving a shared sense of appropriate behavior, these moderator efforts were viewed as a worthwhile expenditure of time, and they often uncovered evidence of worse transgressions than those that had been initially flagged. Similarly, some users who had content removed would find evidence of similar content on the site that was clearly against site policy, but which had not been reported. Strongly negative user reactions to the redesigned site, and the factionalism that followed, tended to amplify these issues, and resulted in more flags of all types. Moderators were swamped.

Several methods were attempted prior to the approach reported here, with little success. An approach focused on sudden pageview increases succeeded primarily in identifying popular topics; traffic spikes often indicate a comment thread where users went completely off topic and had an apparently enjoyable improvisational conversation, but in the vast majority of cases users interacted appropriately within these threads. Some pages where users had posted spam content and directed traffic to it via external links were also identified, but those were already being reported through the regular flag function. Another attempt posited that longtime members were most likely to engage in conflict, but creating a report listing the content around which high-ranking users were contributing succeeded only in duplicating the buzz or "hot topics" algorithm. Not surprisingly, experienced users interacted around a large volume of content, so the report was anything but a time saver for moderators trying to identify unreported inappropriate content.

A solution was needed to supplement user reports of inappropriate content with a way to detect unreported conflict instances, with very limited moderator resources, ideally with the side benefit of learning more about the roots of the conflicts, both of which motivated this study.

The research questions guiding this study are:

- **Which content-bearing terms are associated with instances of reported conflict on this site?**
- **What is the nature of the conflict?**

- To what extent can those content-bearing terms reveal unreported conflicts elsewhere on the site?

4. METHOD

This study is part of a long-term participant observation, and access to the Answerbag Q&A database backend, moderator reports and transaction logs are available. For the purposes of this study, the unit of analysis is a question posted to Answerbag, including all subsequent answers and answer comments, any of which may be reported as a potential instance of conflict. The number and length of answers and comments appended to a given question is highly variable, but since term frequency analysis depends on wordstock quantity, Q&A threads were not normalized for length. Additionally, users may copy and paste content from other sources, and include links, images and embedded video, and threads sometimes diverge from the original topic of the question or answer.

4.1 Operationalizing conflict

Following Shachaf [15], for the purposes of this study, conflict is operationalized as behavior that directly or indirectly threatens the viability of the site. This may include behavior that creates a negative environment for current and future users, diluting the quality of the content and the experience of the site, and diminishes user participation. Differences of opinion, from a single negative comment to a long thread of argument, usually do not meet this standard; indeed, conversations such as these are one of the attractions of social Q&A sites. However, when users attack, stalk or otherwise harass other users, that can not only dissuade continued participation of the participants, but of future visitors who may find the site via a search engine referral, browse through several screens of conflict and click away, never to return. Indicators of conflict in this study include:

- Personal attacks
- Reposting moderator-removed content
- Profanity (including euphemisms) directed at a user or group
- Posting links/screenshots of past conflicts
- Posting attacks on all posts by a particular user
- Vindictively or frivolously flagging content
- Creating multiple accounts to continue/escalate conflict
- Participating in/orchestrating coordinated attacks

Both user-reported flags and the unreported conflict instances discovered in this study were analyzed through these indicators. Elements such as vindictive flagging and creating multiple accounts were identified via transaction logs, and more interpretive indicators such as personal attacks were evaluated via content analysis. Content demonstrating at least one of the above indicators was coded as an instance of conflict.

4.2 Process

Step 1: Harvest wordstock. Content flagged for review as inappropriate by at least two users or moderators from November 2009 through February 2010 was collected. This yielded 2444 user-reported conflict instances connected to a question, answer or comment. Multiple user reports were sometimes connected to the same question; eliminating these duplicates yielded 1890 unique questions associated with user-reported conflict. All words were extracted into a spreadsheet for analysis.

Step 2: Remove non-content-bearing terms, conflate term variants. Stopwords and other terms common in reported conflict instances (e.g. profanity) were removed, since these terms do not help distinguish individual Q&A in a search, and are therefore non-content bearing. A modified Porter stemmer [35] is used to conflate word form variants, primarily via suffix stripping.

Step 3: Relevance rank the remaining terms. Following classical IR, identify the remaining terms which are common in certain instances of reported conflict (term frequency), but otherwise rare across the sample (inverse document frequency). This yields a list of content-bearing terms most highly associated with reported conflicts during the timeframe of the sample. The top seven resulting terms were associated with 880 reported conflict instances.

Step 4: Search content-bearing terms across the entire site. Limiting the expanded search to the timeframe of the sample yields a set of Q&A containing terms associated with reported conflict, but which were not reported.

Step 5: Content analysis of resulting Q&A to identify instances of unreported conflict. The content analysis is conducted as an inductive constant comparison [36, 37, 38]. Transaction logs are consulted to ground instances of suspected conflict, for example by flag history, login times and multiple accounts associated with the same IP address. These top seven terms were associated with an additional 585 questions containing unreported conflicts during the timeframe of the sample.

5. RESULTS AND ANALYSIS

The seven content-bearing terms closely associated with user-reported conflict are listed in ascending order of the ratio of reported conflicts to observed occurrences across the 4-month sample. Unreported conflicts are not included in the percentages, as they were collected and measured outside the original sample.

1. Spam (33.1%)
2. Sockpuppet (37.5%)
3. Troll (40.1%)
4. Bagicide (43.5%)
5. Glitch (47.3%)
6. Rejigger (54.6%)
7. Fluther (59.7%)

A discussion of the content and transaction log analysis around each of these seven terms follows. While the numerical data represents the raw count of observed term occurrences and reported and unreported conflict instances during the period under review, the number of users involved in these conflicts could not be determined with certainty, primarily due to the likelihood that some participants in the conflict used multiple accounts. In rough terms, 75% of the conflict-related reports were associated with unique user accounts, while the remaining 25% involved multiple posts or conflicts by the same user, or were cases where coordinated activity by multiple accounts was suspected.

For the qualitative analyses, both the moderators and the author interpreted the data through their day-to-day familiarity with the site and its users, sometimes incorporating data from past and subsequent interactions outside the sample collected for this study.

5.1 Spam

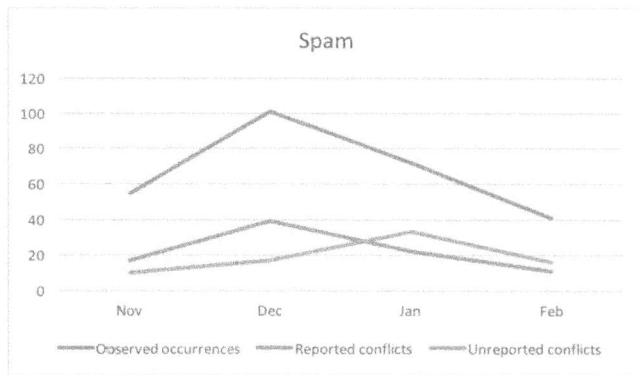

Figure 1. Spam occurrences and surrounding conflicts

The spam flag was conceived by Answerbag designers as a way for users to identify inappropriate ads that slipped through the spam monitoring services and filters used to intercept bot-generated spam attempts. Some would post spam links on random pages throughout the site, others would post spam content on Answerbag, using it as a de facto hosting service, and link to it from elsewhere on the Web. While the latter variety of spamming drove additional traffic to the site, it directly detracted from the site's viability, and Answerbag users caught and reported this activity via the spam flag.

Defining spam as an unwelcome ad is the most common interpretation of the term, but some Answerbag users stretched this definition to include repetitive and/or nonsensical content, leading to conflict over appropriate site usage.

Why is it that when a dingbat comes on and starts spamming with stupid questions one after another, that instead of letting them fade off the main page people keep answering them?

Another user stretched the term even further, to include people who post floods of questions, or who create multiple accounts (sockpuppets, discussed below).

A spammer is someone who posts excessive amounts of the same questions, or questions that are very similar. Or someone who opens up multiple accounts.

However, debate over this term also appeared to bring the community together in some instances, which was a comparatively positive outcome. Users posted examples of appropriate and inappropriate content, compared notes on when to flag a piece of content as spam, and even invoked legal and historical parallels:

Kinda like the Supreme Court ruling on pornography, I know it when I see it.

Figure 1 shows that the term had been associated with conflict prior to the redesign, rose during December along with most reported conflict, then quickly settled back to its previous levels, or slightly below. This may indicate that conflict over what constitutes spam may be relevant to community members under normal circumstances, but when a "force majeure" like a site redesign fragments the community, fewer individuals are concerned about the definition of spam.

5.2 Sockpuppet

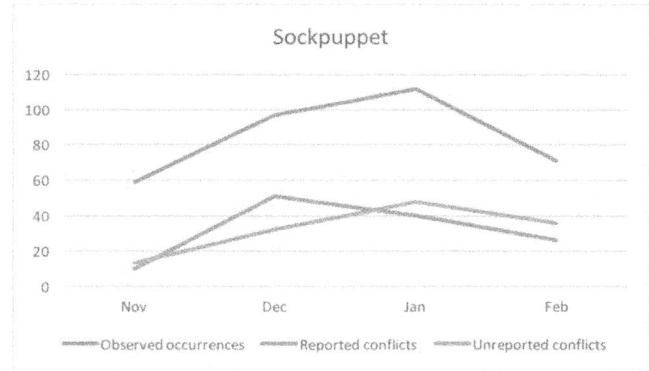

Figure 2. Sockpuppet occurrences and surrounding conflicts

Answerbag policy did not forbid users from creating sock puppets, i.e. alternate accounts on the site. Some users felt it was appropriate to be able to post different content under different accounts, as long as the accounts didn't interact, uprate one another or otherwise game the system. Other users, often those who saw their answers downrated or ridiculed by the same few users, felt certain that sockpuppet accounts were being created by their enemies and used vindictively, which was the source of much of the debate and conflict surrounding this term.

What in the name of Thor is a sock puppet? Is it like a troll?

Q: Is it morally wrong to create a sockpuppet account for the purpose of making you look good and boosting your points?

A: People can do whatever the hell they want, and while I don't find it "morally wrong" per se, I find it to be a pretty sad and pathetic way to boost one's popularity and further a mythos about oneself. No, it just makes you a cheater.

When you accuse someone of being a sock puppet, are you not accusing that person of being a liar, inauthentic, duplicitous and cowardly? If you go by any other name other than that which is yours, you are a coward. What do you think?

Several Answerbag accounts, most notably one using the handle DreAnna, were used to "catfish" other users, usually for expressions of sympathy at their claimed life circumstances. This led to suspicion that some new users were not who they claimed to be.

Besides "DreAnna," do you think there are more ABers among us who are creating elaborate false identities and playing sick games and scams on people here?

After the redesign, many longtime users publicly declared that they would never return to Answerbag via a variety of means: altering their usernames, deleting content from their user profiles, or posting farewell questions. However, examining IP logs revealed that many of these users did return under new accounts, and when a new user posted content others felt only an experienced user would know, conflict would erupt and moderators had to ban several accounts on both sides. Figure 2 shows that in the final two months of the sample, there were more unreported than reported conflict instances related to sockpuppets, indicating that users may have realized that reporting a potential sockpuppet account might not be worthwhile, if it resulted in the reporting user being penalized as well.

5.3 Troll

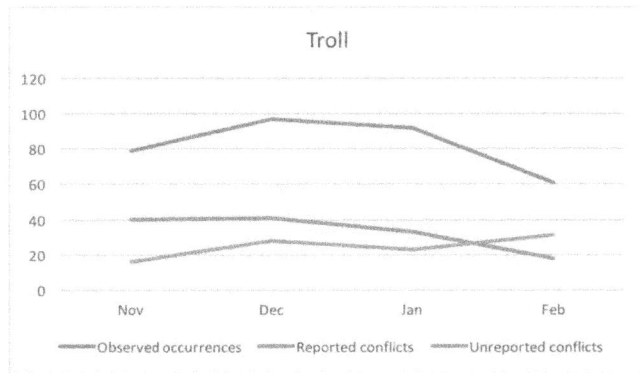

Figure 3. Troll occurrences and surrounding conflicts

In Web parlance, the understanding of trolling lies somewhere between harmless provocation, willful satire and antisocial online behavior, conducted for the "lulz" of generating expressions of frustration from others. The latter can indicate or lead to more serious online attacks such as stalking, bullying or harassment, though these go beyond the generally understood limits of trolling. Donath [39] views trolling as a game of identity deception, where a troll attempts to legitimize their message by first creating the impression that they are members of the community, giving their trolling actions more attention and/or impact. Herring et al. [40] detail the struggle of a feminist online forum to balance anti-trolling policies with freedom of expression, to preserve the online community as a safe space. Figure 3 shows that the term troll was common in conflict instances throughout the period under study, and that Answerbag users showed evidence of struggling with defining the same balance of acceptable and unacceptable conduct.

Conflict surrounding the term troll generally began with a public accusation of improper behavior on the part of another user, labeling it trolling. This would generally result in a redoubling of the behavior by the accused user, with counteraccusations of censorship. Friends and followers of people on both sides would follow their activity notifications into the fray, and thereby create an instance of conflict. Following Donath [39], Answerbag users who conflated trolling with simple disagreement (i.e. anyone who disagrees with me is a troll) tended to include an expression of their legitimacy as a member of the site, in terms of their time as a member, number of contributions or more general "us vs. them" statements.

> Alright, who is the immature troll who is going through ALL my questions and comments and down rating everything? What is your issue? Grow up please!

> How do you feel about short uninformative/uninteresting answers? Do you consider that troll behavior? Because they only want to cause us annoyance and trouble. They are ruining the nice and friendly environment of AB.

Others both claimed site legitimacy and moral high ground by claiming to be above such petty concerns such as points, further escalating the conflict.

> The points are good for creating trolling, vindictiveness, hatred and bigotry. The place would be much better without it. Give insignificant people a little tool of power like stupid points and look at what happens.

In earlier Answerbag iterations, users could rate answers as useful (100%), somewhat useful (75%), or incorrect/not useful (50%). A user's aggregate percentage would be available on their profile page, so other users could evaluate the answerer's history along with the content of their answers. Discussions comparing the current Answerbag implementation to prior versions often led to conversations involving "old-timers" who lamented the loss of a quantitative metric of trolling. Broader conversations took place ascribing increased inappropriate behavior to the loss of the percentage downrating functionality. Through content analysis, several examples of negotiation about the meaning of the term troll were discovered, contextualized by both links to examples of other posted content as well as more abstract discussions about the meaning of the term in other contexts.

> How low does a % need to be for a person to be called a troll? It's my own arbitrary number but my number would be 75%. I'd say anyone between 75% and 90% is a grouch, but perhaps not a troll.

5.4 Bagicide

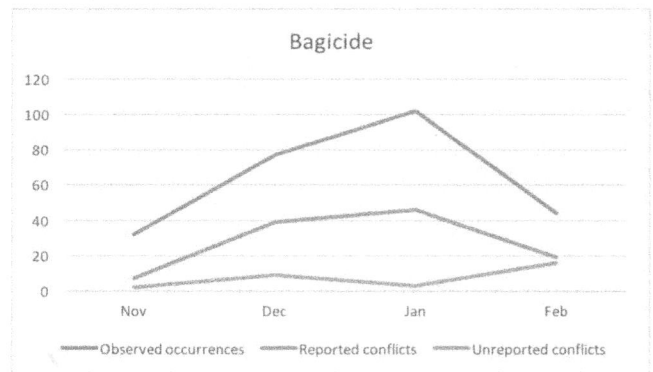

Figure 4. Bagicide occurrences and surrounding conflicts

Bagicide is a user-created portmanteau of Answerbag suicide. Though it generally refers to the act of abandoning or deactivating one's account, it is most often used before the fact, when a user publicly announces their intention to leave the site and request that all their content be deleted. Sometimes users plan to return with new accounts, other times they express disappointment with their experiences on the site and claim they will not return.

The conflicts surrounding the use of this term relate to the sense of a user's responsibility to the Answerbag community. Some view questions of this sort as unseemly attention seeking, and claim that those who propose it are fishing for responses along the lines of "Please don't go!" Others invoke the social responsibility of maintaining a consistent identity, and note that deleting one's content to the extent allowed by the site negatively affects existing discussions, and creates real harm.

> It's been asked before, but how do I do the "Bagicide" thing? I wish to start over as a beginner with no points.

> What would/does committing Bagicide ultimately achieve? Does it award freedom and release from the points obsession, or is it counter-productive in that it may give the impression that points others awarded you are meaningless or not appreciated?

> Drama. Puuuuke. Calls to mind the angsty teenager who commits/attempts suicide as a way of "punishing" their friends

and family for not treating them as they feel they should be treated. Narcissistic, selfish and melodramatic…

The question of whether Bagicide—or the threat of it—is appropriate site behavior is at issue when the term appears. Figure 4 shows that instances of conflict rose in December and January, when some users wished to remove all the content they had contributed as a form of protest in the wake of the redesign. It is notable that a high proportion of conflict instances were reported when this term was used, indicating that users felt that the threat of content removal was worth reporting to moderators. However, Answerbag users demonstrated the ability to have thoughtful and relatively harmonious discussions about Bagicide as well.

The best thing about Bagicide, IMHO, is that it sparks debate about ego and the importance of not allowing yourself to get caught up in points. Seems like a drastic step, though.

5.5 Glitch

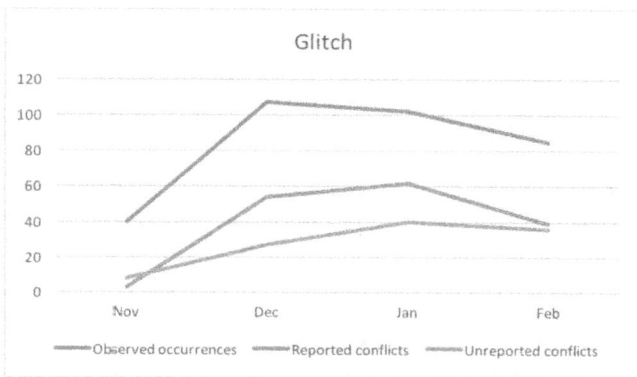

Figure 5. Glitch occurrences and surrounding conflicts

A glitch refers to a site malfunction. In the early days of Answerbag, prior to its sale to Demand Media, users would commonly report and help diagnose bugs and malfunctions, and email the site owner directly. That level of connection created a sense of shared endeavor and ownership, which site bugs arguably enhanced. But as the site grew, and gained the backing and technical resources of a large company, in the eyes of longtime users, malfunctions became less forgivable.

Figure 5 shows that the term "glitch" appeared in the Answerbag database prior to the redesign, but during the period studied here it greatly increased in frequency. Many instances were simply users collectively raging against the site maintainers, who were seen as incompetent and ungrateful. Conflicts occurred when the term became conflated with one's support of the site administrators.

Why didn't you take the hours you put into this "upgrade," fix what we asked nicely to be fixed and made it a better site? All you have done is put all this time into a site that has even more glitches and everyone hates.

Okay Answerbag. Now I am pissed. Why do you glitch me like this? I just tried to ask a long complicated question and it just plain ol' disappeared. You've got to be kidding me. I followed all steps correctly.

Even seemingly positive questions including the term glitch often branched into factionalism and conflict. Responders argued that glitches would never be fixed unless members made a collective

effort to reduce the site's traffic, and that the site owners had not earned such loyalty.

I have officially pronounced myself a glitch-bagger. I will not be happy until all the site glitches are fixed. But I will remain. Are you with me?

Some users attempted to respond with humor, posting questions that made light of the situation and recognized that users were all in this together.

Should there be The Glitch Awards? Categories like Least Frustrating Glitch or Likeliest Glitch to Result in the AB Headquarters Being Burned Down, etc.?

However, as these questions drew more and more responses, users who thought the community had been seriously damaged and disrespected by the site owners tended to "crash the party" on these lighter questions, accusing others of not taking the situation seriously enough, and creating conflict.

5.6 Rejigger

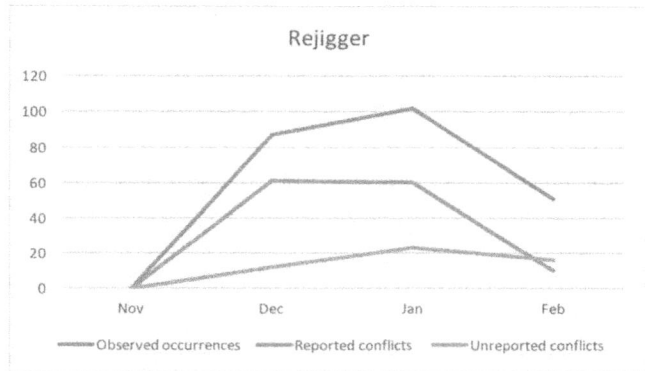

Figure 6. Rejigger occurrences and surrounding conflicts

Part of the 2009 redesign attempted to address the cumulative advantage problem, and establish more equity in points opportunity. The initial points structure allowed users to earn the right to give or take away as much as six points per answer by accumulating positive ratings of their content from other users, while new users could give or take away only one point per answer. Longtime users with large networks of similarly high-ranking friends also had the advantage of the notification function—their friends would receive a notification anytime they posted content, making their posts far more likely to receive large numbers of uprates from large numbers of other high-ranking users, often regardless of the relative quality of their posts. Also, some users had accumulated points by flagging content for removal or recategorization, and had discovered that it was far easier to earn points by clicking once on someone else's content than generating their own. Moderators reported that certain users would submit hundreds of flags in a single session and rise in level while contributing no content.

To address this situation, the redesign included altering the rating structure to more closely resemble that of Facebook—all users regardless of level or experience could bestow one like to a given piece of content. Downrates were seen as the seeds of much site conflict, and eliminated entirely. Importantly, the points users had accumulated under the previous rating scheme would be retroactively converted to the new system using an algorithm that emphasized content contributions and de-emphasized content flagging, but this was not disclosed to users. The new rating system was announced on the site blog by a Demand Media employee, who described the change as "rejiggering" the points structure. Despite assurances that longtime users would not be penalized under the new system, some were.

As Figure 6 shows, the term rejiggering and its variants had not appeared on the site before, but it immediately became code for an unfair rule change, or a too-breezy description of a serious situation. Some new users expressed support for the changes, while some experienced users felt betrayed. The most strident conflicts occurred between experienced users who accused each other of caring too much about points and leaderboard position, the other side took the position that administrators had disrespected the contributors by changing the rules with no consultation or notice.

Q. How long does it take to rejigger points, and how did they get jiggered to start with?

A. You say that nobody has lost a level or anything. As far as I am concerned that is a kick in the guts and a total insult. Especially since the people you put ahead of me have run off to other sites. Maybe it is a ploy to get them back. I was an Illuminati ranked Number 1 with 690+ thousand points and you have screwed me with your lies and promises.

Did Umar Farouk Abdulmutallab attempt to "rejigger" the plane?

The so-called "rejiggering" is, IMO, somehow inequitable and afowl...and certainly has not appropriately rewarded all the work that I, and others, put [in].

In the immediate aftermath of the redesign, one of the few working site functions was the ability for users to change their usernames. Doing so made the new name append to every piece of content the user had ever posted on the site, and some users made it an avenue of protest, generating user-specific conflict appearing across multiple questions, answers and comment, as revealed by transaction logs:

Rejiggering a Fat Baby's Ass (Answerbag member profile)

5.7 Fluther

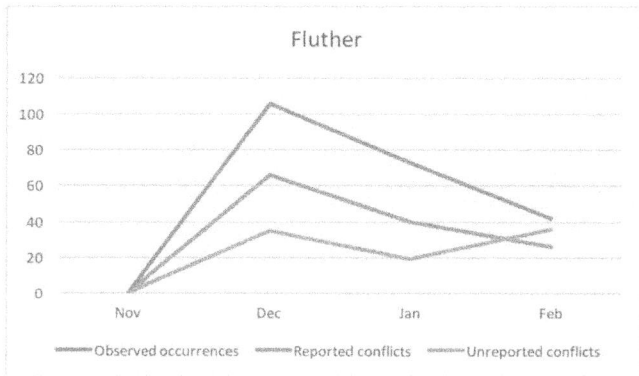

Figure 7. Fluther occurrences and surrounding conflicts

Fluther [41] is another social Q&A site. In the immediate aftermath of the redesign, when communication among users was limited by the site-wide malfunctioning of several new features, some users leveraged their offline connections to notify their friends to migrate to other Q&A sites, Fluther among them.

Figure 7 shows that the term Fluther had not appeared in the Answerbag database before, but its usage spiked in December 2009 and January 2010, and was the term most strongly associated with reported and unreported conflict in this study. Some users felt that it was disloyal to abandon Answerbag for another site, while others argued passionately that implementing a broken site and cutting off people's communication had to be met with a strong collective response.

Some users attempted to start conversations about the plans of other users, but including the phrase "abandoned ship" in this example was viewed as an unwarranted attack, leading to conflict.

Looks like about 80 plus people have abandoned ship and are at Fluther. Are you staying on AB?

In a high percentage of these conflict instances, the cleavage of the community was apparent.

What do you think of all the people who went to Fluther? Apparently there is a Flutherite here who is saying that the flood of ABers to Fluther is rude and disruptive.

Many are using Fluther now and just watching AB fall the hell apart!

I am transitioning from AB to Fluther now. I am going all over AB cussing out and being a bitch to people talking sh-t about people leaving.

I was stunned, shocked and amazed. Not that so many of them chose to leave but that so many of them chose to leave after flinging insults at those of us who chose to stay.

Later in the period studied here, conflict ebbed around the term Fluther, but some users returned with reports and reconnaissance of life in the other community, leading to renewed friction.

Fluther is too much a 'Nanny State' for me. You have to appease the Spanish Inquisition to get a question passed. I got fed up with it. AB will improve I have no doubt.

While some occurrences of the term were in the context of feature comparison rather than conflict between users, this was the term most strongly associated with instances of conflict. Also, Figure 7 shows that while reported conflict instances including the Fluther term fell between January and February, unreported instances rose. This may indicate that those who used the term did not feel that moderator review was effective or worthwhile.

6. CONCLUSION

Identifying conflict and contested terms in an online community is like classic information retrieval in reverse. Instead of users seeking the right terms to identify relevant site documents, the site is seeking the right terms to identify relevant user contributions.

This study addressed the question of whether content-bearing terms could be used to identify instances of conflict on the Answerbag social Q&A site. Returning to the research questions:

Which content-bearing terms are associated with instances of reported conflict on this site? The seven content-bearing terms most strongly associated with instances of reported conflict on Answerbag during the period under study were spam, sockpuppet, troll, bagicide, glitch, rejigger and fluther.

What is the nature of the conflict? Though both the terms and the conflicts tended to be centered around the redesign of the site, the four-month timeframe of the sample also revealed that some terms such as spam and troll were being discussed by the community both before and after the redesign, and that other terms rose and fell in frequency and conflict association as the community acclimated to a particular usage or interpretation, or simply moved on to other things. In other instances, apparent conflict led to positive discussion and negotiation about the meaning of contested terms, and appropriate site behavior.

To what extent can those content-bearing terms reveal unreported conflicts elsewhere on the site? Analyzing content-bearing word occurrences in reported conflict instances and searching them across the entire site yielded additional unreported conflict instances associated with those words in every case. In five of the seven cases, unreported conflicts outnumbered reported conflicts, with a general trend toward fewer reported and more unreported conflicts for the same terms over the duration of the sample.

Analyzing unreported conflicts with content and transaction log analysis revealed users' changing views of appropriate behavior in this online community. By identifying and searching content-bearing terms in this manner, moderators who would normally have to review every user-reported conflict could instead analyze the reported content, extract content-bearing terms, and review those items first, whether reported or not. In this study, the results suggest that by searching these content-bearing terms, moderators could identify conflict instances with 33.1% to 59.7% confidence, allowing them to prioritize reviewing these situations, where community is both created and fragmented.

Beyond managing conflict, this method also shows promise as a way to identify conversations and negotiations around contested terms, perhaps as boundary objects. How community members define appropriate behavior should be of interest to members, moderators and administrators alike in every online community, and future research might attempt to trace a word's introduction, through the negotiation of meaning, and perhaps identify patterns common across online communities.

6.1 Epilogue

On December 15, 2015, Answerbag users who tried to access the site were greeted with a terse message:

> *Answerbag is no longer available. Thank you for your patronage.*

Demand Media, the site owner, did not provide any further explanation. Several days later, the message was replaced by a notice that the domain name was for sale. At this writing, none of the content from the twelve years of the community's existence can be accessed.

However, the viability of the community remains. As they have done before, users connected with one another through alternate means in the wake of the shutdown, and migrated to several new Q&A sites. One of these, Answermug [42], is run by a former Answerbag member.

7. ACKNOWLEDGMENTS

I wish to thank Joel Downs for creating Answerbag and for providing access to its data. I would also like to thank the members of the erstwhile Answerbag community for their contributions and participation. It was a good run.

8. REFERENCES

[1] Carlin, G. 1972. Seven words you can never say on television. *Class Clown* (sound recording). Little David/Atlantic.

[2] Yahoo Answers. 2016. https://answers.yahoo.com/

[3] Quora. 2016. https://www.quora.com

[4] Wilson, G. L. and Kelling, J. Q. 1982. Broken windows: The police and neighborhood safety. *The Atlantic*. http://www.theatlantic.com/magazine/archive/1982/03/broken-windows/4465/

[5] Gazan, R. 2011. Redesign as an act of violence: Disrupted interaction patterns and the fragmenting of a social Q&A community. In *Proceedings of the SIGCHI Conference on Human Factors in Computing Systems* (Vancouver, Canada, May 07-12, 2011). CHI '11. ACM, New York, NY, 2847-56.

[6] Preece, J. and Maloney-Krichmar, D. 2005. Online communities: Design, theory, and practice. *Journal of Computer-Mediated Communication* 10, 4.

[7] Lampe, C., Wash, R., Velasquez, A., and Ozkaya, E. 2010. Motivations to participate in online communities. In *Proceedings of the SIGCHI Conference on Human Factors in Computing Systems* (Atlanta, GA, April 10-15, 2010) CHI '10 ACM, New York, NY, 1927–36.

[8] Ruggiero, T. E. 2009. Uses and gratifications theory in the 21st century. *Mass Communication & Society* 3, 1, 3-37.

[9] Allen, N. J. and Meyer, J. P. 1990. The measurement and antecedents of affective, continuance and normative commitment to the organization. *Journal of Occupational Psychology* 63, 1, 1-18.

[10] Jin, J., Li, Y., Zhong, X., and Zhai, L. 2015. Why users contribute knowledge to online communities: An empirical study of an online social Q&A community." *Information and Management* 52, 7, 840–49.

[11] Gazan, R. 2011. Social Q&A. *Journal of the American Society for Information Science and Technology* 62, 12, 2301-2312.

[12] Raban, D. R. and Harper, F. M. 2008. Motivations for answering questions online. In D. Caspi and T. Samuel-Azran (Eds.), *New Media and Innovative Technologies*, Tel Aviv: Tzivonim Publishing, 73–97.

[13] Bowler, L., Monahan, J., Jeng, W., Oh, J. S., and He, D. 2015. The quality and helpfulness of answers to eating disorder questions in Yahoo! Answers: Teens speak out. Proceedings of the ASIS&T 2015 Annual Meeting. Silver Spring, MD: Association for Information Science and Technology.

[14] Worrall, A. and Oh, S. 2013. The place of health information and socio-emotional support in social questioning and answering. *Information Research* 18, 3. http://www.informationr.net/ir/18-3/paper587.html.

[15] Shachaf, P. 2010. Social reference: Toward a unifying theory. *Library & Information Science Research* 32, 1, 66–76.

[16] Shah, C., Oh, S., and Oh, J. S. 2009. Research agenda for social Q&A. *Library & Information Science Research* 31, 4, 205–9.

[17] Savolainen, R. 2012. The structure of argument patterns on a social Q&A site. *Journal of the American Society for Information Science and Technology* 63, 12, 2536–48.

[18] Toulmin, S. E. 1958. The uses of argument. Cambridge University Press.

[19] Cleverdon, C. W. 1960. ASLIB Cranfield research project on the comparative efficiency of indexing systems. *ASLIB Proceedings* 12, 421-431.

[20] Cleverdon, C. W. 1967. The Cranfield tests on index language devices. *ASLIB Proceedings* 19, 6, 173-194.

[21] Wilson, P. 1973. Situational relevance. *Information Storage and Retrieval* 9, 8, 457–71.

[22] Swanson, D. R. 1986. Subjective versus objective relevance in bibliographic retrieval systems. *The Library Quarterly* 56, 4) 389-398.

[23] Cosijn, E. and Ingwersen, P. 2000. Dimensions of relevance. *Information Processing & Management* 36, 4, 533-550.

[24] Harper, F. M., Moy, D., and Konstan, J. A. 2009. Facts or friends?: Distinguishing informational and conversational questions in social Q&A sites. In *Proceedings of the SIGCHI Conference on Human Factors in Computing Systems* (Boston, MA, April 4-9, 2009) ACM, New York, NY, 759–68.

[25] Liu, Z. and Jansen, B. J. 2015. Subjective versus objective questions: Perception of question subjectivity in social Q&A. *Lecture Notes in Computer Science 9021*. Berlin: Springer International, 131–140.

[26] Mendes Rodrigues, E. and Milic-Frayling, N. 2009. Socializing or knowledge sharing?: Characterizing social intent in community question answering. In *Proceedings of the ACM International Conference on Information and Knowledge Management*. CIKM'09. (Hong Kong, China, November 2-6, 2009). ACM, New York, NY, 1127-36.

[27] Burel, G., Mulholland, P., He, Y., and Alani, H. 2015. Modelling question selection behaviour in online communities. In *Proceedings of the ACM International World Wide Web Conference*, WWW'15, (Florence, Italy, May 18-22, 2015). ACM, New York, NY, 357–58.

[28] Yamamoto, T., Nakamura, S., and Tanaka, K. 2011. Extracting adjective facets from community Q&A corpus. In *Proceedings of the ACM International Conference on Information and Knowledge Management*, ACM, New York NY, 2021–24.

[29] Star, S. and Griesemer, J. 1989. Institutional ecology, 'translations' and boundary objects: Amateurs and professionals in Berkeley's Museum of Vertebrate Zoology, 1907-39. *Social Studies of Science* 19, 3, 387–420.

[30] Bowker, G., and Star, S. L. 1999. *Sorting things out: Classification and its consequences.* Cambridge, MA: MIT Press.

[31] Star, S. 2010. This is not a boundary object: Reflections of the origin of a concept. *Science, Technology, & Human Values* 35, 601-617.

[32] Rehm, S.-V. and Goel, L. 2015. The emergence of boundary clusters in inter-organizational innovation. *Information and Organization* 25, 1, 27-51.

[33] Chen, J., Xu, H., and Whinston, A. B. 2014. Moderated online communities and quality of user-generated content. *Journal of Management Information Systems* 28, 2, 237-268.

[34] Andrews, D. C. 2002. Audience-specific online community design. *Communications of the ACM* 45, 4) 64.

[35] Porter, M. F. 1980. An algorithm for suffix stripping. *Program* 14, 3, 130–137.

[36] Glaser, B. G. 1965. The constant comparative method of qualitative analysis. *Social Problems* 12, 4, 436-445.

[37] Goetz, J. P. and LeCompte, M. D. 1981. Ethnographic research and the problem of data reduction. *Anthropology and Education Quarterly* 12, 5, 51-70.

[38] Lincoln, Y. S. and Guba, E. G. 1985. *Naturalistic Inquiry.* Sage.

[39] Donath, J. 1999. Identity and deception in the virtual community." In P. Kollock & M. Smith (Eds.), *Communities in Cyberspace.* London: Routledge, 29-59.

[40] Herring, S., Job-Sluder, K., Scheckler, R., and Barab, S. A. 2002. Searching for safety online: Managing "trolling" in a feminist forum. *Information Society* 18, 5, 371-384.

[41] Fluther. 2016. http:///www.fluther.com

[42] Answermug. 2016. http://answermug.com

Assessing the Navigational Effects of Click Biases and Link Insertion on the Web

Florian Geigl
KTI, Graz University of
Technology
florian.geigl@tugraz.at

Kristina Lerman
ISI, University of Southern
California
lerman@isi.edu

Simon Walk
IICM, Graz University of
Technology
simon.walk@tugraz.at

Markus Strohmaier
University of Koblenz-Landau
and GESIS
markus.strohmaier@gesis.org

Denis Helic
KTI, Graz University of
Technology
dhelic@tugraz.at

ABSTRACT

Websites have an inherent interest in steering user navigation in order to, for example, increase sales of specific products or categories, or to guide users towards specific information. In general, website administrators can use the following two strategies to influence their visitors' navigation behavior. First, they can introduce *click biases* to reinforce specific links on their website by changing their visual appearance, for example, by locating them on the top of the page. Second, they can utilize *link insertion* to generate new paths for users to navigate over. In this paper, we present a novel approach for measuring the potential effects of these two strategies on user navigation. Our results suggest that, depending on the pages for which we want to increase user visits, optimal link modification strategies vary. Moreover, simple topological measures can be used as proxies for assessing the impact of the intended changes on the navigation of users, even before these changes are implemented.

Keywords

Click Biases, Link Insertion, Random Surfer, Stationary Distribution

1. INTRODUCTION

Millions of people use the Web on a daily basis to buy products in online shops, perform financial transactions via online banking, or simply browse information systems, media libraries or online encyclopedias, such as IMDb, Netflix or Wikipedia. To find and access relevant information on the Web, people either search, navigate, or combine these two activities. A recent study [10] found that 35% of all visits to a website can be attributed to teleports, which are the direct result of clicks on search-engine results, navigation through manually typed URLs, or clicks on browser book-

marks. The remaining 65% of the clicks can be attributed to the task of navigating a webpage. In this paper, we direct our attention towards these 65% of actions and tackle the question what potential effects we can expect if we influence the link selection process of website visitors by simple link modifications. In particular, we are interested in the effects of different link modification strategies on (stochastic) models of Web navigation.

Problem. By inserting new links between webpages of a website, we alter the link structure. This has the potential to change user browsing behavior, since new links create new paths for users to explore the website. Alternatively, without changing the link structure of the website, we might be able to influence the link selection process of visitors. Studies have shown that the decisions of users for where to navigate next can be influenced by the layout and the position of the links on a webpage. In particular, due to position bias [20] users are more likely to select links higher up on webpages [5, 6, 24]. As a result, inducing click biases, such as repositioning links on a webpage, highlighting the links, or even making them visually more appealing, can affect the users' decision of where to click next on a website, similar to the way that adding new links affects browsing.

In this paper we are particularly interested in investigating and comparing the potential consequences of inserting new links and modifying already existing links on the navigational behavior of users. These newly obtained insights are of a significant practical relevance for website owners, as they can be used, for example, by owners of media libraries to increase visits of specific media files in order to reduce the number of different files that need to be cached on fast storage devices. Another example includes online encyclopedias, where operators may want to guide users towards articles of a specific category over some period of time (e.g., the birthday of an inventor). In some of these cases, link insertion might be more time-consuming than simply changing the layout of the website to increase visibility of specific links and vice versa. Theoretically, we would like to analyze and compare the effects of such link modification endeavors. Practically, new tools are needed to assist website operators in deciding which of the two strategies they should deploy to achieve the desired effects.

Methods. In this paper we study the impact of link modifications on the random surfer, which we apply as a proxy for real user behavior. In the past, a user's decision to click on a link on a webpage was successfully modeled using the random surfer [4, 15, 30]. In this model, a user selects one of the links on a webpage uniformly at random and navigates to the page to which the link points. Apart from the huge success of the Google search engine, whose ranking algorithm is based on the random surfer model, empirical studies have shown that this model provides a very precise approximation of real browsing behavior in many situations and for a variety of applications [4, 9]. An important property of a random surfer is its *stationary distribution*, which is the probability distribution of finding a random surfer at a specific webpage in the limit of large number of steps.

In particular, we investigate how the random surfer's stationary distribution of a subset of pages (i.e., *target pages*) of a given website changes as a consequence of (i) modifying already existing links towards them, (ii) introducing new links towards them, or by (iii) combining these two approaches. To that end, we introduce a *click bias*, and a *link insertion* strategy. We model the effects of click biases on the intrinsic attractiveness of a link to the user by increasing the weight of that link. In practice, we may introduce such click biases, for example, by locating the corresponding link on the top of a page. With link insertion, we simply introduce new links between webpages of a website, for example, by linking towards a given target page from the starting page.

We introduce quantitative measures that allow us to address the following research questions:

Navigational Boost. How stable is the stationary distribution with respect to the proposed modification strategies, and what are the limits of stationary distributions that can be achieved for a given set of webpages? Is it (theoretically) possible to achieve a given stationary probability distribution for an arbitrary subset of webpages of a website? What is the connection between simple topological measures of the website network and stationary probability?

Influence Potential. What is the relative gain of the stationary probabilities compared to their unmodified counterparts. This provides us with an answer to the "guidance" potential of a set of webpages, defining to what extent it is possible to increase the relative stationary probabilities as compared to the initial unmodified values.

Combinations. Finally, we are interested how combinations of the two proposed link modification strategies perform in terms of increased stationary probabilities of selected subpages. In particular, we investigate the performance of certain combinations across several different networks and/or selected subpages.

Contributions & Findings. We find that intuitions about how either modification strategy affects navigation are not always correct. Further, our experiments show that the size of a set of targeted subpages is not always a good predictor for the observed effects. Rather, other topological features often better reflect the consequences of a modification. Practically, we provide an open source framework[1] for website administrators to estimate the effects of link modifications on their website.

2. RELATED WORK

The random surfer model has received much attention from the research community [22, 31]. While the model is

---

[1]https://github.com/floriangeigl/RandomSurfers

very simple, it became well-established over the last years. It was applied to a variety of problems from graph generators over graph analysis to modeling user navigation. Furthermore, the model has been applied to calculate structural node properties in large networks. HITS [18] and PageRank [4, 26] rank network nodes according to their values in the stationary distribution of the random surfer model. Especially for the later there exists a detailed analysis ranging from the efficiency of its calculation towards its robustness [3, 19]. Bianchini et al. [3] provided an in-depth analysis of how to tweak the cumulative PageRank of a community of websites. They found that splitting up the content of pages onto more highly interlink pages increases the community's cumulative PageRank—since the community is larger it consists of more pages which are able to trap the random surfer for a longer period of time. Moreover, they suggest to avoid dangling webpages (i.e., pages without links to other pages). In this paper we are also interested in the sum of the random surfers visit probabilities in a community, however we do not use (i) teleportation as in the PageRank model, and (ii) do not modify the network in its size (i.e., number of pages). On the contrary we modify the transition probabilities of certain links and insert new links into the network. Moreover, since all our datasets are strongly connected, we do not face the problem of unwanted high visit probabilities of usually unimportant pages (i.e., dangling nodes) [3].

A random surfer can be steered towards specific nodes in the network by increasing the probability of traversing links towards those nodes. This can be accomplished by biasing random surfer's link selection strategy so that it is not uniformly random anymore, but biased towards specific nodes. For instance, in the field of information retrieval Richardson et al. [28] successfully applied biased random surfers to increase the quality of search results compared to those achieved using a simple PageRank. At the same time Haveliwala [13, 14] biased PageRank towards topics retrieved from a search query to rank the query results. Utilizing this technique the results where more accurate than those produced using a single, generic PageRank. Moreover, Gyongyi et al. [12] successfully used trust as bias to detect and filter out spam pages of search results. However, Al-Saffar and Heileman [1] showed that biased PageRank algorithms generate a considerable overlap in top results with a simple PageRank. Concerning this problem their main suggestion was to use external biases which do not rely onto the underlying link structure of the network. In our paper we randomly decide towards which nodes we bias the random surfer. This allows us to explore the borders of changes in stationary distributions caused by a bias.

In 2013, Helic et al. [15] compared click trails characteristics of stochastically biased random surfers with those of humans. Their conclusion was, that biased random surfers can serve as valid models of human navigation. Further, Geigl et al. [9] validated this by showing that the result vector of PageRank and clickdata biased PageRank have a strong correlation in an online encyclopedia. This is especially interesting, since it creates the connection of our simulation to real human navigation on the web. Additionally, Lerman and Hogg [20] already showed that it is possible to bias the link selection of users. In particular, they came to the conclusion that users are subject to a *position bias*, making the selection of links higher up on webpages up to a factor of 3.5 more likely [5, 20, 24]. Hence, it is of practical relevance to investigate also the effects of *biases* in the link selection process onto the stationary distribution.

Concerning link insertion there already exists work in literature which makes use of statistical methods to suggest new links in network structures to, for instance, increase the performance of chip architectures [25]. In particular, the authors use a standard mesh and insert long-range links, converting the network into a small-world network. This reduced packet latency results in a major improvement in throughput. Another field of research where link insertion is of interest are recommender systems for social friendship networks [2, 21, 23, 29]. For example, Xie et al. [32] characterized interests of users in two dimensions (i.e., context and content) and exploited this information to efficiently recommend potential new friends in an online social network. In this paper we focus on the effects of inserted links onto the typical whereabouts of the random surfer.

3. METHODOLOGY

We base our methodology on the calculations of the stationary distribution of a random surfer on the original and manipulated networks. The networks consist of nodes, which represent webpages and directed links between nodes, which represent hyperlinks between webpages. We first calculate the transition matrix and the stationary distribution for the original network as a baseline for comparing the effects of link modifications. Second, we increase the statistical weight of a random surfer visiting a set of predefined nodes (i.e., *target pages* or *target nodes*). We do that either by increasing the link weights towards selected nodes (click bias) or by adding new links pointing towards those nodes (link insertion). Third, we compute the corresponding transition matrix for the modified network. Fourth, we calculate the stationary distribution of the new transition matrices. Finally, we compare the modified stationary distribution with the original stationary distribution to gain insights into the effects of the different link modifications. Figure 1 illustrates these steps on a toy example.

3.1 Preliminaries

In what follows we formalize our approach algebraically. We represent a website as a directed network with a weighted adjacency matrix $\boldsymbol{W} \in \mathbb{R}^{n \times n}$, where n is the number of webpages in the website under investigation. We define the element W_{ij} of the weighted adjacency matrix $\boldsymbol{W}$ as the sum of edge weights of all links pointing from node j to node i. For example, $W_{ij} = 1$ if there is a single link from page j to page i with weight 1, and $W_{ij} = 3$ if there are three links pointing from page j to page i each with weight 1.

For our analysis we introduce *target nodes* as the nodes whose stationary probability we want to increase. We use vector $\boldsymbol{t} \in \mathbb{R}^n$ to specify them:

$$t_i = \begin{cases} 1 & \text{if } i \text{ is a } target\ node \\ 0 & \text{otherwise.} \end{cases} \quad (1)$$

We further define ϕ as a fraction of target nodes with respect to the total number of nodes n:

$$\phi = \frac{\sum_i t_i}{n} \quad (2)$$

Hence, $\phi = 0.1$ means that 10% of nodes from the network are target nodes.

3.2 Stationary Distribution

The stationary distribution is a probability distribution over nodes that assigns a probability of finding the random surfer on a given node in the limit of large number of steps. To compute the stationary distribution we first need to construct a diagonal out-degree matrix $\boldsymbol{D}$, with the weighted node out-degrees on its diagonal. Using $\text{diag}(\boldsymbol{v})$ to denote diagonal matrices with elements of a vector $\boldsymbol{v}$ on their diagonal we define $\boldsymbol{D}$ as:

$$\boldsymbol{D} = \text{diag}\left(\sum_{i=1}^n W_{ij}\right). \quad (3)$$

Using $\boldsymbol{D}$ matrix we can calculate the transition matrix $\boldsymbol{P}$, which is a left stochastic matrix of $\boldsymbol{W}$ as $\boldsymbol{P} = \boldsymbol{W}\boldsymbol{D}^{-1}$ (in fact this is PageRank matrix without teleportation). The stationary distribution $\boldsymbol{\pi}$ now satisfies the (right) eigenvalue equation for the matrix $\boldsymbol{P}$: $\boldsymbol{\pi} = \boldsymbol{P}\boldsymbol{\pi}$.

3.3 Click Bias

To introduce click biases that influence the link selection strategy of the random surfer, we reweigh the links pointing towards target nodes by multiplying their weight by a constant scalar b, which we call bias strength. For example, a bias strength of $b = 2$ doubles the weight of all links towards target nodes. The final probability of the random surfer to traverse a link is then directly proportional to its weight.

Algebraically, we induce biases with a diagonal bias matrix $\boldsymbol{B}$ which we define as $\boldsymbol{B} = \boldsymbol{I} + (b - 1) \cdot \text{diag}(\boldsymbol{t})$. The adjacency matrix of a biased network is $\boldsymbol{W}' = \boldsymbol{B}\boldsymbol{W}$. To compute the stationary distribution of the biased network, we first calculate the new transition matrix $\boldsymbol{P}' = \boldsymbol{W}'\boldsymbol{D}'^{-1}$ and then its stationary distribution $\boldsymbol{\pi}'$.

Please note that from the technical perspective, inducing a bias is the same as inserting parallel links towards target nodes—it increases the value of specific elements (i.e., those representing links towards target nodes) in the adjacency matrix. The total weight of newly added parallel links $l(b)$ due to an induced bias b is given by:

$$l(b) = \underbrace{\sum_{ij} W'_{ij}}_{\#\ \text{links in } \boldsymbol{W}'} - \underbrace{\sum_{ij} W_{ij}}_{\#\ \text{links in } \boldsymbol{W}} \quad (4)$$

To allow for a fair comparison between the click bias and the link insertion strategy we insert exactly $l(b)$ new links with weight 1 in the latter case.

3.4 Link Insertion

The second link modification strategy consists of inserting new links towards the target nodes from a given set of source nodes. This strategy represents the case where a website administrator inserts links towards target nodes from important subpages of their website. We define the importance of a webpage as its stationary probability in the original network.

To insert a given number $l(b)$ of new links we proceed as follows. We start by sorting nodes by their stationary probability in a descending order. In the next step we insert new links from the top $l(b)/(n \cdot \phi)$ nodes to all target nodes. Here $n \cdot \phi$ is the number of target nodes and we always *ceil* the calculated number of source nodes to ensure that there are enough pairs of nodes. If one of the target nodes

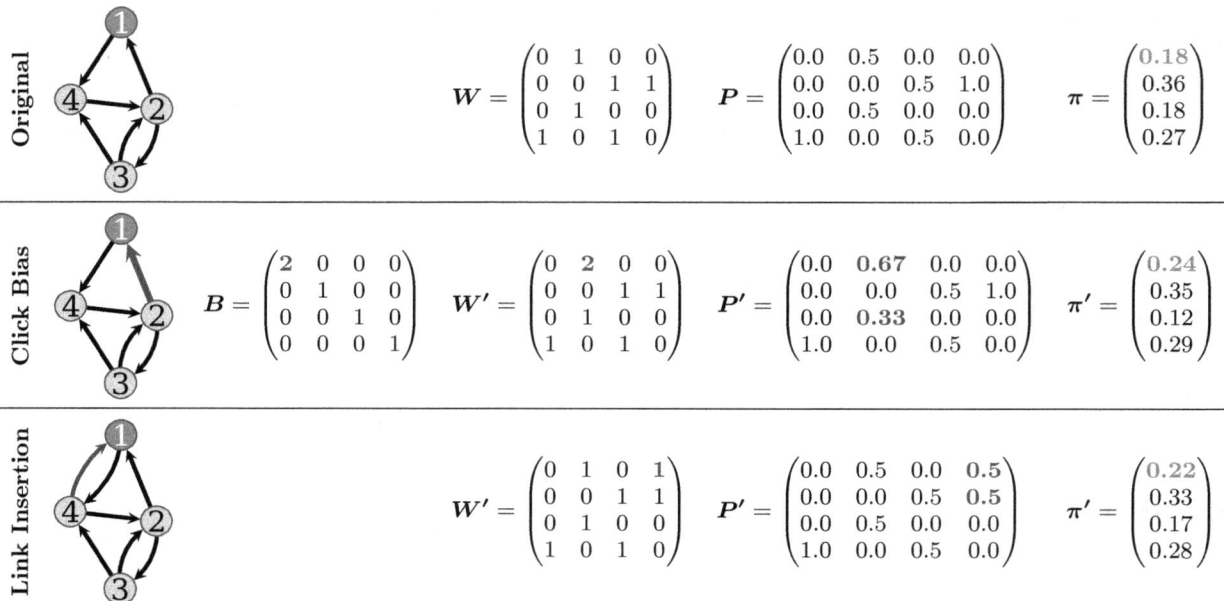

$$
\boldsymbol{W} = \begin{pmatrix} 0 & 1 & 0 & 0 \\ 0 & 0 & 1 & 1 \\ 0 & 1 & 0 & 0 \\ 1 & 0 & 1 & 0 \end{pmatrix} \quad
\boldsymbol{P} = \begin{pmatrix} 0.0 & 0.5 & 0.0 & 0.0 \\ 0.0 & 0.0 & 0.5 & 1.0 \\ 0.0 & 0.5 & 0.0 & 0.0 \\ 1.0 & 0.0 & 0.5 & 0.0 \end{pmatrix} \quad
\boldsymbol{\pi} = \begin{pmatrix} 0.18 \\ 0.36 \\ 0.18 \\ 0.27 \end{pmatrix}
$$

$$
\boldsymbol{B} = \begin{pmatrix} 2 & 0 & 0 & 0 \\ 0 & 1 & 0 & 0 \\ 0 & 0 & 1 & 0 \\ 0 & 0 & 0 & 1 \end{pmatrix} \quad
\boldsymbol{W'} = \begin{pmatrix} 0 & 2 & 0 & 0 \\ 0 & 0 & 1 & 1 \\ 0 & 1 & 0 & 0 \\ 1 & 0 & 1 & 0 \end{pmatrix} \quad
\boldsymbol{P'} = \begin{pmatrix} 0.0 & 0.67 & 0.0 & 0.0 \\ 0.0 & 0.0 & 0.5 & 1.0 \\ 0.0 & 0.33 & 0.0 & 0.0 \\ 1.0 & 0.0 & 0.5 & 0.0 \end{pmatrix} \quad
\boldsymbol{\pi'} = \begin{pmatrix} 0.24 \\ 0.35 \\ 0.12 \\ 0.29 \end{pmatrix}
$$

$$
\boldsymbol{W'} = \begin{pmatrix} 0 & 1 & 0 & 1 \\ 0 & 0 & 1 & 1 \\ 0 & 1 & 0 & 0 \\ 1 & 0 & 1 & 0 \end{pmatrix} \quad
\boldsymbol{P'} = \begin{pmatrix} 0.0 & 0.5 & 0.0 & 0.5 \\ 0.0 & 0.0 & 0.5 & 0.5 \\ 0.0 & 0.5 & 0.0 & 0.0 \\ 1.0 & 0.0 & 0.5 & 0.0 \end{pmatrix} \quad
\boldsymbol{\pi'} = \begin{pmatrix} 0.22 \\ 0.33 \\ 0.17 \\ 0.28 \end{pmatrix}
$$

Figure 1: **Modeling Click Bias and Link Insertion - Illustrative Example.** We intend to use different link modification strategies to steer the random surfer towards the red colored node 1 more often. Hence, our target nodes vector consists of only one node: node 1 ($\boldsymbol{t} = \begin{pmatrix} 1 & 0 & 0 & 0 \end{pmatrix}^{\mathsf{T}}$). In each row we visualize the corresponding network of the website, where nodes represent webpages and links represent hyperlinks between the webpages. Further, for each of them we show how we calculate its stationary distribution. This involves (from left to right) the weighted adjacency matrix $\boldsymbol{W}$ (unmodified network) or $\boldsymbol{W'}$ (modified networks), the corresponding transition matrix $\boldsymbol{P}$ (unmodified network) or $\boldsymbol{P'}$ (modified networks) and finally the corresponding stationary distribution $\boldsymbol{\pi}$ (unmodified network) or $\boldsymbol{\pi'}$ (modified networks). The blue links in the graphs and the blue matrix elements in bold show the link modifications and their effects on the adjacency and the transition matrix. The red vector elements show the effects of the modifications on the stationary probability (energy) of node 1. **Top row.** Here we depict the original and unmodified network. **Middle row.** We modify the network with a *click bias*. We double the statistical weights of links towards target nodes (bias strength $b = 2$). To calculate the modified adjacency matrix we first construct the diagonal bias matrix $\boldsymbol{B}$ and then compute $\boldsymbol{W'} = \boldsymbol{BW}$. We see an increase in energy of node 1 from 0.18 in the unmodified network to 0.24. **Bottom row.** We insert a new link from node 4 to 1 (i.e., blue link in graph and blue element in $\boldsymbol{W'}$) into the original network. Due to the link insertion the energy of node 1 increases from 0.18 in the unmodified network to 0.22 in the modified network. Thus, in this toy example the effects of the click bias are stronger than those of link insertion. Additionally, we see that also elements in the out-component of node 1 (i.e., node 4) profit of an increased energy of node 1 since a significant amount of 1's increased energy flows into node 4.

is itself designated as a source node we do not insert self-loops—from the practical point of view, it does not make sense to link a webpage to itself. In the rare case where we have connected all possible combinations of source and target nodes but did not reach the required number of links, we simply reiterate the list of the source nodes resulting in parallel links between nodes. Please note that we insert parallel links if a link between a source and a target node has already existed in the original network. However, this happens extremely rarely because all of our networks are sparse. In fact, in all our experiments the fraction of inserted parallel links was on average less than 1%.

3.5 Combinations

Finally, we can combine the two link modification strategies and study the effects of such combinations on the stationary distribution and investigate if an optimal combination of strategies exists, which outperforms the individual approaches. From the practical point of view this means that for optimally steering website users, we combine both, the click bias and link insertion mechanisms.

To create a combined link modification method we first introduce $\alpha \in [0, 1]$, which we call the mixing factor. The mixing factor determines how many of the $l(b)$ links are inserted by the click bias. Then, $1 - \alpha$ defines how many links are inserted by the link insertion strategy:

$$
l(b) = \underbrace{\alpha \cdot l(b)}_{\text{\# biased links}} + \underbrace{(1 - \alpha) \cdot l(b)}_{\text{\# inserted links}} \tag{5}
$$

With a combined strategy we cannot bias all links towards target nodes—again, we need to select a subset of links towards target nodes. In analogy to the link insertion method we again preferably select links between nodes having higher stationary probability in the unmodified network. Thus, we first compute the probability distribution over the eligible links in the form of matrix $\boldsymbol{L}$, where $\sum_{ij} L_{ij} = 1$. We define matrix $\boldsymbol{L}$ as:

$$
\boldsymbol{L} = \operatorname{diag}(\boldsymbol{\pi}) \cdot \operatorname{diag}(\boldsymbol{t}) \cdot \boldsymbol{W} \cdot \operatorname{diag}(\boldsymbol{\pi}). \tag{6}
$$

The probability of selecting a link is directly proportional to the product of the unmodified stationary probability of its source and target node. Note that due to the multiplicative factor $\operatorname{diag}(\boldsymbol{t}) \cdot \boldsymbol{W}$ only links towards target nodes have a non-zero probability. With L in place we sample $\alpha \cdot l(b)$ links without replacement and multiply their value in W' by b to induce the click bias. To insert the remaining $(1 - \alpha) \cdot l(b)$ links we adopt the link insertion strategy on the matrix W' as described previously.

3.6 Measuring the Effects

To measure the effects of link modification strategies we quantify how the stationary probabilities of given target nodes change as a function of the modification. In the remainder of this paper we will refer to a node's stationary probability using the, in the literature established, term *energy* [3]. To that end, we calculate the *energy of target nodes* (π'_t), which is the sum of the modified stationary probabilities of target nodes, as following:

$$\pi'_t = \sum_i \pi'_i \cdot t_i, \qquad (7)$$

where π' is the stationary distribution of the modified adjacency matrix.

We further measure the *influence potential*, which is the relative increase in the energy of target nodes due to the modification, as a factor τ:

$$\tau = \frac{\pi'_t}{\pi_t}, \qquad (8)$$

where π_t is the energy of target nodes of the unmodified network (i.e., $\pi_t = \sum_i \pi_i \cdot t_i$).

4. DATASETS

For our experiments we use three datasets: an online encyclopedia Wikipedia for Schools[2] (*W4S*) and two online media libraries ORF TVthek[3] (*ORF*) and Das Erste Mediathek[4] (*DEM*).

We collected the data by crawling the corresponding websites. Starting from the main page of a website we recursively crawled all subpages by following all outgoing links from a given webpage. Note that we did not follow external links, meaning that we skipped links to pages not belonging to a given website. Further, we did not follow links generated via Flash, AJAX or any other client-rendered content.

After collecting the data, we removed self-loops, which are links from a webpage to itself, and special links such as "log-in", "write a review", and all other links that require a session-id. In the next step, we represented each dataset as a directed network—webpages are represented as nodes connected by directed links. For calculating the stationary distribution, we extracted the largest strongly connected component (SCC) of each network, so that in the final network it is possible to navigate from any given node to any other node in the network. These final networks have $4,051$ nodes and $111,795$ links (*W4S*), $9,799$ nodes and $301,844$ links (*ORF*), and $70,063$ nodes and $3,448,513$ links (*DEM*).

5. EXPERIMENTAL SETUP

To investigate the effects of manipulating links we first generate sets of target nodes. For this purpose we draw the desired number of nodes uniformly at random from the network without replacement, creating a synthetic set of nodes

[2]http://http://schools-wikipedia.org/
[3]http://tvthek.orf.at/
[4]http://mediathek.daserste.de/

of a specified size. Note that those sets can consist of unconnected webpages. We conduct all of our experiments with the same initially generated target nodes to reduce the influence of the random node selection process. For making the number of webpages selected as target nodes comparable between datasets we refer to the size of target nodes as ϕ, which is the fraction of target nodes. To generate target nodes we use several values for ϕ which range from 0.01 to 0.2. For each dataset and each ϕ we generate 100 different synthetic sets of nodes (i.e., target nodes).

Limiting (High) Bias Behavior. In our first experiment we are interested in analyzing the impact of an increasing bias strength on the energy of target nodes using either a click bias on already existing links or inserting new links in an informed way. We use bias strengths reaching from $b = 2$ to $b = 200$ to investigate their effects. Note that for the link insertion strategy the number of inserted links is defined by the bias strength b using Equation 4. This ensures a fair comparison between the two methods.

Realistic (Lower) Bias Strengths. In this experiment we investigate practically relevant [17,20] values for the bias strength b. In particular, we iterate over the range 2 to 15 as bias strengths. With this experiment we gain insights into the effects of the proposed modifications, which can be implemented in websites. After the modification of the adjacency matrix we measure the energy of target nodes π'_t. This allows us to investigate the efficiency of both methods for a given bias strength.

Relative Increase in Stationary Probability. With the previous experiments we analyze changes in the energy of target nodes in absolute terms. For instance, we may learn that for a given set of target nodes we may achieve an energy of $\pi'_t = 0.5$. However, we do not know what the relative increase in their energy is. For example, the set of target nodes may have had $\pi_t = 0.49$ in the unmodified network rendering our efforts futile in *relative* terms. Thus, in this experiment we use τ to measure the influence potential. A higher value for τ means a larger *relative* increase in the energy of target nodes. Again, we compare the results for a given bias strength between our two methods.

Combination of Strategies. Finally, we are interested in investigating if and to what extent the energy of target nodes changes if we combine click biases and link insertion. We vary the mixture factor α from 0 to 1 in steps of 0.1 and measure the energy of target nodes π'_t of the modified networks.

6. RESULTS & DISCUSSION

6.1 Saturation

Figure 2 depicts the effects of link modifications in our datasets with increasing values of bias strength b and varying fractions of target nodes ϕ (0.01, 0.1 and 0.2).

In the case of click bias we observe the following situation. For small values of b the energy of target nodes π'_t increases very quickly (navigational boost phase, which we analyze in more detail in Section 6.2)—this energy saturates for larger values of b (i.e., $b > 35$). This holds for larger ϕ values (0.1 and 0.2), whereas for a smaller ϕ, for example $\phi = 0.01$, the initial growth as well as the saturation are significantly slower and lower respectively. Further, for higher ϕ (0.1 and 0.2) π'_t saturates at an almost identical and very high level

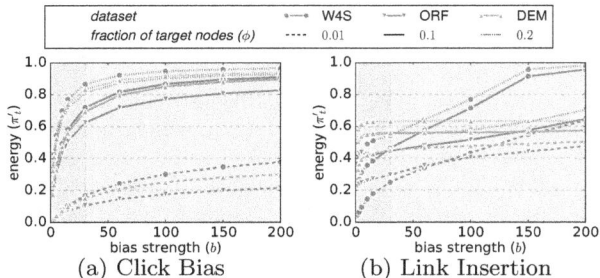

dataset	W4S	ORF	DEM
fraction of target nodes (ϕ)	0.01	0.1	0.2

(a) Click Bias   (b) Link Insertion

Figure 2: **Saturation.** The plots depict the connection between bias strength (x-axis) and the increased energy of target nodes due to an induced click bias (left) or link insertion (right). Each marker type and color refers to one dataset. Dashed, solid and dotted line styles refer to fraction of target nodes ϕ 0.01, 0.1 and 0.2 respectively. We can observe that both link modification strategies reach a certain level of saturation—meaning that further increases in bias strength do not result in an increase in energy of target nodes. Therefore, for both strategies we identify two phases: a (i) *navigational boost* phase in which we observe a rapid increase of the stationary probability (blueish region with small values of the bias strength), and a (ii) *saturation* phase (reddish region with larger values of the bias strength).

(>0.8)—if the click bias is strong enough we can increase the energy of any fraction of target nodes larger than $\phi > 0.1$.

An interesting question in this respect is the height of the energy saturation level. Theoretically, this level is close to 1.0 but as Figure 2 shows, in empirical networks this level can not be fully reached. Essentially, due to the directed nature of the network, the target nodes out-component (i.e., the nodes with incoming links from target nodes) will always act as a drain that will take some energy from the target nodes. That amount depends on the size of the out-component as well as its connectivity with other parts of the network—in particular the existence of back-links towards target nodes. This situation is depicted in our toy example Figure 1 in the middle row. Node 4, which has an incoming link from node 1, profits from an induced click bias towards node 1 (cf. original $\pi_4 = 0.27$ and modified $\pi'_4 = 0.29$). Thus, although π'_1 increases with increasing bias strength, node 1 would never reach energy values close to 1.0 because node 4 attracts a certain amount energy to itself.

In the case of the link insertion strategy the results are more diverse (cf. Figure 2b). For DEM dataset we observe a quick saturation for all values of ϕ. Differently from the click bias the saturation level is significantly lower for this dataset (i.e., 0.6). For the ORF dataset we do not observe saturation but a monotonous increase in the energy of target nodes for increasing values of ϕ. Finally, for the W4S dataset and larger ϕ (0.1 and 0.2) we can observe saturation at levels higher than 0.9.

As previously, the size of the out-component of the target nodes, combined with the size of their in-component (i.e., the source nodes which point towards target nodes), as well as the ratio of these two quantities provide a possible explanation for this behavior. Basically, we can calculate the average number of newly inserted links as $l(b) = \bar{d} \cdot n \cdot \phi \cdot b$, where $\bar{d}$ is the average degree (i.e., in a directed network average degree $\bar{d}$ corresponds to both the average in-degree as well as average out-degree) and n, ϕ, b are as before. Thus, in the networks with a higher average degree we in-

sert more new links. For smaller values of bias strength (blueish region in Figure 2b) these new links lead to a navigational boost, resulting in a quick increase in the energy π'_t of target nodes. The navigational boost is higher in networks with a higher average degree—we observe the highest increase in π'_t in DEM with $\bar{d} = 49.22$, the second highest in ORF with $\bar{d} = 30.8$, and the lowest in W4S with $\bar{d} = 27.6$. As mentioned before, in Section 6.2 we analyze this navigational boost in more detail. However, for larger values of bias strength (reddish region in Figure 2b) the effects of the drain due to the larger size of the out-component become visible—the networks with a higher increase for smaller bias strengths lose their energy now more quickly. Thus, the ordering of the saturation levels for higher bias strengths is reversed to the navigational boost in energy for lower bias strengths, resulting in W4S to now have the highest saturation level, followed by ORF and then by DEM.

To confirm our intuition about the saturation for the link insertion strategy we performed the following analysis. First, we calculated some structural properties for the target nodes. In particular, based on the insights of Ding et al. [7,8], we define the *in-degree* of target nodes as the sum of the weights of links pointing towards target nodes $d_t^- = \sum_{ij} (\operatorname{diag}(\boldsymbol{t}) \cdot \boldsymbol{W})_{ij}$. The *out-degree* of target nodes is the sum of the weights of outgoing links of target nodes $d_t^+ = \sum_{ij} (\boldsymbol{W} \cdot \operatorname{diag}(\boldsymbol{t}))_{ij}$. Finally, the *degree ratio* of target nodes is a ratio between the previous two measurements (i.e., $d_t^r = d_t^+/d_t^-$). Although, it has been shown that properties, such as the simple count of in-links of a node, are bad approximations for PageRank on a large scale [27], they proved to be a good indicator for the random surfer behavior on our datasets.

In our experiments, DEM has on average by one order of magnitude higher both target node in-degree and out-degree than the other two datasets. This explains a quick increase of π'_t for smaller bias strengths. However, degree ratio is typically larger in DEM target nodes than in ORF or W4S target nodes and this explains a higher drain of energy and a lower saturation level in the DEM dataset (cf. Figure 3).

Finding. For larger fractions ϕ of target nodes their energy π'_t achieved through a click bias quickly saturates across all datasets at very high levels (> 0.8). Boost and saturation of the energy is significantly slower for smaller fractions ϕ. The saturation level is determined by the out-degree of the target nodes and reciprocity of outgoing links from the target nodes. For link insertion saturation existence, speed, and levels vary between datasets and ϕ values. The average degree of the original networks as well as the ratio between out-degree and in-degree of target nodes significantly influences those effects.

Implications. In case of medium ($\phi = 0.1$) and large ($\phi = 0.2$) fractions of target nodes we reach high saturation levels with both link modification methods even with small bias strengths. For example, if we would like to increase visibility of a large category in, for example Wikipedia, we can achieve this by either slightly increasing the font size of the links towards the articles of that category or by simple creating some new links towards those articles. Click bias reaches very high visibility levels consistently across several different datasets, whereas link insertion is dependent on the network structure—in datasets with a smaller average number of links we can achieve larger changes. This follows our intuition—in a network with a smaller number of links, each new link affects the network more significantly. How-

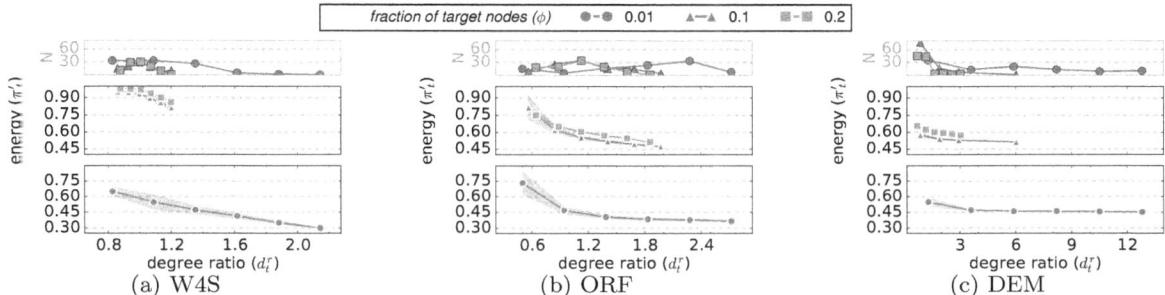

Figure 3: **Influence of Target Nodes Degree Ratio onto the Saturation of their Energy.** The plots depict the due to link insertion achieved energy of target nodes pi'_t as the function of their degree ratio. Each line depicts the results for a given ϕ. For increased readability we group data points into six equally sized bins according to their degree ratio (x-axes). Values on the y-axes represent the averages of the data points falling into the corresponding bin. **Top row.** In the top row we show the distribution of the target nodes degree ratios (in bins; x-axes)—the y-axes denote the number of data points (N) falling into each bin. **Middle row.** Here, we depict the results for medium and large fractions of target nodes. **Bottom row.** For readability we depict small fractions of target nodes separately. Over all datasets and all ϕ we consistently observe a negative correlation between degree ratio and energy π'_t. This means that with an increasing ratio—an increasing out-degree and a decreasing in-degree—the drain of energy increases and this leads to the saturation of the energy of target nodes.

ever, to match the effects of the click bias we need to insert a very large amount of new links. On the other hand, in case of small ($\phi = 0.01$) fractions of target nodes, we can achieve larger changes by using link insertion—we are able to reach higher saturation levels more consistently and more quickly regardless of the dataset. Again, we can explain this intuitively—small fractions of target nodes have, on average, only few links pointing towards them. Hence, inserting a new link from a top webpage achieves larger changes than highlighting an existing (and probably negligible) link.

6.2 Navigational Boost

The blueish region from Figure 2b corresponds to smaller and more realistic bias strengths. In practice, increasing the visibility of a link (e.g., by repositioning or highlighting) by more than a factor of 15, meaning that it would receive 15 times more clicks than before, seems quite unrealistic. In particular, users position bias is estimated to be lower than 3.5 [17,20]. Hence, we focus on bias strengths ranging from 2 to 15 (the blueish region in Figure 2b) where we can observe a phase of quick increase in the energy of target nodes. We call this phase *navigational boost* phase. The results for all bias strengths from 2 to 15 are quite similar and therefore we report only the results for bias strength $b = 5$.

For click bias we observe a robust performance across datasets, see Figure 4. The energy of target nodes π'_t increases almost linearly with the fraction ϕ of target nodes. However, at higher ϕ (i.e., $0.15 \leq \phi \leq 0.2$) the linear trend tends to flatten. This is due to a transition to the stationary phase (cf. Section 6.1). Further, we observe a rather high variance of π'_t over ϕ and different sets of target nodes. For example, we measure the following average standard deviations over ϕ: W4S = 0.023, ORF = 0.103 and DEM = 0.068. This high variance can be attributed to situations in which smaller fractions of target nodes are often able to outperform larger ones. We depict one such extreme situation of two outlier samples marked as A and B in Figure 4. Target nodes depicted with A with $\phi = 0.1$ reach an energy that is almost twice as high as those of the target nodes depicted with B with $\phi = 0.2$.

One potential explanation for these observations is that if the energy of target nodes of the unmodified network is already quite high, that is, the target nodes include one or more nodes with a substantial energy, then the click bias acts as an *amplifier* further magnifying the energy of target nodes. On the other hand, target nodes with a small unmodified energy receive indeed the amplifying effect but are never able to reach the same (high) levels of the modified energy. Therefore, it is possible for smaller fractions of target nodes with one or more nodes with high starting energy to outperform larger fractions of target without such nodes. This can be further attributed to the target nodes structural properties, such as out-degree, in-degree and degree ratio, which we introduced in the previous sections. Basically, starting energy positively correlates with in-degree of target nodes, and therefore we can expect that the click bias is able to amplify target nodes with a higher in-degree more than the target nodes with a lower in-degree. In particular, to confirm this finding we conducted a similar correlation experiment as depicted in Figure 3, but used a combination of the target nodes in-degree and energy achieved due to a click bias. However, due to limitations in space, we do not report the experimental details here.

Finding. The fraction ϕ of target nodes does not have a decisive effect on navigational boost. Often, smaller ϕ exhibit larger effect sizes. Click bias acts as an *amplifier* that only magnifies what is already present in the target nodes.

In the case of link insertion, navigational boost appears to be highly dataset dependent (see Figure 4b). However, the variance of each dataset individually is very low with average standard deviations of 0.017 for W4S, 0.029 for ORF and 0.034 for DEM. Across all datasets we can observe a quick increase in the energy of target nodes with an increasing fraction of target nodes, which then experience a transition towards a stable saturation phase.

To explain the difference in performance between different datasets we have plotted the Lorenz curves of the stationary distributions of our datasets (see Figure 4c). We see that for W4S, a very small fraction of top nodes (0.01) only possesses 0.4 of energy. Diversely, for ORF and DEM the same fraction of top nodes already possesses energy higher than 0.85. As the out-component of a specific set of nodes acts as a drain for the energy of source nodes, connecting source

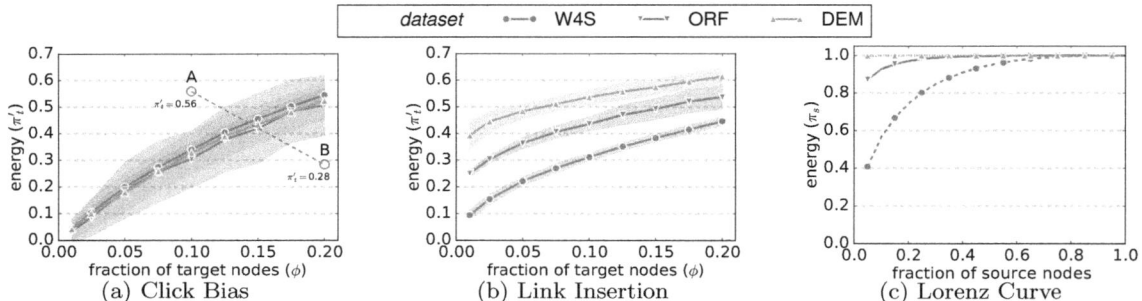

dataset ·—• W4S ▾—▾ ORF ▵—▵ DEM

| (a) Click Bias | (b) Link Insertion | (c) Lorenz Curve |

Figure 4: Navigational Boost. Left center figures depict the energy of target nodes after modifying the network through either inducing a click bias or link insertion respectively. The x-axes correspond to the fraction ϕ of target nodes, whereas on the y-axes we denote the energy of target nodes π_t'. Each line represents the average of 100 samples for each ϕ of one dataset. The areas filled with the same color denote the corresponding standard deviations. **Left.** Inducing a click bias is robust across datasets. However, the variability within values of ϕ is rather high. The high variance is caused by the presence or absence of one or more nodes with high original energy in the target nodes. Thus, in cases where such nodes are present in target nodes (depicted as point A in the plot) even smaller fractions of target nodes are able to outperform larger fractions of target nodes without such a top node (depicted as point B in the plot). **Center.** On the contrary, the performance of link insertion varies over datasets but is stable across various ϕ values, which is signified by the low standard deviation suggests over ϕ. **Right.** We plot the Lorenz curve of the datasets' original stationary distributions. We can observe that for different datasets these distributions are differently skewed. In particular, in DEM the energy of just a few nodes is close to 1, whereas in ORF and W4S we need far more nodes to reach the same level (i.e., 0.4 and 0.7 respectively). This explains why we can achieve the highest effect with link insertion in DEM, followed by ORF and W4S. Thus, the performance of link insertion depends on the initial stationary distribution of the network, whereas click biases are robust across datasets. Moreover, for smaller fractions of target nodes link insertion constantly outperforms click biases.

nodes with high energy to target nodes leads to a flow of energy from those source nodes towards target nodes. Thus, the initial energy of source nodes plays a crucial role in this process. Through link insertion from top source nodes towards target nodes we attach the target nodes as drains to such top nodes. Consequently, target nodes receive a huge amount of energy and experience a large navigational boost (i.e., ORF and DEM). In other words, we can say that link insertion induces *diffusion* of the energy of top nodes towards target nodes. Given the average degree of the network and the fraction of source nodes (which increases with the fraction ϕ of target nodes), we can use the Lorenz curves to approximately predict the point where the performance across datasets becomes similar. For example, the Lorenz curves of DEM and ORF meet around a fraction of 0.4 of source nodes and we can expect that the performance of those two datasets will become similar for all fractions of source nodes larger than 0.4. In the case of W4S, we need a larger fraction of source nodes (0.7) to reach a similar behavior (cf. Figure 4c).

Comparing link insertion with click bias we find that the former outperforms the latter for smaller fractions ϕ of target nodes. For example, in the DEM dataset, link insertion reaches four times higher energy values for the target nodes with $\phi = 0.01$. However, for higher values of ϕ the click bias exhibits a similar performance as link insertion. Further, in the case of the W4S dataset, the click bias even outperforms link insertion (see W4S in Figure 4a and Figure 4b) at $\phi = 0.2$).

Finding. The performance of link insertion varies across the datasets and depends on the skewness of the initial stationary distribution in a dataset. Inserting links from other important webpages towards a given set of webpages results in a higher navigational boost than with the click bias. This is due to the induced *diffusion* of the energy from top nodes towards target nodes.

Implications. If it is possible to insert new links on a website (especially if the fraction of target nodes is small) we should prefer the link insertion over the click bias. However, creation and insertion of such links may be problematic in practice. For example, on Wikipedia it may be difficult and semantically unjustified to insert new links to completely unrelated articles since this may have opposite and contrasting effects on the navigational behavior of users, such as confusion and dissatisfaction. In those cases we may rather choose to increase the transition probability of an already existing link by, for example, highlighting that link (i.e., using CSS[5]) or repositioning it to the webpage's top area. In some other scenarios (i.e., birthdays of famous inventors) implementing a banner which contains links towards a given set of webpages may be an easy way to insert thousands of new links instantly. In those cases, such user interface modifications may prove to have higher lasting effects on the stationary probability than, for example, highlighting links.

6.3 Influence Potential

Figure 5 depicts the effects of link modifications strategies on the relative increase of the energy of target nodes (i.e., influence potential). Again, we concentrated in this experiment on realistic settings for the bias strength from the interval $[2, 15]$. Since we got comparable results over that complete interval we present only the results for bias strength $b = 5$.

The performance of the click bias is robust across datasets and different ϕ with a low variance in both dimensions (cf. Figure 5a). We observe a negative correlation between influence potential and fraction ϕ of target nodes, meaning the smaller fractions of target nodes profit more from an induced click bias than larger fractions. Our calculations of the influence potential confirm once more the results from the previous section, in which smaller fractions with top en-

---

[5]cascading stylesheets

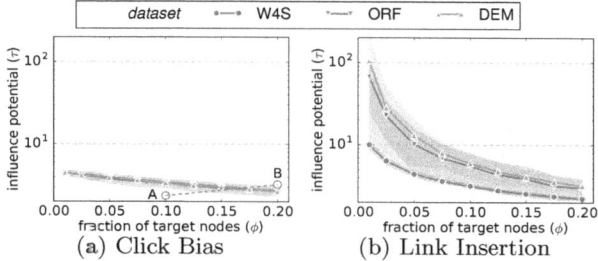

(a) Click Bias   (b) Link Insertion

Figure 5: Influence Potential. The figure depicts the relative increase in the energy of target nodes τ with a fixed bias strength of $b = 5$ over different ϕ and datasets. **Left.** Inducing a *click bias* performs robustly and similarly over all datasets (curves for different datasets overlap each other in the plot). Influence potential correlates negatively with the fraction of target nodes, that is, the relative increase in energy is higher for small fractions of target nodes than for large fractions. **Right.** With *link insertion*, we find a significant variance in performance across our datasets. This confirms our findings from the previous section—the skewness of the original stationary distribution determines the effectiveness of the link insertion strategy in a dataset. Similarly to the click bias, the influence potential decays with an increasing fraction of target nodes.

ergy nodes are able to outperform larger fractions of target nodes without top nodes. We once more depict two such examples from Figure 4a. Target nodes depicted by A with $\phi = 0.1$ reach an energy that is almost twice as high as those depicted by B with $\phi = 0.2$. However, nodes A start with a larger initial energy and nodes B with a smaller one. Therefore, in relative terms nodes B have a higher influence potential than nodes A (cf. Figure 5a).

Performance of link insertion is again strongly dependent of the dataset. However, similarly to the click bias we observe over all datasets that smaller fractions of target nodes profit significantly more from the link insertion than the larger ones. For example, in DEM dataset for $\phi = 0.01$ we measure an average influence potential of more than 100, whereas for $\phi = 0.2$ influence potential is less than 4 (cf. Figure 5b). A similar decay, although not as pronounced as in DEM can be seen in the other two datasets. Similarly to the navigational boost this high influence potential of smaller fractions of target nodes in the case of link insertion can be explained through the skewness of the initial stationary distributions (cf. Figure 4c).

As previously, we investigated more closely the relation between influence potential of small fractions of target nodes and their structural properties such as in-degree, out-degree and degree ratio. Target nodes with a high degree ratio (i.e., a small in-degree, a large out-degree or both) have the largest influence potential. Intuitively, such target nodes start with a very small initial energy and therefore can achieve a significant relative increase. On contrary, in absolute terms such target nodes keep a rather small energy even after the modification, whereas target nodes with a large initial energy (a low degree ratio) are experiencing a significant navigational boost in absolute terms but possess relatively low influence potential.

Finding. The influence potential of small fractions of target nodes is very high regardless of the link modification strategy. For click bias the influence potential is limited by the bias strength, whereas for link insertion we do not observe

such a limit and influence potential can become as high as 100. With increasing fraction of target nodes the influence potential decays drastically.

Implications. As previously, if possible we should prefer link insertion over click bias in cases where we are interested in utilizing the influence potential of the target nodes. Our findings suggest that in practice there is a trade-off that we need to make between optimizing for influence potential and for navigational boost. For the former, we need to aim at target nodes with a high degree ratio and for the latter at target nodes with a low degree ratio.

6.4 Combinations

In the previous experiments we found that in some situations link insertion should be preferred over click bias (e.g., small fraction ϕ of target nodes), whereas sometimes the opposite represents an optimal approach (e.g., large ϕ). For that reason we want now to shed more light onto combinations of both strategies, that is, we are interested in the navigational effects of simultaneously applying click bias and link insertion to varying extent. Figure 6 depicts the results of this experiment. We find consistent best performing mixtures over all datasets. In particular, we observe that for small fractions ϕ of target nodes, exclusive link insertion outperforms any other combination (see Figure 6a). For medium sized target nodes (i.e., $\phi = 0.1$) we observe a shift of best performing combinations towards $\alpha = 0.9$ for higher bias strengths (i.e., $b = 5$ and $b = 15$). This combination consist of 90% click bias and 10% link insertion. For combinations of large fractions of target nodes (i.e., $\phi = 0.2$) and small bias strengths ($b = 2$) the best performing combination is around $\alpha = 0.5$ (50% click bias and 50% link insertion) and further shifts towards $\alpha = 0.9$ (90% click bias and 10% link insertion) with an increased bias strength.

These results confirm our insights from the previous experiments. Thus, click biases act as an amplifier and only work well if target nodes initially possess valuable incoming links. This is highly likely for larger and medium sized fractions of target nodes, and very unlikely for the case of smaller fractions of target nodes. On the other hand, link insertion diffuses a large portion of the energy of top nodes towards target nodes. Hence, it works especially well for combinations of small fractions of target nodes and datasets with a highly skewed stationary distribution.

Finding. For small fractions of target nodes with initially low energy, pure link insertion should be preferred over any other combination. However, with increasing bias strength and larger fraction of target nodes, combinations consisting of 90% click bias and 10% link insertion performs best.

Implications. Smaller sets of webpages (i.e., small ϕ) should focus on introducing new links to achieve the highest browsing guidance. The bigger the set of webpages and the used bias strength becomes, the more this preference shifts towards a combination of 0.9, meaning that 90% of the modifications should be invested in increasing the transition probability of already existing links towards target nodes (e.g., highlighting in the user interface). The remaining 10% should be used to insert new links towards target nodes.

6.5 Stationary vs. Transient User Behavior

The random surfer which navigates forever (stationary behavior) may look like a rather unrealistic behavior of users. More realistically, a single user visits a website clicks a cou-

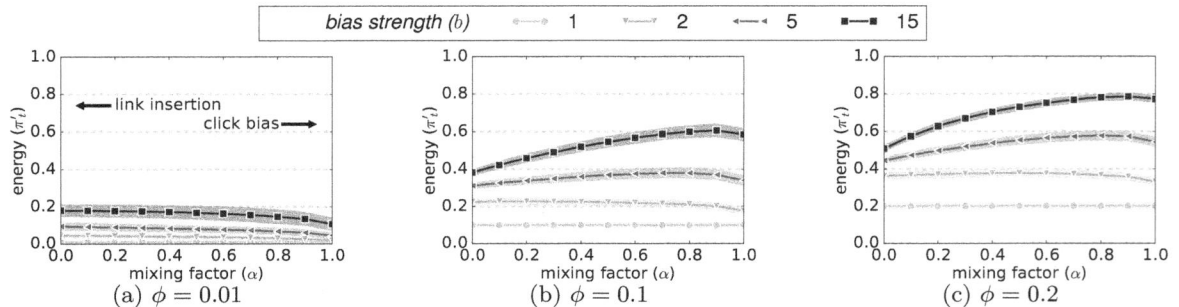

Figure 6: **Combinations of Link Modification Strategies.** The plots depict average results of 100 sets of target nodes of W4S for three ϕ: 0.01 small on the left, 0.1 medium in the middle, and 0.2 large on the right. On the x-axes we denote α, which defines the combination of the two link modification strategies, whereas on the y-axes we denote the energy of target nodes. We see that for smaller values of ϕ $\alpha = 0$ (100% link insertion) outperforms all the others over all used bias strengths. However, for medium and large ϕ values with higher bias strengths this sweet spot shifts towards higher combinations ($\alpha = 0.7$). In the other two datasets we can observe similar results.

ple of times on various links and leaves the website again (transient behavior). However, our calculations of the stationary distribution show that, at least on the networks that we have investigated in this paper these two behaviors are quite similar to each other.

The stationary distribution is calculated with the power-iteration method [11]. Thus, we initialize a probability vector representing an initial probability to find a random surfer on each particular node in the network. We initialize this vector (i) with a uniform distribution and (ii) by setting the visit probability of the home page to 1. The former initialization accounts for the assumption that initially each page is equally likely to be visited by users, whereas the latter models users entering the website over the home page. Afterwards, we iterate by recalculating the probabilities for the next click of the random surfer. Thus, one iteration step of the power-iteration method can be interpreted as a step or a click performed by the random surfer moving from the current node to one of its neighbors. Hence, the number of iteration steps that are needed until there are no significant changes in the node probabilities, that is, the convergence rate of the power-iteration method, can be interpreted as the number of clicks needed to model the stationary user behavior. In other words the random surfer does not need to navigate forever—it only needs to navigate through the network until the point where the next click does not change the observed stationary distribution.

In all our datasets, all networks that we generated and modified for these datasets, all combinations of fractions of target nodes ϕ and the bias strength b our calculations converge within 8 iterations regardless of the initialization. Thus, the stationary user behavior is in fact a behavior of users who navigate 8 pages in a website at most. We believe that these 8 clicks are within realistic boundaries for user behavior in the cases in which users decide to explore and browse a website. However, since many users leave a website immediately upon arrival or within only a single or a small number of clicks this still represents a limitation in our work. This limitation can be easily remedied by introducing a small teleportation probability of jumping to an arbitrary page without following the underlying network structure (i.e., calculating PageRank vector instead of the stationary distribution). We have already experimented with the calculations of PageRank and our first results are quite similar to results that we have presented in this paper.

However, we plan to address this question in more details in our future work.

7. CONCLUSIONS

In this paper we have analyzed the effects of two link modification strategies used to influence the typical whereabouts of the random surfer. We investigated how an induced click bias towards a set of webpages changes the stationary distribution (i.e., energy) of those pages. Additionally, we compared those effects with the consequences of altering the network structure by inserting new links. We find that both strategies have a high potential to modify the stationary distribution and that for certain situations there exist constantly high performing link modification strategy. In particular, click biases work well on sets of webpages containing already highly visible webpages, whereas link insertion should be preferred for sets of webpages consisting of pages with low visibility. Further, we showed that a simple structural property of target nodes, namely degree ratio, provides a valuable basis for the estimation of the effects of both link modification strategies.

Assuming that the random surfer is a realistic model of user behavior on the Web—which previous studies seem to confirm [9,15]—website operators can use our approach and open source framework to determine the best strategy for their settings without having to implement and test all the different strategies. Such strategies include but are not limited to altering link positions [20] (bias) or creating new links using a recommender systems [16] (link insertion).

An important practical issue that we have not addressed in this paper is usability. Usability considerations limit the number of new links that we can insert or how we can reposition links. In future, we plan to account for usability by extending our model and investigating limitations induced by various usability restrictions. Also, including the existing user link selection bias derived from user clickstreams into the model would further improve the practical relevance of our method.

Acknowledgments

This research was in part funded by the FWF Austrian Science Fund research project "Navigability of Decentralized Information Networks" (P 24866).

8. REFERENCES

[1] S. Al-Saffar and G. Heileman. Experimental bounds on the usefulness of personalized and topic-sensitive pagerank. In *Web Intelligence, ACM International Conference on*, pages 671–675. IEEE, 2007.

[2] L. Bian and H. Holtzman. Online friend recommendation through personality matching and collaborative filtering. *Proc. of UBICOMM*, pages 230–235, 2011.

[3] M. Bianchini, M. Gori, and F. Scarselli. Inside pagerank. *ACM Trans. Internet Technol.*, 5(1):92–128, Feb. 2005.

[4] S. Brin and L. Page. Reprint of: The anatomy of a large-scale hypertextual web search engine. *Computer networks*, 56(18):3825–3833, 2012.

[5] G. Buscher, E. Cutrell, and M. R. Morris. What do you see when you're surfing?: using eye tracking to predict salient regions of web pages. In *Proceedings of the SIGCHI conference on human factors in computing systems*, pages 21–30. ACM, 2009.

[6] D. Dimitrov, P. Singer, F. Lemmerich, and M. Strohmaier. Visual Positions of Links and Clicks on Wikipedia. In *Proceedings of the 25th International Conference on World Wide Web*, WWW '16 Companion, New York, NY, USA, 2016. ACM.

[7] C. Ding, X. He, P. Husbands, H. Zha, and H. D. Simon. Pagerank, hits and a unified framework for link analysis. In *Proceedings of the 25th annual international ACM SIGIR conference on Research and development in information retrieval*, pages 353–354. ACM, 2002.

[8] C. H. Ding, H. Zha, X. He, P. Husbands, and H. D. Simon. Link analysis: hubs and authorities on the world wide web. *SIAM review*, 46(2):256–268, 2004.

[9] F. Geigl, D. Lamprecht, R. Hofmann-Wellenhof, S. Walk, M. Strohmaier, and D. Helic. Random surfers on a web encyclopedia. In *Proceedings of the 15th International Conference on Knowledge Technologies and Data-driven Business*, i-KNOW '15, pages 5:1–5:8, New York, NY, USA, 2015. ACM.

[10] D. F. Gleich, P. G. Constantine, A. D. Flaxman, and A. Gunawardana. Tracking the random surfer: empirically measured teleportation parameters in pagerank. In *Proceedings of the 19th international conference on World wide web*, pages 381–390. ACM, 2010.

[11] G. H. Golub and C. F. Van Loan. *Matrix computations*, volume 3. JHU Press, 2012.

[12] Z. Gyöngyi, H. Garcia-Molina, and J. Pedersen. Combating web spam with trustrank. In *Proceedings of the Thirtieth international conference on Very large data bases-Volume 30*, pages 576–587. VLDB Endowment, 2004.

[13] T. H. Haveliwala. Topic-sensitive pagerank. In *Proceedings of the 11th international conference on World Wide Web*, pages 517–526. ACM, 2002.

[14] T. H. Haveliwala. Topic-sensitive pagerank: A context-sensitive ranking algorithm for web search. *Knowledge and Data Engineering, IEEE Transactions on*, 15(4):784–796, 2003.

[15] D. Helic, M. Strohmaier, M. Granitzer, and R. Scherer. Models of human navigation in information networks based on decentralized search. In *Proceedings of the 24th ACM Conference on Hypertext and Social Media*, pages 89–98. ACM, 2013.

[16] J. L. Herlocker, J. A. Konstan, L. G. Terveen, and J. T. Riedl. Evaluating collaborative filtering recommender systems. *ACM Transactions on Information Systems*, 22(1):5–53, 2004.

[17] T. Hogg and K. Lerman. Disentagling the effects of social signals. *Human Computation Journal*, 2(2):189–208, 2015.

[18] J. M. Kleinberg. Authoritative sources in a hyperlinked environment. *Journal of the ACM (JACM)*, 46(5):604–632, 1999.

[19] A. N. Langville and C. D. Meyer. Deeper inside pagerank. *Internet Mathematics*, 1(3):335–380, 2004.

[20] K. Lerman and T. Hogg. Leveraging position bias to improve peer recommendation. *PLoS ONE*, 9(6):e98914, 06 2014.

[21] N. Li and G. Chen. Multi-layered friendship modeling for location-based mobile social networks. In *MobiQuitous, 2009. 6th Annual International*, pages 1–10, 2009.

[22] L. Lovász. Random walks on graphs: A survey. *Combinatorics, Paul erdos is eighty*, 2(1):1–46, 1993.

[23] M. Moricz, Y. Dosbayev, and M. Berlyant. Pymk: Friend recommendation at myspace. In *Proceedings of the 2010 ACM SIGMOD International Conference on Management of Data*, SIGMOD '10, pages 999–1002, New York, NY, USA, 2010. ACM.

[24] J. Murphy, C. Hofacker, and R. Mizerski. Primacy and recency effects on clicking behavior. *Journal of Computer-Mediated Communication*, 11(2):522–535, 2006.

[25] U. Y. Ogras and R. Marculescu. " it's a small world after all": Noc performance optimization via long-range link insertion. *Very Large Scale Integration (VLSI) Systems, IEEE Transactions on*, 14(7):693–706, 2006.

[26] L. Page, S. Brin, R. Motwani, and T. Winograd. The pagerank citation ranking: bringing order to the web. 1999.

[27] G. Pandurangan, P. Raghavan, and E. Upfal. Using pagerank to characterize web structure. In *Computing and Combinatorics*, pages 330–339. Springer, 2002.

[28] M. Richardson and P. Domingos. The intelligent surfer: Probabilistic combination of link and content information in pagerank. In *NIPS*, pages 1441–1448, 2001.

[29] N. Silva, I.-R. Tsang, G. Cavalcanti, and I.-J. Tsang. A graph-based friend recommendation system using genetic algorithm. In *Evolutionary Computation (CEC), 2010 IEEE Congress on*, pages 1–7, 2010.

[30] R. West and J. Leskovec. Automatic versus human navigation in information networks. In *ICWSM*, 2012.

[31] W. Woess. Random walks on infinite graphs and groups-a survey on selected topics. *Bulletin of the London Mathematical Society*, 26(1):1–60, 1994.

[32] X. Xie. Potential friend recommendation in online social network. In *Green Computing and Communications (GreenCom), 2010 IEEE/ACM Int'l Conference on Int'l Conference on Cyber, Physical and Social Computing (CPSCom)*, pages 831–835, 2010.

Guiding Users through Asynchronous Meeting Content with Hypervideo Playback Plans

Andreas Girgensohn[1], Jennifer Marlow[1], Frank Shipman[2], Lynn Wilcox[1]

[1]FX Palo Alto Laboratory
3174 Porter Drive
Palo Alto, CA 94304
{andreasg,marlow,wilcox}@fxpal.com

[2]Department of Computer Science
Texas A&M University
College Station, TX 77843-3112
shipman@cs.tamu.edu

ABSTRACT

We previously created the HyperMeeting system to support a chain of geographically and temporally distributed meetings in the form of a hypervideo. This paper focuses on playback plans that guide users through the recorded meeting content by automatically following available hyperlinks. Our system generates playback plans based on users' interests or prior meeting attendance and presents a dialog that lets users select the most appropriate plan. Prior experience with playback plans revealed users' confusion with automatic link following within a sequence of meetings. To address this issue, we designed three timeline visualizations of playback plans. A user study comparing the timeline designs indicated that different visualizations are preferred for different tasks, making switching among them important. The study also provided insights that will guide research of personalized hypervideo both inside and outside a meeting context.

Author Keywords

Hypervideo; videoconferencing; interactive video; visualization.

1. INTRODUCTION

As the prevalence of distributed work teams increases, the volume of video meetings also grows. This increases the likelihood that not all participants will be able to synchronously converse. Currently, asynchronous review of video-recorded meetings can be a tedious process of going through large sections of irrelevant or old content in order to find a few key relevant points (which may be different from person to person). We identified a series of different meeting-review scenarios and developed an approach for proactively and intelligently inferring users' information-seeking goals. The concepts and design alternatives presented here provide an initial step towards understanding the potential benefits and challenges of enabling personalized information retrieval of relevant meeting details.

We make use of hypervideos that are a form of interactive media with links between a series of videos. With more videos being linked, it becomes difficult to navigate between the content and to keep a coherent awareness of one's place in the flow. If the hypervideo system knows about the user's motivations or information seeking goals, it can anticipate valuable paths through the network of linked videos. Such personalization is particularly valuable for users acquiring knowledge. There are many hypervideo applications aimed at knowledge acquisition, including education and training [5][27] and corporate memory [16].

Our research applies the concept of hypervideos to a video conferencing system that links conceptually related discussions created in a chain of geographically and temporally distributed meetings. Attendees may not attend all meetings, particularly when based in different locations and time zones. The HyperMeeting system introduces a new paradigm for enabling and supporting a sequence of videoconferences involving attendees with differing availability, locations, and participation. It lets attendees record and review a series of videoconference meetings with asynchronous attendance. Attendees of a later meeting simultaneously review video recordings of earlier meetings and add comments. During the course of watching a prior meeting, viewers can pause playback to have a discussion among those present. This creates a hyperlink from the paused video to the video being recorded in the follow-up meeting. In subsequent meetings, further discussions may be added to the hyperlinked meeting content, creating a meeting chain or hypermeeting (see Figure 1).

Viewing the meeting content may be a purely manual interaction where users select hyperlinks to be followed. To address the interaction challenge with complex, branching video topics and threads, we created the concept of playback plans to represent automatic navigation paths through hypervideo. For example, playback plans can help find key action items without having to review all previous meetings [20]. Also, we incorporate novel approaches aimed at improving user understanding of and control over playback plans. This includes a dialog for selecting the most appropriate playback plan, three alternate timeline visualizations of playback plans, transitions between playback plan visualizations, and an interactive recorded history of user interaction and navigation caused by playback plans. Our results inform the visualization of paths through hypervideo more generally.

A prior publication describes the core HyperMeeting system and an early instantiation of playback plans [8]. This paper presents extensions to the capabilities of playback plans, an interface for

HT '16, July 10-13, 2016, Halifax, NS, Canada
© 2016 ACM. ISBN 978-1-4503-4247-6/16/07...$15.00
DOI: http://dx.doi.org/10.1145/2914586.2914597

Figure 1. HyperMeeting with Four Meetings. Meeting Colors above the Videos Are Shown in the Timeline. Video of the Selected Meeting Is Larger.

users to select and tailor playback plans, and an evaluation of different UI design choices aimed at improving user understanding of and control over playback plans. The paper examines and discusses the technical and user-experience aspects of these new contributions.

The next section discusses related work. This is followed by a brief description of the HyperMeeting system. Then, playback plans are introduced including a description of how to generate, visualize, and interact with them. A user study of three timeline visualizations of playback plans is then presented. Finally, we discuss lessons learned and next steps in our research.

2. Related Work

Hypervideo consists of video segments that are connected with links. In the course of watching a video, users navigate to related videos through manually authored or automatically generated links. Early applications of hypervideo include tourism or sightseeing (e.g., Aspen Movie Map [15]), moving between recordings of semi-independent conversations (e.g., HyperCafe [24]), news [2], and education [4]. There are many hypervideo applications aimed at knowledge acquisition, including education and training [5][27] and corporate memory [16]. We focus on hypervideo where links connect video segments rather than media objects (e.g., web pages on topics in the video.) Also, our application focus is teleconference meetings.

Prior work on hypervideo (e.g., [24][25]) has focused on authored content where a person intentionally creates links between video segments. A video-recorded meeting could be taken as the starting point but prior systems lack the ability to identify topics and relations among topics as a way of authoring or generating the hypervideo. Also, they do not include features to support the meeting-specific aspects of the video (e.g., attachment of metadata indicating attendees, topics, and time/date indexing). Hypermedia models such as CHM [23] represent relationships between content elements and definition of presentation arrangements. Such models could be used to represent speaker, topic, and link information. However, none of these systems support geographically distributed synchronous viewing of hypervideos. There has been work to optimize prefetching of video content in anticipation of user-driven navigation [11].

The hyperlinks used in HyperMeeting are similar to those in previous work on detail-on-demand video [10]. Those links are attached to video segments and not to objects depicted in the video. Another similarity is that playback returns automatically to the source link anchor after the linked content is played. A central distinction between the work discussed here and prior research on hypervideo is that prior video players require user interaction to follow a link. The playback plans described in this paper identify the links to be followed automatically. User interests determine which links are followed and which links are ignored when the video player reaches their anchors.

While prior hypervideo research has not addressed distributed meetings, there are a number of teleconference systems that have. They employ a variety of approaches to address the issue of allowing people to asynchronously revisit and review content from discussions or meetings. One class of systems focuses on capturing the content of meetings for later consumption [6][7][12][19]. Such systems record content for later playback and browsing. They take advantage of natural activity during meetings (e.g., slide presentations or activities on an electronic whiteboard) to generate navigation points back into the record. These systems allow users to review and find information in a meeting but do not incorporate

the ability to extend a previous meeting or create links between meetings.

A second class of systems that have supported asynchronous meetings, e.g., Time Travel Proxy [26] and Video Threads [1], include short videos on topics with responses. The model of threaded messages loses the connections between topics and the larger activity context. In particular, each recorded video response is attached to a single prior video discussion. While the work on Time Travel Proxy and Video Threads supports video annotations to prior content and assumes a hierarchy of video recordings and responses, our approach interlinks full meetings with longer recordings with multiple links among pairs of recordings.

A last class of related systems support the synchronous viewing of video content on distributed devices [3][21]. These systems can include additional channels of communication (e.g., chat) for simultaneous viewers to discuss what they are watching. However, the records of communication are, at best, attached as metadata to the video content. Attached metadata related to the synchronous viewing of prior meetings is less powerful than hyperlinking between meetings.

3. The HyperMeeting System

The HyperMeeting system specializes hypervideo capabilities to support distributed meetings. The web-based HyperMeeting user interface is shown in Figure 2. It includes a live video conference and a player for a previously recorded meeting chain. In the depicted meeting chain, a fourth meeting with two participants is currently in progress.

A hypermeeting starts with a video conference where the video of each meeting attendee is recorded. During the meeting, attendees may enter topics and manually mark when a topic starts or ends.

The hypermeeting is continued in a second video conference where the attendees play the video recorded in the original meeting. Playback is synchronized among the recorded streams and across attendees such that all recorded streams play at the same time and all attendees see the same content. Each attendee can control the video playback for the current participants.

When the attendees of the second meeting continue the discussion started in the original meeting, they pause video playback to discuss their response. The action of pausing the playback creates a hyperlink from the first video to the second video.

When reviewing the previous two meetings in a third meeting, attendees may use the hyperlinks to navigate the recorded content. Links may be followed by clicking on them. Following such links allows the viewer to watch the original discussion together with responses from later meeting. Such a viewing pattern provides more continuity for the conversation compared to viewing the meetings in sequence.

Currently, we focus on distributed meetings conducted as a video conference. Separate video recordings of each attendee allow for simple speaker segmentation. As a result, multiple video streams are played together when the recorded meeting is being watched at a later time.

The HyperMeeting client runs in standard web browsers as a single page application. The live video conference among the distributed meeting attendees is maintained using WebRTC (Web Real-Time

Figure 2. HyperMeeting User Interface with Video Players at the Top and Live Video Conference at the Bottom.

Communication)[1] peer-to-peer connections. Meetings are visualized by manipulating the web page with JavaScript. Recorded video is displayed in HTML5 video tags and timelines are drawn in canvases.

The list of meetings, attendees, and topics are shown on the left of the player (see Figure 2). At the top is the bank of video players for the individual video streams that make up the hypermeeting. Below these is the timeline visualization that presents a variety of information about the hypermeeting. Timelines and video players are color-coded to indicate the meeting they belong to. Colored circles represent links that use the color of the meeting they point to. Links are numbered in creation order with the two ends having the same number. Colored regions around link circles indicate link anchors that would be played when traversing links. Video players of non-active meetings are paused and reduced in size.

4. Automatic Navigation via Playback Plans

The focus of this paper is a study of different designs for timeline visualization and the effect they have on user disorientation and comprehension of the video content. Before we discuss the different timeline designs, we present the concept of playback plans that these visualizations are supporting.

While links can be followed manually, it is often convenient to automatically follow relevant links. The system can determine paths through the hypervideo that cover relevant information for the viewers based on their attendance of prior meetings. We

developed the concept of *playback plans* to describe different paths through a hypervideo that are automatically followed during playback. Playback plans for hypermeetings are meant to follow the discussion distributed over multiple recorded meetings by presenting related content together. Additionally, playback plans can be personalized to reduce the quantity of content that is re-watched by individuals.

A playback plan is similar to an edit decision list for video editing. It consists of a sequence of video segments from multiple videos that are played in order. Some plans are a generalization of hypervideo link behaviors [10] – that is they determine what happens at the start or end of a source or destination link anchor during playback. Unlike edit decision lists, playback plans are computed automatically based on previous behavior of the user, available hyperlinks, and specified filter conditions. Filters can identify parts of the videos to include, for example, particular topics, speakers, or non-silent portions.

Different user actions, such as selecting a meeting or a particular link, result in different playback plans. Personalized playback plans can be based on whether the user took part in prior meetings. Consider the case of three meetings shown in Figure 3. An initial meeting is recorded and then additional discussions occur during Meeting 2 and are attached to the initial meeting via two links (Links A and B). A final meeting includes two links connecting the discussions to Meeting 2 (Links C and D). In the case of a user who participated in none of the meetings, it would make sense to play

---

[1] http://www.w3.org/TR/webrtc/

the video of the first meeting and to automatically follow all links to later meetings such that comments could be viewed in context. Such a plan would perform a depth-first traversal on all of the discussion attached to the originally selected meeting. After Segment 2, playback would visit Segments 7, 8, 15, and 9 before continuing with Segment 3. For participants in earlier meetings, an alternative playback would avoid watching recordings of meetings that they were at.

We identified a set of playback plans that are appropriate to particular use scenarios. The plans are divided into two classes: when selecting a whole meeting and when selecting a hyperlink. Playback plans can be used to filter recorded content and are interactive (i.e., users can navigate within a playback plan). For playing one meeting within a hypermeeting, a plan could (a) just play that meeting without following links, (b) follow only links to later meetings, either the next level or all levels, (c) follow only links to earlier meetings, or (d) follow all links. Plans can also be filtered based on who is speaking in each segment or which topics are covered.

In a meeting chain, each meeting may consist of multiple video streams depicting meeting attendees. Those video streams use time-synchronized playback. When user actions result in the generation of a new playback plan, the new plan is distributed to all meeting attendees so that their video playback can be synchronized. The video player of each attendee can follow the same plan independently, requiring only occasional synchronization messages to avoid drift.

4.1 Intelligently Inferring Playback Plans

We conducted informal user studies where remote meeting attendees used different versions of the HyperMeeting system. Those sessions provided guidance for system improvements and helped identify different use scenarios and playback plans appropriate for those scenarios. The plans contain elements from previous work on taxonomies of meeting-search needs (e.g., [22]), but are adapted specifically to the context of asynchronously reviewing a chain of ongoing meetings. Selecting a playback plan takes into account participation in previous meetings. As the system has a record of meeting participation, it can generate all possible playback plans that fit the participation history and present them to the user in order of the likely viewing behavior.

Review all meetings. For a user who has not participated in the meeting chain, one could play the video of the meeting that started the chain and automatically follow all links to subsequent meetings such that those comments can be viewed in context. Such a traversal through the hypervideo would skip the parts of the subsequent meetings that are not linked, presumably because the content in these portions is not related to the older meetings. This plan was described earlier in the context of Figure 3.

Catch-up. For a user who missed a meeting, the missed meeting could be played in the context of the earlier and later meetings. In this case, source anchors of links pointing to the missed meeting would be played before destination anchors in that meeting. Links to subsequent meetings would be followed as before. For example, a viewer who missed Meeting 2 in Figure 3 would see Segments 6, 2, 7, 8, 15, 9, 10, 4, 11, 12, 13, and 17.

Filter. Users may only be interested in particular topics or speakers. Thus, a plan could playback any responses to segments in which the current user was a speaker, first playing the original segment

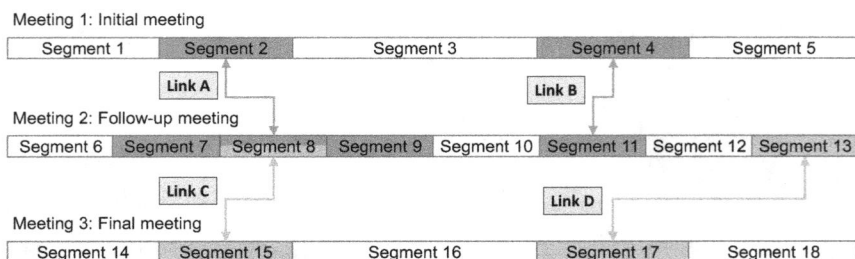

Meeting 1: Initial meeting

| Segment 1 | Segment 2 | Segment 3 | Segment 4 | Segment 5 |

Link A   Link B

Meeting 2: Follow-up meeting

| Segment 6 | Segment 7 | Segment 8 | Segment 9 | Segment 10 | Segment 11 | Segment 12 | Segment 13 |

Link C   Link D

Meeting 3: Final meeting

| Segment 14 | Segment 15 | Segment 16 | Segment 17 | Segment 18 |

Figure 3. Three video meetings interconnected by hyperlinks.

followed by the responses. Similarly, topic-oriented plans can play through segments tagged with particular topics and any content attached to those segments. A common filter can skip silence in the video. Such a filter is useful in situations where meeting attendees are listening to an older meeting without speaking at the same time. Watching the silent part of the meeting would be of little use to the viewer. Because filters may skip passages as short as a few seconds, many video segments could be produced by such filters. Rather than distributing long video segment lists to other meeting participants and storing them in the database, an abstract description of playback plans is used. Each client can compute the video segment list from the abstract description and the currently active filters.

4.2 Selecting Among Playback Plans

Users may select a plan from a set of candidate playback plans. For example, Figure 4 shows a selection based on the user's attendance of meetings. The plan generation uses the earlier discussed patterns and checks which of them are applicable. If different patterns would be instantiated as the same playback plan, only one of the instances is presented.

As the user selects a plan, it is visualized in the timeline. Once the plan is as desired, the user can play the described video. If none of the plans meet the user's needs, they can cancel the plan.

The plan offered first allows the viewer to catch up on the meeting by starting with the earliest meeting that the user did not attend. Whenever a destination link anchor is encountered in that meeting, the source anchor of the link is played first to provide context. If that source anchor contains destination anchors for other links, those links are handled in the same fashion. When a source link anchor is encountered, the corresponding destination link anchor in the later meeting is played next. If it contains links as well, they are followed. Figure 4 shows an example of that plan in combination with filters for skipping silence and for only including the first topic. To review all meetings, users may choose to start with the oldest meeting regardless of attendance.

The effects of the selection choices are visualized in a stacked timeline depicted at the bottom of Figure 4. A red circle indicates the meeting where the playback plan starts. Translucent red overlays mark the parts of the meetings that are included in the playback plan. The selected *catch-up* plan starts with the middle meeting that the user missed and follows encountered hyperlinks to older and newer meetings. In addition, the first topic is selected as a filter and silent passages are skipped. While the start of the green meeting is not silent, it does not have the topic of interest selected so it is skipped. A brief utterance at 2:30 is included. Otherwise, only link anchors inside the first topic are included, with some of them being slightly trimmed due to silence. In each link-anchor pair, the older source anchor is played before the newer destination anchor.

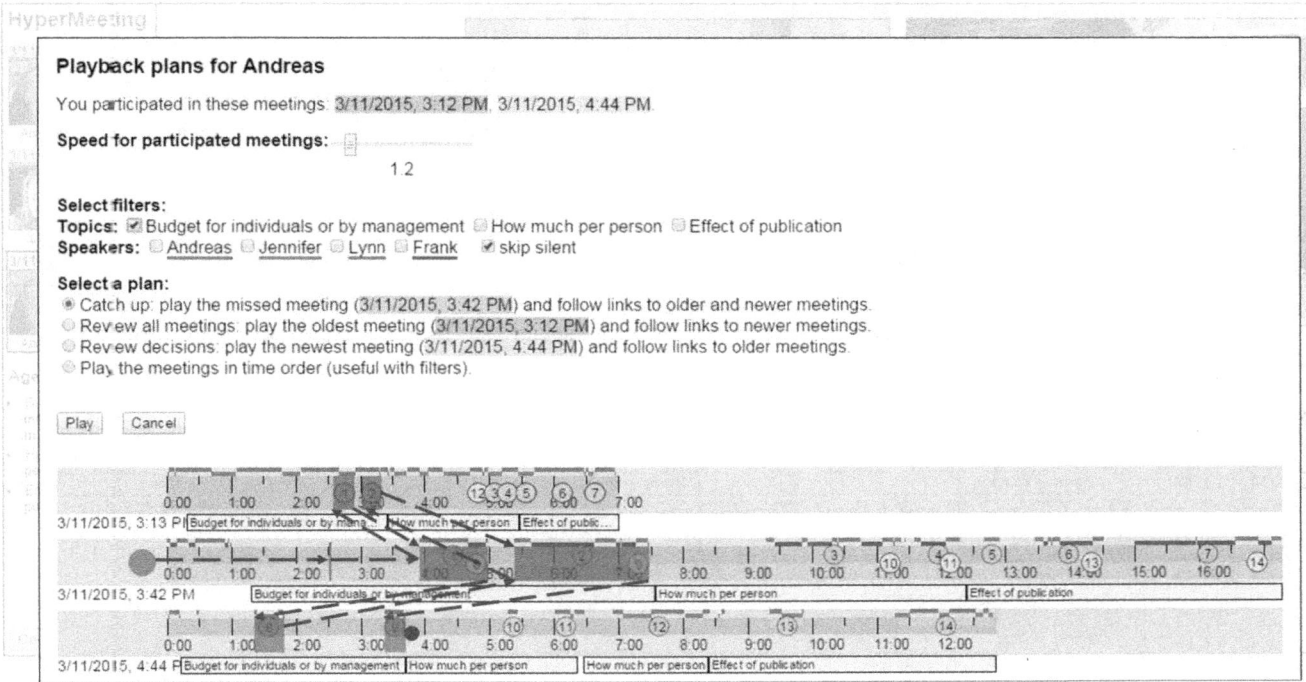

Figure 4. Selected "Catch Up" Playback Plan Combined with Topic and Silence Filters. Red Areas in the Timelines Indicate the Video Included in the Plan Starting at the Red Dot.

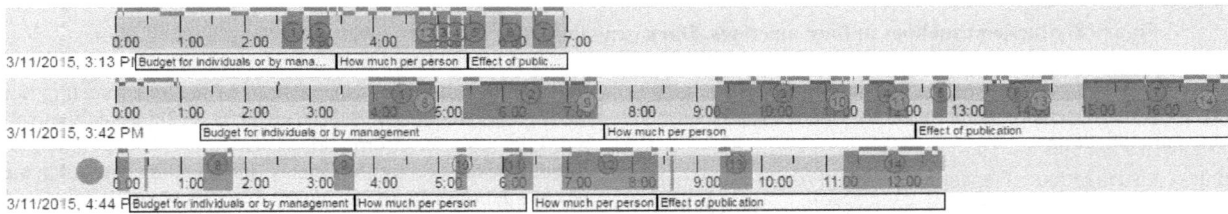

Figure 5. Playback Plan for "Review Decisions" and "Skip Silent" Starting at the Newest Meeting (Red Dot).

Figure 5 shows an example of the *review-decisions* plan for a user who wants to just look at the decisions made in a meeting chain. The plan starts with the newest meeting and plays linked content from older meetings. It is the same as the *catch-up* plan for somebody who missed just the newest meeting. In this example, the plan is combined with a filter for skipping silence.

Link anchors played for context and links to later meetings may refer to meetings that the users attended. Users may play those meetings at a higher speed.

For all meetings in the playback plan, silence may be skipped. Skipping silence is most beneficial when starting with a later meeting in the chain because time in those meetings is spent listening to earlier meetings. Most of the non-silent meeting content may be hyperlinked. However, new topics may be introduced in later meetings that would not have links to earlier meetings.

Users may play only the content that they missed and not follow links leading to meetings they attended. This can be controlled via an age cutoff, e.g., by skipping all known content from the past week.

In addition to selecting the general playback plan strategy, users may indicate that they are only interested in certain topics or people. Check boxes can be used to turn topics or particular speakers on or off. For speakers, one can select to also include adjacent passages from other speakers to provide some context. When selecting only one topic, automatic link following may be less important because the topic provides the context. In such a situation, selecting to play the parts of the meetings tagged with the topic in time order may be more desirable.

Overall, the selection of a playback plan combines automated decisions based on the user's prior participation with options for user adaptation. By associating playback plans with goals and visualizing the plans, HyperMeeting supports user understanding of the effect of their selections.

5. Plan Visualization and Control

In an initial study [8], participants found hyperlinks between meeting discussions to be useful. However, usability issues arose regarding the different playback plans invoked during interaction with a hypermeeting. A common complaint was feeling lost, not knowing where in the meeting chain you were after following hyperlinks. Participants suggested improvements to link behavior such as visualizing the parts of the meeting that had been seen and providing a back button to undo the effect of automatic link following.

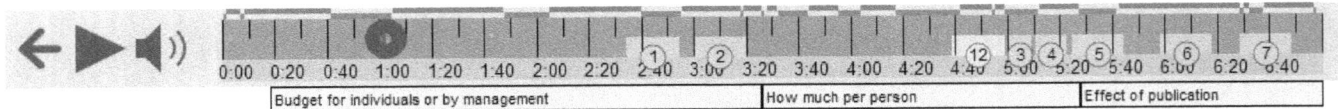

Figure 6. Single timeline showing the oldest meeting of three meetings. Colors above the timeline indicate speaker changes.

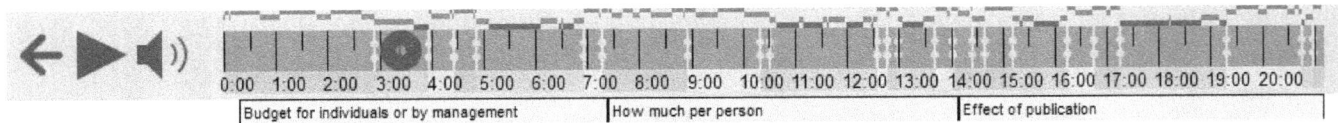

Figure 7. Merged timeline for a playback plan covering oldest meeting and links from it. Colors indicate the meetings.

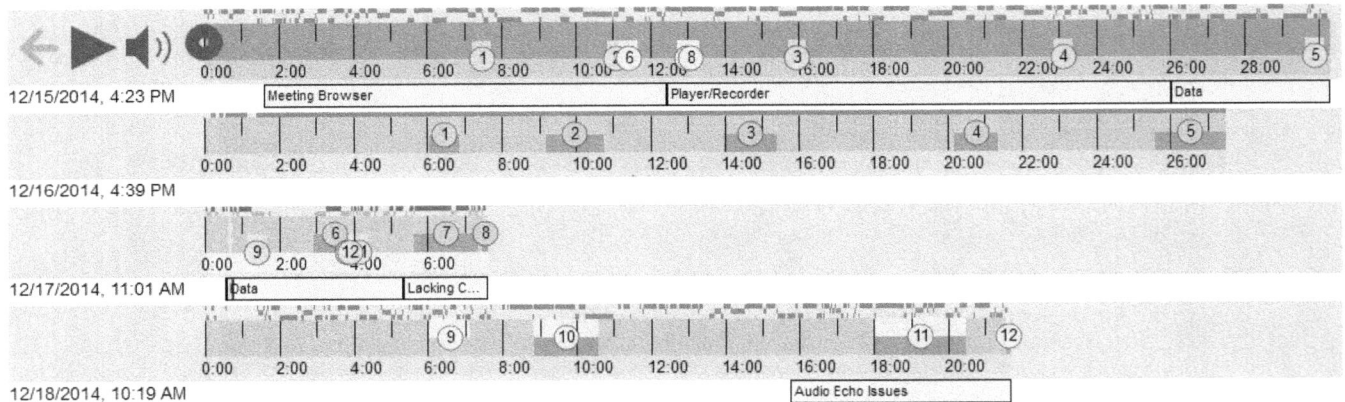

Figure 8. Stacked timelines of four meetings. Dark gray indicates the parts covered by the playback plan.

To improve the use of playback plans, we built on initial findings from [8] to further explore techniques for their visualization, transition, and interaction.

Designing a visualization of a complex set of time-distributed conversations across topics and people can be challenging. There is a tradeoff to be made between providing a great degree of detail (which can be informative but cognitively challenging to interpret) and hiding this detail from the user (which can be easier to visually parse but may obscure useful connections between topics).

No single visualization is likely to be best in all use contexts. Hence, there needs to be a user selectable and automatic way of transitioning between the views of the playback plan. HyperMeeting includes a toggle for users to switch between the views (see checkbox "merge timeline" at the center of Figure 2. HyperMeeting User Interface with Video Players at the Top and Live Video Conference at the Bottom.). Furthermore, double-clicking on the timeline toggles between a merged and non-merged timeline from the other two views.

Prior work in information visualization has explored ways of depicting the flow of events or information over time (e.g., [17][22][29]). However, these visualizations focus on static (non-animated) displays of information. When the information visualized is dynamic and presented in video format, additional cues such as changing speakers, voices, and content being discussed add additional complexity and cognitive load. We focused on three different visualizations of playback plans that revolve around timelines. These timelines show information such as speaker and topic changes and indicate the presence of hyperlinks.

In designing alternate visualizations of the hypermeeting timeline, we incorporated Wang Baldonado et al.'s [28] guidelines for using multiple views for information visualization. These guidelines were initially developed for the display of a complex data set in multiple representations. In the context of HyperMeeting, we apply the design principles to address various tradeoffs in providing multiple views of multiple meetings and helping guide viewers interested in following multiple topics over time. In particular, we incorporated the principles of parsimony, self-evidence, decomposition, consistency, and attention management in different combinations to compare and contrast the relative advantages and disadvantages of each. These principles are elaborated in their application for the respective visualizations that are described in the next subsections.

5.1 Single Timeline

The first visualization, shown in Figure 6, is the standard view of the timeline. This timeline follows the principle of self-evidence [28] and employs perceptual cues (in this case, colored and numbered circles) to make the relationships among the multiple meetings evident. In this view, the hypervideo structure (a set of recorded synchronous meetings and a set of links between segments of these recordings) is presented to the user with one recorded meeting being visualized at a time. After navigating to another meeting, the timeline for that meeting is shown. The playback control to the left of the timeline controls the currently shown meeting. In this view, there is no visualization of the overall playback plan generated by the user's most recent navigation action (e.g., selection of a meeting, link or topic or navigation within the current meeting) as meetings that are not currently being viewed are not visualized.

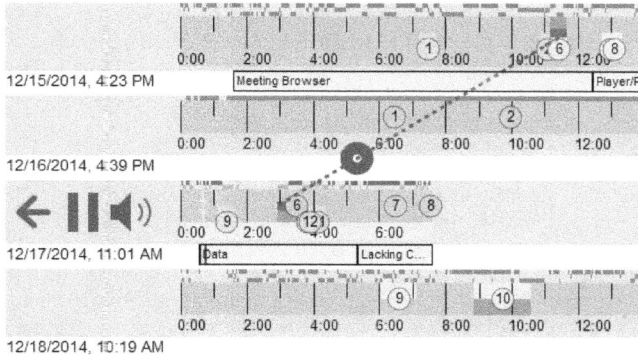

Figure 10. Animation of playback indicator along dashed line during link traversal.

Early users of this timeline design did not have an accurate mental model of the relationships among meetings and topics. Although the single timeline took up less display space, it presented challenges with context switching as the meeting shifted.

5.2 Merged Timeline

To improve users' expectations of what they are going to see, we developed the merged timeline shown in Figure 7. Like the single timeline, the merged timeline is also parsimonious and consistent by using a single view to provide a user with a stable context for analysis [28]. Specifically, the merged timeline does not change as the meeting progresses. This design uses the attention management principle by showing only the relevant parts of the timelines. A benefit of such a design is that the need for display space is reduced. However, a potential drawback is usability issues with memory, comparison, and context switching. This timeline concatenates the portions of the recorded meetings that will be shown based on the current playback plan. Links are not visualized because the automatic link traversal is implied in the playback plan. Links outside the playback plan cannot be selected in this view. Color is used to indicate which meeting will be shown when. Colors are also merged and standardized for the meeting attendees so the same person has the same color across meetings when presenting speaker segmentation information along with the merged timeline.

It has been suggested to us to create a variant of the merged timeline in form of a Gantt chart[2] that would make it look similar to the stacked timeline described in the next section. While such a variant would introduce redundant coding for the meeting a video segment belongs to, it adds no other advantage and takes up more space. We chose not to test this variant in the interest of time.

5.3 Stacked Timeline

A weakness of the merged timeline is that it does not provide information about the material not included in the current playback plan. Hence, users do not know how much of the content they are seeing relative to the amount available and the relative positions of the segments in the meetings. Thus, we designed a third visualization to display this content. It does so at the cost of providing multiple timelines simultaneously rather than a single timeline as in the two previous visualizations. By using the rule of decomposition to visually split the individual meeting timelines from each other, the problems of cognitive overload of a single complex view could be reduced. Multiple views can help the user to "divide and conquer" by reducing the amount of data they need to process at one time [28]. The stacked timeline shows the

hypervideo structure (as in the single timeline) but also shows the segments of all meetings that are part of the current playback plan (as in the merged timeline). The coverage of the playback plan is indicated by a darker shade of gray. Figure 8 uses a chain of four meetings instead of the earlier used chain of three meetings to better illustrate the concept of the stacked timeline. The three-part stacked timeline can be seen in Figure 4.

Unlike the other two timeline designs, the user's attention has to shift when playback moves to another meeting. In the stack of timelines shown in Figure 8, the playback control moves to the timeline of the meeting currently being played. While following a link, the playback indicator is animated in its path from one meeting to the other (see Figure 10). This animation was designed to use the rule of attention management to help ensure that the user focuses on the right view at the right time [28].

6. Evaluation Setup and Participants

A study comparing the three timeline visualizations was performed to assess their relative impact on user disorientation, comprehension, and satisfaction when watching an automatic meeting playback. We used the *review-all-meetings* playback plan in the study because that would be the plan used most frequently by viewers who did not attend any of the meetings. Watching previous meetings as an observer is a common playback plan use case, especially for viewers who did not attend those meetings. The plan starts at the oldest meeting and follows all links to newer meetings. The study was a within-subjects design where each participant was exposed to the three different timeline visualizations and provided comments on the advantages and disadvantages of each.

6.1 Method

This study was conducted using an Amazon Mechanical Turk Human Intelligence Task (HIT). Each participant watched a hypermeeting and answered questions about their experience with each of the three designs. The study was developed using best practices from the literature [13][14][18].

The overall structure of the HIT was training followed by three sections for the three designs. There was additional training between sections. Each section consisted of two halves of watching video followed by questionnaires.

Because hypervideo is not a common concept, training included several instructional resources beginning with a textual description of the task. This was followed by a storyboard explaining how the hypervideo was recorded (shown in Figure 9). Finally, a video was presented introducing the interface and its features containing scenes from a similar hypermeeting to the one they would see in the actual task.

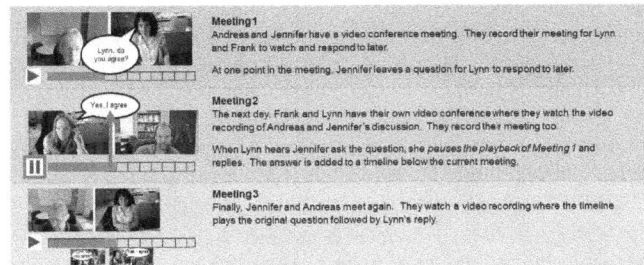

Figure 9. Storyboard for study.

---

[2] https://en.wikipedia.org/wiki/Gantt_chart

Before switching to a different timeline design, participants were shown a video explaining the features in the particular timeline design. During training, participants answered seven questions about the videos to ensure attention and comprehension.

The hypermeeting in the actual task consisted of three separate meetings between two pairs of individuals and covered three topics. While the order of topics was fixed – participants saw the meetings from beginning to end – the order of designs was counterbalanced using a Latin Square design to account for learning and fatigue effects. There were six possible orders for viewing the timelines: two in which each design (single, merged, or stacked) appeared first, two in which each design appeared second, and two in which each design appeared third.

The overall goal of the presented hypermeeting was to establish a conference travel policy for a research lab. The three topics were (1) whether to have individual budgets or budgets controlled by managers, (2) how much per person, and (3) what effect having publications at the conference should have, if any.

To make sure that all participants experienced the playback plan in the same way, we recorded a screen-capture movie of the playback of the hypermeeting in each timeline design. This gave participants experience with each design while minimizing the required time. The playback speed was set to 1.2 times real-time. Participants could not pause or rewind the movie. The movie paused twice for each topic/design. At each pause, the participant was asked 3-4 questions about the content of the segment they had just watched.

After the second segment on a topic, participants were asked to answer eight 5-point Likert-scale questions (*strongly disagree* to *strongly agree*) about the usability, understandability, and design of the visualization (see Table 1). Finally, after watching the last segment of the hypermeeting, participants were asked which were their favorite and least favorite interfaces and why. They were also asked to provide feedback on the trade-offs between the designs and any other comments they might have on their experience.

6.2 Participants

The 126 participants in the study were part of the US Mechanical Turk population who had at least a 95% acceptance rate for their past work. They were paid $4.50 for the approximately half hour it took to take part in the study regardless of whether we used their data or not. Nine participants who made eight or more errors on the 26 factual questions (seven from training and 19 from actual meeting footage) were removed from consideration to ensure data was from participants who paid attention to the content and activity. To ensure proper balance, data for the first 18 of the remaining participants in each of the six orders of exposure to the designs were included in the final analysis. Thus the remaining discussion concerns data from 108 participants.

The participants included 43 women and 65 men. Most of the participants were in their 20s (47) or 30s (39) although there were also participants in their 40s (13), 50s (5), teens (3), and 60 or over (1). All but 16 participants had at least some college education with 12 having graduate degrees, 47 having Bachelor degrees and 11 having Associates degrees. Nine of the 22 participants reporting some college time but no degree were among the 16 current students.

We also asked about participant experience with videoconferencing as that is the most common related class of system to the one being viewed in the study. 61 reported at most infrequent use. This included 13 reporting never using videoconferencing software, 22 reporting use of a couple times, and 26 reporting a few times a year. There were 47 participants that reported regular use including 25

reporting a few times a month, 16 reporting weekly use, and 6 reporting daily use. While only half the participants regularly use videoconferencing software, the assessments of the other participants are still valuable because the use of videoconferencing in the office increases at a rapid pace.

7. Results

Results are presented regarding usability assessments for the designs, the favorite and least favorite designs as identified by participants, and comments on trade-offs between designs or other suggestions/feedback. Participants were also asked to answer comprehension questions about the content of the meeting but there was no effect of design on the correctness of answers so that data is not reported further.

7.1 Usability Assessments

To analyze the effect of timeline type on user experience, we combined the responses to the eight Likert-scale questions (see Table 1) into an overall "usability" scale with a maximum score of 40. We inverted the scores of the odd-numbered questions such that a score of 5 was always most positive. We then performed a within-subjects analysis, using a 3x6 repeated measures mixed-model ANOVA where usability was the dependent measure and the three timeline types, six possible timeline orders, and the interaction between timeline type and order were independent measures. We also included participant familiarity with video conferencing as a covariate, and Participant ID was modeled as a random effect.

There was a significant main effect of timeline type on usability ($F(2,204)=13.53$, $p<.001$). A Tukey HSD post-hoc test revealed the merged timeline was rated as significantly more usable ($M=29.69$) than either the single timeline ($M=27.52$) or the stacked timeline ($M=26.44$).

We also expected that there would be some learning effects as participants gradually gained familiarity and confidence with hypermeetings. There was a significant main effect of the order in which participants experienced the timelines on perceived timeline usability ($F(5,102)=2.7$, $p=.02$). People who saw the single timeline first rated all timelines (on average) as significantly more usable than people who saw the stacked timeline first.

Prior experience has shown that it can take users some time to understand the structure of a hypermeeting. This challenge likely affected participant experience during the study. As a result, we compared the usability results between the 36 participants that saw each design last. In this case, the people who saw the merged timeline last rated it as significantly better ($M=29.47$) than those

1. The timeline helped me understand the flow of the conversation between people.
2. The timeline distracted me from the content of the meeting.
3. The timeline helped me understand relationships between the meetings.
4. The timeline was confusing.
5. I expect I could use the timeline to accurately find a particular point in the discussion.
6. The timeline hid information I would find valuable.
7. The order of the segments of meetings played made sense to me.
8. The transitions between meetings were confusing.

Table 1. Likert-scale questions about each timeline design

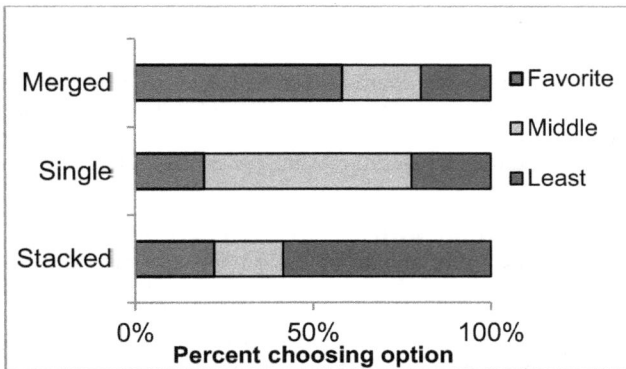

Figure 11. Relative preferences of each timeline design.

who saw the single timeline last (M=25.67) ($F(2,105)$=3.08, p=.04).

There was a near-significant interaction between timeline type and order on usability ($F(10,204)$=1.78, p=.06). In this case, the single timeline was rated as significantly more usable (M=30) when it came first in the order of timeline evaluation compared to when it came last in the order (M=22.66). This suggests that when participants had more experience with the system and with other alternative designs, the single timeline was viewed as even worse.

Finally, there was a significant effect of familiarity with video conferencing; as participants' prior experience using video conferencing tools increased, it had a positive effect on overall perceptions of timeline usability ($F(1,101)$=16.26, p<.001).

7.2 Favorite and Least Favorite Designs

At the end of the study, we had participants compare the three timelines against each other and discuss their favorite and least favorite designs (and why). This was done to mitigate the impact of potential order effects. These comments provided more insight into the design elements that worked and were challenging across the different designs.

The merged timeline was identified by 63 of the 108 participants as their favorite. Stacked was favored by 24 and single was favored by 21. Figure 11 shows the percentages of respondents who chose each timeline type as their favorite, middle, and least favorite design. The open-ended comments gave further insights into the most prevalent positive and negative aspects of the various designs.

7.2.1 Merged Timeline

The most positive aspect of the merged timeline was its general ease of interpretation. 19 of the 63 participants who chose it as their favorite mentioned that it was easy to tell where the meeting would switch and who would be speaking next. We initially expected that the parsimonious nature of the merged timeline design would create a stable context for interpretation that was also not too complex. Multiple comments echoed agreement with these principles. The merged timeline was described as straightforward or easy to follow and understand by 14 individuals. 14 respondents also mentioned it was compact, simple, or consolidated.

For me it was easiest to follow. I always knew when it would transition and could anticipate which group would be speaking. I could also see what the conversation was about if I looked at the bottom. With this timeline I could skip around and still know where to find the information I needed.

Another positive aspect of the merged timeline was that it presented a continuous view of the meetings (5), and unlike the other two

views, there was no movement (5). This made it less distracting (4) and less intimidating (1).

It made the most sense for someone watching the entire set of meetings in one shot, as for the viewer, it's just one meeting that jumps around.

There were several negative comments about the merged timeline. Seven people found the view to be too crowded, with too much information in too little space.

One conceptual challenge in the design of timeline visualization was how to avoid creating distractions with a lot of movement and visual cues jumping around in the timeline making it confusing to anticipate when the meeting would change and when. The merged design avoided this issue by signaling when a change would occur without using visual motion over several areas of the screen.

7.2.2 Single Timeline

Overall, the single timeline fell between the merged and stacked timeline in terms of preference. Positive aspects of this design also focused around the relative simplicity of the design, which was seen as being clean and digestible (5) and easy to follow and understand (5).

However, unlike the merged timeline, that showed all the information in a single view, the single timeline transitioned between three individual meeting timelines. This led some people to feel as though information was being hidden from them since they could only see one meeting at a time (5). Also, unlike the merged timeline, more people found it difficult to know when the meeting would jump and where it would jump to (5).

7.2.3 Stacked Timeline

The stacked timeline was the most detailed and also required the most screen real estate to show the individual meeting timelines all in one place. As a result, it was also necessary to use attention management principles to help users understand where they were at any given point and where they were going when a jump occurred. This attention management device was implemented as a moving gray circle that showed the flow of the conversation. Eight people appreciated the use of the circle to show the flow of conversation. The use of decomposition to divide up the different meeting timelines was also a frequent positive aspect mentioned by five people who preferred the stacked timeline. One person appreciated that this timeline showed the "most data."

However, while some people appreciated the gray dot moving between individual timelines, nearly twice as many disliked this feature. In particular, many viewed the moving dot as distracting, which made it hard to follow the conversation with the visual movement. Additionally, eight users found the information density to be too great, describing it as "too spread out" or "cluttered and messy." The following quotes illustrate some of the frequently-mentioned negatives about the stacked timeline:

I found this to contain too much extraneous information and it was difficult to really piece together the timeline of when it was going to jump to another meeting and where in the meeting it would jump to. There is way too much clutter and confusion in this design. More is better in most cases, but not here. It didn't really make intuitive sense and all of that information is not only confusing, but also distracting.

It was confusing to try to look at the timeline and understand what was going on and follow a coherent discussion at the same time.

This presentation can get busy, and it feels too easy to get lost in the flow of the different responses and answers to one another. It feels like something a physics professor would love, though! It's like some play of linear time presented across three separate possibilities.

Our initial hypothesis was that the stacked timeline would be preferred because it provides the clearest visualization of the playback plan within the context of the whole hypermeeting. As the study participants could not access the video outside the playback plan, this information may not have been relevant for them. Also, the comments make clear that dividing attention between the video and the timeline was difficult. Further studies will investigate whether the stacked timeline is more useful for information seeking tasks.

7.3 Comments on Trade-Offs

After they had experienced all three timelines, users were asked to comment on the trade-offs between each version. Overall, there is a tradeoff between decomposition and providing too much information (the main complaint for the stacked timeline). Also, there is a tradeoff with using parsimony to visually navigate the user through multiple streams without being distracting, but essentially hiding most of the information from the user (the complaint with the single timeline). Many of the users realized the tradeoffs between a large amount of detailed information (which could induce cognitive load) and a summary of the information, which is less informative but easier to mentally follow.

You can get more information in a design like Design 2 [stacked], but you keep it less confusing if you limit it to one timeline (like in 1 [single] and 3 [merged]). Loss of information isn't great but the simplicity of the system is apparent in both 1 [single] and 3 [merged]. While the advantages of more information is obvious, the information needed in these types of meeting timelines can definitely be condensed.

The merged and single timelines can create clutter that the stacked timeline alleviates, but the stacked timeline introduces a flow problem.

The merged is easy to see everything all at once while it may take some time to figure it out. The stacked is easier to see where things come from but it's very hard to put it together mentally and the single is basic and easy to understand but feels like its missing things.

For many users, the merged timeline seemed to be a happy medium between these two extremes: *I thought that the merged design had the best of both worlds.*

However, at the same time, the relative advantages or disadvantages of the different timelines could vary depending on the user's goals and tasks in using the timeline to review a meeting. For example, if the goal is not to passively watch and follow the meeting but to understand the evolution of a specific discussion topic, the decomposed view of the stacked timeline could be helpful. As one participant explained,

I think it might be easiest to find a specific and particular piece of a conversation or response using the exploded, stacked visual representations of conversation. I think if you were sitting do [sic] to watch this as a unified whole to have it make sense, that the merged would be best. Merged definitely, I think, gave me the best feel for the different meeting flows.

Another also mentioned the potential need to find a specific point in the conversation:

The single is simple, but maybe too simple. If I was looking for a specific conversation that was being had in the conference it might be a little more difficult to spot that exact moment. The merged was

a great balance between the stacked and single with minimizing the timeline without cutting out too much of the important details.

In future work, we will evaluate the timeline design in a variety of information-seeking use case scenarios with different playback plans to see how a system might dynamically support the same user performing different types of meeting review and comprehension tasks.

8. Conclusions and Future Directions

Reviewing a chain of meetings that span time and location is not well-supported by existing systems. Using a series of different review scenarios, we built upon prior work [8] by intelligently inferring playback plans that express users' information-seeking goals. We provided an in-depth description of alternative ways of generating, visualizing and playing back a series of linked asynchronous meetings. We created three visualizations of the hypermeeting timeline, incorporating guidelines for using multiple views for information visualization. These visualizations help users understand automatic link following within a sequence of meetings.

We conducted a user evaluation of the *review-all-meetings* playback plan. Watching previous meetings as an observer is a common use case, especially for viewers who did not attend those meetings. The results showed that the merged timeline design was the most beneficial presentation. This design presented all information, including transitions, in a single condensed view. However, this visualization required users to make tradeoffs between obscuring details of the topics and limiting distraction during navigation flow. Participants indicated that switching among visualizations would be beneficial for different tasks.

This result generalizes to additional hypervideo contexts. In particular, the visualizations studied are reasonable choices for adaptive hypervideo when providing paths through educational or how-to content. Playback plans in such contexts would reason about the user's understanding of prerequisite knowledge and the need for detailed description of a how-to process much as they reason about prior knowledge of meetings in our context.

By building on the design insights uncovered in this work, we can continue to explore how to design personalizable hypervideo tools. In particular, such tools should enable users to quickly and easily extract even more fine-grained and useful information from a time-distributed series of videos, both in the context of reviewing meetings and beyond. For example, we will explore the interaction between timeline visualizations and alternate types of information-seeking scenarios, such as finding a particular topic in the meeting.

We will also explore more organic user behavior when navigating through the meeting using various approaches. An example is to use the timeline versus the navigation history stack to have more user-defined control in moving back and forth throughout the content.

Lastly, we plan to add support for other types of meetings, such as local meetings recorded by a single video camera or video conferences between two hubs. In both cases, there would be more than one person per video feed requiring more advanced approaches to participant and speaker identification.

9. REFERENCES

[1] Jeremy Barksdale, Kori Inkpen, Mary Czerwinski, Aaron Hoff, Paul Johns, Asta Roseway, and Gina Venolia. 2012. Video threads: asynchronous video sharing for temporally distributed teams. *Proceedings of the ACM 2012 conference on Computer Supported Cooperative Work*, ACM, 1101–1104.

[2] Guillaume Boissière. 1998. Automatic creation of hypervideo news libraries for the World Wide Web. *Proceedings of the ninth ACM conference on Hypertext and hypermedia*, ACM, 279–280.

[3] Jonathan J. Cadiz, Anand Balachandran, Elizabeth Sanocki, Anoop Gupta, Jonathan Grudin, and Gavin Jancke. 2000. Distance learning through distributed collaborative video viewing. *Proceedings of the 2000 ACM conference on Computer supported cooperative work*, ACM, 135–144.

[4] Teresa Chambel, Carmen Zahn, and Matthias Finke. 2004. Hypervideo design and support for contextualized learning. *IEEE International Conference on Advanced Learning Technologies*, IEEE, 345–349.

[5] Brian Dorn, Larissa B. Schroeder, and Adam Stankiewicz. 2015. Piloting TrACE: Exploring Spatiotemporal Anchored Collaboration in Asynchronous Learning. *Proceedings of the 18th ACM Conference on Computer Supported Cooperative Work & Social Computing*, ACM, 393–403.

[6] Lutz Gericke, Matthias Wenzel, and Christoph Meinel. 2014. Asynchronous understanding of creative sessions using archived collaboration artifacts. *International Conference on Collaboration Technologies and Systems (CTS)*, IEEE, 41–48.

[7] Werner Geyer, Heather Richter, and Gregory D. Abowd. 2005. Towards a smarter meeting record—capture and access of meetings revisited. *Multimedia Tools and Applications* 27, 3: 393–410.

[8] Andreas Girgensohn, Jennifer Marlow, Frank Shipman and Lynn Wilcox. 2015. HyperMeeting: supporting asynchronous meetings with hypervideo. *Proceedings of the 23rd ACM international conference on Multimedia*, ACM, 611-620.

[9] Andreas Girgensohn, Frank Shipman, and Lynn Wilcox. 2011. Adaptive clustering and interactive visualizations to support the selection of video clips. *Proceedings of the 1st ACM International Conference on Multimedia Retrieval*, ACM, Article 34.

[10] Andreas Girgensohn, Lynn Wilcox, Frank Shipman, and Sara Bly. 2004. Designing affordances for the navigation of detail-on-demand hypervideo. *Proceedings of the working conference on Advanced visual interfaces*, ACM, 290–297.

[11] Romulus Grigoras, Vincent Charvillat, and Matthijs Douze. 2002. Optimizing hypervideo navigation using a Markov decision process approach. *Proceedings of the tenth ACM international conference on Multimedia*, ACM, 39–48.

[12] Seth Hunter, Pattie Maes, Stacey Scott, and Henry Kaufman. 2011 MemTable: an integrated system for capture and recall of shared histories in group workspaces. *Proceedings of the SIGCHI Conference on Human Factors in Computing Systems*, ACM, 3305–3314.

[13] Markus Jakobsson. 2009. Experimenting on Mechanical Turk: 5 how tos. *ITWorld, September* 3: 2009.

[14] Aniket Kittur, Ed H. Chi, and Bongwon Suh. 2008. Crowdsourcing user studies with Mechanical Turk. *Proceedings of the SIGCHI conference on human factors in computing systems*, ACM, 453–456.

[15] Andrew Lippman. 1980. Movie-maps: An application of the optical videodisc to computer graphics. *ACM SIGGRAPH Computer Graphics*, ACM, 32–42.

[16] Franz Lehner, Michael Langbauer, and Nadine Amende. 2014. Measuring success of enterprise social software: the case of hypervideos. *Proceedings of the 14th International Conference on Knowledge Technologies and Data-driven Business*, ACM, 3.

[17] Shixia Liu, Yingcai Wu, Enxun Wei, Mengchen Liu, and Yang Liu. 2013. Storyflow: Tracking the evolution of stories. *IEEE Transactions on Visualization and Computer Graphics*, 19, 12: 2436–2445.

[18] Catherine C. Marshall and Frank M. Shipman. 2013. Experiences surveying the crowd: Reflections on methods, participation, and reliability. *Proceedings of the 5th Annual ACM Web Science Conference*, ACM, 234–243.

[19] Thomas P. Moran, Leysia Palen, Steve Harrison, Patrick Chiu, Don Kimber, Scott Minneman, William van Melle, and Polle Zellweger. 1997. "I'll get that off the audio": a case study of salvaging multimedia meeting records. *Proceedings of the ACM SIGCHI Conference on Human factors in computing systems*, ACM, 202–209.

[20] Mukesh Nathan, Mercan Topkara, Jennifer Lai, Shimei Pan, Steven Wood, Jeff Boston, and Loren Terveen. 2012. In case you missed it: benefits of attendee-shared annotations for non-attendees of remote meetings. *Proceedings of the ACM 2012 conference on Computer Supported Cooperative Work*, ACM, 339–348.

[21] Juan Pan, Li Li, and Wu Chou. 2012. Real-Time Collaborative Video Watching on Mobile Devices with REST Services. *Third FTRA International Conference on Mobile, Ubiquitous, and Intelligent Computing (MUSIC)*, IEEE, 29–34.

[22] Adam Perer and Fei Wang. 2014. Frequence: Interactive mining and visualization of temporal frequent event sequences. *Proceedings of the 19th international conference on Intelligent User Interfaces*, ACM, 153–162.

[23] Madjid Sadallah, Olivier Aubert, and Yannick Prié. 2014. CHM: an annotation-and component-based hypervideo model for the Web. *Multimedia tools and applications* 70, 2: 869–903.

[24] Nitin Sawhney, David Balcom, and Ian Smith. 1996. HyperCafe: narrative and aesthetic properties of hypervideo. *Proceedings of the the seventh ACM conference on Hypertext*, ACM, 1–10.

[25] Frank Shipman, Andreas Girgensohn, and Lynn Wilcox. 2008. Authoring, viewing, and generating hypervideo: An overview of Hyper-Hitchcock. *ACM Transactions on Multimedia Computing, Communications, and Applications (TOMM)* 5, 2: 15.

[26] John Tang, Jennifer Marlow, Aaron Hoff, Asta Roseway, Kori Inkpen, Chen Zhao, and Xiang Cao. 2012. Time travel proxy: using lightweight video recordings to create asynchronous, interactive meetings. *Proceedings of the SIGCHI Conference on Human Factors in Computing Systems*, ACM, 3111–3120.

[27] Claudio AB Tiellet, André Grahl Pereira, Eliseo Berni Reategui, José Valdeni Lima, and Teresa Chambel. 2010. Design and evaluation of a hypervideo environment to support veterinary surgery learning. *Proceedings of the 21st ACM conference on Hypertext and hypermedia*, ACM, 213–222.

[28] Michelle Q. Wang Baldonado, Allison Woodruff, and Allan Kuchinsky. 2000. Guidelines for using multiple views in information visualization. *Proceedings of the working conference on Advanced visual interfaces*, ACM, 110–119.

[29] Krist Wongsuphasawat, John Alexis Guerra Gómez, Catherine Plaisant, Taowei David Wang, Meirav Taieb-Maimon, and Ben Shneiderman. 2011. LifeFlow: visualizing an overview of event sequences. *Proceedings of the SIGCHI Conference on Human Factors in Computing Systems*, ACM, 1747–1756.

Patterns of Sculptural Hypertext in Location Based Narratives

Charlie Hargood
Electronics and Computer
Science
University of Southampton
Southampton, United Kingdom
cah07r@ecs.soton.ac.uk

Verity Hunt
Department of English
University of Southampton
Southampton, United Kingdom
v.hunt@soton.ac.uk

Mark J. Weal
Electronics and Computer
Science
University of Southampton
Southampton, United Kingdom
mjw@ecs.soton.ac.uk

David E. Millard
Electronics and Computer
Science
University of Southampton
Southampton, United Kingdom
dem@ecs.soton.ac.uk

ABSTRACT

Location based narratives are an emerging form of digital storytelling that use location technologies to trigger content on smart devices according to a user's location. In previous work on the Canyons, Deltas and Plains (CDP) model we argued that they are best considered as a form of sculptural hypertext, but sculptural hypertext is a relatively unexplored medium with few examples, and limited critical theory. This means that there is little guidance for authors on what is possible with the medium, and no common authoring tools, both of which impede adoption and experimentation. In this paper we describe our work to tackle this problem by working with creative writing students to create 40 location based sculptural hypertexts using an approach similar to paper-prototyping, and then analysing these for common patterns (structures of nodes, rules, and conditions used for a poetic purpose). We present seven key patterns: Parallel Threads, Gating, Concurrent Nodes, Alternative Nodes, Foldbacks, Phasing, and Unlocking. In doing so we see some overlap with the patterns identified in traditional (calligraphic) hypertext, but in many cases these patterns are particularly suited to sculptural hypertext, and hint at a different poetics for the form. Our findings refine our original CDP model, but also present a starting point for educating writers on how to approach sculptural stories, and form a foundation for future location-based authoring tools.

Categories and Subject Descriptors

H.1 [**Models and Principles**]: General

HT'16, 10–13 July, 2016, Halifax, Canada.

© 2013 Copyright held by the owner/author(s). Publication rights licensed to ACM.
ISBN 978-1-4503-4247-6/16/07...$15.00

DOI: http://dx.doi.org/10.1145/2914586.2914595

Keywords

Narrative, Narrative Systems, Location Based Narrative, Mobile Narrative

1. INTRODUCTION

The increasing availability of location-aware smart devices, particularly smartphones, has led in recent years to experimental forms of context-aware entertainment. One such form is Location Based Narrative - a type of dynamic storytelling where content is triggered by location. Location based narratives have been studied by the research community for some time but focus has mostly been on individual bespoke location aware systems, typically developed and supported by a dedicated research team, and outside the reach of much of the creative community. However, many of these systems have commonalities, and a better understanding of the core patterns and uses of location-based narratives could potentially lead to standard platforms and expectations, unlocking the form for a wider variety of writers.

Towards this goal in 2013 we published a general model of location based narrative [19] which identified three high level structures which we called Canyons, Deltas, and Plains (CDP), when used individually, or when combined, these structures could be used to express the structural forms of existing systems. We then showed that a general Sculptural Hypertext model could be used to build all of these CDP forms, including the hybrid ones.

While the sculptural hypertext model is a powerful one it is very low level (we doubted that authors would think about their stories in the form of multi-dimensional states and state transitions), so we also suggested a number of mid-level structures that would make more sense to authors, these included chapters, stacks and timers. These were inspired by our earlier work on sculptural hypertext [7] but we had no way of knowing if these were the most useful mid-level structures for authors.

A better term for these mid-level structures is *Patterns*. Bernstein's key 1998 paper analysed some of the patterns that he had observed in traditional node/link hypertext [5] (sometimes called Calligraphic in contrast to Sculptural) but no similar work has been done on sculptural hypertext, probably due to the scarcity of examples, and the lack of common format. This is a circular problem that affects new forms of hypertext [15], as without a clear idea of the sorts of patterns that authors want to employ it is difficult to design effective authoring tools, and without effective authoring tools there is no method by which to create example works, and thus analyse patterns.

In this paper we attempt to tackle this problem, and build on our CDP model to define a number of sculptural patterns that could be used to support authors of location-based narratives.

To achieve this we took a paper-based prototyping approach, and as part of the StoryPlaces project worked with 40 creative writing students to have them each create a short location aware narrative for us based around a common location (in this case the old town area of Southampton, UK). We were then able to perform a structural analysis of the resulting stories, in order to identify common patterns and the ways in which they were used.

Our goal is to bootstrap the understanding of location based narrative, and work towards authoring tools that are aware of the common goals of location-based narrative authors. While we do not claim to have an exhaustive set of patterns for sculptural hypertext, there are echoes of Bernstein's calligraphic patterns and the mid-level structures of CDP, and we believe that this initial analysis does move beyond our original CDP model to a more mature understanding of location based narrative.

2. BACKGROUND

Our work draws on two principle existing areas: Location Based Narrative systems, being the application space, and Sculptural Hypertext, being part of our solution to the problem and relevant to our structural analysis.

2.1 Sculptural Hypertext

Sculptural hypertext is an approach to hypermedia where by structure is created through the removal (or blocking) of links between nodes rather than their creation [6][28]. In his work on Card Shark and Thespis [6] Bernstein describes his systems as "sculptural" because of the way all nodes are linked together, but these links are then prohibited by rules and constraints (such as the requirement that a different node be visited first) sculpting away the links into an eventual structure. In contrast he describes the more traditional hypertext where nodes are unconnected and links are then explicitly added as "calligraphic".

Sculptural hypertext lends itself to broad open narratives with a high degree of potential interconnectivity as only the restrictions must be defined, not the connections, in contrast calligraphic hypertext lends itself to more controlled linear experiences where the number of possible connections is smaller. Referencing his earlier patterns of hypertext [5] Bernstein points out that "The tangle, not the link" is the primitive in sculptural hypertext. Location based narrative, with its common focus on open narratives encouraging exploration is a natural fit for sculptural hypertext, where the locations are modelled as additional constraints on nodes, and the requirement to construct links for all possible reading patterns and routes is avoided. A number of existing location aware systems discussed in the following section such as Chawton House [27][26], and the Ambient Wood

[24] use a sculptural engine to support them, and the rule based structures of other systems such as Riot! [8] and San Servolo [23] also echo the sculptural approach of defining what is not linked, as supposed to what is linked.

2.2 Location Based Narrative

A range of bespoke location based narrative systems have been built, both within and outside the Hypertext research community. These systems employ subtly different structures and technologies, but can be best classified by their application. We divide existing systems into *Tour Guides*, *Educational Tools*, *Location Aware Fiction*, *Location Aware Games*. While some fall outside this (such as the Geo-Spatial Hypermedia information systems by Grønbæk [14][13]), the majority fall within these four types.

2.2.1 Tour Guides

A common application of location based narrative is within location aware tour guides, which seek to inform and engage their audience in their surroundings, often accompanied by a historical narrative. These guides can take both an open form (encouraging the user to explore), or a linear structure guiding the user through exhibits.

Typical of this are the Louvre tour developed within the HIPS system [9] and REXplorer [3]. HIPS is designed to allow for a range of location aware tour guides that are also connected to knowledge bases, and while this is demonstrated with a more open guide more structured guides are also possible. REXplorer is more tightly suited to structured tours, taking a more playful, almost game-like approach to tour guides, and encouraging the collection of artefacts throughout the tour.

There is a broad range of bespoke location aware tour guides that have been used to explore the field. Riot! [8] employs an open narrative structure where visitors to Queen's Square in Bristol were invited to listen to a location sensitive interactive play about a famous riot during their visit. The open structure encouraged the users to explore the area playing sounds clips contains parts of the narrative as they entered relevant areas. The work by Nisi on HopStory [22], and The Media Portrait of the Liberties [21] also explores a range of different ways of presenting location aware tour guides. HopStory, a linear dramatized brewery guide, includes the exploration of time based narratives similar to that of Riot!, where nodes are only accessible within a given time frame. Media Portrait is by contrast an combination of both open and linear narratives exploring stories contributed by people living in an area of Dublin, and distributed to immerse visitors in the culture of that space. Its combination of two different types of high level structure (open and linear) is typical of a great many systems, and an important part of our Canyons, Deltas, and Plains model.

2.2.2 Educational Tools

While location aware guides could be considered educational, some location based applications focus more carefully on the educational process of learning rather than just exploring a space. These include interactive educational tools such as Gaius' Day in Egnathia [2] and 'edutainment' systems such as Geist [18].

Location aware educational tools are also well represented in sculptural hypertext. The Ambient Wood project [24] utilises a card and deck metaphor for children exploring educational nodes in a wood. The users are encouraged to collect artefacts while participating (similar to the way REXplorer and HopStory do) and engage in multimedia educational activities using a range of sensors. Similarly the Chawton House project [27][26] adopts a similar card based approach to support an educational experience for children set around a period home, but with more interactive cards and a more structured direction of participants around the space.

2.2.3 Location Aware Games

Location aware games is a broad classification that includes systems with game mechanics connected to player context as well as augmented reality experiences such as Can You See Me Now? [4], Viking Ghost Hunt [20], TimeWarp [16], or University of Death [10]. Can You See Me Now? makes use of a mapping between a players real and virtual locations as part of an exciting chase between participants. Viking Ghost Hunt and TimeWarp take a more visual augmented reality approach to hunting ghosts and Heinzelmännchen of Cologne (small virtual elves) respectively - leading players on a branching trail of clues and narratives and using interactive mini games and camera overlays to allow the player to achieve their objectives.

2.2.4 Location Aware Fiction

Location Aware Fiction can be used to increase the immersion of a reader within a story setting. While the distinction between these and both tour guides, and games, can be blurred at times the important defining feature here is the focus on delivering an engaging story, as supposed to location description or interactive play. The iLand of Madeira exposes an oral history of the island of Madeira through an open narrative of content tied to locations, not unlike Riot! as discussed previously [12]. Similarly "San Servolo, travel into the memory of an island"[23] is a location aware work of fiction set around an island based sanatorium. Pittarello's narrative framework for San Servolo is based on earlier work on machine readable models of narrative carried about by Carnielli [11], and focuses of the delivery of "situations" based on a variety of contextual checks. These "situations" are sections of textual narrative shown to user based on the decisions of an intelligent director agent that assess suitability of the content based on contextual data recorded on the user as they travel the island such as location, weather, and content previously read.

3. MODELLING LOCATION BASED NARRATIVE

In our work on Canyons, Deltas, and Plains (CDP) [19] we explored a general model of location based narrative that could be supported by an underlying sculptural hypertext engine. Our CDP model proposed that location based narratives such as the ones described above could be described in terms of Canyons, Deltas, and Plains - representing Linear, Branching, and Open narratives respectively. Linear narratives being an ordered sequence of nodes, branching narratives being those where the sequence of nodes diverged and split based on reader interaction (which could be simply choosing a direction to physically move), and open narratives being a collection of nodes that could be explored in any order. These structures are presented in figure 1. A

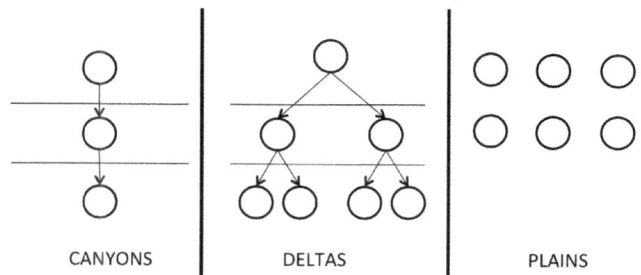

Figure 1: Nodes arranged in Canyons (Linear), Deltas (Branching), and Plains (Open) structures. As presented in [19]

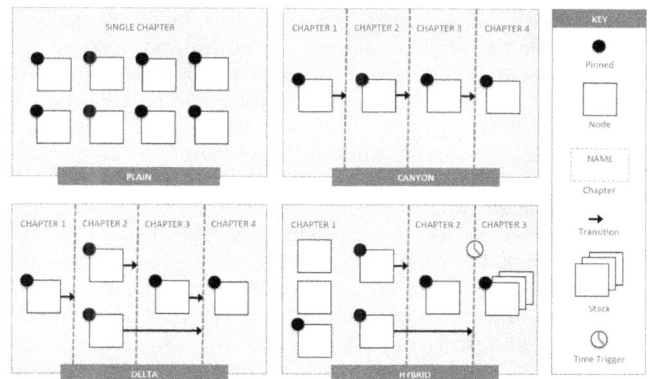

Figure 2: Canyons, Deltas, Plains, and Hybrids may be constructed out of nodes, chapters, and transitions. As presented in [19].

location based narrative could be built of a composite of these structures to create a hybrid of different structures - it might start as a linear narrative but later branch, or begin as an open story that leads to a number of different discoverable linear narratives. We showed that this was sufficient to model a number of different location based narrative examples from the literature.

Key to the CDP model was the realisation that location based narratives were better considered as sculptural rather than calligraphic. This is because location can be modelled as part of the user's state, and in sculptural hypertext it is state changes, rather than explicit link following, that move a reader through the hypertext.

We suggested a number of mid-level structures that could be built on top of a sculptural hypertext engine to make things easier for authors: nodes that could be pinned to locations, chapters that gather nodes that are concurrently available (subject to location changes), transitions between chapters (triggered by reading specific nodes), timers that trigger transitions, and stacks that provide an easy way of creating a simple sequence. Through these mid-level structures the higher level structures of canyons, deltas, and plains could emerge. Figure 2 depicts how a combination of these mid-level structures can be used to build canyons, deltas, plains, or a hybrid combination of more than one.

4. METHODOLOGY

The StoryPlaces project aims to build a framework for understanding the poetics of location based narrative that can support critical analysis, author education, and lead to improved authoring systems. To achieve this the project has adopted a co-design approach where we work directly with both writers and literary experts in three consecutive story projects to develop both our models and systems, and our understanding of location based narrative as a form. This paper reports the work of the first story project to investigate the sorts of stories that authors might create, and identify the sculptural patterns that emerge. The intention being that this understanding can support writers in the later story projects, and lead directly to better authoring tools.

This investigation requires us to observe a broader range of stories then those we sampled from the literature in our work on CDP. It also requires writers working with real purpose, as the patterns are not just structural, but also poetic, in the sense that they are used for particular poetic purpose within the stories, and this is an important part of the description of the pattern. The difficulty is that there is no large group of authors working with sculptural hypertext, location-based or not, and thus finding a suitable set of rich stories is challenging.

To address this as part of the first story project (set in the old town of Southampton) we approached a group of creative writing students on a higher education course about writing and place, and for their assessment asked them to create location based narrative using an approach inspired by paper prototyping. The students all had experience with writing, but didn't have particular experience with writing hypertext, meaning that they had no pre-conceptions of what sculptural or location based narratives should be, but also that they needed some guidance on what was possible. The students were therefore given an introductory explanation of location aware narratives and introduced to short overviews of a few examples[1] in order to give them an appreciation of the sorts of things that were possible.

We were very conscious in this stage that by providing explanation and examples we might lead the students, but previous experience has shown that without basic training in a new form authors resort to simplistic and safe approaches that do not best show what is possible [15]. Thus our approach here is similar to that found in participatory and co-design [25], where domain experts (in this case the authors) are brought into a conversation about what they want to achieve, and how the technology might enable it, without dictating to them what should be done.

Using a paper prototype supported this approach as we could allow authors to express their ideas freely, without the constraints of a digital authoring system, in the end we used a digital document format (Microsoft Word) rather than paper, as the students preferred to write digitally and were able to submit their stories remotely. However, the core principles of paper prototyping remained: that the authors were able to construct the content and the associated rules and locations, but with minimal restrictions, to avoid preventing the authors from creating something we might not have anticipated.

Consequently, we provided the students with a Word document in the shape of a simple form, in which they could write their annotated story - the form had three columns: a large one for content, and two smaller ones for locations and rules. We did not separate the form into rows for nodes, but allowed students to indicate this however they wished (typically with whitespace). This way the authors could write their stories but also annotate the content with location restrictions and story logic throughout as they saw fit. The students were also encouraged to "write over" the form if they wished to annotate or explain something that didn't fit the form. In order to foster stories of appropriate size and complexity they were also given guidelines that individual story nodes should be less than 200 words (to account for the common mobile delivery platform of location aware narratives) and that they should aim for a total story length of at least 2000 words.

5. RESULTS AND ANALYSIS

In total the study had 40 participants, each submitting a location aware narrative in the annotated format specified (an example of which is depicted in figure 3) and with a broad range of structures, location types, features, and genres. Figure 4 depicts a Venn diagram of the frequencies of different CDP structures and hybrids of multiple structures; authors more commonly wrote open or linear stories but there were also a range of hybrid structures that included branching. Our authors used a range of locations, mostly local around the city of Southampton in the UK (although one global story was written), and stories evenly ranged from using a small tight area that could be traversed with less than 15 minutes walking to large distributed stories that would involve multiple hours walking to finish. The majority of locations were outside (however three stories made use of inside locations), and there was a broad variety of locations used including residential, commercial, waterfront, entertainment, and religious spaces - with a slight preference for public and historical spaces such as parks and monuments. The genre of the stories varied widely, but dramatized tour guides, thrillers, and historical dramas accounted for a large number of the pieces. Our story set had an average length of 2311 words, and were made up of an average of 11 story nodes (range 4-19), most were roughly in line with the guidelines we had set out.

The stories created by the authors demonstrate the structures identified in our original CDP model, however the purpose of the exercise was to explore the mid-level structures, or patterns, that the authors used in their work.

In 1998 Bernstein wrote about the "Patterns of Hypertext" [5] that he had observed in the key hypertext literature of the time: Cycle, Counterpoint, Mirrorworld, Tangle, Sieve, Montage, Split/Join, Missing Link, and Feint. A key question for our analysis was whether we would see similar patterns emerge (but expressed in terms of sculptural state changes rather than links) or whether there are different sculptural patterns altogether.

5.1 Patterns of Sculptural Hypertext

We manually analysed each of the submitted stories, looking for common structures and mechanisms. In total we identified seven patterns: Parallel Threads, Concurrent Nodes,

---

[1]Examples were HopStory [22], San Servolo [23], The Chawton House Project [26], Viking Ghost Hunt [20], and Riot![8]

Location	Content	Conditions
Avenue Campus	 Just a quick detour – heading right onto Highfield Lane, up that all the way until you get to Lover's Lane (the reader is advised to maybe avoid this road at night – also to keep an eye out for militant cyclists). From there, it should be pretty clear when you've arrived at Avenue (there'll be nice big signs, and also it looks like the picture). After looking around a bit, maybe having some lunch at the café, if you're so inclined, and deciding that all in all it's much better than Highfield, it's time to turn around and head on down to Page Five. But, before you go...	Have to have read Pages Two-Point-Five, Three, and Three-Point-Five
	Page Four	

Page Four-Point-Five		
Location	Content	Conditions
Anywhere	Having stumbled out of a lecture, caught in the stream of people headed for various doors, you're momentarily bewildered. The *thing* you were supposed to do has dropped out of your head, and it's tempting just to leave it where it is and carry on regardless. You catch yourself, though, and turn your head casually (or, rather, with more effort than pretty much anything you've ever done to date)	Have to have read Page Four, and all the previous Point-Five pages

Figure 3: An example screenshot from a submitted story showing the annotated narrative.

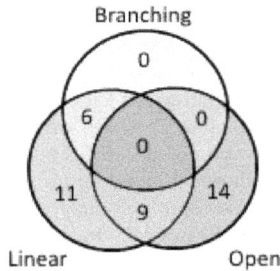

Figure 4: A Venn diagram of the frequencies of CDP structures and hybrids observed in our story set.

Alternative Nodes, Foldbacks, Phasing, Unlocking, and Gating. As previously described these patterns exist within the greater CDP structures, and form a middle layer between these and the underlying sculptural hypertext engine, this is depicted in Figure 5.

5.1.1 Parallel Threads

Parallel Threads allow for stories with parallel subplots that may progress at different rates depending on the actions of the reader (at any time a node is available from each thread, and by activating that node by visiting its location the reader moves that particular subplot forward). Figure 6 shows this pattern. In this diagram (and the subsequent diagrams in this section) content nodes are shown as circles, and prerequisites are shown as arrows between nodes. A node only becomes available once its prerequisite has been

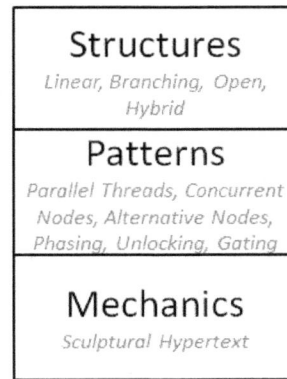

Figure 5: Patterns of authorship between higher CDP structures and the sculptural engine.

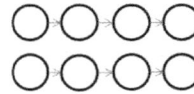

Figure 6: Parallel Threads

activated, and only activate themselves once the reader visits the location associated with that node.

Parallel Threads enable a reader to jump back and forth between the two threads in a way that is not dissimilar to Bernstein's Counterpoint pattern, but unlike calligraphic hypertext the threads are independent and it is equally possible that a reader could read one thread entirely before another. The examples of Parallel Threads we saw in our stories were all of the form of 2 or 3 parallel linear threads, but in principle any number of linear or branching threads could be involved in the pattern.

Parallel Threads are introduced in one of two different ways. In an *open introduction* each of the threads is available from the outset. Alternatively some stories demonstrate a *staged release* where there is at first only a single thread and then more threads become available as the story progresses.

5.1.2 Gating

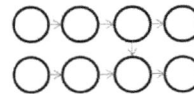

Figure 7: Gating

Gating (shown in Figure 7) represents a sub pattern of Parallel Threads and is related to staged release. Gating occurs where parallel threads are present, but there are dependencies between those threads meaning that the reader must reach a particular stage in one of the threads, before the next node in the other thread becomes available (this manifests as a requirement on a node within one thread for the reader to have previously visited a particular node in another thread). Staged release can thus be seen as a kind of simplistic gating, where a second thread only starts once the first has reached a particular point. Gating allows the author to control the freedom of the reader and ensure that they catch up with a particular thread, potentially to ensure certain characters have been introduced or certain events have transpired, before progressing further in another. It is therefore a mechanism that brings the parallel threads patterns closer to calligraphic counterpoints, which manage the same problem through link structures.

5.1.3 Concurrent Nodes

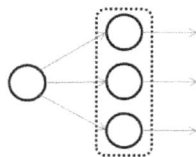

Figure 8: Concurrent Nodes

The sculptural structure of our location aware stories means that it is possible for more than one node to be active at the same time, a pattern we call Concurrent Nodes (shown in Figure 8, where a dotted lines surrounds the nodes that appear concurrently). How this is handled from a presentational perspective is down to the interpretation of client software, the nodes available may be summarised for a user to select, or they might be presented side by side (in which case they are analogous to Bernstein's Montage pattern). The creation of concurrent nodes in location aware sculptural hypertext must consider two types of restriction in that the nodes must satisfy both narrative rules (such as the prerequisite to have visited a given node) but also be collocated in a given location (to be read in the same place). We had anticipated that this would make Concurrent Nodes rarer in location based narrative than other forms of sculptural hypertext (where collocation is not necessarily a restriction), but multiple examples were found within our set of stories.

5.1.4 Alternative Nodes

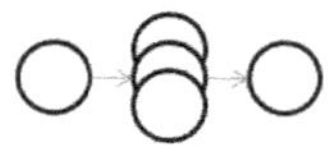

Figure 9: Alternative Nodes

Alternative nodes (shown in Figure 9, where overlapping nodes are the alternatives) are when a set of nodes are available in a particular point in the story but rather then appearing concurrently they account for each of the possibilities of a particular state check. For example there might be one that is valid on a Saturday, another on a Sunday, and another on any other day. Alternative nodes were often used in conjunction with contextual conditions such as those based on time, weather, or other aspects outside of the readers direct control to provide a story that varies according to the conditions in which it is read

Alternative Nodes are structurally a localised form of Bernstein's Split-Join, however their use is to account for contextual variation rather than interactivity.

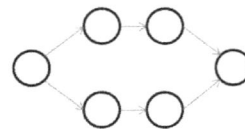

Figure 10: Foldback

5.1.5 Foldbacks

Foldbacks (shown in Figure 10) are similar to Alternative nodes but differ in their use and scale. In a foldback the reader's choice of location triggers a temporary alternative thread of one or more nodes before re-joining the central thread. Choosing one of these threads (in this case by activating one of the optional nodes by moving to its location) will invalidate the other thread. These are more similar to Bernstein's split-joins in their use, in that both allow a hypertext author to manage the agency of their reader, and avoid the exponential complexity that would result from continual branching.

5.1.6 Phasing

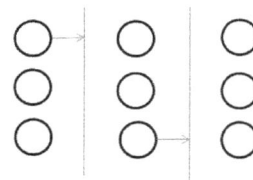

Figure 11: Phasing

The phasing pattern (shown in Figure 11, where solid lines separate the different phases) arises when nodes, each with their own conditions and constraints, can be clustered into a number of different phases dependent on a significant change in state that shifts the available nodes from one cluster to another. It is typically used in open narratives where the story moves through a series of phases, but within each phase a number of nodes may be openly explored. The phase is advanced by either the reader visiting a key node, or a specific contextual state (such as the passing of time) being satisfied.

The phasing pattern matches the original mid-level structures of Chapters, Transitions and Timers that we proposed in the original CDP model, but do not necessarily have to perform the narrative function of chapters in the story. In fact in our story set they tended to be used in a more coarse-grained way to manage a three act structure (of beginning, middle and end).

While the phases we saw are typically sequential they don't have to be and a branching or open phasing structure could be possible (similar to deltas and plains but with whole phases taking the place of single nodes). The open nature of phasing patterns makes them inherently suited to sculptural hypertext engines, with little in the way of a calligraphic hypertext equivalent (the equivalence would be a set of nodes that were exhaustively interlinked, in such a way that any node was navigable from any other, this has superficial similarities to Bernstein's Tangle pattern, but fulfils a very different narrative function).

5.1.7 Unlocking

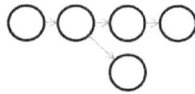

Figure 12: Unlocking

Satisfying constraints in order to "unlock" a node is a fundamental part of sculptural hypertext structure, and by itself does not constitute a particular pattern. However an Unlocking pattern is sometimes used (shown in Figure 12) to go beyond the simple linear story progression of one node after the other and instead build more complicated constraints where a range of different nodes must be visited to unlock a particular node. This could be used to progress the story (in which case it is related to Gating, but in this case the unlocking threads end at the unlock event), but in our story set it was typically used to open a additional diversionary node. These hidden diversionary nodes are similar to "easter eggs" seen sometimes in games or other interactive media in that they represent non-essential but additional bonus content to be sought out by the reader.

5.2 Story Examples

All seven patterns manifested in our story set, some manifesting multiple patterns within a single short story, as demonstrated in table 1 which summarises the stories collected and their structure and patterns.

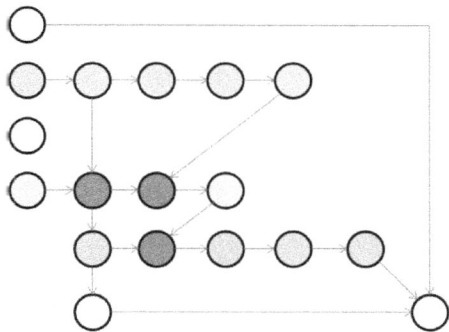

Figure 13: The story structure for 'A Walk in the City', arrows denote nodes being made available. Each parallel thread is highlighted a different colour, darker colours signify gated nodes.

In figure 13 the structure for the story 'A Walk in the City' is presented demonstrating triple Parallel Threads with Gating. A Walk in the City uses its Parallel Threads to deliver three separate short stories that the reader may switch between at will, while using gating to control the release of parts of the story until ideas and themes have been introduced in other threads. The story represents a collision of two genres: that of a tour guide (introducing parts of the city) and a romantic drama (taking place in the locations explained) and the two are interwoven across all three threads. The doubling/blurring of the text's genre identity is symbolically paralleled in the description of the landscape when an occurrence of two streets with the same name in the city results in a miscommunication between the protagonists.

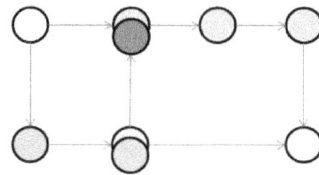

Figure 14: The story structure for 'Through the Years', arrows denote nodes being made available. Each parallel thread is highlighted a different colour, and darker colours signify gated nodes. Alternative nodes are present.

Figure 14 shows the story structure of 'Through the Years', which uses Parallel Threads but also makes use of Alternative Nodes. Through the Years uses its Parallel Threads to display the story from three different POV characters, it also makes restrictions on some content being available only in certain weather conditions but uses Alternative Nodes to allow the story to progress if these are not satisfied. The POV characters for the story are handled in two parallel threads with a third character existing only as alternative nodes for poor weather in the other 2 threads. This makes the third POV optional (and somewhat glum and dour in tone), and its presence as optional nodes in the other threads necessitates the use of a gate to control the order in which it is read. Each of the characters explores the city in a different time period and by using the parallel threads to allow the reader to jump between two of the POV's the author highlights and sometimes exaggerates the differences between the periods of time.

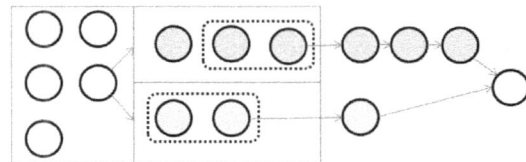

Figure 15: The story structure for 'Our Journey', arrows denote nodes being made available, dotted lines encircle concurrent nodes, and solid lines encircle phases. Each parallel thread is highlighted a different colour.

"Our Journey" is depicted in figure 15 and also makes use of Parallel Threads, but also Phasing, and Concurrent Nodes. The Parallel Threads are used to follow two different POV's once again, but also two different themes - one educational, the other more emotional. Allowing the reader to shifts between these allows them to access the tone and perspective they prefer. The story makes use of concurrent nodes and open phases early on to allow the reader to explore in a way that suits them, and potentially to allow them to decide which perspective they find more interesting, before locking them in to a much more linear series of nodes leading to conclusion.

Title*	Nodes	Genre	Structure	Patterns Present
That ship sailed a long time ago	10	Drama	Open/Linear	Unlocking
A Walk in the Park	17	Thriller	Open/Linear	
The History of Jesters ...	10	Biopic	Open	
The Biography of Mankind	10	Biopic	Linear	Alternative Nodes
A Shadow on the Wall	10	Biopic	Linear/Branching	Unlocking, Foldback
Do you see me yet?	12	Drama	Linear	
The Ghosts	11	Horror	Linear/Branching	Unlocking
A Walk in the City ...	19	Tour Guide/Drama	Open/Linear	Unlocking, parallel Threads, Gating
The Spirit of Southampton	4	Drama	Open	
Notes on an illegible city ...	8	Tour Guide	Open	
Sailing in the Wake	18	Tour Guide	Open	Unlocking, Concurrent Nodes
The Ballad of Elizabeth Loder	10	Thriller	Open	Concurrent Nodes
The Titanic Criminal in Southampton	8	Thriller	Open	Concurrent Nodes
Hollybrook	11	Drama	Open/Linear	Unlocking
An Unbreakable Bond	8	Drama	Linear	
Our Journey	16	Biopic	Open	Phasing, Concurrent Nodes, parallel Threads
The Saints of the City	10	Biopic	Linear	Alternative Nodes
Jane Austen's Days in Southampton	10	Drama	Linear/Branching	
A Place With a Dark Side ...	11	Thriller	Linear/Branching	Foldback
Ballad for a Knight	10	Poetry	Open/Linear	
Lights	14	Biopic	Open	Concurrent Nodes
Six Stories of Southampton	8	Tour Guide	Open	Phasing
The Ever Changing City	10	Tour Guide	Open	Unlocking, Concurrent Nodes
On the Wrong Side of the Wrong Town	17	Thriller	Linear	
(think of one)	9	Biopic	Open/Linear	parallel Threads
A glimmer of a past Southampton	10	Tour Guide	Open/Linear	
untitled	11	Tour Guide	Linear	Alternative Nodes
Through the Years ...	10	Drama	Open/Linear	Alternative Nodes, Parrallel Threads, Gating
Discovering Mary	10	Biopic	Open	Unlocking, Phasing
The Lost Letters of RMS Titanic	5	Drama	Open	Phasing
Waiting For News	8	Drama	Open	Unlocking
Edytki	17	Drama	Linear/Branching	
A Century Ago From Today	10	Tour Guide	Open/Linear	Unlocking
Ship In a Bottle	6	Drama	Linear/Branching	
The Witch's Curse	16	Horror	Open	Unlocking, Concurrent Nodes
Homage To The Vagrants ...	8	Drama	Open/linear	Concurrent Nodes, parallel Threads
Lost in the crowd	11	Drama	Linear	
Just Google It	10	Tour Guide	Linear	
The Green	9	Poetry	Open	
The Tale Of Molly DeVito	10	Biopic	Open/Linear	Unlocking

* Some long titles have been abbreviated or shortened.

Table 1: Story set, including title, size in nodes, genre, and patterns present.

5.3 Discussion

Table 2 summarises the patterns that we found in our story set, their frequency, and the calligraphic pattern to which they are best compared.

The patterns we have identified are a mixture of those that lend themselves to the mechanics of sculptural hypertext (such as Parallel Threads, Gating, Concurrent Nodes, and Phasing), and patterns that emerge from working with the context sensitive nature of location based narrative (such as Alternative Nodes, and Foldbacks). Sculptural hypertext represents a loss of control for authors when compared to calligraphic hypertext, and it could be argued that some of these patterns represent ways to get control back (so for example, using gating to manage the progression of multiple story threads, in the absence of explicit link structures).

On the other side of the comparison we find that Phasing, Gating, and Unlocking are unrepresented amongst the calligraphic patterns. All three of these patterns control the rate of progress within a story. It could be argued that such structures are necessary within sculptural hypertext to control or limit the way in which a reader moves through the content in the same way that a more explicit network of links in calligraphic hypertext might limit navigation.

It is also notable that several calligraphic patterns are missing. Sieves, while absent from our patterns are directly analogous to the branching we see at a higher level, and Tangles are similar to the open structures we see in that there is a collection of nodes with a high degree of interconnectivity. However, Cycles, and Contours are important calligraphic patterns but are entirely missing from our story set; while a complex phasing arrangement could be constructed in order to achieve the same effect, the carefully constructed explicit link structures these patterns require are arguably better suited to calligraphic hypertext rather than sculptural.

This then seems to be the main difference in the patterns we observe in sculptural as opposed to calligraphic hypertexts, calligraphic patterns tend towards managing a reader's path which is easily achieved with explicit links (for example, causing her to revisit previously visited nodes in a Cycle pattern), whereas sculptural patterns tend towards enabling openness (for example, by allowing a reader to follow multiple stories at once in a Parallel Thread, or by shifting the story in its entirety through different phases).

Pattern	Frequency	Calligraphic Pattern
Parallel Threads	5	Potential Counterpoint*
Gating	2	
Concurrent Nodes	8	Potential Montage*
Alternative Nodes	4	Split-Join
Foldbacks	2	Split-Join
Phasing	4	
Unlocking	13	

*Similarity can be rendering or reading dependant

Table 2: Pattern Frequencies within the set of 40 stories and their Calligraphic counterpart.

6. CONCLUSIONS AND FUTURE WORK

The Canyons, Deltas and Plains model framed location-based narratives as a form of sculptural hypertext, providing a theoretical framework in which different examples of the medium could be explained and understood in a coherent and comparable way. Unfortunately, sculptural hypertext is itself a relatively unexplored form, with few examples, and little critical theory to explain how authors might use it to express their ideas and realise their stories. This is a serious barrier to both the education of sculptural writers and the design of authoring tools.

In this paper we tackled this problem by working with 40 creative writing students, using an approach inspired by co-design and paper-prototyping, in order to create location-based sculptural hypertexts that we could analyse for common structures and approaches. The stories created demonstrate the high level story structures identified in our earlier work on the CDP model (linear, branching, open, and hybrid stories), but also authoring patterns that offer a more descriptive vocabulary for the structures that authors create, and the poetic effects that they engender.

The seven patterns we identify are Parallel Threads, Gating, Concurrent Nodes, Alternative Nodes, Foldbacks, Phasing, and Unlocking. Some of these demonstrate similarities with Bernstein's calligraphic patterns of hypertext, but others are more unique to sculptural hypertext.

Our work is based on a relatively small sample, and while we were careful not to lead authors, it is inevitable that our interactions will have impacted their choices. The patterns we have identified are thus clearly not exhaustive, and may be unrepresentative in terms of their frequency of use. Nevertheless, they represent the first serious attempt to understand the possible intentions of authors working in this space, and shed light on the poetic differences between calligraphic and sculptural hypertext. In particular the difference in emphasis between constrained and open exploration, the lack of cycles in sculptural hypertext, and the use of patterns such as gating and phasing (in place of link structures) to enable managed progression through a narrative.

It has been observed that building a richer vocabulary for patterns based on observations from actual hypertexts enables richer and more effective criticism [5]. It also provides a basis for educating new authors, and has the potential to inspire new ideas and support the creative process. From a technical standpoint this translates directly into the design of authoring tools. The challenges of building domain specific authoring tools are well documented[29][1][17]. By identifying these sculptural patterns we gain some insight into the techniques behind the creation of location aware narrative which could be used to create more effective and engaging authoring tools.

Thus having identified these patterns our future work will focus on the development and evaluation of authoring tools that embed them in the author's workflow, making them easier to employ within a given story. This in turn will enable further exploration of critical theory around sculptural hypertext, and hopefully lead to a new poetical understanding of location aware narrative.

7. ACKNOWLEDGEMENT

This work was undertaken as part of the StoryPlaces project funded by The Leverhulme Trust (RPG-2014-388). All experimental work was approved under University of Southampton ethics review (ethics ID: 18364).

8. REFERENCES

[1] V. Aleven, B. M. McLaren, J. Sewall, and K. R. Koedinger. The cognitive tutor authoring tools (ctat): preliminary evaluation of efficiency gains. In *Intelligent Tutoring Systems*, pages 61–70. Springer, 2006.

[2] C. Ardito, P. Buono, M. F. Costabile, R. Lanzilotti, and T. Pederson. Mobile games to foster the learning of history at archaeological sites. In *Proceedings of the IEEE Symposium on Visual Languages and Human-Centric Computing*, VLHCC '07, pages 81–86, Washington, DC, USA, 2007. IEEE Computer Society.

[3] R. Ballagas, A. Kuntze, and S. P. Walz. Gaming tourism: Lessons from evaluating rexplorer, a pervasive game for tourists. In *Proceedings of the 6th International Conference on Pervasive Computing*, Pervasive '08, pages 244–261, Berlin, Heidelberg, 2008. Springer-Verlag.

[4] S. Benford, R. Anastasi, M. Flintham, C. Greenhalgh, N. Tandavanitj, M. Adams, and J. Row-Farr. Coping with uncertainty in a location-based game. *Pervasive Computing, IEEE*, 2(3):34–41, 2003.

[5] M. Bernstein. Patterns of hypertext. In *Proceedings of the Ninth ACM Conference on Hypertext and*

Hypermedia : Links, Objects, Time and Space—structure in Hypermedia Systems: Links, Objects, Time and Space—structure in Hypermedia Systems, HYPERTEXT '98, pages 21–29, New York, NY, USA, 1998. ACM.

[6] M. Bernstein. Card shark and thespis: exotic tools for hypertext narrative. In *Proceedings of the twelfth ACM conference on Hypertext and Hypermedia*, 2001.

[7] M. Bernstein, D. E. Millard, and M. J. Weal. On writing sculptural hypertext. In *Proceedings of the Thirteenth ACM Conference on Hypertext and Hypermedia*, HYPERTEXT '02, pages 65–66, New York, NY, USA, 2002. ACM.

[8] M. Blythe, J. Reid, P. Wright, and E. Geelhoed. Interdisciplinary criticism: analysing the experience of riot! a location-sensitive digital narrative. *Behaviour & Information Technology*, 25(2):127–139, 2006.

[9] J. Broadbent and P. Marti. Location aware mobile interactive guides: usability issues. In *Proceedings of the Fourth International Conference on Hypermedia and Interactivity in Museums (ICHIM97)*, pages 162–172, 1997.

[10] B. Bunting, J. Hughes, and T. Hetland. The player as author: Exploring the effects of mobile gaming and the location-aware interface on storytelling. *Future Internet*, 4(1):142–160, 2012.

[11] E. Carnielli and F. Pittarello. Interactive stories on the net: a model and an architecture for x3d worlds. In *Proceedings of the 14th International Conference on 3D Web Technology*, pages 91–99. ACM, 2009.

[12] M. Dionisio, V. Nisi, and J. P. Van Leeuwen. The iland of madeira location aware multimedia stories. In *Proceedings of the Third Joint Conference on Interactive Digital Storytelling*, ICIDS'10, pages 147–152, Berlin, Heidelberg, 2010. Springer-Verlag.

[13] K. Grønbæk, J. F. Kristensen, P. Ørbæk, and M. A. Eriksen. "physical hypermedia": Organising collections of mixed physical and digital material. In *HYPERTEXT '03: Proceedings of the fourteenth ACM conference on Hypertext and Hypermedia*, pages 10–19, New York, NY, USA, 2003. ACM Press.

[14] K. Grønbæk, P. P. Vestergaard, and P. Ørbæk. Towards geo-spatial hypermedia: Concepts and prototype implementation. In *Proceedings of the thirteenth ACM conference on Hypertext and Hypermedia*, pages 117–126. ACM Press, 2002.

[15] C. Hargood, R. Davies, D. E. Millard, M. R. Taylor, and S. Brooker. Exploring (the poetics of) strange (and fractal) hypertexts. In *Proceedings of the 23rd ACM Conference on Hypertext and Social Media*, HT '12, pages 181–186, New York, NY, USA, 2012. ACM.

[16] I. Herbst, A.-K. Braun, R. McCall, and W. Broll. Timewarp: Interactive time travel with a mobile mixed reality game. In *Proceedings of the 10th International Conference on Human Computer Interaction with Mobile Devices and Services*, MobileHCI '08, pages 235–244, New York, NY, USA, 2008. ACM.

[17] S. Kim, J. Mankoff, and E. Paulos. Sensr: evaluating a flexible framework for authoring mobile data-collection tools for citizen science. In *Proceedings of the 2013 conference on Computer supported cooperative work*, pages 1453–1462. ACM, 2013.

[18] R. Malaka, K. Schneider, and U. Kretschmer. Stage-based augmented edutainment. In *Smart Graphics*, pages 54–65. Springer, 2004.

[19] D. E. Millard, C. Hargood, M. O. Jewell, and M. J. Weal. Canyons, deltas and plains: Towards a unified sculptural model of location-based hypertext. In *Proceedings of the 24th ACM Conference on Hypertext and Social Media*, HT '13, pages 109–118, New York, NY, USA, 2013. ACM.

[20] K. Naliuka, T. Carrigy, N. Paterson, and M. Haahr. A narrative architecture for story-driven location-based mobile games. In *New Horizons in Web-Based Learning-ICWL 2010 Workshops*, pages 11–20. Springer, 2011.

[21] V. Nisi, I. Oakley, and M. Haahr. Location-aware multimedia stories: turning spaces into places. *Universidade Católica Portuguesa*, pages 72–93, 2008.

[22] V. Nisi, A. Wood, G. Davenport, and I. Oakley. Hopstory: An interactive, location-based narrative distributed in space and time. *Technologies for Interactive Digital Storytelling and Entertainment*, pages 132–141, 2004.

[23] F. Pittarello. Designing a context-aware architecture for emotionally engaging mobile storytelling. *Human-Computer Interaction–INTERACT 2011*, pages 144–151, 2011.

[24] Y. Rogers, S. Price, G. Fitzpatrick, R. Fleck, E. Harris, H. Smith, C. Randell, H. Muller, C. O'Malley, D. Stanton, et al. Ambient wood: designing new forms of digital augmentation for learning outdoors. In *Proceedings of the 2004 conference on Interaction design and children: building a community*, pages 3–10. ACM, 2004.

[25] E. B.-N. Sanders and P. J. Stappers. Co-creation and the new landscapes of design. *Co-design*, 4(1):5–18, 2008.

[26] M. Weal, D. Cruickshank, D. Michaelides, D. Millard, D. Roure, K. Howland, and G. Fitzpatrick. A card based metaphor for organising pervasive educational experiences. In *Pervasive Computing and Communications Workshops, 2007. PerCom Workshops' 07. Fifth Annual IEEE International Conference on*, pages 165–170. IEEE, 2007.

[27] M. Weal, D. Michaelides, D. Millard, D. De Roure, and G. Fitzpatrick. Observations on pervasive information systems design. In *Workshop on Principles of Pervasive Information Systems Design in conjunction with Pervasive 2007*, Toronto, Ontario, Canada, 2007.

[28] M. J. Weal, D. E. Millard, D. T. Michaelides, and D. C. De Roure. Building narrative structures using context based linking. In *Proceedings of the 12th ACM Conference on Hypertext and Hypermedia*, HYPERTEXT '01, pages 37–38, New York, NY, USA, 2001. ACM.

[29] W. M. Zhang, T. Tsang, E. Cheow, S. C. Ho, B. N. Yeong, and C. R. Ho. Enabling psychiatrists to be mobile phone app developers: Insights into app development methodologies. *JMIR mHealth uHealth*, 2(4):e53, Nov 2014.

Teens Engage More with Fewer Photos: Temporal and Comparative Analysis on Behaviors in Instagram

Jin Yea Jang[1], Kyungsik Han[2], Dongwon Lee[1], Haiyan Jia[1], & Patrick C. Shih[3]

[1]Pennsylvania State University, [2]Pacific Northwest National Laboratory, [3]Indiana University

{jzj157, dongwon, hjia}@psu.edu, kyungsik.han@pnnl.gov, patshih@indiana.edu

ABSTRACT

Research has suggested that teens are more active and engaged than adults on social media. Most of such observations, however, have been made through the analysis of limited ethnographic or cross-sectional data. Using a temporally extended, large-scale dataset and comparative analyses to remedy this shortcoming, we examined how and why the age difference in the behaviors of users in Instagram might have occurred through the lenses of social cognition, developmental psychology, and human-computer interaction. We proposed two hypotheses — *teens as digital natives* and *the need for social interactions* — as the theoretical framework for understanding the factors that help explain the behavioral differences. Our computational analysis identified the following novel findings: (1) teens post fewer photos than adults; (2) teens remove more photos based on the number of Likes the photos received; and (3) teens have less diverse photo content. Our analysis was also able to confirm prior ethnographic accounts that teens are more engaged in Liking and commenting, and express their emotions and social interests more than adults. We discussed theoretical and practical interpretations and implications as well as future research directions from the results. Our datasets are available at: https://goo.gl/LqTYNv

Keywords

Teens; age difference; comparative analysis; Instagram.

1. INTRODUCTION

Social media has been widely adopted in people's daily lives, especially through the help of mobile devices, allowing them to access, create, and interact with a wide range of information. In particular, teens are known to be highly engaged in social media [1][15]. According to Pew Research reports, 73 percent of all American teens now use a smartphone, 81 percent of them use social media, and 92 percent of them are online daily with their smartphone [11][24][27]. Most noteworthy is the phenomenon that teens and young adults appear to be early adopters — and arguably the most active users — of social media [8]. For them, social media has become a new channel and a new way of representing themselves [31] to share their everyday activities and thoughts with friends [12] to establish and maintain social connections and networks [30], and to learn something new and useful [19].

Research has studied several factors that drive such uses of social media by teens. On the one hand, being acclaimed as the "digital natives" [37], teens grow up with an abundance of communication

HT '16, July 10-13, 2016, Halifax, NS, Canada
© 2016 ACM. ISBN 978-1-4503-4247-6/16/07...$15.00
DOI: http://dx.doi.org/10.1145/2914586.2914602

technology and are believed to be more technologically-savvy than adults. On the other hand, from a developmental perspective, teens may consider social media as an exciting opportunity for social interaction space [19] and self-display [25], while adults may be more concerned about their information privacy in online disclosure. Given that socialization is an especially influential process in childhood and adolescence, interaction with their peers through social media plays an important role in teens' life and has a significant impact on teens' self-esteem and psychological well-being [45]. Their social media use is driven by their needs — they would stay active online to build and maintain connections with their peers through online interactions.

However, both the assumption of teens being active users in social media and the rationale behind this assumption have not been sufficiently studied and validated through their actual use of social media. First, despite the growing body of work that examines teens' online behaviors and technology use, little effort has been put into directly comparing teens' and adults' social media use and activities. Thus, it is difficult to determine if teens' actual use of social media is unique compared to other age groups. Second, existing studies of social media use have been mostly limited to ethnographic accounts (e.g., interviews, focus groups, etc.) or self-reported survey studies, while empirical investigation of large-scale user data is lacking. The latter is particularly useful for developing an understanding of behavioral patterns of teens in social media and the underlying strategies that they may use to manage their online activities. However, such an approach faces technical challenges. For example, identifying teens versus adults in social media is non-trivial, because many users often do not publicly reveal their age information nor, in many cases, do social networking sites (SNS) ask for user's age information at the time of registration.

In this regard, we seek to address the aforementioned limitations of social media studies and investigations. We strive to better understand and articulate teens' behavioral characteristics in social media by augmenting theoretical understandings of teens as well as additional behavioral patterns in social media. This paper is the extension of our previous work [20], which presented two main contributions. First, we introduced our hybrid method of textual pattern matching and facial recognition to detect users' age information in a large scale, and collected user information and usage data from a total of 27,000 teens and adults in Instagram, an online photo sharing site. Second, we presented some preliminary comparative analyses between teens and adults. We found that teens tended to have fewer photos than adults because of limited topics and photo removal. We also found that teens tended to have more selfies exhibiting a higher level of self-representation.

This paper significantly extends our previous work [20] in the following four important ways:

- First, our previous study lacked theoretical understanding of the underlying factors for behavioral differences that teens and adults showed. Thus, in this paper, we outline our two hypotheses based on the developmental literature and related work, serving as the theoretical foundation for explaining how age factors in social media behaviors.

- Second, our study significantly extends some of the previous findings by presenting the difference in the number of users who posted and removed photos as well as in the total number of posted and removed photos based on the topics. We add an additional behavioral difference — relationship between removed photos and the number of Likes — to strengthen our finding.

- Third, our study employs a comprehensive temporal analysis using time series dataset to empirically analyze the way teens and adults use Instagram over time, and examine the different interaction patterns with other users that teens and adults show.

- Finally, based on the empirical findings, we draw theoretical, practical interpretations and implications that may provide useful insights and guidance for future research and design.

Compared to existing research in this domain, this paper presents an analysis with large-scale user activity data to extensively reveal online behavioral patterns and empirical understandings as well as to identify potential factors that drive these patterns. Our analysis is guided by the following research questions:

- RQ1: *Do teens behave differently from adults in Instagram? Are teens more active users than adults?*

- RQ2: *If behavioral differences from different age groups are identified, what are social, psychological or technological factors that may explain such behavioral differences?*

Regarding RQ1, our study shows mixed findings. Comparatively, it appears that adults post more photos, whereas teens engage more in interactions with their social networks through Liking, commenting, and expressing more emotional and social interests. Regarding RQ2, we develop two hypotheses — *teens as digital natives* and *the need for social interactions* — based on previous literature and interpret behavioral and social aspects from the results of RQ1. We identify behavioral patterns which indicate that, while self-representation seems to be universally important for social media users irrespective of age, teens tend to show more behavioral activities in social media, manage their social media content to meet their social needs, and interact with more diverse users. On the other hand, adults tend to focus on expressing their identity and engagement through content creation (e.g., adults tend to post more photos than teens) and to interact with relatively smaller number of and less diverse users.

2. RELATED WORK

In this section, we present two hypotheses grounded by previous theoretical insights and implications to better understand how age factors in social media behaviors.

2.1 Perspectives on teens in social media

The notion of "digital natives" was first proposed by Prensky [37], which describes a new generation who has spent their entire lives surrounded by technologies and tools of the digital age. This notion has sparked a wide range of debate. Much of the opposition argues that the so-called digital natives do not necessarily possess the natural fluency and technological skills that they are assumed to, nor are they necessarily more intensive users of digital media than many so-called "digital immigrants" — people of the older generation who transitions from traditional media to new [44].

However, although the term may exaggerate the inter-generational gap and overlook the intra-generational digital divide, research has shown that young people in general, especially teens, are highly tech-savvy [23]. When it comes to social media contexts, studies show that teens tend to be early and fast adopters of newer or better online social space [5]. They also show that teens tend to use multiple social media sites and maintain different forms of communication [39], and can quickly switch between different platforms to take advantage of their unique features [38].

As a result of the digital proficiency and skillfulness, teens are likely to be active users of digital media. For instance, a national survey of teens in 2009 confirmed that age and Internet access are positively associated with digital literacy and Internet use [26]. Thus, we hypothesize that teens would exhibit more behavioral activities in social media, and would be capable of utilizing more technological features afforded by the platform:

- H1: *Teens are more active users of social media than adults, because they will be engaged in more behavioral activities and utilize more technological affordances on the social media (in this paper, Instagram).*

2.2 Teens & other age groups in social media

Some of the differences in social media use between teens and adults can be explained by their different levels of digital literacy and perceived competence. However, as discussed above, this assumed generational digital divide is rather ambiguous in reality. As the design of social media interfaces has become increasingly intuitive and easy to use, adults are quickly catching up in number when it comes to the use of some of the most popular social media websites, such as Facebook and Pinterest [11]. If technological literacy is not the determining factor, what other factors might lead to the unique behavioral patterns of the different age groups?

Social media offers abundant opportunities for social connections and social interactions; therefore, it serves to provide a virtual "social context" [1], an immediate social environment in which social and situational variables can greatly shape individual behavior. Therefore, individuals would behave in accordance with the social norms and in response to social influence they experience in social media. Previous developmental literature suggests that teens are particularly prone to such social influence. Consistent with such theoretical assertions, uses and gratification research [32][33] has also found that individuals use social media mainly for relationship maintenance, social surveillance, and social interaction, among other purposes (e.g., entertainment, self-status seeking, information seeking, etc.).

However, especially for teens, communication with their peers emerges as the single most important motivation for SNS use [4]. Ethnographic data have shown high teen engagement in online socialization opportunities and social behaviors unique to the mediated environment [8]. Teens also tend to maintain a social network with a large number of users [36] and consider social media a place for self-representation and for establishing their own identity [20][25].

In this regard, we hypothesize that teens would show more social activities than adults to stay connected with their peers through various means that are unique to the social media site:

- **H2:** *Teens are more engaged with social interactions with other users than adults through communication features (e.g., Likes, comments, tags, etc.) offered by Instagram.*

Overall, there have been a lot of research efforts on studying teens and generational perspectives in social media. However, very few studies have explicitly articulated differences from a large, data-driven longitudinal and comparative analysis. To fill this gap, this paper introduces a new method and presents less explored aspects, and a comprehensive picture of teens' social media behaviors.

In the following section, we will describe our method and process of data collection.

3. DATA COLLECTION

Instagram was chosen for data collection for two main reasons. First, Instagram is one of the most popular SNS with users who create and share mainly photos every day. Because of its high popularity, there has been a great volume of research studies on Instagram. Examples include exploring the relationship between photo content and engagement [3], analyzing photo content and user types [18], studying Like activities through the structural, influential, and contextual perspectives [21], and studying tag-based Like networks formed by Instagram users who have the same tags [16]. Second, given the fact that more than 90 percent of Instagram users are under the age of 35 [11], it is suitable to study our target age groups of teens and adults. By following Erikson's eight stages of psychosocial development[1], we define our target user populations as follows (note that we intentionally add a five-year gap between two age groups to minimize the ambiguity in estimating ages):

- *Teens*: people who are between 13 and 19 years old.
- *Adults*: people who are between 25 and 39 years old.

We used the programming API[2] to extract usage data for all users. The data collection was done between April and May 2014. We first chose one random seed user and crawled the followers of the seed user until we collected 150,000 users. We then randomly chose 1,000 users from the pool of 150,000 users and again crawled the followers of 1,000 users until we reached 2 million unique users. We used this two-step and random-seed crawling process in order to minimize the bias in sampling a homogenous population.

The dataset includes various pieces of user information, such as name, the number of photos posted, the number of Likes, tags and comments in the photo, the number of followers and followings, and a bio description, which are all associated with the individual accounts (Figure 1). From this data, we found some trends of teens in Instagram, which motivated us to investigate reasons behind those trends.

Classifying users to a specific age group was challenging. Most social media platforms, including Instagram, neither collect nor publicly disclose users' age information. To address this challenge, in our prior paper, we proposed a method that leverages two existing media contents (i.e., bio descriptions and profile images) with existing APIs [20]. First, we applied textual pattern

[1] https://goo.gl/dYfXYZ

[2] https://www.instagram.com/developer/

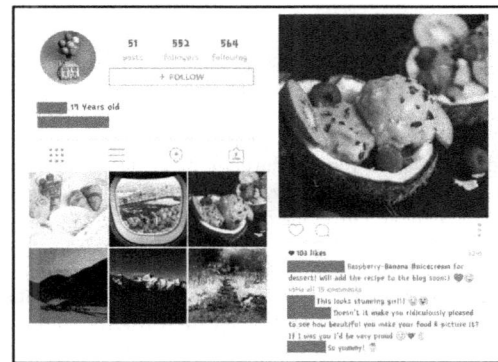

Figure 1. Mock-up Instagram page (username anonymized), illustrating poster-related information (e.g., # posts, # followers, # following, bio, etc.) and photo-related information (e.g., # Likes, tags, comments, etc.).

recognition algorithms to parse a list of patterns that specifically describe users' age in the bio (e.g., "I am 17 years old," "I'm 23"). Second, we used a facial recognition technique, Face++[3], to auto-detect the age information from people's profile images, which has been utilized and showed a high accuracy in another study [3]. Figure 2 illustrates the method and process of data collection.

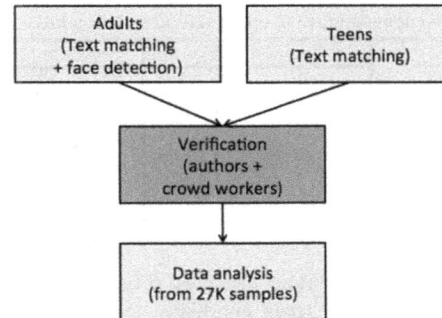

Figure 2. Data collection method and process.

With the data collected, we manually verified the age of all users to make sure that the data accurately represented each group from a total of five human judges (i.e., two authors and three crowd workers in Amazon Mechanical Turk). We finally had a total of 26,885 teens and adults for the analysis. See [20] for the more detailed process of data collection.

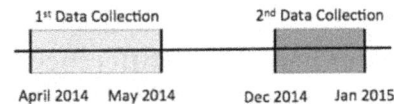

Figure 3. We found a trend from the 1st dataset and temporally extended it to create the 2nd dataset with the same number of users (13,533 teens and 13,352 adults).

We additionally collected the dataset from the same 26,885 users in 12-hour intervals over 12 days (from Dec. 26, 2014 to Jan. 6, 2015) to investigate the patterns of usage and engagement over time in Instagram. Figure 3 illustrates the construction of two datasets. For the analysis, we calculated the delta of photo counts in every two consecutive time slots and checked the total number of photos that users have posted, the number of users who added photos, and the number of users who removed their photos in 12 hours.

[3] http://www.faceplusplus.com/

Lastly, in order to protect the privacy and confidentiality of the Instagram users in our sample, privacy-preserving measures were taken throughout different stages of this study. More specifically, during the process of manual age verification, we removed all identifiable and sensitive information (i.e. name, ID, and email address) from the profiles and photos before they were presented to crowd workers. Moreover, during data analysis, we removed all user identifiable information (except for age), and aggregated and analyzed the data at a group level.[4]

4. RESULTS

In this section, we report our analyses on the usage data from a total of 26,885 teens and adults. We first briefly summarize our previous findings about the two primary usage differences (i.e., teens tend to post less and be engaged more than adults) between two groups [20], and then introduce and explain several factors that may influence those two findings.

4.1 Teens' behavioral differences

Our analysis on the usage of Instagram from all users showed that teens tend to post fewer Photos but show more activities in Liking, Tagging, and Commenting (see Table 1). As all variables show a long-tailed distribution, we used the median value for the analysis.

Table 1. Summary of activities by two groups. Teens tend to post less but be engaged more in other activities than adults [20].

	Teens (13,533)		Adults (13,352)	
	Median	SD	Median	SD
# Photos	110	272	175	487
# Likes	3,293	29,851	2,150	24,829
# Tags	446	2,595	294	2,511
# Comments	175	1,016	35	1,023
# Followers	401	3,683	348	5,700
# Followings	286	2,045	272	2,699

We also calculated the ratio of Likes, Tags, and Comments to Photos and found that teens are likely to receive more Likes (teens: 56.10; adults: 40.03; we used eta-square (η^2) for the effect size: 0.09), add more tags (teens: 6.34; adults: 4.70; η^2: 0.01), and have more comments (teens: 2.52; adults: 1.06; η^2: 0.07) per photo than adults (statistically, all showed significant differences; $p < 0.001$). This indicates that the way of using and engaging in Instagram between teens and adults is different. In the following sections, we investigated several factors that might lead to having these results.

4.2 Factors of behavioral differences: (1) teens have fewer photos in Instagram

4.2.1 Lack of topic diversity in photos

We first examined the list of topics that are presented in teens' and adults' photos. We assumed that, for teens, activities and topics of photos might be limited, because they are financially or culturally dependent on their parents to venture outside of their daily activities compared to adults. To test our assumption, we used tags in both posted and removed photos in order to find the topics of photos that users have or used to have (but removed).

Table 2. LDA-discovered topics from all users (N=26,885). Tags were used for topic discovery [20].

Topic	Tag examples

---

[4] Our datasets are available at: https://goo.gl/LqTYNv

Arts/photos/design	photo, interior, architect, design, building
Entertainment	music, movie, pop, rock, song, star, dance
Fashion/beauty	makeup, model, fashion, jewelry, beauty
Follow/like	followme, followback, follow, tagsforlike
Foods	food, coffee, yummy, delicious, dessert
Instagram-tags	instagood, instalove, instadaily, instashare
Locations	nyc, boston, spain, brazil, dutch, europe
Mood/emotion	love, happy, depressed, bored, sad, great
Nature	sky, sun, ocean, beach, flower, sunset
Social/ people	family, girlfriend, friends, folks, gay, pets
Sports/wellness	hiking, biking, fitness, cleaneating, soccer

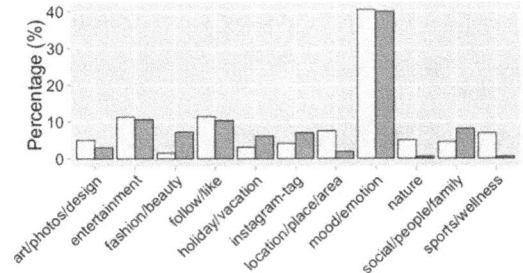

(a) Teens (N=13,533)

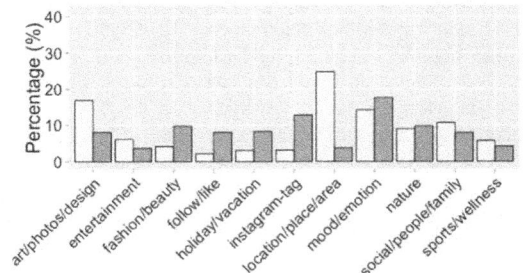

(b) Adults (N=13,352)

▨ Posted ▨ Removed

Figure 4. Percentage of the posted and removed photos based on LDA-discovered topics (x-axis), where N=26,885. Teens show a very high result in the mood/emotion topic both for posted and removed photos whereas adults show more diverse topics.

We identified latent topics from the tags of users' photos through an LDA analysis [6] using Mallet [28]. We used tags to infer photo content, because research has found that people tend to add tags that represent the photos they post [17]. We also obtained a list of ground-truth tag topics from two popular websites (i.e., tagsforlikes.com and tagstragram.com). We manually coded the types of photo topics from Mallet's output into those topics. Table 2 summarizes the 11 topics extracted from our dataset. We then calculated the percentage of topics from posted and removed photos for each group, as presented in Figure 4.

Figure 4 shows a clear difference between two groups in terms of topic types. On the one hand, for teens, more than half of posted and removed photos were in "Mood/emotion" and "Follow/Like." These topics are not necessarily tied to the content of photos but rather describe one's emotional status or intention to have more followers. In addition, topics of posted and removed photos for teens are highly correlated ($r = 0.92$, $p < 0.001$), indicating that teens show quite similar patterns when managing their photos. On the other hand, adults showed a high ratio in more diverse topics from their photos, including "Arts/photos/design," "Locations," "Mood/emotion," "Nature," and "Social/people."

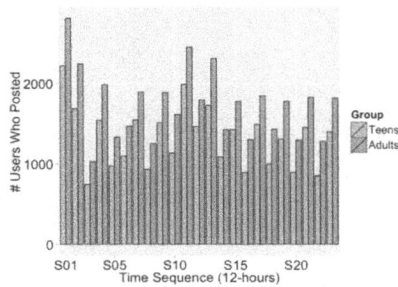

(a) # users who posted photos

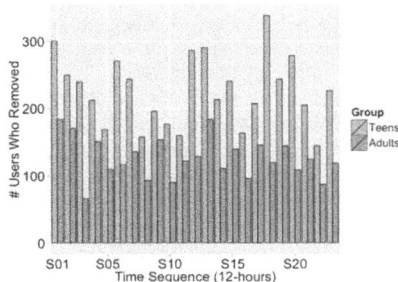

(b) # users who removed photos

Figure 5. Number of users who (a) posted or (b) removed photos over 12 days (N=26,885). More adults post and more teens remove photos.

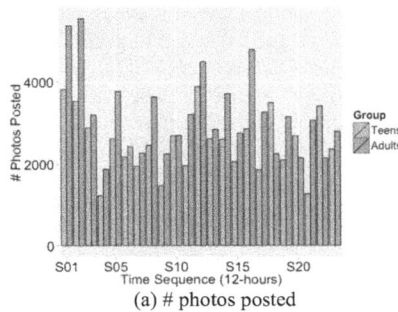

(a) # photos posted

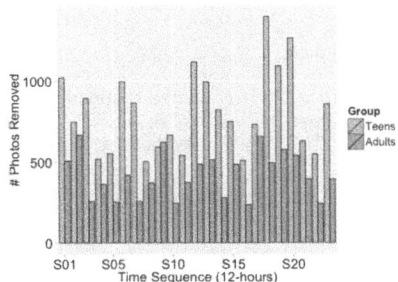

(b) # photos removed

Figure 6. Number of photos (a) posted and (b) removed over 12 days (N=26,885). More photos posted by adults and more photos removed by teens.

Unlike popular topics presented in teens' photos, these topics imply more diverse content in the photos, such as photos that depict different facets of cities and countries around the world, photos of arts and design (some of them were taken professionally), photos of a variety of people, and so on. Similarly, adults present quite diverse topics from removed photos, and, unlike teens, topics from posted and removed photos do not correlate with each other (r = 0.09, p = 0.77). In summary, it appears that teens' posted and removed photos have less diverse topics compared to adults' ones.

4.2.2 Post fewer and remove more photos

In addition to the topics of photos, we used the data showing the temporal usage reports (collected in the second phase) to measure the number of users who posted or removed photos, and that of posted or removed photos. For removed photos, we checked if each individual photo still existed by comparing a list of photos every 12-hours.

Figures 5 and 6 show the number of photos posted or removed and the number of users who posted or removed photos over time, respectively. From almost the same number of users in each group, the results show that fewer teens tend to post photos (t(42) = -3.89, p < 0.001), but more teens tend to remove photos than adults (t(42) = 8.01, p < 0.001). Regarding the total number of photos posted and added, teens posted fewer photos (t(42) = -3.76, p < 0.001) and removed more photos than adults (t(42) = 6.14, p < 0.001).

4.2.3 Remove photos with fewer Likes

Prior research has found that many teens tend to manipulate their photo content to receive as many Likes as possible or sometimes remove some photos that have received too few Likes [8][27]. Because there has been no attempt to examine this phenomenon through a large-dataset analysis, we measured whether the usage data from our sample showed a similar perspective, which also supports the idea of teens having fewer photos.

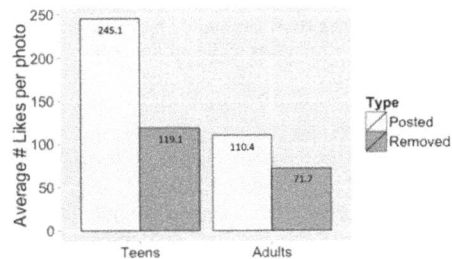

Figure 7. Average number of Likes per photo for posted and removed photos (N=26,885). Removed photos from adults have 35.0% fewer Likes than posted photos, whereas teens show 51.4% fewer Likes. Teens remove more photos that have fewer Likes than adults.

We first measured the number of Likes that the removed photos received and compared it to the number of Likes that all posted photos received. As we had the usage data 12-days in a row, we could calculate how many Likes had been in the removed photos. We then checked if teens removed photos that had relatively fewer Likes compared to the average of all of their photos. Figure 7 shows the result of the differences. The average number of Likes per posted photo is 245.1 for teens and 110.4 for adults. The average of Likes per removed photo is 119.1 for teens and 71.7 for adults. Then adults' removed photos have 35.0 percent fewer Likes than the posted (and kept) photos, whereas teens' removed photos have 51.4 percent fewer Likes than their posted (and kept) photos (t(44) = 7.08, p < 0.01). This result indicates that both user groups tend to remove photos that have fewer Likes than their overall photos, but teens show larger differences.

4.3 Factors of behavioral differences: (2) teens engage more in Instagram

To understand the level of engagement, we examined four aspects of teens and adults including: (1) how many Likes and comments they have had over time, which implies a level of activities in Liking and commenting; (2) how fast they replied to other users' comments added to their photos, which implies a level of one's interest in interacting with other users; (3) how they engaged with other users through comments, which implies a level of their engagement; and (4) what they wrote in their comments, which implies their intention through commenting.

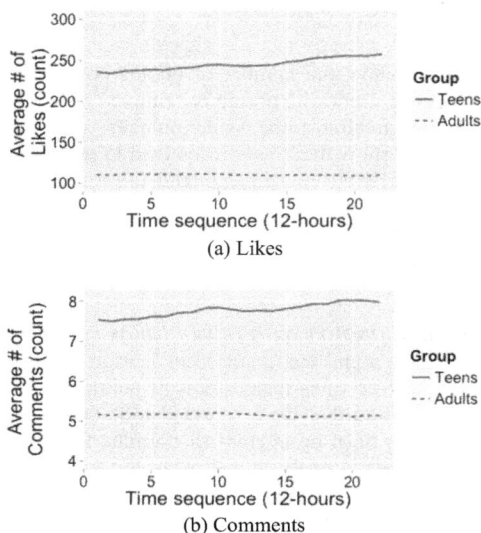

(a) Likes

(b) Comments

Figure 8. The average number of Likes and comments in every 12 hours (N=26,885). Teens show the steady increase over time for both Likes and comments while adults remain flat.

4.3.1 Teens have more Likes and comments over time
We measured the average number of Likes and comments teens and adults have had over time. Figure 8 illustrates the average number of Likes and photos over 12 days. Not surprisingly, teens showed the higher number of Likes and comments every day than adults (p < 0.0001). However, a more interesting aspect is that teens presented an overall increase, especially in Likes. In addition, when we consider this as a cumulative result, a total number of Likes for teens will be much higher than adults, which also implies high engagement in Liking. On the other hand, for adults, the average number of Likes and that of comments do not seem to be changed a lot. This implies that adults are likely to receive the similar number of Likes, even after they add new photos (i.e., in the previous section, we found that more adults post more photos than teens as shown in Figures 5 and 6). This further means that adding more photos does not necessarily lead to having more Likes or comments in adults' case. Figure 8 does not show a saturation point (i.e., no increase after reaching the certain number of Likes) for teens. However, for adults, the number seems to reach the threshold of having around 110 Likes and 5 comments. In summary, this result supports well the idea of teens engaging more in Instagram activities than adults.

4.3.2 Teens reply to others' comments more quickly
Adding user's name right after the "@" symbol has been widely used in social media for replying to another user and helping establish a language for communicating. We can think about a scenario where an original photo poster, @robinson, checked one comment (e.g., "Nice pic, where did you take it?") added to his photo by another user, @johndoe. Then, @robinson added a new comment (e.g., "@johndoe, I took this photo when I visited New York") and mentioned @johndoe in his comment.

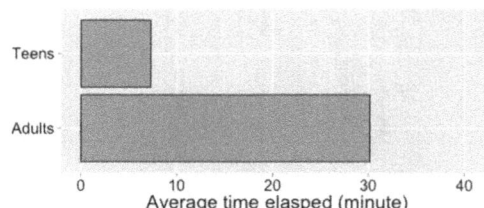

Figure 9. Avg. time elapsed when the original photo posters (N=26,885) commented and mentioned @name_of_previous_commenter right after @name_of_previous_commenter's comment. Teens tend to reply more quickly than adults.

Based on the scenario above, we measured how quickly the original photo posters replied to other users' comments that were added to their photos. As shown in figure 9, we found that teens replied to the previous comments from other users in around 7.2 minutes, which is significantly shorter than adults who replied in around 30.0 minutes.

4.3.3 Teens engage with more diverse users through commenting activities
To measure a number of other users that our sample users are engaging with through their comments, we first calculated the ratio of the number of comments with @others_username to that of all comments for each group. We found that teens showed a higher ratio result (45.2%) than adults (34.1%). This indicates that more teens are adding @username in their comments in order to, for example, call other users, or start and maintain conversations.

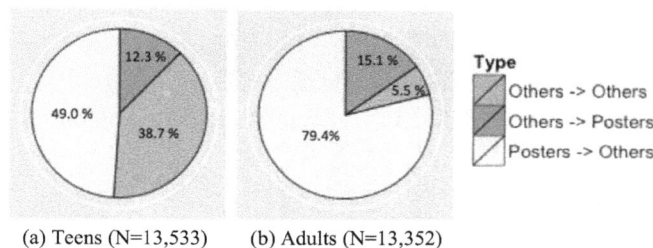

(a) Teens (N=13,533) (b) Adults (N=13,352)

Figure 10. Results of three types of adding comments with @. Teens show a higher result in "others→others" than adults, and adults show a higher result in "posters→others" than teens.

We further examined additional types of commenting with respect to two dimensions: (1) "users in the comments" — those who added comments and those who were mentioned in the comments — and (2) "user types" — original photo posters and other users. By combining these two dimensions, then, we derived three directional aspects of commenting with @: (1) original photo posters mentioned other users (posters → others); (2) other users mentioned the original photo posters (others → posters); and (3) other users mentioned other users (others → others), excluding the original photo posters, in their comments.

Figure 10 shows the break-downs of three types. First, teens have fewer cases (49.0%), where the original photo posters commented @others (posters → others) in their comments, than adults (79.4%). Second, teens have fewer cases (12.3%), where other users mentioned @photo_posters in their comments (others → posters), than adults (15.1%). Third, teens show more cases (38.7%) where other users mentioned @others in their comments (others → others) than adults (5.5%).

When we consider these results together, most comments (79.4% + 15.1% = 94.5%) in adults' photos are associated with the adult photo posters, whereas more than half of the comments (49.0% + 12.3% = 61.3%) in teens' photos are associated with teen photo posters. It is interesting to note that many other users who commented on teens' photos mentioned other "third users" in their comments (38.7%), whereas only very few cases of others → others are observed (5.5%) in adults' photos.

In order to gain a more concrete idea of patterns of commenting, we further measured the percentage of (non-overlapping) unique users who were mentioned in photo poster's comments, and the percentage of unique users who mentioned the photo poster in their comments.

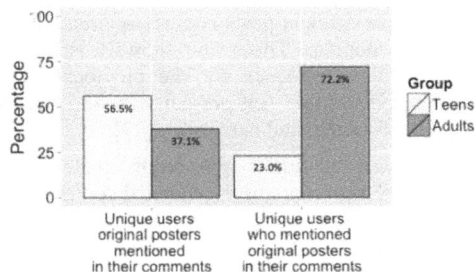

Figure 11. Percentage of (non-overlapping) unique users whom photo posters mentioned in their comments and unique users who mentioned the photo posters in their comments with @. For teens, (1) the original photo posters mentioned more unique users in their comments and (2) other users who added comments to teens' photos mentioned more third users. However, these were opposite in adults' comments.

Figure 11 shows the results with two interesting insights. First, teens mentioned other users in their comments (56.5%) more than adults (37.1%). Second, a majority (72.2%) of the comments on adults' photos were directed toward the original photo posters by mentioning their usernames, whereas less than a quarter (23.0%) of the comments on teens' photos were directed toward the original photo posters. Instead, 77.0% of the comments on teens' posts mentioned other people's usernames.

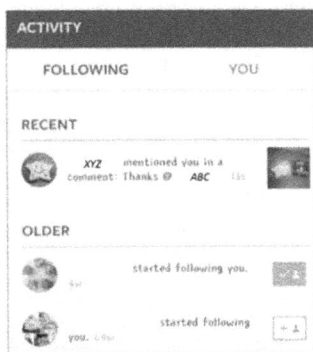

Figure 12. Instagram interface that shows one's activity. When a user (named *XYZ; anonymized*) adds *@ABC (anonymized)* in his comment, a notification will be sent to *ABC* as well as added to her activity page, indicating her name was mentioned in *@XYZ's* comment.

Given that comments and mentions can reach users instantly through push notifications (Figure 12) and are therefore effective communication tools on Instagram, this result shows the different communication patterns between teens and adults. Teens are known to be highly active in being connected with others [8][15]

through texts, emails, and social media [7][34] and responding quickly (Figure 9), thus it is reasonable enough to assume that they utilize a notification feature for communication. The comparison in Figure 11 reveals that teens tend to use the comment section to reach out to and interact with a more diverse and bigger network of users, while adults tend to use comments and mentions to have a more direct and interpersonal interaction (with fewer other users), showing more person-to-person or individual-oriented interactions.

4.3.4 Teens post emotional, social interests
Lastly, we measured the words in the comments with @ by teens and adults as the response to others' comments. We utilized Linguistic Inquiry and Word Count (LIWC) [35] in order to parse words representing tones and psychological components in the comments. We first randomly chose a total of around 6,000 teens and adults and compared word count (i.e., related to talkativeness and verbal fluency), the number of words longer than six letters (i.e., the higher it is, the less emotional and connected), and a level of social interests and that of emotionality.

Table 3. Analysis on comments from randomly selected teens (N=2,927) and adults (N=2,928) using LIWC. Teens show a higher result in social and emotional connection in their comments. Eta-square (η^2) was used for the effect size.

	Teens	Adults	Effect size (η^2)
Word count*	86.4	191.9	0.04
Words > 6 letters*	9.1	10.4	0.02
Social interests*	13.7	11.2	0.01
Emotionality*	38.0	31.0	0.07

*p < 0.001.

Table 3 summarizes the result. The word count and words longer than 6 letters for teens were lower than for adults. However, social interests and emotionality were higher for teens than for adults. It shows that although adults add longer comments, their comments are less emotional and oftentimes psychologically distant. Teens' comments were shorter but more emotional and embodied social aspects. Teens might spend less time on commenting because they have shorter texts. This perhaps implies that promptness is an important factor for teens when interacting with others as shown in Figure 9.

5. DISCUSSION
In this paper, we have presented an in-depth analysis on the social media usage of two different age groups – teens and adults. We primarily focused on investigating the factors that may affect the earlier findings where teens tend to have fewer photos but be more engaged in Instagram. We attempted to detail the reasons behind these trends based on the theoretical foundations and the analysis on the large datasets collected from a total of 26,885 teens and adults through mixed methods (i.e., text matching, face detection, and crowd workers). In this section, we first summarize two trends and the underlying factors, which we assumed and found through the analysis, and then discuss those factors within a lens of our hypotheses. We finally discuss study limitations and future work.

5.1 Two trends and the corresponding factors identified from the data analysis
For the first trend, where teens have fewer photos than adults, we have identified the following insights that explain it:

- Having fewer topics to post seems to lead teens to post fewer photos over time. Teens are likely to add and remove topics that mostly describe their emotional status or their intention to have more followers, while adults showed more diversity.

- Teens tend to add fewer photos and remove more photos than adults based on the analysis on the temporal usage dataset.
- Teens tend to remove photos that have relatively fewer Likes compared to adults.

For the second trend, where teens engage more than adults, we have discovered the following insights:

- Teens have more Likes and comments per photo than adults, and our analysis from the temporal usage dataset shows that teens are likely to receive more of them.
- Teens tend to reply more quickly to others' comments added to their photos than adults.
- Teens tend to add more comments with @username and have more non-overlapping (unique) users mentioned in their comments. Users who added comments to teens' photos also mentioned many diverse third-users in their comments. Thus, given that users will receive a push notification whenever there is a new message added to their photos or comments, it is likely that the original photo posters (teens) will see and be aware of the user names mentioned in the comments. Teens tend to add more comments that show social interests and emotionality. Conversely, adults tend to post fewer comments with @ and mention fewer unique users in their comments. Users who commented on adults' photos mentioned the original photo posters more than teens.

5.2 Theoretical and practical interpretation and implications

5.2.1 Hypothesis on digital natives

First of all, H1 (digital native hypothesis) was partially supported. Teens in Instagram were fairly active in all activity categories but were not necessarily more active than adult users in all aspects. In particular, they were found to create less content than adult users, despite their high engagement in commenting, Liking and tagging activities.

This finding has several implications. First, it shows that social media engagement is a multi-facet concept that encompasses not only content creation but also social interactions in various means.

Second, it indirectly supports the assumption of tech-savvy teens [5][23] in the sense that teen users were more likely to utilize the diverse features afforded by the interface for social networking purposes. Both hashtags and Likes are unique features of the new social media, which may be unfamiliar to some of the adult users. However, teens in our sample effectively utilized such features for proactive socialization.

Third, while examining teens' activities in Instagram, we identified an interesting pattern that they tend to manage their personal profile through content removal. This could also be an indicator of their skilled use of social media, where we found a possible link to a privacy aspect. For instance, teen privacy research has suggested that technology-savvy and -native teens would limit or remove their online postings (often after the fact) as a privacy protection mechanism rather than limiting their overall online activities and information revelation [22]. Similarly, based on the survey result out of 622 teens, research has found that 62 percent of teens (382) deleted or edited their content posted in the past as a way of their privacy strategy [14][46]. This unique strategy shows how today's teens manage their online content in different ways than older generations. In addition, content deletion could be a novel way to manage teens'

online self-representation, and this is also related to our second hypothesis.

5.2.2 Hypothesis on social interactions

Secondly, H2 (social interaction hypothesis) was supported. Our findings showed that social interaction was the primary motive for teens and had significantly shaped their behaviors in Instagram. Not only did teens receive more Likes and comments than adults — and following the social rule of reciprocity [13], we could assume that they left more Likes and comments on other users' profiles prior and/or in return — but their content deletion appeared to be associated with a lack of Likes. Teens' content management strategy appears to be for the purpose of self-presentation: compared to adults, teenagers especially may want to display the "popular self" [19]. For them, they would think that only keeping the most Liked posts could help create a perception that the profile is popular. This result shows a strong empirical and longitudinal field evidence for the previously established relationship between online self-presentation and psychological factors such as self-esteem and narcissism [29].

Our analyses showed that adults appeared to create more original content and to have kept more user-generated content (UGC) than teens. This finding shows some interesting perspectives. On the one hand, adults may have access to more resources and life experiences, which serve well as their source of content creation, while such resources and experiences are lacking for teens. On the other hand, existing research has suggested that, different from consumption and participation in UGC, the production of UGC is primarily driven by the needs of self-actualization [41].

Such needs can be more salient for adults as they have well-established identities and confidence in voicing their identity. Shao [41] pointed out that participation in UGC, in forms such as commenting and Liking, is associated with social needs. Given that social needs are more salient for teen social media users, it would be reasonable to see the result where teens were more engaged in these social interactions than content creation. From the social capital perspective, despite the fact many scholars believe the active use of SNS is more effective in achieving social capital, some research indicates that passive use (e.g., Liking, commenting, or just lurking) of SNS can also function as a form of social investment and therefore contributes to social capital [10].

Another insight can be revealed from the finding in which teens tend to use limited tags (mood/emotion or follow/like) and topics (i.e., we can assume that topics would be limited from those tags compared to the tags from adults) when they did create content in Instagram. The limitation might be explained by the hypothesis of online environment as an "echo chamber," referring to a situation in which information, ideas, or beliefs are amplified or reinforced by transmission and repetition inside an enclosed system [42]. In our study, the highly personalized content consumption enabled by online services allows users, young adults and adolescents in particular, to select only the content that they are interested in and the opinions that they agree with. Such selective exposure may lead to their limited scope of interest and topic diversity.

Lastly, our findings about comments and mentions in comments revealed the different strategies that teens and adults utilize to interact with their social networks. The fact that the mentions in comments on adults' profiles were used more frequently for direct communication with the original photo posters shows the adult users' preference for having or maintaining close, interpersonal interactions. Teens, however, tend to use the comment space to reach more and other users. They also responded more quickly to these comments through the Instagram notifications. This shows that teens maintained wider and more timely interactions with a large network of people. The social interaction that takes place in the comment space may have compensated for the limited content posted onto Instagram as well. This also in part affects the increase in Liking that teens showed compared to adults as teens make more new friends while adults seem to be more interested in interacting with established friend groups.

In summary, our data-driven temporal and comparative analysis unearths several new and unique insights on teens and their behaviors in social media. At the same time, the analysis substantiates the idea that teens leverage social media primarily as a "conversation space" [8] and use many features the platform provides in order to create connections and facilitate conversations and interactions [19]. Teens engage in social media not only because they are well aware of the intention of those activities, but also because they are familiar with technology use and the "tagging culture" in online space, which reinforces their social practice [1].

5.2.3 Practical interpretations and implications
Along with many theoretical insights, there are some practical interpretations and implications especially about the design of social media sites (in particular, Instagram).

There is a design opportunity where social networking sites can provide users with a summary of their usage. Several activity variables that are used for the analysis in this paper can be considered including the number of photos, Likes, comments, tags that users added, photo topics identified from the system, most popular photos based on the total number of Likes and comments, and etc. Then the social networking sites can leverage this design idea to provide one with a recommendation of other users who have shown similar activities or photos. This feature is expected to create interactive social space, which is beyond the one with simply one's followers/followings or location. As we found that teens and adults show distinctive usage differences in Instagram, this feature will give them chances to discover, meet and interact with new people who show similar interests and activities and/or are in the similar age. For example, teens and adults may find a list of users in their age groups more interesting and meaningful and want to check their photos, follow them, share messages or interests, because they may have more personal connections to peers. Yet, due to privacy concern, obviously, a careful design of supporting this new feature; for example, allowing users to control the visibility of some of their usage reports, should be taken into account.

5.3 Limitations and future work
Although we presented a number of insights, we acknowledge some limitations that can be handled in future studies.

First, errors may exist in the detection of age information even if we manually verified them. Many users provide additional social media links (e.g., Facebook, Twitter, etc.) in their profiles that we can leverage. Future studies that apply our method should obtain and corroborate additional age information from those sites.

Second, the age information auto-detected from users' bios or profile images could be incorrect when users have not updated them for a long period. This could affect the analysis of behavior differences by age. A possible remedy is, for instance, to double-check users' age information by comparing a user's "selfie" photos with the user's profile photos. However, a further study to validate its accuracy will be necessary.

Third, the results from our dataset may not represent the whole social media platforms and may only be limited to teens and adults in Instagram [40]. We plan to extend our study to other social media sites (e.g., Facebook, Flickr, etc.) to validate our method and compare results.

Lastly, we are very aware of the potential privacy issues that may arise from the analyses like ours if conducted improperly, and call on researchers to pay more attention to the ethical implications of collecting and using social media data for research purposes. Even if the data being gathered and analyzed are publicly available and accessible, users usually have no way to know about whether their data are used in research or about how to opt out. As boyd and Crawford [9] suggest, social media scholars need to be aware of the "considerable difference between being in public and being public," and should therefore carefully consider privacy and ethical implications when collecting and analyzing publicly available data. Especially if the data concern teenage users, as in our study, we recommend researchers to take the best measures to minimize potential risk and harm, remove personally identifiable information, aggregate and analyze data at a group level, and adopt systematic data management strategies to ensure data security.

6. CONCLUSION
This paper contributes to deeper analyses on age differences in Instagram, more broadly in social media. Based on comparative analysis methods using large-scale datasets that represent teens' and adults' Instagram usage, we tested our hypotheses developed through the lenses of social cognition, developmental strategy, and human-computer interaction in order to explain how age factors in social media behaviors. Our computational analysis identified the following novel findings: (1) teens post fewer photos than adults; (2) teens remove more photos based on the number of Likes the photos received; and (3) teens have less diverse photo content. Our analysis also confirmed prior ethnographic accounts that teens are more engaged in Liking and commenting, and express their emotions and social interests more than adults. These behavioral patterns show the age differences in online communication strategies such that teens and adults adopt to meet their social, self-expression needs and to accommodate with their technological skills and preferences. Our study presents a number of new and theoretically, practically meaningful insights and guidelines for ongoing research studies in social media.

7. ACKNOWLEDGMENT
This research was in part supported by NSF CNS-1422215, NSF IUSE-1525601, and Samsung GRO 2015 awards.

8. REFERENCES
[1] Adams, G. R. & Marshall, S. K. (1996). A developmental social psychology of identity: Understanding the person-in-context. *Journal of adolescence*, 19(5), 429-442.

[2] Agosto, D. E., Abbas, J., & Naughton, R. (2012). Relationships and social rules: Teens' social network and other ICT selection practices. *Journal of the Association for Information Science and Technology*, 63(6), 1108-1124.

[3] Bakhshi, S., Shamma, D. A., & Gilbert, E. (2014). Faces Engage Us: Photos with Faces Attract More Likes and Comments on Instagram. *Proceedings of the International Conference on Human Factors in Computing Systems*, ACM, 965-974.

[4] Barker, V. (2009). Older adolescents' motivations for social network site use: The influence of gender, group identity,

and collective self-esteem. *Journal of CyberPsychology & Behavior*, 12(2), 209-213.

[5] Birnholtz, J. (2010). Adopt, adapt, abandon: Understanding why some young adults start, and then stop, using instant messaging. Journal of Computers in Human Behavior, 26(6), 1427-1433

[6] Blei, D. M., Ng., A. Y., & Jordan, M. I. (2003). Latent dirichlet allocation. *Journal of Machine Learning Research*, 3, 993-1022.

[7] Boase J. & Kobayashi, T. (2008). Kei-Tying teens: Using mobile phone e-mail to bond, bridge, and break with social ties – a study of Japanese adolescents. *Journal of Human-Computer Studies*, 66, 930-943.

[8] boyd, d. (2008). Why Youth (Heart) Social Network Sites: The Role of Networked Publics in Teenage Social Life. *MacArther Foundation Series on Digital Learning - Youth, Identity, and Digital Media*, 119-142.

[9] boyd, D., & Crawford, K. (2012). Critical questions for big data: Provocations for a cultural, technological, and scholarly phenomenon. *Information, communication & society*, 15(5), 662-679.

[10] Burke, M., Kraut, R., & Marlow, C. (2011). Social capital on Facebook: Differentiating uses and users. *Proceedings of the International Conference on Human Factors in Computing Systems*, ACM, 571-580.

[11] Duggan, M. & Brenner, J. (2013). The Demographics of Social Media Users. *Pew Research Center's Internet & American Life Project.*

[12] Ellison, N. B., Steinfield, C., & Lampe, C. (2007). The benefits of Facebook "friends:" Social capital and college students use of online social network sites. *Journal of Computer-Mediated Communication*, 12, 1143–1168.

[13] Falk, A. & Fischbacher, U. (2006). A theory of reciprocity. *Journal of Games and Economic Behavior*, 54(2), 293-315.

[14] Feng, Y. & Xie, W. (2014). Teens' Concern for Privacy When Using Social Networking Sites: An Analysis of Socialization Agents and Relationships with Privacy-Protecting Behaviors. *Journal of Computers in Human Behavior*, 33, 153-162.

[15] Grinter, R.E., Palen, L., & Eldridge, M. (2006). Chatting with teenagers: Considering the place of chat technologies in teen life. *ACM Transactions on Computer-Human Interactions*, 13(4), 423-447.

[16] Han, K., Jang, J., & Lee, D. (2015). Exploring Tag-based Like Networks. *Proceedings of the International Conference on Human Factors in Computing Systems*, ACM, 1941-1946.

[17] Hollenstein, L. & Purves, R.S. (2010). Exploring place through user-generated content: Using Flickr tags to describe city cores. *Journal of Spatial Information Science*, 1(1), 21-48.

[18] Hu, Y., Manikonda, L., & Kambhampati, S. (2014). What we Instagram: A first analysis of Instagram photo content and user types. *Proceedings of the International Conference on Web and Social Media*, AAAI.

[19] Ito, M., Horst, H., Bittanti, M., boyd, d., Herr-Stephenson, B., & Lange, P., et al. (2008). Living and learning with new media: Summary of findings from the Digital Youth Project.

MacArthur Foundation Reports on Digital Media and Learning.

[20] Jang, J., Han, K., Shih, P. C., & Lee, D. (2015). Generation Like: Comparative Characteristics in Instagram. *Proceedings of the International Conference on Human Factors in Computing Systems*, ACM, 4039-4042.

[21] Jang, J., Han, K., & Lee. D. (2015). No Reciprocity in "Liking" Photos: Analyzing Like Activities in Instagram. *Proceedings of the International Conference on Hypertext and Social Media*, ACM, 273-282.

[22] Jia, H., Wisniewski, P., Xu, H., Rosson, M.B., & Carroll, J.M. (2015). Risk-taking as a learning process for shaping teen's online information privacy behaviors. *Proceedings of the International Conference on Computer-Supported Cooperative Work and Social Computing*, ACM, 583-599.

[23] Kennedy, G. E., Judd, T. S., Churchward, A., Gray, K., & Krause, K. L. (2008). First year students' experiences with technology: Are they really digital natives?. *Australasian journal of educational technology*, 24(1), 108-122.

[24] Lenhart, A. (2015). "Teen, Social Media and Technology Overview 2015". *Pew Research Center.*

[25] Livingstone, S. (2008). Taking risky opportunities in youthful content creation: teenagers' use of social networking sites for intimacy, privacy and self-expression. *Journal of New media & society*, 10(3), 393-411.

[26] Livingstone, S., & Helsper, E. (2009). Balancing opportunities and risks in teenagers' use of the internet: The role of online skills and internet self-efficacy. *Journal of New Media & Society*, 12(2), 309-329.

[27] Madden, M., Lenhart, A., Cortesi, S., Gasser, U., Duggan, M., Smith, A., & Beaton, M. (2013). Teens, Social Media, and Privacy. *Pew Research Center's Internet & American Life Project.*

[28] McCallum, A. K. (2002). *"Mallet: A Machine Learning for Language Toolkit".*

[29] Mehdizadeh, S. (2010). Self-presentation 2.0: Narcissism and self-esteem on Facebook. *Cyberpsychology, Behavior, and Social Networking*, 13(4), 357-364.

[30] Muscanell, N. L. & Guadagno, R. E. (2011). Make new friends or keep the old: Gender and personality differences in social networking use. *Journal of Computers in Human Behavior*, 28(1), 107-112.

[31] Ong, E., Ang, R., Ho, J., et al. (2011). Narcissism, extraversion and adolescents' self-presentation on Facebook. *Journal of Personality and Individual Differences*, 50(2), 180-185.

[32] Papacharissi, Z. & Mendelson, A. (2011). *Toward a new(er) sociability: Uses, gratifications and social capital on Facebook.* in Papathanassopoulos, S. ed. Media perspectives for the 21st century, Routledge, New York, 212-230

[33] Park, N., Kee, K. F., & Valenzuela, S. (2009). Being immersed in social networking environment: Facebook groups, uses and gratifications, and social outcomes. *Journal of CyberPsychology & Behavior*, 12(6), 729-733.

[34] Pater, J. A., Miller, A. D., & Mynatt, E. D. (2015). This Digital Life: A Neighborhood-Based Study of Adolescents' Lives Online. *Proceedings of the International Conference on Human Factors in Computing Systems*, ACM, 2305-2314.

[35] Pennebaker, J. W. & Francis, M. E. (1999). *Linguistic inquiry and word count (LIWC)*. Mahwah, NJ: Erlbaum.

[36] Pfeil, U., Arjan, R., & Zaphiris, P. (2009). Age differences in online social networking - A study of user profiles and the social capital divide among teenagers and older users in MySpace. *Journal of Computers in Human Behavior*, 25(3), 634-654.

[37] Prensky, M. (2001). Digital natives, digital immigrants. *On the Horizon*, 9(5), 1-6.

[38] Quan-Haase, A. & Young, A. L. (2010). Uses and gratifications of social media: A comparison of Facebook and instant messaging. Bulletin of Science. *Journal of Technology and Society*, 30(5), 350-361.

[39] Quinn, D., Chen, L., & Mulvenna, M. (2011). Does Age Make A Difference In The Behaviour Of Online Social Network Users? *Internet of Things*, IEEE, 266-272.

[40] Ruths, D. & Pfeffer, J. (2014). Social media for large studies of behavior. *Science* 28, 346 (6213), 1063-1064.

[41] Shao, G. (2009). Understanding the appeal of user-generated media: a uses and gratification perspective. *Journal of Internet Research*, 19(1), 7-25.

[42] Sunstein, C. R. (2002). *Republic.com*. Princeton University Press.

[43] Tausczik, Y. R., & Pennebaker, J. W. (2010). The Psychological Meaning of Words: LIWC and Computerized Text. *Journal of Language and Social Psychology*, 29(1), 24-54.

[44] Thomas, M. (Ed.). 2011. *Deconstructing Digital Natives: Young people, technology, and the new literacies*. Taylor & Francis.

[45] Valkenburg, P. M., Peter, J., & Schouten, A. P. (2006). Friend networking sites and their relationship to adolescents' well-being and social self-esteem. *Journal of CyberPsychology & Behavior*, 9(5), 584-590.

[46] Xie W. & Kang, C. (2015). See you, see me: Teenagers' self-disclosure and regret of posting on social network site. *Journal of Computers in Human Behavior*, 52, 398-407.

Friendship Maintenance and Prediction in Multiple Social Networks

Ka-Wei Roy Lee and Ee-Peng Lim
School of Information Systems
Singapore Management University
{roylee.2013, eplim}@smu.edu.sg

ABSTRACT

Due to the proliferation of online social networks (OSNs), users find themselves participating in multiple OSNs. These users leave their activity traces as they maintain friendships and interact with other users in these OSNs. In this work, we analyze how users maintain friendship in multiple OSNs by studying users who have accounts in both Twitter and Instagram. Specifically, we study the similarity of a user's friendship and the evenness of friendship distribution in multiple OSNs. Our study shows that most users in Twitter and Instagram prefer to maintain different friendships in the two OSNs, keeping only a small clique of common friends in across the OSNs. Based upon our empirical study, we conduct link prediction experiments to predict missing friendship links in multiple OSNs using the neighborhood features, neighborhood friendship maintenance features and cross-link features. Our link prediction experiments shows that unsupervised methods can yield good accuracy in predicting links in one OSN using another OSN data and the link prediction accuracy can be further improved using supervised method with friendship maintenance and others measures as features.

Categories and Subject Descriptors

H.2.8 [**Database Applications**]: Data Mining

Keywords

Multiple Social Networks, Twitter, Instagram, Link Prediction

INTRODUCTION

Motivation. According to the recent Pew Social Media Usage report [4], 52% of online users now use two or more online social networking sites (OSNs). As such, users today may find themselves engaging friends using a number of OSNs. For example, they may "like" their friends' posts on Facebook, retweet their friends' tweets on Twitter, and

HT '16, July 10 - 13, 2016, Halifax, NS, Canada

© 2016 Copyright held by the owner/author(s). Publication rights licensed to ACM.
ISBN 978-1-4503-4247-6/16/07...$15.00

DOI: http://dx.doi.org/10.1145/2914586.2914593

share photos on Instagram. The participation in multiple OSNs implies that users have to stretch and spread their already limited time and attention over the networks, which results in new dynamics in maintenance of friendships. For instance, a user may choose to connect to the same group of friends in multiple OSNs for ease of friendship maintenance, or conversely a user may partition and maintain different groups of friends in different OSNs while keeping only a smaller group of close friends overlapped in multiple OSNs.

This similarity of user's friendship in multiple OSNs also has impact on the evenness of user's friendship in multiple OSNs. For example, a user who maintains high similarity of friendship in multiple OSNs may or may not choose to partition and distribute his friends evenly across multiple OSNs. Our goal in this paper is to investigate the how users maintain friendships in multiple OSNs. Specifically, we study the similarity of users' friendship and the evenness in user's friendship distribution in multiple OSNs.

The study on users' friendship maintenance behavior may provide some new insights to other user behavior studies in multiple OSNs. Lim et al. conducted an empirical study on user's information sharing behavior in six OSNs and found users exhibited varied information sharing behaviors on different OSNs [9]. They postulated that this was due to the difference in user's usage for different OSNs. From friendship maintenance perspective, a possible explanation could be the users were varying their sharing of information to cater for the different groups of "audience" (i.e. friends) in different OSNs. Thus, research on friendship maintenance behavior of users can potentially help to provide new insights to other user's behaviors in these OSNs.

The study on friendship in multiple OSNs have real-world applications. In the second part of our study, we extend our empirical research on user's friendship maintenance in multiple OSNs and propose friendship maintenance related features to predict missing links (i.e. friendship) in multiple OSNs. There have been few recent link prediction studies done on *multidimensional networks* which refers to networks with multiple types of links between nodes. Researchers applied neighborhood features such as Common Neighbors and Adamic-Adar on a dimension of network to predict user's links in another dimension within the same network [15]. However, it is important to point out that there are differences between multidimensional networks and in multiple OSNs. For example, the users need to be matched across different networks in multiple OSNs, while users account matching is not required in multidimensional networks. Also, for multiple OSNs, user behaviors in one network are only observed by neighbors in the same network but not the same users's neighbors in another network, while in multidimensional networks, user behaviors are observed by all neighbors of the multidimensional network. As such, the link prediction in our study is different from the previous link prediction studies in multidimensional networks.

Research Objectives and Contributions. This research is conducted on a large real world dataset consisting of about 100,000 users on both Twitter and Instagram with tens of millions online friends. Our research in this paper is divided into two main parts addressing different research questions. In the first part, the research question is how users maintain friendship across networks. We focus on friendship maintenance measures that allow us quantify *friendship overlapping* and *friendship distribution*. In the second part of our study, we address the research question of how one conducts friendship prediction in the context of multiple social networks. In particular, we would like to explore using the friendship maintenance measures as features to improve the *friendship prediction* accuracy.

As shown in Figure 1, our proposed research framework begins with data crawling from both Twitter and Instagram to assemble a dataset of base users. For this set of users, we perform *cross-network friend matching* to identify the Twitter and Instagram friends of the same users. We then propose several measures for their friendship maintenance behavior. Finally, we use our findings to design both unsupervised and supervised friend prediction methods.

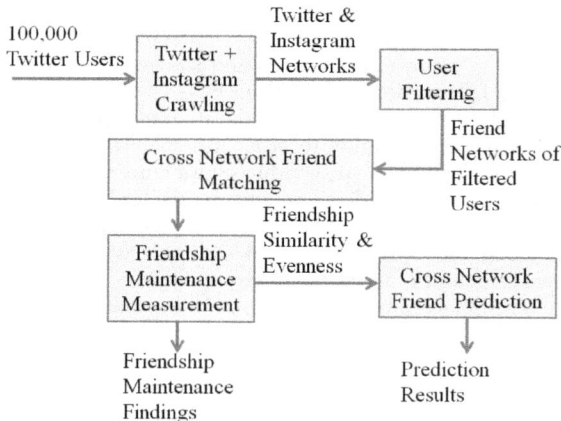

Figure 1: Research Framework

This work improves the state-of-the-art of social network analysis and link prediction in multiple OSNs. We establish a novel research framework to compare friends in two OSNs. Included in the framework are the measures for evenness of friendship distribution and similarity of friendship across multiple OSNs, as well as the prediction of links in the multiple OSNs settings. The interesting findings derived from our work include:

- Most users prefer to maintain roughly the same number of friends in Twitter and Instagram. i.e. evenly distributed friendship across multiple OSNs.

- Most users prefer to maintain different friendships in Twitter and Instagram, while keeping only a small clique of common friends across the two OSNs. i.e. low similarity in friendship across multiple OSNs.

- Unsupervised methods can yield good accuracy predicting friendship in one network using neighborhood properties of another network. In particular, the Jaccard Coefficient of two users computed in Instagram network can quite accurately predict the link between the two users in Twitter (average F1 score of 0.882).

- Supervised method with friendship maintenance measures as features can further improve the accuracy in friendship prediction across multiple OSNs (average F1 score of 0.93).

Paper Outline. The rest of the paper is organized as follows. We first describe the construction of our Twitter and Instagram datasets. Next, we propose measures that quantify the evenness of user's friendship distribution and similarity of friendship in multiple OSNs. We then apply the proposed measures to analyse the users' friendship maintenance in Twitter and Instagram networks. Subsequently, we describe the friendship link prediction experiments conducted using friendship features and present the results. Finally, we review related research to this study and conclude this work with possible future research.

BASE USER DATASET

In order to study the user friendships in multiple OSNs, we first need to construct a dataset of users who have accounts with both Twitter and Instagram, a popular microblogging site and a photo-sharing social media site respectively. As the two selected OSNs serve different purposes, it is unlikely that the two OSNs cannibalize each other's users. Furthermore, the two OSNs are highly complementary and popular among teen users [4]. We therefore expect a user on both Twitter and Instagram would generally have the interest to include the same friends in both networks.

We begin by gathering a set of 100,000 Twitter users who have declared their Instagram accounts in their Twitter biography description from *Followerwonk* [1], a Twitter analytic platform. Subsequently, the Twitter and Instagram followers and followees of these 100,000 users were crawled using the Twitter and Instagram APIs. However, as some of these Twitter and Instagram accounts have set their privacy settings to "private", we are not able to obtain all the followers and followees of the users. We are also only interested in analyzing friendship of average OSN users, thus we further filter away celebrity or popular users who have more than 2,000 followers. At the end, we manage to obtain 97,978 users who have declared both their Twitter and Instagram accounts, and these users constituted the **base user set**.

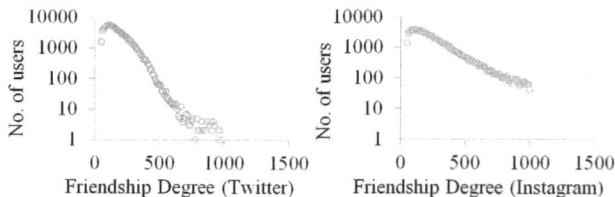

Figure 2: Twitter and Instagram Friendship Distribution

Next, we retrieve the Twitter and Instagram friends of the users in *base user set*. As Twitter and Instagram only cap-

---
[1]https://moz.com/followerwonk/

ture follower and followee relationships, we define the *friend* of a user to be someone who follows and is followed by the user [20, 6]. An estimated 17 million Twitter friends and 24 million Instagram friends are finally obtained. Figure 2 shows the Twitter and Instagram friendship degree distributions. The average Twitter and Instagram friendship degrees for these users are 171 and 245 respectively.

USER FRIEND MATCHING

Before we can study how the users maintain friendships in their Twitter and Instagram accounts, we are required to match the friend accounts in the two OSNs. Unfortunately, very few of the friends have declared both their Twitter and Instagram accounts. Hence, in this section, we present a few simple but effective ways to match users between OSNs by adapting the methods proposed by Zafarani and Liu [21] and Vosecky et al. [18], which are quite effective in this context. We match the Twitter and Instagram friends of our base user set using three levels of user matching methods:

1. **Self-Report Matching.** This method matches the Twitter and Instagram friends of the base user set if these friends declare both their Twitter and Instagram accounts.

2. **Username Matching.** Past research has reported that 59% of users prefer to use the same username repeatedly on different OSNs for easy recall [21]. Instead of matching all our Twitter and Instagram users by their usernames, we match Twitter users with Instagram users by username when they are the friends of the same user in our base set. This minimizes the possibility of two users being matched because they adopt more popular username.

3. **Username Bigram Matching.** Users may tweak their usernames slightly across different OSNs due to the unavailability of their usual usernames. To cater for such situations, we introduce an approximate method which matches the Twitter and Instagram friends of the base users using username bigrams. Each username is now represented by a vector of bigram weights each of which is the number of occurrences of the bigram in the username. Cosine similarity is then applied on two username bigram vectors to determine if the two usernames are sufficiently similar. If the cosine similarity score exceeds a threshold, the two usernames are considered matched. We adopt a threshold value of 0.63 which is derived by taking the median cosine similarity values of Twitter and Instagram username bigrams of the base users.

Table 1: Number of users and friends matched using different methods

Methods	Self-Report	Username	Username Bigram	Total
# Users Matched	17,236	1,473,217	1,546,645	3,037,098
# Friends Matched	22,234	1,735,719	1,798,457	3,556,410

Table 1 shows the number of friends matched using the above three methods. As expected, the self-report method returns the smallest number of matched friends. A total of 22,234 friends were matched using this method giving an average of $\frac{22,234}{97,978} = 0.23$ matched friends per user. In other words, vast majority of base users do not have their Twitter and Instagram friends matched using self-report. User name matching method, on the other hand, is able to match a total of 1,735,719 friends (in addition to those matched by self-report) or an additional 17.72 friends per user, representing $\frac{17.72}{171} = 10.4\%$ and $\frac{17.72}{245} = 7.2\%$ of all Twitter and Instagram friends of the base users respectively. Finally, the username bigram matching method returns yet an additional 1,798,457 matched friends, or 18.36 matched friends per user. This corresponds to 10.7% and 7.5% of all Twitter and Instagram friends respectively. Combining all methods, we are able to match 3,556,410 friends, or 36.3 matched friends per user. Henceforth, we will use all these matched friends in the subsequent analysis.

As there are no ground truth for the validation of the matched friends, we randomly inspected Twitter and Instagram profiles of 100 pairs of matched friend pairs using the username matching and another 100 pairs of matched friends using combined method. We then looked at the visual cues such as their profile photos to assess whether the matching methods are accurate. Among the inspected 100 pairs of matched friends using the exact username matching method, we observed that 77 of the pairs have (i) matching profile photos for their Twitter and Instagram accounts, or (ii) their Twitter profile photos matched with some of the photos posted by the Instagram accounts. Majority of the non-matched friend profiles are due to the users not setting profile picture for their Twitter accounts, thus the actual number of matched pair could be higher than 77. For the username bigram method, 68 of the pairs meet the matching profile photos criteria. This suggests that the user matching methods were able to match the user friends with good accuracy.

FRIENDSHIP MAINTENANCE MEASUREMENT

Before we study how users maintain friendship in Twitter and Instagram, we first propose two measures, *friendship similarity* and *friendship evenness*, to quantify the similarity of user's friendship and the evenness of user's friendship distribution in multiple OSNs respectively.

Friendship Similarity

To ease friendship maintenance, users may choose to overlap their friendships in multiple OSNs. We adapt the *D-Correlation* approach by Berlingerio et. al [3] to measure this overlap or similarity of friendship across multiple OSNs. D-Correlation was originally designed for multi-dimensional networks where it measures how redundant are two dimensions for existence of a node or an edge.

We use $\mathbb{N}$ to denote a set of OSNs $\{N_1, N_2, \cdots, N_n\}$. We denote the set of friends of a user x in a OSN N_i by $FR(x, N_i)$. We define the friendship similarity of user x among these OSNs, $F_{Sim}(x, \mathbb{N})$, to be the ratio of common friends of x across all OSNs as shown in Equation 1.

$$F_{sim}(x, \mathbb{N}) = \frac{|\cap_{N_i \in \mathbb{N}} FR(x, N_i)|}{|\cup_{N_i \in \mathbb{N}} FR(x, N_i)|} \quad (1)$$

Example. Figure 3 illustrates the an example of user distributing his friends in two OSNs, A and B. The user x

have a total of 25 friends; 10 friends in A, 20 friends in B and 5 of the friends are overlap two OSNs. Thus, the user x's friendship similarity in OSN A and B will be computed as $F_{sim}(x, \mathbb{N}) = 5/25 = 0.2$.

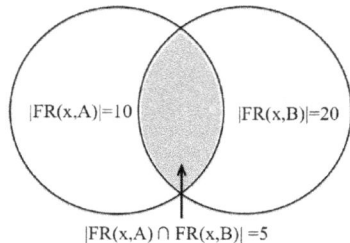

Figure 3: Example of user's friendship in two OSNs

Upper Bound of Friendship Similarity. The maximum Friendship Similarity value is only achieved when x has the same friends in all OSNs.

The maximum value of for a user's friendship similarity in multiple OSNs is equal to ratio between the minimum and maximum number of friends added to a OSN among the OSNs that the user has participated (as shown in Equation 2). Referencing to the earlier example in Figure 3, the maximum possible F_{sim} value for user x would be $10/20 = 0.5$. i.e. user x added all his friends in OSN A in OSN B as well.

$$max(F_{sim}(x, \mathbb{N})) \leq \frac{\min\limits_{N_i \in \mathbb{N}} |FR(x, N_i)|}{\max\limits_{N_i \in \mathbb{N}} |FR(x, N_i)|} \qquad (2)$$

Friendship Evenness

Suppose that a user x divides all his friends among all the n OSNs without overlap, we expect $\frac{1}{n}$ of his friends in each OSN. Suppose there is a non-zero overlap among his friends across all the OSNs but negligible overlap between subsets of OSNs, and $F_{sim}(x, \mathbb{N}) > 0$, the *expected ratio of friends* x *adds to each OSN* is then estimated by $\frac{1}{n} + \frac{F_{sim}(x, \mathbb{N})}{n}$ as shown in Equation 3.

$$F_{equal}(x, \mathbb{N}) = \frac{1 + (n-1) \cdot F_{sim}(x, \mathbb{N})}{n} \qquad (3)$$

Proof. Suppose x has N unique friends in $\mathbb{N}$. Assume that x distributes her friends evenly across the OSNs. Let N_u be the number of unique friends in each OSN and let F denote $F_{sim}(x, \mathbb{N})$. We then expect x to have $N \cdot F$ common friends across the OSNs. In other words, x has $N_u + F \cdot N$ friends in each OSN. As $N = n \cdot N_u + F \cdot N$, we obtain $N = \frac{n \cdot N_u}{1-F}$. Each OSN is then expected to have $N_u + F \cdot \frac{n \cdot N_u}{1-F}$ friends in each OSN. The expected ratio of friends in each OSN is therefore

$$\frac{N_u + F \cdot N}{N} = \frac{N_u + F \cdot \frac{n \cdot N_u}{1-F}}{\frac{n \cdot N_u}{1-F}} = \frac{1 + (n-1) \cdot F}{n} \qquad (4)$$

When $F = 0$, the above ratio degenerates to $\frac{1}{n}$ implying that all friends of x are equally divided among OSNs exclusively. When $F = 1$, the ratio also becomes 1 implying that every OSN covers all friends of x. When there are only two OSNs, i.e., $n = 2$, the expected ratio of friends in each OSN is $\frac{1+F}{2}$.

However, we would expect that in many circumstances, unevenness exists among the friend counts of the OSNs. For example, a user may maintain a larger group of friends in an OSN N_i while keeping a smaller clique in another network. We thus define the *ratio of friends of a user x in OSN N_i relative to all friends* in Equation 5.

$$F_{in}(x, N_i, \mathbb{N}) = \frac{|FR(x, N_i)|}{|\cup_{N_i \in \mathbb{N}} FR(x, N_i)|} \qquad (5)$$

Finally, we then define the *evenness of user's friendship distribution* in multiple OSNs as the inverse of summation of difference between the ratio of friends added in each OSN and the expected ratio of friends a user adds to each OSN when the friends are evenly distribution as shown in Equation 6.

$$F_{even}(x, \mathbb{N}) = 1 - \sum_{i=1}^{n} \left| F_{in}(x, N_i, \mathbb{N}) - F_{equal}(x, \mathbb{N}) \right| \qquad (6)$$

Example. Referring to our earlier example in Figure 3, $F_{in}(x, A, \{A, B\})$ is $10/25 = 0.4$ and $F_{in}(x, B, \{A, B\})$ is $20/25 = 0.8$. User x's evenness of friendship distribution in OSN A and B is $F_{even}(x, \{A, B\}) = 1 - (|0.4 - \frac{1+0.2}{2}| + |0.8 - \frac{1+0.2}{2}|) = 0.6$.

Note that $F_{even}(x, \{A, b\})$ measure is also in the range of 0 to 1. Suppose that a user add equal number of friends in the two OSNs with any number of overlap friends among the two OSNs, the user's friendship evenness value will 1. The value for friendship evenness will be 0 is no friend in one of the two networks.

Relationship between Measures. There is also an interesting relationship between the upper bound of Friendship Similarity and Friendship Evenness. Based on Equation 2, in order to achieve a maximum friendship similarity value of 1 (i.e., $max(F_{sim}(x, \mathbb{N})) = 1$), the minimum and maximum numbers of friends in all the OSNs are identical. That is, user x distributes friendships evenly among all the OSNs ($F_{even}(x, \mathbb{N}) = 1$). Thus, the more evenly distributed the friends among OSNs, the higher the $max(F_{sim}(x, \mathbb{N}))$.

EMPIRICAL RESULTS

In this section, we apply the friendship similarity and evenness measures to analyze how the 97,978 *base users* maintain their friendships in Twitter and Instagram.

Distribution Analysis

Figure 4 shows the distribution of friendship similarity. The average friendship similarity is 0.104. The 1st, 2nd and 3rd quartile friendship similarity values are 0.046, 0.09 and 0.148 respectively. This left-leaning bell shape distribution suggests that there are very few users who maintained similar friendship in their Twitter and Instagram accounts. Interestingly, this is contrary to our initial hypothesis that user would prefer to have a high friendship similarity for ease of maintenance. There could be a few reasons for the low average friendship similarity; for instance, the users may have maintained low evenness for their friendship in the two OSNs, thus limiting the maximum possible friendship similarity value for the users, or the users simply prefer to maintain different groups of friends in different OSNs.

Figure 5 depicts the distribution of friendship evenness of the base users. The average friendship evenness is 0.648,

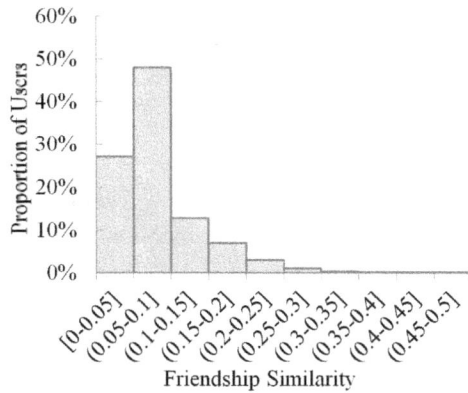

Figure 4: Friendship Similarity Distribution

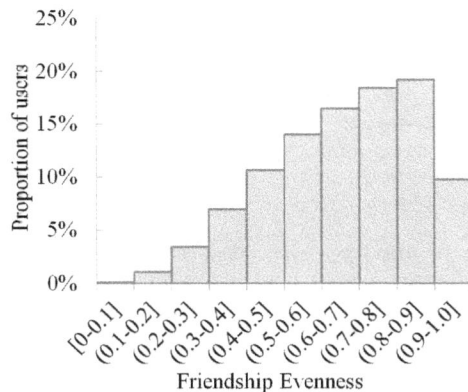

Figure 5: Friendship Evenness Distribution

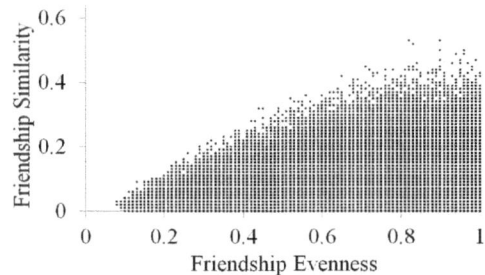

Figure 6: Friendship Similarity and Friendship Evenness

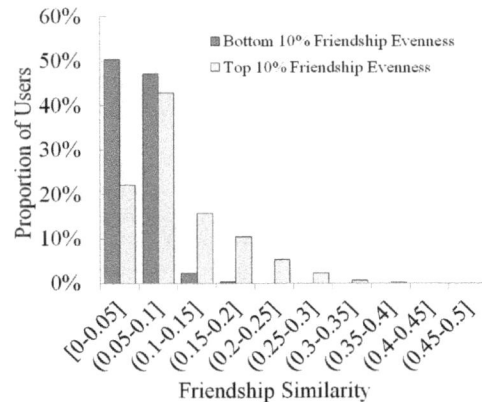

Figure 7: Friendship Similarity of Top and Bottom 10% Friendship Evenness Users

a value much higher than the average friendship similarity. The 1st, 2nd and 3rd quartile evenness values are 0.534, 0.705 and 0.856 respectively. The distribution is right-leaning, suggesting that most users may prefer to have not overly uneven friendship counts in different OSNs. Also, the right-learning friendship evenness distribution further strengthens our earlier finding that the users tend to prefer to maintain different groups of friends in different OSNs. There could be many reasons for users preference to maintain different friendship in different OSNs. One of the possible reasons could be as suggested by Lim et al. [9], that users use different OSNs for different purposes or interests, which indirectly motivates the users to connect to different friends in different OSNs. To explain the the user's friendship maintenance behavior, we will study beyond the structural properties of multiple OSNs and investigate the differences in the user interests across different OSNs in our future works.

Relationship Between Measures

We also examine the relationship between friendship similarity and friendship evenness of users in Figure 6 where each point in the figure represents a user with his friendship similarity and evenness values.

Figure 6 shows that as the user's friendship evenness increases, friendship similarity seems to increase its range of values. This supports what we have highlighted in our earlier discussion that the friendship similarity is limited by

the friendship evenness. We also further investigate this by showing the friendship similarity distribution of users with top and bottom 10% friendship evenness in Figure 7. The top 10% friendship evenness users have friendship similarity distribution similar to the overall friendship similarity distribution (as shown in Figure 4), while the bottom 10% friendship evenness users have a more left-leaning friendship similarity distribution. The top 10% friendship evenness users also have an average of friendship similarity of 0.124, slightly higher than the 0.104 friendship similarity of an average user, while the bottom 10% friendship evenness users have an average of 0.055 friendship similarity, significantly lower than the average user. However, it is observed that there are quite still a number of users who have high friendship evenness but low friendship similarity.

To investigate the dependency between friendship evenness and similarity, we performed a Chi-squared Test of Independence on the two measures. The test result shows p-value $< 2.2e{-}16$, which is lesser than the 0.05 significance level, therefore we reject the null hypothesis that friendship similarity is independent of friendship evenness. The two measures also shows a positive weak correlation of 0.277.

FRIENDSHIP LINK PREDICTION

We now examine how the link prediction in multiple social networks can leverage on the links across networks. Link prediction can come in two forms, namely, prediction of future links and prediction of missing links [8, 5, 17]. In our research, we focus on the latter which is useful in applications such as friend recommendations. As this is the first attempt to conduct link prediction for multiple social networks, we also want to answer the following research questions:

- *Can we predict the link between two users in one network using the structural information of the two users in another network?* Suppose that two users have many common friends in a single OSN, it is likely the they are friends in the OSN. Intuitively, the existence of a link between the two users in one OSN should also increase the likelihood of a link between the users in another OSN.

- *Can the friendship maintenance features improve the accuracy of link prediction in multiple online social networks?* Now that we have the friendship similarity and evenness measures, we would like to know if they can make good features for link prediction.

Task Definitions

There are two prediction tasks to be performed: (a) **Twitter Link Prediction (TWLP)** where we predict if two users are friends in Twitter; and (b) **Instagram Link Prediction (INLP)**, where we predict if two users are friends in Instagram.

We now describe the setup of the training and test data in our the link prediction task. Let V_{Both} be the 97,978 base users who exist in both Twitter and Instagram. For our base users in Twitter, we define the set of positive instances to be (u, v) pairs such that both u and v are in V_{Both} and (u, v) is an observed link in Twitter. We denote this set of positive instances by $E_{pos}(TWT)$. The set of negative instances, denoted by $E_{neg}(TWT)$, is the set of (u, v) pairs with both u and v from V_{Both} but are not friends in Twitter. The sets of positive and negative instances for our base users in Instagram are defined in a similar manner.

With the above definitions, we derive 17,651 and 26,241 positive instances for base users in Twitter and Instagram respectively, i.e., $|E_{pos}(TWT)| = 17,651$ and $|E_{pos}(INT)| = 26,241$. The numbers look small compared with the size of base users largely because the base users which are selected based on having both Twitter and Instagram accounts do not come from the same user community. Hence, only very few of them know each other on Twitter or Instagram. In other words, there are many more negative instances making the link prediction tasks highly imbalanced. Furthermore, there are additional overheads crawling additional data (e.g., friends of neighbors) for each positive and negative instance in the prediction task. In order to keep the number of instances manageable for the prediction methods, we randomly select 5,000 positive instances and 25,000 negative instances for each run in our prediction tasks. The negative instances are kept to five times that of positive instances. To make the prediction harder, we also check that at least 5,000 negative instances have at least 1 common neighbor in Twitter or Instagram.

Unsupervised Prediction task. For this task, we rank the 5,000 positive and 25,000 negative instances by some ranking measure. We expect the top ranked instances to be positive if the prediction method works accurately. In the ideal case, all positive instances are ranked above all negative ones.

Supervised Prediction Task. For this task, we select set of training and test datasets. Each dataset consist of 5,000 positive instances and 25,000 negative instances which

are randomly selected. We also check that the instances selected for testing dataset does not exist in the training dataset. We then train a classifier using the training dataset and apply the trained classifier on the test dataset. This experiment is repeated three times and the results reported are the average of the three runs.

Unsupervised Link Prediction Methods

We propose to use several unsupervised link prediction methods using different *neighborhood features* as ranking measures[12, 1]. These measures involve using the common neighbors between a pair of users u and v to derive some affinity score for ranking the user pair. These measures are also based on the triadic closure principle in social network analysis [16]. In this work, the following measures are used:

- **Common Neighbors (CN)**: This measure counts the number of common neighbors between u and v.

- **Jaccard Coefficient (JC)**: This measure returns the fraction of common neighbors between u and v.

- **Adamic-Adar (AA)**: This measure considers the popularity of common neighbors. The less popular common neighbors are given larger weights as they are added together to derive an affinity score.

The above measures are chosen as they were commonly used in link prediction experiments. More formal definitions of them are given at the top of Table 2. In Table 2, $FR(u, T)$ and $FR(u, I)$ denotes the friends of u in Twitter and Instagram respectively. While applied to score each of the 5,000 positive and 25,000 negative instance, the measures are computed using all observable link instances in our dataset, i.e., all links excluding those used as positive instances.

There were also recently studies that applied these neighborhood measures in multidimensional networks, where links between users in one dimension are ranked using the neighborhood features of users in another dimension of the same network [15]. Unlike these existing link prediction works on multidimensional networks, we are now using these neighborhood measures for unsupervised link prediction between users in multiple social networks where users may not have accounts on both networks and users having accounts on both networks may not have their accounts matched.

Performance Evaluation. We use *F1 at Top K* to evaluate each unsupervised link prediction method. We first rank all given 30,000 instances by the method's measure in decreasing order. The *Precision* and *Recall at Top K* are computed by:

$$Prec@K = \frac{\# \text{ correct predictions among top K ranked instances}}{K}$$

$$Rec@K = \frac{\# \text{ correct predictions among top K ranked instances}}{1000}$$

$$F1@K = \frac{2 \cdot Prec@K \cdot Rec@K}{Prec@K + Rec@K}$$

Experiment Results. Figure 8 shows F1@K of unsupervised link prediction methods in TWLP and INLP tasks. We introduce a baseline method which returns randomly selected K instances as predicted links. We vary K from 1000 to 10,0000 to examine the performance of each method.

Unsupervised TWLP

Unsupervised INLP

Legend:
- Common Neighbor (Twitter)
- Jaccard Coefficient (Twitter)
- Adamic Adar (Twitter)
- Common Neighbor (Instagram)
- Jaccard Coefficient (Instagram)
- Adamic Adar (Instagram)
- Baseline

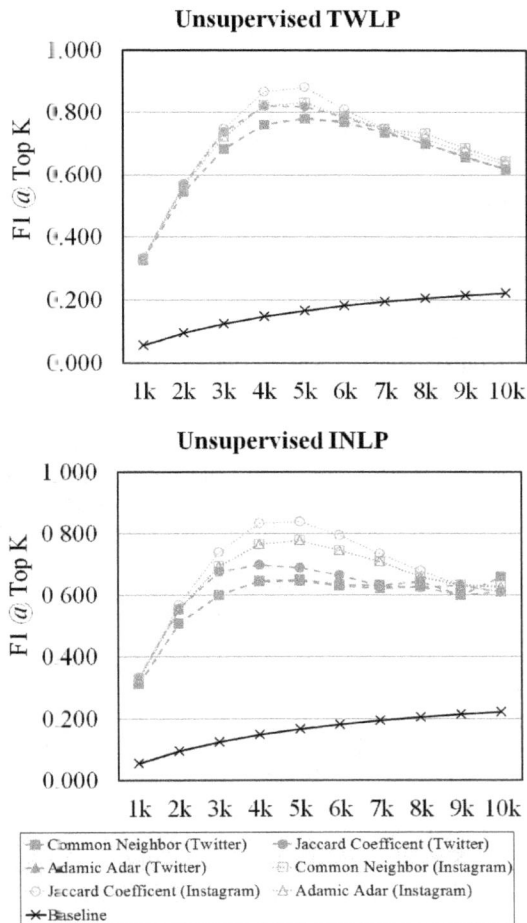

Figure 8: F1 scores @ Top K for TWLP and INLP

Table 2: Link Prediction Features

Feature	Description
Neighborhood features	
$\mathbf{CN}_T$	$|FR(u,T) \cap FR(v,T)|$
$\mathbf{JC}_T$	$\frac{|FR(u,T) \cap FR(v,T)|}{|FR(u,T) \cup FR(v,T)|}$
$\mathbf{AA}_T$	$\sum_{z \in FR(u,T) \cap FR(v,T)} \frac{1}{\log |FR(z,T)|}$
$\mathbf{CN}_I$	$|FR(u,T) \cap FR(v,I)|$
$\mathbf{JC}_I$	$\frac{|FR(u,I) \cap FR(v,I)|}{|FR(u,I) \cup FR(v,I)|}$
$\mathbf{AA}_I$	$\sum_{z \in FR(u,I) \cap FR(v,I)} \frac{1}{\log |FR(z,I)|}$
Common Neighbor Friendship Maintenance features	
$\mathbf{HFHS}_T$	$\frac{|\{z \in FR(u,T) \cap FR(v,T) | F_{sim}(z) \text{ is high}, F_{even}(z) \text{ is high}\}|}{|FR(u,T) \cup FR(v,T)|}$
$\mathbf{HELS}_T$	$\frac{|\{z \in FR(u,T) \cap FR(v,T) | F_{sim}(z) \text{ is low}, F_{even}(z) \text{ is high}\}|}{|FR(u,T) \cup FR(v,T)|}$
$\mathbf{LEHS}_T$	$\frac{|\{z \in FR(u,T) \cap FR(v,T) | F_{sim}(z) \text{ is low}, F_{even}(z) \text{ is low}\}|}{|FR(u,T) \cup FR(v,T)|}$
$\mathbf{LELS}_T$	$\frac{|\{z \in FR(u,T) \cap FR(v,T) | F_{sim}(z) \text{ is high}, F_{even}(z) \text{ is low}\}|}{|FR(u,T) \cup FR(v,T)|}$
$\mathbf{HEHS}_I$	$\frac{|\{z \in FR(u,I) \cap FR(v,I) | F_{sim}(z) \text{ is high}, F_{even}(z) \text{ is high}\}|}{|FR(u,I) \cup FR(v,I)|}$
$\mathbf{HELS}_I$	$\frac{|\{z \in FR(u,I) \cap FR(v,I) | F_{sim}(z) \text{ is low}, F_{even}(z) \text{ is high}\}|}{|FR(u,I) \cup FR(v,I)|}$
$\mathbf{LEHS}_I$	$\frac{|\{z \in FR(u,I) \cap FR(v,I) | F_{sim}(z) \text{ is high}, F_{even}(z) \text{ is low}\}|}{|FR(u,I) \cup FR(v,I)|}$
$\mathbf{LELS}_I$	$\frac{|\{z \in FR(u,I) \cap FR(v,I) | F_{sim}(z) \text{ is high}, F_{even}(z) \text{ is low}\}|}{|FR(u,I) \cup FR(v,I)|}$
Cross Network features	
CL	$\begin{cases} 1 & \text{if } (u,v) \text{ exists in another network} \\ 0 & \text{otherwise} \end{cases}$

As shown in the figure, all the unsupervised methods perform significantly (3 to 4 folds) better than the random baseline in both TWLP and INLP tasks. While the baseline method increases gradually with larger K values due to increasing recall, most of the other methods improve their F1@K only up K=4000 or K=5,000. Beyond which, their F1@K drops. This is because these methods are able to rank positive instances more highly than negative instances.

Interestingly, the figure also shows that the prediction methods using Instagram links outperform those using Twitter links even when the prediction task involves Twitter link prediction i.e., TWLP. In particular, the method using Jaccard Coefficient on Instagram links (i.e., $\mathbf{JC}_I$) outperforms the rest for almost all K values, achieving the highest F1 scores of 0.882 and 0.838 for TWLP and INLP tasks respectively for top 5,000 ranked results. A possible explanation of the above findings could be that the users have higher friendship degrees in Instagram than Twitter. Two users who are friends in Twitter are likely to have common friends in Instagram. Even though the Twitter neighborhood measures performed worse than Instagram neighborhood measures, they still yield good results (up to 0.689 for F1@5K) in predicting links between users in Instagram. This suggests that predicting links in one OSN using the neighborhood information of another OSN can yield very respectable accuracy.

Supervised Link Prediction Methods

For supervised link prediction, we use Support Vector Machine (SVM) with linear kernel as the binary classifier trained with each instance represented as a feature vector. SVM is chosen because of its relatively good results in other link prediction tasks. We also consider three types of features as shown in Table 2. The **neighborhood features** are the scores from different measures used in unsupervised link prediction methods. By including the neighborhood features, the supervised methods can hopefully achieve at least the good accuracy of the unsupervised methods.

We introduce a binary **cross network feature CL** which returns 1 if the users of the instance are friends in another network, and 0 otherwise. For example, in the case of TWLP task, a (u, v) instance is assigned a CL feature value of 1 if and only if u and v are friends in Instagram. This feature is included because having a friendship in another OSN should increase the odd of the users having friendship in the target OSN.

Finally, we also include a group of features known as **common neighbor friendship maintenance features**. While the neighborhood features in one OSN yield reasonable or even good results in unsupervised link prediction in another OSN, the features may not work very well when the common neighbors demonstrate friendship maintenance behavior that prevent friendship inference across OSNs. For example, a common neighbor between users u and v in Instagram who maintain separate friends in Twitter and Instagram does not increase the likelihood of friendship between u and v in Twitter. The common neighbor friendship maintenance features are obtained by dividing all common neighbors who are present in both Twitter and Instagram into four different categories: namely: (a) high friendship evenness and high friendship similarity; (b) low friendship evenness and high friendship similarity; (c) high friendship evenness and low friendship similarity; and (d) low friendship evenness and low friendship similarity. We say that a user has high (or low) friendship evenness if her friendship evenness is greater than (or not greater than) the average friendship evenness value. We define the user with high or low friendship similarity in the same way. These common neighbor friendship maintenance features are shown in Table 2.

We use six different feature configurations in our supervised link prediction methods as follows:

- **NBO**: Neighborhood features only

- **NFM**: Common Neighbor Friendship Maintenance features only

- **NBOFM**: Neighborhood and Common Neighbor Friendship Maintenance features

- **NBCL**: Neighborhood and Cross Network features

- **NFMCL**: Common Neighbor Friendship Maintenance and Cross Network features

- **ALL**: All features

Performance Evaluation. We conduct three runs of TWLP and INLP experiments and report the average precision, recall and F1 score of each method. For each run, we use a sample of 5,000 user pairs with friendship and 25,000 user pairs without friendship as the positive and negative instances respectively for training a SVM classifier, and another sample of 5,000 user pairs with friendship and 25,000 user pairs without friendships for testing. We conducted altogether three runs of training and test evaluation.

Table 3: Link Prediction Results by Supervised Methods

Tasks	Methods	Avg Prec.	Avg Recall	Avg F1
TWLP	**NBO**	0.954	0.873	0.911
	NFM	0.955	0.830	0.888
	NBOFM	0.953	0.875	0.912
	NBCL	0.976	0.887	0.929
	NFMCL	**0.979**	0.861	0.916
	ALL	0.973	**0.891**	**0.930**
	JC$_I$	0.882	0.882	0.882
INLP	**NBO**	0.942	0.832	0.883
	NFM	0.959	0.721	0.823
	NBOFM	0.942	0.833	0.884
	NBCL	0.958	0.838	0.894
	NFMCL	**0.971**	0.74	0.84
	ALL	0.956	**0.841**	**0.895**
	JC$_I$	0.838	0.838	0.838

Experiment Result. Table 3 shows the results of supervised link prediction for TWLP and INLP tasks. In these experiments, all the feature configurations yield better precision than recall. Most of them have F1 higher than the best F1 scores of the unsupervised methods (i.e., **JC**$_I$). Generally, according to F1, the configuration using all features outperforms other methods. Although the Common Neighbor

Friendship Maintenance (**NFM**) features performed slightly worse than the Neighborhood (**NBO**) features, the **NFM** features still managed to achieve a reasonably good F1 score of 0.888 and 0.823 for TWLP and INLP tasks respectively. This suggests that we are able to predict, with reasonable accuracy, the friendship between users using the common neighbor's friendship maintenance behavior as features. The addition of Cross Network (**CL**) feature also improves the results of **NFM** and **NBO** features. Interestingly, the configuration with Common Neighbor Friendship Maintenance and Cross Network features (i.e., **NFMCL**) yield the best precision result in both TWLP and INLP task. This suggests that the existence of a link between the two users in one OSN increases the likelihood of a link between the users in another OSN.

A possible reason for Common Neighbor Friendship Maintenance (**NFM**) features performing slightly worse than the Neighborhood (**NBO**) features could be due to the lack of common neighbors with friendship maintenance measures who are also base users. Thus we re-examined the supervised link prediction results and determined the accuracy of link prediction for test instances that have at least one common neighbor who is also a base user.

Table 4: Link Prediction Results of Test Instances with at Least 1 Base User Common neighbor

Task	Methods	Avg Prec.	Avg Recall	Avg F1
TWLP	**NBO**	0.948	0.970	0.959
	NFM	**0.971**	**0.994**	**0.982**
INLP	**NBO**	0.938	0.959	0.949
	NFM	**0.976**	**0.999**	**0.987**

As shown in Table 4, our **NFM** features only method outperformed the method using **NBO** features by precision, recall and F1 score in both TWLP and INLP tasks. This suggests that there were several occasions where the **NBO** features only method wrongly labeled a positive instance as negative but these instances are correctly labeled by **NFM** features.

Upon further examination of these test instances, we found that although each user pair have very few common neighbors, the common neighbors actually falls in the *low friendship evenness and high friendship similarity* friendship maintenance category (i.e., LEHS). The users in LEHS connect to more friends in either Twitter or Instagram, while keeping a smaller and potentially closer clique of common friends across the two OSNs. Thus, a pair of users with a LEHS common neighbor are more likely to be friends especially when they belong to the smaller clique of friends in one of the OSNs.

RELATED WORKS

In this section, we review thee groups of existing research works related to our research. The first group is the research studies on structural properties and user behaviors in multiple OSNs. The second group discusses link prediction conducted in multidimensional networks. Finally, the last group focuses on triadic closure property in OSNs, which is often used in link prediction.

The study on structural properties and user behaviors in multiple OSNs is an emerging topic and the research subject has been gaining attractions in recent years. Magnani and Rossi [11] did a study on the structural properties in multiple OSNs and proposed to represent multiple OSNs as a *multi-layer network*. They had also extended the degree and closeness centrality measures to multi-layer network. Their work however did not consider other network structural properties or behaviors such as the friendship similarity and evenness across networks. The linkage of user accounts across multiple OSNs belong to the same person is also a widely studied topic [21, 23]. With wider adoption of the new user linkage methods by proposed by previous research works, researchers also studied user behaviors across multiple OSNs. Benevenuto, et. al, performed a macro-level analysis of user behaviors such as browsing and content posting at different OSNs [2]. Zafarani and Liu conducted an empirical study on users in 20 social media sites and showed that the most users join and stay active in less than 3 social media sites [22]. Kumar et al. analyzed the user migration patterns across seven OSNs [7].

Unlike the existing works on user behaviors across multiple OSNs, our study focuses on the friendship maintenance behavior of users when they join multiple OSNs. Our study analyzes if a user would prefer to add a friend in multiple OSNs or simply maintain and restrict the friend to a particular OSN only. The findings of our work provide new perspectives to the existing studies on user behaviors in multiple OSNs. For instance, Ottoni et al. studied the users' activities across Twitter and Pinterest and found that the user usage patterns across the two OSNs differ significantly [13]. They found that users tend to post items to Pinterest before posting them on Twitter. Using the insights from our studies, a possible explanation for the observed user behaviors in Ottoni et al's study could be due to the low user friendship similarity across the multiple OSNs and the users were maintaining different groups of friends in different OSNs, thus there was a need for users to re-post the content on multiple OSNs so as to disseminate the information to all friends in different OSNs. Similar explanation could also be made for the study conducted by Lim et al. where they found that users exhibited varied information sharing behaviors on different OSNs [9]; the users, who may maintained low friendship similarity, were catering for the different group of "audience" (i.e. friends) in different OSNs. Future works could be done to investigate the impact of friendship maintenance on other user behaviors such as information adoption and diffusion.

There were few link prediction studies done on multidimensional networks. Rossetti et. al performed supervised and unsupervised multidimensional link predictions on the DBLP and IMDb networks [15]. In that study, the researchers used neighborhood features such as Common Neighbors and Adamic-Adar to predict user collaboration in the different dimensions of a network. For example, they predicted the collaboration of authors in DBLP with the publishing venues defined as the dimensions. Our link prediction experiment differs from the previous study as we predict friendship of users in different OSNs instead of different dimensions of the same network. Multiple OSNs is quite different from multidimensional networks as there are unmatched user accounts across multiple OSNs while user accounts matching is not required in multidimensional OSN. Furthermore, our friendship link prediction methods not only consider friendship neighborhood features but also friendship maintenance features.

Another related field of work is the study on triadic closure property in social networks. The triadic closure property been widely studied for many years even before the rise of OSNs [16, 19]. In recent years, researchers modeled and studied the process of triadic closure in OSNs. For example, Romero and Kleinberg had empirically investigated the triadic closure process in Twitter network [14]. Lou, et. al, performed prediction of reciprocal relationships and triadic closure process in Twitter. They also developed a model to accurately predict 90% of the reciprocal relationships in Twitter and to predict the triadic closure process among users [10]. Our study builds on the existing works and focus on how similarity and evenness of friendship across OSNs affect the likelihood of the triadic closure.

CONCLUSION AND FUTURE WORKS

In this paper, we studied how users manage and maintain friendships across multiple social networks. We constructed a base set of about 100,000 users with Twitter and Instagram accounts and studied the friendship of these users in the two OSNs. We introduced friendship similarity to measure the similarity of friendships between two OSNs. A friendship evenness measure was also defined to quantify the degree of balance a user maintains for the number of friendships in different OSNs. We shown that most users prefer to maintain different friendships in different OSNs, while keeping only a small clique of common friends across OSNs.

We also investigated link prediction in multiple OSNs using unsupervised and supervised methods. We shown that the conventional unsupervised methods using neighborhood features perform well even when we predicted links in one OSN using only the network structural properties from another OSN. We also proposed a set of network features and applied them to supervised link prediction method. The experiments shown that the supervised methods with suitable feature sets improved the accuracy over that of unsupervised methods.

To conclude, we note that this research is among the very few conducted on multiple social networks. While we have shown that the concepts of friendship similarity and evenness are important, they need to be generalized beyond just two OSNs. As part of the future work, we plan to expand the study to include larger and more diverse OSNs with overlapping user communities. The content generated by users can be further studied so as to provide more insights about the way users manage the different OSNs.

ACKNOWLEDGEMENTS

This work is supported by the National Research Foundation under its International Research Centre@Singapore Funding Initiative and administered by the IDM Programme Office, and National Research Foundation (NRF).

REFERENCES

[1] Lada A. Adamic and Eytan Adar. Friends and neighbors on the web. *Social Networks*, 2001.

[2] Fabrício Benevenuto, Tiago Rodrigues, Meeyoung Cha, and Virgílio Almeida. Characterizing user behavior in online social networks. In *ACM IMC*, 2009.

[3] Michele Berlingerio, Michele Coscia, Fosca Giannotti, Anna Monreale, and Dino Pedreschi. Foundations of multidimensional network analysis. In *ASONAM*, 2011.

[4] Pew Research Center. Social media site usage 2014. Technical report, Jan 2015.

[5] Debra S. Goldberg and Frederick P. Roth. Assessing experimentally derived interactions in a small world. 100(8), 2003.

[6] Akshay Java, Xiaodan Song, Tim Finin, and Belle Tseng. Why we twitter: Understanding microblogging usage and communities. In *SNA-KDD*, 2007.

[7] Shamanth Kumar, Reza Zafarani, and Huan Liu. Understanding user migration patterns in social media. In *AAAI*, 2011.

[8] David Liben-Nowell and Jon Kleinberg. The link prediction problem for social networks. *JASIST*, 58(7), 2007.

[9] Bang Hui Lim, Dongyuan Lu, Tao Chen, and Min-Yen Kan. # mytweet via instagram: Exploring user behaviour across multiple social networks. In *Proceedings of the 2015 IEEE/ACM International Conference on Advances in Social Networks Analysis and Mining 2015*. ACM, 2015.

[10] Tiancheng Lou, Jie Tang, John Hopcroft, Zhanpeng Fang, and Xiaowen Ding. Learning to predict reciprocity and triadic closure in social networks. *TKDD*, 7(2), 2013.

[11] M Magnani and L Rossi. The ml-model for multi-layer social networks. In *ASONAM*, 2011.

[12] M.E.J. Newman. Clustering and preferential attachment in growing networks. *Physical Review E*, 64(2), 2001.

[13] Raphael Ottoni, Diego B Las Casas, Joao Paulo Pesce, Wagner Meira Jr, Christo Wilson, Alan Mislove, and Virgilio Almeida. Of pins and tweets: Investigating how users behave across image-and text-based social networks. In *ICWSM*, 2014.

[14] Daniel Mauricio Romero and Jon Kleinberg. The directed closure process in hybrid social-information networks, with an analysis of link formation on twitter. In *ICWSM*, 2010.

[15] Giulio Rossetti, Michele Berlingerio, and Fosca Giannotti. Scalable link prediction on multidimensional networks. In *Data Mining Workshops (ICDMW), 2011 IEEE 11th International Conference on*, 2011.

[16] Georg Simmel. *The Sociology of Georg Simmel*. Simon and Schuster, 1950.

[17] Ben Taskar, Ming-Fai Wong, Pieter Abbeel, and Daphne Koller. Link prediction in relational data. In *NIPS*, 2003.

[18] Jan Vosecky, Dan Hong, and Vincent Y Shen. User identification across multiple social networks. In *ICNDT*, 2009.

[19] Stanley Wasserman. *Social Network Analysis: Methods and Applications*, volume 8. Cambridge University Press, 1994.

[20] Wei Xie, Cheng Li, Feida Zhu, Ee-Peng Lim, and Xueqing Gong. When a friend in twitter is a friend in life. In *ACM WebSci*, 2012.

[21] Reza Zafarani and Huan Liu. Connecting users across social media sites: A behavioral-modeling approach. In *KDD*, 2013.

[22] Reza Zafarani and Huan Liu. Users joining multiple sites: Distributions and patterns. In *ICWSM*, 2014.

[23] Haochen Zhang, Min-Yen Kan, Yiqun Liu, and Shaoping Ma. Online social network profile linkage. In *Information Retrieval Technology*. Springer, 2014.

Where is the Goldmine? Finding Promising Business Locations through Facebook Data Analytics

Jovian Lin, Richard Oentaryo, Ee-Peng Lim, Casey Vu, Adrian Vu, Agus Kwee
Living Analytics Research Centre, Singapore Management University, 80 Stamford Road, Singapore
jovian.lin@gmail.com, {roentaryo, eplim, caseyanhthu, adrianvu, aguskwee}@@smu.edu.sg

ABSTRACT

If you were to open your own cafe, would you not want to effortlessly identify the most suitable location to set up your shop? Choosing an optimal physical location is a critical decision for numerous businesses, as many factors contribute to the final choice of the location. In this paper, we seek to address the issue by investigating the use of publicly available Facebook Pages data—which include user "check-ins", types of business, and business locations—to evaluate a user-selected physical location with respect to a type of business. Using a dataset of 20,877 food businesses in Singapore, we conduct analysis of several key factors including business categories, locations, and neighboring businesses. From these factors, we extract a set of relevant features and develop a robust predictive model to estimate the popularity of a business location. Our experiments have shown that the popularity of neighboring business contributes the key features to perform accurate prediction. We finally illustrate the practical usage of our proposed approach via an interactive web application system.

Keywords

Location analytics, Facebook, feature extraction, machine learning

1. INTRODUCTION

Motivation. Location is a crucial factor of retail success, as 94% of retail sales are still transacted in physical stores [24]. To increase the chance of success for their stores, business owners require not only the knowledge of *where* their potential customers are, but also their surrounding competitors and complementary businesses. From the property owners' standpoint, it is also important to assess the potential success values of their property locations so as to determine the appropriate businesses to lease the locations to and for the right amounts. However, assessing and picking a store location is a cumbersome task for both business and property owners.

To carry out the above tasks well, many factors need to be taken into account, each of which requires gathering and analyzing the relevant data. Traditionally, business and property owners conduct surveys to assess the value of store locations [3]. Such surveys,

however, are costly and do not scale up well. With fast changing environments (*e.g.*, neighborhood rental, local population size, composition, etc.) and emergence of new business locations, one also needs to continuously reevaluate the value of store locations.

Fortunately, in the era of social media and mobile apps, we have an abundance of online user-generated data, which capture both activities of users in social media as well as offline activities at physical locations. Facebook is one of the world's largest social media platforms, with more than 1 billion active users everyday [21]. From the business standpoint, the massive availability of user, location, and other behavioral data in Facebook is attractive, and has changed the way people do businesses. For instance, many small/medium business owners are now setting up Facebook Pages to: (i) allow customers to find their businesses on Facebook; (ii) connect with customers via "likes" and "check-ins"; (iii) reach out to more customers through advertising their business pages on Facebook; and (iv) conduct analytics of their pages to get a deeper understanding of their customers and marketing activities.

Consumers are also adapting both their online and offline behaviors to the introduction of Facebook Pages for businesses. Other than "liking" businesses on their Facebook Pages, they can do a "check-in" whenever they physically visit the respective business stores. Facebook Pages have turned many offline signals into online behavior that can be analyzed for business insights. In particular, features such as "likes" and "check-ins" can be used as indicators of popularity, and by extension, success. Similarly, Instagram, Twitter, and Foursquare also have variants of these quantitative signals that can be retrieved from their geotagged photos, tweets, and tips. These data allow us to study the dynamics of brick-and-mortar stores and discover meaningful patterns and insights that will help retail and property owners make better decisions.

Objective. In this work, we make use of data collected from Facebook Pages to answer important research questions such as: *"Where should an owner set up his physical retail store at, so as to optimize the store's popularity?"*, *"What are the important factors influencing a store's popularity?"*, and *"Is there a "local" effect, whereby businesses can benefit from the presence of more popular/established neighbors?"* To this end, we propose a new location analytics framework that operates on top of Facebook Pages data. The centerpiece of our current framework is the following prediction task: *Given a target location that a business/property owner wants to hypothetically set his/her store at, how can we extract the relevant data of businesses within the vicinity of the target location and use them to estimate the popularity of the target location?*

As an illustration, Figure 1 shows a visualization of our web application system that realizes our location analytics framework. For the system's input, a business/property owner first drops a blue pin on the map that indicates the hypothetical location of his/her new

HT '16, July 10-13, 2016, Halifax, NS, Canada
© 2016 ACM. ISBN 978-1-4503-4247-6/16/07. . . $15.00
DOI: http://dx.doi.org/10.1145/2914586.2914588

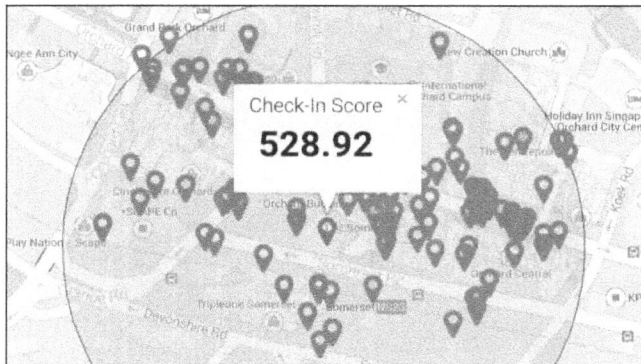

Figure 1: Prediction of "check-ins" based on the location indicated by the blue pin. The red pins represent nearby existing businesses.

store. Our system then retrieves the relevant information about the area nearby, which are also occupied by the existing businesses as indicated by the red pins. Based on these inputs, the system extracts a set of features and invokes a machine learning algorithm to predict the "check-in" score for the target location, which in turn serves as an indicator for the potential popularity of that location.

Contributions. In this paper, we show how publicly available Facebook Pages data can be analyzed and used to predict the potential popularity of a business location. To our best knowledge, this is the first work that demonstrates the feasibility of using Facebook data for business location analytics and, in particular, for aiding business and property owners to evaluate the value of a store location. It is also worth noting that our work presents a *fine-grained* approach that allows the business/property owners to estimate the popularity of *any* point on the city map. Our approach can be easily extended to predict multiple points simultaneously as well. We summarize our main contributions as follows:

- We present a new study on business location analytics using Facebook Pages data. Specifically, we conduct detailed analyses on 20,877 Facebook Pages of food-related businesses in Singapore, which constitute one of the largest business types in the city with generally healthy visitor traffic. Based on the analyses, we identify key features that can be used to extract insights, as well as suitable metric for business popularity.

- We develop a location analytics framework that includes a rich feature extraction module as well as a fast and accurate predictive model based on gradient boosting machine (GBM) [8]. Unlike the previous close work on optimal store placement [13] that outputs a ranked list of discretized areas (circles) with fixed radius, our approach is much more fine-grained. That is, our model can estimate on the fly the popularity of any arbitrary point on the map—which can be the location of an existing or a new/hypothetical business—without needing the locations to be discretized a priori.

- Based on our (trained) predictive model, we analyze the contribution of key features that are crucial in predicting the popularity of a retail business—at both *chunk* (*i.e.*, a group of features) and *individual* feature levels. In particular, we discover that distance-dependent features such as the total "check-ins" of businesses within certain radius are of utmost importance. We then provide an in-depth investigation on whether businesses, particularly smaller ones, benefit from the existence of other popular businesses within its vicinity.

- To concretely realize our idea, we have built an interactive web application that allows a business/property owner to drop a pin on the map and obtain a predicted "check-in" score for that location. The application is available at http://research.larc.smu.edu.sg/bizanalytics/.

Paper outline. Section 2 first provides an overview of related works. In Section 3, we describe the Singapore Facebook Pages data we use in our experiments. We subsequently elaborate our proposed location analytics approach in Section 4. Section 5 presents our experimental setup, followed by the results and analyses in Section 6. We present our web application prototype in Section 7, and finally conclude the paper in Section 8.

2. RELATED WORK

Our work can be viewed as a new type of *location analytics* [11], which is an emerging area related to business intelligence (BI) [2]. In recent years, organizations have relied on BI tools to delve into their data and reveal key insights that can aid their decision-making processes. With these tools, businesses have been able to make informed decisions based on what happened and when — typically pertaining to sales figures and supplier transactions. Lately, there is an important trend for organizations to address the question of *where*. Conventional BI systems, however, lack location-related analytics capabilities, and thus do not consider geographic and demographic factors crucial for consumer analysis, *e.g.*, where to set up stores, warehouses, or marketing campaigns.

Previously, combining separate BI and location-based approaches such as geographic information systems (GIS), was privileged only to large enterprises such as oil/gas-exploration companies, transportation companies, or government agencies [2]. These technologies involve costly data acquisition processes and specialized labor skills. Moreover, their integration requires complex and time-consuming implementation. A recent survey by ESRI and IT Media firm TechTarget [4] discovered that many organizations now believe that it is important to look at business data in a geographical context. Today, location-based data are abundant, thanks to the large volumes of user traces available from social media (such as Foursquare and Facebook) as well as mobile devices. However, many organizations are still unaware of the value of location-based data and struggle to put them to effective use.

Using data from social media to understand the dynamics of a society has always been a popular research theme, particularly, in recommending a new location to a user. For example, Facebook researchers Chang and Sun [1] analyzed Facebook users' "check-ins" data to develop models that predict where users will "check-in" next. They were able to predict user-to-user friendships (*i.e.*, friend recommendation) just by the "check-in" data alone. Gao *et al.* [9] explored the use of Foursquare "check-ins" and temporal effects for the task of location-recommendation; subsequently, the data were also used to predict a user's location [10].

Recent works on social media-based location analytics largely focus on detecting events and predicting user mobility patterns, although their use for BI applications are still limited so far. For instance, Li *et al.* [14] presented a machine learning method to discover and profile the user's location based on their following network and tweet contents. Noulas *et al.* [17] used Foursquare data to study the problem of predicting the next venue a mobile user will visit, by exploiting transitions between types of venues, mobility flows between venues, and spatio-temporal patterns of user "check-ins". Also based on Foursquare data, Karamshuk *et al.* [13] demonstrated the power of geographic (*e.g.*, types and density of nearby places) and user mobility (*e.g.*, transitions between venues or incoming flow of users) features in predicting the best placement of retail stores. In a similar vein, Georgiev *et al.* [12] conducted a study to predict the rise and decline of popularity of the local retail shops during the 2012 London Olympic Games. Most recently, Zhang *et al.* [25] extracted traffic and human mobility features from Manhattan restaurants data and studied how static and dynamic factors affect the economic outcome of local businesses in the city.

Our approach. Our work differs from all the above studies in several ways. Firstly, to our best knowledge, our work is the first to explore the use of Facebook data in business-location analytics. With 1.55 billion monthly active users and 50 million business pages [21], Facebook can provide a more comprehensieve database of crowdsourced locations than other platforms (by comparison, Foursquare only has 55 million monthly active users and 1.3 million business pages [22]). Secondly, instead of recommending places for users to establish retail stores or analyze on how unique events will affect businesses,we predict the popularity score of a user-selected venue, giving the user more freedom to choose *anywhere* he/she wants to set up his/her business. Thirdly, among all the works, Karamshuk *et al.*'s [13] is the closest to ours. But the key difference is that their work *discretized* the city into multiple circles with fixed radius and treated the issue as a "ranking problem", *i.e.*, producing a ranked list of discretized circles. In contrast, we view it as a "prediction problem" and provides a much more *fine-grained* approach of estimating the popularity of *any* point on the map. Our method also works robustly on a range of radius values, instead of relying on a single predefined radius as in [13].

3. FACEBOOK PAGES DATASET

In this section, we first provide an overview of the data that we collected from Facebook, and then describe the important attributes found in the data. We then conduct a simple analysis on the two popularity measures—"check-ins" and "likes"—to determine the better metric for quantifying the popularity of a business.

3.1 Data Harvesting

In this paper, we focus our studies on food-related businesses found in the Facebook of Singapore. We choose food because it constitutes one of the largest business types in Singapore with generally healthy visitor traffic ("check-ins" and "likes"). The food-related businesses were defined based on a manually-curated list that consists of 133 food-related categories of business, such as those containing the words "restaurant", "pub", "bar", etc. In particular, we consider food-related businesses in Singapore Facebook Pages that explicitly specify latitute-longitude coordinates, and these coordinates must be within the physical boundaries of Singapore. Using Facebook's Graph API [6], we obtained a total of 82,566 business profiles within Singapore boundaries, of which we categorically filtered 20,877 (25.2%) profiles that are food-related. All business data were analyzed in aggregate, and no personally-identifiable information was used.

Figure 2 shows an example of one such business profile, *Wimbly Lu Chocolates*, with important attributes (highlighted in bold) such as: (*i*) ID, (*ii*) category (*i.e.*, the primary-category), (*iii*) category list (*i.e.*, the sub-categories), (*iv*) "check-in" count, (*v*) "like" count, and (*vi*) location (including latitude and longitude). Figure 3 shows the corresponding Facebook Page of the business profile.

3.2 Categories Data

From the 20,877 food-related businesses, we retrieved a total of 357 unique categorical labels (as standardized by Facebook) from the attribute "category list", which represents the sub-categories of a business. These categories contain not only food-related labels


```
{
  "id": "200823339955298",
  "attire": "Casual",
  "can_post": false,
  "category": "Restaurant/cafe",
  "category_list": [
    {
      "id": "197871390225897",
      "name": "Cafe"
    }
  ],
  "checkins": 22811,
  "cover": {
    "cover_id": 465179196853043,
    "offset_x": 0,
    "offset_y": 24,
    "source": "https://fbcdn-sphotos-g-a.akamaihd.net/hphotos-ak-xaf1/t31.0-8/s720x720/471918_465179196853043_134634759_o.jpg",
    "id": "465179196853043"
  },
  "description": "Chocolate cafe.",
  "general_manager": "Rachel Foo",
  "has_added_app": false,
  "hours": {
    "tue_1_open": "12:30",
    "tue_1_close": "22:30",
    "wed_1_open": "12:30",
    "wed_1_close": "22:30",
    "thu_1_open": "12:30",
    "thu_1_close": "22:30",
    "fri_1_open": "12:30",
    "fri_1_close": "23:00",
    "sat_1_open": "09:00",
    "sat_1_close": "23:00",
    "sun_1_open": "09:00",
    "sun_1_close": "22:30"
  },
  "is_community_page": false,
  "is_published": true,
  "likes": 8134,
  "link": "https://www.facebook.com/WimblyLuChocolates",
  "location": {
    "city": "Singapore",
    "country": "Singapore",
    "latitude": 1.3474290978105,
    "longitude": 103.86750392653,
    "street": "15-2, Jalan Riang",
    "zip": "358987"
  },
  "name": "Wimbly Lu Chocolates",
  "parking": {
    "lot": 0,
    "street": 1,
    "valet": 0
  },
  "payment_options": {
    "amex": 0,
    "cash_only": 0,
    "discover": 0,
    "mastercard": 1,
    "visa": 1
  },
  "phone": "(65) 62891489",
  "price_range": "$ (0-10)",
  "public_transit": "Nearest MRT Serangoon: Take bus 105 from bus interchange or take bus 58 from the bus stop. Alight on the second stop and turn into Jalan Girang road. Take the first left and the second right.\nNearest MRT Lorong Chuan: Exit the MRT and walk towards NYJC and turn into Jalan Girang.\nSee you! :)",
  "restaurant_services": {
    "delivery": 0,
    "catering": 0,
    "groups": 0,
    "kids": 0,
    "outdoor": 0,
    "reserve": 0,
    "takeout": 1,
    "waiter": 1,
    "walkins": 1
  },
  "restaurant_specialties": {
    "breakfast": 0,
    "coffee": 1,
    "dinner": 0,
    "drinks": 1,
    "lunch": 0
  },
  "talking_about_count": 185,
  "username": "WimblyLuChocolates",
  "website": "www.wimblylu.com",
  "were_here_count": 22811
}
```


Figure 2: Facebook Graph API provides a JSON-formatted data of a business. Shown here is the Facebook Page of the *Wimbly Lu Chocolates* cafe in Singapore. Source: `https://graph.facebook.com/200823339955298/`

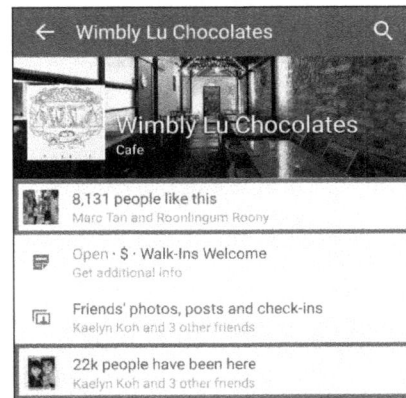

Figure 3: The Facebook page of *Wimbly Lu Chocolates* that shows key popularity metrics such as 8.131 "likes" and 22K "check-ins".

(*i.e.*, "bakery", "bar", "cafe", "coffee shop"), but also non-food labels such as "movie theatre", "shopping mall", and "train station." The existence of non-food related labels within food businesses is Facebook's way of allowing business owners to choose more than one categorical label for their business profile. For example, a Starbucks outlet located at a train station in an airport would likely have a mixture of food and non-food labels, such as "airport", "cafe", "coffee shop", and "train station." In addition, there is an intimate relationship between the categories of a target business and those of its neighbors. For instance, a family-run cafe will unlikely set itself next to an established coffee franchise like Starbucks, whereas a dessert shop may be located near complementary dining places.

Table 1 shows the top 25 categories of the food businesses in Singapore, their expected "check-ins", and the percentage of businesses that perform better than expectation. The proportion of businesses performing better than expectation ranges from 6 to 28%. The largest category is "food and restaurant", which is the most common category-type. From the low percentages of those that actually perform better than the expectation, we can tell that businesses obey a *long-tail* distribution, with the majority of businesses being unable to achieve the expected "check-ins" or more.

Table 1: Top 25 categories of food-businesses, their expected "check-ins", and those that perform better than the expectation.

Categories	Businesses count	Total "check-ins"	Expected "check-ins" per business	% of Businesses that have "check-ins" above the expected "check-ins"
Food & Restaurant	6,758	5,771,148	853.97	13.36%
Restaurant	5,233	8,195,356	1,566.09	16.09%
Cafe	3,126	3,799,849	1,215.56	19.10%
Shopping Mall	3,101	5,772,105	1,861.37	15.90%
Coffee Shop	2,959	2,395,000	809.40	13.99%
Fast Food Restaurant	2,840	3,447,999	1,214.08	19.12%
Food & Grocery	1,449	1,055,175	728.21	6.21%
Bakery	1,338	394,982	295.20	11.58%
Chinese Restaurant	1,157	2,376,432	2,053.96	23.16%
Food Stand	1,099	1,454,820	1,323.77	10.92%
Bar	956	3,234,860	3,383.74	20.08%
Japanese Restaurant	922	1,297,228	1,406.97	22.02%
Train Station	879	429,740	488.90	26.17%
Nightlife	744	866,619	1,164.81	10.62%
Movie Theater	717	1,015,632	1,416.50	9.09%
Cafeteria	661	421,774	638.08	11.20%
Seafood Restaurant	629	1,786,933	2,840.91	22.58%
Italian Restaurant	459	735,620	1,602.66	27.67%
Thai Restaurant	437	593,546	1,358.23	26.32%
Ice Cream Parlor	413	744,514	1,802.70	18.40%
Sushi Restaurant	380	741,305	1,950.80	26.58%
Pub	369	513,009	1,390.27	20.33%
Night Club	361	1,416,278	3,923.21	14.40%
Indian Restaurant	350	538,624	1,538.93	18.00%

3.3 Location Data

Each business profile has a *location* attribute that contains the physical address and latitude-longitude coordinates (hereafter known as "lat-long"). Knowing the location of every business allows us to calculate the neighborhood of a selected business through the spatial distribution of other businesses around the vicinity. Specifically, we consider the set $P_l = \{p | dist(p, l) \leq r\}$ of places p that lie in a radius r around a target location l. The term $dist(p, l)$ denotes the *Haversine distance* [20] between two locations p and l. We can then create a two-dimensional *distance matrix* containing the distance between every pair of business. For efficiency, we only consider a maximum radius of 1km (*i.e.*, $r \leq$ 1km). This allows us to quickly retrieve the k nearest neighbors of any location.

3.4 Visitor Data

Ideally, we would like to analyze customer information, such as *who* commented on or "liked" a business' Facebook post, and match/recommend some user profiles to some businesses. However, due to privacy concerns, Facebook does not allow us to identify *who* has checked-in or liked a particular business. Although one can still crawl the posts on a business' wall, as of Facebook's Graph API v2.0 [5] (released in 2014), Facebook no longer supplies a user's actual ID. Instead, Facebook uses the concept of "app-scoped user IDs", whereby a user's ID is unique to each app and cannot be used across different apps. As our crawler is considered an app, and Facebook limits the number of user posts that an app can query in a day, we are unable to gather enough posts—and by extension user IDs—to cover all (food-related) businesses in Singapore. Having multiple crawlers will not work either, as the same user ID will be different for any two crawlers.

3.5 Popularity Indicator: "Check-in" vs "Like"

Facebook provides two possible indicators for a business page's popularity: "check-in" and "like". The "check-in" metric is common in location-based social media like Facebook and Foursquare. Meanwhile, the "like" metric (shown as a "thumbs up" button) is

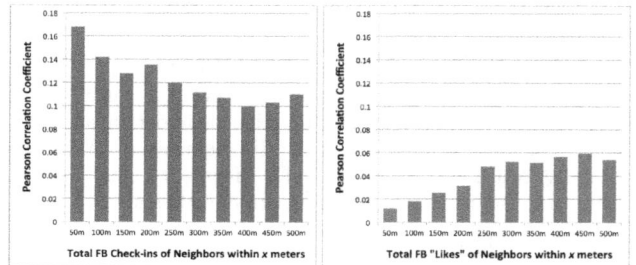

(a) Target business' total "check-ins" vs. neighbors' total checkins

(b) Target business' total "check-ins" vs. neighbors' total likes

Figure 4: Pearson correlation coefficient (PCC) of neighboring total "check-ins" (in red) and neighboring total "likes" (in blue).

more unique to Facebook, allowing users to express their recommendation/support for an entity. A "check-in" is the action of registering one's physical presence, and the total number of "check-ins" received by a business gives us a rough estimate of how popular and well-received it is. In contrast, the number of "likes" literally reflects an online vote for the business. Intuitively, therefore, a "check-in" should be a more suitable measure of a physical store's popularity, as it indicates a physical presence. Furthermore, "check-in" can be repeated, *i.e.*, a user could "check-in" to a place on Monday and do so again on Tuesday. By contrast, "likes" cannot be done repeatedly—it is a one-time event.

To prove this point, we compute the Pearson correlation coefficient (PCC) on two pairs: (*i*) the target business' "check-ins" w.r.t. its neighbors' total "check-ins", and (*ii*) the target business' "check-ins" w.r.t. its neighbors' total "likes". We only use the number of "check-ins" for the target business because we are only interested in the physical presence of customers for the target business. But for the target business's neighbors, we use both "check-ins" and "likes", as they reflect the popularity—physical or metaphysical—

of the area in which the target business is located. For the neighbors' total "check-ins" and total "likes", we further partitioned them based on the relative distance from the target business. Specifically, for every target business, we calculate the PCC between its "check-ins" and the total "check-ins" or "likes" of its neighbors within radius r, where $r = \{50, 100, 150, 200, \ldots, 500\}$.

Figure 4 shows the PCC of the two popularity indicators, broken down by the relative distance. It is evident that, between the neighbors' "check-ins" and the neighbors' "likes", the "check-in" feature is the better indicator as it has a higher PCC score than "likes." Furthermore, nearer "check-ins" (*e.g.*, 50 meters) have better PCC than further "check-ins", which suggests that the nearer a target business is to a popular neighbor, the more "check-ins" it reaps. On the contrary, the PCC score for "likes" increases as the distance between a target business and its surrounding neighbors increases. This can be attributed to the nature of "likes", which reflects an online support for the business and is not limited to physical proximity, whereas "check-ins" represent the registration of a person's physical presence, which is determined by physical proximity.

4. PROPOSED FRAMEWORK

Our location analytics framework, as illustrated in Figure 5, consists of two phases: *training* and *prediction*. The training phase involves extracting a set of features from the existing business profiles and feeding them to a machine learning algorithm (*i.e.*, gradient boosting [8]; see Section 4.3) in order to a predictive model for the "check-in" count. In turn, the prediction phase involves extracting features from a target business profile and invoking the trained predictive model to generate a (predicted) "check-in" count for that profile. Note that the training phase is carried out *offline*, whereas the prediction phase is done *on the fly* for a (new) target profile.

The modules in our proposed framework consist of three main types: (*i*) *input profiles*, (*ii*) *feature extractor*, and (*iii*) *predictive model*. We shall describe each module type in turn.

4.1 Input Profile

The input profile represents a physical business, and is used in both *training* (Figure 5(a)) and *prediction* (Figure 5(b)) phases. An input profile contains several attributes of a business, namely:

- **The lat-long coordinate of the business**. This is used in both training and prediction phases. Note that, during training, we only use the lat-long of the existing business profiles, whereas during prediction the lat-long being queried can be at an arbitrary (new or existing) location.

- **The business categories**. Examples include "bar", "cafe", "dining", "train station", etc.. This information is also used in both training and prediction phases.

- **The "check-in" counts**. In the training phase, we feed the actual "check-in" counts of the existing businesses as the target variable of our algorithm. In the prediction phase, the "check-in" counts of the queried locations are assumed to be unknown and our algorithm is supposed to predict them, whether it is for an existing or a new location.

All input profiles of the existing businesses are stored in a database of place profiles (*cf.* Figure 5). Using this database, we can extract a set of features for a given business, which include features derived from its own (input) profile as well as features from its neighbors (computed based on a range of radius as described in Section 3.3). The next section describes our feature extraction procedure.

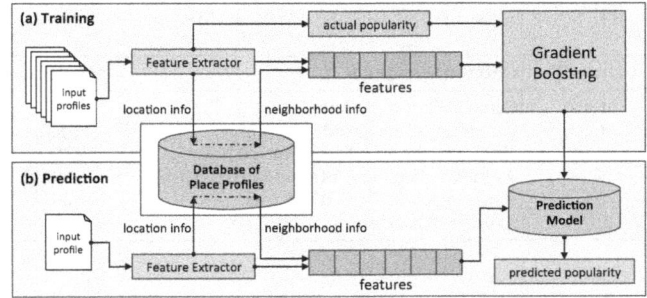

Figure 5: Our location analytics framework.

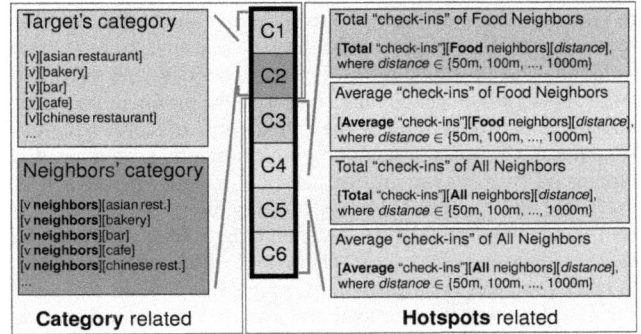

Figure 6: A break down of the feature vector into six chunks.

4.2 Feature Extraction

The feature extraction module serves to construct a feature vector representing a particular business. In this work, we divide our feature vector into six *chunks*, which represent different aspects of a target business. Figure 6 summarizes our feature chunks. The first two are associated with *categorical* data, while the remaining four are about *hotspots* (*i.e.*, location and "check-ins") data. Table 2 summarizes the unique identifier (ID), description, and the number of features of each chunk. We describe each chunk below.

Chunk C_1: The categories of the target business. This chunk is represented using a binary feature vector. For example, a categorical variable with four possible values: "A", "B", "C", and "D" is encoded using four binary features: $[1, 0, 0, 0]$, $[0, 1, 0, 0]$, $[0, 0, 1, 0]$, and $[0, 0, 0, 1]$, respectively. To represent multiple categories, we simply use "0" and "1" to indicate the absence and presence of each category label respectively. For example, we represent a profile with categories "A, C" and another with categories "A, B, C, D" as $[1, 0, 1, 0]$ and $[1, 1, 1, 1]$, respectively. In other words, we use a one-vs-all scheme where we convert multi-class labels to binary labels (*i.e.*, belong or does not belong to the class). As there are a total of 357 unique categories in the dataset of food venues, the binary feature vector will have 357 elements.

Chunk C_2: The categories of the target business' neighbors. We first select—from our database of place profiles—the neighboring food businesses within r meters from the target business, after which we extract and sum up the category feature vectors of the neighbors. To define category neighborhood, we use $r = 200$ meters, which we found to give optimal performance in our experiments. Similar to C_1, chunk C_2 is also a 357-long feature vector that corresponds to the same number of unique categories, except that each feature value is now an integer. Returning to our toy example of the four categories "A", "B", "C", and "D", if a profile

Table 2: Feature chunks used in our location analytics work.

Chunk ID	Chunk Description	#Features
C_1	Categories of the profile	357
C_2	Categories of the profile's neighbors	357
C_3	Total "check-ins" of food-related hotspots	20
C_4	Average "check-ins" of food-related hotspots	20
C_5	Total "check-ins" of all hotspots	20
C_6	Average "check-ins" of all hotspots	20

only has 5 neighbors of category "A" and 7 neighbors of category "B", its integer feature vector will be $[5, 7, 0, 0]$.

Chunks C_3 and C_4: Food-related hotspots. The two chunks are related in that both only use *food-related* neighbors. In other words, they exclude neighbors that have no relevance to food, such as clothing and electronic stores. For each chunk, we are interested in "hotspots", which are circular areas with the profile in the center and each area is quantified by the "popularity" of stores within it. We define 20 hotspots around the profile whereby each hotspot is demarcated by a maximum distance of r meters, of which $r \in \{50, 100, 150, \ldots, 1000\}$. Finally, the only difference between C_3 and C_4 is in how "popularity" is defined; the former computes the (natural) logarithm of the *total* "check-ins" within a hotspot, while the latter computes the logarithm of the *average* "check-ins".

It must be noted that the total and average "check-ins" include only the "check-in" counts of the neighbors and not the count of the target business itself (which is assumed to be unknown). Also, the purpose of applying logarithmic transformation to the "check-in" counts is to reduce the *skewness* in the counts distribution (*i.e.*, most businesses have small "check-ins" counts, but there is a handful number of businesses with unusually large "check-ins"). In other words, applying logarithm transformation would allow us to mitigate the impact of (unusually) high "check-ins" for popular businesses. Previously, we conducted an experiment that used the *raw* "check-ins" instead of the logarithmic values. Indeed, we observed that using the logarithm values yielded lower prediction errors than using the raw counts. As such, we shall focus on the results of the logarithm-scaled "check-ins" throughout the rest of this paper.

Chunks C_5 and C_6: All (food + non-food) hotspots. These chunks are similar to C_3 and C_4, respectively. The only difference is that, instead of solely using *food-related* neighbors, chunks C_5 and C_6 use food *and* non-food neighbors together. The non-food neighbors include bookshops, transportation facilities like bus and train stations, furniture stores, universities, etc. We include non-food hotspots so as to capture the *complementary* (non-food) businesses within the neighborhood of a target business.

4.3 Predictive Model

In order to learn the association between the extracted features and "check-in" scores of a given business. we train a supervised regression model called gradient boosting machine (GBM) [8]. GBM is a machine learning algorithm that iteratively constructs an ensemble of weak decision tree learners through *boosting* mechanism. Specifically, the boosting procedure consists of training weak learners and adding them into a final strong model in a forward stage-wise manner. By combining many weak learners that have high bias (*i.e.*, high prediction error), GBM yields an accurate and robust predictive model that has a lower bias than its constituent weak learners [16]. The GBM allows for the optimization of arbitrary differentiable loss functions for classification and/or regression task. For the purpose of "check-in" regression, however, we shall focus on the *least square* loss function [8] in this work.

Another major benefit of using GBM is that it can automatically derive the so-called *feature importance* metric [8, 16]. This provides an important mechanism to interpret the trained model and identify the key features that contribute substantially to the prediction of the target variable (*i.e.*, "check-in" score). In particular, each decision tree in the GBM intrinsically performs feature selection by choosing the appropriate split points. This information can then be used to measure the importance of each feature. That is, the more often a feature is used in the split points of a tree, the more important that feature is. This notion can be extended to the tree ensemble by averaging the feature importance of each tree. We further elaborate our feature importance analysis in Section 6.3.

5. EVALUATION PRELIMINARIES

We preface our evaluation proper by detailing the evaluation metrics and procedure, the baseline models against which we compare GBM, as well as the model variations we considered in our study.

5.1 Evaluation Metrics and Procedure

To measure how accurate our predicted "check-in" scores differ from the actual (observed) scores, we use two popular regression quality metrics: *mean-squared logarithmic error* (MSLE) and *mean absolute logarithmic error* (MALE). The MSLE and MALE metrics are respectively defined as:

$$MSLE = \frac{1}{n} \sum_{i=1}^{n} (\log(p_i + 1) - \log(a_i + 1))^2 \qquad (1)$$

$$MALE = \frac{1}{n} \sum_{i=1}^{n} |\log(p_i + 1) - \log(a_i + 1)| \qquad (2)$$

where n is the number of samples in the test set, p is the predicted "check-ins", and a is the actual "check-ins". The MSLE metric measures the averaged squared errors, which gives a higher penalty to large logarithmic differences $|\log(p_i + 1) - \log(a_i + 1)|$. On the other hand, the MALE metric measures the averaged absolute errors, whereby all the individual differences are weighted equally.

To assess the performance of our predictive model, we perform a 10-fold cross-validation procedure whereby the dataset is randomly partitioned into 10 equal sized subsamples. A single subsample is retained as the validation data for testing our models, while the remaining 9 subsamples are used as training data. The cross-validation process is then repeated 10 times, with each of the 10 subsamples used exactly once as the validation data. We then report the averaged performance.

Finally, to test for the statistical significance of our results, we utilize the *independent two-sample t-test* [19]. In particular, we look at the p-value of the t-test involving two performance vectors, at a significance level of 0.01. If the p-value is less than 0.01, we can conclude the performance difference is statistically significant.

5.2 Baselines

We compare GBM with several regression baseline algorithms. To foster reproducibility of this work, our implementations of all these algorithms (including GBM) are based on the *scikit-learn* library [18]. The following baselines are used in this work:

- **Distance-based nearest neighbors (DNN).** This is a simple baseline that takes the logarithm of the average "check-ins" of the neighbors that reside within some radius r of a target business location. DNN works based on a simple intuition: "*the more popular the neighborhood, the more popular the target location is going to be, all else being equal*". We test on $r \in \{50, 100, \ldots, 500\}$ and found that DNN with $r = 100$m brings about the best results.

- **Support vector regression with linear kernel (SVR-Linear)** [7]. This method produces a linear regression model that depends only on a subset of the training data, since the cost function for building the model ignores any data points close to the model prediction. For this method, we set the cost parameter to $C = 1$ and the epsilon parameter (for controlling epsilon-insensitive loss) to $\epsilon = 0.1$, which give the best performance in our experiments.

- **Support vector regression with radial basis function kernel (SVR-RBF)** [23]. This is the same as SVR-Linear, except that now it uses a radial basis function (Gaussian) kernel. As with SVR-Linear, we use $C = 1$ and $\epsilon = 0.1$, which again constitute the optimal configuration for SVR-RBF.

Last but not least, we configure our GBM algorithm using the "least squares" loss function, a learning rate of 0.1, a maximum tree depth of 10, and a maximum tree width of "sqrt" (*i.e.*, the square root of the total number of features). For the number of boosting iterations N, we perform an exhaustive *grid search* on $N \in \{100, 200, \ldots, 5000\}$ and found that $N = 1000$ produces the best results. Note that, in each boosting iteration, a new tree is created and added into the ensemble. As such, the number of boosting iterations N is equal to the number of trees constructed.

5.3 Model Variations

To evaluate the contributions of different feature chunks, we construct a variation of the predictive models by enumerating all possible combinations of the six chunks (see Section 4.2). That is, we construct all possible $2^6 - 1 = 63$ chunk combinations and build a predictive model for each combination. We represent a model variant using a binary array of length six, where chunk C_i maps to the ith element in the array. We use the notation "[model_name]$_{xxxxxx}$" to represent a particular model variant, where $x \in \{0, 1\}$. For example, a GBM model using C_1, C_2, and C_4 is denoted as GBM$_{110100}$. Note that DNN does not use this notation, since it works based on spatial distance only, instead of feature chunks. For SVR-Linear, SVR-RBF and GBM, we run experiments on all 63 variants and report the best results for each of the three methods.

6. RESULTS AND ANALYSIS

We now present our main experimental results. Our experiments seek to answer several key research questions (RQs):

RQ1: How well can our predictive model (GBM) estimate the popularity (*i.e.*, "check-in" scores) of business locations?

RQ2: What are the contributions of different feature chunks? How robust is our model against different feature combinations?

RQ3: Do the important features found by our model make sense? What can we learn/conclude from them?

6.1 Performance Assessment (RQ1)

Table 3 compares the cross-validation performances (*i.e.*, averaged MALE and MSLE) of different regression methods. For SVR-Linear and SVR-RBF, we show both the "full variant" (*i.e.*, SVR-Linear$_{111111}$ and SVR-RBF$_{111111}$) as well as the variants that give the best results for the same method (*i.e.*, SVR-Linear$_{111000}$ and SVR-RBF$_{100011}$). We observe that GBM consistently and significantly outperforms other models (at $p < 0.01$), particularly against SVR-RBF$_{100011}$, which is the best among all the baselines.

Table 3: Performance comparisons of different models.

Model	Feature Chunks	MALE	MSLE
DNN$_{r=100m}$	-	1.99305	7.27499
SVR-Linear$_{111000}$	$\{C_1, C_2\}$	1.59072	4.25301
SVR-Linear$_{111111}$	$\{C_1, C_2, C_3, C_4, C_5, C_6\}$	2.12345	7.35446
SVR-RBF$_{100011}$	$\{C_1, C_5, C_6\}$	1.47518	3.61863
SVR-RBF$_{111111}$	$\{C_1, C_2, C_3, C_4, C_5, C_6\}$	1.53067	3.92219
GBM$_{111111}$	$\{C_1, C_2, C_3, C_4, C_5, C_6\}$	**1.16362***	**2.56924***

*: significant at 0.01 with respect to SVR-RBF$_{100011}$

We can explain the results in terms of model complexity. For instance, we can expect the simplest nearest neighbor method (*i.e.*, DNN) to be beaten by other methods, as it only uses spatial distance. We can also anticipate that SVR-RBF would outperform SVR-Linear, as the RBF kernel maps the original features into a high-dimensional space. This expanded feature space provides SVR-RBF with a greater representation power to model a much more complex relationship than SVR-Linear. Finally, as GBM combines weak learners into a strong learner, the aggregate prediction of the ensemble is more accurate than the prediction of any of its constituent learners. This aggregation also provides GBM with more robustness to data overfitting, as compared to SVM-RBF.

Additionally, the results in Table 3 suggest that the two SVR methods are more sensitive to the variation of feature chunks, particularly to the presence of less relevant (or irrelevant) features. This can be attributed to the fact that each tree in GBM intrinsically performs feature selection, for which less important features are unlikely to be chosen and used in the ensemble. Indeed, we can see that SVR-Linear with all six chunks (*i.e.*, SVR-Linear$_{111111}$) is outperformed by the simpler SVR-Linear variant (*i.e.*, SVR-Linear$_{111000}$) that uses only three chunks. Surprisingly, the former is also outperformed by even the DNN method. The same conclusion can be made by comparing SVR-RBF$_{111111}$ and SVR-RBF$_{100011}$. On the contrary, GBM is more robust against inconsequential features. In fact, GBM generally improves its performance as we add more chunks, as we will see shortly in Section 6.2.

6.2 Contribution of Feature Chunks (RQ2)

The partitioning of the feature vectors into six chunks allows us to investigate the contribution of each feature group. Table 4(a) lists the top 10 GBM variants (out of 63 possible variants), sorted in an ascending order of their MALE scores. Similarly, Table 4(b) lists the top 10 GBM variants, sorted in ascending order of their MSLE scores. Note that the top 10 GBM variants happen to be the same for the two tables, except that they have slightly different ordering. From the results, it is evident that GBM$_{111111}$ does not significantly outperform the other nine variants (at a significance level of 0.01). This shows that GBM is robust against the variation of feature chunks. We can also see that the performance of the GBM improves as we add more feature chunks. Again, this can be attributed to the feature selection mechanism of each tree in the ensemble, which helps exclude irrelevant features.

Based on the binary representation of the six chunks, we can also calculate the relative significance of a chunk by counting the number of times in which it is present (*i.e.*, when the chunk is assigned the value of 1). The sum of each chunk's presence in the 10 GBM variants is shown at the last row of Tables 4(a) and 4(b), entitled "Count". We see that the categories of the target business (*i.e.*, chunk C_1) is present in all the top 10 GBM variants, indicating that it is an essential feature. This may seem to suggest that the nature

Table 4: Cross-validation results of the top 10 GBM variants.

(a) MALE results of the top 10 GBM variants.

Model	Feature Chunks						MALE
	C_1	C_2	C_3	C_4	C_5	C_6	
GBM_{111111}	Yes	Yes	Yes	Yes	Yes	Yes	**1.163618**
GBM_{111100}	Yes	Yes	Yes	–	–	–	1.172693
GBM_{111010}	Yes	Yes	Yes	–	Yes	–	1.173910
GBM_{110011}	Yes	Yes	–	–	Yes	Yes	1.175062
GBM_{101111}	Yes	–	Yes	Yes	Yes	Yes	1.177136
GBM_{101100}	Yes	–	Yes	Yes	–	–	1.182053
GBM_{100011}	Yes	–	–	–	Yes	Yes	1.184053
GBM_{111000}	Yes	Yes	Yes	–	–	–	1.184895
GBM_{110010}	Yes	Yes	–	–	Yes	–	1.189258
GBM_{101010}	Yes	–	Yes	–	Yes	–	1.191831
Count	10	6	7	4	7	4	

(b) MSLE results of the top 10 GBM variants.

Model	Feature Chunks						MSLE
	C_1	C_2	C_3	C_4	C_5	C_6	
GBM_{111111}	Yes	Yes	Yes	Yes	Yes	Yes	**2.569236**
GBM_{111010}	Yes	Yes	Yes	–	Yes	–	2.608927
GBM_{101111}	Yes	–	Yes	Yes	Yes	Yes	2.609254
GBM_{111100}	Yes	Yes	Yes	Yes	–	–	2.610255
GBM_{110011}	Yes	Yes	–	–	Yes	Yes	2.615818
GBM_{101100}	Yes	–	Yes	Yes	–	–	2.627101
GBM_{100011}	Yes	–	–	–	Yes	Yes	2.628505
GBM_{111000}	Yes	Yes	Yes	–	–	–	2.653032
GBM_{110010}	Yes	Yes	–	–	Yes	–	2.660369
GBM_{101010}	Yes	–	Yes	–	Yes	–	2.667292
Count	10	6	7	4	7	4	

of the business itself plays a pivotal role. However, as described in Section 3.2, food businesses on Facebook may contain non-food labels such as "airport" and "shopping mall" (*e.g.*, for a cafe located in the shopping mall of an airport). In turn, this suggests that the "environment" around a selected business is also a key factor. The method of chunk counting presented in this section is a coarse-grained analysis and is not sufficient to validate this conjecture. We will further analyze this in Section 6.3, where we employ a more fine-grained analysis of the individual feature's importance.

Moving on, we also notice that the total "check-ins" chunks (*i.e.*, chunks C_3 and C_5) are ranked higher than the average "check-ins" (*i.e.*, C_4 and C_6), *i.e.*, the counts are 7/10 vs. 4/10. This suggests that the total "check-ins" have more discriminatory power than the average "check-ins", which could be due to the averaging failing to account for the number of business nearby. On the other hand, total "check-ins" (of an area) gives a more accurate reflection of the *potential human traffic* that an area has. Finally, we see no substantial performance difference between *food-related* hotspots and *all* (*i.e.*, food + non-food) hotspots (both have a count sum of $7 + 4 = 11$). This implies that the presence of non-food-related categories does not contribute significantly to the prediction quality.

6.3 Analysis of Feature Importance (RQ3)

The analysis of the six *chunks* of the feature vectors in the previous section represents a coarse-grained analysis. To perform a more fine-grained analysis, we look into the full feature vector (with all six chunks included) in the GBM_{111111} model and try to compute the *relative importance* of each individual feature. GBM derives this automatically, by measuring how many times a feature is used in the split points of a tree [8] (see also Section 4.3).

Figure 7(a) shows the relative importance of the top 20 features in descending order of importance, while Figure 7(b) shows the relative importance of the 71st to the 90th features. (We do not include the results for the 21st to 70th features here, as the changes in the feature importance score are fairly smooth.) Accordingly, we can make the following observations:

- Chunks C_3 to C_6 (black bars in Figure 7) dominate the top 80 feature importance positions (not fully shown in Figure 7), and it is not until the 81st top feature that chunks C_1 and C_2 show up. This suggests that *hotspot* features play a very crucial role: the more "check-ins" a target business' neighbors have, the more popular the target business is likely to be.

- From Figure 7(a), 14 out of 20 hotspot features are below 500m, suggesting that nearer "check-ins" are used as a strong signal to make a split in the decision tree. This is not surprising, as it may be physically tiring for customers to travel farther than 500m, and most will settle all their outdoor needs in a specific area, such as a shopping mall.

- Comparing the *total* and *average* "check-ins" in Figure 7(a), 14 out of 20 features belong to the former. This indicates that *total* "check-ins" is a better input feature/signal for split points in the GBM's trees. This finding is generally in agreement with what we have found in Section 6.2.

- Figure 7(a) also shows that the *type* of neighbors (*i.e.*, "food-only" or "all") are equally matched with 10 counts each. Again, this finding conforms with the earlier finding in Section 6.2. Note that, despite the different approaches in Sections 6.2 and 6.3, both arrived at the similar conclusion with regard to the type of "check-in" and the type of neighbor.

- From the colored bars (*i.e.*, chunks C_1 and C_2) in Figure 7(b), we see that C_1 is dominated by the C_2. This suggests that categories of the neighboring businesses are more important than those of the target business (C_1). Together with the "hotspot" features in Chunks C_3 to C_6, this reinforces the idea of a "local effect" whereby business benefit by being close to more established neighbors.

- Finally, we notice a significant and faster drop in the *importance* scores from the 81st to 90th features (as compared from the 1st to 80th). In this case, places or franchises that typically attract general (and larger) crowd, such as "restaurant", "coffee", or "shopping mall"-related categories, take the first top spots among the neighbors' categories. This suggests that food-related categories (of the neighbors) are more important than the non-food categories.

7. WEB APPLICATION PROTOTYPE

We implement our location analytics framework as an interactive web application service, which can be accessed at: `https://research.larc.smu.edu.sg/bizanalytics/`.

Technologies. We employ the following technologies to build our web application: (*i*) Python (implementing the predictive model and feature extraction), (*ii*) RabbitMQ (a messaging passing system that allows querying the predictive model), (*iii*) Node.js (for processing users' queries and returning the prediction results to the front-end), (*iv*) ElasticSearch (a distributed search engine for querying the database of place profiles), and (*v*) Google Maps (for visualization at the front-end). This configuration provides an efficient and scalable way to process a user's location query (via Node.js and

Figure 7(a) feature labels (descending order of importance):

1. [FOOD-ONLY] [TOTAL CHECKINS] [250m]
2. [FOOD-ONLY] [TOTAL CHECKINS] [300m]
3. [FOOD-ONLY] [TOTAL CHECKINS] [200m]
4. [ALL] [TOTAL CHECKINS] [600m]
5. [FOOD-ONLY] [TOTAL CHECKINS] [550m]
6. [ALL] [TOTAL CHECKINS] [200m]
7. [ALL] [AVERAGE CHECKINS] [50m]
8. [FOOD-ONLY] [TOTAL CHECKINS] [750m]
9. [ALL] [TOTAL CHECKINS] [550m]
10. [ALL] [AVERAGE CHECKINS] [250m]
11. [ALL] [TOTAL CHECKINS] [350m]
12. [FOOD-ONLY] [AVERAGE CHECKINS] [50m]
13. [FOOD-ONLY] [TOTAL CHECKINS] [450m]
14. [FOOD-ONLY] [TOTAL CHECKINS] [150m]
15. [FOOD-ONLY] [TOTAL CHECKINS] [600m]
16. [ALL] [AVERAGE CHECKINS] [150m]
17. [ALL] [TOTAL CHECKINS] [100m]
18. [ALL] [AVERAGE CHECKINS] [550m]
19. [ALL] [AVERAGE CHECKINS] [350m]
20. [FOOD-ONLY] [TOTAL CHECKINS] [100m]

(x-axis: Feature Importance Score, 0 to 0.01)

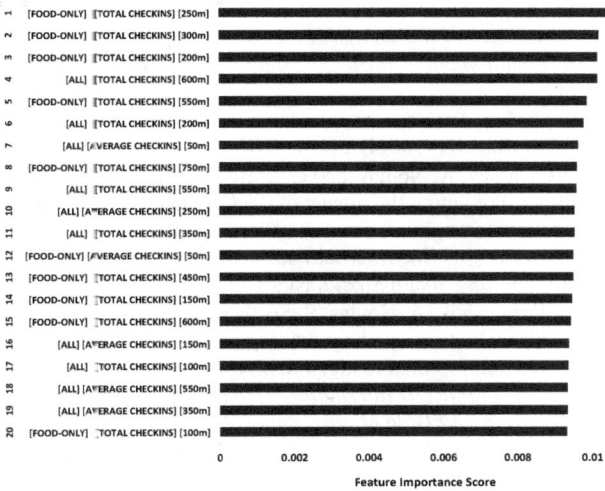

(a) Feature importance of the top 20 features descending order of importance. The top 20 happen to consists of Chunks C_3 to C_6.

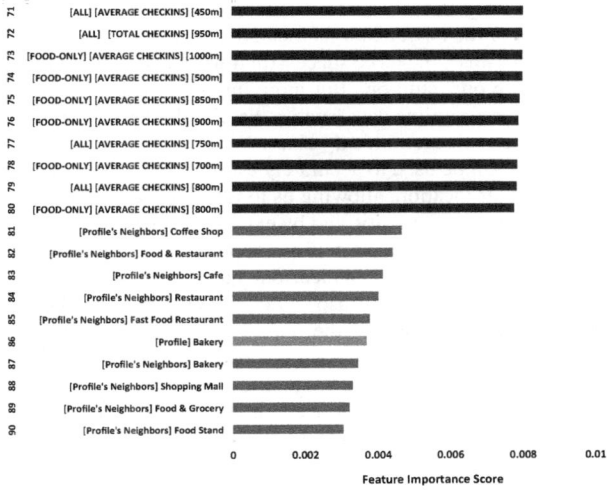

Figure 7(b) feature labels (71st to 90th):

71. [ALL] [AVERAGE CHECKINS] [450m]
72. [ALL] [TOTAL CHECKINS] [950m]
73. [FOOD-ONLY] [AVERAGE CHECKINS] [1000m]
74. [FOOD-ONLY] [AVERAGE CHECKINS] [500m]
75. [FOOD-ONLY] [AVERAGE CHECKINS] [850m]
76. [FOOD-ONLY] [AVERAGE CHECKINS] [900m]
77. [ALL] [AVERAGE CHECKINS] [750m]
78. [FOOD-ONLY] [AVERAGE CHECKINS] [700m]
79. [ALL] [AVERAGE CHECKINS] [800m]
80. [FOOD-ONLY] [AVERAGE CHECKINS] [800m]
81. [Profile's Neighbors] Coffee Shop
82. [Profile's Neighbors] Food & Restaurant
83. [Profile's Neighbors] Cafe
84. [Profile's Neighbors] Restaurant
85. [Profile's Neighbors] Fast Food Restaurant
86. [Profile] Bakery
87. [Profile's Neighbors] Bakery
88. [Profile's Neighbors] Shopping Mall
89. [Profile's Neighbors] Food & Grocery
90. [Profile's Neighbors] Food Stand

(x-axis: Feature Importance Score, 0 to 0.01)

(b) Feature importance of the top 71st to 90th features. Besides Chunks C_3 to C_6, it also contains Chunks C_1 and C_2, in red and blue, respectively.

Figure 7: Top features from the feature importance of the GBM_{111111} model.

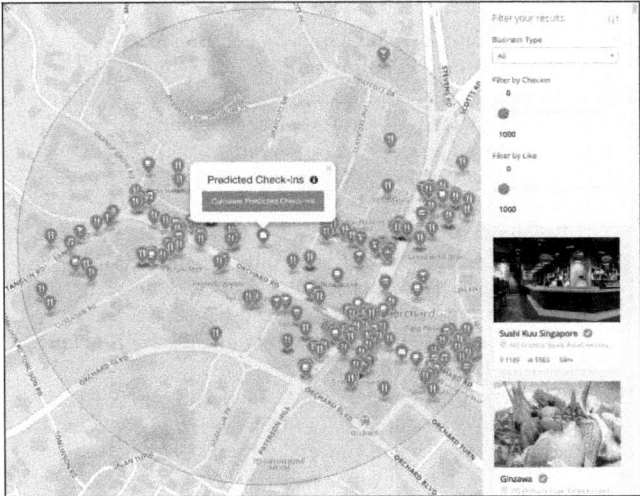

Figure 8: Our online interactive location analytics system.

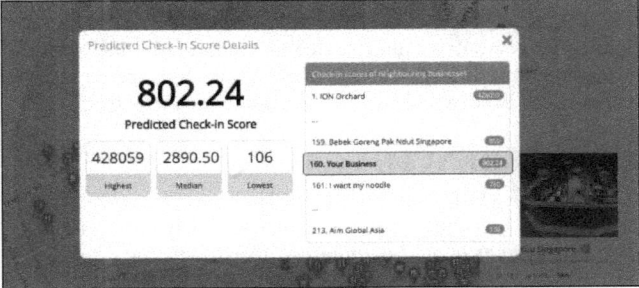

Figure 9: After computing the predicted "check-in" score, users can compare their target location with the surrounding businesses.

RabbitMQ), retrieve the relevant neighbors (via ElasticSearch), involve feature extraction and predictive models (in the Python component), and finally display the prediction results to the users (again via Node.js and RabbitMQ, along with Google Maps).

User interaction. Figure 8 shows an example of how our web application works. A user drops a pin (*i.e.*, the blue pin in the middle of the screen) to indicate where his (hypothetical) store location would be. Depending on the location, the interface also dynamically shows the neighboring businesses on the right panel and their respective information, such as (*i*) the distance from the drop-pin, and (*ii*) the number of physical "check-ins" and "likes". When the user is ready, he/she may click the "Calculate Predicted Check-ins" button, which will then calculate the predicted "check-in" score on the fly. After presenting the predicted "check-in" score, the user can also open a new panel, showing a ranked list of his/her target location relative to the nearby businesses (Figure 9). The rank-

ing allows users to understand how their target location would fare against the neighboring businesses. The panel also shows the highest, lowest, and the median scores of these neighbors.

Qualitative study. Figures 8 and 9 demonstrate the on-the-fly prediction of our web application, where it is able to predict the "check-in" score of a hypothetical, inexistent target business. For this example, the score of 802.24 in Figure 9 represents a fairly conservative prediction of the potential "check-ins" in the target location (*i.e.*, the blue pin) and the selected type of business. This hypothetical business is ranked 160th among 213 businesses, with the lowest "check-ins" being 106. This is a reasonable prediction. On the one hand, because the place is near places with consistent human traffic, such as the Hilton Hotel and several other shopping malls, it should garner a decent amount of check-ins. On the other hand, as there are many other businesses in the area (the area is a renowned shopping paradise in Singapore), it may be challenging for the hypothetical business to compete with these businesses.

8. DISCUSSION AND FUTURE WORK

In this work, we investigate whether businesses can benefit from other (popular) businesses within its vicinity. Our results show not only a positive correlation between the popularity of a target business and its neighbors, but also the critical importance of the "hotspot" features: the nearer a target location is to a popular place with larger "check-ins", the more successful it would be. This finding conforms with our intuition. But more importantly, it demonstrates that ubiquitous online data (such as Facebook Pages) can be used to gauge the socioeconomical values. We also show how our predictive model can be used to accurately estimate the "check-in" score of a particular location, allowing us to identify the best locations that would bring popularity, and by extension, success.

Despite the promising potentials of our approach, there remains room for improvement. For instance, our current work has not taken into account the temporal aspects of the business popularity, such as modeling the trend of the "check-in" scores over time. Further quantitative and qualitative studies may also be needed in the future to compare our work with other location-based services such as Foursquare. To facilitate more comprehensive location analytics, we can extend our approach by building a two-level location recommendation system, whereby we first (coarsely) recommend a city district [15] and then pinpoint (multiple) promising locations within that district. As we include more data, such as non-food categories and auxiliary data that reflect the human flow of different areas of an urban city, we will be able to further improve on our current model and findings. To address all these, we plan to develop a new *spatiotemporal* predictive model that integrates a richer set of residential, demographics, and other social media data.

Acknowledgements. This research is supported by the National Research Foundation, Prime Minister's Office, Singapore under its International Research Centres in Singapore Funding Initiative.

9. REFERENCES

[1] J. Chang and E. Sun. Location3: How users share and respond to location-based data on social networking sites. In *Proceedings of the International AAAI Conference on Weblogs and Social Media*, pages 74–80, 2011.

[2] H. Chen, R. H. L. Chiang, and V. C. Storey. Business intelligence and analytics: From big data to big impact. *MIS Quarterly*, 36(4):1165–1188, 2012.

[3] N. Cohen. Business location decision-making and the cities: Bringing companies back. Technical report, Brookings Institution Center on Urban and Metropolitan Policy, 2000.

[4] ESRI. Revealing the "where" of business intelligence using location analytics. http://www.esri.com/library/whitepapers/pdfs/business-intelligence-location-analytics.pdf, 2012.

[5] Facebook. Facebook platform upgrade guide. https://developers.facebook.com/docs/apps/upgrading, 2016.

[6] Facebook. Graph API reference. https://developers.facebook.com/docs/graph-api/reference/page, 2016.

[7] R.-E. Fan, K.-W. Chang, C.-J. Hsieh, X.-R. Wang, and C.-J. Lin. LIBLINEAR: A library for large linear classification. *Journal of Maching Learning Research*, 9:1871–1874, 2008.

[8] J. H. Friedman. Greedy Function Approximation: A Gradient Boosting Machine. *The Annals of Statistics*, 29:1189–1232, 2001.

[9] H. Gao, J. Tang, X. Hu, and H. Liu. Exploring temporal effects for location recommendation on location-based social networks. In *Proceedings of the ACM Conference on Recommender Systems*, pages 93–100, 2013.

[10] H. Gao, J. Tang, X. Hu, and H. Liu. Modeling temporal effects of human mobile behavior on location-based social networks. In *Proceedings of the ACM Conference on Information and Knowledge Management*, pages 1673–1678, 2013.

[11] L. Garber. Analytics goes on location with new approaches. *IEEE Computer*, 46(4):14–17, 2013.

[12] P. Georgiev, A. Noulas, and C. Mascolo. Where businesses thrive: Predicting the impact of the Olympic Games on local retailers through location-based services data. In *Proceedings of the International AAAI Conference on Weblogs and Social Media*, pages 151–160, 2014.

[13] D. Karamshuk, A. Noulas, S. Scellato, V. Nicosia, and C. Mascolo. Geo-spotting: Mining online location-based services for optimal retail store placement. In *Proceedings of the ACM SIGKDD International Conference on Knowledge Discovery and Data Mining*, pages 793–801, 2013.

[14] R. Li, S. Wang, and K. C.-C. Chang. Multiple location profiling for users and relationships from social network and content. *Proceedings of the International Conference on Very Large Data Bases*, 5(11):1603–1614, 2012.

[15] J. Lin, R. J. Oentaryo, E.-P. Lim, C. Vu, A. Vu, A. T. Kwee, and P. K. Prasetyo. A business zone recommender system based on Facebook and urban planning data. In *Proceedings of the European Conference on Information Retrieval*, pages 1–7, 2016.

[16] A. Natekin and A. Knoll. Gradient boosting machines: A tutorial. *Frontiers in Neurorobotics*, 7(21):1–21, 2013.

[17] A. Noulas, S. Scellato, N. Lathia, and C. Mascolo. Mining user mobility features for next place prediction in location-based services. In *Proceedings of the IEEE International Conference on Data Mining (ICDM)*, pages 1038–1043, 2012.

[18] F. Pedregosa, G. Varoquaux, A. Gramfort, V. Michel, B. Thirion, O. Grisel, M. Blondel, P. Prettenhofer, R. Weiss, V. Dubourg, J. Vanderplas, A. Passos, D. Cournapeau, M. Brucher, M. Perrot, and E. Duchesnay. Scikit-learn: Machine learning in python. *Journal of Machine Learning Research*, 12:2825–2830, 2011.

[19] W. H. Press, B. P. Flannery, S. A. Teukolsky, and W. T. Vetterling. *Numerical Recipes in C: The Art of Scientific Computing*. Cambridge University Press, 1988.

[20] R. W. Sinnott. Virtues of the haversine. *Sky and Telescope*, 68(2):159, 1984.

[21] C. Smith. 200+ amazing facebook user statistics. http://expandedramblings.com/index.php/by-the-numbers-17-amazing-facebook-stats/, 2016.

[22] C. Smith. By the numbers: 17 important Foursquare stats. http://expandedramblings.com/index.php/by-the-numbers-interesting-foursquare-user-stats/, 2016.

[23] A. J. Smola and B. Schölkopf. A tutorial on support vector regression. *Statistics and Computing*, 14(3):199–222, 2004.

[24] B. Thau. How big data helps chains like starbucks pick store locations—an (unsung) key to retail success. http://onforb.es/1iijr2o, 2015.

[25] Y. Zhang, B. Li, and J. Hong. Understanding user economic behavior in the city using large-scale geotagged and crowdsourced data. In *Proceedings of the International World Wide Web Conference*, 2016.

Comparing Community-based Information Adoption and Diffusion Across Different Microblogging Sites

Xiaozhong Liu
Dept. of Information and
Library Science
Indiana University
Bloomington
liu237@indiana.edu

Xing Yu
Dept. of Human-Centered
Computing
Indiana University
Indianapolis
yu64@umail.iu.edu

Zheng Gao
Dept. of Information and
Library Science
Indiana University
Bloomington
gao27@umail.iu.edu

Tian Xia
School of Information
Resource Management
Renmin University of China
xiat@ruc.edu.cn

Johan Bollen
Dept. of Informatics
Indiana University
Bloomington
jbollen@indiana.edu

ABSTRACT

The proliferation of social media is bringing about significant changes in how people make sense of their world and adopt new information. However, social, cultural and political divisions continue to separate users and information into different social media systems. Twitter and Facebook, for example, are strictly forbidden in mainland China. As a result, 21.97% of all world-wide Internet users are thus excluded from participating in these platforms. In this study, we investigate whether the dynamics of information diffusion, modeled as the adoption patterns of topical hashtags, differ between the communities of the mentioned social media sites as a result of this separation. Specifically, we compare Weibo and Twitter, the two largest micro-blogging sites serving respectively the Chinese population and the rest of the world, by exploring the similarities and differences of how their respective users adopt new information. By leveraging sophisticated community detection algorithms and heterogeneous graph mining methods, we investigate and compare how the different characteristics of these communities influence information diffusion and adoption. Experimental results show that while community-specific information influences topic diffusion and adoption in both environments, novel features, extracted from heterogeneous graph based communities, have a greater effect on Weibo information adoption than Twitter. We also find that users sharing hashtags is an important factor in information diffusion on both Twitter and Weibo, whereas user mentions are important for Weibo, but less so for Twitter. Overall, we conclude that Weibo and Twitter differ sharply in how their users adopt information in response to similar factors.

HT '16 July 10-13, 2016, Halifax, NS, Canada

© 2016 ACM. ISBN 978-1-4503-4247-6/16/07. . . $15.00

DOI: http://dx.doi.org/10.1145/2914586.2914665

Categories and Subject Descriptors

H.3.3 [**Information Storage and Retrieval**]: Information Search and Retrieval

Keywords

Information Diffusion, Social Media, Information Comparison

1. INTRODUCTION

Social media is bringing about significant changes in how people perceive and make sense of their world [24]. Millions of individuals now communicate with each other through a variety of social media platforms, sharing pertinent information about the world as well as the most minute details of their social lives, thereby collectively shaping each others' culture and worldview. This has led to a surge in the development of algorithms and methods for social media mining that leverage social media data to study long-standing questions in social science [1, 12, 22, 35].

Unfortunately, significant sample bias may occur when researchers rely on social media data that is generated by any particular social media platform. Social media users are frequently separated along cultural, linguistic, and political divisions. For example, Twitter and Facebook are blocked in mainland China for political reasons [40], thus excluding 21.97%[1] of Internet users from these systems. Similarly, the world's second largest microblogging system, Sina Weibo[2], had more than 113 million active users by 2013. However, since Sina Weibo's default system language is Chinese and the system is solely designed for Chinese users, almost all its users are Chinese and speak Chinese. This situation leads to separate semantic, political, and linguistic "bubbles" that bias how users perceive and understand their world, and may in fact shape the topics they discuss and are interested in, leading to "culture bubbles". As a result, social media analytics based on a single social media system can be strongly biased as a result of the particular linguistic, social, political, and topical "bubbles" of that particular social media system. To achieve a user sample that is truly representative of the

---

[1]Statistics of China Internet Users (2014): http://www.internetlivestats.com/internet-users/china/

[2]Now the largest Chinese microblogging system http://www.weibo.com/

world's population, one can therefore not rely on a single source of social media data.

To better understand the effects of the aforementioned user bubbles, this paper presents results that address two issues related to how information is disseminated and adopted across different social media systems and networks.

First, users from different social networks (bubbles) can become interested in and adopt new topics in different ways. For instance, Weibo users could adopt new topics by relying mostly on personal features, e.g., user hashtags, user mentions, and user in- and out-degree, while Twitter users might rely on entirely different features, due to cultural and social differences. In this study, by using Weibo and Twitter data (representing users from China and the rest of the world) and various machine-learning methods, e.g., random forest classification and factor analysis, we compare which explicit features and implicit factors account for differences in information adoption across these different social networks.

Second, we investigate the effects of heterogeneous community-based features on information adoption and diffusion. We use community detection [29] and heterogeneous graph mining [20] methods to detect different kinds of communities on the Twitter and Weibo social networks using heterogeneous graph representations that allow different types of nodes and edges. For instance, we can define edges that represent a relationship between 2 users based on their sharing of hashtags. A random walk probability can be calculated from one user to another following these types of relationships (ignoring link direction). These user-to-user probabilities can then support the detection of distinct user communities. Note that, on a heterogeneous graph, one user can reach another via different kinds of paths, and therefore community detection results can differ, i.e., the same user may belong to different kinds of communities. In this study, we extract various kinds of community-based features to enhance the prediction performance of our information adoption models where community-based features can help us better explore the in-depth differences between information diffusion and adoption in Twitter and Weibo.

The contribution of the paper is threefold. First, we compare Twitter and Weibo information adoption and diffusion patterns, i.e., we show significant differences in how Weibo and Twitter users adopt new topics and consume new information through social network communication. Second, we characterize how community features affect information adoption and diffusion. Last but not least, by using a heterogeneous network representation, we can generate different types of communities by leveraging different kinds of paths and relations between user pairs. A large-scale dataset, including 9 days Twitter and Weibo messages (with 2,222,163 Twitter users + 211,816 Weibo users), is used in these experiments.

In the remainder of this paper, Section 2 reviews relevant literature; Section 3 proposes our novel method and hypotheses for information adoption/diffusion comparison and community-based feature extraction; Section 4 describes the experiment setting and evaluation results; and Section 5 discusses the findings of the study and identifies subsequent research steps.

2. LITERATURE REVIEW

2.1 Filter Bubbles in Social Media

When Pariser defined the concept of filter bubbles [25], this notion referred to the phenomenon of users becoming isolated in terms of the information they are exposed to as a result of algorithmic curation (filtering). Yet, equally significant filter bubbles can exist due to users getting trapped in specific social media platforms due to "walled garden" policies, language barriers, and national poli-

cies. Prior studies show that users are restricted in their exposure to conflicting points of view and are isolated intellectually in their own informational bubble [37] as a result of this. From the viewpoint of social media and social networking, these filter bubbles dominate the acquisition and distribution of information by sharply reducing the range and nature of information that users are exposed to [26].

Filter bubbles exist across different social media platforms. Tim Berners-Lee, in his 2010 report [2], claimed that social media sites, like Facebook, are threatening the open nature of the Internet by walling off content from other competing sites. As a result social media users become increasingly locked into restricted online environments that limit the information that they are exposed to. These filter bubbles do not merely present a societal challenge, but jeopardize the scientific study of online information diffusion. When researchers rely on data acquired from a single social media platforms, the results of their investigations may be biased and may generalize poorly. A recent study [32] shows significant differences in how users consume and adopt the same kind of information in different online environments.

In this study, we attempt to characterize the filter bubble phenomenon across different, but comparable social media sites used by individuals across different nations and cultures. Our results provide important information on how information adoption and diffusion patterns can differ significantly across platforms due to cultural, national, and linguistic differences that call into question the common assumption that our online activities are becoming increasingly globalized.

2.2 Social Media Mining and Information Diffusion on Social Network

The proliferation of social media does not only revolutionize the way people communicate, perceive, and understand the world, but also provides a treasure trove of new large-scale data for scientists across many domains, including computer science, sociology, mathematics, and business. There has been extensive research on the development of algorithms and methods for social media mining [1, 12, 22, 35]. Microblogging systems such as Twitter are common targets for this type of analysis due to their public nature and the relative simplicity of their services. For instance, methods on various topics such as user interest modeling [19, 31], sentiment analysis [1, 24], social network analysis [13], event prediction [3, 27, 38], and information diffusion [28] have been well documented in previous studies.

As tools mature, researchers have begun to address more challenging questions in the area of information diffusion and dissemination, using increasingly sophisticated textual and graphical features in social media data [39, 41]. However, there is increasing concern with respect to how well many results and findings generalize across disconnected online communities separated by cultural, linguistic, national, social, and corporate boundaries. Here we investigate the possibility of social media analytics that acknowledges these boundaries and leverages them to conduct computational social science [34] across a multitude of online information bubbles. We combine large-scale data from two comparable online social media platforms that are mainly used in two very different cultural spheres.

From prior studies, we found that community detection is an important tool for social media mining [33, 36]. However, few studies have utilized community information to enhance information diffusion analysis or the prediction of information adoption. For instance, Yang et al., [41] extracted comprehensive features from the Twitter retweet network to predict information adoption. However, they did not investigate community features relevant to targeted users although they could conceivably provide relevant information to explore information dissemination among users in microblogging environments [14, 36].

As another limitation of existing work, most existing information diffusion studies, e.g., [23,28], utilize homogeneous social network representations, which solely depend on one type of relationship between users. However, in the real world, social media users may be interconnected via a plurality of different kinds of explicit or implicit relationships. For instance, users could be connected via retweet, mention, or share-the-same-hashtag relationships, each carrying information that could be useful to model and characterize information adaption and diffusion.

2.3 Comparing Twitter and Weibo

The number of Chinese Internet users has been growing rapidly. Presently more than 20% of all Internet users are Chinese, making the Chinese Internet community an increasingly important target for social media studies [8, 44]. The use of Twitter data to characterize real world events is well documented, but its Chinese counterpart, Weibo, is becoming an important means to understand the Chinese community. For instance, Zhao et al. [45] employed Weibo data to investigate event discussions by using the term-message-user network. They used random-walk algorithms to study the temporal event information diffusion with event information that was pre-defined by domain expert. Similarly, Guan et al., [11] studied 21 (expert pre-defined) trending events on Weibo by studying the behavior of 32 influential users.

In the context of filter bubbles, Twitter and Weibo, the most popular microblogging systems, have been successfully used to represent and investigate Western and Chinese communities, respectively. Due to language and political barriers, users from each platform are largely restricted to exclusive use of either system. And it posts a significant challenge to algorithms [16, 42, 43] that attempt to identify users across both platforms.

While most previous studies treated Twitter and Weibo as the same kind of social media platforms except for language, some have found features that uniquely characterize Weibo [10, 17, 32]. Not until recently did some researchers become aware of the importance of comparing the Weibo and Twitter corpora. For instance, Gao et al., [10] compared Twitter and Weibo corpora from sentiment, entity, system access perspectives. A list of comparison indicators were listed in Table 1.

Table 1: Twitter and Weibo comparison in previous studies

Comparison Indicator	Previous Studies	Findings
HashTag distribution	[10,17]	Weibo users are interested in entertainment and sports topics, and Weibo users like more joke related content compared with Twitter users.
URL distribution	[10]	Weibo users post less URLs compared with Twitter users.
Forward distribution	[17]	Weibo users forward message slower than Twitter.
Follow distribution	[17]	Twitter users number of actions will have a more significant effectiveness on the number of "Followers" than that of Weibo.
Gender distribution (for 32 users)	[11]	Male users are more likely to be involved.
Picture distribution (for 32 users)	[11]	Messages containing pictures are more likely to be posted.
Sentiment distribution	[10]	Weibo users post more positive messages compared with Twitter users.
System access distribution	[10]	On Twitter, more than 95% of the users use more than one client application while on Sina Weibo around 65% of the users switch between different clients.
Entity distribution	[10]	Weibo users post more entity information than Twitter users.

Most comparative studies focus on a limited set of statistical features or properties (hashTags, forwarding linkages, following linkages, etc.) of microblogging platforms. The lack of community-relevant features however provides very limited information about the differences and similarities between Chinese and Western users. More recently, Shuai et al., [32] investigated topical or categorical Twitter and Weibo comparison during hot events. And they found that the responses of Weibo (or Twitter) to *Political* news can be very different from that of *Science* news.

This paper investigates the similarity and difference between Weibo and Twitter from the viewpoint of information diffusion and adoption. We utilize novel features extracted from community detection analysis in conjunction with heterogeneous graph representations to enhance the performance of our information adoption and diffusion models. We hypothesize that heterogeneous community-based features extracted from Twitter and Weibo platforms can help us better understand and compare how information is adopted across different microblogging sites.

3. METHODOLOGY

In this section, we discuss our research method in detail, which includes: constructing heterogeneous graphs for feature extraction (3.1), extracting novel community-based features for information adoption models generation (3.2), and comparing multiple information adoption models (3.3). We will also propose a number of hypotheses in this section, which will be verified in the experiment section.

3.1 Topic Adoption Model on Heterogeneous Social Network

We operationalize topic adoption and diffusion in terms of how users generate, adopt, communicate, and share *hashtags*. Hashtags are chosen because they are explicitly intended to represent a user-chosen topic, e.g., *#obama*, in the online communication ecology. When a user introduces a new hashtag and includes it in their social media messages, we say that the user has adopted a new hashtag. More formally, in this study, we use a number of indicators to quantify the event that a user, u_i, adopts a new topic, h_j, at time t. Each topic is represented by a hashtag. Unlike earlier studies, we use a directed heterogeneous graph, $G = (\mathcal{V}, \mathcal{E})$, representation. On this graph, we define an object (node) type mapping function $\tau : \mathcal{V} \rightarrow \mathcal{A}$ and a link type mapping function $\phi : \mathcal{E} \rightarrow \mathcal{R}$, where each object $v \in \mathcal{V}$ belongs to one particular object type $\tau(v) \in \mathcal{A}$, and each link $e \in \mathcal{E}$ belongs to a particular relation $\phi(e) \in \mathcal{R}$. If two links belong to the same relation type, the two links share the same starting object type as well as the ending object type. The types of nodes and edges are presented in Table 2. Note that Twitter and Weibo graphs are constructed separately for subsequent step in which we carry out the model comparison.

Table 2: Nodes and relations in the heterogeneous graph

	Type	Description
Node	u	User node
	h	Hashtag node
Edge	$u_i \xrightarrow{m} u_j$	User to user via mention relation
	$u_i \xrightarrow{r} u_j$	User to user via retweet relation
	$u_i \xrightarrow{rp} u_j$	User to user via reply relation
	$u_i \xrightarrow{u} h_j$	User use hashtag

For any node on the graph, the sum of the same type of outgoing links equals 1 yielding a transition probability (of the same edge type) from one node to another. For instance, the weight of the link

105

from $user_i$ to $hashtag_j$ is defined as $w(u_i \overset{u}{\to} h_j) = \frac{d(u_i \overset{u}{\to} h_j)}{d(u_i \overset{u}{\to} \{h\})}$, where $d(u_i \overset{w}{\to} h_j)$ is the total number of $hashtag_j$ that $user_i$ used in her messages and $d(u_i \overset{w}{\to} \{h\})$ is the total number of (any) hashtags that $user_i$ used in her messages. Similarly, we defined the weights of edges in $u_i \overset{r}{\to} u_j$ and $u_i \overset{m}{\to} u_j$. For instance, $w(u_i \overset{r}{\to} u_j) = \frac{d(u_i \overset{r}{\to} u_j)}{d(u_i \overset{r}{\to} \{u\})}$ indicates the probability that u_i retweeting u_j on the heterogeneous graph.

In this heterogeneous network, users can be connected via different types of relationships, and various kinds of relationships can be important to predict the information diffusion/adoption on microblogging sites. In the study, we will verify:

Hypothesis 1 *Given that in the Twitter and Weibo platforms users will be explicitly or implicitly connected via different kinds of relations or paths, the features extracted from these different kinds of relations or paths between users are important to predict the degree to which information is adopted for either group of users.*

In this study, we investigate four types of relations between users:

1. $u_i \overset{r}{\to} u_j$ **denoted as (ufu):** User to user relation induced from *retweeting*. Comparing with the following-followee relationship, a retweeting relationship can be a much stronger indicator of social influence, which is a major factor in information cascades in online communities [9, 41].

2. $u_i \overset{rp}{\to} u_j$ **denoted as (uru):** User to user relation induced from *reply*. A reply on Twitter or Weibo means responding to a message or tweet from a person while to retweet is to broadcast a message posted by a person to others.

3. $u_i \overset{m}{\to} u_j$ **denoted as (uau):** User to user relation induced from *mentions*. In a "mention", a user embed user names (@username) in his or her Twitter or Weibo message thus publicly signaling the message is directed at or submitted to the attention of the mentioned user. Celebrities are frequently mentioned due to their popularity, without their messages necessarily being retweeted [7].

4. $u_i \overset{u}{\to} h \overset{u}{\leftarrow} u_j$ **denoted as (uhu):** User to user relation induced from *sharing-the-same-hashtag*. Unlike retweeting and mention relations, u_i and u_j sharing the same hashtag(s) doesn't mean that they have a social relationship. Instead, they may share similar interests in the social network, and they do not necessarily know each other.

For each kind of relationship, $\Re$, in order to quantify the relation probability score $P_\Re(u_i \to u_j)$ between users, a random walk based measure is proposed:

$$P_\Re(u_i \to u_j) = \sum_{t=u_i \rightsquigarrow u_j} RW(t|\Re)$$

where t is a path from u_i to u_j following the specific relationship, $\Re$, and $RW(t|\Re)$ is the random walk probability of the path t. Suppose $t = u_i \overset{u}{\to} h_x \overset{u}{\leftarrow} u_j$, the random walk probability is then given by $RW(t|\Re) = w(u_i \overset{u}{\to} h_x) \cdot w(u_j \overset{u}{\to} h_x)$. Note that this is an asymmetric measure, where $P_\Re(u_i \to u_j)$ does not necessarily equal $P_\Re(u_j \to u_i)$.

For each relationship $\Re$, we can generate a homogeneous graph $G_\Re$ where each node on the graph represents a user. The edge between users has a weight $P_\Re(u_i \to u_j)$. So, we generate three distinct user graphs on the basis of three kinds of relationships. For each graph, a number of features can be extracted to characterize a different model of information adoption. One example is depicted in Figure 1 by following $u_i \overset{m}{\to} u_j$ relationship. Clearly,

Table 3: Feature Description for Each Community Type

Type	Feature	Symbol
personal	degree	Degree
	unique hashtag used	UniqueHashtag
	pagerank	Pagerank
local	number of users use hashtag in community	NuserLoc
	ratio of users use hashtag in community	RatioLoc
	average page rank score	AvgLoc
	max pagerank score	MaxLoc
global	average number of users use hashtag in community	NuserGlob
	global ratio of users use hashtag	RatioGlob
	global average page rank score	AvgGlob
	global max pagerank score	MaxGlob

based on the example heterogeneous graph (on the left of Figure 1), but using different kinds of relationship, we can construct different homogeneous graphs. For graph $G_\Re$, we extract k features $F_{\Re_1}, F_{\Re_1} \dots F_{\Re_k}$, allowing us to build a topic adoption model using regression methods. Isolated nodes will be removed from the graph. Note that the total number of users on different homogeneous graphs can be different. For instance, if a user never uses any hashtag, we cannot find this user on the $u_i \overset{u}{\to} h \overset{u}{\leftarrow} u_j$ graph.

For Weibo and Twitter, we construct two information adoption models, $\Phi_{twitter}(\{F\})$ and $\Phi_{weibo}(\{F\})$, to predict and compare topic adoption, where $\{F\}$ is the feature set extracted from three homogeneous user graphs. Note that the feature space of Twitter and Weibo are exactly the same, which means we can compare the impact of each feature in the information adoption models. In this study, we will verify:

Hypothesis 2 *The contributions of the target feature to Twitter and Weibo information adoption models are different for the same feature $F_{\Re_p}, t$.*

For Twitter and Weibo, given a feature $F_{\Re_i}$, we can compare the values of $\beta_{F_{\Re_i}}$ (weight of feature $F_{\Re_i}$) in $\Phi_{twitter}(\{F\})$ and $\Phi_{weibo}(\{F\})$. More detailed model construction will be presented in section 3.3.

3.2 Feature Extraction via Community Detection

In [41], Yang et al., investigated a number of features for Twitter hashtag adoption modeling, and a number of features are extracted from the user retweeting network. In this study, we leverage similar kinds of features for Twitter and Weibo comparison. The model predicts if user u_i will adopt hashtag h_j in the future (in either Twitter or Weibo network):

1. **Indegree/Outdegree:** The number or ratio of users that u_i retweeted and the number of users who retweeted u_i.
2. **Unique hashtags:** The number of unique hashtags that u_i used.
3. **Popularity:** the number of times a hashtag has been posted; or the number of users who adopted the hashtag.
4. **Prestige:** The prestige of a hashtag as measured by the average and maximum PageRank scores of all the users who adopted the target hashtag.

All these features have been proved useful for information adoption [41]. In this study, we will propose a novel feature set by using community information while we hypothesize:

Hypothesis 3 *For user u_i, if u_i belongs to a community C_k, the characters and features extracted from C_k are statistically useful to predict information adoption for u_i.*

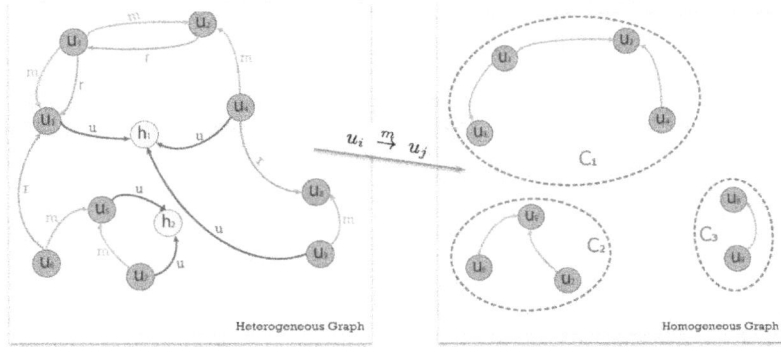

Figure 1: User Graph Construction and Community Detection Example by Using $u_i \xrightarrow{r} u_j$ Relationship.

As Figure 1 shows, for each relationship $\Re$ and corresponding homogeneous graph $G_\Re$, we can generate different kinds of communities based on the network topology. For $u_i \xrightarrow{r} u_j$ (retweeting) and $u_i \xrightarrow{m} u_j$ (mention), users from the same community are more likely to know each other. The case of $u_i \xrightarrow{u} h \xleftarrow{u} u_j$ (sharing-the-same-hashtag) is different, whereas users from the same community may share the similar interests.

In this study, we use the InfoMap algorithm [29], a well-performing community detection algorithm [15], to identify communities from 3 homogeneous user graphs. The InfoMap algorithm generates communities via a nomenclature based on Huffman coding, which identifies the best community structure by minimizing the quantity of information needed to represent random walks in the network using this nomenclature. Partitions containing few inter-community links will result in walkers spending more time inside communities.

Subsequently, we can split the feature set into two groups: (1) features related to user community, and (2) features only related to target users:

- **Community-based Features**: *1. Number of users adopting the target hashtag h_j, 2. Ratio of users adopting the target hashtag h_j, 3. Average user prestige scores[3] and 4. Maximum users' prestige scores (who adopted the target hashtag h_j).*
- **User-based Features**: *5. Indegree, 6. Outdegree, and 7. Number of unique hashtags used.*

For each community-based feature, we can also generate intra- and extra-community values. More detailed feature information is presented in Table 3. The intra-community value represents the community that the target user belongs to, and the extra-community value is defined for communities that the target user doesn't belong to. For example, for *"number of users adopting the target hashtag h_j"*, if u_i belongs to a community C_k, we can generate the intra-community value for this feature by using community C_k, while the extra-community value represents the average score for other communities that u_i doesn't belong to. In this study, we will verify the following hypothesis:

Hypothesis 4 *Intra- and extra-community feature values of the same community-based feature are useful and important to predict the information adoption in social network since they represent internal and external information of the community that the target user belongs to. The contributions of intra- and extra-community values are different.*

---

[3]User prestige score is represented by users' PageRank scores on the target homogeneous user graph.

3.3 Information Adoption Model Construction, Validation and Comparison

For Weibo and Twitter data, we first construct two classifiers using the random forest algorithm [18], $\Phi_{twitter}(\{F\})$ and $\Phi_{weibo}(\{F\})$, to predict information adoption in the target social media environment, where $\{F\}$ is the feature set extracted from four user graphs (presented in section 3.1 and 3.2). From the classifiers, we extract variable importance measurements (VIE) to evaluate the importance of each feature in terms of their impact on the adoption decision. Note that there can be two types of features, explicit and latent features (like a kind of community). Hence, we also trained two sets of classifiers, one with explicit features and the other with latent features, to compare their performance.

The random forest algorithm [4] offers various benefits that make it suitable for our study. First, the algorithm does not have a linear assumption between the predictors and the outcomes, which makes it perform better than linear-based methods (e.g., logistic regression) in complex cases. Second, the random sampling mechanism and the out-of-bag estimation approach used in the algorithm make our models less prone to overfitting. Last but not least, unlike many machine-learning algorithms that work in a black-box style, the random forest model allows us to evaluate the individual importance of each predictor, which helps us further explore and understand the potential causal relation between the predictors and the outcome.

The random forest algorithm has two common variable importance metrics to measure the influence of predictors: 1) the mean decrease in accuracy, and 2) the total decrease in node impurities [5]. In this study, we adopt the second metric since it has been proven to be more stable [6] than the first one. Meanwhile, in order to avoid the potential bias, which would be in favor of variables that have either more distinct numerical values or fewer missing instances, we use the heuristic correction strategy proposed by Sandri and Zuccolotto [30] to estimate the overall importance of the predictors. Later on, we train and tune the classifiers based on the overall accuracies and report the final rankings of the features based on the VIEs in the final model.

In order to better test hypothesis 1, we apply an unsupervised machine-learning technique–factor analysis–to explore the latent factors that potentially cause the explicit features we observe. The analysis can be described as a two-step process. First, we apply an exploratory factor analysis (EFA) to explore the underlying constructs. During this step, no prior assumption of the structure regarding the dataset will be applied. Once we have the result from the EFA analysis, the factor loadings will be examined. From there we will decide whether to carry out the next step, in which we examine whether the assume latent variables–the four ways that we group different kind of communities–could explain the explicit features. To do that, we will conduct a confirmatory factor analysis (CFA) using structural equation modeling (SEM) [21]. In addition, we are also very interested to see to what extent that the latent factors can be used to predict the hashtag adoption behavior of the online users. So we will train classifiers using the latent features instead of the explicit features to see how they perform.

For these classifiers, the training graphs (homogeneous user graphs extracted from heterogeneous graphs) are generated by using a time period of (Weibo and Twitter) data - $[t_1, t_2]$, noted as T. By using the features extracted from these graphs, we train the Twitter and Weibo classifiers to predict the information (hashtag h_j) adoption for each user u_i in a future time period $(t_2, t_3]$, noted as ΔT. The dependent variable is boolean: 1 indicates the user u_i adopts the target topic (hashtag u_j) in ΔT, and 0 means him/she does not. In both cases, the user did not use (adopted) the target hashtag h_j in the training time period T (before ΔT), which means the model is to predict the new information that the user is likely to adopt.

For each feature F_t in the classifiers trained from Twitter data and Weibo data, we can compare the importance of β_{F_t} (VIE of feature F_t) in $\Phi_{twitter}(\{F\})$ and $\Phi_{weibo}(\{F\})$. Larger β values indicate features' stronger impact on the adoption model.

In order to verify the usefulness of community information (Hypothesis 3), we build different adoption models by using vs. not using community information. In baseline models, we consider all users on the target graph to generate community based features, a.k.a. all the users in the baseline models belong to the same community. As a result, all features in the baseline models are community independent. The values of Correctly Classified Rate (CCR) and Brier Scores will be utilized to compare the performance of different models. If community-based models outperform baseline models (information adoption models without community-based features for both Twitter and Weibo), then it is taken to support our hypothesis.

3.4 Hypothesis Summarization

In this section, we proposed four different but related hypotheses. On microblogging sites, users can be interconnected via different kinds of explicit or implicit relationships, i.e., retweet ($u_i \xrightarrow{r} u_j$), mention ($u_i \xrightarrow{m} u_j$), or share hashtag ($u_i \xrightarrow{u} h \xleftarrow{u} u_j$) relationships. While different relationships provide information on user relatedness from various perspectives, we hypothesize that features extracted from these relationships can be potentially useful to predict Twitter and Weibo information adoption (Hypothesis 1). For the same feature, we hypothesize that its contribution for Twitter and Weibo information adoption can be quite different (Hypothesis 2). By training information adoption models using an ensemble learning method, we can verify these hypotheses.

By using a novel community detection method, we propose two additional hypotheses. First, we hypothesize that for the target user, the features extracted from the community that this user belongs to can be important to predict the information adoption (Hypothesis 3). Note that as we extracted various kinds of relationships from the heterogeneous networks, one user may belong to more than one kind of community. Meanwhile, we verify the usefulness of the intra- (the community that user belong to) and extra-community (the communities that user doesn't belong to) features. We hypothesize that the contribution of the intra- and extra-community features can be different for information adoption (Hypothesis 4).

4. EXPERIMENTS

4.1 Datasets

In our experiments, we extract Twitter and Weibo users, hashtags, and various kinds of relationship information from a large number of Twitter and Weibo messages (46,390,456 Twitter messages and 12,362,489 Weibo messages). The training data (to generate Twitter and Weibo heterogeneous social networks as well as extracting all the features to train classifiers) covers the time period T from September 17, 2012 to September 23, 2012 (7 days). The testing data (to verify classifiers and estimate features' performance) were recorded from September 24 to 25, 2012 (ΔT for 2 days). As discussed in Section 3.2, we use the InfoMap community detection algorithm to extract community information from three types of Twitter and Weibo user graphs. And the user graphs are generated based on the method of section 3.1. More detailed data comparison is presented in Table 3. Hashtags that appeared in fewer than ten messages and users that composed fewer than ten messages were removed from the datasets.

4.2 Experimental Results

From these datasets, we initially extract 7,028,200 instances in Twitter and 21,252,000 instances in Weibo. However, the number of negative instances (where a user did not use the target hashtag in T, and did not adopt the hashtag in ΔT) is much larger than the positive ones (a user did not use the target hashtag in T, but adopted the hashtag in ΔT). To ensure classifier quality, we first pick up all the positive instances from the datasets, and then we performed the under-sampling technique (simple random sampling without replacement) on the negative instances to sample a subset that matches the number of positive instances we have. Finally, we got 9,446 instances from Twitter and 9,494 instances from Weibo, both contain 50% positive instances and 50% negative instances, for information adoption models generation and validation. Every one of the selected instances has less than four missing values in the feature space.

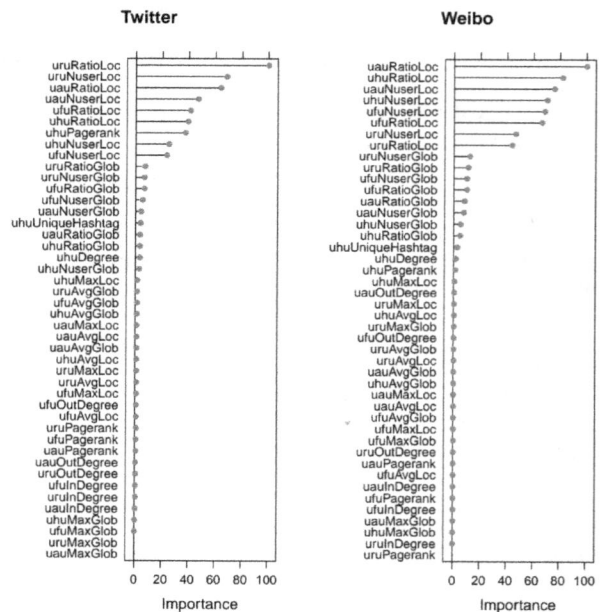

Figure 2: VIE of Twitter and Weibo Models.

Table 4: Summary of dataset

	Twitter		Weibo	
Number of users	2,222,163		211,816	
Number of tweets	46,390,456		12,362,489	
Number of hashtags	1,065,600		201,740	
Scheme Info	**Number of Users**	**Number of Communities**	**Number of Users**	**Number of Communities**
$u_1 \xrightarrow{r} u_2$	1,791,600	152,646	328,065	32,223
$u_1 \xrightarrow{rp} u_2$	1,697,115	176,061	85,104	13,661
$u_1 \xrightarrow{m} u_2$	1,440,992	240,044	986,703	65,699
$u_1 \xrightarrow{u} h \xleftarrow{u} u_2$	1,579,750	239,891	93,270	30,624

Table 5: Evaluation Results of Community Methods and Baseline Models

	Twitter Community Method	Twitter Baseline Model	Weibo Community Method	Weibo Baseline Model
Correctly Classified Rate (CCR)	99.2237%	93.7544%	99.9306%	65.4407%
Incorrectly Classified Rate	0.7763%	6.2456%	0.06940%	34.5593%
Brier Score	0.0123	0.0570	0.0006	0.2411

Explicit Feature Testing: To assess the usefulness of community-based features, we generate 4 different random forest classifiers for Twitter and Weibo. To build the classifiers, we randomly sampled (without replacement) 70% instances for model training and 30% for model testing. For each classifier that we build, we used 10-fold cross-validation with 15 repetitions to obtain the best model in the training session. In the testing session, we put the testing dataset into the classifier to generate a confusion matrix, based on which we calculate the sensitivity, specificity, and the overall accuracy. Overall, when we apply both the community-based and user-based features to the training and testing datasets, the model prediction performance peaks, with accuracy of 99.2237 for Twitter and 99.9306 for Weibo. However, after we remove the community-based features, the model performance decrease, especially for Weibo. The results are shown in Table 5. Both corrected classified rate (CCR) and Brier Scores (Brier) indicate that community-based features indeed enhance the performance of information adoption prediction models (especially for Weibo). In addition, community-based features improve prediction accuracy more so for Weibo than Twitter, indicating the features play different roles or to different degrees for the two microblogging environments. Overall, Weibo prediction performance is higher than that for Twitter, and community-based features are more critical for Weibo.

Followingly, we report the variable importance measurements (VIE) in Fig. 2. Although the two classifiers performed well, they produce different rankings for the importance of the features. The (normalized) VIE results are depicted in Fig. 2 and Table 6. Based on the VIE and average VIE result (for each kind of community), we found that first, the local (intra-community) features are of the most important ones in both models. Second, although local features are important in both models, different communities show different impact. The *uru* (user-reply-user community) generates the most important features in the Twitter model while the *uau* (user-mention-user community) and *uhu* (user-hashtag-user community) generate the most important features in the Weibo model. The *uau* (user-mention-user community) seems to be important in both models. And *ufu* (user-retweet-user community) is more important in the Weibo model. Overall, both models provide strong evidence of the relation between the community-based features and the hashtag adoption behavior.

Latent Variable Testing: In order to explore the latent factors of the hashtag adoption behavior, we perform an exploratory factor analysis to exam the latent constructs of the data. We set the number of latent factors to assuming the existence of 4 latent factors

that each corresponds to one community type. The result is illustrated in diagrams (Fig. 3), which show the factor loadings of each explicit feature over the latent factors.

We can see that we identified a very unexpected structure. In the Twitter diagram, based on EFA, we find that most of the global features group together into a factor (MP1), and **uru**, **uhu**, and **uau** features can be projected to factor 2, 3, and 4. One the other hand, the Weibo CFA model shows that most of the global features and one local feature can be grouped into factor 1. Factor 4 consists of 6 **uhu** features, while factor 3 accounts for three **uru** features. Factor 2 is a combination of **uau** and **ufu** features. Meanwhile, based on the EFA results, we find the local features are more sparse in each factor, which means they are more independent compared with global features.

A confirmatory factor analysis was carried out afterwards. As expected, after fixating the factor loadings between the communities and the corresponding explicit features, the model will not converge. This further confirmed that the assumed structure does not fit our observation. First, most of the global features, despite from different communities, have heavy loadings on latent factor 1. The rest three factors are responsible for part of the **uhu** features, **uru** features, and **uau** features, however, they only account for a small part of the features that we extracted from each community settings. It is safe to say that despite community-like factors (**uhu**, **uru**, **uau**, but not **ufu**) do play certain causal effect on the explicit features, there are certain factors, which we did not take account for is the assumption, that has more important effect over the three community-like factors.

Based on the EFA models, latent variables can predict Twitter hashtag adoption with 0.866 accuracy, and 0.879 for Weibo.

4.3 Hypothesis Verification

In this study, we examine 4 different hypotheses through experimental results that are outlined in this section. Detailed information is summarized in Table 7.

For H1, the high accuracies of the classifiers we have trained based on the extracted features strongly support our hypothesis. We have achieved an accuracy of 99.22% for Twitter and an accuracy of 99.93% for Weibo, which are extremely high.

From the classifiers we find that the contributions of most features to Twitter and Weibo information adoption vary significantly. For instance, while *Ratio of users for h* and *Degree* (intra-community) are important for both Twitter and Weibo, other top ranked features differ for Twitter and Weibo. Based on these results, we conclude that *maximum and average users' prestige scores and aver-*

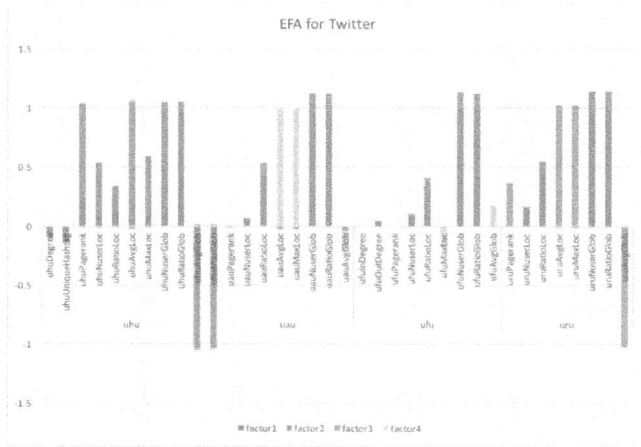

((a)) EFA for Twitter

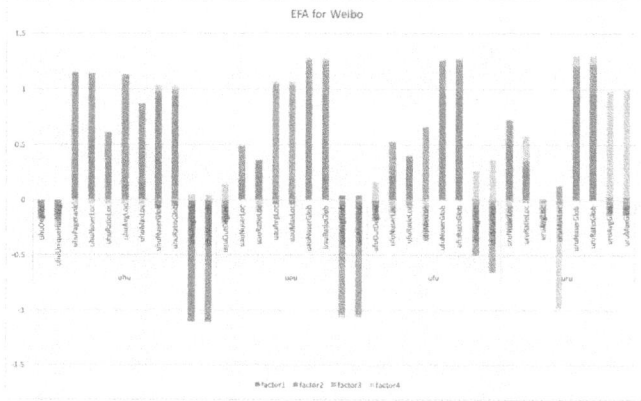

((b)) EFA for Weibo

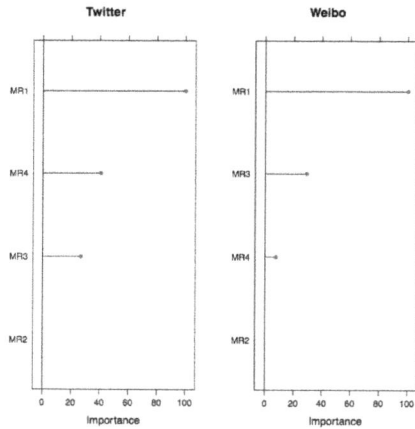

((c)) Comparison

Figure 3: Exploratory Factor Analysis (EFA) comparison for Twitter and Weibo.

Table 6: (Normalized) VIE Comparison

Scheme	Feature type		Feature	Twitter	Weibo
ufu	community based	intra	Number of users for hashtag h	23.39	68.55
			Ratio of users for h	41.15	66.43
			Average users' pagerank scores	1.01	0.12
			Maximum users' pagerank scores	1.08	0.14
		extra	Average number of users for h	5.33	10.01
			Ratio of users for h	6.56	9.99
			Average users' pagerank scores	1.47	0.17
			Maximum users' pagerank scores	0.01	0.14
	personal-based		Indegree	0.67	0.09
			Outdegree	1.07	0.42
			Pagerank score	0.86	0.09
	Averaged VIE			**7.51**	**14.20**
uru	community based	intra	Number of users for hashtag h	68.42	46.53
			Ratio of users for h	100.00	43.88
			Average users' pagerank scores	1.17	0.34
			Maximum users' pagerank scores	1.22	0.53
		extra	Average number of users for h	6.65	12.14
			Ratio of users for h	7.13	10.95
			Average users' pagerank scores	1.47	0.38
			Maximum users' pagerank scores	0.00	0.48
	personal-based		Indegree	0.64	0.00
			Outdegree	0.70	0.13
			Pagerank score	1.01	0.00
	Averaged VIE			**17.13**	**10.49**
uau	community based	intra	Number of users for hashtag h	47.19	75.95
			Ratio of users for h	64.10	100.00
			Average users' pagerank scores	1.30	0.19
			Maximum users' pagerank scores	1.34	0.21
		extra	Average number of users for h	4.29	7.65
			Ratio of users for h	3.48	8.26
			Average users' pagerank scores	1.26	0.25
			Maximum users' pagerank scores	0.00	0.04
	personal-based		Indegree	0.52	0.09
			Outdegree	0.72	0.65
			Pagerank score	0.83	0.12
	Averaged VIE			**11.37**	**17.58**
uhu	community based	intra	Number of users for hashtag h	24.95	70.59
			Ratio of users for h	39.34	82.18
			Average users' pagerank scores	1.24	0.51
			Maximum users' pagerank scores	1.54	0.72
		extra	Average number of users for h	3.05	5.21
			Ratio of users for h	3.37	4.89
			Average users' pagerank scores	1.36	0.22
			Maximum users' pagerank scores	0.10	0.03
	personal-based		Degree	3.33	1.61
			Number of unique hashtags used	3.78	2.72
			Pagerank score	37.37	1.38
	Averaged VIE			**10.86**	**15.46**

age users' pagerank scores are important to predict information adoption for Twitter, whereas extra-community *ratio of users for h* are important for Weibo thus verifying the H2 that the same features affect the Twitter and Weibo networks communities differently.

In terms of the usefulness of community information to predict information adoption, we find, overall, community-based features can be helpful to predict the information adoption/diffusion for both Twitter and Weibo. However, the contribution of community-based features affects our Weibo observations more strongly than Twitter, i.e., for Twitter, the community-based model outperforms our baseline model by 5.47% (for CCR) whereas for Weibo this number is 34.49%. However, the usefulness of each explicit community-based features cannot be explained by the four latent community

Table 7: Hypothesis Verification

	Content	Verification	Twitter	Weibo
H1	Given that in the Twitter and Weibo platforms users will be explicitly or implicitly connected via different kinds of relations or paths, the features extracted from these different kinds of relations or paths between users are important to predict the degree of to which information is adopted for either group of users.	Features, from 4 different user graphs, contribution to the adoption models	True, the *uru* (user-reply-user community) generates the most important features in the Twitter model.	True, the *uau* (user-mention-user community) and *uhu* (user-hashtag-user community) generate the most important features in the Weibo model.
H2	For the same feature $F_{\Re_p}$, the contributions of the target feature to Twitter and Weibo information adoption models are different.	Compare VIE for random forest regression models	True. For feature $F_{\Re_i}$, $VIE_{F_{\Re_i}}$ to Twitter and Weibo models can be different.	
H3	For user u_i, if u_i belongs to a community C_k, the characters and features extracted from C_k are statistically useful to predict the information adoption for u_i.	Compare baseline models (without community-based features) and community based models	True, for community-based models, CCI +5.47%, Brier Score -0.0447%	True, for community-based models, CCI +34.49%, Brier Score -0.2405
H4	Intra- and extra-community feature values of the same community-based feature are useful to predict the information adoption in social network since they represent internal and external information of the community that the target user belongs to. The contributions of intra- and extra-community values are different.	Compare VIE of the intra and extra-community based features	For all 4 groups of features, intra-community features are more important than extra-community features for information adoption.	

variable that we assumed (via SEM modeling). This finding is supported by both exploratory and confirmatory factor analysis.

For different kinds of features, based on average VIE, $u_i \xrightarrow{rp} u_j$ (user-reply-user) relation is more important for Twitter, while $u_i \xrightarrow{m} u_j$ (user-mention-user) and can be more significant for Weibo. Meanwhile, for our Weibo observations, $u_i \xrightarrow{u} h \xleftarrow{u} u_j$ (user-share-hashtag-user) is more important than it is for Twitter information adoption. By using community information, we extract intra-community and extra-community features. In this study, intra-community features can be more important for both Twitter and Weibo information adoption prediction.

5. CONCLUSION AND FUTURE WORK

In this paper, we explore and compare Twitter and Weibo information adoption models via novel community-based features extracted from heterogeneous social networks. Different kinds of schemes on the graph depict various kinds of relationships between users. Among the investigated user relations, as Table 6 shows, we find that $u_i \xrightarrow{rp} u_j$ is important for Twitter but $u_i \xrightarrow{m} u_j$ is more significant for Weibo, which means that user information adoption behavior on Twitter and Weibo can differ significantly.

We also find local information extracted from the target user's community (intra-community features) to be a significant predictor of information adoption for both Twitter and Weibo. Experimental results show that $u_i \xrightarrow{m} u_j$ (mention relation) is a more useful feature for the Weibo network, which indicates that Weibo user are more likely to be influenced by others who frequently mention each other. The picture that emerges is that the information adoption models for Twitter and Weibo are quite different, indicating that the adoption of new information by Chinese and Western internet users are driven by different processes.

In this study, we also found that Weibo hashtag quality can be lower than that of Twitter. In particular, we found a number of advertisements or spam hashtags in the Weibo dataset that might pollute the experiment dataset. In the future, in order to address this limitation, we intend to use named-entity recognition to extract important entities from the Twitter and Weibo messages for information adoption model construction.

In addition, we aim to develop more sophisticated hierarchical community detection methods to enhance the performance of our information adoption model through the extraction of additional features from the resulting hierarchical community information. Last but not least, assuming that user information adoption models may vary depending on broad information categories we may need to classify hashtags and entities into different categories for comparison following [32].

6. REFERENCES
[1] Eric Baucom, Azade Sanjari, Xiaozhong Liu, and Miao Chen. Mirroring the real world in social media: twitter, geolocation, and sentiment analysis. In *Proceedings of the 2013 international workshop on Mining unstructured big data using natural language processing*, pages 61–68. ACM, 2013.

[2] Tim Berners-Lee. Tim berners-lee: Facebook could fragment web.

[3] Johan Bollen, Huina Mao, and Xiaojun Zeng. Twitter mood predicts the stock market. *Journal of Computational Science*, 2(1):1–8, 2011.

[4] Leo Breiman. Random forests. *Machine learning*, 45(1):5–32, 2001.

[5] Leo Breiman. Manual on setting up, using, and understanding random forests v3. 1. *Statistics Department University of California Berkeley, CA, USA*, 2002.

[6] M Luz Calle and Víctor Urrea. Letter to the editor: Stability of random forest importance measures. *Briefings in bioinformatics*, 12(1):86–89, 2011.

[7] Meeyoung Cha, Hamed Haddadi, Fabricio Benevenuto, and P Krishna Gummadi. Measuring user influence in twitter: The million follower fallacy. *ICWSM*, 10(10-17):30, 2010.

[8] Surajit Chaudhuri, Raghu Ramakrishnan, and Gerhard Weikum. Integrating db and ir technologies: What is the sound of one hand clapping? In *Conference on Innovative Data Systems Research*, pages 1–12, 2005.

[9] David Easley and Jon Kleinberg. *Networks, crowds, and markets: Reasoning about a highly connected world*. Cambridge University Press, 2010.

[10] Qi Gao, Fabian Abel, Geert-Jan Houben, and Yong Yu. A comparative study of users' microblogging behavior on sina weibo and twitter. In *User Modeling, Adaptation, and Personalization*, pages 88–101. Springer, 2012.

[11] Wanqiu Guan, Haoyu Gao, Mingmin Yang, Yuan Li, Haixin Ma, Weining Qian, Zhigang Cao, and Xiaoguang Yang. Analyzing user behavior of the micro-blogging website sina weibo during hot social events. *Physica A: Statistical Mechanics and its Applications*, 395:340–351, 2014.

[12] Bernard J Jansen, Mimi Zhang, Kate Sobel, and Abdur Chowdury. Twitter power: Tweets as electronic word of mouth. *Journal of the American society for information science and technology*, 60(11):2169–2188, 2009.

[13] Haewoon Kwak, Changhyun Lee, Hosung Park, and Sue Moon. What is twitter, a social network or a news media? In *Proceedings of the 19th international conference on World wide web*, pages 591–600. ACM, 2010.

[14] Renaud Lambiotte and Pietro Panzarasa. Communities, knowledge creation, and information diffusion. *Journal of Informetrics*, 3(3):180–190, 2009.

[15] Andrea Lancichinetti and Santo Fortunato. Community detection algorithms: a comparative analysis. *Physical review E*, 80(5):056117, 2009.

[16] Chung-Yi Li and Shou-De Lin. Matching users and items across domains to improve the recommendation quality. In *Proceedings of the 20th ACM SIGKDD international conference on Knowledge discovery and data mining*, pages 801–810. ACM, 2014.

[17] Daifeng Li, Jingwei Zhang, Gordon Guo-zheng Sun, Jie Tang, Ying Ding, and Zhipeng Luo. What is the nature of chinese microblogging: Unveiling the unique features of tencent weibo. *arXiv preprint arXiv:1211.2197*, 2012.

[18] Andy Liaw and Matthew Wiener. Classification and regression by randomforest. *R news*, 2(3):18–22, 2002.

[19] Xiaozhong Liu and Vadim von Brzeski. Computational community interest for ranking. In *Proceedings of the 18th ACM conference on Information and knowledge management*, pages 245–254. ACM, 2009.

[20] Xiaozhong Liu, Yingying Yu, Chun Guo, Yizhou Sun, and Liangcai Gao. Full-text based context-rich heterogeneous network mining approach for citation recommendation. In *ACM/IEEE Joint Conference on Digital Libraries*, 2014.

[21] Keith A Markus. Principles and practice of structural equation modeling by rex b. kline. *Structural Equation Modeling: A Multidisciplinary Journal*, 19(3):509–512, 2012.

[22] Evgeny Morozov. *The net delusion: The dark side of Internet freedom*. PublicAffairs Store, 2012.

[23] Seth A Myers, Chenguang Zhu, and Jure Leskovec. Information diffusion and external influence in networks. In *Proceedings of the 18th ACM SIGKDD international conference on Knowledge discovery and data mining*, pages 33–41. ACM, 2012.

[24] Alexander Pak and Patrick Paroubek. Twitter as a corpus for sentiment analysis and opinion mining. In *The International Conference on Language Resources and Evaluation*, 2010.

[25] Eli Pariser. *The filter bubble: What the Internet is hiding from you*. Penguin UK, 2011.

[26] J Pfeffer, T Zorbach, and KM Carley. Understanding online firestorms: Negative word-of-mouth dynamics in social media networks. *Journal of Marketing Communications*, 20(1-2):117–128, 2014.

[27] Joshua Ritterman, Miles Osborne, and Ewan Klein. Using prediction markets and twitter to predict a swine flu pandemic. In *1st international workshop on mining social media*, 2009.

[28] Daniel M Romero, Brendan Meeder, and Jon Kleinberg. Differences in the mechanics of information diffusion across topics: idioms, political hashtags, and complex contagion on twitter. In *Proceedings of the 20th international conference on World wide web*, pages 695–704. ACM, 2011.

[29] Martin Rosvall and Carl T Bergstrom. Maps of random walks on complex networks reveal community structure. *Proceedings of the National Academy of Sciences*, 105(4):1118–1123, 2008.

[30] Marco Sandri and Paola Zuccolotto. A bias correction algorithm for the gini variable importance measure in classification trees. *Journal of Computational and Graphical Statistics*, 17(3), 2008.

[31] Xin Shuai, Xiaozhong Liu, and Johan Bollen. Improving news ranking by community tweets. In *Proceedings of the 21st international conference companion on World Wide Web*, pages 1227–1232. ACM, 2012.

[32] Xin Shuai, Xiaozhong Liu, Tian Xia, Yuqing Wu, and Chun Guo. Comparing the pulses of categorical hot events in twitter and weibo. In *ACM Hypertext*, 2014.

[33] Lei Tang and Huan Liu. Community detection and mining in social media. *Synthesis Lectures on Data Mining and Knowledge Discovery*, 2(1):1–137, 2010.

[34] Zeynep Tufekci. Engineering the public: Big data, surveillance and computational politics. *First Monday*, 19(7), 2014.

[35] Sherry Turkle. *Alone together: Why we expect more from technology and less from each other*. Basic Books, 2012.

[36] Yu Wang, Gao Cong, Guojie Song, and Kunqing Xie. Community-based greedy algorithm for mining top-k influential nodes in mobile social networks. In *Proceedings of the 16th ACM SIGKDD international conference on Knowledge discovery and data mining*, pages 1039–1048. ACM, 2010.

[37] Jacob Weisberg. Bubble trouble: Is web personalization turning us into solipsistic twits. *Slate. com*, pages 10–06, 2011.

[38] Lilian Weng, Filippo Menczer, and Yong-Yeol Ahn. Virality prediction and community structure in social networks. *Scientific reports*, 3:2522, 2013.

[39] Lilian Weng, Filippo Menczer, and Yong-Yeol Ahn. Predicting successful memes using network and community structure. In *The 8th International AAAI Conference on Weblogs and Social Media (ICWSM'14)*. AAAI, 2014.

[40] Wikipedia. List of websites blocked in china, 2014. [Online; accessed 2014-02-07].

[41] Lei Yang, Tao Sun, Ming Zhang, and Qiaozhu Mei. We know what@ you# tag: does the dual role affect hashtag adoption? In *Proceedings of the 21st international conference on World Wide Web*, pages 261–270. ACM, 2012.

[42] Reza Zafarani and Huan Liu. Connecting users across social media sites: a behavioral-modeling approach. In *Proceedings of the 19th ACM SIGKDD international conference on Knowledge discovery and data mining*, pages 41–49. ACM, 2013.

[43] Reza Zafarani and Huan Liu. Finding friends on a new site using minimum information. In *International Conference on Data Mining*. SIAM, 2014.

[44] Fareed Zakaria. *The post-American world: release 2.0*. WW Norton & Company, 2011.

[45] Bin Zhao, Zhao Zhang, Yanhui Gu, Xueqing Gong, Weining Qian, and Aoying Zhou. Discovering collective viewpoints on micro-blogging events based on community and temporal aspects. In *Advanced Data Mining and Applications*, pages 270–284. Springer, 2011.

Assessing Review Recommendation Techniques under a Ranking Perspective

Luciana B. Maroun, Mirella M. Moro, Jussara M. Almeida, Ana Paula C. Silva
Universidade Federal de Minas Gerais, Belo Horizonte, Brazil
{lubm,mirella,jussara,ana.coutosilva}@dcc.ufmg.br

ABSTRACT

Reading online reviews before a purchase is a customary action nowadays. Nevertheless, the increasing volume of reviews works as a barrier to their effectiveness so that many approaches try to predict reviews' quality, which is *not* standardized to all users due to different backgrounds and preferences. Thus, recommending reviews in a *personalized* fashion is probably more accurate. Here, we analyze methods for recommending reviews that have not been compared against each other yet. Our experiments consider parameter tuning and comparison through statistical tests. Such study allows to understand the state-of-the-art and to evidence potential improvement directions. Our results show that assessing under a ranking perspective, model simplicity and observed features are important traits for this problem, being Support Vector Regression the best solution.

Keywords

Review Helpfulness, Top-n Recommendation Task, Review Recommendation, Ranking

1. INTRODUCTION

Online reviews platforms, such as Yelp[1], Amazon[2], TripAdvisor[3] and Ciao UK[4], play an important role on users' buying experience. A study conducted in the United States in 2014 pointed out that 88% of consumers have read online reviews before a purchase (vs. 85% in 2013) and 39% read them regularly (vs. 32% in 2013) [3]. Besides, 72% of interviewees said that positive reviews increase their trust in a local business, and 88% trust in online reviews as much as personal recommendations. The impact on sales was also measured quantitatively: increasing half star on Yelp raises businesses' sells by 19 percentage points [4].

Although consumers depend upon reviews to make decisions, searching for suitable ones is not easy. The great adherence of users submitting reviews derive an intractable amount of information with high variability in style and quality. Indeed, Yelp has more than 90 million reviews[5]; and TripAdvisor, more than 290 million with an average of 55 reviews per business[6], both by the end of the third quarter of 2015. On the other hand, a survey indicates that 67% users read up to 6 reviews, 85% read up to 10, 93% read up to 20 and only 7% read more than 20 [3]. Thus, whereas users are not willing to read many reviews, a lot of them are being produced such that extracting relevant information from this extensive volume of data becomes imperative.

To solve this problem, review-enabled applications allow users to assess the quality of reviews through a positive or negative vote or in a range (e.g., from 0 to 5). Still, there are many reviews without evaluation and more being produced every day. In Amazon, for instance, only 10% of reviews have at least 10 helpfulness evaluations[7]. Hence, having all of them evaluated by a representative amount of users is practically impossible. Also, reviews with many positive votes are often ranked on top, in a rich-get-richer effect, so that new reviews are hardly considered useful [29].

Several approaches try to overcome the sparseness and the rich-get-richer effect in a non-personalized fashion [20, 24, 27, 41]. They predict a global helpfulness score by considering aspects such as author's reputation and length, part-of-speech tagging and sentiment statistics from the review text. Nonetheless, users have different backgrounds and preferences. Hence, the helpfulness of a review is unlikely to be equally perceived by all readers. Despite the efforts to design personalized recommendations in other domains (e.g., product recommendation [5, 18, 26]), only recent works [29, 35] consider *personalized* solutions for review recommendation.

Despite a couple of techniques for review recommendation exist, their experimental evaluations have not considered yet other important baselines nor the best configuration of each under a unified statistical experimental project. Therefore, we compare approaches for review recommendation, both generic and specialized ones, under five paradigms: (*i*) mean-based predictors; (*ii*) regressors; (*iii*) learning to rank methods; (*iv*) general-purpose recommender systems; and (*v*) review recommender systems.

---

[1]YELP: www.yelp.com

[2]Amazon: www.amazon.com

[3]TripAdvisor: www.tripadvisor.com

[4]Ciao UK www.ciao.co.uk

HT '16, July 10-13, 2016, Halifax, NS, Canada

© 2016 ACM. ISBN 978-1-4503-4247-6/16/07. . . $15.00

DOI: http://dx.doi.org/10.1145/2914586.2914598

---

[5]Yelp – About Us: http://www.yelp.com/about

[6]TripAdvisor – Fact Sheet: http://www.tripadvisor.com/PressCenter-c4-Fact_Sheet.html

[7]A Statistical Analysis of 1.2 Million Amazon Reviews: http://minimaxir.com/2014/06/reviewing-reviews

Our experiments differ from others in four ways. First, we are the first to compare specialized solutions for review recommendation and to use personalized features for regressors. BETF [29] and CAP [35] (specialized approaches) were not compared against each other in their original publications. Also, Linear Regression [30] and Support Vector Regression (SVR) [34] were considered for predicting review helpfulness [29, 35, 37], but using *only* non-personalized features (i.e., information that is the same for all users). Thus, baseline approaches were not considered in their full potential.

Second, our evaluation considers parameter configurations for each algorithm. Current evaluation of specialized review recommenders have not covered several configurations: only sensitivity analysis was performed on the number of latent dimensions [29] or a cross-validation was used for setting parameters [35]. Still, the versions of the baseline algorithms are not clear in existing evaluations. Also, sophisticated strategies are yet to be considered, such as learning to rank algorithms and state-of-the-art recommenders.

Third, our experimental evaluation considers multiple runs; then, our results provide confidence intervals of the measured performance (with 95% of confidence). Specialized approaches are non-deterministic and, yet, repetition of executions and variability were not reported on the experiments previously conducted with them [29, 35].

Finally, we consider a ranking metric for performance evaluation, since the ultimate goal is to display reviews sorted decreasingly by helpfulness. Recommendation of reviews is intrinsically a top-N recommendation task [13], whose goal is to compose a selection of items, preferentially ranked, and should be evaluated as such. Evaluating recommender systems through ranking metrics is not a new proposal [5, 13, 18], whereas regression metrics are still common [19, 29, 35]. However, such metrics aim at *exact* prediction of item ratings, then becoming too restrictive for recommender systems, for which a good *ordering* of items is typically enough. In spite of that, no review recommender was previously evaluated for ranking. Overall, our contributions are:

- Overview of the main techniques for review recommendation grouped into five classes;
- Comparison of personalized review recommender systems in a unified statistical experimental design;
- Modeling and evaluation of review recommendation task from a ranking perspective;
- Implementation (with public available source code) of specialized and general-purpose solutions for review recommendation task.

The remainder of the paper is organized as follows. Section 2 explains concepts and states our target problem. Section 3 overviews the techniques considered. Section 4 presents the unified experimental design. Section 5 presents and discusses our results. Finally, Section 6 concludes this work.

2. CONCEPTS AND PROBLEM DEFINITION

We first introduce basic concepts, both for generic and review recommendation, and then state the problem.

2.1 Recommender Systems Basics

A recommender system is traditionally divided into two types: content-based and collaborative filtering [23]. The first suggests items to a user based on the kind of items he

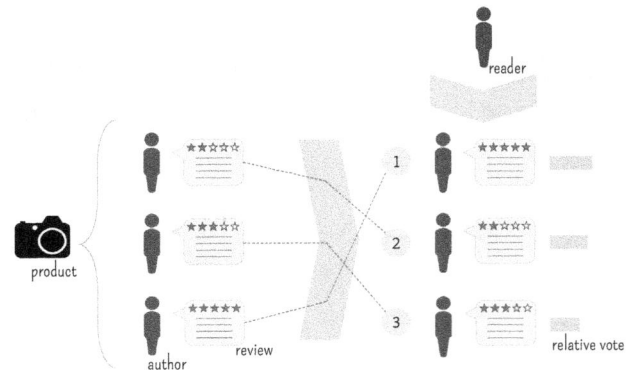

Figure 1: Review Recommender System – given a reader and a product (e.g., a camera) with reviews written by authors, the system retrieves a personalized ranking of reviews.

liked in the past, represented by observed features. The second consists of methods that suggest items liked by similar users or similar items of the ones previously liked. When both item profiles and collaborative information of similar users or items are considered, then a *hybrid* recommender system is composed [32].

Recommender systems techniques typically rely on existing labeled data, the *training set*, which contains historical examples of truth labels for the level of interest of users to items. Using this set and assuming that past patterns are repeated in the future, a *predictor* is built as a function that, given an input user, returns a set of suggested items. Predictors' components (e.g., coefficients, latent factors) are typically adjusted to optimize prediction in the training set. Then, unseen data is used for assessing the method, the *test set*. Sometimes, a portion of the training set is left out for parameter tuning, the *validation set*.

Cold-starts represent a challenging for recommender systems [2, 19]. A *cold-start* refers to a user or item whose past transactions are scarce or not available while learning the predictor, whereas the opposite is called *warm-start*. Under a cold-start circumstance, finding similar items or users in collaborative filtering and profile for user tastes in content-based is not possible, thus such systems fail to predict.

Part of the rating value is commonly not explained by interaction but by user and item biases. An entity's bias represents its tendency of giving or receiving high or low ratings, computed by the average deviation of its ratings from the mean of ratings [19]. Any method can add bias awareness by fitting a bias baseline predictor and removing the portion of the ratings explained solely by bias.

2.2 The Review Recommendation Problem

In a website of reviews, a user may perform different roles. As an *author*, the user writes a *review* about a *product* (we use product as naming convention, but it may be any object in a review platform). As a *reader*, the user simply reads through existing reviews of a product. Then, as a *voter*, the user evaluates the helpfulness of existing reviews. Specifically, a *review* is composed by a *text* (describing features about the product, e.g., experience of usage, pros and cons and any other comment the author considers relevant), and a *rating* (giving a grade to how much the author liked the product, e.g., 0 to 5 stars). Rating differs from *vote*, the grade given by a voter to a review.

Ideally, a review recommender system provides a ranking of reviews in descending order of helpfulness for a given user and product (Figure 1). Thereafter, whenever a reader accesses a product, the most helpful reviews are on top, eliminating the burden to manually look for suitable ones.

Formally, this scenario considers a set of products $\mathcal{P} = \{p_1, p_2, ..., p_i\}$, a set of users $\mathcal{U} = \{u_1, u_2, ..., u_j\}$, a set of reviews $\mathcal{R} = \{r_1, r_2, ..., r_k\}$, and a set of helpfulness votes $\mathcal{H} = \{h_1, h_2, ..., h_l\}$. We define two functions to state relationships between elements: $\pi_r : \mathcal{R} \mapsto \mathcal{P} \times \mathcal{U}$ such that $\pi_r(r) = (p, a)$ states that r was written by author a about product p; and $\pi_h : h \in \mathcal{H} \mapsto \mathcal{R} \times \mathcal{U}$ such that $\pi_h(h) = (r, v)$ defines that h was given by voter v to review r. Note that both author a and voter v belong to set $\mathcal{U}$.

The goal of a recommender system is to compose an utility function [1], restricted here for the specific case of review recommendation. Accordingly, the purpose of a *review recommender system* is to derive an utility function $\tau : \mathcal{U} \times \mathcal{R} \to \mathbb{R}$ such that, given an input (u, r), it measures the *relative helpfulness* of review r for a user u. Fitting τ may require a training set $\{\mathcal{P}_0, \mathcal{U}_0, \mathcal{R}_0, \mathcal{H}_0\} : \mathcal{P}^0 \in \mathcal{P}, \mathcal{U}^0 \in \mathcal{U}, \mathcal{R}^0 \in \mathcal{R}, \mathcal{H}^0 \in \mathcal{H}$.

After the utility function is built, given a product p and a reader u, we may obtain a set of reviews associated to product p, defined as $\mathcal{R}_p = \{r \in R \mid \exists a \in \mathcal{U} : \pi_r(r) = (p, a)\}$, and derive a ranking of reviews $r \in \mathcal{R}_p$ in decreasing order of $\tau(u, r)$. The utility function is optimal when rankings are generated in decreasing order of the ground-truth of helpfulness given by the users to reviews in $\mathcal{R}_p$.

3. OVERVIEW OF TECHNIQUES

Existing works on predicting review global helpfulness state the problem as a classification [20, 24] or a regression [40] task, or both [22, 27]. These approaches consider that all users have a common perception of helpfulness and are limited to discovering helpfulness for an average person. Only a few works [29, 35] deal with the problem in a personalized fashion, considering users' idiosyncrasy.

We present a comparison of algorithms that predict review helpfulness in a personalized fashion of different paradigms. We describe some of them using naming conventions from the original scenario, which Table 1 maps to the corresponding name in review recommendation. The paradigms considered are the following:

- *Mean-Based Predictors* (MBP) compute mean statistics from the training set and use them for prediction;
- *Regressors* (REG) predict a real value for each instance, represented by a set of features;
- *Learning to Rank Predictors* (LTR) determine a ranking of documents for a query given observed features;
- *General-Purpose Recommender Systems* (GRS) predict a ranking of items by utility for each user;
- *Review Recommender Systems* (RRS) obtain a ranking of reviews by helpfulness for a reader-product pair.

Such classes are defined with increasing specialization, e.g., regressors may be applied in place of general-purpose review recommender systems, but not the other way around.

3.1 Mean-Based Predictors

Mean-Based Predictors are basic: they compute mean values in the training set and use them as predictions. When the mean is not available (e.g., the training set does not have

Table 1: Mapping of naming conventions between the original definition of LTR and GRS classes (generic) and applied to review recommendation scenario (specific).

Class	Generic	Specific
LTR	document	review
	query	reader-product pair
	relevance	helpfulness vote
GRS	item	review
	user	reader
	rating	helpfulness vote

the votes of an author when using author's mean), it uses the overall mean. The techniques in this class are as follows.

Overall Mean Vote (OM) predicts every helpfulness vote as the mean value of all votes in the training set.

Author's Mean Vote (AM), for each author, computes the mean of votes associated to all reviews written by that author in the training set. Then, any vote associated to a review is predicted as the mean of review's author.

Voter's Mean Vote (VM), for each voter, computes the mean of all votes given by that voter in the training set. Any vote given by a voter is predicted as the voter's mean.

3.2 Regressors

Regressors use a set of features to predict an approximation of the review's true helpfulness for a given user. Solutions of this type consider the ordinal nature of the output. When used for ranking, REG is called *pointwise* due to learning scores for a query-document pair in isolation [21].

Using regressor for review recommendation requires to apply a transformation to the input as $f_{REG} : \mathcal{U} \times \mathcal{R} \mapsto \mathbb{R}^n$, representing a mapping to a vector of n features. The utility function τ is derived with image close to the range of votes as algorithms in this class make absolute predictions. We consider three representatives of this class.

Linear Regression (LR) learns a linear model to compute a vote given features related to a reader and a review. The predicted vote is a linear combination of these feature values added to a constant, the intercept. The coefficients are learned minimizing a loss function in the training set.

Support Vector Machine Regression (SVR) corresponds to the regressor version of Support Vector Machine classifier (SVM) [36]. A predictor is built by minimizing both model complexity (represented by the norm of the vector of coefficients) and absolute errors of data points outside a margin of tolerance ϵ. As a consequence, the model focuses on minimizing large errors only. The trade-off between model complexity and intolerable errors is determined by parameter C, the penalty factor. The higher the value of C, the more complex is the learned function.

Gradient Boosting Regression Trees (GBRT) is an algorithm with high performance for ranking [25], also known as Multiple Additive Regression Trees (MART) [14]. GBRT combines functions (i.e., an ensemble) whose weight sum of returned values provides the final prediction. The model is built stage-wise by extending the current function through adding a new decision tree using as ground-truth the pseudo-residuals, which are the negative of the loss function's derivative evaluated at each instance. A model update simulates a gradient descent step, which changes the current function towards the negative of the gradient in order to reduce the error. In this case, an approximation of the gradient is computed through fitting a decision tree on pseudo-residuals.

3.3 Learning to Rank Predictors

Learning to Rank approaches build a model for predicting rankings of documents given a query. Using features of a query-document pair, the model outputs a relevance of the document for the query. We evaluate two methods: SVMRank [11] and LambdaMART [8]. They build predictive models using different strategies – pairwise and listwise, respectively – that represent a fair coverage of existing approaches. A *pairwise* approach optimizes a loss defined over pairs of documents, typically as a classification problem for one being above or below the other. In turn, a *listwise* method tries to directly optimize a ranking loss function computed on all queries' rankings.

A LTR predictor employs an input transformation $f_{LTR} : \mathcal{U} \times \mathcal{R} \mapsto \mathcal{Q} \times \mathbb{R}^n$, where $\mathcal{Q}$ is a set of query identifiers and n is the number of features. The set $\mathcal{Q}$ is only used during the training phase for grouping reviews into rankings. The utility function τ provides outputs not necessarily in the same range of votes, since this class aims at position correctness, not absolute predictions.

RankSVM (RSVM) is a learning to rank version of SVM such that the number of inversions between documents in the same query is minimized. As it is a pairwise technique, the problem becomes a classification in which SVM builds a hyperplane dividing the two classes with maximal margin.

LambdaMART is a combination of GBRT and LambdaRank [8] and has a central role in the winner technique of Yahoo! Learning to Rank Challenge [9, 10]. LMART empirically optimizes an arbitrary ranking function, e.g., the normalized Discounted Cumulative Gain at position p ($nDCG@p$), which distinguishes this technique as listwise [6]. Like LambdaRank, a document relevance is updated based on the presence of an inversion and proportionally to the score gain after swapping documents. Using these updates, an ensemble is built in a stage-wise fashion, as GBRT.

3.4 General-Purpose Recommender Systems

General-Purpose Recommender Systems learn a model for suggesting items, preferentially in a personalized fashion. Fitting such model often requires a set of previous ratings given by users to items, composing a *user-item matrix* of ratings with missing values. We chose two representatives: Matrix Factorization [19], a collaborative filtering technique, and RLFM [2], a hybrid method.

A GRS method requires an identity transformation of input as $f_{GRS} : \mathcal{U} \times \mathcal{R} \mapsto \mathcal{U} \times \mathcal{R}$. The utility function t is obtained trying to minimize ordering error of item's ranking. Although we define as a top-N recommender task, the methods described here predict an exact rating.

Matrix Factorization (MF) models user and items in a K-dimensional space of latent factors. The inner product of user and item vectors of latent factors estimates the rating given by a user to an item. The meanings of learned vectors' dimensions are unknown, but they represent properties of items and users that explain existing ratings. They might correspond, for instance, to category, style, and even depth of characters [19]. MF may easily account for biases by adding a bias variable for each entity and optimizing them jointly with the latent factors [32].

Regression-Based Latent Factor Model (RLFM) is a hybrid technique that combines both the benefits of accuracy from collaborative filtering and the ability of recommending for cold-starts from content-based methods [2].

Table 2: Definition of variables used by RLFM.

K	Number of dimensions of all latent vectors.
α_i	Latent variable for user i with a gaussian distribution centered on the linear regression of user features.
β_j	Latent variable for item j with a gaussian distribution centered on the linear regression of item features.
$\mathbf{u}_i$	Latent vector $K \times 1$ for user i with a gaussian distribution centered on a vector of K linear regressions of user features.
$\mathbf{v}_j$	Latent vector $K \times 1$ for item j with a gaussian distribution centered on a vector of K linear regressions of item features.
$\mathbf{x}_{ij}$	Vector with dyadic features, i.e., related to user-item pair.
$\mathbf{b}$	Linear regression coefficients for $\mathbf{x}_{ij}$.

The rating given by user i to item j is predicted as follows:

$$\hat{H}_{ij} = \mathbf{x}_{ij}^T \mathbf{b} + \alpha_i + \beta_j + \mathbf{u}_i^T \mathbf{v}_j,$$

where the variables are detailed in Table 2. Since RLFM is not specialized for review recommendation, author information is not considered separately, but as item features. Regression term $\mathbf{x}_{ij}^T \mathbf{b}$ builds the base prediction value. Variables α_i and β_j are a representation of user and item biases, respectively, tied with regression on features. The inner product $\mathbf{u}_i^T \mathbf{v}_j$ represents interaction strength of user and item. Whenever a cold-start entity is encountered, the regression is used in place of the corresponding latent variable.

Latent variables and parameters are learned through a Monte Carlo Expectation Maximization (MCEM) method [7], which comprises a series of iterations refining the maximization of the log-likelihood. An iteration is divided in two phases: E-step computes the expectation of the log-likelihood on posterior distribution of latent factors, and M-step finds the parameter values that maximize the expectation. In E-step, the expectation is not in closed form due to latent vectors inner product term $\mathbf{u}_i^T \mathbf{v}_j$, with an unknown distribution. Gibbs Sampler, a Monte Carlo method, is applied to overcome that [30]. Then, the empiric mean of latent factors are an approximation for the expectation. In M-step, parameters are adjusted through regression on empirical means, using any fitting procedure.

3.5 Review Recommender Systems

Recent works have explored the hypothesis that users do not perceive helpfulness in the same way by incorporating relevant personalized information for review recommendation. We compare two representatives: BETF [29] and CAP [35]. No previous work, to the best of our knowledge, compares representatives of this class against each other.

A Review Recommender System applies the identity transformation: $t_{RRS} : \mathcal{U} \times \mathcal{R} \mapsto \mathcal{U} \times \mathcal{R}$. The utility function t returns a value indicating a relative helpfulness and aiming at the lowest error for rankings of reviews. Similarly to GRS, techniques considered in this class compute absolute predictions, but they could calculate only a relative score.

UnBiased Extended Tensor Factorization (BETF) is derived from MF with the extensions: (*i*) review dimension is replaced by product and author, becoming a Tensor Factorization; (*ii*) the sum of squared differences of each rating and the dot product of author and product latent factors is added to the loss; (*iii*) biases are added for all entities [29]. The prediction for user i, author k and product l is:

$$\hat{H}_{ikl} = g(\mu + q_{\bar{u}_i} + q_{\bar{r}_{kl}} + \mathbf{s} \times_u \mathbf{u}_i \times_v \mathbf{v}_k \times_p \mathbf{p}_l),$$

Table 3: Definition of variables used by BETF.

K	Number of dimensions of all latent vectors.
μ	Overall mean of helpfulness in the training set.
$\mathbf{s}$	Central tensor $K \times K \times K$ with relevance of dimensions.
$\mathbf{u}_i$	Latent vector $K \times 1$ for user i with a gaussian distribution centered on a zero-vector.
$\mathbf{a}_k$	Latent vector $K \times 1$ for author k with a gaussian distribution centered on a zero-vector.
$\mathbf{p}_l$	Latent vector $K \times 1$ for product l with a gaussian distribution centered on a zero-vector.
q_{u_i}	Bias of user i as his average deviation from the mean.
$q_{r_{kl}}$	Bias of review r_{kl}, such that $\pi_r(r_{kl}) = (p_l, a_k)$, as its average deviation from the sum of the mean and voter bias.
g	Logistic or sigmoid function, computed as $g(x) = \frac{1}{1+e^{-x}}$.

Table 4: Definition of variables used by CAP.

K	Number of dimensions of all latent vectors.
α_i	Latent variable for user i with a gaussian distribution centered on the linear regression of voter features.
β_j	Latent variable for review j with a gaussian distribution centered on the linear regression of review features.
ξ_k	Latent variable for user k with a gaussian distribution centered on the linear regression of author features.
$\mathbf{u}_i$	Latent vector $K \times 1$ for user i with a gaussian distribution centered on K linear regressions of voter features.
$\mathbf{v}_j$	Latent vector $K \times 1$ for review j with a gaussian distribution centered on K linear regressions of review features.
δ_1	Indicator function that, given input (i,k), is 1 if user i is similar (using cosine of ratings) to user k above the average of i with all the other users, and 0 otherwise.
δ_2	Indicator function that, given input (i,k), is 1 if user i trusts user k in trust network, and 0 otherwise.
γ_i^k	Latent variable for voter i and author k with a gaussian distribution centered on the sigmoid function of the linear regression of author-voter similarity features.
λ_i^k	Latent variable for voter i and author k with a gaussian distribution centered on the sigmoid function of the linear regression of author-voter connection features.

where the variables are explained in Table 3. Bias variables are calculated in a preprocessing step; they are related to voter and review in vote values, and to author and product in rating values (not used in prediction, only in fitting). Moreover, tensor factorization uses a Tucker model by incorporating a central tensor [33]. Latent variables are fitted using stochastic gradient descent for minimizing the error [29], composed of: (*i*) sum of squared errors on vote prediction; (*ii*) sum of squared errors on rating prediction; and (*iii*) regularization of latent factors and central tensor.

Context-Aware Review Helpfulness Rating Prediction (CAP) extends RLFM to review recommendation context [35]. The vote of user i to review j is predicted as:

$$\hat{H}_{ij} = \mathbf{u}_i^T \mathbf{v}_j + \alpha_i + \beta_j + \xi_k + \delta_1(i,k)\gamma_i^k + \delta_2(i,k)\lambda_i^k,$$

whose variables are defined in Table 4. CAP differs from RLFM in four ways: (*i*) author and review variables are considered separately in β_j and ξ_k; (*ii*) author features are not used for computing $\mathbf{v}_j$ mean; (*iii*) dyadic features x_{ij} are split into two linear regressions with a logistic transformation; (*iv*) dyadic regressions are wrapped into latent variables γ_i^k and λ_i^k and only added under conditions through indicator variables.

MCEM is employed to learn latent variables and parameters as in RLFM. However, the procedure conducted by CAP differs from RLFM since parameters are adjusted in M-step using specific regression fitting procedures. Ordinary Least Squares (OLS) [30] is used for regression parameters related to latent variables α_i, β_j, ξ_k, $\mathbf{u}_i$ and $\mathbf{v}_j$. Newton-Raphson (NR) [39] is applied for adjusting γ_i^k and λ_i^k parameters as they apply a sigmoid transformation to the regression.

4. UNIFIED EXPERIMENTAL DESIGN

We propose a unified evaluation design of review recommendation techniques that allows evaluating any kind of method using parameter tuning, ranking or regression metric and different scenarios. Previous experiments did not use all these resources nor reported a reproducible design.

4.1 Methodology

We assess the variability of each method through execution in five different splits of the dataset with sliding windows over votes disposed chronologically. A window size is fixed with 60% of votes, shifting 10% of votes each time. For each window, the first 40% represent the training set, the next 10% the validation set, and the last 50% the test

set. We use a larger test than training set because the former is further reduced by eliminating votes from voter-product pairs grouping less than 5 votes. This filtering procedure is required for meaningful evaluation using a ranking metric. For non-deterministic techniques (MF, RLFM, BETF and CAP) the performance is computed as the average of three runs for the same split. Under this setting, we assess both contextual and stochastic variability through different splits and repetitions, respectively.

We use a chronological opposed to a random split of the data (as many prior studies [24, 29, 41]) to respect temporal constraints when building the prediction model. Specifically, by doing a chronological split, we avoid using future information to build the predictor (e.g.: feature values computed over data observed after the prediction time) [2].

For every algorithm configuration, we compute the confidence interval (CI) with 95% of confidence relative to the results on different training-test splits. We compare any two solutions using a paired t-test [16]. To apply this test, we assume performance results are normally distributed.

4.2 Evaluation Metrics

The goal of a review recommender is to generate a total ordering of reviews for each reader-product pair. However, the dataset does not contain all reviews of a product with helpfulness votes from all users. Under this restriction, we only evaluate ordering of reviews with available votes for each reader-product pair. This is a subset of the intended ranking, but whose relative positioning shall be good.

In our evaluation, we consider two metrics: Root Mean Squared Error (RMSE) and normalized Discounted Cumulative Gain at position p (nDCG@p), defined as follows:

$$RMSE(V) = \sqrt{\frac{1}{|V|} \sum_{v \in V} (q_v - t_v)^2},$$

$$DCG@p(R_{u,p}) = \sum_{i=1}^{p} \frac{2^{t_{r_i}} - 1}{log_2(i+1)},$$

$$nDCG@p(R_{u,p}) = \frac{DCG@p(R_{u,p})}{DCG@p(R_{u,p}^*)},$$

where, V is a set of votes, v is a vote, q_v is the predicted value for vote v, t_v is the true value of vote v, $R_{u,p}$ is a ranking of reviews for user u and product p, t_{r_i} is the true vote given by user u to the review ranked at position i in $R_{u,p}$, and $R_{u,p}^*$ is the ranking of reviews in $R_{u,p}$ sorted by decreasing true votes t_{r_i}, $\forall r_i \in R_{u,p}$, the best ranking possible. For a set of rankings, nDCG@p is reported as their average.

RMSE is used in all previous evaluations of specialized methods [29, 35] and is a standard metric for recommender systems [18]. However, the purpose of most recommendation tasks is to compose a ranking of items to a user; so, a ranking metric is more adequate and we focus on nDCG@p [5].

4.3 Dataset

We use a publicly available dataset from Ciao UK[8], a platform that displays the helpfulness given by each voter (not available in Amazon, TripAdvisor nor Yelp). No other platform or dataset with such information was found. The crawling used a breadth-first search from active users [35].

The dataset was filtered as follows: we disregard instances with empty fields, invalid value/format and texts with more than 40% of words outside WordNet [28]; and we keep only votes from reader-product pairs with at least ten members (ranking metrics require rankings with reasonable sizes). Table 5 contains statistics of the final dataset.

Table 5: Statistics of the filtered dataset.

# Reviews	58,826
# Users	8,511
# Author	8,065
# Voters	1,737
# Authors	1,291
# Products	1,908
# Helpfulness Votes	457,679
Mean # Votes / Review	8.05
Reviews' Time Span	05.31.00 - 09.25.11

Figure 2a shows that a lot of authors have a few reviews, and a few authors have a lot of reviews; the same occurs for votes. The number of votes given by voters (Figure 2b) and the number of votes for a review (Figure 2c) also follow this trend. Then, recommender systems are relevant as, otherwise, the vast amount of unpopular reviews in Figure 2c would not be easily discovered [38]. On the other hand, recommending for such distinct users is a challenge.

Figure 2d contains the CCDF of vote Coefficient of Variation (CV) [16] distribution grouping by author, review and author-reader. We note that, while reviews quite reduce the CV, author-reader shrinks even more, thus demonstrating the potential of explaining votes in a personalized way.

Figure 3 presents the distribution of users' evaluation as ratings and votes. Both are very concentrated, with clear peaks around high ratings/votes and the latter even more severe. A reason for such unbalance may be that users are more compelled to evaluate when they like a product or a review. In such scenario, any predictor outputting values close to 4 has a reasonably low regression error, another motivation for prioritizing ranking metrics. The most frequent vote is 4, opposed of 5 for ratings, suggesting that users easily consider reviews as helpful, but hardly as perfect.

---

[8]www.jiliang.xyz/Ciao.rar

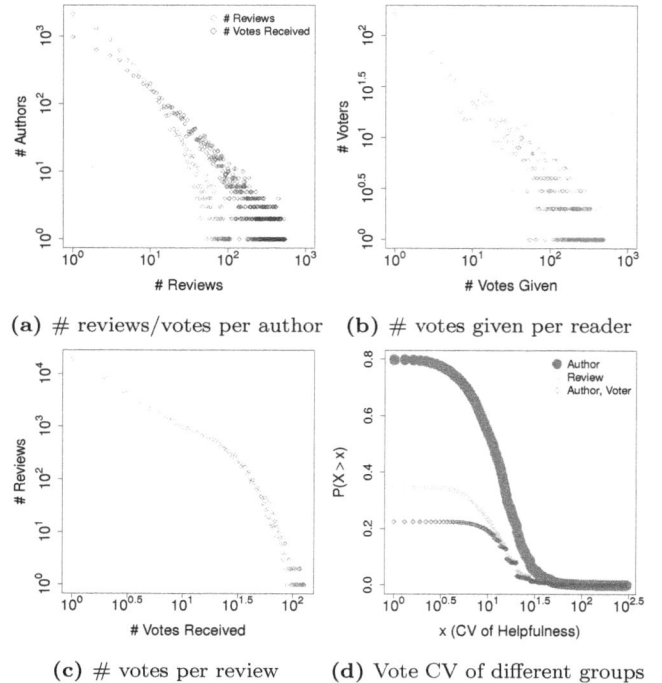

(a) # reviews/votes per author (b) # votes given per reader

(c) # votes per review (d) Vote CV of different groups

Figure 2: Distributions describing the dataset.

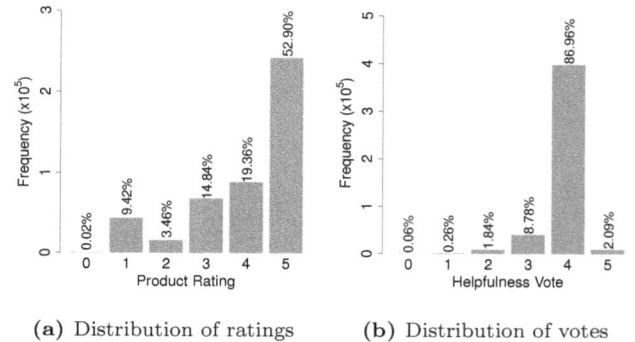

(a) Distribution of ratings (b) Distribution of votes

Figure 3: Distributions of evaluation values.

Although we use only one dataset, it is representative due to resembling the dynamics of other platforms. For instance, an analysis of a dataset from Epinions[9] includes a heavy tail distribution of users/reviews participation and popularity, and a highly unbalanced distribution of helpfulness [29].

As argued above, chronologically dividing the dataset into training and test sets is important. However, this dataset does not contain votes' timestamps to obtain a chronological split. Hence, we use the time the review was created as an approximation. Consequently, in a chronological split, votes from the same review lie in the same set – training or test – configuring all reviews as cold-starts, and severely penalizing some approaches as further discussed in Section 5.1.

4.4 Features

Some techniques (all but MBP methods, MF and BETF) use features for prediction. We used the set of features defined for CAP [35], the most recent specialized technique.

---

[9]The link for such dataset is no longer available.

Table 6: List of features with a brief description. Each feature is derived from an entity or relationship, represented in fragment headers.

Feature	Description
	REVIEW
num_tokens	Number of tokens.
num_sents	Number of sentences.
uni_ratio	Unique words ratio.
avg_sent	Average sentence length.
cap_sent	Number of capitalized sentences.
noun_ratio	Ratio of tokens classified as nouns.
adj_ratio	Ratio of tokens classified as adjectives.
comp_ratio	Ratio of tokens classified as comparatives.
verb_ratio	Ratio of tokens classified as verbs.
adv_ratio	Ratio of tokens classified as adverbs.
fw_ratio	Ratio of tokens classified as foreign words.
sym_ratio	Ratio of tokens classified as symbols.
num_ratio	Ratio of tokens classified as numbers.
punct_ratio	Ratio of tokens classified as punctuation.
kl	KL divergence of text from all texts of product.
pos_ratio	Ratio of sentences tagged as positive.
neg_ratio	Ratio of sentences tagged as negative.
	AUTHOR
num_reviews	Number of reviews written by the author.
avg_rating	Average rating given by the author.
num_trustors	Number of users who trust in the author.
num_trustees	Number of users trusted by the author.
pagerank	Author's pagerank score in trust network.
	READER
num_trustors	Number of users who trust in the voter.
num_trustees	Number of users trusted by the voter.
pagerank	Pagerank score of the voter in trust network.
avg_rat	Average rating given by the voter.
avg_rat_soc	Average rating of the social network.
avg_rat_sim	Average rating of similar users.
avg_help	Average vote given by the voter.
avg_help_tru	Average vote given by trust network.
avg_help_sim	Average vote given by similar users.
	AUTHOR-READER SIMILARITY
comm_rated	Number of products rated in common.
jacc_rated	Jackdaw coefficient of ratings.
cos_ratings	Cosine similarity of ratings.
pear_ratings	Pearson correlation of ratings.
diff_avg_rat	Difference of author and voter average ratings.
diff_max_rat	Difference of author and voter maximum ratings.
diff_min_rat	Difference of author and voter minimum ratings.
	AUTHOR-READER CONNECTION
jacc_trustors	Jaccard coefficient of trustors of users.
jacc_trustees	Jaccard coefficient of trustees of users.
adam_trustees	Adamic-Adar score of common trustors.
adam_trustees	Adamic-Adar score of common trustees.
katz	Katz index of paths from voter to author.

Table 6 briefly describes all features. Review features are derived from review text, containing length-based, part-of-speech tagging and sentiment statistics. Author features capture their reputation and past behavior. These first two sets contain non-personalized information (i.e., they are the same for all readers) and are from an earlier work [24]. Reader features include historical data of the target user of recommendation. Author-reader similarity features capture the similarity level of author and reader. Author-reader connection features measure the connection strength between author and reader, in a social recommendation fashion [26].

5. EXPERIMENTAL EVALUATION

In this section, we present the results from the unified statistical design of experiments. The implementation of methods required several considerations, exposed first.

5.1 Implementation Remarks

The implementation of most approaches considers available sources: LR, SVR, RFR and GBRT use Scikit-learn for Python [31]; RSVM uses SVMRank built upon SVM-Light[10] [17]; LMART employs RankLib[11]; RLFM has an available source code[12]. The other algorithms – MF, BETF and CAP – were implemented from scratch and are publicly available[13]. Implementation specifics are presented next.

Preprocessing. All parameter values are scaled within $[0, 1]$ and mean imputation is performed for feature values that are undefined in training set.

Initial values. We determine the most suitable range of initial values empirically. The best result for BETF occurs with initial values randomly in the range $(0, 1)$. For CAP and MF, a smaller range is required for convergence and we use the range $(10^{-10}, 10^{-8})$.

Bias baseline. Such method consists of decomposing prediction value into mean, user bias and item bias [32]. We consider the addition of bias for all techniques, except those that already acknowledge it (RLFM, BETF, CAP). First, biases are computed using stochastic gradient descent, then techniques are fitted on remaining unexplained values. We replace review bias by author and product.

MF. Since all reviews are cold-start, we model authors of reviews as items under evaluation. Previous studies validated the Author Consistency Hypothesis, which claims that authors tend to write reviews of similar quality [24]. Bias variables are optimized jointly with latent factors [32]. The mean of votes is applied for cold-starts.

BETF. This method requires normalization in $[0, 1]$ range for applying sigmoid function. We scale the input to be in such range and rescale the results back to $[0, 5]$, which is the range of votes. Unlike MF, bias variables are considered static since the original definition does not include them in the optimization formula [29]. We replaced review bias by product and author. The overall mean is used for cold-starts.

5.2 Parameter Tuning

The best parameter is defined by the value that maximizes nDCG@5 or minimizes RMSE, but we only present results for the former due to space constraint (Table 7).

Observing the parameters of REG class for nDCG@5, better performance occurs for simpler models, with low $C = 10^{-2}$ and linear kernel for SVR, and high regularization $\beta = 10^3$ for LR. Also, in any method from this class, accounting for *bias* causes a worse performance. For GBRT, we note that the best loss function is least squares (ls), which penalizes high deviations more. The optimal value for bias in LTR class is *true*, in opposite to REG. Small optimal values of T and L for LMART indicates that simpler models, with fewer rules, are more efficient. For MF, jointly updating bias as additional variables in the model is a good strategy. For both GRS methods, more iterations does not represent an improvement in accuracy. The same occurs for the number of Gibbs and burn-in samples. In general, such values provide a more stochastic model and less prone to overfitting. Finally, the best parameters of techniques in RRS class also indicates that the simpler the model, the better: we observe

---

[10] www.cs.cornell.edu/people/tj/svm_light/svm_rank.html
[11] sourceforge.net/p/lemur/wiki/RankLib
[12] github.com/yahoo/Latent-Factor-Models
[13] github.com/lucianamaroun/review_recommendation

Table 7: List of parameters with evaluated range (or set) and the best value for ranking (Opt).

Symbol	Description	Range	Opt
	LR		
β	Regularization	$(10^{-6}, 10^6)$	10^3
$bias$	Addition of bias	$\{true, false\}$	$false$
	SVR		
C	Penalty	$(10^{-4}, 10)$	10^{-3}
ker	Kernel	$\{poly1/2/3, rbf, sig\}$	$poly1$
ϵ	Addition of bias	$(10^{-4}, 10)$	10^{-1}
$bias$	Addition of bias	$\{true, false\}$	$false$
	GBRT		
α	Learning rate	$(10^{-4}, 1)$	10^{-1}
T	# Trees	$(10, 10^3)$	10^2
D	Depth of trees	$(1, 5)$	4
ls	Loss function	$\{ls, lad, hub, .5/.9qt\}$	ls
S	Subsample/tree	$(0.2, 1)$	1
F	Max. features/tree	$(10, 43)$	43
$bias$	Addition of bias	$\{true, false\}$	$false$
	RSVM		
C	Penalty	$(10^{-3}, 10)$	10^{-2}
$bias$	Addition of bias	$\{true, false\}$	$true$
	LMART		
α	Learning rate	$(10^{-5}, 10^{-1})$	10^{-5}
T	# Trees	$(10, 10^3)$	10
L	# Tree leaves	$(5, 25)$	5
$bias$	Addition of bias	$\{true, false\}$	$true$
	MF		
K	# Latent dim.	$(5, 50)$	25
I	# Iterations	$(10, 50)$	10
tol	Convergence tol.	$(10^{-6}, 10^{-2})$	10^{-4}
α	Learning rate	$(10^{-5}, 1)$	10^{-1}
β	Regularization	$(10^{-4}, 1)$	10^{-4}
	RLFM		
K	# Latent dim.	$(5, 50)$	15
I	# Iterations	$(5, 25)$	20
G	# Gibbs samples	$(10, 10^3)$	30
B	# Burn-in samples	$(0, 20)$	0
	BETF		
K	# Latent dimensions	$(3, 20)$	4
I	# Iterations	$(5, 25)$	15
tol	Convergence tol.	$(10^{-6}, 10^{-2})$	10^{-4}
α	Learning rate	$(10^{-4}, 10)$	10^{-3}
β	Regularization	$(10^{-4}, 10)$	1
	CAP		
K	# Latent dim.s	$(3, 25)$	5
I	# Iterations	$(5, 25)$	5
G	# Gibbs samples	$(10, 10^2)$	50
N	# NR iterations	$(10, 50)$	10
α	NR learning rate	$(10^{-5}, 10^{-1})$	10^{-2}
η	OLS constant	$(10^{-6}, 10^{-2})$	10^{-6}

low to moderate values for K, I, G, and I_N. Moreover, a high regularization $\beta = 1$ is the best for BETF.

In general terms, optimal RMSE values provide more complex models, for instance, with higher number of iterations, lower regularization and higher penalty factor.

5.3 Comparison of Techniques

We compare techniques within the classes for nDCG@p, and then we contrast the best one of each class to identify the overall best method. Table 8 presents the 95% confidence intervals for nDCG@5 and RMSE. For each metric, the best of each class is shown in bold, along with statistical ties. An asterisk suffix represents the overall best of a metric and

Table 8: Evaluation of techniques for the metrics considered, with respective optimal parameters. For nDCG@5, higher values are better and for RMSE, lower.

Technique	nDCG@5	RMSE
OM	0.8808 ± 0.0265	$\mathbf{0.4148 \pm 0.0489}$
AM	$\mathbf{0.8944 \pm 0.0278}$	0.4394 ± 0.0624
VM	0.8808 ± 0.0265	0.4323 ± 0.0681
LR	0.9269 ± 0.0178	$\mathbf{0.3916 \pm 0.0463^*}$
SVR	$\mathbf{0.9362 \pm 0.0132^*}$	$\mathbf{0.3997 \pm 0.0524^*}$
GBRT	0.9233 ± 0.0185	$\mathbf{0.3621 \pm 0.0354^*}$
RSVM	0.8790 ± 0.0279	—
LMART	$\mathbf{0.8929 \pm 0.0277}$	—
MF	0.8886 ± 0.0286	0.4370 ± 0.0621
RLFM	$\mathbf{0.9229 \pm 0.0197}$	$\mathbf{0.4167 \pm 0.0235}$
BETF	0.8869 ± 0.0281	$\mathbf{0.4161 \pm 0.0509}$
CAP	$\mathbf{0.9213 \pm 0.0196}$	0.4354 ± 0.0462

Table 9: Result of paired t-test, represented by p-values, for each class regarding both metrics. The null hypothesis corresponds to equality of performance for a pair of methods.

	p-value	
Hypothesis	**nDCG@5**	**RMSE**
OM = AM	< 0.0001	$\mathbf{0.0107}$
OM = VM	< 0.0001	0.1188
AM = VM	< 0.0001	0.2659
LR = SVR	$\mathbf{0.0067}$	0.0883
LR = GBRT	$\mathbf{0.0104}$	0.1847
SVR = GBRT	$\mathbf{0.0040}$	0.1064
RSVM = LMART	< 0.0001	—
RLFM = MF	$\mathbf{0.0005}$	0.3095
CAP = BETF	$\mathbf{0.0004}$	$\mathbf{0.0407}$

statistical ties. We also evaluate with Expected Reciprocal Rank (ERR) [12], with mostly similar results of nDCG@p.

Table 9 shows paired t-test p-values. We apply a Holm-Bonferroni correction [15] for the hypothesis within each class aiming at 95% of confidence, and significant p-values are shown in bold. We note that AM significantly surpasses OM and VM for ranking, while OM is significantly the best for regression. OM and VM do not generate meaningful rankings of reviews as their predictions are constant for a reader-product pair. All three methods in the REG class produce statistically different average of nDCG@5, but are statistically tied using RMSE. For nDCG@5, SVR is the best followed by LR and GBRT. For RMSE, such an order is inverted, although no difference is significant. Regarding LTR, LMART has significantly the best performance in nDCG@5. We do not evaluate these predictors considering RMSE as they only output relative values. In GRS, RLFM is significantly better than MF for ranking, but statistically tied for regression. For RRS, CAP significantly outperforms BETF in nDCG@5 and the opposite occurs for RMSE.

Figure 4a compares the nDCG@p for the best of each class, Figure 4d compares all methods but LTR in RMSE, and Table 10 and 11 show p-values for nDCG@5 and RMSE, respectively. Similarly, a Holm-Bonferroni correction is applied and significant p-values are displayed in bold. Note that, regarding nDCG@5, all methods are significantly different, while no pair is statistically distinguishable for RMSE. SVR is significantly the overall best for ranking, followed by LR, RLFM, CAP, AM e LMART. LR was included due to better performance than all other classes. GBRT is the best one for regression, tied with OM, RLFM and BETF. It is

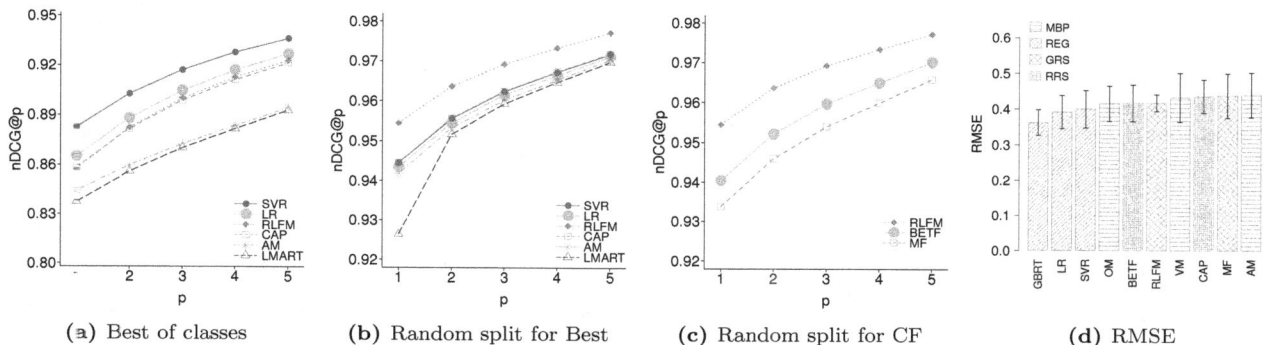

(a) Best of classes   **(b)** Random split for Best   **(c)** Random split for CF   **(d)** RMSE

Figure 4: Comparison of Techniques regarding nDCG@p, with $p \in \{1, ..., 5\}$, for the best of each class in Figure **(a)**, on random split in Figure **(g)**, for collaborative filtering (CF) and RLFM on random split in Figure **(c)**, and RMSE of all approaches in Figure **(d)**, except for LTR class.

Table 10: Obtained p-values from paired t-test of best of classes for nDCG@5 by comparing a technique defined in the column with the one in the row upon equality.

	LR	RLFM	CAP	LMART	AM
SVR	0.0067	0.0053	0.0037	0.0012	0.0014
LR		0.0046	0.0013	0.0008	0.0010
RLFM			0.0219	0.0006	0.0008
CAP				0.0007	0.0010
LMART					0.0010

Table 11: Obtained p-values from paired t-test of best of classes for RMSE by comparing a technique defined in the column with the one in the row upon equality.

	OM	RLFM	BETF
GBRT	0.0210	0.0125	0.0227
OM		0.8994	0.1940
RLFM			0.9696

remarkable how a very basic solution as OM reaches a good performance in RMSE.

For the top 3 methods among best of classes, we compare the performance under cold and warm-start scenario for readers, as shown in Table 12. All methods are different in performance when comparing under paired t-tests and applying Holm-Bonferroni correction. SVR is significantly the best in both scenarios, with a higher gain for cold-start case. Nonetheless, RLFM is more effective than LR for cold-starts, opposed to warm-starts; this is probably due to its more sophisticated way of learning parameters through linking warm and cold-start cases. In spite of SVR being the best overall methods, under restricted resources, LR or RLFM may be more suitable: in our experiments, LR is around 46 times faster and RLMF, 17%.

We also compare the techniques by considering random splits of training and test sets (Figure 4b). Even though such split is often employed by previous works [24, 29, 41], we argue that it is not a valid approach, as future data is used in the learning process. Figure 4b shows that this favorable setting may indeed lead to incorrect conclusions: SVR is not the best approach, being outperformed by RLFM. In fact, all methods are outperformed by RLFM significantly on paired t-tests. Although the performance of collaborative filtering techniques (BETF and MF) improve, they still do

Table 12: Top 3 methods for cold and warm-start readers.

	Warm-Start	Cold-Start
SVR	**0.936262 ± 0.013216**	**0.927939 ± 0.015284**
LR	0.928612 ± 0.019309	0.907157 ± 0.029005
RLFM	0.922199 ± 0.019730	0.912220 ± 0.029250

not overcome RLFM, which uses observed features (Figure 4c). Moreover, under such a setting, the performance of all methods are somewhat inflated (though not proportionally), when compared to the results obtained with a chronological split. Such results serve to show the importance of the chronological for a solid evaluation of recommendations.

Furthermore, we have not observed the same relative performance of BETF surpassing SVR and LR in RMSE, as claimed in the original paper [29]. Our experiments are different due to four reasons: (i) we consider such baselines with not only non-personalized features, but also personalized; (ii) we evaluate using a chronological split while the authors used random split, in a different dataset; (iii) we use around the same amount of data for training and test, while the authors used 90% for training and the remainder for test; (iv) we compare solutions through a statistical test.

Previous comparison of CAP with LR and MF yields different results with respect to RMSE, as reported in the original paper [35]. Specifically, the authors reported that CAP outperforms LR and MF on RMSE; but here, we observe that LR overcomes CAP and a statistical tie with MF, when performing paired t-tests. We believe such difference may be explained by the following facts: we use MF with review replaced by author dimension (to overcome cold-starts) and with incorporated bias; we apply LR with personalized features; and we apply statistical tests under five scenarios.

5.4 Discussion of Results

Based on the experimental results, we observe that simpler models are usually more efficient than complex ones, as suggested by high regularization factors, low penalty factors, and reasonably good performance of simple personalized models, such as LR. Such models often encounter better generalization patterns and suffer less from overfitting.

Our results also indicate that adding a bias factor is *not* a good practice for REG, unlike for LTR and GRS. This is possibly due to the presence of a large fraction of cold-starts, causing bias distributions in training and test to be discrepant. Then, test performance is degenerated, specially for absolute predictions. In other words, our evaluation shows that traditional assumptions such as accounting for bias in recommender systems are *not* prevalent in this scenario, which has plenty of cold-starts.

We also note that collaborative filtering techniques, very popular in recommender systems, do not perform as well for review recommendation. Sparseness is increased for reviews as recommendable items, since their volume is uncontrollably increasing. Including observed features is very important to complement historical behavior in this case, as shown by higher performance of CAP and RLFM than their counterparts. Differently from MF, RLFM incorporates observed features into the model, then allowing prediction for cold-starts. Also, BETF, another collaborative filtering approach, is outperformed by CAP using nDCG@5, despite being significantly better in RMSE.

Although review recommendation is intrinsically a ranking problem, our results reveal that LTR methods are not the best performers. The main problem seems to be the enormous amount of ties in pairs of reviews. By enumerating all pairs in all ranking in each split, only 11,5%, in average, have different relevance values. Thus, from all data in training set, pairwise techniques, such as RankSVM, only uses around one tenth as they disregarded tied pairs. Despite being listwise, LambdaMART uses pairs to compute changes in ranking metrics after swaps, which in this case provides no change many times. Learning from a very small training set makes it difficult to derive a good predictor.

On the other hand, SVR overcomes such sparseness by performing a pointwise learning to rank. In fact, when regression responses are integer values, a perfect SVR model (i.e., with no error) has a perfect ranking $\forall \varepsilon < 0.5$. For such ε, each integer response has a margin of predicted values that does not overlap with another. When responses are not integer values, SVR does not generate a perfect ranking under a perfect model, allowing inversions in the buckets defined by ε tolerance. A perfect LR model also implies in a perfect ranking, but it is much more challenging to linearly model all responses perfectly. By introducing a ε relaxation, SVR becomes much more robust.

We note that CAP produces results that are statistically worse with RLFM using nDCG@5 (they were tied for ERR). Thus, the new model structure proposed in CAP does not improve upon RLFM. In fact, adding dyadic features with plain regression, as RLFM does, is sufficient. In fact, CAP only adds regression on interaction features under restrictions and forces a positive contribution through sigmoid transformation. Nonetheless, a weak interaction may be useful as a negative contribution to helpfulness.

It is also important to notice that ranking and regression are clearly uncorrelated problems for review recommendation, noted by very different results and conclusions addressed by nDCG@p and RMSE. Even naive predictors perform well for RMSE, then making difficult to distinguish the methods with statistical significance. Since the ultimate goal is to provide an ordering of reviews to a reader, finding good predictors using ranking performance is a priority.

5.5 Impact of Features

Table 13 shows the performance by removing a single set of features belonging to certain entity or interaction. Significant changes in performance are presented in bold. Review features are the ones that impact the most. Indeed, con-

Table 13: SVR performance for one set of features removed at a time. A paired t-test is performed between each new version and the original.

Removed Feature Set	nDCG@5	p-value
Review	**0.9078 ± 0.0256**	0.0040
Author	**0.9356 ± 0.0130**	0.0253
Reader	0.9117 ± 0.0433	0.1300
Author-Reader Similarity	0.9364 ± 0.0130	0.0973
Author-Reader Connection	**0.9356 ± 0.0130**	0.0056

tent explains great part of helpfulness, even when it consists of simple textual statistics. Voter features are the second ones that reduces the average performance the most, but such difference is not significant. In fact, removing voter features is better in some cases and worse in others, probably working well only for certain users. Similarity also does not significantly worsen the results. This is an evidence that the similarity used, related to ratings given, does not represent well users' common interests. The remaining author and connection features impact the result in a similar way and significantly. Thus, author's reputation and connection interaction are important, although the ranking metric decreases only a little in average. We believe there is still a great potential in exploiting better interaction features, specially similarity ones.

6. CONCLUSIONS AND FUTURE WORK

There is a large volume of reviews available representing a challenge for readers seeking useful information. A common solution is to rank the reviews according to their global quality. However, recent works model the task as a *personalized* problem. In such a context, we presented and compared a rich and heterogeneous set of personalized solutions, from five paradigms, that had not been previously compared against each other. Unlike previous work, we modeled review recommendation as a *ranking task* and compared all techniques under a *unified* statistical experimental design.

We analyzed the best parametric configuration for each method and evaluated through RMSE and nDCG@p. SVR was the best performer, becoming close to ranking purpose for integer responses and revealing robust by introducing ε relaxation. In general terms, simplicity and incorporating observed features are good design decisions. Albeit having a ranking goal, LTR suffers from tied pairs of reviews, then providing poor results. Specialized solutions are not the best for regression nor ranking. Finally, RMSE, a regression metric leads to very different conclusions than nDCG@p, a ranking one, whereas a ranking metric is more suitable as it represents well the purpose of filtering reviews for a user.

Future work includes exploring new observed features (specially personalized ones and related to review-reader interaction) and taking more advantage of the ranking purpose (e.g., adding a ranking loss error in the recommendation) as it may improve performance. Additionally, our results are bound to a limited scope, concerning the specific dataset used. Hence, repeating the experiments for a new dataset, especially one containing votes' timestamps, is another future step. At last, we address the promising course of analyzing what predictor works well for each type of user.

Acknowledgments. Work partially funded by CNPq, CAPES and FAPEMIG, Brazil.

7. REFERENCES

[1] G. Adomavicius and A. Tuzhilin. Toward the next generation of recommender systems: A survey of the state-of-the-art and possible extensions. *IEEE Trans. on Knowl. and Data Eng.*, 17(6):734–749, 2005.

[2] D. Agarwal and B.-C. Chen. Regression-based latent factor models. In *Procs. of KDD*, Paris, France, 2009.

[3] M. Anderson. Local consumer review survey 2014, 2014. https://www.brightlocal.com/2014/07/01/local-consumer-review-survey-2014.

[4] M. L. Anderson and J. R. Magruder. Learning from the crowd: Regression discontinuity estimates of the effects of an online review database. *Economic Journal*, 122(563):957–989, 2012.

[5] S. Balakrishnan and S. Chopra. Collaborative ranking. In *Procs. of WSDM*, Seattle, WA, USA, 2012.

[6] K. Balog and H. Ramampiaro. Cumulative citation recommendation: Classification vs. ranking. In *Procs. of SIGIR*, Dublin, Ireland, 2013.

[7] J. G. Booth and J. P. Hobert. Maximizing generalized linear mixed model likelihoods with an automated monte carlo em algorithm. *JRRS: B*, 61(1):265–285, 1999.

[8] C. J. Burges. From RankNet to LambdaRank to LambdaMART: An overview. Technical Report MSR-TR-2010-82, Microsoft Research, 2010.

[9] S. D. Canuto et al. A comparative study of learning-to-rank techniques for tag recommendation. *JIDM*, 4(3):453–468, 2013.

[10] O. Chapelle and Y. Chang. Yahoo! learning to rank challenge overview. In *Procs. of the Yahoo! Learning to Rank Challenge - ICML*, Bellevue, WA, USA, 2011.

[11] O. Chapelle and S. S. Keerthi. Efficient algorithms for ranking with SVMs. *IR*, 13(3):201–215, 2010.

[12] O. Chapelle, D. Metlzer, Y. Zhang, and P. Grinspan. Expected reciprocal rank for graded relevance. In *Procs. of CIKM*, Hong Kong, China, 2009.

[13] P. Cremonesi, Y. Koren, and R. Turrin. Performance of recommender algorithms on top-n recommendation tasks. In *Procs. of RecSys*, Barcelona, Spain, 2010.

[14] J. H. Friedman. Greedy function approximation: A gradient boosting machine. *The Annals of Statistics*, 29(5):pp. 1189–1232, 2001.

[15] S. Holm. A simple sequentially rejective multiple test procedure. *Scandinavian Journal of Statistics*, 6(2):65–70, 1979.

[16] R. Jain. *The art of computer systems performance analysis - techniques for experimental design, measurement, simulation, and modeling.* Wiley, 1991.

[17] T. Joachims. Training linear SVMs in linear time. In *Procs. of KDD*, Philadelphia, PA, USA, 2006.

[18] Y. Koren. Factorization meets the neighborhood: A multifaceted collaborative filtering model. In *Procs. of KDD*, Las Vegas, NV, USA, 2008.

[19] Y. Koren, R. Bell, and C. Volinsky. Matrix factorization techniques for recommender systems. *Commun. ACM*, 42(8):30–37, 2009.

[20] S. Lee and J. Y. Choeh. Predicting the helpfulness of online reviews using multilayer perceptron neural networks. *Expert Syst. Appl.*, 41(6):3041–3046, 2014.

[21] H. Li. A short introduction to learning to rank. *IEICE Transactions*, 94-D(10):1854–1862, 2011.

[22] Y. Liu, X. Huang, A. An, and X. Yu. Modeling and predicting the helpfulness of online reviews. In *Procs. of ICDM*, Miami, FL, USA, 2008.

[23] W. Lu, S. Chen, K. Li, and L. V. S. Lakshmanan. Show me the money: Dynamic recommendations for revenue maximization. *PVLDB*, 7(14):1785–1796, 2014.

[24] Y. Lu et al. Exploiting social context for review quality prediction. In *Procs. of WWW*, Raleigh, NC, USA, 2010.

[25] C. Lucchese et al. Quickscorer: A fast algorithm to rank documents with additive ensembles of regression trees. In *Procs. of SIGIR*, Santiago, Chile, 2015.

[26] A. Machanavajjhala, A. Korolova, and A. D. Sarma. Personalized social recommendations: Accurate or private. *PVLDB*, 4(7):440–450, Apr. 2011.

[27] L. Martin and P. Pu. Prediction of helpful reviews using emotions extraction. In *Procs. of AAAI*, Québec City, Canada, 2014.

[28] G. A. Miller. WordNet: A lexical database for english. *Commun. ACM*, 38(11):39–41, 1995.

[29] S. Moghaddam, M. Jamali, and M. Ester. ETF: Extended Tensor Factorization model for personalizing prediction of review helpfulness. In *Procs. of the WSDM*, Seattle, WA, USA, 2012.

[30] K. P. Murphy. *Machine Learning: A Probabilistic Perspective.* The MIT Press, 2012.

[31] F. e. a. Pedregosa. Scikit-learn: Machine learning in Python. *JMLR*, 12(Oct):2825–2830, 2011.

[32] F. Ricci et al. *Recommender Systems Handbook.* Springer-Verlag, 1st edition, 2010.

[33] Y. Shi, M. Larson, and A. Hanjalic. Collaborative filtering beyond the user-item matrix: A survey of the state of the art and future challenges. *ACM Comput. Surv.*, 47(1):3:1–3:45, 2014.

[34] A. J. Smola and B. Schölkopf. A tutorial on support vector regression. *Statistics and Computing*, 14(3):199–222, 2004.

[35] J. Tang et al. Context-aware review helpfulness rating prediction. In *Procs. of RecSys*, Hong Kong, China, 2013.

[36] V. N. Vapnik. *The Nature of Statistical Learning Theory.* Springer-Verlag, 1995.

[37] M. Vasconcelos, J. M. Almeida, and M. A. Gonçalves. Predicting the popularity of micro-reviews: A foursquare case study. *Information Sciences*, 325:355–374, 2015.

[38] H. Yin et al. Challenging the long tail recommendation. *PVLDB*, 5(9):896–907, 2012.

[39] T. J. Ypma. Historical development of the Newton-Raphson method. *SIAM Rev.*, 37(4):531–551, Dec. 1995.

[40] K. Zhang, R. Narayanan, and A. Choudhary. Voice of the customers: Mining online customer reviews for product feature-based ranking. In *Procs. of the WOSN*, 2010.

[41] R. Zhang and T. Tran. An information gain-based approach for recommending useful product reviews. *Knowl. Inf. Syst.*, 26(3):419–434, 2011.

Download and Cache Management for HTML5 Hypervideo Players

Britta Meixner[1,2], Christoph Einsiedler[1]
[1]University of Passau, Innstrasse 43, 94032 Passau, Germany
[2]FX Palo Alto Laboratory, 3174 Porter Drive, Palo Alto, CA 94304, USA
meixner@fxpal.com, einsied@fim.uni-passau.de

ABSTRACT

Web videos are becoming more and more popular. Current web technologies make it simpler than ever to both stream videos and create complex constructs of interlinked videos with additional information (video, audio, images, and text); so called hypervideos. When viewers interact with hypervideos by clicking on links, new content has to be loaded. This may lead to excessive waiting times, interrupting the presentation – especially when videos are loaded into the hypervideo player. In this work, we propose hypervideo pre-fetching strategies, which can be implemented in players to minimize waiting times. We examine the possibilities offered by the HTML5 <video> tag as well as the Media Source Extensions (MSE). Both HTML5 and MSE allow element pre-fetching (video and additional information) up to a certain granularity. Depending on the strategy and technology used, beginning scene waiting times and the overall download volume may increase. The strategies presented in this paper allow the number of delays during playback and the overall waiting time of a video to be reduced significantly from an average of 8.1 breaks to less than one break. The overall waiting times can be reduced by one third, to less than 18 seconds improving the hypervideo watching experience.

Keywords

Pre-fetching; Download; Cache; HTML5; Media Source Extensions; Hypervideo; Quality of Experience

1. INTRODUCTION

Videos on the Web are becoming more and more popular. According to the Cisco Visual Networking Index, "mobile video traffic exceeded 50 percent of total mobile data traffic by the end of 2012 and grew to 55 percent by the end of 2014" [7]. "Globally, consumer Internet video traffic will be 80% of consumer Internet traffic in 2019, up from 64% in 2014" [8]. These statistics show how important video is on the Internet in daily life.

HT '16, July 10-13, 2016, Halifax, NS, Canada
© 2016 ACM. ISBN 978-1-4503-4247-6/16/07... $15.00
DOI: http://dx.doi.org/10.1145/2914586.2914587

Technologies like HTML5, JavaScript, and CSS allow the creation of annotated, interactive, non-linear hypervideos. These consist of linked video scenes and may contain additional information like video, audio, images, text, and other media, which can be selected by the viewer via hyperlinks, or are displayed in parallel with the main video scenes. This type of video allows a high level of interaction and non-linear navigation during playback, where every user can chose her/his own path through the hypervideo. A detailed description of annotated interactive non-linear video can be found in [16, 17]. These hypervideos can be used in several scenarios, like instructional videos [29], medical training [21], and walks through cities or buildings [19]. In the remainder of this work, we use the term "annotated interactive non-linear video" as synonymous with "hypervideo".

Hypervideos have metadata which define the underlying scene graph and link structures between videos and additional information. The metadata are needed by the player before the playback of the video may start. Analyzing the structures described in these metadata, the next possible displayable contents are known. This knowledge can be used to pre-fetch and cache future elements (video and additional information) and make them available before the viewer selects them. Accordingly, the waiting times are reduced which results in a better user experience. Furthermore, breaks during playback can be limited or avoided. While it may be a suitable strategy to download and cache the whole hypervideo on a desktop computer with an unlimited internet connection, data plans for mobile phones often limit the amount of high speed data. Consequently, downloading a whole video where huge parts will not be watched is not an option. New strategies need to be found to provide a good viewer experience while keeping the overall download volume as small as possible. Experiments in a simulation environment showed promising results for several algorithms and strategies for download and cache management [16, 17], but no implementation for real world players exists. In this work, we adapt, rewrite, and implement the strategies and algorithms described in [16, 17] with HTML5 [36] and the Media Source Extensions (MSE) [37, 38]. Thereby, we make the following research contributions:

- We transform findings from a simulation framework for download and cache management in hypervideos into efficient pre-fetching strategies for real-world hypervideo web players using HTML5 and MSE.
- We outline the limitations that appear when using HTML5 and MSE for implementing hypervideo players for the Web.

- We show that using the right combination of framework and algorithm, we can achieve smaller waiting times before and during playback, as well as overall waiting times compared to implementations using the standard HTML5 video-tag. We show that we can limit the number of breaks during playback to zero in most of the times. While limiting waiting times and pauses we also achieve the smallest possible overall download volumes.
- We provide guidelines for future implementations in this area using HTML5 and MSE.

The remainder of this work is structured as follows: In the following section, an overview of related work in adjoining areas is given and discussed. Section 3 describes algorithms used and their implementation in different web frameworks. The results of a comprehensive evaluation with patterns most frequently appearing in hypervideos are described in Section 4. A summary of the results and an outlook on future work can be found in Section 6.

2. RELATED WORK

Related work exists in the areas of web video frameworks, hypervideo players on the Web, and pre-fetching strategies for hypervideos. To the best of the authors' knowledge no related work exists combining these three aspects. Therefore, we will discuss the most important work from all areas.

2.1 Web Video Frameworks

Frameworks and standards for embedding video into a website are SMIL [35], the Adobe Flash Player [3], Microsoft Silverlight [22], and HTML5 [36].

The first public release of the SMIL Specification was in 1997 [32]. Its final version (SMIL 3.0) from 2008 [35] "allows authors to write interactive multimedia presentations. Using SMIL, an author may describe the temporal behaviour of a multimedia presentation, associate hyperlinks with media objects and describe the layout of the presentation on a screen" [35]. "In June of 2000, Microsoft Internet Explorer version 5.5 was the first product to support SMIL 2.0 technology" [31]. A true subset of SMIL 2.0, SMIL Animation [33] in SVG is supported by Firefox 41, Chrome 46, Safari 9, and Opera 32 [1]. However, none of the current browsers supports the whole standard in its final version.

The first version of the browser plug-in Flash Player was released by Macromedia in 1997. The first version capable of playing video was Flash 6 released in March 2002 [39]. Buffering and caching of videos at player side is possible in current versions using ActionScript 3 [2].

Another browser plug-in is Microsoft Silverlight, which was released in September 2007 [23]. As with the Adobe Flash Player, Silverlight is also capable of controlling its cache up to a certain degree. A comparably new way of embedding video into a website is provided by HTML5 [36].

In contrast to the already described plug-ins, HTML5 is implemented by the browsers directly. While the video element was in the standard since the first working draft from January 2008 [34] it was not implemented in the browsers at that time. The first browsers capable of interpreting the video element were Safari 3.1 (2008), Chrome 3.0 (2009), Firefox (Gecko) 3.5 (1.9.1) (2009), Opera 10.5 (2009), and Internet Explorer 9.0 (2011) [24]. Predefined settings and states for pre-loading and buffering are available for the video element, but a fine grained manual control of the download and cache is not possible.

While Flash was widely used for the playback of video on the Web before the introduction of HTML5 video [4], the "general trend for Flash usage is downward" [41]. Throughout the Web, different prognoses can be found claiming that HTML5 will be the main method to embed video into a website [28, 30] in the future. Silverlight has never played an important role in video playback on the Web compared to Flash. Therefore, we will focus on an implementation in HTML5 in the remainder of this paper.

2.2 Hypervideo Player for the Web

With growing bandwidths in the Internet and the availability of HTML5 in all important browsers, more and more hypervideo players are available. Each of them provides different functions offering more or less liberties and possibilities to the authors of hypervideos. Since January 2010, YouTube uses HTML5 video [27]. The YouTube player [42] provides functions to link videos with each other using buttons. The video selected by the button then opens in a new web-page which ruins the perception of a self-contained presentation. Besides the linking of videos, text boxes and speech bubbles can be added to provide additional information. This player does not cache or pre-fetch contents due to its loading behavior.

Linius [15] is a Wordpress-theme [40] for linear video with additional navigational features. Extended navigation in the video is possible. Scenes can be skipped using a table of contents. Each "chapter" of a Linius video may contain videos, text, images, audio files, interactive graphics, and more. Linius executes an initial pre-fetch before playback. Thereby, all images of the presentation are pre-fetched as well as the video of the first chapter (if it exists). Videos and audio files of the remainder of the presentation are loaded when they are selected during playback. While the initial pre-fetch may take some time, its loading progress is displayed.

A very similar player to Linius is Pageflow [9]. It is a content management system designed for the creation of multimedia stories. The navigation in Pageflow is similar to Linius. Chapters can be skipped by using the mouse wheel, the arrow keys, or by using the table of contents. As in Linius, chapters may contain videos, text, image, audio files, interactive graphics, and more, but a temporal synchronization of the contents with a video is not possible. Pre-fetching works the same way as described for Linius, where only metadata are pre-fetched for future chapters.

The Klynt player [12] is used for the playback of videos created with the Klynt authoring tool. In contrast to linked videos on YouTube, the hypervideo is presented in one player without loading a new page. Navigation between videos and additional information is possible. Compared to the YouTube player, this player offers a huge variety of additional information like text, Wikipedia-articles, info-graphics, or maps. To the best of the author's knowledge, it is not possible to customize the caching behavior of this player.

The SIVA HTML5 Player (for a detailed description see [20], a revised version with a GUI redesign is described in [21]) is used for the playback of hypervideos exported from the associated authoring tool (SIVA Producer, described in [19]). This player provides different ways to navigate in the hypervideo like button panels (to select the next scene from the underlying scene graph), a table of contents, or a keyword search. Additional information is synchronized and displayed with the video in panels in the player or as overlays over the video. No pre-fetching is implemented in the current version of the player, but the availability of all elements is checked before the playback of each scene starts.

Summing up, many players provide interactivity and non-linear navigation in (hyper)videos, but none of them provides a comprehensive download and cache management strategy covering the whole video.

2.3 Pre-fetching Strategies for Hypervideos

Pre-fetching strategies can mainly be found for the streaming of linear videos in multicast environments or on different types of underlying networks. Fei et al. [10] describe an active buffer management for partitioned video multicast systems. Their client pre-fetches segments from broadcast channels and is thus able to provide VCR actions to the viewers. Laraspata et al. [13] describe an algorithm for variable bit rate video transmission over UMTS networks, which helps to reduce delays by taking user interactivity into account. Both works only deal with interactivity in a linear video. None of them takes additional information that has to be displayed with the video into account.

Grigoras et al. propose an adaptive approach to "stream hypervideo that takes into account user behavior" [11] reducing network induced latency. Their "technique is based on a model provided by a Markov Decision Process approach" [11]. Doing this, they describe two different methods. These are tested under stochastic network conditions. Their approach only takes video into account. Additional information like images, text, audio files, or other videos which are played parallel to the main video are not taken into consideration.

A simulation framework for download and cache management algorithms in annotated interactive non-linear videos is presented in [16, 17]. Strategies for pre-fetching, scheduling, and downloading elements of annotated interactive non-linear videos are presented as well as algorithms for the deletion of elements from the cache. This frameworks allows the simulation of videos linked in a scene graph which are extended with additional information displayed with main video scenes. Different bandwidth and cache settings can be used for the simulations. An initial set of algorithms is tested using patterns that often appear in hypervideos, like sequences, cycles, and tree-like structures with branches. Some algorithms show promising results in the framework and will therefore be integrated in the SIVA HTML5 hypervideo player [20, 21] as described hereafter.

3. HTML5 HYPERVIDEO

In this section we will give a deeper overview of the underlying software and algorithms for this work. We first describe the existing HTML5 hypervideo player. Then we introduce the implementation of the algorithms as tested in our simulation framework [16, 17]. We then describe how we adapted, rewrote and implemented these strategies with recent web technologies (HTML5 and MSE) to integrate them into the existing HTML5 hypervideo player [20, 21].

3.1 HTML5 Hypervideo Player

The basis of this work is the SIVA HTML5 hypervideo player from our previous work [20, 21]. This player has a video area (Figure 1, left side) where the main video scenes

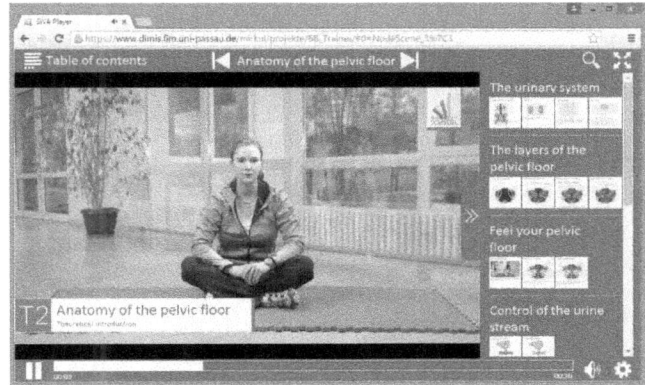

Figure 1: Screenshot of the SIVA HTML5 player with main video area and a fold-out panel for annotations.

are displayed. The annotation area 1, right side) may contain different types of annotations like images, image galleries, text, audio files, or additional videos. These annotations can be displayed for the whole duration of a scene or only for a defined time range within the scene. The annotation area in Figure 1 shows four image galleries. At the end of a scene, either the next scene is loaded automatically by the player (because the scene has only one successor) or a panel folds out from the right side which provides buttons for the selection of the next scene (in case the scene has more than one successor). The player provides all standard control elements as known from traditional video players at the bottom and additional control elements needed for hypervideos at the top of the player. These are a table of contents, buttons to jump to the next or previous scene, a keyword search, and a button for the full-screen mode. The structure of the video is read from a JSON file which is structured as described in [18].

This player provides all functions needed to read and process the metadata and display the media at the right place and time in the player. However, there are no pre-fetching functions implemented in this player so far. The buffering of each scene and its annotations starts when the scene is selected by the viewer at a button panel or when the scene is selected by the player in case of a sequence of scenes. How and when to buffer the media is left to the browser. This may lead to delays and scene transition waiting times.

3.2 Pre-fetching - Theory

As described in the previous section, each scene of a hypervideo consists of a main video (then again consisting of frames), and additional information which are displayed during a certain continuous range of frames in a scene. In order to provide all necessary contents at the time of display without further loading times (thus causing breaks in the flow during playback), strategies for pre-fetching and download scheduling are needed. We first implemented these strategies in a simulation framework to get a better feeling for the inter-dependencies between cache size, bandwidth, user interaction, and settings in a hypervideo like probabilities for choosing a certain scene, durations of scenes, numbers and sizes of annotations, sizes of the videos, and certain perennial structures each hypervideo contains. For an overview

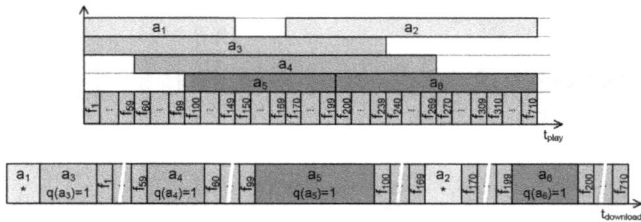

Figure 2: Playback schedule (top) and resulting linear download schedule (bottom) of a scene.

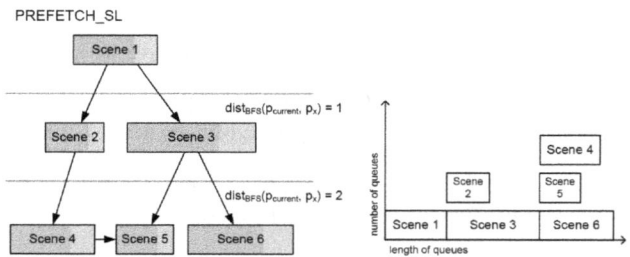

Figure 3: Download queues for the PREFETCH_SL strategy of a sub-part of a scene graph (left) with six scenes resulting in three layers (right).

of the framework and its results please refer to [16, 17]. We want to outline the most important concepts and algorithms from this work hereafter to show the difficulties and differences in a real-world implementation thereafter.

3.2.1 Scheduling a Scene

Taking a closer look at a scene, each one has two schedules: one for playback and one for download. The playback schedule of a scene containing six annotations and 710 frames is illustrated in Figure 2 (top). Annotations a_1 and a_3 are displayed from the beginning, then annotation a_4 is shown from frame f_{60} and so on. Taking a look at a possible linear download schedule, the annotations are scheduled before the frames they are displayed with to make sure they can be displayed immediately. This results in a schedule where annotations a_1 and a_3 are scheduled before frame f_1. Then all frames up to frame f_{59} are scheduled followed by annotation a_4 and frame f_{60} and so on. The resulting linear download schedule is shown in Figure 2 (bottom).

3.2.2 Scheduling a Sub-graph

With the graph structure of the scenes known from the metadata of a hypervideo, it is possible to calculate which elements may be selected by the viewer in the future course of the hypervideo. Different ways of scheduling elements for pre-fetching and download are possible. One strategy would be to analyze all possible paths from a certain point in the hypervideo and download all elements of the paths up to a certain time limit (like a sliding window, but over different paths). This method downloads whole scenes leaving no elements out, which is bandwidth consuming. It ensures that all elements are cached for future playback which avoids breaks in the video flow. In our tests in previous work [16, 17], a strategy ("PREFETCH_SL") which schedules and downloads only the part of the scene that is needed to start playback while also loading the missing data of a scene wherein no breaks during playback occur, showed good results. The scheduling of the single scenes is done for each layer. The layers are calculated from a certain scene onward with a breadth first search noting the distances to the current scene. An illustration of the PREFETCH_SL schedule for six scenes can be found in Figure 3. Outgoing from scene 1, scenes 2 and 3 can be reached with one step and are therefore on the second level. Scenes 4, 5 and 6 can be reached with two steps are therefore on the third level. Thereby, scene 5 has two ingoing edges, one with a distance of two steps and one with a distance of three steps. Using a breadth first search, the smaller of the two distances is used for further processing.

Different probabilities can be applied to the single paths

depending on the previous user behavior or other settings in the hypervideo defined in the metadata. For the creation of a linear schedule of a level of the scene graph, a slightly modified version of the round robin algorithm described by Shreedhar and Varghese [26] is used where the probability of selecting a scene is applied to the quantum size of the queue.

3.2.3 Calculation of the Start Frame for Playback

When the playback schedule for one scene is known, the point in time from which the scene can be played without breaks after downloading a certain amount of data from the download schedule can be calculated. Doing that, we first calculate the download time $t_{download}$ for the given schedule. Next, the elements of the schedule are downloaded step-by-step. The remaining time for the download $t_{download}$ is reduced with every downloaded element. In parallel, the already downloaded frames are counted and we calculate how much time of the scene can be played back $t_{playback}$. We then compare both values, and if $t_{playback} > t_{download}$, the playback can be started.

3.3 Pre-fetching - Realization in Browsers

The theoretical background and calculations on the definitions described in Section 3.2 help to understand the connections between different algorithms for pre-fetch, download scheduling, cache management, and deletion from the cache. Cache management and deletion from the cache will not be examined in more detail in this work, because it is mainly executed by the Web browser and cannot be influenced by our implementation. The results in [16, 17] showed that the deletion of elements from the cache only has a greater influence in the cycle pattern but does not affect the overall performance significantly.

Trying to "translate" the algorithms and strategies from the simulation framework into a real-world player in a browser, we were facing the following problems:

- Frames could not be downloaded one-by-one, neither in HTML5 nor in the MSE.
- The creation of linear schedules was not possible in HTML5.
- A linear scheduling of a sub-graph was not possible in HTML5 due to the aforementioned limitations.
- The calculation of the start frame for playback could not be implemented on a frame basis.

Most of the problems resulted from the fact that it is not possible to apply such a fine granularity of pre-fetch and download scheduling as used in the simulation framework to currently existing web technologies. In the following, we will describe how the algorithms introduced in Section 3.2 can be modified and realized with HTML5 [36] and the MSE [37, 38]. See Table 1 for an overview and comparison.

3.3.1 Implementation in HTML5

Using the standard HTML5 video tag, different attributes can be set and properties can be queried. The relevant ones are:

- `preload (auto|metadata|none)`: Setting `preload` to "none", no pre-loading is performed. Using "metadata", only the metadata of the video but not the video itself is loaded. The standard setting is "auto", it triggers an optimistic pre-fetching of the whole video.
- `buffered`: The `buffered` property contains the time ranges (start and end times) of parts of the video that are already loaded into the browser cache.
- `readystate`: The `readystate` property indicates the state of the video:
  - HAVE_NOTHING: No data were loaded so far.
  - HAVE_METADATA: The metadata are loaded.
  - HAVE_CURRENT_DATA: The currently needed frame was loaded.
  - HAVE_FUTURE_DATA: Future frames were loaded.
  - HAVE_ENOUGH_DATA: Enough data were loaded to be able to most likely play the video without any breaks.

The initial version of the HTML5 hypervideo player did not analyze the video in any manner. Therefore, the player was extended with two new components, the "fork analyzer" and the "pre-fetcher". The fork analyzer analyzes the scene graph of the hypervideo and determines which scenes may be played in the future course of playback. It also identifies how many layers are between the current scene and possible future scenes. When a viewer selects one of the scenes, the pre-fetcher determines which scenes will be scheduled for pre-load, performs the pre-load, and calculates the time from which the scene can be played without breaks.

Accordingly, the player first gets the scene graph from the metadata. When a scene is selected, the fork analyzer determines the next possible scenes. Then the scene is analyzed by the pre-fetcher and the download from the server starts. When enough data are available (as calculated by the pre-fetcher), the playback starts. If there is still bandwidth available after all elements of the scene are downloaded, the pre-loading of future scenes is started.

However, some adjustments of the algorithms described in Section 3.2 are necessary:

- **Scheduling a scene**: Using HTML5, it is not possible to implement a linear schedule for a scene. For pre-fetching a scene, it is only possible to chose between the `preload` options `auto`, `metadata`, or `none`. A higher granularity is not possible. Furthermore, it is not possible to pause the buffering of a video. For that reason, additional information is downloaded in parallel with the main video when the (already buffered) main video reaches the point where the additional information should be displayed. Thereby the guarantee is lost that annotations are pre-fetched for display and can be displayed immediately. The main video pre-fetch as well as the handling of parallel downloads may be different using different web browsers.

- **Scheduling a sub-graph**: It is possible to determine the levels of the scene graph. Accordingly a pre-fetch of selected scenes is realizable. However, as described for scheduling a scene, the same restrictions apply for scheduling a sub-graph. This results in parallel downloads for scenes of one level. Furthermore, the prioritization of scenes can not be realized. In order to adapt to the viewer behavior, we pre-fetch all scenes with a priority higher than the average priority. If all scenes have the same priority, all are pre-fetched.

- **Calculation of the start frame for playback**: An approximation of the calculations described in Section 3.2 can be used to determine the point in time for starting the playback. However, different browsers handle the pre-fetch of elements differently. Accordingly, the calculated point in time to start playback may never be reached and thus the playback of the video will never be started. A work-around is checking the `readystate` and waiting for the event `canplaythrough`. This does not ensure the availability of the annotations and may result in a displaying delay. Like the handling of the pre-fetch of elements, the browsers are also handling the throwing of events differently.

3.3.2 Implementation with Media Source Extensions

The Media Source Extensions (MSE) allow a smaller deviation from the algorithms described in Section 3.2 in contrast to the previously described implementation of the buffering in HTML5. Currently, the MSE are in the state of a W3C Candidate Recommendation [37] or rather a W3C Editor's draft [38]. The two most important features of this future standard are client sided buffering and adaptive streaming via HTTP (DASH). Client sided buffering allows the pre-fetching of parts of the video, which can than be added to the video tag in the form of byte streams. For the realization of our algorithms, a separation of the video into downloadable "clusters" is necessary. "Clusters" of frames are a specified set of consecutive frames of a single video file - or with regard to hypervideo in a single scene. While the WebM container already provides clusters, MP4 files need to be modified because the internal structure of the container must be adapted. The buffering is then done by MSE. First a new MediaSource object is created which is then used as a source for the HTML5 video tag. A source buffer is added to the MediaSource object. Then video clusters are added and the buffer is filled.

In order to extend the existing HTML5 hypervideo player with a pre-fetching strategy using MSE, three new components ("scene analyzer", "fork analyzer", and "pre-fetcher") were added. The scene analyzer calculates linear download schedules and the overall download volume for individual scenes. The fork analyzer calculates the distances to possible future scenes. It calculates a complete download schedule for the current situation. The pre-fetcher calculates the start point for the playback and applies the download schedule calculated by the fork analyzer.

Accordingly, first schedules for scenes are created, then the structure of the scene graph is fetched as well as information about the different elements. After selecting a scene, possible next scenes are analyzed and the schedule is refreshed. Then the schedule (of the current and possible future scenes) is applied and the elements are downloaded

Table 1: Comparison of the implementations.

	Status quo HTML5		MSE immediately	wait	wait no break
Calculate start frame for play-back	start playback depending on imple-mentation in browser	approximated calculation as described in Section 3.2.3 in combination with checking the ready-state for the `can-playthrough` event (imple-mentation browser depen-dent)	similar to im-plementation in HTML5	as described in Section 3.2.3 but based on clus-ters instead of frames	more optimistic than the "wait no break" strategy but may lead to breaks; differentiates between main video and annotations; takes into account that down-loaded clusters lead to more available playback time
Schedule scene	no pre-fetch imple-mented	preload options: `auto`, `meta`, `none`; additional information downloaded parallel with main video; no guarantee for immediate display of anno-tations	linear scheduling of clusters (instead of frames) of scene as de-scribed in Section 3.2.1 - more pessimistic calculation of start frame		
Schedule sub-graph	no pre-fetch imple-mented	parallel download of scenes on one level of the graph; if same prio, all scenes down-loaded parallel; if one scene has higher prio, only this scene downloaded	scheduling based on clusters, not frames - priorities applied to clusters in scenes, not frames		

from the HTTP server. Playback starts when enough ele-ments are in the buffer.

As described for the implementation in HTML5, MSE also needs adjustments to the algorithms described in Sec-tion 3.2:

- **Scheduling a scene**: Due to the fact that a sepa-ration of the video into clusters is possible, a linear download schedule can be calculated for a scene. The schedule is calculated as described in Section 3.2.1 with the difference that the scheduling is not based on sin-gle frames but on available clusters. This may lead to a little more pessimistic calculation of the start time as the calculations based on frames.
- **Scheduling a sub-graph**: Like the scheduling of scenes, the scheduling of parts of the graph is also pos-sible, again with the limitation on clusters instead of individual frames. It is possible to realize the prioriti-zation of scenes by adding more clusters to a schedule for higher prioritized scenes.
- **Calculate start frame for playback**: We introduce three different ways to calculate the start frame:
  - **MSE immediately**: This strategy is similar to the one described for the HTML5 implementation.
  - **MSE wait no break**: This strategy is implemented as described in Section 3.2.3 with the limitation of using clusters instead of individual frames.
  - **MSE wait**: The "MSE wait no break" strategy may result in comparably long waiting times. For that reason we implemented a further variant to calcu-late the start frame. It cannot guarantee a playback without breaks, but limits them to a minimum with significantly lower beginning scene waiting times. This strategy differentiates between the download of additional information and the main video of a scene and takes into account the fact that down-loaded clusters of the video result in further avail-able playback time.

4. EVALUATION

In the following, we present our evaluation results. To measure the quality of our algorithms, we defined metrics for the analysis of the quality of the algorithms. We test or algorithms using patterns which occur in scene graphs. We present and discuss our results at the end of this section.

4.1 Metrics

In order to determine the quality of our algorithms, we use five metrics, namely:

- **Wait start**: sum of waiting times from selecting a scene until the playback starts
- **Wait playback**: sum of waiting times during playback after breaks if needed elements are not in buffer
- **Wait total**: *wait start + wait playback*
- **Breaks**: occurrence of a break in the video flow for more than 500 ms
- **Download volume**: overall data volume, sum of file sizes of all downloaded files

For a more formal definition of the metrics, please refer to [16, 17]. The metrics commonly used for web caching (see [25] for an overview) have only little informative value in the area of hypervideos.

4.2 Patterns

Dealing with hypervideo, two different sub-patterns ex-ist for each pattern: the structure pattern (black colored arrows in our figures) and the user-path pattern (blue col-ored dashed arrows in our figures). The structure pattern describes the connections between the video scenes and the additional information representing the edges of the scene graph. The user-path pattern is the sequence of scenes from the structure pattern describing the path that was selected through the scene graph by the viewer.

Testing on patterns instead of complete hypervideos has the advantage of measuring relevant data without having to test on a large number of different hypervideos, which

Table 2: **Settings for video and additional information for the patterns.**

Scene name	dur. [sec]	size [MB]	add. info	display [sec]	sizes [MB]
S01	10	0.54			
S02	32	29.8	A02	10-20	6.37/7.18/5.68/5.36
S03	60	60.3	A03	30-40	8.06/6.83/9.57
S04	41	28.5			
S05	45	56.7	A05	00-10	7.40/5.51
S06	4	2.1	A06	00-04	2.32
S07	30	15.9	A07	00-10	1.21
S08	42	44.8	A08	00-10	1.39
S09	60	53.1	A09	10-20	3.24/5.92
S10	59	53.7	A10	20-30	2.24/2.80/2.76/2.62
S11	37	72.4	A11	10-20	3.13/1.35
S12	46	36.8			
S13	60	36.7	A13	30-40	4.96/6.51
S14	61	55.6	A14	20-30	3.88/5.48/4.71

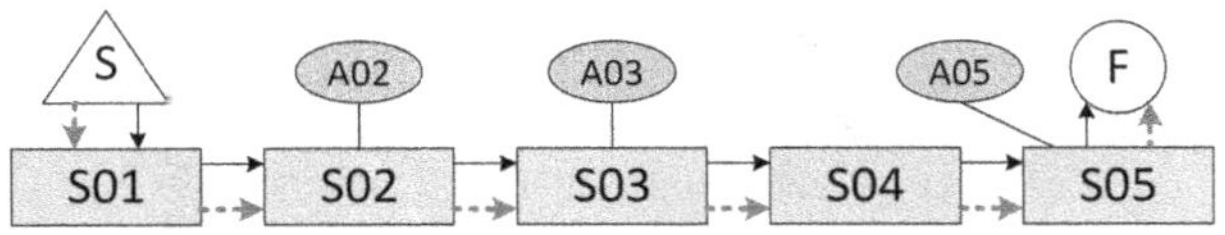

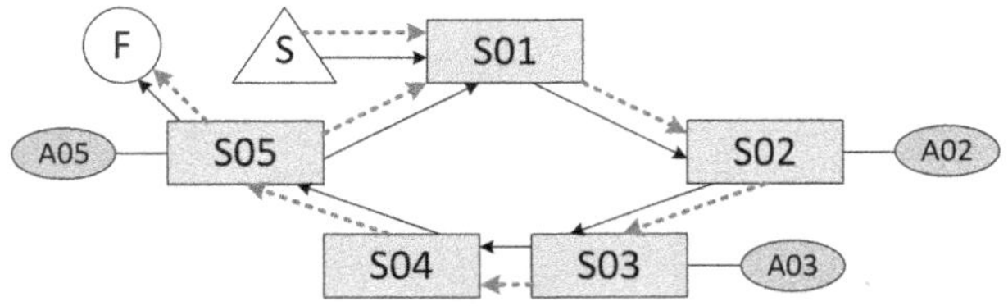

Figure 5: Cycle pattern with five scenes and three blocks of additional information.

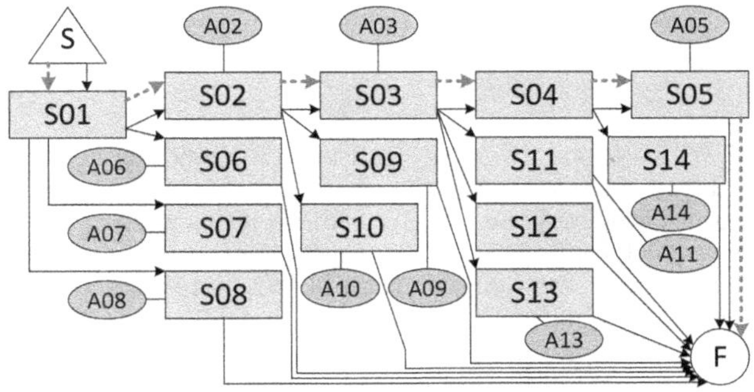

Figure 6: Split pattern with 14 scenes and eleven blocks of additional information.

Figure 4: Sequence pattern with five scenes and three blocks of additional information.

would be necessary to get reliable results due to their large variance in structure, depending on the usage scenario. All hypervideos contain the same sub-patterns. The test-results for the sub-patterns can then be combined into a recommendation for a specific hypervideo. The patterns used in our evaluation are derived from the analysis of existing scene graphs that were created for different scenarios using our software (see [19, 21, 29] for further descriptions). We also analyzed the work of Bernstein [6] for the suitability of the patterns in hypertext for structures in hypervideos. Basically three patterns reoccur and will therefore be analyzed in detail:

- **Sequence pattern:** The sequence pattern provides a linear series of scenes from the start to the end of the video. Hereby, every scene is watched by the viewer. This results in the same user-pattern as the structure pattern. The sequence pattern used in the tests in this work has five video scenes. Three of them have annotations. An illustration of this pattern can be found in Figure 4. The exact durations of scenes, files sizes, and display times of annotations can be found in Table 2.
- **Cycle pattern:** The cycle pattern has two or more scenes which can be watched more than once. Every scene is watched by the viewer. At the last scene of the cycle, the viewer can decide if she/he wants to watch the scenes one more time. Hereby, the user-pattern may even be larger than the structure pattern. The cycle pattern used in our tests contains the same scenes and annotations as the sequence pattern (see Figure 5). The exact durations of scenes, files sizes, and display times of annotations can be found in Table 2. The cycle is taken three times by the viewer in our tests. It gives hints on how the cache is managed internally.

- **Split pattern:** The scenes in the split pattern have at least two successor scenes of which one can be selected by the viewer. The viewer usually only watches a small subset of the scenes of the structure pattern, resulting in a much smaller user-path pattern than the structure pattern. The split pattern in our tests contains 14 scenes whereof eleven have annotations. Only five scenes are selected, see Figure 6. The exact durations of scenes, files sizes, and display times of annotations can be found in Table 2. We apply different probabilities to the paths in this pattern resulting in three different sub-tests. One test is performed with equal probabilities for all scenes at a fork in the scene graph. A test with very low probabilities for the selected user-path is performed with the following settings: S1 → S2: 7%, S2 → S3: 5%, S3 → S4: 5%, and S4 → S5: 10%. The test with high probabilities for the selected user-path uses these settings: S1 → S2: 70%, S2 → S3: 80%, S3 → S4: 85%, and S4 → S5: 90%. This pattern gives hints about the quality of the pre-fetching algorithms.

To provide a comparability between the patterns, the same five scenes are always selected for playback, S01 to S05, resulting in a playback time of 188 sec. This playback time is enough because the relative results for the metrics that emerge from the scene changes do not change if they are measured for longer playback paths. These scenes have the same additional information in each scenario resulting in the same minimum download volume for each test. The videos were VP8 encoded WebM videos with a 720p HD resolution. All additional information were JPG images.

4.3 Test Environment

Each pattern is tested with the bandwidths 11 Mbit/s,

Table 3: Statistics: split pattern, MSE immediately, bandwidth 11 Mbit/s, 50 runs

	Wait start [ms]	Wait playback [ms]	Breaks [count]	Download volume [Mbit/s]
Minimum	227	26771	4	292.47
Maximum	359	27356	4	293
Average	261.14	27048.82	4	292.74
SD	20.07	118.64	0	0.13
1st quart.	249.5	26973.25	4	292.63
2nd quart.	260	27037	4	292.72
3rd quart.	268	27115	4	292.86

Table 4: Number of playback breaks (0-0.9 → green, 1-3.9 → yellow, 4-9.9 → orange, ≥ 10 → red)

Pattern	Bandwidth	status quo	HTML5	MSE imm.	MSE wait	MSE w.n.b.	$\bar{x}$
Sequence	11	12	5	1	0	0	3.6
	13.5	8	1	1	0	0	2.0
	16	4	0	0	0	0	0.8
	$\bar{x}$	8	2	0.67	0	0	2.1
Cycle	11	10	5	2	1	0	3.6
	13.5	7	1	0	0	0	1.6
	16	6	0	0	0	0	1.2
	$\bar{x}$	7.67	2	0.67	0.33	0	2.1
Split high	11	13	6	2	1	0	4.4
	13.5	7	1	1	1	0	2.0
	16	5	0	0	0	0	1.0
	$\bar{x}$	8.33	2.33	1	0.67	0	2.5
Split avg	11	12	9	4	2	0	5.4
	13.5	7	6	2	1	0	3.2
	16	6	5	1	1	0	2.6
	$\bar{x}$	8.33	6.67	2.33	1.33	0	3.7
Split low	11	13	13	2	1	0	5.8
	13.5	7	7	2	1	0	3.4
	16	4	4	1	1	0	2.0
	$\bar{x}$	8	8	1.67	1	0	3.7
$\bar{x}$		8.1	4.2	1.3	0.7	0.0	

13.5 Mbit/s, and 16 Mbit/s. These bandwidths were derived from currently available exemplary average connection speeds throughout the world [5]. 16 Mbit/s represent an average speed available in Norway or Switzerland, 13.5 Mbit/s is available in Denmark or the UK, and 11 Mbit/s is, on average, reached in Slovakia or Hungary. To provide these bandwidths, we used a local web server and the maximum bandwidth was limited using the NetLimiter tool [14] (version 4.0.13.0) at client side. All tests were performed in an automated way, with the waiting time for selecting the next scene set to three seconds. The values were logged for the evaluation. All test runs were performed on a Windows 8.1 computer using the Chrome Browser (version 42.0.2311.152 m) and a browser cache size setting of 209.71 MB. With a minimum download volume of 239 MB for a user-path, not all elements fitted into the cache accordingly. The files used in the evaluation can be requested from the authors of this paper.

4.4 Statistics

Each of the 75 test runs (5 pattern * 3 download speeds * 5 algorithm settings) is performed in real time, resulting in a playback time of 188 seconds. Adding waiting times, download times, and times for test setup we wanted to minimize the time needed for the tests. Accordingly, we performed a pre-test of 50 test runs in one representative setting (split pattern, average probabilities, MSE immediately, bandwidth 11 Mbit/s) to evaluate the variations of the result values. The results showed that the variations were very small to non-existent (see Table 3 for the exact values). The difference between the first and the third quartile for the waiting time before playback is 17.5 ms which is less than the display duration of a frame. The difference between the first and the third quartile for the waiting time during playback is 0.14 sec, which is less than 0.5 sec (the duration for recognizing a break). The number of breaks is the same for all test runs. The difference between the first and the third quartile for the download volume is 0.22 MB which is one sixth of the smallest used annotation size. Having shown that the variances between the different test runs are very small, we concluded that one run per test setting is enough to get meaningful results (using the same preconditions in the test environment as for the statistics test).

4.5 Breaks During Playback

Taking a look at the number of breaks during scenes, it can be stated that the status quo has by far the most breaks for each bandwidth, pattern, and on average ($\bar{x} = 8.1$ breaks).

The best results are achieved for the "MSE wait no break" implementation which has no breaks in any of the test cases. Slightly worse results are achieved by the "MSE wait" implementation with a maximum of two breaks during playback on average and for all patterns, except the sequence pattern where both implementations show the same results. A maximum of four breaks is achieved by the "MSE immediately" implementation which achieves on average slightly worse results than the "MSE wait" implementation ($\bar{x} = 1.3$ breaks vs. $\bar{x} = 0.7$ breaks). The HTML5 implementation shows worse results than all of the MSE implementations, but better results than the status quo except for the split pattern with low probabilities on the user path, where both implementations show the same number of pauses. Using the pre-fetching in HTML5 can reduce the breaks by half ($\bar{x} = 4.2$ breaks) compared to the status quo without any pre-fetch. The exact results are given in Table 4.

4.6 Waiting Times

Taking a look at the waiting times in the different patterns, we distinguish between the waiting time at the beginning of scenes, the time to wait after a break during a scene, and the sum of both times. The lowest waiting time at the beginning of scenes was achieved by the improved HTML5 implementation for each of the patterns as well as on average. Similarly low beginning scene waiting times were also measured using the status quo and the "MSE immediately" strategies. The lowest waiting time during scenes was reached by the "MSE wait no break" strategy for all patterns as well as on average. The lowest overall waiting time

132

Table 5: Waiting times at different bandwidths, at the beginning and during scenes (0-3 → green, 3.1-6 → yellow, 6.1-12 → orange, ≥ 12.1 → red), as well as summarized waiting times (0-6 → green, 6.1-12 → yellow, 12.1-24 → orange, ≥ 24.1 → red).

Pattern	Bandw.	status quo			HTML5			MSE immediately			MSE wait			MSE wait no break			$\overline{x}(sum)$
		start	during	sum	start	during	sum	start	during	sum	start	during	sum	start	during	sum	
Sequence	11	0.3	42.5	42.8	0.1	10.3	10.3	0.3	7.1	7.4	17.8	1.2	19.0	31.6	0.6	32.3	**22.4**
	13.5	0.3	22.6	22.9	0.1	1.9	1.9	0.2	1.7	2.0	0.9	1.1	2.1	10.4	0.6	11.0	**8.0**
	16	0.3	11.3	11.6	0.1	0.6	0.7	0.3	1.1	1.3	0.8	0.7	1.5	3.1	0.7	3.8	**3.8**
	$\overline{x}$	0.3	25.5	25.8	0.1	4.3	4.3	0.3	3.3	3.6	6.5	1.0	7.5	15.0	0.6	15.7	**11.4**
Cycle	11	0.8	44.8	45.8	0.1	14.1	14.3	0.8	14.7	15.5	35.1	3.2	38.3	69.2	2.0	71.2	**37.0**
	13.5	0.8	27.2	27.9	0.1	3.5	3.7	0.8	4.1	4.8	2.8	2.4	5.3	22.6	1.9	24.5	**13.2**
	16	0.8	16.6	17.4	0.1	2.1	2.3	0.9	3.5	4.3	2.3	2.2	4.52	7.9	1.9	9.8	**7.7**
	$\overline{x}$	0.8	29.5	30.4	0.1	6.6	6.8	0.8	7.4	8.2	13.4	2.6	16.0	33.2	1.9	35.2	**19.3**
Split high	11	0.3	41.6	41.9	0.1	10.5	10.6	0.3	16.4	16.7	29.9	1.5	31.4	45.6	0.7	46.3	**29.4**
	13.5	0.3	24.6	24.9	0.1	2.0	2.1	0.3	6.2	6.5	4.9	3.0	7.9	29.0	0.6	29.6	**14.2**
	16	0.3	11.4	11.7	0.1	0.6	0.7	0.2	1.8	2.0	0.8	1.2	2.0	12.9	0.7	13.5	**6.0**
	$\overline{x}$	0.3	25.9	26.2	0.1	4.4	4.5	0.3	8.1	8.4	11.9	1.9	13.8	29.2	0.7	29.8	16.5
Split avg.	11	0.3	40.9	41.2	0.0	30.0	30.0	0.3	27.0	27.3	37.6	2.0	39.6	71.7	0.6	72.3	**42.1**
	13.5	0.3	24.0	24.4	0.0	15.1	15.1	0.3	14.2	14.4	18.7	3.2	22.0	47.4	0.7	48.0	**24.8**
	16	0.3	15.4	15.7	0.1	8.9	8.9	0.3	9.0	9.3	7.6	1.7	9.2	24.3	0.7	25.0	**13.6**
	$\overline{x}$	0.3	26.8	27.1	0.0	18.0	18.0	0.3	16.7	17.0	21.3	2.3	23.6	47.8	0.7	48.4	**26.8**
Split low	11	0.3	42.0	42.3	0.3	42.3	42.6	0.3	28.1	28.4	41.3	1.7	43.0	78.2	0.6	78.8	**47.0**
	13.5	0.3	24.0	24.3	0.3	24.6	24.9	0.3	16.0	16.3	20.5	3.3	23.8	53.1	0.7	53.8	**28.6**
	16	0.3	11.2	11.6	0.3	12.6	12.9	0.3	10.9	11.2	9.5	1.7	11.1	33.9	0.6	34.5	**16.3**
	$\overline{x}$	0.3	25.7	26.1	0.3	26.5	26.8	0.3	18.3	18.6	23.8	2.2	26.0	55.1	0.6	55.7	**30.6**
	$\overline{x}$	0.4	26.7	27.1	0.1	11.9	12.1	0.4	10.8	11.2	15.4	2.0	17.4	36.1	0.9	37.0	

depends on the underlying structure pattern. The "MSE immediately' implementation achieves the best results for the sequence pattern, the split pattern with average or low probabilities on the user path, as well as on average. The HTML5 implementation performs better for the Cycle pattern and especially for the split pattern with high probabilities on the user path.

The highest beginning scene waiting times are reached by the "MSE wait no break" strategy for all patterns individually and averaged. This results from the pre-fetch behavior and the calculation of the start frame which makes sure that no breaks occur during playback. Most of the content loaded into the cache results in high to very high beginning scene waiting times. The highest during scenes waiting times are achieved by the status quo on average and for all patterns except for the split pattern with low probabilities on the user path. The highest overall waiting times are reached by the "MSE wait no break" implementation on average and for all patterns except for the sequence pattern, where the status quo achieves longer waiting times.

To summarize these findings, it can be noted that the HTML5 or the "MSE immediately" implementations achieve the shortest overall waiting times, but show longer waiting times during the scenes, especially for the split pattern with average or low probabilities on the user path. The "MSE wait" implementation has slightly longer overall waiting times, where only a very small amount of time has to be waited during playback. The status quo has the shortest beginning scene waiting times, but very long during scene waiting times. "MSE wait no break" represents the opposite behavior, having very long beginning scene waiting times

and very short during scene waiting times. Another finding is that the number of breaks correlates with the waiting times after a break. Accordingly, it can be noted that each break leads to a certain waiting time. An overview of all results is given in Table 5.

4.7 Overall Download Volume

The overall download volume is always the lowest for the status quo implementation on average and for all patterns, because no pre-fetching is done and all elements are downloaded when they are needed. The minimum download volume for all patterns is 239 MB, which is also the size of all scenes and annotations together for the sequence and the cycle pattern. The size of all elements for the split pattern is about three times as high (663.42 MB). Equal results are achieved by the HTML5 implementation with pre-fetch for the sequence, the cycle, and the split pattern with high priorities for the user path. All MSE strategies achieve the minimum available download volume of 239 MB for the sequence pattern. The download volumes are higher for each of the MSE implementations for the split pattern, while the "MSE immediately" implementation requires less volume ($\overline{x} = 358.7MB$) than the "MSE wait" ($\overline{x} = 377.8MB$) and the "MSE wait no break" ($\overline{x} = 384.5MB$) implementation. An overview of all results is given in Table 6.

The values for the cycle pattern are much higher for the MSE implementations compared to the other patterns. The available buffer size in the tests is 209 MB. The amount of data of one cycle is 239 MB, which is slightly higher than the overall available buffer size. One could assume that all implementations result in a higher download vol-

Table 6: Overall download volume in MB (239 MB → green, 239.1-318.7 MB → yellow, 318.8-398.3 MB → orange, ≥ 398.4 MB → red)

Pattern	Bandwidth	status quo	HTML5	MSE imm.	MSE wait	MSE w.n.b.	$\bar{x}$
Sequence	11	239	239	239	239	239	**239.0**
	13.5	239	239	239	239	239	**239.0**
	16	239	239	239	239	239	**239.0**
	$\bar{x}$	239.0	239.0	239.0	239.0	239.0	**239.0**
Cycle	11	239	239	570	662	664	**474.8**
	13.5	239	239	654	672	541	**469.0**
	16	239	239	570	672	672	**478.4**
	$\bar{x}$	239.0	239.0	598.0	668.7	625.7	**474.1**
Split high	11	239	239	267	281	289	**263.0**
	13.5	239	239	283	283	324	**273.6**
	16	239	239	333	333	346	**298.0**
	$\bar{x}$	239.0	239.0	294.3	299.0	319.7	**278.2**
Split avg.	11	239	272	293	309	336	**289.8**
	13.5	239	285	337	346	367	**314.8**
	16	239	296	363	363	386	**329.4**
	$\bar{x}$	239.0	284.3	331.0	339.36	363.0	**311.3**
Split low	11	239	272	294	313	345	**292.6**
	13.5	239	272	330	346	376	**312.6**
	16	239	272	370	370	404	**331.0**
	$\bar{x}$	239.0	272.0	331.3	343.0	375.0	**312.1**
	$\bar{x}$	**239.0**	**254.7**	**358.7**	**377.8**	**384.5**	

ume, because the buffer is eventually full and has to be deleted. But the status quo and the HTML5 implementation only need the minimum download volume. This can be explained by the fact that the Chrome Browser has a media cache in addition to the standard cache. A large amount of the downloaded data is moved into this media cache and not kept in the standard browser cache, thus retransmissions are avoided. Using MSE, the downloaded clusters are not recognized as media files and therefore stored in the standard browser cache. The data of one cycle exceeds the cache size, resulting in a deleting of the elements from the cache and a repeated download during the next cycle. Knowing this for the Chrome Browser, we also examined the caching behavior for other available browsers for the cycle pattern. The Opera Browser (version 31.0) shows the same behavior as the Chrome Browser. Internet Explorer (version 11.0.9.600.17905) has no dedicated media cache. Its standard cache size is 250 MB, so the data of the whole cycle fit into the cache and nothing has to be deleted. The Firefox Browser (version 39.0) also only has one cache with a standard cache size of 367 MB. Tests showed that not all data are stored in the cache, which resulted in higher values for the download volume for all implementations using Firefox.

5. GUIDELINES

From the findings of the previous section and the results in [16, 17], we can derive the following guidelines for the implementation of hypervideo web players with HTML5 or MSE:

- *Minimization of breaks:* Use the "MSE wait" implementation as described in this paper. It does not avoid breaks at all costs but keeps the waiting time at the beginning of scenes as low as possible.
- *Minimization of waiting times before scenes:* Use "MSE immediately" or HTML5. The "MSE immediately" implementation provides a solution for less breaks during scenes and the HTML5 implementation results in a lower download volume.
- *Minimization of the download volume:* Use the HTML5 implementation. It needs a little more volume than the "status quo", but provides much better results for waiting times and breaks during scenes.
- *Hypervideo with mainly sequences or many splits of paths:* Use HTML5 or "MSE immediately".
- *Hypervideo with many circles:* Use the HTML5 implementation because it performs better if the browser provides a separate media cache (see Section 4.7).

6. CONCLUSIONS

In this work we presented hypervideo download and cache management algorithms implemented in HTML5 and MSE. We compared our new implementations to the status quo of an HTML5 hypervideo player. We tested the implementations with three different patterns (sequence, cycle, and split pattern), at three different bandwidths (11 Mbit/s, 13.5 Mbit/s, and 16 Mbit/s), and one set of video scenes and annotations. We tested larger file sizes with higher bandwidth in our previous work [16, 17] and discovered that if file size and bandwidth increase linearly the effects of our strategies stay the same.

The results show that significantly lower overall waiting times can be achieved if either HTML5 pre-fetching or MSE is used. We implemented three different versions of the algorithms for MSE ("MSE immediately", "MSE wait", and "MSE wait no break") that balance the beginning and during scene waiting times differently. "MSE immediately" and HTML5 with pre-fetching show similar results in many test settings. The overall waiting time of the "MSE wait" implementation is higher than for the "MSE immediately" and the HTML5 with pre-fetching implementations. It shows longer beginning scene waiting times, but results in no, or only very few, breaks. With much shorter overall waiting times, the "MSE wait" implementation is preferable to the "MSE wait no break" implementation. Overall download volume strongly depends on the browser used and its internal cache management. It is especially relevant when the hypervideo has many cycles which may be viewed more than once. Due to the caching behavior of the browsers using HTML5, retransmissions are avoided.

In future work, we want to test our algorithms in hypervideos that contain a table of contents and a keyword search function. In order to be able to deal with random jumps in a hypervideo's structure we want to see how the algorithms described in this work need to be improved.

7. ACKNOWLEDGMENTS

This work was funded by the Bundesministerium für Bildung und Forschung (German Federal Ministry of Education and Research) (BMBF) under project number 03V0633.

8. REFERENCES

[1] Svg smil animation. Website (accessed October 17, 2015), 2015. http://caniuse.com/feat=svg-smil.

[2] Adobe Systems Incorporated. Actionscript 3.0 reference for the adobe flash platform. Website (accessed October 12, 2015), 2015. http://help.adobe.com/en_US/FlashPlatform/reference/actionscript/3/index.html.

[3] Adobe Systems Incorporated. Adobe flash professional cc. Website (accessed October 12, 2015), 2015. http://www.adobe.com/products/flash.html.

[4] Adobe Systems Software Ireland Ltd. Adobe flash platform runtimes. statistics : Pc penetration. Website (accessed October 12, 2015), 2011. http://www.adobe.com/de/products/flashplatformruntimes/statistics.html.

[5] Akamai Technologies. akamai's [state of the internet] - q3 2015 report. Website (accessed January 13, 2016), 2015. https://www.akamai.com/us/en/multimedia/documents/report/q3-2015-soti-connectivity-final.pdf.

[6] M. Bernstein. Patterns of hypertext. In Proceedings of the Ninth ACM Conference on Hypertext and Hypermedia: Links, Objects, Time and Space - structure in Hypermedia Systems: Links, Objects, Time and Space - structure in Hypermedia Systems, HYPERTEXT '98, pages 21–29, New York, NY, USA, 1998. ACM.

[7] Cisco. Cisco visual networking index: Global mobile data traffic forecast update 2014-2019 white paper. Visual networking index (vni), white paper, CISCO, February 2015.

[8] Cisco. Vni forecast highlights. Website (accessed October 13, 2015), 2015. http://www.cisco.com/web/solutions/sp/vni/vni_forecast_highlights/index.html.

[9] Codevise Solutions Limited. Pageflow. das tool für multimediales storytelling. Website (accessed October 12, 2015), 2015. http://pageflow.io/de.

[10] Z. Fei, M. Ammar, I. Kamel, and S. Mukherjee. Providing interactive functions through active client-buffer management in partitioned video multicast vod systems. In L. Rizzo and S. Fdida, editors, Networked Group Communication, volume 1736 of Lecture Notes in Computer Science, pages 152–169. Springer Berlin Heidelberg, 1999.

[11] R. Grigoras, V. Charvillat, and M. Douze. Optimizing hypervideo navigation using a markov decision process approach. In Proceedings of the Tenth ACM International Conference on Multimedia, MULTIMEDIA '02, pages 39–48, New York, NY, USA, 2002. ACM.

[12] Honkytonk Films. Klynt. Website (accessed October 12, 2015), 2015. http://www.klynt.net/.

[13] R. Laraspata, D. Striccoli, and P. Camarda. A scheduling algorithm for interactive video streaming in umts networks. In Computers and Communications (ISCC), 2010 IEEE Symposium on, pages 997–1002, June 2010.

[14] Locktime Software. Welcome to netlimiter. netlimiter is an ultimate internet traffic control and monitoring tool designed for windows. Website (accessed August 30, 2015), 2015. http://www.netlimiter.com/.

[15] mc-quadrat. Linius. das storytelling-tool. Website (accessed October 12, 2015), 2015. http://linius-storytelling.de/.

[16] B. Meixner. Annotated Interactive Non-linear Video - Software Suite, Download and Cache Management. Phd thesis, Universität Passau, 2014.

[17] B. Meixner. A pattern-based evaluation of download and cache management algorithms for annotated interactive non-linear videos. Multimedia Systems, pages 1–35, 2016.

[18] B. Meixner and H. Kosch. Interactive non-linear video: Definition and xml structure. In Proceedings of the 2012 ACM Symposium on Document Engineering, DocEng '12, pages 49–58, New York, NY, USA, 2012. ACM.

[19] B. Meixner, B. Siegel, G. Hölbling, F. Lehner, and H. Kosch. Siva suite: Authoring system and player for interactive non-linear videos. In Proceedings of the International Conference on Multimedia, MM '10, pages 1563–1566, New York, NY, USA, 2010. ACM.

[20] B. Meixner, B. Siegel, P. Schultes, F. Lehner, and H. Kosch. An html5 player for interactive non-linear video with time-based collaborative annotations. In Proceedings of International Conference on Advances in Mobile Computing & Multimedia, MoMM '13, pages 490:490–490:499, New York, NY, USA, 2013. ACM.

[21] B. Meixner, K. Tonndorf, S. John, C. Handschigl, K. Hofmann, and M. Granitzer. A multimedia help system for a medical scenario in a rehabilitation clinic. In Proceedings of the 14th International Conference on Knowledge Technologies and Data-driven Business, i-KNOW '14, pages 25:1–25:8, New York, NY, USA, 2014. ACM.

[22] Microsoft. Microsoft silverlight. Website (accessed October 12, 2015), 2015. http://www.microsoft.com/silverlight/.

[23] Microsoft Corporation. Microsoft silverlight release history. Website (accessed October 12, 2015), 2015. http://www.microsoft.com/getsilverlight/locale/en-us/html/Microsoft%20Silverlight%20Release%20History.htm.

[24] Mozilla Developer Network. <video>. Website (accessed October 12, 2015), 2015. https://developer.mozilla.org/en-US/docs/Web/HTML/Element/video.

[25] S. Podlipnig and L. Böszörmenyi. A survey of web cache replacement strategies. ACM Comput. Surv., 35(4):374–398, Dec. 2003.

[26] M. Shreedhar and G. Varghese. Efficient fair queueing using deficit round robin. SIGCOMM Comput. Commun. Rev., 25(4):231–242, Oct. 1995.

[27] M. Silverman. The history of html5. Website (accessed October 12, 2015), 2012. http://mashable.com/2012/07/17/history-html5.

[28] Stack Exchange Inc. (User: AndreaC). Code::trends - a visualization of the stackoverflow dataset. Website (accessed October 12, 2015), 2012. http://stackapps.com/questions/3509/codetrends-a-visualization-of-the-stackoverflow-dataset.

[29] K. Tonndorf, T. Knieper, B. Meixner, H. Kosch, and F. Lehner. Challenges in creating multimedia instructions for support systems and dynamic

problem-solving. In *Proceedings of the 12th International Conference on Knowledge Management and Knowledge Technologies*, i-KNOW '12, pages 33:1–33:4, New York, NY, USA, 2012. ACM.

[30] E. Trautman. Rip flash: Why html5 will finally take over video and the web this year. Website (accessed October 12, 2015), 2014. http://thenextweb.com/dd/2014/04/19/rip-flash-html5-will-take-video-web-year/.

[31] W3C. Smil 2.0 testimonials. Website (accessed October 17, 2015). http://www.w3.org/2001/08/smil2-testimonial.

[32] W3C. Synchronized multimedia integration language. w3c working draft 09-november-97. Website (accessed October 17, 2015), 1997. http://www.w3.org/TR/WD-smil-971109.

[33] W3C. Smil animation. w3c recommendation 04-september-2001. Website (accessed October 17, 2015), 2001. http://www.w3.org/TR/2001/REC-smil-animation-20010904/.

[34] W3C. Html 5. a vocabulary and associated apis for html and xhtml. w3c working draft 22 january 2008. Website (accessed October 12, 2015), 2008. http://www.w3.org/TR/2008/WD-html5-20080122/.

[35] W3C. Synchronized multimedia integration language (smil 3.0). w3c recommendation 01 december 2008. Website (accessed October 17, 2015), 2008. http://www.w3.org/TR/SMIL3/.

[36] W3C. Html5. a vocabulary and associated apis for html and xhtml. w3c recommendation 28 october 2014. Website (accessed October 12, 2015), 2015. http://www.w3.org/TR/html5/.

[37] W3C. Media source extensions. w3c candidate recommendation 31 march 2015. Website (accessed October 15, 2015), March 2015. http://www.w3.org/TR/media-source/.

[38] W3C. Media source extensions. w3c editor's draft 13 october 2015. Website (accessed October 15, 2015), March 2015. http://w3c.github.io/media-source/.

[39] Wavelength Media. Flash player version history. Website (accessed October 12, 2015), 2015. http://www.mediacollege.com/adobe/flash/player/version/.

[40] WordPress.com. Wordpress.com. Website (accessed October 12, 2015). https://wordpress.com/.

[41] S. Yegulalp. Adobe flash: Insecure, outdated, and here to stay. Website (accessed October 12, 2015), 2014. http://www.infoworld.com/article/2610420/adobe-flash/adobe-flash--insecure--outdated--and-here-to-stay.html.

[42] YouTube Engineering and Developers Blog. Youtube now defaults to html5 <video>. Website (accessed October 12, 2015), 2015. http://youtube-eng.blogspot.de/2015/01/youtube-now-defaults-to-html5_27.html.

Summarizing Situational Tweets in Crisis Scenario

Koustav Rudra
IIT Kharagpur, India
koustav.rudra@cse.iitkgp.ernet.in

Siddhartha Banerjee
The Pennsylvania State University, USA
sub253@ist.psu.edu

Niloy Ganguly
IIT Kharagpur, India
niloy@cse.iitkgp.ernet.in

Pawan Goyal
IIT Kharagpur, India
pawang@cse.iitkgp.ernet.in

Muhammad Imran
Qatar Computing Research Institute, HBKU, Doha, Qatar
mimran@qf.org.qa

Prasenjit Mitra
Qatar Computing Research Institute, HBKU, Doha, Qatar
pmitra@qf.org.qa

ABSTRACT

During mass convergence events such as natural disasters, microblogging platforms like Twitter are widely used by affected people to post situational awareness messages. These crisis-related messages disperse among multiple categories like infrastructure damage, information about missing, injured, and dead people etc. The challenge here is to extract important situational updates from these messages, assign them appropriate informational categories, and finally summarize big trove of information in each category. In this paper, we propose a novel framework which first assigns tweets into different situational classes and then summarize those tweets. In the summarization phase, we propose a two stage summarization framework which first extracts a set of important tweets from the whole set of information through an Integer-linear programming (ILP) based optimization technique and then follows a word graph and content word based abstractive summarization technique to produce the final summary. Our method is time and memory efficient and outperforms the baseline in terms of quality, coverage of events, locations et al., effectiveness, and utility in disaster scenarios.

Keywords: Disaster events; Twitter; situational information; classification; summarization.

1. INTRODUCTION

In response to an event, a lot of short messages are posted on social media. Specifically, microblogging platforms such as Twitter provide rapid access to situation-sensitive messages that people post during mass convergence events such as natural disasters. Studies show that these messages contain situational awareness and other useful information such as reports of urgent needs, missing or found people that, if processed timely, can be very effective for humanitarian organizations for their disaster response efforts [27]. Enabling rapid crisis response requires processing of these messages as soon as they arrive. However, typically the volume and velocity of these messages during big disasters can go beyond hu-

man processing capacity. For instance, the largest observed peak was during the Sandy hurricane in which around 16 thousands messages per minute were posted using hashtag #Sandy.

Typically, the first step in extracting situational awareness information from these tweets involves classifying them into different informational categories such as infrastructure damage, shelter needs or offers, relief supplies. For instance, one such application is AIDR [10] that performs real-time classification of Twitter messages into different categories. However, even after the automatic classification step, each category still contains thousands of important messages—also increasing each passing minute, which requires further in-depth analysis to make a coherent situational awareness summary for disaster managers to understand the situation.

To get a quick overview of the event and what tweeters are saying about it, a summary of these tweets is very valuable. To deal with the information overload issue and to extract time-sensitive information, in this work, we propose to generate automatic summaries using messages that are classified as useful.

To this end, a straightforward and fast way would be to pick the messages that maximize the coverage of the content words (extractive summarization) [22]. However, to maximize the coverage of information within the specified word limit, it may be necessary to combine related information from several messages (abstractive summarization). For example, consider the following tweets from Nepal earthquake that happened in 2015:

1. Dharara Tower built in 1832 collapses in Kathmandu during earthquake

2. Historic Dharara Tower Collapses in Kathmandu After 7.9 Earthquake

Both tweets provide information about the collapsing of the Dharara tower. Our objective is to combine important information from both of these tweets and generate a single meaningful situational tweet that contains all the relevant information like, Dharara tower built in 1832 collapses in Kathmandu after 7.9 earthquake.

Tweet summarization is a hard problem because given thousands of tweets identifying which tweets are the most important and informative is a subjective problem difficult for even humans to solve. One needs to cover the entire information yet be concise. Even if the most important tweets are chosen, we need to automatically piece them together to create a coherent readable summary. De-

HT '16, July 10-13, 2016, Halifax, NS, Canada

© 2016 ACM. ISBN 978-1-4503-4247-6/16/07...$15.00

DOI: http://dx.doi.org/10.1145/2914586.2914600

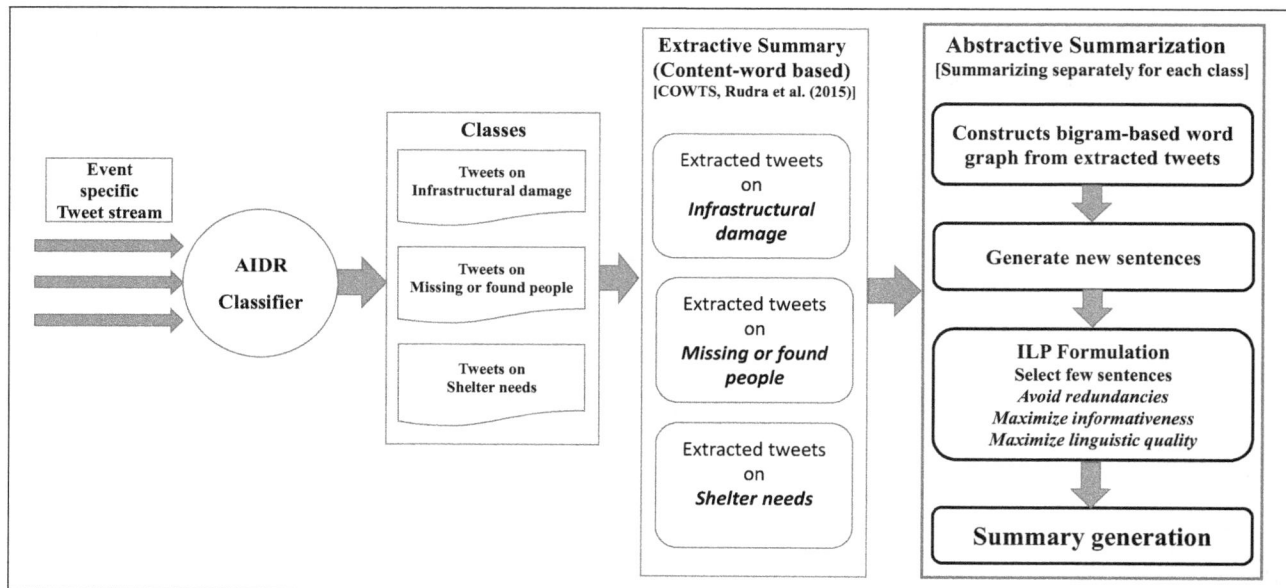

Figure 1: Our proposed framework for Abstractive Summarization of disaster-specific tweets

spite progress in natural language generation, generating abstractive summaries remains a hard problem. Although abstractive summarization [16] produces more compact and informative sentences, the algorithms in general are time-consuming. Hence if the abstractive approach is run over entire incoming set of tweets, it may not be possible to produce the results in run-time (which is one of the important requirements during disaster).

In order to circumvent this problem, first we extract a set of important tweets from the whole set using a fast but effective extractive summarization. In the second step, we use abstractive summarization to choose and rewrite the most important tweets among them, remove redundancy and improve the readability of these tweets.

Figure 1 provides an overview of our proposed approach. We test our proposed approach over Nepal earthquake dataset [14]. In the first step, messages are classified into appropriate classes by AIDR (Artificial Intelligence for Disaster Response) platform [10]. We focus on three information classes, i). *infrastructure and utilities damage*, ii). *missing, trapped, or found people*, and iii). *shelter and supplies needs or offers*. In the summarization phase, first we extract an important set of informative messages from the whole set. Then we propose a word graph based abstractive summarization technique which combines information from semantically similar tweets and finally apply ILP-based[1] content word coverage method to generate final summary for each of the classes respectively.

Our contribution lies in the two-step extractive-abstractive summarization strategy (section 4) that is efficient and yet, generates better summaries with respect to information coverage, diversity, redundancy, coherence, and readability. Experimental results in section 5 confirm that the extractive-abstractive summarization model performs better than state-of-the-art Twitter specific real time summarization models in terms of ROUGE-1 recall and F-scores in most of the cases. We also perform crowdsourcing based experi-

ment and find that our algorithm is superior in terms of readability, information coverage, redundancy and information diversity.

2. RELATED WORK

Twitter has evolved as one of the most significant sources of information during disaster-specific events. Real-time information posted by affected people on Twitter help improve disaster relief operations [4, 9]. However, it is important to extract the crucial information from the tweets for effective planning by relief organizations [12]. Summarization of Twitter information is significantly more challenging than news articles. The difficulty arises due to two important reasons. First, tweets provide continuous stream of data and therefore it requires real-time processing. Second, the tone of the tweets is different from the formal language used in news articles.

Kedzie, et al. [11] proposed an extractive summarization [6] method to summarize disaster event-specific information from news articles. In contrast, several researchers have attempted to utilize information from Twitter to retrieve important situational updates from millions of posts on disaster-specific events [23, 26, 28, 31]. More recently, sophisticated methods for automatically generating summaries by extracting the most important tweets on the event [15, 22] have been proposed. To generate summaries in real-time, a few approaches for online summarization of tweet streams have recently been proposed [24, 32, 30]. Osborne *et al.* [17] proposed a real event tracking system using greedy summarization. Shou et al. [24] used clustering and LexRank [2] based extractive summarization technique to generate summaries from Twitter.

All the above mentioned methods generate summaries that are merely a collection of tweets. An abstractive summary is desirable because it can generate a summary by collecting important content from the tweets and not including entire tweets. Such a summary should also be more readable than a collection of tweets. Furthermore, the summaries should not contain redundant information. To this end, Olariu [16] proposed a bigram word-graph-based summarization technique that is capable of handling online stream of tweets in real-time and also generate summaries that are abstrac-

---

[1]Henceforth we represent integer linear programming approach as ILP-based approach

tive [18] in nature. Each bigram represents a node in the graph and new words are added real-time from incoming new tweets. However, the method does not consider POS-tag information of nodes and thus can create spurious fusions of tweets having the same bigram but used in a different context. Furthermore, it is a generalized method and does not take into consideration the typicality of disaster related tweets. Banerjee, *et al.* [1] proposed a graph-based abstractive summarization method on news articles. Several new sentences are generated using the graph and an optimization problem is formulated that selects the best sentences from the new sentences to optimize the overall quality of the summary. The optimization problem ensures that redundant information is not conveyed in the final generated summary. However, the graph construction and path generation is computationally expensive in real-time.

In this work, we combine the positive aspects of the above studies - (a) we use a variant of [1] for tweet fusion but employ an extractive step initially to enable the graph to generate new sentences in real-time, (b) we use POS tags along with the words in each bigram to avoid spurious fusions and (c). we also employ disaster-specific content words to determine the importance of a disaster-related tweet [22]. Details of the methodology will be elaborated subsequently.

3. DATASET AND CLASSIFICATION OF MESSAGES

We use the crisis-related messages collected and classified by the AIDR platform [10] from Twitter posted during the 2015 Nepal Earthquake. More than 27 million messages were collected from April 25th to April 27th using different keywords (e.g. "Nepal Earthquake, NepalQuake, NepalQuakeRelief, NepalEarthquake, KathmanduQuake, QuakeNepal, EarthquakeNepal, ⋯ "). AIDR is used to classify tweets into several categories (see below); we seek to develop summaries of tweets belonging to each category automatically. For example, for the Nepal earthquake crisis, around 9,000 messages were labeled by the volunteers of the Standby Task Force (SBTF), into the classes/categories specified below. AIDR uses these human-labeled messages to train classifiers that automatically classify subsequent messages collected from Twitter in real-time.

The classes used are as follows:

1. **Injured or dead people:** Casualties due to the crisis

2. **Missing, trapped, or found people:** Questions and/or reports about missing or found people

3. **Displaced people:** People who have been relocated due to the crisis, even for a short time (includes evacuations)

4. **Infrastructure and utilities:** Buildings or roads damaged or operational; utilities/services interrupted or restored

5. **Shelter and supplies:** Needs or donations of shelter and/or supplies such as food, water, clothing, medical supplies or blood

6. **Money:** Money requested, donated or spent

7. **Volunteer or professional services:** Services needed or offered by volunteers or professionals

8. **Animal management:** Pets and animals, living, missing, displaced, or injured/dead

9. **Caution and advice:** Warnings issued or lifted, guidance and tips

10. **Personal updates:** Status updates about individuals or loved ones

11. **Sympathy and emotional support:** Thoughts and prayers

12. **Other relevant information:** Other useful information that helps one understand the situation

13. **Not related or irrelevant:** Unrelated to the situation or irrelevant

In this work, we selected AIDR classified messages from three categories for which the machine confidence was ≥ 0.80. The selected classes and messages in each of the three classes are as follows:

1. **Missing, trapped, or found people** (10,751 machine classified messages)

2. **Infrastructure and utilities** (16,842 machine classified messages)

3. **Shelter and supplies** (19,006 machine classified messages).

4. AUTOMATIC SUMMARIZATION

Given the categorized messages by AIDR for which the machine-confidence score is ≥ 0.80 (as described in section 3), in this section we present our two step automatic summarization approach to generate summaries from each class. We consider the following key characteristics/objectives while developing an automatic summarization approach:

1. A summary should be able to capture most situational updates from the underlying data. That is, the summary should be rich in terms of information coverage.

2. As most of the messages on Twitter contain duplicate information, we aim to produce summaries with less redundancy while keeping important updates of a story.

3. Twitter messages are often noisy, informal, and full of grammatical mistakes. We aim to produce more readable summaries as compared to the raw tweets.

4. The system should be able to generate the summary in real-time, i.e., the system should not be heavily overloaded with computations such that by the time the summary is produced, the utility of that information is marginal.

The first three objectives can be achieved through abstractive summarization and near-duplicate detection, however, it is very difficult to achieve that in real-time (hence violating the fourth constraint). In order to fulfill these objectives, we follow an extractive-abstractive framework to generate summaries. In the first phase (extractive phase), we improve the approach proposed by Rudra et al. [22] and select a sub-set of tweets that cover most of the information produced and then run abstractive summarization over that.

4.1 Extractive Summarization Approach

Disaster-related tweets have distinct features that we use to construct our extractive summaries.

Content Words: As identified in earlier studies [15, 22], in crisis scenarios some specific type of words can play a key role by capturing important events and snapshots. Such useful words which we term as *content words* are as follows:

- Numerals (number of casualties, missing or found people, emergency helpline and ambulance numbers)

- Nouns (capturing important disaster specific context words such as 'hospital', 'ambulance' etc.)

- Information about locations/places surrounding the disaster affected area

- Main verbs ('collapsed', 'destroyed', 'killed', 'trapped' etc.), capturing most of the event phrases

Duplicates: Moreover, a large proportion of messages on Twitter contain redundant information. For instance, in the following five tweets, the same information related to the closure of Kathmandu airport and flights cancellation is conveyed in different ways:

1. Nepal quake , Kathmandu airport shut, flights from India cancelled via @timesofindia

2. Flights to Kathmandu put on hold following powerful earthquake Read more here

3. Kathmandu airport shut, flights from India cancelled

4. K'mandu airport shut, flights from India cancelled via @timesofindia

5. After massive 7.9 earthquake, commercial flights to Kathmandu put on hold

To handle duplicate or near duplicate information in the messages and to find disaster specific content words we follow two schemes — (i) we remove duplicate and near-duplicate tweets (using the technique developed by Tao, et al., [25]), and (ii) we focus on the content words during summarization as proposed by Rudra, et al. [22].

We consider each class (infrastructure and utilities, missing, trapped or found people, shelter and supplies) separately and try to extract concise summaries for these classes. Specifically, we take day-wise snapshots of each class, i.e., the system produces a summary of the desired length (number of words) over each day for each of the classes using an improved version of COWTS [22]. First we extract a set of content words i.e. words with numeral, noun or verb pos-tags from the messages and try to maximize the coverage of these set of content words. In this phase, our main objective is to capture all the content words within a small number of tweet set such that the next phase of abstractive summarization can generate paths from these tweets and also rank those paths in near real-time. On an average within 1,000 words limit, majority of the content words (present in the entire tweet set) can be covered within the chosen limited set of tweets. We illustrate the rationale behind the 1000 word limit as follows.

Role of *content words* during disaster We want to check whether content words play a different role in disaster scenario or not. We observed that number of content words grow very slowly compared to other general events like sports, music or politics. To understand this, we compare tweet streams posted in above mentioned three different disaster classes (infrastructure, missing, shelter) with those posted during two sports, and specific datewise events;

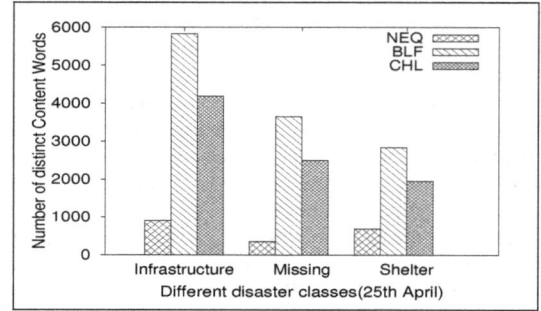

Figure 2: Variation in the number of distinct content words with the number of tweets shown for three disaster classes during Nepal earthquake(NEQ), and two other types of events(BLF, CHL)

these streams were made publicly available by [24]. we have measured the number of content words present in the above mentioned classes. In order to compare their variation with general events, we random sample same number of tweets(as respective disaster classes) from two general events — i) blackfriday (BLF), (ii) chelsea (CHL). Figure 2 shows that number of content words increase very slowly during disaster events compared to any other general event. This observation indicates that capturing such content words can provide an effective coverage of disaster events.

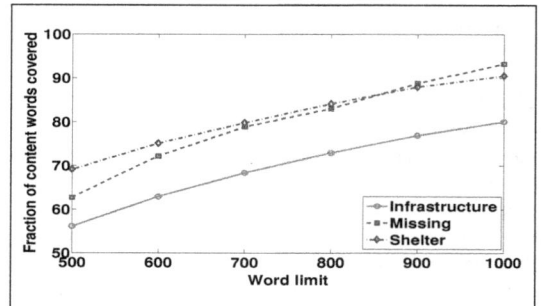

Figure 3: Variation in the coverage of content words with number of extracted tweets.

Content-word coverage vis-a-vis length In Figure 3, we show how the coverage of content words varies with number of tweets extracted from the whole dataset for three different classes of tweets posted on 25th April, 2015. We observe a similar pattern for the other days. An informative set of 1,000 words may be sufficient for the next stage of summarization; hence, we extract a set of tweets with 1,000 word limit constraint in our initial extractive phase of summarization.

After extracting a set of important and informative tweets we try to prepare a more concise and comprehensive summary through a COntent Words based ABstractive Summarization (**COWABS**) approach using these tweets (described next).

4.2 Abstractive Summarization

The goal of this step is to generate an abstractive summary by combining information from multiple tweets. The generated summary must be comprehensive in the sense that it contains more information than extractive summaries of the same length (in words). Our abstractive summarization method is aimed at maximizing the informativeness of tweets and avoiding redundancy of information jointly. We follow an over-generate and select [29] strategy where we combine multiple tweets to generate a new sentence. Our method tries to select the best sentences from the set of generated sentences and create a summary by optimizing three factors: **Informativeness, Redundancy** and **Readability**. Informativeness and readability have to be maximized, while redundancy is required to be minimized. *Informativeness* is defined as the amount of information in the summary, measured using a centroid-based ranking score. *Redundancy* is minimized such that we do not convey same or similar information in multiple sentences in the summary. We use a trigram-based log-likelihood score using a language model as a dummy representative of the *Readability* of the generated content. We adapt the ILP-based method for summarization proposed by Banerjee, et al. [1] for news summarization; however, we make several modifications to make it usable for tweet summarization. Instead of a unigram-based sentence generation technique, we employ a bigram-based method. This adaptation improves the grammaticality of the resulting summaries. We also introduce a content-word based parameter in the ILP to tackle informativeness and redundancy.

Sentence Generation Process: In order to generate sentences, we **build up a word-graph** [3] with the entire tweet set where each tweet is iteratively added to the graph with the bigrams (adjacent words along with their parts-of-speech (POS) tags[2]) representing the nodes. An edge in the graph represents consecutive words in a sentence. When a new tweet is added to the graph and it contains a bigram that already exists in the graph, the nodes of the new tweet are merged with the existing nodes. We merge the nodes if the words in the bigrams have the same lexical form as well as the same POS tag. POS tags help maintain grammaticality and avoid potentially spurious fusions.

An example of our bigram-based word-graph construction is shown in Figure 4. Each node has been labeled with the form $w1 \parallel w2$, where $w1$ and $w2$ refer to the first and the second word in every bigram, respectively. We mark two nodes as the start and the end nodes that indicate the beginning and end of the tweets. The graph is generated considering the following two tweets that were tweeted on a particular day and were assigned to the infrastructure class by the AIDR system — (i) *dharara tower built in 1832 collapses in kathmandu during earthquake*, and (ii) *historic dharara tower collapses in kathmandu after 7.9 earthquake*. We lower-case all words during the graph construction.

Once the graph is formed, sentences, which we term as *tweet-paths* are generated by **traversing paths in the graph** between the dummy *Start* and the *End* nodes. For example, from the graph in Figure 4, we can easily generate a *tweet-path* such as *dharara tower built in 1832 collapses in kathmandu after 7.9 earthquake*. Several such sentences might hold more information than the original tweets, yet containing the same or similar number of words.

We set a minimum (10 words) and maximum (16 words) length for a sentence to be generated. We apply such constraints to avoid very long sentences that might be grammatically ill-formed and very short sentences that are often incomplete. In a real-scenario, the number of generated *tweet-paths* can be several thousands, be-

Table 1: Notations used in the summarization technique

Notation	Meaning
L	Desired summary length (number of words)
n	Number of *tweet-paths* considered for summarization (in the time window specified by user)
m	Number of distinct content words included in the n *tweet-paths*
i	index for *tweet-paths*
j	index for content words
x_i	indicator variable for *tweet-paths* i (1 if *tweet-paths* i should be included in summary, 0 otherwise)
y_j	indicator variable for content word j
$Length(i)$	number of words present in *tweet-paths* i
$I(i)$	Informativeness score of the *tweet-paths* i
$LQ(i)$	Linguistic quality score of a *tweet-paths*
T_j	set of *tweet-paths* where content word j is present
C_i	set of content words present in *tweet-paths* i

cause there can be multiple points of merging across several tweets. Our goal is to select the best paths from these generated paths with the objective of generating a readable and informative summary. We formulate an ILP problem to select final paths and construct the summary.

ILP Formulation

The ILP-based technique optimizes based upon three factors - (i) Presence of content words (this is similar to that adopted during the extractive phase): The formulation tries to maximize the number of content words in the final summary. Consequently, maximizing content words automatically implies tackling *redundancy* as constraints avoid choosing the same content words from the set of generated paths. (ii) Informativeness of a path i.e. importance of a path, and (iii) *Linguistic Quality Score* that captures the readability of a path using a trigram confidence score.

Informativeness($I(i)$)**:** We use a centroid based ranking as a proxy of sentence importance as one of the system configurations in our experiments. Centroid-based ranking [19] implies selection of sentences that are more central to the topic of the document. Each sentence is represented as a TF-IDF vector. The centroid is basically the mean of the TF-IDF vectors of all the sentences. Cosine similarity value between the sentences and the centroid is computed and used as the informativeness component in the ILP formulation.

Linguistic Quality Score ($LQ(i)$) : The linguistic quality score is computed using a language model. A language model assigns probabilities to the occurrences of words. We use a Trigram language model [8] to compute a score with the goal of assigning higher scores to more probable sequences of words.

$$LQ(s_i) = \frac{1}{(1 - ll(w_1, w_2, w_3, \cdots, w_q))} \quad (1)$$

where $ll(w_1, w_2, w_3, \cdots, w_q)$ is computed as:

$$ll(w_1, w_2, w_3, \cdots, w_q) = \frac{1}{L} log_2 \prod_{t=3}^{q} P(w_t | w_{t-1} w_{t-2}) \quad (2)$$

Assuming the sentence consists of the words $w_1, w_2, w_3, \cdots w_q$, the value of $LQ(i)$ is computed using the above two equations

The summarization of L words is achieved by optimizing the following ILP objective function, whereby the highest scoring *tweet-*

---

[2]We employed a Twitter specific POS tagger [5]. In addition to the regular parts-of-speech tags, it also tags hashtags, retweet mentions, URLs separately. We ignore such words that have these specific hashtags because they are not important in the context of summarization as it might affect readability.

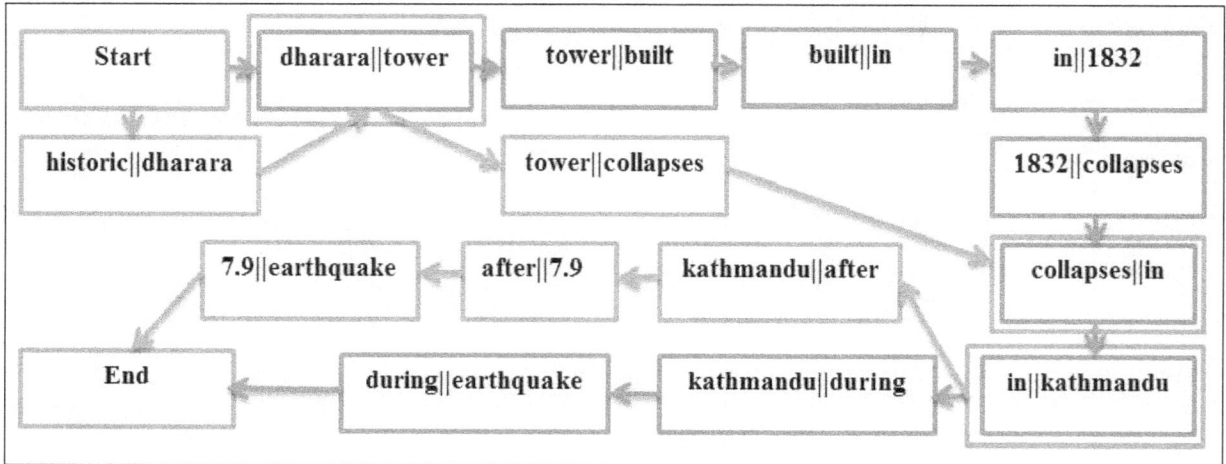

Figure 4: Bigram word graph generated using above two tweets. (We do not show POS tags in the figure for clarity). Nodes from different tweets are represented by different colors. Common nodes contain both the colours. Start and End are special marker nodes.

paths are returned as output of summarization, The equations are as follow:

$$max(\sum_{i=1}^{n} LQ(i).I(i).x_i + \sum_{j=1}^{m} y_j) \quad (3)$$

subject to the constraints

$$\sum_{i=1}^{n} x_i \cdot Length(i) \leq L \quad (4)$$

$$\sum_{i \in T_j} x_i \geq y_j, j = [1 \cdots m] \quad (5)$$

$$\sum_{j \in C_i} y_j \geq |C_i| \times x_i, i = [1 \cdots n] \quad (6)$$

where the symbols are as explained in Table 1. The objective function considers both the number of *tweet-paths* included in the summary (through the x_i variables) as well as the number of important content-words (through the y_j variables) included. The constraint in Eqn. 4 ensures that the total number of words contained in the *tweet-paths* that get included in the summary is at most the desired length L (user-specified) while the constraint in Eqn. 5 ensures that if the content word j is selected to be included in the summary, i.e., if $y_j = 1$, then at least one *tweet-path* in which this content word is present is selected. Similarly, the constraint in Eqn. 6 ensures that if a particular *tweet-path* is selected to be included in the summary, then the content words in that *tweet-path* are also selected.

We use the GUROBI Optimizer [7] to solve the ILP. After solving this ILP, the set of *tweet-paths* i such that $x_i = 1$, represent the summary at the current time.

5. EXPERIMENTAL SETUP AND RESULTS

In this section, we compare the performance of our proposed framework with state-of-the-art abstractive and disaster-specific summarization techniques. We first describe the baseline technique as well as the experimental settings.

5.1 Experimental Settings

Given the AIDR classified messages from three classes i.e. (1) *infrastructure and utilities damage*, (2) *missing, trapped, or found*

people, and (3) *shelter and supplies*, we perform date-wise split starting from 25th April to 27th April, 2015 of the messages.

Establishing gold standard summaries: We take summaries generated by experts from the disaster management domain. During Nepal earthquake, UN OCHA (United Nations Office for the Coordination of Humanitarian Affairs) among other humanitarian organizations used AIDR's output (i.e. machine classified messages) for their disaster response efforts. In this case, the experts were given the machine classified messages that they analyzed to generate a situational awareness report for each informational category. We consider these reports as our gold standard summaries, which contain 498, 4,609, and 6,826 words for infrastructure, missing, and shelter classes respectively. Following their standard practice, the experts also incorporated useful information from other social media sources such as Facebook in the reports.

Baseline approaches: We use three state-of-the-art summarization approaches as our baseline that are described below:

1. **COWTS:** is an extractive summarization approach specifically designed for generating summaries from disaster-related tweets [22].

2. **APSAL:** is an affinity clustering based summarization technique proposed by Kedzie et al. [11]. It mainly considers news articles and focuses on human-generated information nuggets to assign salience score to those news articles while generating summaries.

3. **TOWGS:** is an online abstractive summarization approach proposed by Olariu [16]. It is designed for informal texts like tweets. They consider bigrams as nodes and build word graph using these nodes. To generate a summary, they start from most frequent bigrams to explore different paths. However, TOWGS method is not proposed to generate event-specific summaries. In our case, we modified it to generate event-specific summaries. While generating a path, we start with most frequent bigram node, and subsequently expand the path by finding most promising adjacent node based on co-occurrence frequency etc. as proposed by Olariu. We prepare a final summary by coalescing the generating paths,

Table 2: Comparison of ROUGE-1 recall (with classification, Twitter specific tags, emoticons, hashtags, mentions, urls, removed and standard rouge stemming(-m) and stopwords(-s) option) for COWABS (the proposed methodology) and three baseline methods (COWTS, APSAL, TOWGS) on the same situational tweet stream across three different classes (infrastructure, missing, shelter) over three different dates.

Step size	ROUGE-1 recall Score											
	Infrastructure				Missing				Shelter			
	COWABS	COWTS	APSAL	TOWGS	COWABS	COWTS	APSAL	TOWGS	COWABS	COWTS	APSAL	TOWGS
25th	**.0972**	.0678	.0588	.0656	**.0206**	.0189	.0131	.0156	**.0189**	.0185	.0131	.0181
26th	**.1018**	.0927	.0520	.0588	**.0201**	.0168	.0147	.0140	**.0211**	.0173	.0168	.0152
27th	**.0882**	.0791	.0610	.0701	**.0196**	.0131	.0126	.0138	**.0198**	.0176	.0155	.0141

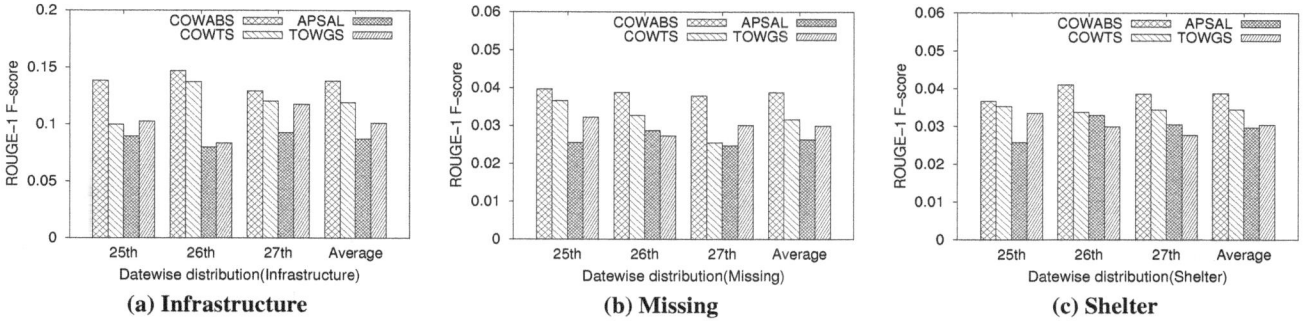

(a) Infrastructure   (b) Missing   (c) Shelter

Figure 5: ROUGE-1 F-scores of the date wise summaries of different classes, generated by the proposed methodology (COWABS) and three baseline methods from 25th to 27th April, 2015.

Table 3: Summary of length 50 words(excluding #,@,RT,URLs), generated from the situational tweets of the infrastructure class (26th April) by (i) COWABS (proposed methodology), (ii) COWTS.

Summary by COWABS	Summary by COWTS
Times of india live blog earthquake in katmandu , 25 04 2015. Chairs follow-up meeting to review situation following earthquake in decades. 5 commercial flights have landed in kathmandu was painted in 1850 ad. Iaf's c-130j aircraft carrying 55 passengers , including four infants , lands at delhi's palam airport. Nepal quake photos show historic buildings reduced to rubble as survivor search continues.	#PM chairs follow-up meeting to review situation following #earthquake in #Nepal @PMOIndia #nepalquake. @SushmaSwaraj @MEA-controlroom Plz open help desk at kathmandu airport. @Suvasit thanks for airport update. #NepalQuake. Pakistan Army Rescue Team comprising doctors, engineers & rescue workers shortly after arrival at #Kathmandu Airport http://t.co/6Cf8bgeort. RT @cnnbrk: Nepal quake photos show historic buildings reduced to rubble as survivor search continues. http://t.co/idVakR2QOT http://t.co/Z.

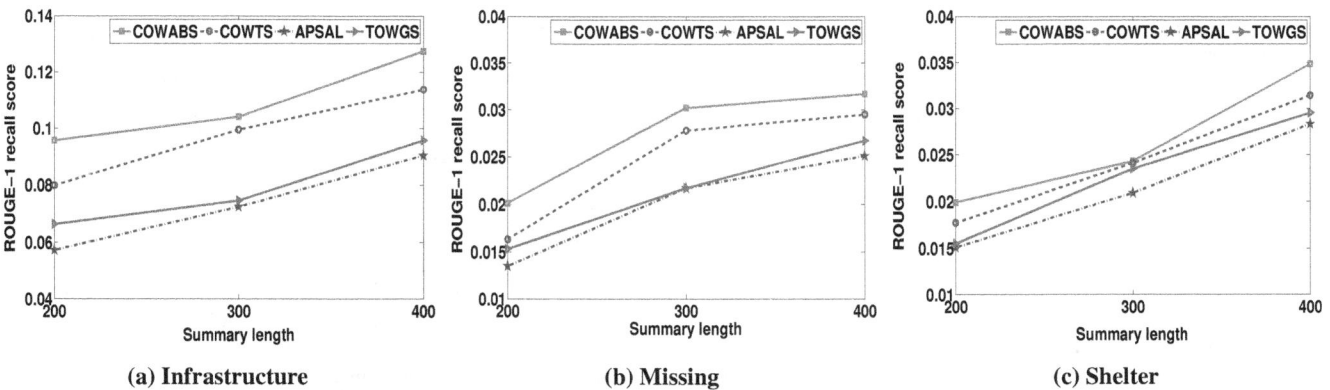

(a) Infrastructure   (b) Missing   (c) Shelter

Figure 6: Variation in ROUGE-1 recall scores with system summary length

however, similar tweet-paths are removed based on cosine similarity.

Evaluations: We perform two types of evaluations. First, we use the standard ROUGE [13] metric for evaluating the quality of summaries generated using the proposed as well as the baselines methods. In this case, due to the informal nature of tweets, we consider the recall and F-score of the ROUGE-1 variant only. Second, we perform user studies using paid crowdsourcing (described below).

5.2 Performance comparison

Table 2 and Figure 5 depict the ROUGE-1 recall and F-scores for the three algorithms for each class and day. *Note that the low recall values correspond to the mismatch in the length of the system generated summary (200 words) and gold standard summary (ranging from 500 to 7000 words).* We can see that COWABS performs significantly better compared to other three baselines - the improvement ranges from 20% to 40%.

Further in order to test the robustness of COWABS, we compare the performance of the baselines by increasing the summary length. To perform this experiment, we vary summary length in the range of 200 to 400 for all the different classes. From figure 6, it is observed that as summary length increases, COWABS is increasingly able to capture more informative content compared to other baseline approaches.

To give a flavor of the kind of summaries produced by the proposed summarization approach, Table 3 shows summaries generated by COWABS and COWTS (both disaster-specific methodologies) from the same set of messages (i.e tweets form infrastructure class posted on 26th April). The two summaries are quite distinct. We find that summary returned by COWABS is more informative and diverse in nature compared to COWTS. For instance, we can see the COWABS summary contains information about flights, damages of buildings, and information sources.

Redundancy in summaries: Apart from ROUGE-1 score, we also measure redundancy score of the summaries as this can indicate if the summaries contain distinct or redundant information. We compute redundancy score for a summary as follows: For each sentence included in the summary (a sentence can be a tweet or a path), we assign it a *sentence redundancy score* as its maximum cosine similarity (excluding #,@,URLs,stopwords) with any other sentence in the summary. Finally, we take an average of the individual sentence redundancy scores to compute the redundancy value for the summary. Table 4 shows redundancy values of different methods across each of the three classes. Through abstraction, we can reduce redundancy by 30.11%, 27.75%, 47.95% respectively for each of the three classes.

Table 4: Redundancy score for different methods of summarization (lower is better)

Method	Redundancy score		
	Infrastructure	Missing	Shelter
COWABS	0.1775	0.2099	0.1433
COWTS	0.1833	0.2122	0.2112
APSAL	0.2986	0.3797	0.3731
TOWGS	0.3205	0.3222	0.3336

Evaluation using crowdsourcing: Next, we perform crowdsourced evaluation using the CrowdFlower [3] crowdsourcing platform. We

[3] http://www.crowdflower.com/

take summaries generated from each class using our proposed method and all three baselines for each day—in total we use 9 summaries. A crowdsourcing task, in this case, consists of four summaries (i.e. one proposed and three from baseline methods) and the four criteria with their description (as described below) along with a scale from 1 (very bad) to 5 (very good) for each criterion. For each task, we asked five different annotators to read each summary carefully and provide scores for each criterion. The exact description of the crowdsourcing task is as follows: *"The purpose of this task is to evaluate machine-generate summaries using tweets collected during the Nepal Earthquake happened in 2015. Each task given below has 4 summaries of length 200 words generated by 4 different algorithms on same set of tweets (thousands in this case) belong to a particular topic. Given the summaries and their topic, we are interested in comparing them based on the following criteria: Information coverage, Redundancy, Diversity and Readability".* We provide details analysis of our crowdsourcing task in the following section:

Information coverage corresponds to the richness of information a summary contains. For instance, a summary with more informative sentences (i.e. crisis-related information) is considered better in terms of information coverage. Our proposed method is able to capture very good situational information/updates in case of Infrastructure and Missing class for both of the days chosen while it performs fairly in the shelter class. However, in 5 cases it performs better than the three competing techniques and for rest of the 4 cases it performs equally well to some baseline technique. Figure 7 shows details ranking of users for 25th and 26th April [4].

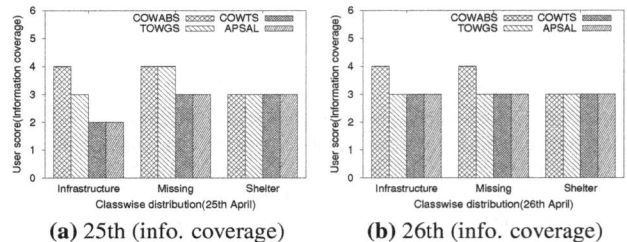

(a) 25th (info. coverage)   **(b)** 26th (info. coverage)

Figure 7: Results of the crowdsourcing based evaluation based on the information coverage

Redundancy corresponds to the duplication of same information. A good summary should be representative of underlying data and should have less redundant information. COWABS outperforms other baselines in case of 6 summaries and in rest of the cases it performs equally well to some other baseline. In our first phase of extractive summarization technique, we try to remove similar tweets to reduce redundancy and user observations suggest that COWABS is taking advantage of that phase to reduce redundancy in final summary. We provide details of user ranking in figure 8.

Diversity corresponds to the novelty of sentences in a summary. A good summary should contain diverse informative sentences. Although we do not apply any direct parameter in our ILP framework to control diversity, but in our abstractive ILP method, we not only rely on importance score of paths but also coverage of different content words which helps in capturing information from various

[4] We only keep two dates to maintain clarity and brevity

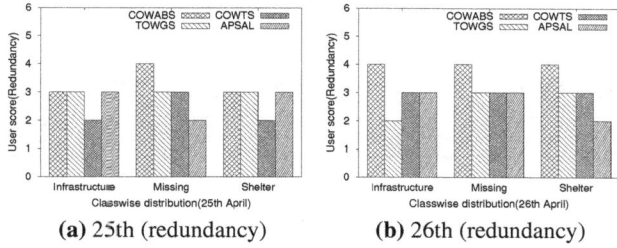

(a) 25th (redundancy)   **(b)** 26th (redundancy)

Figure 8: Results of the crowdsourcing based evaluation based on the redundancy

dimensions. This is also quite clear from figure 9. Out of 9 summaries, COWABS appeared to be more diverse in 4 cases and in all other cases it performs equally well as others.

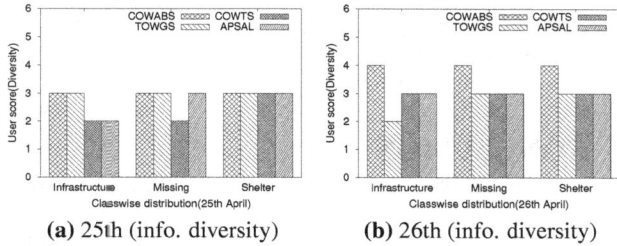

(a) 25th (info. diversity)   **(b)** 26th (info. diversity)

Figure 9: Results of the crowdsourcing based evaluation based on the information diversity

Readability corresponds to the overall readability of the content in a summary. For instance, a good summary should be easily readable, well formed, having less grammatical mistakes. One of our main focus in this summarization technique is to make summaries more readable and coherent. For that, we have applied linguistic quality score in our final ILP framework and prefer those paths which have higher linguistic scores. According to user evaluations, COWABS appears to be more readable compared to other baselines in 6 cases. Figure 10 reveals that readability wise our summaries get lowest score as 3, the performance is particularly good on 26th April where it is marked 4 (good) for all the cases.

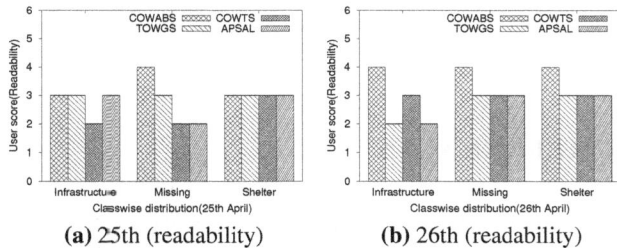

(a) 25th (readability)   **(b)** 26th (readability)

Figure 10: Results of the crowdsourcing based evaluation based on the readability

In particular, COWABS outperforms other baseline techniques in most of the cases and rest of the cases it is a tie but it never performs poorly compared to any baseline method.

Evaluation in terms of time taken: During such crisis scenario, time is very critical and one of our main focuses is on real-time

summarization. Hence, we analyze the execution times of the various techniques. Table 5 provide details information about run-time of our proposed COWABS method and other three baselines. The time taken is comparable with other real-time summarization approaches like COWTS [22] and TOWGS [16]. APSAL requires more time due to non-negative matrix factorization and affinity clustering approach over large dataset. COWABS is taking slightly higher running time compared to COWTS and TOWGS, but it is at par with these two baselines. However, COWABS performs much better compared to COWTS and TOWGS in terms of information coverage, readability, redundancy, diversity.

Quality of Information Summarized: Beyond the mere numbers proving our superiority, we also looked into the tweets and checked its quality with respect to (a). number of distinct places mentioned (b). number of event phrases used and (c). extent of numbers present in the summary. Details of which follow -

Location coverage: During large scale disaster like earthquake, flood *et al.* several parts of a country are damaged and coverage of information from these different places are necessary. Location coverage corresponds to the information about different places a summary contains. For instance, a summary with diverse information from many locations is considered better in terms of location coverage. The problem is challenging in the sense that there is overwhelmingly more information about big cities/towns in the tweet. For example, during Nepal earthquake most of the information are available in Twitter from its capital city **Kathmandu** but there is a scarcity of information from local villages like **Barpak**, **Lamjung** etc. Our proposed method COWABS is able to capture information about more number of locations in 7 cases. Figure 11 shows number of locations captured by different methods.

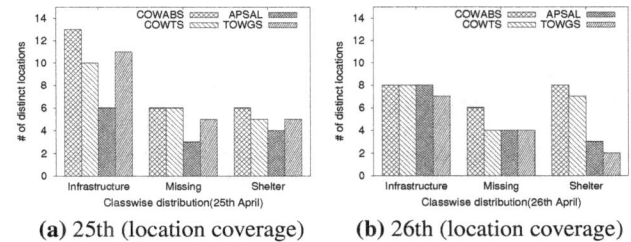

(a) 25th (location coverage)   **(b)** 26th (location coverage)

Figure 11: Coverage of locations in summaries by COWABS (proposed) and three baselines (COWTS, APSAL, TOWGS)

Event coverage: To extract event phrases, we have used a named entity recognition tool designed explicitly for tweets [20, 21], which tags the words in a tweet with event. For instance, in the tweet "180 Bodies Retrieved From Debris of Nepal's Historic Tower", the word 'Retrieved' is tagged as an event phrase. A good summary should contain more number of distinct events. Out of the 9 cases, our proposed method is able to capture more number of events in 7 cases. We provide details information about event coverage in figure 12.

Numerical coverage: As identified in earlier studies [22, 15] numerals play a key role in disaster scenario as they contain information about casualties, injured or missing people, tracking numbers, helpline information etc. Summary which contains more numer-

145

Table 5: Runtime (seconds) of different algorithms for each of the three classes (infrastructure, missing, shelter).

Date	Infrastructure					Missing					Shelter				
	#Tweets	COWABS	COWTS	APSAL	TOWGS	#Tweets	COWABS	COWTS	APSAL	TOWGS	#Tweets	COWABS	COWTS	APSAL	TOWGS
25/04	9371	25.57	23.46	1187.19	19.34	3953	14.98	11.15	35.20	7.10	2593	11.21	8.68	96.95	7.22
26/04	5036	19.14	17.21	4507.50	18.91	5668	16.98	14.89	504.41	14.24	11178	42.45	40.24	16002.47	29.84
27/04	2435	11.07	8.76	533.62	14.17	1130	7.90	5.54	21.70	4.90	5267	23.94	21.21	7653.34	22.73

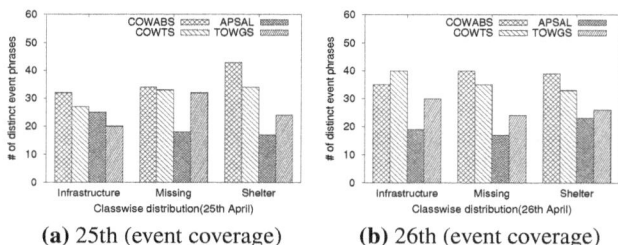

(a) 25th (event coverage)   **(b)** 26th (event coverage)

Figure 12: Coverage of event phrases in summaries by COWABS (proposed) and three baselines (COWTS, APSAL, TOWGS)

ical information is more useful during disaster scenario, specially for certain types of disaster classes like 'missing or trapped people', 'injured or dead people' etc. Our proposed method is able to capture more number of numerical information in 8 cases. Figure 13 provides details about numerical information coverage of different summarization techniques.

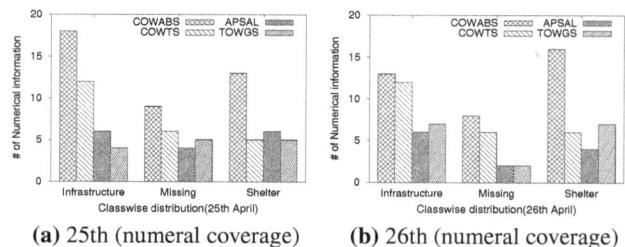

(a) 25th (numeral coverage)   **(b)** 26th (numeral coverage)

Figure 13: Coverage of numerals in summaries by COWABS (proposed) and three baselines (COWTS, APSAL, TOWGS)

It is quite clear that COWABS is able to capture more microlevel information compared to other baseline techniques which is a crucial requirement of summarization process.

5.3 Reason behind better performance

We try to dissect the three baseline algorithms and identify their limitations and thus understand the reason behind COWABS superior performance.

TOWGS, proposed by Olariu [16], ranks different paths based on normal term frequency of each node (bigram) constituting a path. However, term weight might not clearly justify relevancy of a term. Besides this, Olariu's technique does not employ any grammaticality or linguistic quality check; as a result, TOWGS suffers due to poor readability as evident from our crowdsourcing experiments. Our other baseline, APSAL, is a semi-supervised technique which also maintains clusters of related information and finally chooses one exemplar tweet from each cluster. All clusters are assumed to have equal importance which might not always be applicable. Fur-

thermore, the method was originally proposed for summarization on formal news articles where clusters are more coherent as compared to clusters of tweets. Due to mismatch in reality, it is not able to generate summaries with high informative content (as evident from ROUGE-1 scores). Furthermore, as can be seen from the human judgments, APSAL summaries also contain significant redundancies. COWTS although extractive performs the best among all the baselines according to the ROUGE-1 scores perhaps due to its simplicity. However, COWTS suffers from the fundamental problem of extractive summarization namely redundancy. Same or similar information might exist in two different tweets, yet they can be the part of the summary. As a result, information is repeated as evident from our crowdsourcing experiments.

6. CONCLUSION

A large number of tweets are posted during disaster scenarios and a concise, categorical representation of those tweets is necessary. In this paper, we develop a complete system to generate summaries in real time from the incoming stream of tweets. We specifically take the tweets generated during Nepal Earthquake and generate comprehensive abstractive summaries for three most important classes - infrastructure, missing and shelter. We perform an extensive evaluation of our algorithm by roping in disaster-related experts in the loop - results show that our method - COWABS perform significantly better than all competing baselines. We also perform crowd-sourcing experiment asking the crowd to rank our algorithm compared to baselines – in all the cases ours is ranked higher. Also independently the crowd comments that our summaries are high-quality thus satisfying the purpose for which the entire exercise has been undertaken. We would strive to deploy the system so that it can be practically used for any future disaster event.

Acknowledgement: This research was partially supported by a grant from the Information Technology Research Academy (ITRA), DeITY, Government of India (Ref. No.: ITRA/15 (58)/ Mobile/ DISARM/ 05) Additionally, K. Rudra was supported by a fellowship from Tata Consultancy Services. The authors thank the anonymous reviewers whose suggestions greatly helped to improve the paper.

7. REFERENCES

[1] S. Banerjee, P. Mitra, and K. Sugiyama. Multi-document abstractive summarization using ilp based multi-sentence compression. In *Proceedings of the 24th International Joint Conference on Artificial Intelligence (IJCAI)*, 2015.

[2] G. Erkan and D. R. Radev. LexRank:Graph-based lexical centrality as salience in text summarization. *Artificial Intelligence Research*, 22:457–479, 2004.

[3] K. Filippova. Multi-sentence compression: finding shortest paths in word graphs. In *Proceedings of the 23rd International Conference on Computational Linguistics*, pages 322–330. Association for Computational Linguistics, 2010.

[4] H. Cao, G. Barbier, and R. Goolsby. Harnessing the crowdsourcing power of social media for disaster relief. *Intelligent Systems, IEEE*, 26(3):10–14, 2011.

[5] K. Gimpel, N. Schneider, B. O'Connor, D. Das, D. Mills, J. Eisenstein, M. Heilman, D. Yogatama, J. Flanigan, and N. Smith, A. Part-of-speech tagging for twitter: Annotation, features, and experiments. In *Proc. ACL*, 2011.

[6] V. Gupta and G. S. Lehal. A survey of text summarization extractive techniques. *Journal of Emerging Technologies in Web Intelligence*, 2(3):258–268, 2010.

[7] Gurobi – The overall fastest and best supported solver available, 2015. http://www.gurobi.com/.

[8] K. Heafield. Kenlm: Faster and smaller language model queries. In *Proceedings of the Sixth Workshop on Statistical Machine Translation*, pages 187–197. Association for Computational Linguistics, 2011.

[9] M. Imran, C. Castillo, F. Diaz, and S. Vieweg. Processing social media messages in mass emergency: a survey. *ACM Computing Surveys (CSUR)*, 47(4):67, 2015.

[10] M. Imran, C. Castillo, J. Lucas, P. Meier, and S. Vieweg. AIDR: Artificial intelligence for disaster response. In *Proceedings of the companion publication of the 23rd international conference on World wide web companion*, pages 159–162. International World Wide Web Conferences Steering Committee, 2014.

[11] C. Kedzie, K. McKeown, and F. Diaz. Predicting salient updates for disaster summarization. In *Proceedings of the 53rd Annual Meeting of the Association for Computational Linguistics and the 7th International Joint Conference on Natural Language Processing (Volume 1: Long Papers)*, pages 1608–1617, Beijing, China, July 2015. Association for Computational Linguistics.

[12] B. Klein, X. Laiseca, D. Casado-Mansilla, D. López-de Ipiña, and A. P. Nespral. Detection and extracting of emergency knowledge from twitter streams. In *Ubiquitous Computing and Ambient Intelligence*, pages 462–469. Springer, 2012.

[13] C.-Y. Lin. ROUGE: A package for automatic evaluation of summaries. In *Proc. Workshop on Text Summarization Branches Out (with ACL)*, 2004.

[14] 2015 Nepal earthquake – Wikipedia, April 2015. http://en.wikipedia.org/wiki/2015_Nepal_earthquake.

[15] M.-T. Nguyen, A. Kitamoto, and T.-T. Nguyen. TSum4act: A Framework for Retrieving and Summarizing Actionable Tweets during a Disaster for Reaction. In *Proc. PAKDD*, 2015.

[16] A. Olariu. Efficient online summarization of microblogging streams. In *Proc. EACL*, pages 236–240, 2014.

[17] M. Osborne, S. Moran, R. McCreadie, A. V. Lunen, M. Sykora, E. Cano, N. Ireson, C. Macdonald, I. Ounis, Y. He, T. Jackson, F. Ciravegna, and A. OBrien. Real-Time Detection, Tracking, and Monitoring of Automatically Discovered Events in Social Media. In *Proc. ACL*, 2014.

[18] D. R. Radev, E. Hovy, and K. McKeown. Introduction to the special issue on summarization. *Computational linguistics*, 28(4):399–408, 2002.

[19] D. R. Radev, H. Jing, M. Styś, and D. Tam. Centroid-based summarization of multiple documents. *Information Processing & Management*, 40(6):919–938, 2004.

[20] A. Ritter, S. Clark, Mausam, and O. Etzioni. Named entity recognition in tweets: An experimental study. In *EMNLP*, 2011.

[21] A. Ritter, Mausam, O. Etzioni, and S. Clark. Open domain event extraction from twitter. In *KDD*, 2012.

[22] K. Rudra, S. Ghosh, N. Ganguly, P. Goyal, and S. Ghosh. Extracting situational information from microblogs during disaster events: a classification-summarization approach. In *Proc. CIKM*, 2015.

[23] T. Sakaki, M. Okazaki, and Y. Matsuo. Earthquake shakes Twitter users: real-time event detection by social sensors. In *Proc. World Wide Web Conference (WWW)*, pages 851–860, 2010.

[24] L. Shou, Z. Wang, K. Chen, and G. Chen. Sumblr: Continuous summarization of evolving tweet streams. In *Proc. ACM SIGIR*, pages 533–542, 2013.

[25] K. Tao, F. Abel, C. Hauff, G.-J. Houben, and U. Gadiraju. Groundhog Day: Near-duplicate Detection on Twitter. In *Proc. World Wide Web Conference (WWW)*, pages 1273–1284, 2013.

[26] S. Verma, S. Vieweg, W. J. Corvey, L. Palen, J. H. Martin, M. Palmer, A. Schram, and K. M. Anderson. Natural Language Processing to the Rescue? Extracting "Situational Awareness" Tweets During Mass Emergency. In *Proc. AAAI ICWSM*, 2011.

[27] S. Vieweg, C. Castillo, and M. Imran. Integrating social media communications into the rapid assessment of sudden onset disasters. In *Social Informatics*, pages 444–461. Springer, 2014.

[28] S. Vieweg, A. L. Hughes, K. Starbird, and L. Palen. Microblogging During Two Natural Hazards Events: What Twitter May Contribute to Situational Awareness. In *Proc. ACM SIGCHI*, 2010.

[29] M. A. Walker, O. Rambow, and M. Rogati. Spot: A trainable sentence planner. In *Proceedings of the second meeting of the North American Chapter of the Association for Computational Linguistics on Language technologies*, pages 1–8. Association for Computational Linguistics, 2001.

[30] Z. Wang, L. Shou, K. Chen, G. Chen, and S. Mehrotra. On summarization and timeline generation for evolutionary tweet streams. *IEEE Transactions on Knowledge and Data Engineering*, 27:1301–1314, 2015.

[31] W. Xu, R. Grishman, A. Meyers, and A. Ritter. A preliminary study of tweet summarization using information extraction. *NAACL 2013*, page 20, 2013.

[32] A. Zubiaga, D. Spina, E. Amigo, and J. Gonzalo. Towards Real-Time Summarization of Scheduled Events from Twitter Streams. In *Hypertext(Poster)*, 2012.

Spatio-Temporal Parsing in Spatial Hypermedia

Thomas Schedel
thomas.schedel@iisys.de

Claus Atzenbeck
claus.atzenbeck@iisys.de

Institute of Information Systems (iisys)
Hof University
Alfons-Goppel-Platz 1
95028 Hof, Germany

ABSTRACT

Spatial hypertext represents associations between chunks of information by spatial or visual attributes (such as proximity, color, shape, etc.). This supports expressing information structures implicitly and in an intuitive way. However, automatic recognition of such informal, implicitly encoded structures by a machine (a so-called *spatial parser*) is still a challenge.

Conventional parsers are conceptually restricted by their underlying source of information. Due to this limitation there are various possible structures that cannot be recognized properly, as the machine has no means to detect them. This inevitably limits both the quality of parser output and hence parser performance. In this paper we show that considering temporal aspects in spatial parser design will lead to significant increase in parsing accuracy, detection of richer structures and thus higher parser performance. We call machines that consider such spatial and temporal information *spatio-temporal parsers*.

For the purpose of providing evidence, parsers for recognizing spatial, visual, and temporal object relations have been implemented and tested in a series of user surveys. One aim was to find out how "close" the machine interpretetation of structures get to human interpretation. It turned out that in none of the test cases pure spatial or visual parser could outperform the spatio-temporal parser. Instead, the spatio-temporal parser was able to compensate limitations of conventional parsers. Furthermore, we have statistically tested parsing accuracy. The results indicate a non-trivial effect that is recognizable by humans. This shows that spatio-temporal parsers produce output that is significantly closer to what knowledge workers intend to express compared to traditional spatial parsers.

Categories and Subject Descriptors

Human computer interaction (HCI) [**Interaction paradigms**]: Hypertext/hypermedia; Artificial intelligence [**Knowledge**

representation and reasoning]: Reasoning about belief and knowledge

Keywords

time, hypertext, spatial hypertext, spatial parsing, spatio-temporal parsing

1. INTRODUCTION

Unlike the *World Wide Web*, in which links between webpages are set explicitly, so-called *spatial hypertext* represents associations between chunks of information by spatial and visual attributes (e. g., proximity, shape, color, etc.) [9, 16]. This supports expressing information structures implicitly and in an intuitive way. Following a "cards on a table" metaphor, humans can easily use spatial hypertexts for organizing information or interpreting visual expressions. Humans easily can encode and decode spatial hypertext by using their natural ability to perceive visual structure. However, automatic recognition of such informal and implicitly encoded structure by a machine (a so-called *spatial parser*) is still a challenge. Apart from few exceptions (e. g., [17, 7, 12]) only little research has been done on spatial parsing. This paper aims to fill this gap building on [14].

What makes a good spatial parser? Good spatial parsers can be expected to operate *efficiently* and produce *high-quality output*. The parser's output should be as close to the human's interpretation of the spatial hypertext as possible. A better parsing algorithm will lead to fewer differences between both interpretations. Ideally, spatial parsers extract *only* structures that were intended by the authors.

Both objectives, maximized efficiency and effectiveness are inherently difficult to reconcile. They often are seen as competing aims in particular in computer science. In this paper we focus only on improving the *accuracy* of spatial parsers.

Conventional non-adaptive parsing strategies (as described in [17, 16, 6, 2, 13, 12, 11, 7]) are based on the assumption that "snapshots" of visual information spaces include sufficient information for inferring correct structural meaning. However, this is not always the case. Instead, single spatial hypertexts rarely provide means for detecting *what* the author intended to express. This could be solved by providing a clear and explicitly defined visual language. This, however, would contradict the *implicit* and *ambiguous* nature of spatial hypertext.

Spatial hypertext structure can be categorized as follows: (a) destroyed structures; (b) ambiguous structures; (c) temporal structures and (d) combinations of all or part of them.

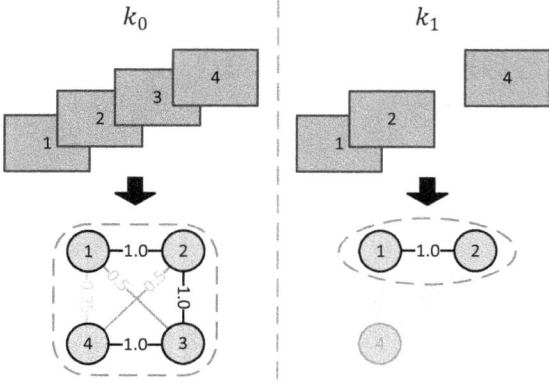

Figure 1: partly destroyed list-structure of diagonally aligned rectangles

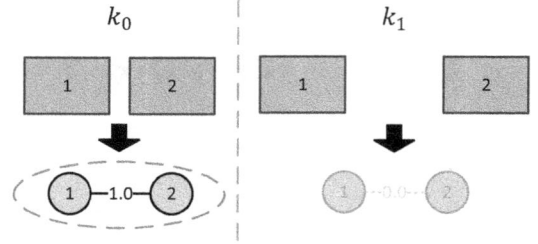

Figure 2: fully destroyed object relation

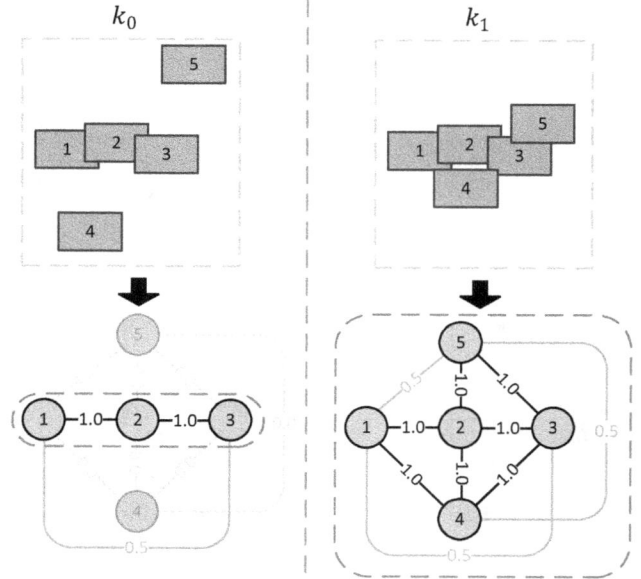

Figure 3: example: list-structures formed by ambiguously aligned rectangles

They are results of an informal process of creating and arranging nodes without following specific semantic rules. They need to be considered for spatial parsing. In the following, we will describe those in greater detail.

1.1 Destroyed Structures

Destroyed structures are information structures described spatially or visually, which used to exist in the past, but have been *partly* or *fully* destroyed in the course of an editing process. This includes all information structures that could have been automatically detected at a given time in the past, but are not (fully) visible anymore at present.

A very simple example which illustrates the nature of such *destroyed structures* is given in Fig. 1: There is a diagonal aligned list of rectangular shaped information objects and the interpretation by a spatial parser at two different points in discrete time (k_0 and k_1). Interpretations of such spatial structures are represented here as complete, undirected, and weighted graphs. Weights are assigned to edges (i.e., associations) between information units in the range from 0.0 to 1.0. Those indicate the strength of certain relationships (in this case the strength of spatial dependencies). The interpretation of the given spatial hypertext at k_0 comprises a single information structure including all four information units. At k_1, however, unit number 3 is missing. This causes that the dependency between units 1/2 and unit 4 is no longer recognizable. Only units 1 and 2 remains as the recognized information structure. This is geometrically correct, however, may not be valid from a user's perspective. Possibly when the user removed object number 3, he/she simply forgot to move 4 closer to the other two nodes. Then, units 1, 2 and 4 would still form a list. Without this correction, however, a conventional spatial parser would not recognize the relation between the three remaining nodes anymore. A similar example is mentioned in [15].

This becomes even more obvious in cases when information structures are *fully* destroyed. Figure 2 shows two consecutive snapshots of a sample hypertext together with the interpretation of a spatial parser. Due to their spatial proximity at time point k_0, both objects 1 and 2 are considered as being strongly related. The parser recognizes the spatial relation with a strength of one-hundred percent. A single time step later, however, both objects 1 and 2 have moved

too far away from each other. The parser does no longer recognize this association. This may not match the author's intention. Possibly the change between k_0 and k_1 happened accidentally as a side effect of another editing operation. Another issue may be that the parser configuration does not match the author's understanding of proximity. We do not consider heuristics used for spatial parsing to be universally correct. Thus, there are multiple reasons that would cause conventional parsers to not detect any association in k_1.

1.2 Ambiguous Structures

Ambiguous structures are networks of information objects which were not modified substantially, but still cannot be recognized anymore. These are structures which do still exist at present, however, due to an increase of ambiguity, they cannot be *uniquely* identified by a parser.

Figure 3 illustrates how a clear separation from other structures and therefore unique identification gets more difficult when additional spatial ambiguities are introduced. Starting at k_0, a well structured spatial hypertext shows an obvious separation of a horizontal list of rectangles (1 to 3) in the middle of the canvas. Unit 4 and 5 are yet unaligned.

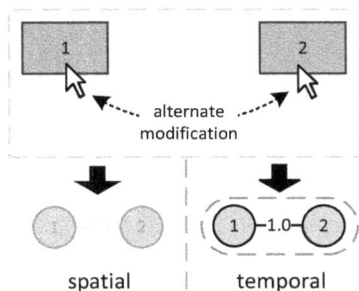

Figure 4: pure temporal structure formed by alternate modification of rectangular information objects

The spatial parser's interpretation, depicted bottom left of Fig. 3, includes the structural counterpart to that horizontal list. Moving the two unaligned nodes closer together results in an ambiguous structure, as illustrated as k_1. By considering the spatial arrangement only it is not possible anymore to decide which nodes belong to the list and which objects do not. The graph in the bottom right of Fig. 3 shows the corresponding information structure, including *all five* objects. The list-structure formed by objects 1, 2 and 3, which could be recognized at state k_0, is still part of this big structure, but (since all the delimiting zero-weightings have been gone) cannot be uniquely identified anymore. The user, however, may still remember the horizontal list as a discrete unit.

1.3 Temporal Structures

As argued above, neither destroyed nor ambiguous structures can be detected properly by conventional spatial parsers. This includes structures using spatial arrangement as well as size, shape, color, etc. In the following we discuss another, only little researched aspect in spatial hypertext: *temporal structures*.

Figure 4 shows a characteristic example of this type of structures. Two rectangular information units are located too far away from each other to be considered spatially associated. The strength of spatial dependency would be 0.0. Thus, a conventional spatial parser would not detect any relation. However, there still might be an association between unit 1 and 2, as (if you analyzed the edit history) it could be recognized that both objects were repeatedly modified in an alternate fashion. This operation pattern might indicate that the author considers object 1 and 2 as associated.

These examples show that there are cases for which traditional spatial parsers would not be sufficient. Besides position, size, shape, color, etc. further information must be considered for a more complete interpretation and better parser design. We claim that adding *temporal aspects* to spatial hypertext will solve the kind of problems described above and thus improve conventional spatial parsers significantly.

A spatial parser which is "aware" of previous structures (i.e., information structures which used to exist but are not visible anymore) and "knows" about temporal dependencies between information units could (a) detect discrete structures that are closer to what humans would see; (b) complete corrupted structures and (c) detect associations that are purely temporal.

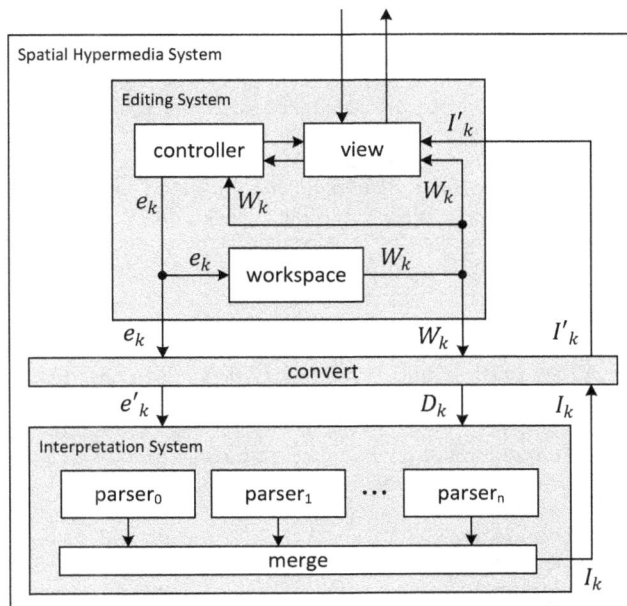

Figure 5: abstract spatial hypermedia system model

Although the idea of enhancing spatial parsing by temporal information was proposed already earlier [10, 15, 1] it has never been implemented. Until now, there was neither a complete and coherent algorithmic design for such a temporal extension nor a working software prototype.

In the following we will discuss our spatio-temporal parser that is based on (to our knowledge) the first complete and coherent formal description of spatial hypertext. We will show that the spatio-temporal parser will significantly increase in parsing accuracy and thus outperform conventional spatial parsers.

2. METHODS AND MATERIALS

Research results only applicable in a single application's context are very limited in general, as conclusions cannot be applied to other contexts. Therefore, we planned our investigation to be context and implementation independent. In order to achieve that, our algorithm design was driven by a generic spatial hypermedia system model. From that we have developed our prototype. Since a complete formal specification of our system model would go beyond the scope of this paper, we will focus on conceptional descriptions only. A complete formal definition can be found in [14].

2.1 Spatial Hypermedia System Model

We define spatial hypermedia systems as composites of two sub-systems, as depicted in Fig. 5: (a) *Editing System* and (b) *Interpretation System*.

Editing systems support creation of visual information structure, whereas interpretation systems perform automatic structural analysis. Linked together they realize interactive structure creation loops. This represents the functional core of spatial hypermedia systems.

Editing system models define how spatial hypertext can evolve and thus form the basis for any spatial hypermedia

151

system. Using the MVC pattern we can summarize the basic behavior of such systems as follows: Viewing components receive user activities and pass them on to a controlling module. The controller transforms those activities into adequate editing events (or commands) which are then forwarded as input signals to a workspace model. That model switches to a new state and finally publishes the updated hypermedia workspace W_k to its observers. Thus, this is an event-driven, dynamic system, which transforms incoming sequences of user activities into output sequences of edit events e_k and workspaces W_k (see Fig. 5).

One of our major design goals was to keep our system components as application independent as possible. However, since both e_k and W_k strongly depend on the definition of the workspace model and thereby on the concrete editing system, it was necessary to extend our model by conversion functionality. For that the system model includes functions (in the block-diagram denoted as "convert"), which take incoming edit steps (e_k, W_k) and transform them into some common representation form. Those do not include any workspace-specific information. The resulting sequence of edit events e'_k (e.g., creation, deletion, spatial or visual modification, etc.) and object properties D_k (e.g., bounds, layer, shape, color, etc.) can then be used as input for the so-called interpretation system.

The interpretation system essentially forwards incoming edit steps (e'_k, D_k) to internal parsing components (e. g., spatial parser, visual parser, etc.), merges their interpretations together and provides that mixed result as output I_k. It thereby forms a dynamic system, which transforms ingoing sequences of edit steps $((e'_0, D_0), (e'_1, D_1), \ldots, (e'_{k_e}, D_{k_e}))$ into outgoing sequences of interpretations $(I_0, I_1, \ldots, I_{k_e})$. Interpretations generated this way are converted back to application-specific representation form, which then can be used again as input for diverse application services.

Following this definition, one could understand spatial hypermedia applications as dynamic, graphical and intelligent systems that only come to life through user interaction (i. e., the "pulse" of the system).

We define *interpretations* I_k of spatial hypertext artifacts as complete, undirected, and weighted graphs. Each weight is represented as a member in $\{\varepsilon, 0.0, \ldots, 1.0\}$ and describes the strength of relations between information units. This information can be used later for the identification of structures. For example, a weight of 0.0 would mean that there is no immediate relationship between two objects; a weight of ε indicates an unknown association. Simple examples of such weighted graphs are shown in Figures 1, 2, 3, and 4.

In summary, we can define interpretations as collections of information *structures*, which are represented as networks of meaningfully connected information *objects*.

Based on this it becomes obvious, that our notion of interpretation is much more general than what is known today as the state-of-the-art [17, 6, 7, 12] in spatial parsing. We regard spatial parsers as machines *detecting* the strength of object relations instead of simply searching the workspace for *pre-defined* structural patterns. As such, spatial parsing becomes rather a matter of *interpretation* than *pattern recognition*. Therefore, our parsers operate on a higher level of abstraction compared to common parser implementations. This opens new opportunities with respect to theoretical investigations, but also practical applications.

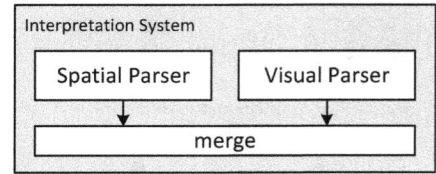

Figure 6: spatio-visual interpretation system

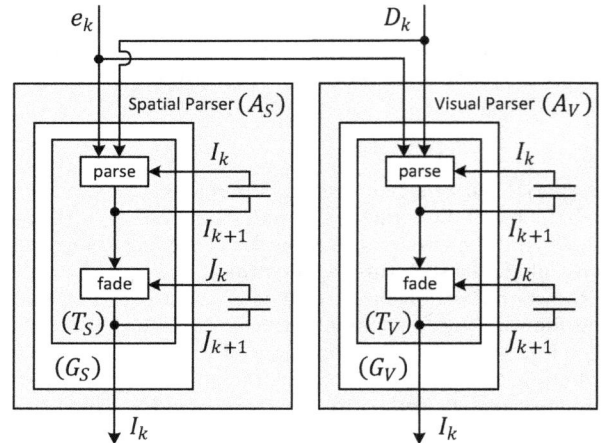

Figure 7: spatial and visual parser extended by fading subsystem

As discussed in Sect. 1 our goal is to design a parser capable of detecting destroyed, ambiguous, and temporal structures. In other words, our parser needs to "remember" previous associations and "knows" about temporal dependencies. We call this machine a *spatio-temporal parser*.

2.2 Spatio-Temporal Parsing

Spatio-temporal parsers are extensions of spatio-visual interpretation systems (see Fig. 6) and hence build on two connected sub-systems: spatial parser and visual parser. Spatial parsers detect the strength of spatial dependencies (given by proximity, alignment, etc.) and visual parsers scan the canvas for visual similarities (e. g., similar shape, color, size, proportions etc.). When mixing both outputs in the right proportions (in Fig. 6 depicted as system block "merge") we can not only detect spatial structures, but also visual relationships or nuances.

For the detection of destroyed structures we suggest extending spatial and visual parser by a post-processor that we call "fade". Patching in such a post-processor after the core parsing algorithms (as illustrated in Fig. 7) enhances the parser's behavior as follows: If a parser cannot detect a relation between two objects, the fading module checks whether there is still a connection known from a previous parser run. If the parser can "remember" a relationship with a weight > 0.0, then that old weight gets multiplied by a given fading factor and is treated as the current parse result. If, however, there is no such relationship, or if the product of previous weight and fading factor reaches a predefined fading threshold, then we accept the result of the

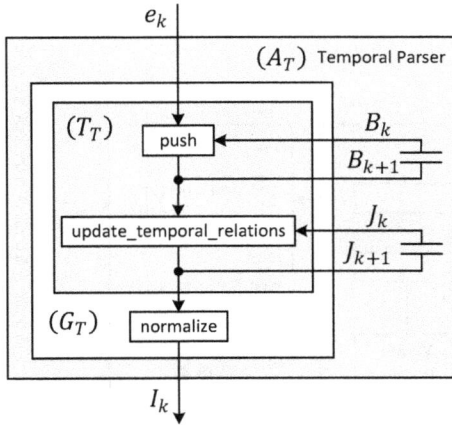

Figure 8: abstract block-diagram of a temporal parsing system (i. e., the temporal parser)

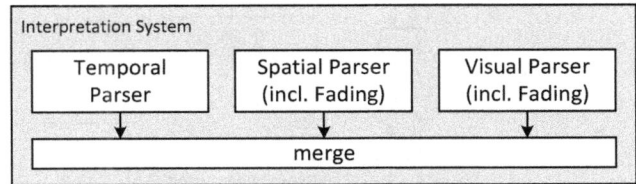

Figure 9: spatio-visual interpretation system extended by temporal parser and fading

current parser run. In short, the fading feature makes it possible, that associations which are not recognized anymore, do not get omitted. Instead, they *fade* away and thus can still be used some more time to improve the parser's quality. In other words, the parser slowly "forgets" outdated associations. A similar aging feature for objects, viewport positions, and motion paths has been proposed earlier in [1].

Fading helps to solve the "destroyed structures problem". Detecting ambiguous (Sect. 1.2) and temporal structures (Sect. 1.3), however, requires a different approach. We propose a separate parsing system with a slightly different architecture that can process temporal dependencies. We call it the *temporal parser*, depicted in Fig. 8.

Like spatial and visual parser, also the temporal parser in Fig. 8 measures the strength of relationships between information objects. However, it does not operate in geometrical 2D space or in color space, but considers *time*. Temporal parsers do not parse a canvas or a workspace, instead they analyze streams of edit events in order to detect the strength of relationships between objects.

Since there is no single natural order in which people create spatial hypertext, it would be impossible to predict users' behavior. Therefore, universal default activities (e. g., constructor or destructor patterns for lists, tables, etc.) cannot be defined. Due to that the temporal parser is based on temporal heuristics and does not perform pattern matching on pre-defined activity patterns.

In a nutshell, our algorithm design was driven by the following rule: *pairs of objects that are frequently modified at short time intervals have a stronger temporal connection than objects touched less frequently or in longer intervals.*

Following this principle it becomes possible to recognize temporal dependencies between information objects, even without considering user profiles or application contexts.

Summarizing the above, we can say, that spatio-temporal parsers extend spatio-visual interpretation systems by "short-term memory" (see Fig. 6 vs. Fig. 9). Basically, this corresponds to the state memory of temporal parsers (Fig. 8) and fading sub-systems (Fig. 7).

Both, temporal parser and fading were implemented in a spatial hypermedia prototype, strictly following the model presented in Fig. 5. A detailed and complete formal definition can be found in [14].

Synergies between spatial, visual and temporal parser have been examined under laboratory conditions. However, fading functionality was not yet included in the analysis, because the fading feature is only relevant for long time use scenarios. Fading could be tested in long-term studies, where heavy restructuring of spatial hypertexts lead to accidentally or unnoticably destroyed structures. In such a scenario fading may help to parse structures more effectively. In our current studies, however, we focus on short-term tests only.

In principle this limitation also applies to the evolution of temporal dependencies and therefore on the temporal parser. Most likely, many structures will emerge only after a certain period of time. Nevertheless, we will show that the temporal parser will also show its benefits in short-term tests.

2.3 Test Run

In order to compare the spatial, visual, and temporal parsers we had to collect adequate reference data. We decided to do that by user surveys in a laboratory setting. Tests took around 20 minutes or slightly more minutes, which was accepted by most subjects. Longer tests would have had mostly a deterrent effect.

A total of 50 German native speakers joined the survey. All participants had a technical background in computer sciences, ranging from bachelor to PhD level. None of the participants had used a spatial hypermedia system before.

Each participant was placed in front of a 65 inch computer monitor and then informed about the basic test conditions. After that, subjects were told about the prototype's user interface. Even though we have implemented only a small number of common GUI features in our prototype, we decided to still demonstrate each of those features to every single test person. For this purpose we prepared a simple sample hypertext that consists of random objects. These objects neither had any visual nor semantic relation with the hypertext used for the test. During the demonstration, subjects were requested to actively try out each interface feature to ensure that they had understood its functionality. After the subject had explicitly confirmed that there were no open questions regarding the interface usage, the actual test hypertext was loaded into the prototype application. Fig. 11 shows the initial display as seen by the subjects.

Each test person was presented 24 rectangular objects, each labeled with a term (in German) related to a common subject area. Participants were then asked to restructure those objects so that the resulting diagram reflected their basic comprehension of the given terms and their relations. This means, subjects should rearrange, scale, color, etc. the

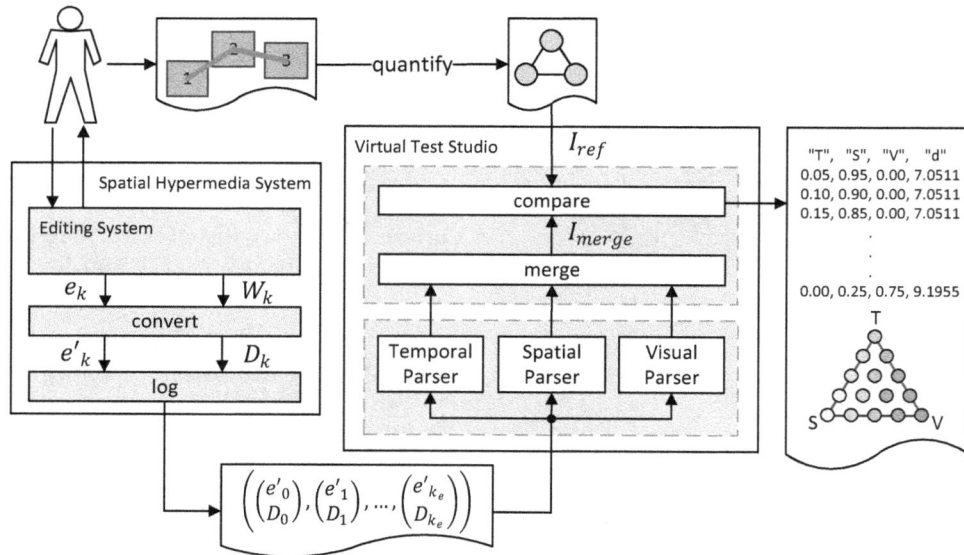

Figure 10: overview of the entire test run

Flora	Tierwelt	Pilze	Blumen
Beschreibung	Region	Wissenschaft	Fauna
römische Göttin	Vögel	Pflanzenarten	Bakterien
Bestimmung	Pflanzenwelt	Organismen	Gesamtheit
Vegetation	Jugend	Reptilien	Erde
Tiere	Arten	Fungi	Insekten

Figure 11: initial display as seen by subjects

given terms to express their (individual) structural understanding of the given topic area. Participants were explicitly told to continue with their work until the result would make most sense to them.

After the structuring task has been completed, each subject has been asked to explain what they intended to express. For this purpose they received a hard copy of their work and a pen. The person then marked associations between objects (by drawing lines, circles etc.). Figure 12 shows an example of such a marked document. The user's feedback received in this graphical form was then quantified, in order to make it comparable by a machine. For this purpose we wrote a small visual analysis tool as a means to transform handwritten user feedback into a weighted graph. These graphs formed the reference data for our automated analysis.

In addition to the graphical user feedback we also recorded each subject's interface activities. To achieve that, we substituted the interpreter component in our prototype with a special logging module that was designed for recording streams of edit operations. This made it possible to persistently store full test sessions and to "replay" it later in a virtual test environment.

Once we had collected the user's edit process (i.e., what the participant did) and reference interpretation (i.e., what the participant intended to express), we proceeded as follows: An interpreter was instantiated that was build from only temporal, spatial, and visual parser. Fading and im-

plicit merging were deactivated, since those features were not part of the analysis. Then, the reference interpretation graph and the recorded stream of edit steps were loaded into memory and passed through all three parser components. The resulting temporal, spatial and visual interpretations were merged together in varying ratios $(T, S, V) \in \Delta^2$, with an increment of five percent (i. e., weighting factors T, S, and V were multiples of 0.05 and summed up to 1.0).

Each merge result was then compared with the given reference interpretation. For this comparison we used a statistical divergence function which shows numerically how close a merged interpretation graph is to the respective reference interpretation graph. The smaller such numerical divergence values are, the closer the parse result is to what a user intended to express. For example, an optimal value of 0.0 indicated that model and observation were identical; that is, our merge result represented exactly what the user had in mind.

Having repeated this test procedure for each of our test candidates, we finally got 50 result sets. Fig. 10 illustrates the entire process.

3. EVALUATION

Our virtual test run resulted in 50 CSV lists (one per test person). Each of those lists included 231 tuples of weighting factors for temporal, spatial and visual parser together with the respective divergence value (the number 231 comes from our chosen weighting factor increment of five percent).

Demonstrated with an example, each of those 50 tabular listings was of the following form:

```
#0    "T" , "S" , "V" , "d"
#1    0.05, 0.95, 0.00, 7.05113242479466400000
#2    0.10, 0.90, 0.00, 7.20835108739322600000
#3    0.15, 0.85, 0.00, 7.32986400847126800000
...
#231 0.00, 0.25, 0.75, 9.19552448851569300000
```

154

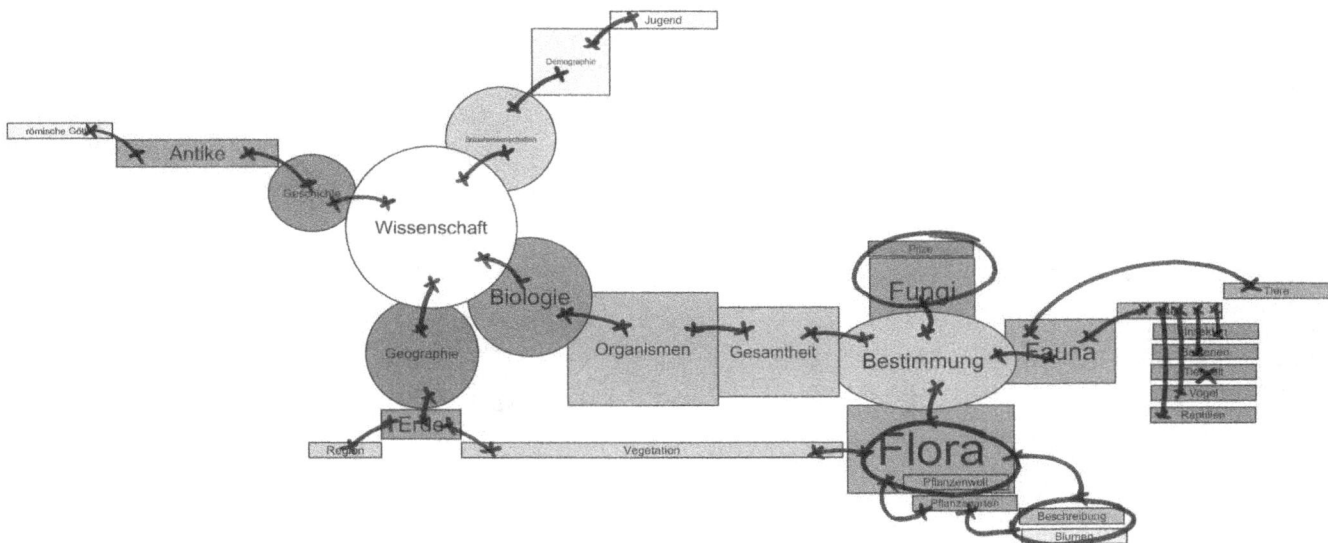

Figure 12: sample feedback provided by one of our participants

"T", "S", and "V" label the weighting factors for temporal, spatial and visual parser by mixed ratios. The divergence of each ratio is labeled as "d".

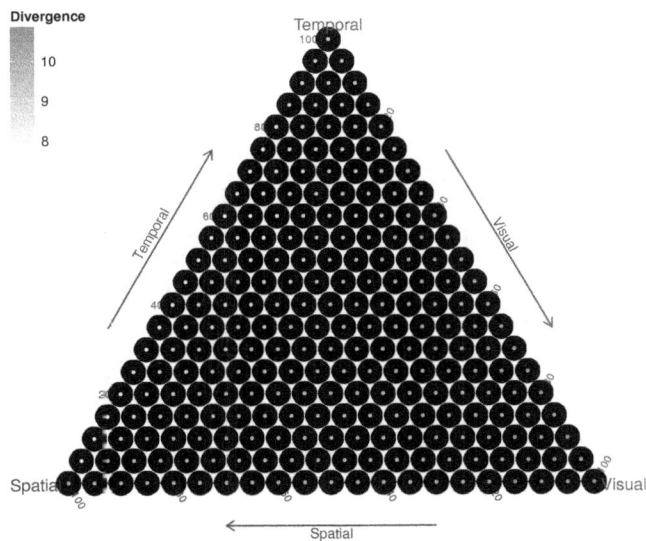

Figure 13: sample ternary plot

As an initial step, we illustrated our results as colored ternary diagrams. In ternary plots the ratios of three variables correspond to positions within a triangle. As such, they are well suited for visualizing the given triples of weighting factors. Figure 13 shows an example of such a colored ternary diagram. The colored circles in the triangle represent different parser combinations or triples $(T, S, V) \in \Delta^2$ and therefore are evenly distributed over the simplex. The triangle's vertices $((1, 0, 0), (0, 1, 0), \text{and} (0, 0, 1))$ are special cases where only spatial, temporal, or visual parser are included. The divergence values d assigned to the ratios

throughout the triangle are expressed as colors with a color scale ranging from yellow to red. Pure yellow indicates the smallest divergence value whereas pure red the biggest one in a sample. Brighter colors indicate better results.

Drawing ternary plots for each of the 50 sample cases has not shown a uniform picture. We could not spot a single connected area of optimal ratios of parser configurations throughout all 50 diagrams. In contrary, we have indicated various patterns in analyzing the ternary plots. Nevertheless this analysis has provided some important insights regarding the relationship of spatial, visual, and temporal parsers:

The more explicit a spatial structure was (e. g., in form of lists, trees, mind maps, etc.) the more the optimum has moved towards $(T, S, V) = (0.0, 1.0, 0.0)$ and thus put the focus on the spatial parser. The more dominant visual attributes have been used in a meaningful manner (e. g., for highlighting different object categories, etc.) the more the optimum has been shifted towards $(T, S, V) = (0.0, 0.0, 1.0)$ and hence towards the visual parser. In other words, the "easier" it was for the spatial and visual parsers to detect clear structures, the more weight they have got in the optimal solution. This is the expected behavior and hence not surprising. It is interesting to note, though, that even in such extreme cases pure spatial and visual parser could not outperform the spatio-temporal parser; that is, there always was at least one temporal mixture which performed at least as good as the best without temporal component.

Furthermore, we made the important observation that the impact of the temporal parser was higher for more ambiguous and "uncommon" structures. We assume the reason to be in the spatial and visual parser's limitations and lack of heuristic definitions. Thus, the temporal parser became important in cases when spatial and visual parser failed to recognize accurate structures. One could argue that the *temporal parser complemented spatial and visual parsers beyond their limits*.

To some extent this could eliminate the need for manually tuning parsers to specific users. Instead, limited precision caused by inadequate parser configurations or heuristics could be partly compensated by adding our temporal parser. Even though this could not reach the same high level of accuracy as it may be possible with highly customized parsers, the addition of our temporal parser still provided better results than pure spatial or visual parsers while being *fully independent of user profiles and application contexts*. This was the most promising finding related to our temporal parser.

Ternary plots are good for an initial assessment, but do not permit reliable conclusions about significance. A statistical approach was required.

To compare spatio-visual and spatio-temporal parsers statistically we had to determine optimal merging ratios with and without the temporal component. We regard ratios of temporal, spatial, and visual parser combinations as *optimal* if they generate results at consistently high level of accuracy. It is neither optimal to constantly produce output of low quality nor to generate perfect results for a single or a few persons only. Divergence values should be as low as possible, not varying between different users. Ideally they reach the value zero.

Since our ternary plots did not show a uniform picture it was not possible to identify single connected areas of optimal ratios. Thus, we had to determine temporal and non-temporal optima numerically rather than visually.

In order to identify good candidates for temporal and non-temporal configurations we calculated for each merging ratio the median and the standard deviation of their assigned divergence values and mapped them to the value range $[0, 1]$. This lets us represent them as points in $\{0.0, \ldots, 1.0\}^2$. Sorting these two-dimensional vectors in ascending order according to their Euclidean norm resulted in two ranking lists: one for temporal and one for non-temporal configuration candidates. The first entries in these lists represented optimal merging ratios. These were $(0.00, 0.45, 0.55)$ and $(0.75, 0.25, 0.00)$.

As both divergence samples were normally distributed, dependent and metric samples with equal variances we used the *two-tailed paired Student's t-test* for analysis.

Our null hypothesis H_0 stated that there is no effective difference between the non-temporal sample mean and the temporal sample mean. That is, any measured difference in divergence would be only due to chance and including the temporal parser would have no effect. The opposite of our null hypothesis H_0 was our experimental (or alternative) hypothesis H_1, which assumes that means would not be equal and that including the temporal parser would change the mean accordingly. As a level of significance we selected the widely adopted $\alpha = 0.05$.

Applying the paired Student's t-test on non-temporal divergence sample as first and temporal sample as second condition resulted in:

$$t = 3.0635, \ df = 49, \ p = 0.00355$$

with a 95 percent confidence interval ranging from 0.1325554 to 0.6380730

Because $p < \alpha$ (0.00355 < 0.05) we can conclude, that there is a significant difference between temporal and non-temporal means. The fact that the t-value is positive ($t = 3.0635$) shows that the non-temporal divergence sample has a larger mean than the temporal one and so divergences are smaller when using the temporal parser.

In order to determine whether this difference in parsing accuracy was substantive we converted our t-statistics into a standard effect size. To avoid overestimation we used the rather conservative d_{rm} [5, 8]. For our t-statistics we got:

$$|d_{rm}| = 0.39$$

Preferably, effect sizes should be interpreted by comparing them to related effects in literature. Since, however, in our special case there are no such references we decided to use the benchmarks defined in [3] instead where effect sizes are classified as *small* ($|d| = 0.2$), *medium* ($|d| = 0.5$), and *large* ($|d| = 0.8$). According to [4] *medium* $|d|$ represents an effect visible to the human eye, *small* $|d|$ is noticeably smaller than *medium* but not trivial, and a *large* $|d|$ has the same distance above *medium* as *small* has below.

Our effect size $|d_{rm}| = 0.39$ lies between 0.2 and 0.5 and therefore between the thresholds for *small* and *medium* effects (with a slight tendency towards *moderate*). Therefore, besides *statistical significance*, our detected *effect is non-trivial and recognizable by humans*.

Finally, we can summarise our findings as follows: On average, divergence from user intention when adding our temporal parser ($M = 8.9335$, $SE = 0.1412$) was significantly lower than when using only spatial and visual parser ($M = 9.318871$, $SE = 0.136446436$); $t(49) = 3.0635$ and $p < 0.05$. The 95 percent confidence interval for the mean difference between the two conditions was 0.1325 to 0.6380. The effect size estimate $|d_{rm}| = 0.39$ indicates a non-trivial effect that is recognizable by humans.

From this we conclude, that *the addition of a temporal parser shifts machine detected structures significantly closer to what knowledge workers intend to express*.

4. CONCLUSION AND FUTURE WORK

Conventional spatial parsers are conceptually limited by their underlying source of information. Due to this limitation there are several types of structures that cannot be recognized properly by a machine. This limits both quality of parser output and hence parser performance.

In order to overcome this issue we suggest considering not only spatial and visual properties, but also temporal aspects in spatial parser designs. A spatial parser that is "aware" of previous structures and "knows" about temporal dependencies between objects could (a) complete corrupted structures; (b) remove ambiguous relationships and (c) detect associations that are pure temporal. We expect this to increase parsing precision and hence parser performance.

In order to show that adding a temporal extension provides better results than a conventional parser, algorithms for the detection of spatial, visual, and temporal object relations have been implemented and tested. Reference data used for the test has been collected by surveys in which subjects were asked to solve a simple structuring task using a prototypical spatial hypermedia system. After that they were asked to indicate explicitly what they intended to express. That qualitative feedback was then quantified in order to make it comparable to machine-generated results. With this data at hand we finally determined to what extent the spatio-temporal parser performed better than spatial or visual parser.

It turned out, that in none of the test cases pure spatial or visual parsers have outperformed the spatio-temporal parser. Instead, the spatio-temporal parser compensated limitations of conventional parsers and hence provided better results. Differences in parsing accuracy were successfully tested for statistical significance. Converted into a standard effect size our statistics indicated a non-trivial effect that is recognizable by humans.

Thus, we have shown that considering *time* in combination with spatial and visual attributes shifts machine-detected structures significantly closer to user's intended structures.

Even though both temporal parser and fading have been already implemented, the latter has not been tested under controlled conditions. So far we have analyzed synergy effects between pure spatial, visual, and temporal parsers only in short-term tests, using a prototypical spatial hypermedia application. As a next step we are planning to integrate those parsers into a productive system for performing long-term tests. This will provide information about positive effects of temporal parsers and fading under real working conditions.

5. REFERENCES

[1] C. Atzenbeck and D. L. Hicks. Integrating time into spatially represented knowledge structures. In *Proceedings of the 2009 International Conference on Information, Process, and Knowledge Management*, pages 34–42. IEEE Computer Society, 2009.

[2] D. Bucka-Lassen, C. Pedersen, and O. Reinert. *Cooperative Authoring Using Open Spatial Hypermedia*. Aarhus University, Department of Computer Science, 1998.

[3] J. Cohen. *Statistical Power Analysis for the Behavioral Sciences*. L. Erlbaum Associates, 1988.

[4] J. Cohen. Quantitative methods in psychology: A power primer. *Psychological Bulletin*, 112(1):155–159, 1992

[5] W. P. Dunlap, J. M. Cortina, J. B. Vaslow, and M. J. Burke. Meta-analysis of experiments with matched groups or repeated measure designs. *Psychological Methods*, 1(2):170–177, 1996.

[6] L. Francisco-Revilla and F. Shipman. Parsing and interpreting ambiguous structures in spatial hypermedia. In *Proceedings of the sixteenth ACM conference on Hypertext and hypermedia*, HYPERTEXT '05, pages 107–116, New York, NY, USA, 2005. ACM.

[7] T. Igarashi, S. Matsuoka, and T. Masui. Adaptive recognition of implicit structures in human-organized layouts. In *Visual Languages, Proceedings., 11th IEEE International Symposium on*, pages 258–266, Sep 1995.

[8] D. Lakens. Calculating and reporting effect sizes to facilitate cumulative science: A practical primer for t-tests and ANOVAs. *Frontiers in Psychology*, 4(863), 2013.

[9] C. C. Marshall and F. M. Shipman, III. Spatial hypertext: designing for change. *Commun. ACM*, 38(8):88–97, Aug. 1995.

[10] C. C. Marshall, F. M. Shipman, III, and J. H. Coombs. VIKI: spatial hypertext supporting emergent structure. In *Proceedings of the 1994 ACM European conference on Hypermedia technology*, ECHT '94, pages 13–23, New York, NY, USA, 1994. ACM.

[11] M. B. Nielsen and P. Ørbæk. Finding hyper-structure in space: Spatial parsing in 3d. In *THE NEW REVIEW OF HYPERMEDIA AND MULTIMEDIA*, pages 153–183. Taylor & Francis, Inc., 2001.

[12] M. B. Nielsen and P. Ørbæk. Spatial parsing within the Topos 3d environment. In *IN THE FIRST WORKSHOP ON SPATIAL HYPERTEXT*, 2001.

[13] O. Reinert, D. Bucka-Lassen, C. A. Pedersen, and P. J. Nürnberg. CAOS: a collaborative and open spatial structure service component with incremental spatial parsing. In *Proceedings of the tenth ACM Conference on Hypertext and hypermedia : returning to our diverse roots*, HYPERTEXT '99, pages 49–50, New York, NY, USA, 1999. ACM.

[14] T. Schedel. *Spatio-Temporal Parsing in Spatial Hypermedia*. PhD thesis, Aalborg University, 2016.

[15] F. M. Shipman, III and H. Hsieh. Navigable history: a reader's view of writer's time. *The New Review of Hypermedia and Multimedia*, 6:147–167, 2000.

[16] F. M. Shipman, III, H. Hsieh, P. Maloor, and J. M. Moore. The visual knowledge builder: a second generation spatial hypertext. In *Proceedings of the 12th ACM conference on Hypertext and Hypermedia*, HYPERTEXT '01, pages 113–122, New York, NY, USA, 2001. ACM.

[17] F. M. Shipman, III, C. C. Marshall, and T. P. Moran. Finding and using implicit structure in human-organized spatial layouts of information. In *Proceedings of the SIGCHI Conference on Human Factors in Computing Systems*, CHI '95, pages 346–353, New York, NY, USA, 1995. ACM Press/Addison-Wesley Publishing Co.

Social Media-Based Collaborative Information Access: Analysis of Online Crisis-Related Twitter Conversations

Lynda Tamine
IRIT, University of Toulouse,
UPS
118 Route de Narbonne
Toulouse, France
tamine@irit.fr

Laure Soulier
Sorbonne Universités,
UPMC Univ Paris 06,
CNRS UMR 7606, LIP6
F-75005 Paris, France
laure.soulier@lip6.fr

Lamjed Ben Jabeur
IRIT, University of Toulouse 3,
UPS
118 Route de Narbonne
31062 Toulouse, France
jabeur@irit.fr

Frederic Amblard
IRIT, University of Toulouse 1
Capitole
2 rue du Doyen Gabriel Marty
31042 Toulouse Cedex,
France
amblard@irit.fr

Chihab Hanachi
IRIT, University of Toulouse 1
Capitole
2 rue du Doyen Gabriel Marty
31042 Toulouse Cedex,
France
hanachi@irit.fr

Gilles Hubert
IRIT, University of Toulouse,
UPS
118 Route de Narbonne
Toulouse, France
hubert@irit.fr

Camille Roth
Centre Marc Bloch Berlin,
UMIFRE CNRS-MAE
Berlin, Germany
roth@cmb.hu-berlin.de

ABSTRACT

The notion of implicit (or explicit) collaborative information access refers to systems and practices allowing a group of users to unintentionally (respectively intentionally) seek, share and retrieve information to achieve similar (respectively shared) information-related goals. Despite an increasing adoption in social environments, collaboration behavior in information seeking and retrieval is mainly limited to small-sized groups, generally restricted to working spaces. Much remains to be learned about collaborative information seeking within open web social spaces. This paper is an attempt to better understand either implicit or explicit collaboration by studying Twitter, one of the most popular and widely used social networks. We study in particular the complex intertwinement of human interactions induced by both collaboration and social networking. We empirically explore explicit collaborative interactions based on focused conversation streams during two crisis. We identify structural patterns of temporally representative conversation subgraphs and represent their topics using Latent Dirichlet Allocation (LDA) modeling. Our main findings suggest that: *1)* the *critical mass* of collaboration is generally limited to small-sized flat networks, with or without an influential user, *2)* users are active as members of weakly overlapping groups and engage in numerous collaborative search and sharing tasks dealing with different topics, and *3)* collaborative group ties evolve within the time-span of conversations.

HT '16, Jul- 10-13, 2016, Halifax, NS, Canada
© 2016 ACM. ISBN 978-1-4503-4247-6/16/07...$15.00
DOI: http://dx.doi.org/10.1145/2914586.2914589

CCS Concepts

•**Information systems** → **Collaborative and social computing systems and tools;** *Information systems applications;* Social networking sites;

Keywords

Information Access; Social Networks; Twitter; Topic Models; Collaboration

1. INTRODUCTION

Using social networking platforms for information seeking and sharing is an increasingly common practice [28]. Although previous research [7] and various services, such as Aardvark [20], have investigated the use of social media for information access, the underlying paradigm still relies on individual search. In this setting, the information access is generally enriched by cues stemming from a seeker's social relationships (e.g., so-called "friends" or "followers"). However, recent studies highlighted the fact that a significant portion of information searches remains unsolved within the user's social neighborhood [23]. To address this issue, we believe that search engines could support the creation of social ties between users or groups of users aiming at carrying out similar search tasks. The long-term goal is to favor both explicit and implicit collaboration. In explicit collaborative search scenarios, two or more individuals (say, a work team) are engaged in the search process and intentionally combine their knowledge and skills to solve a shared information need. In contrast, implicit collaboration refers to scenarios where users might unintentionally share their experience with other users to satisfy their own information needs [16].

A sizable literature has shown that explicit collaboration within small-sized groups is beneficial to information search [36]. Yet, a research topic which is still under exploration deals with the opportunities of large-scale explicit collaboration supported by social networking platforms [30, 32]. We aim to contribute to this emerging topic by studying the properties of groups of users with shared interests emerging from online social conversations, viewed here as collaboration signals. We empirically explore explicit collaborative interactions based on focused conversation streams during two crisis. We identify structural patterns of temporally representative conversation subgraphs and represent their topics using Latent Dirichlet Allocation (LDA) modeling. We focus on a crisis management scenario based on two Twitter-based datasets collected during critical circumstances (Hurricane Sandy[1] and Ebola[2]). The reasons for choosing specifically this scenario are twofold: *1)* social media platforms are increasingly used by citizens during crisis situations [21] to make helpful information and knowledge available (events, video, expertise, etc.), to ease crises awareness, to accept or distribute tasks to volunteers, and to share their opinions on the way crises are managed by official responders, *2)* crisis-related situations lead to the emergence of spontaneous groups of users willing to collaborate (through online communications) in order to provide resources and help victims [18].

Our main contributions include:

- Characterizing both the structural and semantic patterns of explicit collaboration, based on information seeking and sharing traces as well as signals left by groups of users who are jointly engaged in temporally tight conversations.

- Exploring whether and how much groups of users with similar interests may be more likely to explicitly collaborate with each other.

Our findings provide a number of significant opportunities for future research on collaboration in the social Web. More precisely, they may guide designers of social media-based information search tools to connect users to a wide and relevant audience in accordance with their search goals and interests

The remainder of this paper is organized as follows. In section 2, we give an overview of the relevant literature on social and collaborative information search, and then focus on the main challenges and research advances in social-media based crisis management. Section 3 details the data acquisition and processing methods. In section 4, we present and discuss the results. Section 5 highlights the broader implications of our study in terms of social-media collaboration resarch, while section 6 outlines its limitations and future research directions. Some concluding remarks follow in section 7.

2. BACKGROUND AND RELATED WORK

This paper is related to two lines of previous work that we overview. We first focus on the social and collaborative information access using social media platforms and then, investigate the use of social media services during crisis situations.

[1]https://en.wikipedia.org/wiki/Hurricane_Sandy
[2]https://en.wikipedia.org/wiki/West_African_Ebola_virus_epidemic

2.1 Collaborative and social media information seeking: two sides of the same coin?

Although generally perceived as a solitary process, information seeking and retrieval increasingly imply collaboration with others either within small-sized work teams [36] or open social web spaces [30]. The first research initiative dealing with the use of social media and favoring large-scale collaboration has been raised by the DARPA challenge aiming at identifying ten red balloons across the USA [40]. Collaboration could be defined according to various dimensions: namely, intent, depth, concurrency, and location, leading to fundamentally distinct processes (e.g., recommendantion, task-based search) and research challenges [16, 33]. With respect to the above-mentioned objectives, we focus in this paper on the intent dimension which can be either explicit or implicit.

Explicit collaboration has commonly been addressed in the area of collaborative information seeking and retrieval [14, 36]. In this context, an important paradigm for the optimization of the collaborators' search actions is the *division of labor*. This could be traced to three types of mediation which, in turn, correspond to specific user behaviors: *1)* user-based mediation through explicit discussions or exchanges between the collaborators using interfaces [36], *2)* system-based mediation supported by search algorithms which transfer the results to the right collaborators, generally according to their predefined roles [38], *3)* hybrid mediation that learns and assigns evolving roles to users and adapts the search accordingly [37]. Implicit collaboration has traditionally been addressed in algorithms and applications such as collaborative filtering [6].

Recently, social media platforms have given rise to both explicit and implicit collaborative search under the umbrella of "social search" [13, 29, 30]. Authors in [29] broadly define social search as *"the process of finding information online with the assistance of other social resources as well as search over collections of socially-generated content"*. While some works exploit social signals (*like/dislike*, comments) [2] or social features (engagement, trust) [24] to enhance implicit collaborative search models, other research strands closer to ours focusing on how users appropriate social media platforms to explicitly collaborate. The main findings may be subsumed as follows: *1)* seeking and sharing information are the two basic forms of online explicit collaboration using social networks [10, 29], *2)* the main motivations of users to explicitly ask their social network are trust, awareness (social support), searching for opinionated information and reaching specific audience [29, 23] and that *3)* a significant part of the questions asked to social networks did not receive answers mostly because of the low social activity of askers or the limited size of their social neighborhood [23].

In this paper, we reveal some characteristics about the behavioral facets of users engaged in social-media based explicit collaboration. Unlike previous work [9, 10, 23, 29], our study specifically focuses on: *1)* the characterization of the group patterns of users engaged in explicit collaboration supported by topically focused online conversations that express shared information goals and interests; *2)* the examination of the social connectivity between these groups in order to have a picture of their interplay regarding both the generation of content and the social interactions. In addition, different from the study presented in [9], our study focuses on the group level rather than the user level. More specifically, rather than aiming to discover the user-to-user interaction graph structure regardless of the users' intent, our goal here is to give an abstracted picture of the collaborative group patterns that emerge from the user-to-user social interactions regarding shared information needs and interests.

2.2 Social-media based collaboration in emergency situations

Besides conventional social media (e.g., Facebook, Twitter, etc.) that are commonly used in crisis management, new dedicated platforms have recently emerged (Sahana, Ushahidi, OneResponse, Tweet4Act, Google Crisis Response. etc.). Some tools (i.e., NYPA) offer several functions while interfacing with conventional tools and Geographic Information Systems. In terms of use, these tools allow 1) citizens to geo-locate elements (events, victims, demands, resources, etc.) in order to be informed and active in resolving the crisis as well as 2) stakeholder organizations to collaborate and be more efficient, which results in accelerating decision making and therefore action. In this context, Twitter, Facebook, and Ushahidi are the most used social platforms in crisis situations notably during the earthquake in Haiti in 2010 and the Fukushima nuclear accident in 2011 [42]. A detailed review of social-media processing in crisis-management can be found in [21].

Based first and foremost on Twitter streams, a large amount of research studies proposed approaches to predict crises [19, 26] and model information spread [35]. This enables to improve communication channels or understand users' individual and collective behaviors that highlight situational awareness [1, 17, 41]. Heverin and Zach [17] highlighted the collective effort made by users to produce information that could be identified within "the chaos" through the hashtag stream, aiming at forging a global picture of the overall crisis-related information. Vieweg et al. [41] distinguished among various content-based tweet features those which could be used to identify ad hoc audiences viewed as potential collaborators. The topical analysis of tweets showed that different types of information may be broadcasted depending on the role of those seeking information. For instance, *Preparation* and *Response to warning* concern both individual and organizational audiences. However confidence-related challenges remain, especially with respect to the reliability of both partners' commitment and shared information. On the whole, they limit the use of social-media based technologies to enhance citizen-to-organization and organization-to-organization collaboration [25].

Our work extends previous work [17, 41] about users' involvement in crisis-related social-media streams by giving a picture of the structure of the *intra* and *inter* collaboration between user groups with the aim of highlighting collaboration opportunities.

3. STUDY DESIGN

3.1 Definitions and assumptions

We introduce here the basic definitions and assumptions:

- *Collaboration.* Collaboration allows people to create and share collective knowledge within a work team to identify and solve a shared complex problem [34]. From the social web point of view, the collaboration

concept is closely related to the notion of wisdom of crowds, i.e., how large groups of people are better at solving problems and fostering innovation [39].

- *Collaboration signals in the social web.* To detect collaboration intent of active users in the social web, we use the following assumption:

  Assumption 1. *Providing assistance to others by means of social signals like answering, sharing, and propagating information through the social network is a form of online collaboration [13].*

- *Collaborative information search and sharing task.* We consider here that a collaborative search and sharing task is implicitly performed through a conversation started by a seed tweet, whereby other participants are trying to address the same issue. All of them strive to achieve a common task that consists, for instance, in the retrieval of a specific information or the synchronization around a particular action. Accordingly, we will later consider in our study the following assumption:

  Assumption 2. *Online conversations are timely bounded and could convey different subtopics and subtasks alongside their lifetime [9].*

- *Collaborative group.* We consider the active users involved in a conversation as the members of the collaborative group.

3.2 Twitter Datasets

We selected two datasets obtained by constantly monitoring Twitter's stream via Twitter Streaming API using appropriate tracking keywords during a critical period of two different crises. In particular, we used the *filter* method of streaming API that delivers tweets which imperatively contain tracked keywords. The *filter* method enables to gather a higher number of tweets about the monitored crises in comparison to the *sample* method that randomly pushes 1 % from all tweets. Although the *filter* method could gather all tracked tweets, this must not exceed the limit rate of 1 % of the whole Twitter stream. We note that only the paid *Firehose* method of Twitter API guarantees the delivery of 100 % of all tweets. However, previous work has shown that such obtained samples are close to the random samples over full Twitter stream [31]. We analyzed two tweet collections, restricted to English-language tweets, related to two crises:

1. *Sandy*: A dataset of tweets about Hurricane Sandy which was the most destructive hurricane in United States history with more than 230 deaths and 75 billion of damages. This dataset were collected from 29th October 2012 to 31st October 2012 using the 3 keywords: *"sandy"*, *"hurricane"* and *"storm"*.

2. *Ebola*: A dataset of tweets about West African Ebola virus epidemic which is the most widespread epidemic of Ebola virus disease. The epidemic began in Guinea in December 2013 and lasted for two years. World government agencies report more than $11,295$ deaths. The dataset were collected from July 29th 2014 to August 28th 2014 using *"ebola"* as a keyword.

The two datasets *Sandy* and *Ebola* have similar sizes with the number of tweets reaches $4,853,345$ and $4,815,142$, respectively.

The first key challenge was to select a sub-sample of informative tweets and filter out noisy ones. To tackle this issue, we processed the datasets using the methodology introduced in [8] for automatic data reliability detection. Practically, unreliable tweets are filtered using an automatic classifier. Based on regression logistic model, the automatic classifier maps tweets into two categories: *useful* and *useless*. The dataset processing is conducted into three steps:

- *Step 1: Building the training dataset.* A manual annotation task was assigned to 10 human assessors who were independently provided with *1)* instructions about the categorization task: a tweet is assessed as *useful* if it is related to the crisis and brings relevant information that helps to understand the tweet context or the situation. The tweet is *useless* otherwise; *2)* a set of manually annotated examples of each category (*useful* and *useless*), and *3)* a set of tweets from each crisis-related collection. The assessors were asked to choose a single category that best matched the content of the tweet. This task results in a training dataset including $1,800$ labeled tweets and two dictionaries containing the 100 most frequent terms (resp. less frequent) from each category of manually annotated tweets (*useful* terms resp. *useless* terms). Using term frequencies extracted from annotated tweets would allow us to filter the most vs. less frequent topics embedded in the datasets.

- *Step 2: Training the classification model.* We used the training dataset to learn the automatic classification model based on a logistic regression. To achieve this goal, we set up a feature-based representation of the manually annotated tweets based on 12 features that we classify into 3 categories: *1)* content features (e.g., number of hashtags, number of mentions), *2)* typographical features (e.g., number of punctuation characters, number of emoticons), *3)* vocabulary features (e.g., number of *useful* terms, number of *useless* terms). Since this feature is based on a statistical distribution of terms over the collection, as indicated above, we expect filtering useful tweets dealing with representative topics. This does not imply that useless tweets include only irrelevant tweets to the emergency situation. The performance of the training model was higher than 80% for both datasets with a Mean Absolute Error (MAE) of 18%.

- *Step 3: Filtering the datasets.* For the remaining analysis in this study, we only consider tweets classified as *useful* using the automatic classification model built in the previous step. Statistics about the resulting datasets are presented in Table 1.

We can see from Table 1 that both datasets contain more than 40% of retweets, 64% of mentions, and between 28% and 46% of shared URL. These statistics clearly show the engagement of the users involved in these datasets to explicitly collaborate through conversation built as detailed below.

Dataset	Sandy	Ebola
Tweets	2,119,854	2,872,890
Microbloggers	1,258,473	750,829
Retweets	963,631	1,157,826
Mentions	1,473,498	1,826,059
Reply	63,596	69,773
URLs	596,393	1,309,919
Pictures	107,263	310,581

Table 1: Descriptive statistics of each crisis-related dataset.

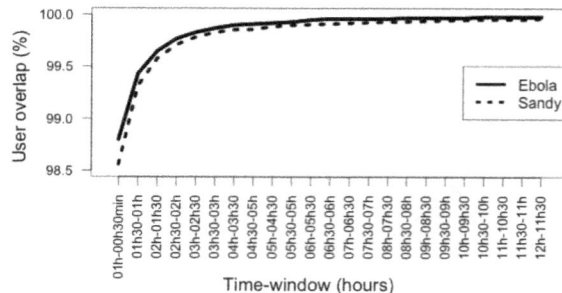

(a) Overlap ratio over all conversations

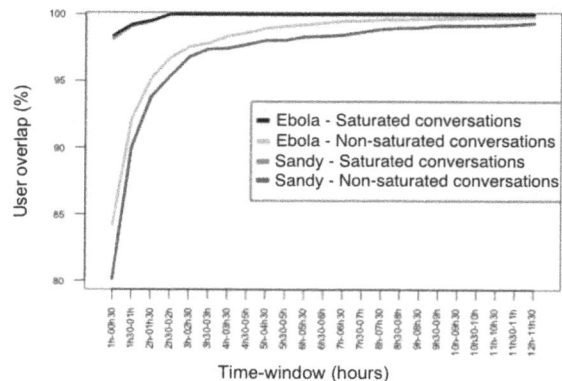

(b) Overlap ratio over saturated and non-saturated conversations

Figure 1: Tuning the temporal parameter.

3.3 Conversation Datasets

We assume that explicit collaboration in online social networks is channeled by a certain type of interactions. With respect to the definitions presented in section 3, we aim at describing and differentiating interactional patterns which we deem to be typically collaborative. According to Assumption 1, we built the set of conversations, based on the vocabulary of Twitter user interactions, namely *replying*, *mentioning* or *retweeting*, all mediated by the use of the @ symbol which conveys a collaboration manifestation [11]. Practically, the @ symbol is followed by the user handle (username) and thereby defines a link from tweet to tweet and, further, from user to user.

In order to characterize such conversations, we applied the algorithm proposed by Cogan et al. [9] on the cleaned data sets including only useful teweets. The algorithm works in two steps: starting from a given tweet, it first goes upstream by recursively discovering tweets in an ascending manner until it finds the root tweet. It then goes downstream, in a descending manner, to explore the subset of tweets related

Dataset	Sandy - 2 hours		Ebola - 2 hours	
# tweets	758,887	(79.83%)	878,171	(79.27%)
# user	1,020,213	(84.24%)	1,102,895	(83.17%)
# *retweet*	702,227	(78.75%)	825,642	(78.77%)
# *reply*	56,682	(96.28%)	52,624	(88.06%)
# *mention*	90,370	(83.51%)	157,457	(80.23%)
# conversation	240,991	(100.00%)	196,005	(100.00%)
Average number of tweets per conversation	3.15	(79.83%)	4.48	(79.27%)
Average number of users per conversation	4.23	(84.24%)	5.62	(83.17%)
Average number of *retweets* per conversation	2.91	(78.75%)	4.21	(78.77%)
Average number of *reply* per conversation	0.24	(96.28%)	0.27	(88.06%)
Average number of *mention* per conversation	0.37	(83.51%)	0.80	(80.23%)
Average length of the conversation	1.10	(99.68%)	1.23	(98.83%)

Table 2: Descriptive statistics for the 2 hours conversations for Sandy and Ebola datasets. Percentage (%) represents the divergence index between temporally truncated trees and complete trees, using 100.00 as a basis for complete trees. Most index are close to 100.00.

to this root tweet. Put differently, it reconstructs the whole tree of conversation in which the original tweet is embedded. On the Sandy and Ebola datasets, we respectively gather 240, 991 and 196, 005 conversation trees.

According to Assumption 2, a conversation may diverge progressively towards subgroups of users and topics, long after it started, plausibly far from the original collaborative search and sharing task goal. Indeed, in graph-theoretical terms, conversation trees are downstream connected components which can grow very large in practice. The chain of interactions may go deep and it is reasonable to put a boundary on long-lasting discussions: explicit collaboration should a priori correspond to compact interaction patterns, both structurally, temporally, and topically. A conversation may indeed diverge progressively towards subgroups of users, topics, long after it started plausibly far from the original collaboration goal.

To deal with this issue, we introduce a simple criterion to limit the conversation tree exploration: we require downstream tweets to be sufficiently close in time to the root tweet, whereby no more than T minutes should separate the last tweet from the root. This approach relies on the notion that conversations reach a point of saturation hereafter the explicit collaboration group is relatively stable. To check this, we examine the social content of trees as a function of time from the root tweet. More precisely, we look at the temporal evolution of participant lists when choosing a longer exploration period. We compute the average ratio of overlap between user lists, for a same conversation collected until t from the root seed and $t + 30$ minutes.

Figure 1 shows the distribution of the collaborative group overlaps over time for both Sandy and Ebola datasets. The x-axis represents the two successive temporal constraints (t and $t + 30$), while the y-axis corresponds to this *overlap ratio*. We notice that fixing T at 120 minutes yields an average overlap ratio of more than 99 %, for both datasets. We thus distinguish *"saturated"* from *"non-saturated"* conversations by considering trees which exhibit an overlap ratio of 100 % after 120 minutes (or not). Even for non-saturated conversations, we observe an average overlap ratio around 95 %. When comparing temporally-truncated trees with complete trees (see Table 2), we still observe a strong similarity in terms of structural features which further justifies the choice of this constraint. Truncated trees constitute the basic structural pattern of user groups engaged in explicit

collaboration bounded by a relatively tight time constraint. We can now analyze both their social and semantic configurations.

4. RESULTS

4.1 Characterization of the Collaborative Groups

Our objectives here are twofold: *1)* identifying the structural patterns of the users' collaboration networks and *2)* identifying the topics of the conversation threads that might make sense of the crisis situation for the users engaged in conversations.

4.1.1 Structure of the collaborative group networks

To have a picture of the collaboration structure, we derive the interaction subgraphs from the conversation trees. Nodes of the subgraph are conversation tree participants, while links correspond to at least one interaction between two users. We are particularly interested in the shape of these subgraphs and their distribution as done in [27, 15] for the study of diffusion cascade patterns in blog post networks. However, we are dealing here with conversation patterns, i.e., social subgraphs based on mentions, retweets and replies, in order to eventually describe distinct conversation roles and configurations [12].

To start with, we introduce a nomenclature defining a subgraph by a pair of numbers (x, y) where x represents the number of users and y the number of links. An analysis of this simple notation already makes it possible to describe and discriminate a wide range of different subgraphs. Table 3 gathers the most frequent interaction subgraphs and their graphical representations. Interestingly, this taxonomy is roughly identical for both Ebola and Sandy datasets, both in terms of rank and order of magnitude of the respective patterns. There are essentially two main types of subgraphs which appear to be meaningful in terms of potential collaboration configurations, involving between 2 and 7 users:

1. *Star-shaped networks* (patterns $(2, 1)$, $(3, 2)$, $(4, 3)$, $(6, 5)$, etc.). These subgraphs feature the prominence of a central person, and subsequent discussants which are all linked to her. Qualitatively, they correspond to information relaying subgroups where peripheral indi-

Setting	#Sandy	#Ebola	Pattern	Setting	#Sandy	#Ebola	Pattern
2;1	157,687	96,573		3;2	36,929	35,694	
4;3	12,124	11,639		5;4	5,568	6,058	
4;4	2,767	4,342		6;5	3,394	3,855	
7;6	2,177	2,862		8;7	1,528	2,434	
5;6	1,446	2,322		3;3	750	2,181	

Table 3: Most frequent collaboration patterns in Sandy and Ebola datasets, for saturated conversations.

viduals all cite or retransmit the content published by the central person.

2. *Flatter networks* (patterns $(4,4)$, $(3,3)$ or $(5,6)$, i.e., which respectively look like a square, a triangle, or a square and a triangle). These subgraphs indicate a more horizontal, collective discussion structure where more users interact with each other in a relatively decentralized manner, that is, without the existence of a central user.

Overall, we can see that collaborative groups are quite small without necessarily involving central users.

4.1.2 Content of the intra-group interactions

With respect to our second goal related to the topical analysis of the conversation streams, we applied the Latent Dirichlet Allocation (LDA) model [4] to the meta-documents built from the conversations and then tuned the optimal number of parameters using the perplexity measure [4]. We reached a minimal perplexity at 16 topics for the Ebola collection and 21 topics for the Sandy collection. Three assessors made a manual unsupervised annotation of the topics automatically extracted with the LDA model, to define topic labels. In case of disagreement on topic labels, a consensus has been reached between the three assessors. As shown by the labels listed in Table 4, the topics extracted from both collections are mostly related to crisis management except some of them (e.g., Obama and the Benghazi attack) which could be due to classification errors (18 %). We outline that these topics are quite different from those identified in similar emergency situations [22] extracted from the tweet streams, regardless of the groups' conversations. This observation is expected since topics extracted from conversations are likely to be more focused.

In order to relate the group structure to the underlying task topic, we associated each conversation with a topic through the maximal probability assignment criteria in the distribution conversation-topic resulting from the LDA model. Table 5 shows statistics about conversations by topic. We can notice that the most represented topics according to conversation numbers (#Conv.) related to crisis management are *1)* prayers, negative thoughts

Dataset	Topics
Sandy	(1) State of New York City; (2) Negative thoughts; (3) Donations/aids; (4) Thanks; (5) Explanations; (6) Water/Flood; (7) Insults; (8) Photos/Videos; (9) Dead persons/Deaths; (10) After Sandy; (11) Damages; (12) Missing people; (13) Prayers; (14) Obama and the Benghazi attack; (15) Weather alerts and nuclear alerts; (16) Humor; (17) Fear/Terror; (18) Financial impact; (19) Report/Inventory of fixtures; (20) Communication tools; (21) Information via the media
Ebola	(1) Prevention; (2) Actions/Thoughts to people; (3) Official reports; (4) Personal thoughts; (5) Dead persons/Deaths; (6) Worldwide urgency; (7) Exile; (8) Propagation; (9) Clinical tests; (10) Drug/Vaccine research; (11) Treatments; (12) First case in the US; (13) Disease/Fear in the US; (14) Victims and quarantine; (15) Action plan in Africa; (16) Propagation control

Table 4: Extracted conversation topics from Sandy and Ebola datasets.

and thanks, for the Sandy collection, and prevention, victims/quarantine, and *2)* actions/thoughts to people, for the Ebola collection.

To characterize the network of the collaborative groups related to each topic, we computed the modularity measures. This metric measures the relationship density between and within users' modules obtained by a classification algorithm. We found a high average modularity value that reaches 0.96 for Sandy dataset and 0.88 in the case of Ebola dataset. These modularity values reflect a higher density between the users of collaborative groups but -in contrast- sparse connections between users of different collaborative groups. The computation of the ratio between the number of identified modules and the number of conversations for each topic revealed a high ratio (0.8) for Sandy and a low ratio for Ebola (0.3). The results obtained on the Sandy dataset suggests that conversation networks are highly disconnected while those obtained on the Ebola dataset sug-

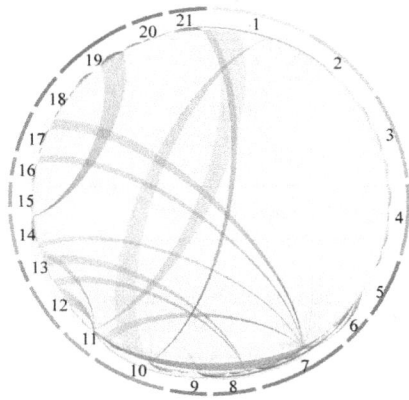

(a) Sandy dataset   (b) Ebola dataset

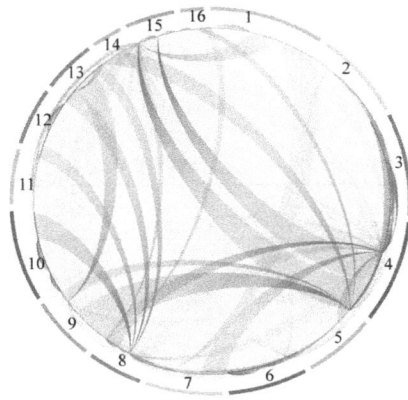

Figure 2: Collaboration networks

	Sandy				Ebola		
	#Conv.	#Users	#Tweets		#Conv.	#Users	#Tweets
1	12,325	49,979	36,618	1	42,811	238,022	188 987
2	17,857	74,853	55,493	2	13,282	71,808	56,656
3	12,573	55,557	41,938	3	10,640	56,377	44,240
4	13,779	56,475	41,509	4	9,846	54,375	43,153
5	9,743	41,583	30,974	5	10,103	54,849	43,166
6	10,365	41,108	29,887	6	9,041	51,871	41,478
7	38,781	163,959	121,852	7	12,950	75,458	60,597
8	10,152	41,505	30,482	8	8,719	49,632	39,629
9	8,297	34,678	25,642	9	7,081	38,012	29,932
10	8,928	36,354	26,703	10	11,294	64,080	51,103
11	6,842	28,256	20,818	11	5,762	32,750	26,151
12	9,642	42,084	31,557	12	11,383	70,132	57,151
13	23,329	102,708	77,465	13	6,925	41,058	33,032
14	9,477	41,560	31,273	14	20,594	114,007	90,347
15	11,672	51,118	38,489	15	8,374	49,266	39,660
16	4,663	19,199	14,234	16	7,202	41,200	32,888
17	5,461	24,195	18,339				
18	8,278	35,337	26,313				
19	5,897	23,053	16,666				
20	6,817	29,855	22,496				
21	6,164	26,797	20,138				

Table 5: Statistics of the collaborative groups sharing similar interests.

gest that a high ratio of conversations are subsumed. The difference in these observations could be explained by the differences in the life-spans of the datasets as explored in the next section. It seems that long-time social interactions lead to create user-to-user connections and bridge the gap between some of the collaborative groups.

In summary, these results outline that many collaborative groups deal with the same topic, but these groups are not totally connected as they form distinct ones, particularly within a short-term period. This may be explained by the fact that the conversations were held synchronously or asynchronously by users with similar interests who fail to connect with each other. To get a deeper understanding of this observation, we focus below on the connectivity between the collaborative groups.

4.2 Examination of the Connectivity between the Collaborative Groups

We believe that an interesting analysis concerns the exploration of the global collaboration network in order to highlight whether and how groups of users with similar interests (or not) are likely to explicitly collaborate with each other. Therefore, it seems interesting to identify relationships (reply, retweet, and mention links) between conversations, whether they share similar interests or not.

Respectively for Sandy and Ebola datasets, Figures 2a and 2b illustrate the collaboration networks inferred from users' social interactions considering their LDA topic-based assignation (see Section 4.1). These networks include the whole overlapping conversations, from the user belonging perspective, dealing with the same topic. Since the datasets include a large amount of users and social interactions, and in order to favor a better readability, we have represented these collaboration networks by filtering the three most populated conversations within each LDA topic. In each figure, collaboration topics are scattered around the perimeter of the circle and two types of relationships are characterized:

1. The *"intra-topic"* relationships between users engaged in conversations addressing the same topic, illustrated by arcs around and external to the perimeter. These relationships as illustrated in these figures are not particularly dense. We remember that Figure 2.a and Figure 2.b illustrate only the top three conversations of each topic which explain the low visible density. With all conversations considered, the number of average of "intra-topic" relationships exceeds $47,700$ relations for Sandy data and $36,300$ relations of Ebola dataset. Moreover, the degree of density varies across topics. These results added to structural analysis of the collaboration structure (see 4.1) corroborates the lack of social connectivity between users engaged in similar search/sharing tasks.

2. The *"inter-topic"* relationships between users engaged in distinct conversations dealing with distinct topics, symbolized by arcs inside the circle, are more prevalent for Sandy dataset whereas Ebola is characterized by a greater number of "inter-topic" relationships.

Considering the fact that Figures 2a and 2b show a sub-representation of the overall collaboration networks, we first

	Sub-Dataset 1	Sub-Dataset 2	Sub-Dataset 3
Period	07/29/2014 07:23 am - 07/31/2014 9:59 pm	08/07/2014 9:39 am - 08/08/2014 5:54 pm	08/14/2014 10:00 pm - 08/17/2014 9:59 pm
#Tweets	394,399	311,340	326,985
#Users	165,764	137,398	123,260
Cohesion value	1.418	1.309	1.958

Table 6: Analysis of the impact of the time-window on the cohesion metric.

Sandy	Ebola
(7) Exile - (13) Disease/Fear in the US	(1) Prevention - (14) Victims and quarantine
(7) Exile - (1) State of New York City	(1) Prevention - (2) Actions/Thoughts to people
(7) Exile - (2) Negative thoughts	(1) Prevention - (7) Exile
(7) Exile - (3) Donations/aids	(1) Prevention - (12) First case in the US
(2) Negative thoughts - (13) Disease/Fear in the US	(2) Actions/Thoughts to people - (14) Victims and quarantine

Table 7: Top pairwise topics assigned to users and inferred from their conversations.

judge the generalizability of our observations by the use of the cohesion metric [5] estimated over the collaboration network obtained with the whole datasets characterized by topical clusters associated to the LDA topics. This metric estimates the ratio between the strength of "*intra-topic*" user relationships (within topical cluster) and the strength of the "*inter-topic*" user relationships (between topical clusters), where a value higher than 1 highlights the preponderance of "*intra-topic*" relationships. We obtained a cohesion metric value equals to 1.43 for Sandy and 0.63 for Ebola, suggesting that the previous observed statements on the network sub-representation could be generalized to the overall collaboration network.

The differences between the Ebola and Sandy collaboration networks could be explained with respect to the duration of the social activity traced to the beginning of the crisis, at least starting from the oldest timestamp of the tweets in the crisis-related datasets. Indeed, both datasets, although characterized by similar collaboration patterns in individual conversations (see Table 3), have contrasted results in terms of cohesion metric values. Due to the collect time-periods (3 days for the Sandy dataset and 1 month for the Ebola one), we could infer that collaboration relationships of those datasets are respectively performed in short and long-term. Accordingly, the cohesion metric suggests that short-term interactions between users are more likely to focus on few topics ("*intra-topic*" relationships), in contrast to long-term interactions that seem to provide a wider range of topics and favor "*inter-topic*" social interactions. This result is consistent with previous findings [17] which indicate that the nature and intensity of communication between users change over-time according to the crisis phases. We expect that the latter has a significant effect on the degree of diversity of the sub-topics since an increasing number of users are involved during the evolving sense-making process.

To deepen our understanding of the differences between both datasets according to the time period parameter, we split the Ebola dataset into several sub-datasets in which the collect period is relatively equivalent to the one of the Sandy dataset. We randomly selected 3 sub-datasets in order to identify conversations, extract topics and finally built the collaboration network. We present in Table 6 the characteristics of these 3 sub-datasets and the obtained cohesion met-

rics. We notice that the cohesion metric values are higher than 1 (respectively equals to 1.418, 1.309 and 1.958 for the 3 sub-datasets), reinforcing our intuition that short-term interactions favor collaboration around few and more focused topics, with less interest sharing with the other users. This observation leads us to argue that large-scale collaboration is timely influenced by the emergence (or not) of users playing roles of intermediaries between distinct groups of users.

Moreover, we highlight that users are generally implied in different conversations, which might favor the diversity of the topic assignment at the user level. Indeed, for the Ebola dataset, a user is assigned on average to 7 topics while this value is lower (equals to 4) in the Sandy dataset. Therefore, it seems reasonable to assume that a user engaged in multiple conversations with different topics is more likely to create "*inter-topic*" relationships than a user engaged in few or a unique conversation. For instance, the most identified pairwise topics assigned to users within each dataset are represented in Table 7. We notice that for both datasets, one topic remains predominant in pairwise associations, respectively topic 7 and 1 for Sandy and Ebola, highlighting its exploratory aspect. This is mostly identifiable for Ebola since prevention might be carried according to several dimensions. This topic connectedness highlights the fact that some topics (likely exploratory topics) include a wide range of sub-topics (connected topics), leading to consider sub-topics as micro-tasks built naturally over users' conversations.

5. IMPLICATIONS FOR SOCIAL MEDIA COLLABORATION RESEARCH

We believe that our findings have important implications relevant for the research in social web collaboration, including:

• *Recommendation of collaborators.* Our findings indicate that the social graph of collaborative groups of users engaged in similar or shared search and sharing tasks is a set of weakly connected (or disconnected) small-sized sub-graphs. People are likely to be connected with a small audience while, being involved in an open social web space, they believe that they are connected to the crowd. One relevant research opportunity would be to enhance the collaboration mediation between users by designing information seeking algorithms able to automatically enhance user's seeking tweets with mentions leading to collaborator recommendation. This would allow creating social collaborative ties between users in order to overpass the small-sized collaboration network restricted to the user's neighborhood guided by his mentions and followers. Such algorithms would *1)* tackle the issue mentioned in [23] related to unanswered seeking tweets and *2)* constitute a valuable support for users who explicitly asked the questions to the crowd using the hashtag rather than their followers' network, as revealed in [17]. In addition, algorithms could be created to identify long-term group members who reinforce collaboration by providing advice or help through the identification of appropriate contributors for solving topically-related search and sharing tasks. The presence of a strong social support on the network is likely to encourage low-activity users to be better engaged towards a larger audience and benefit from it.

• *Enhancement of social awareness.* The analysis of collaborative groups connectivity demonstrated that active users are involved in many conversations with distinct topics, either sub-topics of the root search/sharing task topic or even other tasks dealing with other topics. Thus, another interesting implication for future research would be to design algorithms that enhance the information seeking process by detecting complex information needs and tasks. These would then be rooted to users engaged in different collaborative groups of users through conversations gathering shared or complementary topical facets of the original information need and task. Such users, viewed here as valuable intermediaries, could better transfer the need or task through the social network and increase more quickly the situational awareness rate over the whole social network. In turn, this would enhance the self-engagement of users, which is particularly desired in emergency situations. More generally, algorithmic mediation on the social web would create social ties between users or turn social ties into collaborative ties, tackling the problem of the so-called *"digital desert"* [3].

6. STUDY LIMITATIONS AND FUTURE WORK

The study faces some limitations. First, we acknowledge that the generalization of our findings requires further work. One limitation is the non-diversity and size of samples used in the study. For future research, we plan to perform our study across large-scale collections of User Generated Content (e.g., forums) within different application domains or search and sharing intents–beyond crisis-management–(e.g., health concerns). This would provide additional insights into how social media-based collaboration occurs.

We also note the lack of data about users. That is, based on our findings, we are not able to characterize group patterns according to the social neighborhood of the group members. This requires tracking users' personal profiles as well as those of their followers and those of users they mention or retweet. We intend to collect these data in the future to evaluate the ratio of strangers and their adequacy, compared to social neighbors, to solve the search topic. User-centric data would likely help us better explain the absence of explicit collaboration from a user perspective.

We finally point out that while previous works have shown that seeking and sharing information are the two basic forms

of online explicit collaboration using social networks [10, 29], we analyzed them in this study without distinction. The latter would be possible by building distinct conversation trees considering tweet-question seeds vs. non tweet-question seeds. Hence, we were not able to determine the differences that these two forms of collaboration might exhibit in both structural patterns and topics. We plan to overcome this limitation in the near future and explore the statistical differences between the corresponding social graphs.

7. CONCLUDING REMARKS

We studied explicit collaborative information search/sharing practices supported by social media. We used data from two crisis-related Twitter datasets. We first generated conversation datasets built upon a target collaboration concept and then analyzed their social structure and content. The results of the analyses reported here particularly highlight that *1)* collaboration is generally limited to small-sized flat networks, with or without a central user, based on user's explicit mentions, replies, and retweets, *2)* users are often engaged in distinct conversations involving different users, members of disconnected or weakly connected groups, and dealing with both distinct and shared topics, and that *3)* the time factor impacts the structure of the collaboration network; more particularly, we show the existence of a robust threshold in the time-span of conversation trees.

Based on our findings, we provided relevant research opportunities that would enable the emergence of a new generation of social collaborative information sharing and search systems.

8. ACKNOWLEDGMENTS.

This research was supported by the French CNRS PEPS research program under grant agreement EXPAC (CNRS/PEPS 2014-2015).

9. REFERENCES

[1] A. Acar and Y. Muraki. Twitter for crisis communication: Lessons learned from japan tsunami disaster. *Int. J. Web Based Communities*, 7(3):392–402, 2011.

[2] I. Badache and M. Boughanem. Harnessing social signals to enhance a search. In *WI*, volume 1, pages 303–309, Aug 2014.

[3] R. Baeza-Yates and D. Saez-Trumper. Wisdom of the crowd or wisdom of a few? an analysis of users' content generation. In *Hypertext and Social Media*, pages 69–74. ACM, 2015.

[4] D. M. Blei, A. Y. Ng, and M. I. Jordan. Latent dirichlet allocation. *J. Mach. Learn. Res.*, 3:993–1022, 2003.

[5] R. D. Bock and S. Z. Husain. An adaptation of holzinger's b-coefficients for the analysis of sociometric data. *Sociometry*, 13(2):pp. 146–153, 1950.

[6] F. Cacheda, V. Carneiro, D. Fernández, and V. Formoso. Comparison of collaborative filtering algorithms: Limitations of current techniques and proposals for scalable, high-performance recommender systems. *ACM Trans. Web*, 5(1):2:1–2:33, Feb. 2011.

[7] D. Carmel, N. Zwerdling, I. Guy, S. Ofek-Koifman, N. Har'el, I. Ronen, E. Uziel, S. Yogev, and

S. Chernov. Personalized social search based on the user's social network. In *CIKM*, pages 1227–1236. ACM, 2009.

[8] C. Castillo, M. Mendoza, and B. Poblete. Information credibility on twitter. In *WWW*, pages 675–684. ACM, 2011.

[9] P. Cogan, M. Andrews, M. Bradonjic, W. S. Kennedy, A. Sala, and G. Tucci. Reconstruction and analysis of twitter conversation graphs. In *HotSocial Workshop*, pages 25–31. ACM, 2012.

[10] M. De Choudhury, M. R. Morris, and R. W. White. Seeking and sharing health information online: Comparing search engines and social media. In *CHI*. ACM, 2014.

[11] K. Ehrlich and N. S. Shami. Microblogging inside and outside the workplace. In *ICWSM*. The AAAI Press, 2010.

[12] I. Eleta and J. Golbeck. Multilingual use of twitter: Social networks at the language frontier. *Computers in Human Behavior*, 41:424–432, 2014.

[13] B. M. Evans and E. H. Chi. Towards a model of understanding social search. In *CSCW*, pages 485–494. ACM, 2008.

[14] J. Foster. Collaborative information seeking and retrieval. *Annual Rev. Info. Sci & Technol.*, 40(1), Dec. 2006.

[15] L. Franco and H. Kawai. News detection in the blogosphere: Two approaches based on structure and content analysis. In *ICWSM*, 2010.

[16] J. P. Gene Golovinsky and M. Back. A taxonomy of collaboration in online seeking. In *arxiv.org/pdf/0908.0704*, CoRR abs/0908.0704, 2009.

[17] T. Heverin and L. Zach. Use of microblogging for collective sense-making during violent crises: A study of three campus shootings. *JASIST*, 63(1):34–47, 2012.

[18] S. R. Hiltz, P. Diaz, and G. Mark. Introduction: Social media and collaborative systems for crisis management. *ACM Trans. Comput.-Hum. Interact.*, 18(4):18:1–18:6, 2011.

[19] T. Holderness and E. Turpin. *PetaJakarta.org: Assessing the Role of Social Media for Civic Co-Management During Monsoon Flooding in Jakarta, Indonesia.* SMART Infrastructure Facility, University of Wollongong, 2015.

[20] D. Horowitz and S. D. Kamvar. The anatomy of a large-scale social search engine. In *WWW*, pages 431–440. ACM, 2010.

[21] M. Imran, C. Castillo, F. Diaz, and S. Vieweg. Processing social media messages in mass emergency: A survey. *ACM Comput. Surv.*, 47(4):67:1–67:38, June 2015.

[22] M. Imran, S. Elbassuoni, C. Castillo, F. Diaz, and P. Meier. Practical extraction of disaster-relevant information from social media. In *WWW*, pages 1021–1024, 2013.

[23] J.-W. Jeong, M. R. Morris, J. Teevan, and D. Liebling. A crowd-powered socially embedded search engine. In *ICWSM*. AAAI, 2013.

[24] B. Karweg, C. Huetter, and K. Böhm. Evolving social search based on bookmarks and status messages from social networks. In *CIKM*, pages 1825–1834. ACM, 2011.

[25] A. Kavanaugh, S. D. Sheetz, F. Quek, and B. J. Kim. Cell phone use with social ties during crises: The case of the virginia tech tragedy. *Using Social and Information Technologies for Disaster and Crisis Management*, (84), 2013.

[26] V. Lampos, T. De Bie, and N. Cristianini. Flu detector: Tracking epidemics on twitter. In *ECML PKDD*, pages 599–602. Springer-Verlag, 2010.

[27] J. Leskovec, M. McGlohon, C. Faloutsos, N. Glance, and M. Hurst. Cascading behavior in large blog graphs. 2007.

[28] J. T. Meredith Ringel Morris and K. Panovitch. What do people ask their social networks, and why? a survey study of status messages q&a behaviour. In *CHI*, pages 1739–1748. ACM, 2010.

[29] M. R. Morris. Exploring the complementary roles of social networks and search engines. In *ICWSM*, 2011.

[30] M. R. Morris. Collaborative search revisited. In *CSCW*, pages 1181–1192. ACM, 2013.

[31] F. Morstatter, J. Pfeffer, and H. Liu. When is it biased?: assessing the representativeness of twitter's streaming api. In *WWW*, 2014.

[32] L. Palen and K. Starbird. Working and sustaining the virtual disaster desk. In *CSCW*, 2013.

[33] J. Pickens. Social and collaborative information seeking: Panel. In *CIKM*, pages 2647–2648, New York, NY, USA, 2011. ACM.

[34] S. Poltrock, J. Grudin, S. Dumais, R. Fidel, H. Bruce, and A. M. Pejtersen. Information seeking and sharing in design teams. In *SIGGROUP*, pages 239–247, 2003.

[35] A. Sadilek, H. A. Kautz, and V. Silenzio. Modeling spread of disease from social interactions. In *ICWSM*, 2012.

[36] C. Shah. *Collaborative Information Seeking - The Art and Science of Making the Whole Greater than the Sum of All*, volume 34 of *The information retrieval series*. Springer, 2012.

[37] L. Soulier, C. Shah, and L. Tamine. User-driven system-mediated collaborative information retrieval. In *SIGIR*, pages 485–494, 2014.

[38] L. Soulier, L. Tamine, and W. Bahsoun. On domain expertise-based roles in collaborative information retrieval. *IP&M*, 50(5):752 – 774, 2014.

[39] J. Surowiecki. The Wisdow of crowds: Why the many are smarter than the few and how collective wisdom shapes business, economies, societies and nations. *Random House*, pages 78–85, 2004.

[40] J. C. Tang, M. Cebrian, N. A. Giacobe, H.-W. Kim, T. Kim, and D. B. Wickert. Reflecting on the DARPA Red Balloon Challenge. *Commun. ACM*, 54(4):78–85, 2011.

[41] S. Vieweg, A. L. Hugues, K. Starbird, and L. Paeln. Microblogging during two natural hazards events: What twitter may contribute to situational awareness. In *CHI*, 2010.

[42] C. Wendling, J. Radisch, and S. Jacobzone. The use of social media in risk and crisis communication. *OECD Working Papers on Public Governance*, (24), 2013.

Can Disputed Topic Suggestion Enhance User Consideration of Information Credibility in Web Search?

Yusuke Yamamoto
Kyoto University
Yoshida-honmachi, Sakyo, Kyoto, Japan
yamamoto@gsm.kyoto-u.ac.jp

Satoshi Shimada
Kyoto University
Yoshida-honmachi, Sakyo, Kyoto, Japan
shimada@gsm.kyoto-u.ac.jp

ABSTRACT

During web search and browsing, people often accept misinformation due to their inattention to information credibility and biases. To obtain correct web information and support effective decision making, it is important to enhance searcher credibility assessment and develop algorithms to detect suspicious information. In this paper, we investigate how credibility alarms for web search results affect searcher behavior and decision making in information access systems. This study focuses on disputed topic suggestion as a credibility alarm approach. We conducted an online user study in which 92 participants performed a search task for health information. Through log analysis and user surveys, we confirmed the following. (1) Disputed topic suggestion in a search results list makes participants spend more time browsing pages than ordinary search conditions, thereby promoting careful information seeking. (2) Disputed topic suggestion during web browsing does not change participant behaviors but works as complementary information. This study contributes to system designs to enhance user engagement in critical and careful information seeking.

CCS Concepts

•Information systems → Search interfaces; *Web searching and information discovery;* •Human-centered computing → Empirical studies in HCI;

Keywords

Web search; careful information seeking; credibility; decision making; behavior analysis

1. INTRODUCTION

Currently, people frequently rely on web pages to acquire various types of information. Such information varies from lightweight reading to significant information that can affect their lives. However, if people do not consider information credibility, they can be misled easily. Several studies have reported that people often trust web information without considering its credibility. Nakamura et

HT '16, July 10-13, 2016, Halifax, NS, Canada

© 2016 ACM. ISBN 978-1-4503-4247-6/16/07...$15.00

DOI: http://dx.doi.org/10.1145/2914586.2914592

al. reported that more than 50% of people perceive web pages retrieved by search engines as credible [17]. Lindgaard et al. claimed that people often trust visually appealing web pages based on initial impressions [13]. Morris et al. stated that many people trust information from social network services more than search engine results [16], even though false information is often spread on social networks [14].

Unlike information published or broadcast by conventional media, information in web pages is rarely verified before publication. The Pew Research Center reports that more than 70% of American Internet users searched for health information in the period 2011-2012[1]. However, according to Sillence et al., less than 50% of medical websites have been authenticated by medical experts [22]. There is a great deal of unverified information on the web, and many people accept such information without careful consideration. Therefore, it is important to create an information access environment where people can obtain credible information to support effective decision making. In this paper, we study one possible approach to support the assessment of information credibility.

Various types of support systems have been proposed, including evidence information search [11], disputed sentence suggestion [7, 26], and systems that provide scores according to credibility criteria [27, 21]. These systems are helpful if people can use them to support decision making. However, people often search for, interpret, and favor information that confirms their pre-existing beliefs and biases [10]. Therefore, some people accept information as credible when systems provide complementary information conforming to their pre-existing beliefs. In addition, people often do not feel the need for support systems because they assume the information on the web is credible [17], and others believe that they can identify correct information effectively [25]. Thus, we must consider how to enhance "careful" information seeking. Unless people are careful, they will not read web pages critically or compare multiple information sources, and they may accept suspicious information as credible information. Developing careful information seeking enables people to use the above mentioned support systems more appropriately and effectively in order to enhance decision making.

In this paper, we study the relationship between credibility warnings and user behavior. This relationship has implications for the design to enhance user engagement in careful information seeking. In the field of communication and persuasion, researchers have discussed threat appeal as a possible approach to change people's attitudes [20]. Our study focuses on the suggestion of disputed topics as a type of threat appeal. Here, disputed topics are those that some people claim are suspicious, regardless of whether the topics are actually true or not. In this study, we focus on two situations to

---

[1]PewResearchCenter's Health Fact Sheet, http://www.pewinternet.org/fact-sheets/health-fact-sheet/

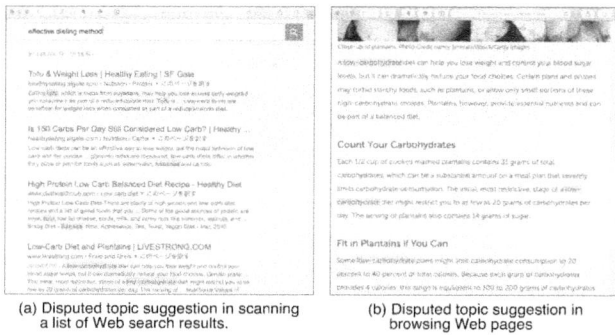

(a) Disputed topic suggestion in scanning a list of Web search results.

(b) Disputed topic suggestion in browsing Web pages

Figure 1: Examples of disputed topic suggestion during search and browsing

suggest disputed topics: *scanning a list of web search results* and *browsing web pages in the list* (Figure 1). We conducted an online user study where participants search for health information using our experimental system. Based on the results, we examine how disputed topic suggestion during web search influences user search behavior and attitude under both conditions.

Our primary contributions are as follows.

- The effect of disputed topic suggestion depends on suggestion timing even though the same disputed topic is highlighted.

- Disputed topic suggestion while scanning a list of search results has significant influence on user attitude toward information seeking, leading them to slow search and browsing.

- When users see disputed topics when browsing web pages, they often use them as complementary information to support decision making. The suggestions do not affect user search behaviors significantly.

2. RELATED WORK

2.1 Measuring correctness and credibility of web information

One possible approach against suspicious web information is measuring the correctness or credibility of the given information. Several studies have presented algorithms to measure the correctness probability of information. Galland and Pasternack et al. developed algorithms to measure the credibility of information by aggregating multiple sources that support or contradict the given information [8, 18]. Dong et al. described a method to evaluate web page information credibility assuming that credible web pages have few false facts or claims [6]. Although these algorithms appear hopeful, they only work well for domains where prior knowledge is available.

Rather than measuring correctness, some researchers have developed methods to measure the credibility of web information from specific sources, such as Wikipedia, Twitter, claims, and web pages. Adler et al. proposed an algorithm to measure the credibility of sentences in Wikipedia articles under the hypothesis that sentences are credible if they have not been edited [1]. Castillo et al. studied a method to automatically judge the credibility level of news propagated through Twitter by analyzing tweets and re-posts

about news [3]. These algorithms focus on various criteria that comprise credibility, such as objectivity, authority, and freshness [15]. However, credible information is not always correct and vice versa. Measuring credibility is inappropriate for misinformation detection, although the calculated scores can help people assess the credibility of web information.

2.2 Supporting user credibility judgment on the web

Some studies have focused on helping users judge credibility. Suh et al. introduced WIKIDASHBOARD, a system to visualize edit histories in Wikipedia articles [24]. Pirolli et al. examined how WIKIDASHBOARD affects user credibility assessment of Wikipedia articles [19]. Leong et al. developed an algorithm to retrieve evidence information from the web so that users can verify the credibility of suspicious statements [11]. Some researchers have proposed prototype systems that visualize scores of web search results according to various credibility criteria [21, 27]. Measuring the credibility of web information can be useful if users are willing to filter out non-credible web information according to their own credibility criteria. Regarding the credibility of multimedia data, Diakopoulos et al. introduced a system to support credibility judgment of video content by visualizing user evaluations and comments about the content [5].

Some studies have focused on dispute suggestion to notify which information users should consider. Our study extends this approach. DISPUTE FINDER developed by Ennals et al. highlights suspicious sentences in actively browsed web pages [7]. Yamamoto proposed suspicious sentence suggestion as a new type of query suggestion in web search engines [26]. These studies conducted qualitative user studies to evaluate the usefulness of the proposed systems. However, little attention has been paid to how such systems actually influence user attitudes and behaviors. In this paper, we study the effects of suspicious information suggestion on user search attitudes and behaviors.

2.3 Bias in web search and browsing

If all people were strongly motivated toward careful and critical information seeking on the web, the previously described measurements and support systems would be useful. However, few people are conscious of information credibility in web search and browsing. As stated in the previous section, Nakamura et al. reported that many search engine users inherently perceive web pages in search result lists as somewhat credible [17].

Furthermore, even if people are aware of suspicious information, they often make mistakes in credibility judgment owing to the use of incorrect heuristics, which is known as cognitive bias [10]. Some types of cognitive bias have been found in the information retrieval field. Leong et al. revealed the existence of domain bias whereby searchers often believe that relevant web pages are authorized by particular domains [9]. Clarke et al. analyzed the clickthrough logs of a commercial web search engine. They indicated that searchers are more likely to select search results that present more readable snippets [4]. White et al. studied the relation between pre-existing beliefs about search topics and search behaviors [25]. They showed that, if searchers have weak belief in search topics, they are likely to change their belief after performing a search. They also indicated that, if searcher belief in the search topic is strong, it is difficult to shift their belief after search and browsing.

These studies suggest that focusing on credibility and avoiding cognitive biases are important issues to prevent people from consuming incorrect information.

(a) SERP-d UI

(b) Page-d UI

Figure 2: Overviews of (a) SERP-d UI behavior and (b) Page-d UI behavior (each UI highlights disputed topics in red)

3. METHODS

We conducted an online study with 92 participants to understand how different disputed topic suggestion styles affect search behaviors. In the study, we asked participants to search the web for effective treatment or prevention of several health problems using three search user interfaces (UIs). Our study was conducted to address the following questions.

- Does disputed topic suggestion focus searcher attention on suspicious topics on the web?

- Which disputed topic suggestion style encourages searchers to scrutinize web search results in order to obtain the most credible information?

- How do searchers use suggested disputed topic information for their final decision making in search tasks?

The primary objective of this study is to determine whether disputed topic suggestion encourages web searchers to engage in careful information seeking. Therefore, we do not focus on improving search task efficiency and preciseness.

3.1 Conditions

This study adopted a one-way factorial design with three search UI conditions: **Control**, **SERP-d**, and **Page-d**. In the Control UI, our experimental search system simply returns a list of search results for a given query. Each search result contains a title, a snippet (content summary), and a URL, similar to conventional search engines. The SERP-d UI highlights disputed topics only in search engine result pages (SERP). If disputed topics about a given query exist, disputed topics appearing in titles and snippets on SERPs are highlighted in red, as shown in Figure 2(a). In the Page-d UI, disputed topics are highlighted while web pages are being browsed (Figure 2(b)). Note that participants using Page-d cannot notice which topics are considered disputed before visiting the web pages.

Table 1: Search topics and disputed topic examples

Search topic	Disputed topic example
Cancer	Avastin, BCG[2], MTX[3], macrobiotic, carbohydrate, hormone therapy, vitamin C
Dieting (weight loss)	karaoke, banana, water, soda, half-body bathing, low-carbohydrate, tofu
Acne	acerola, olive, steroid, yogurt, Vaseline, water face-wash, laser
Hangover	turmeric, caffeine, sauna, aquarius, cyrenidae, honey, salt plums
Atopy	BCG, eel, chocolate, bread, baby oil, Grifola frondosa, antihistamine
Depression	SNRI[4], SSRI[5], Inderal, screening, alcohol, exercise, mental therapy
Constipation	konjac, sesame, prune, lactobacillales, bok choy laxative, enzyme diet
Pollen allergy	protein, smoking, alcohol, margarine, Celestamine, roe, Chinese herb
Asthma	β2-adrenergic agonists, alcohol, APAP[6], Meptin, smoking, sugar, milk

3.2 Materials

3.2.1 Topics for search tasks

We selected nine search topics about health. The topics are listed in Table 1. These search topics are popular in Japan; however, many web pages about the topics contain suspicious approaches to cures and prevention (e.g., home remedies and urban legends).

3.2.2 Disputed topics

We define a disputed topic as having negative comments on some web pages. To collect disputed topics related to the chosen search topics, we used WISDOM X, a semantics-oriented web mining service by National Institute of Information and Communications Technology, Japan[7]. WISDOM X provides a question answering function that provides answer candidates using natural language questions. WISDOM X applies natural language processing techniques to indexes of 100 million Japanese web pages to extract a list of answer candidates (e.g., *What is effective for weight loss?* → *low-carb diet*) [2].

To obtain disputed topic candidates for each search topic shown in Table 1, we issued the query "What is not effective for {*search topic*}" into WISDOM X. Then, we filtered out unknown or meaningless topic candidates from the gathered candidates manually. Examples of the obtained disputed topics are given in Table 1.

3.2.3 Web page collection for search tasks

Web pages displayed during each task were gathered using the Microsoft Bing Search API[8] before the online study. We gathered two types of web pages: (1) pages containing disputed topics

---

[2]BCG: Bacillus Calmette Guerin
[3]MTX: Methotrexate
[4]SNRI: Serotonin & Norepinephrine Reuptake Inhibitors
[5]SSRI: Selective Serotonin Reuptake Inhibitors
[6]APAP: parracetamol
[7]WISDOM X: http://wisdom-nict.jp (in Japanese)
[8]Microsoft Bing Search API:
https://datamarket.azure.com/dataset/bing/search

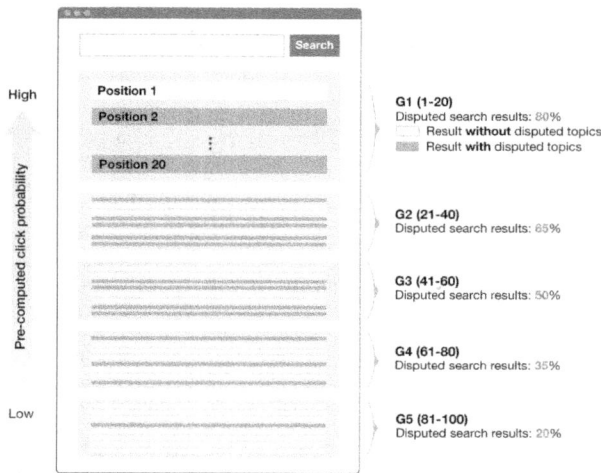

Figure 3: Manipulation of search result listing. Disputed and non-disputed pages are allocated to red and white slots, respectively. web pages with higher click probability appear at higher ranks.

(*disputed web pages*) and (2) pages not containing disputed topics (*non-disputed web pages*). To collect 100 disputed web pages for search topic q and disputed topic d, we issued the query "*effective* $\land$ $q \land d$" to the Bing API. Hundred non-disputed web pages were collected with the query "*effective* $\land$ q." We checked the relevance of the obtained search results for the given query manually and stored the titles, snippets, URLs, and raw HTML of the relevant results as our test set.

3.2.4 Listing search results

For any UI condition, immediately after beginning search tasks, our experimental system presented a controlled list of search results for a pre-defined initial query. As is well known, most users look at the first 10 search results only [23]. However, the number of displayed search results was fixed to 100 per query in this experiment. This manipulation was intended to enable participants to investigate as many web pages as possible for obtaining credible information. Each search result comprised a title, a snippet, and a URL. The same list of search results was displayed for the same search topic under each UI condition. Note that the participants were not permitted to change the initial query. They selected and browsed web pages from the fixed list. Furthermore, link navigation was disabled in order to track participant behavior.

Note that we selected search results to display and adjusted the rank position of each result prior to conducting the user study. This was done to avoid cases in which (1) few disputed topics in SERPs would attract participant attention with the SERP-d UI and (2) participants using the Page-d UI would visit few pages with disputed topics.

For case 1, we manipulated lists of search results such that more search results whose titles or snippets contained disputed topics would appear at higher ranks. As shown in Figure 3, the list of search results for each search topic was divided into five groups (G1, G2, G3, G4, and G5). In each group, 80%, 65%, 50%, 35%, and 20% of the search results had disputed topics in their title or snippet, respectively. We randomized the positions of the slots

where disputed web pages and *non-disputed web pages* were allocated within each group.

For case 2, we computed the clickthrough probability of the *disputed web pages* and *non-disputed web pages*. We then positioned the pages into the slots for *disputed web pages* (red slots in Fig 3) and *non-disputed web pages* (white slots in Fig 3) in order of clickthrough probability. For this clickthrough probability pre-computation, we used Lancers.jp[9], a crowd sourcing service in Japan. We asked workers on the crowdsourcing service to scan lists of our collected web pages about the search topics and find the web pages to satisfy information needs behind the search topics. The order of the web pages in the list was randomized for each worker. In this task, disputed topics were not highlighted (i.e., the Control UI). The workers' clickthrough logs were stored during their tasks. More than 100 workers were allocated to a single search topic. A total of 1012 workers participated in this preliminary investigation task. Finally, we computed the clickthrough probability of the collected web pages using the obtained logs.

3.3 Participants

A total of 121 participants were recruited via Lancers.jp. None participated in the preliminary investigation tasks. All participants reported that they were familiar with searching and browsing the web. They were randomly assigned to one of 27 groups (3 UIs x 9 topics) per task. Note that the maximum number of tasks each participant could perform was limited to nine. The participants received 50 Japanese yen (around 50 cents) for each response as compensation.

In this study, we collected 507 responses from the 121 participants. We omitted 27 responses for which the participants did not complete the tasks and 180 responses for which the participants' behavior data was not monitored due to browser Javascript settings. Finally, we used 310 valid responses from 92 participants.

3.4 Procedure

The online study consisted of four parts: (1) registration, (2) task introduction, (3) search task, and (4) questionnaire.

First, participant candidates checked a recruiting message on Lancers.jp. The recruiting message stated that the study's objective was to survey what people considered effective for health. The message also showed that the required time per task would be between 5 and 10 minutes. Once participant candidates agreed to participate in the study, they enrolled and proceeded to our study's website.

When the participants visited the website, we randomly allocated them a search topic and a UI condition. The participants were asked to read a brief introduction to the task procedure. Furthermore, for the participants allocated the SERP-d UI or Page-d UI, the website described that disputed topics would be highlighted during the search task using an example about an athlete's foot remedy. The description explained that when some web pages suggested that a topic was ineffective for a target health problem, the system would highlight the topic in red. After the brief introduction, the participants were presented with the following task scenario.

> *You have troubles with your health and want to lose weight. You are about to search the web for effective weight loss diet methods. Please start a web search from the following link, and then find and report effective methods.*

After reading this scenario, the participants clicked a link to start the web search. Once moving to the web search page, a list of

---

[9]Lancers.jp: http://www.lancers.jp/

Table 2: Mean and standard error of the mean (SEM) of pageviews for the three UIs

UI condition	Control	Page-d	SERP-d
Mean pageviews	5.24	5.55	4.64
(SEM)	(0.634)	(0.537)	(0.547)

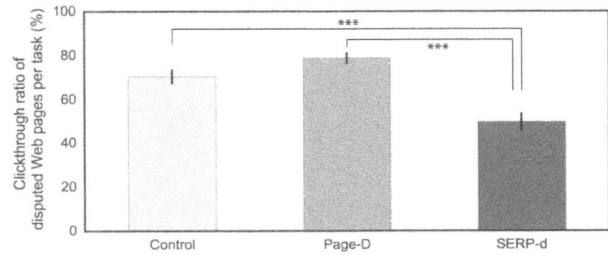

Figure 4: Clickthrough ratio of disputed web pages per task for the three UIs (significant differences are shown by lines)

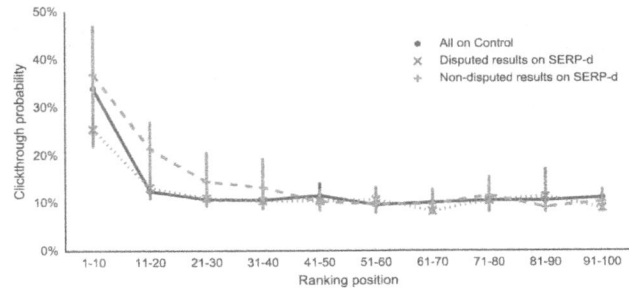

Figure 5: Clickthrough probability for disputed/non-disputed web search results in each ranking position group

100 search results was presented, similar to conventional search engines. The participants were asked to browse the web pages in the list without time limitation. When they found their answer (effective method for the target health problem), they finished the search and reported the answer on the study's website. If they did not find satisfactory answers, they were allowed to report "nothing effective." During the search tasks, the participants' clickthroughs and dwell times on web pages were stored using Javascript.

Finally, the participants using the SERP-d UI or Page-d UI were asked to fill out questionnaire about the usefulness and useful aspects of the UIs. The survey about usefulness was answered on a 5-point Likert scale (1 = never useful, 3 = neutral, 5 = very useful). For the useful aspect survey, the participants were asked to make multiple selections from the following list.

- **Attention calling for credibility-aware search**: to become more conscious of information credibility during web search

- **Notification of information to be checked**: to find which disputed topics should be examined in detail

- **Suspicious topic filtering**: to filter out suspicious topics

- **Others**: unlisted useful aspects

- **Nothing**: no useful aspects

After the search task and survey, a unique confirmation code was issued to the participants. The participants copied and pasted the code to Lancers.jp, thereby allowing us to pay task rewards.

4. RESULTS

Here, we present our results for the behavior analysis and post questionnaire. Our analytical results show that SERP-d had a more significant impact on participant behaviors in search tasks than Page-d.

For statistical testing, we utilized a one-way analysis of variance (ANOVA) with the three UI conditions as factors. For post-hoc pairwise comparisons, we used the Tukey–Kramer test. The analysis of the post questionnaire used Pearson's χ^2 test.

4.1 Pageviews

To evaluate whether Page-d and SERP-d encouraged participants to check multiple information sources for careful decision making, we examined the number of web pages (pageviews) that participants viewed in the three UIs using clickthrough logs. The results are given in Table 2. Our ANOVA results revealed no statistical difference between the mean pageviews per task for the participants using Control (5.24, SEM = 0.634), SERP-d (4.64, SEM = 0.547), and Page-d (5.55, SEM = 0.537) ($F(2, 307)$=0.638, $p = 0.529$, η^2 = 4.14-3).

To determine how Page-d and SERP-d influenced participant page selection, we measured the mean clickthrough ratio of disputed web search results per task with the three UIs. The clickthrough ratio means how much percentage of web search results which a participant clicked during his/her task contained disputed topics in the SERPs. Although Control and Page-d did not highlight disputed topics in the SERPs, we checked and computed how often the participants using these UIs clicked disputed web search results that SERP-d highlighted in the SERPs. There was a significant difference between the three UIs for the clickthrough ratio of disputed web pages ($F(2, 307)$=19.8, $p^{**} < .01$, $\eta^2 = 0.114$). Figure 4 shows that our post-hoc pairwise comparison analyses reported that the mean clickthrough ratio of SERP-d was much less than that of Control (49.7% < 70.5%; $p^{**} < .01$) and Page-d (49.7% < 78.9%; $p^{**} < .01$). This indicates that the disputed topic highlighting in SERPs helped participants avoid disputed web pages before visiting them.

We also analyzed the clickthrough probability for web search results in each ranking position by comparing SERP-d and Control. Here, the clickthrough probability of a web search result means the percentage of participants that clicked the given search result. As seen in Figure 5, when the participants used SERP-d, non-disputed web pages were clicked in SERPs with higher probability than disputed web pages in the 1–40 rank positions. In particular, for the 1–20 positions, the clickthrough probability for non-disputed web pages was more than 10% higher than that of disputed web pages. These results support the finding about clickthrough ratio per task, indicating that participants clicked non-disputed web search results more frequently than disputed results. Furthermore, as shown in Figure 5, in contrast to Control, the clickthrough probability for non-disputed web pages with SERP-d decreased gradually to lower-ranked results. This suggests that participants using SERP-d tried to check the middle-positioned search results as well as the high-positioned group, because the middle-positioned one had fewer disputed search results than the high-positioned one. On

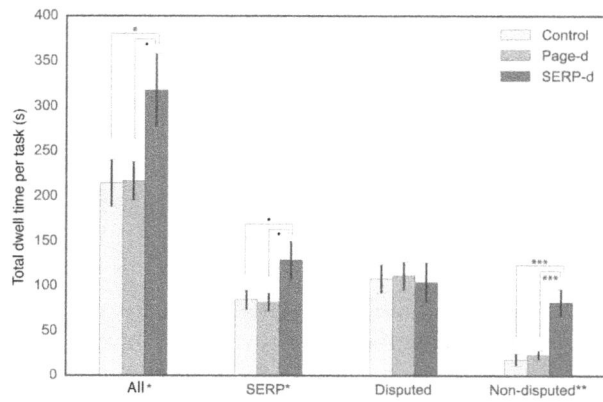

Figure 6: Total dwell time per task for all pages, SERPs, disputed pages, and non-disputed pages with the three UIs (significant differences are indicated by lines ($\cdot$=p < 0.1, *=p < .05, **=p<.01))

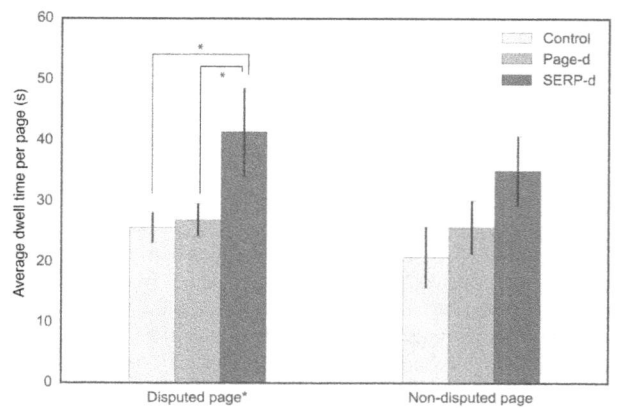

Figure 7: Average dwell times per disputed and non-disputed web pages for the three UIs

the other hand, participants using Control often concentrated on browsing high-ranked web search results.

4.2 Dwell time

To observe how Page-d and SERP-d enhanced participant engagement in careful reading of web information, we examined dwell time while viewing SERPs and web pages with the three UIs. Figure 6 shows the mean total dwell times per task for viewing SERPs, disputed web pages, non-disputed web pages, and all pages. The total dwell times for disputed/non-disputed web pages for Control were measured by checking how long a participant stayed on web pages where disputed topics would/would not have been highlighted when using SERP-d or Page-d. In terms of total dwell time for all web pages (session time), there was significant statistical difference between the three UIs ($F(2,307)$=3.75, p^* < .05, η^2 = 2.38e-2). Furthermore, as shown in Figure 6, the session time for SERP-d was significantly longer than that for Control (317.8s > 214.7s; p^* < .05). A marginal trend toward significance was found between SERP-d and Page-d (317.8s > 217.0s p=.056 < 0.1). In terms of total dwell time on SERPs, the time for SERP-d was longer than that of the other UIs. ANOVA results revealed a significant difference between the three UIs ($F(2,307)$=3.27, p^* < .05, η^2 = 2.09e-2). The post-hoc pairwise comparisons suggested marginal trends toward significance between SERP-d and Control and between SERP-d and Page-d (129.4 > 84.8 s; p=.081; 129.4 s > 82.1 s; p=.056, respectively). This indicates that participants using SERP-d might tend to take more time to scan a list of search results than with the other UIs.

With respect to total dwell time on disputed web pages, there was no statistical difference between the three UIs (Control = 117.2 s, SERP-d = 104.3 s, and Page-d = 111.5 s; p = .961; η^2 = 2.60e-4). On the other hand, in terms of dwell time on non-disputed web pages, there was statistical significance between the three UIs ($F(2,307)$=13.0, p^{**} < .01, η^2 = 7.78e-2). The post-hoc pairwise comparisons indicated that participants using SERP-d viewed non-disputed web pages longer in total than participants using Control (81.6 s > 18.2 s, p^{***} = 8.89e-5) and Page-d (81.6 s > 23.4 s, p^{***} = 1.83e-5). When the findings for dwell time on SERPs were combined, the results indicate that SERP-d made participants spend longer time staying in SERPs and non-disputed web pages than Control and Page-d.

Furthermore, we calculated the average dwell times per disputed and non-disputed web pages. In this calculation, we did not consider participants who did not visit disputed/non-disputed web pages. For the average dwell time per disputed web page, the analytical results show a significant difference between the three UIs ($F(2,260)$ = 4.13, p^* < .05, η^2 = 3.08e-2). Moreover, as shown in Figure 7, the post-hoc pairwise tests indicate that SERP-d made participants view each disputed web page longer than Control and Page-d at a significance level of 0.05 (41.4 s > 25.7 s, p^* = .022; 41.4 s > 27.0 s, p^* = .038). Figure 6 shows that total dwell time for the disputed web pages were shorter than that of non-disputed web pages. However, the results on Figure 7 indicate that once participants using SERP-d visited disputed web pages, they viewed the pages more carefully than participants using Control and Page-d. Regarding non-disputed web pages, we found no significant difference between the three UIs ($F(2,170)$ = 1.83, p = .164, η^2 = 2.10e-2), although the mean average dwell time for SERP-d appeared greater than that of Control and Page-d (SERP-d = 35.1s, Control = 20.8s, Page-d = 25.8s).

4.3 Search task answer

To analyze how SERP-d and Page-d affected the participants' final decisions, we evaluated the 310 answers reported as effective health methods. We compared the reported answers with the disputed topics the system highlighted during the tasks by manually classifying them into two groups: *disputed answers* and *non-disputed answers*. During the classification process, we removed five answers that were too ambiguous to judge.

Figure 8 shows the ratio of participant answers classified as *disputed answer* and *non-disputed answer*. According to Figure 8, more participants using Page-d and SERP-d reported non-disputed answers than those using Control (69.5%, 69.4% > 56.9%). A Pearson's χ^2 test revealed marginal trends toward significance between Page-d and Control (χ^2 = 3.57, p = 5.88e-2 < 0.1, Cramer's V = 1.31e-1) and between SERP-d and Control (χ^2 = 3.36, p = 6.67e-2 < 0.1, Cramer's V = 1.30e-1). These results indicate that SERP-d and Page-d were likely to influence the participants' final decisions in such a way to avoid suspicious topics.

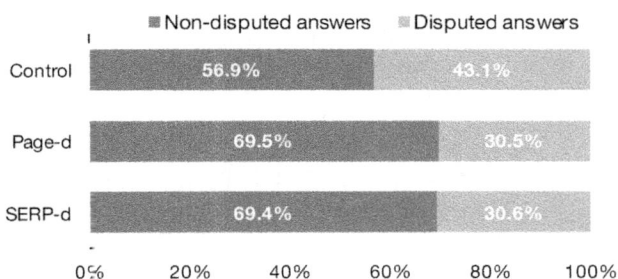

Figure 8: Ratio of participant answers contained/not contained in disputed topic list

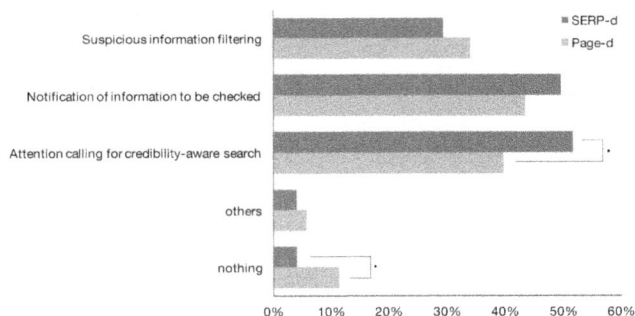

Figure 9: Ratio of participants who thought each factor was useful (marginal trends toward significance are illustrated by lines)

Table 3: Mean and SEM of usefulness rating score for SERP-d and Page-d

UI condition	SERP-d	Page-d
Mean usefulness	4.02	3.74
(SEM)	(9.30e-2)	(1.01e-1)

Table 4: Features of SERP-d UI and Page-d UI

Effect	SERP-d	Page-d
Prevention of suspicious topic	X	
Reinforcing critical info. seeking	X	
Seeking complementary information	X	X

4.4 Usability of disputed topic suggestion

To investigate the participants' subjective evaluations and use of Page-d and SERP-d, we analyzed the answers to the post questionnaire. Table 3 shows how useful SERP-d and Page-d were to search for effective health methods. The usefulness of SERP-d and Page-d were 4.02 and 3.74, respectively, and there was statistical significance between the two UIs ($F(1, 203) = 4.23$, $p^* < .05$, $\eta^2 = 2.04e-2$). This indicates that both UIs were considered useful on average. Another finding is that the participants thought that SERP-d was more useful for searching for effective health methods than Page-d.

Figure 9 shows which factors of SERP-d and Page-d participants considered useful for search tasks. The two most useful factors of SERP-d and Page-d were attention calling for credibility-aware search (SERP-d = 51.5%; Page-d = 39.6%) and notification of information to be checked (SERP-d = 49.5%; Page-d = 43.4%). With respect to the attention calling aspect, there was a marginal trend toward significance between participants using the two UIs ($\chi^2 = 2.92$, $p < 3.74e-2 < 0.1$, Cramer's $V = 1.19e-1$). Fewer participants indicated that suspicious information filtering was a useful factor than the previous two aspects for both of the UIs (SERP-d = 29.3%; Page-d = 34.0%). 11.3% of participants using Page-d and 4.04% of participants using SERP-d indicated that the UI was not useful. Regarding this "nothing useful" factor, there was a marginal trend toward significance between participants using the two UIs ($\chi^2 = 3.77$, $p < 5.22e-2 < 0.1$, Cramer's $V = 1.36e-1$). Note that Page-d was considered less useful than SERP-d.

5. DISCUSSION

Through our study of 92 participants' behaviors and subjective evaluations, we obtained the following findings for disputed topic suggestion in web search.

1. Participants using SERP-d often spent more time performing tasks than when using Control and Page-d, especially when viewing SERPs and non-disputed web pages.

2. When scanning a search results list with SERP-d, participants clicked more search results without disputed topics than those with disputed topics.

3. Once participants visited web pages whose disputed topics were highlighted by SERP-d, they often spent more time viewing them than with the other UIs.

4. With respect to search behaviors (i.e., dwell time and click-through ratio), there was no difference between Page-d and Control.

5. SERP-d and Page-d made fewer participants select disputed topics as their task answers than Control.

6. Page-d and SERP-d obtained good evaluations from participants on average.

From these findings, we examine the potential of the two dispute suggestion styles from three aspects: (1) preventing users from browsing suspicious topics, (2) reinforcing careful information seeking, and (3) seeking complementary information for decision making. These are summarized in Table 4.

Disputed topic suggestion in SERPs notifies searchers which search results contain suspicious information before they click the results. It can be presumed from some of our findings that, rather than simply filtering out suspicious information, the SERP-d suggestion style has a significant impact on searcher consideration of information credibility on the web. As shown in Figure 4, SERP-d prevented participants from clicking disputed web search results. In addition, SERP-d appeared to make the participants more careful in web search. This can be interpreted from three findings: (a) participants using SERP-d spent more time performing tasks, (b) they selected web search results more carefully for a longer time (Figure 6), and (c) SERP-d encouraged them to read disputed web pages more carefully once visiting them as well as non-disputed pages (Figure 7). These results indicate that SERP-d influenced the entire search process so that the participants examined the credibility of web pages, regardless of whether the pages contained disputed topics on their SERPs. Therefore, we conclude that disputed topic suggestion in SERPs promotes careful information seeking.

On the other hand, it can be presumed that disputed topic suggestion on visited web pages could be used as complementary information for decision making rather than strongly restraining checking suspicious information and promoting careful information seeking. If the Page-d suggestion style prevented checking suspicious information, participants using Page-d would have spent less time dwelling on disputed web pages than with Control because the participants would have immediately left the pages after seeing disputed topic suggestions. However, the average dwell time on disputed web pages for Page-d was as long as that for Control (Figure 7). Furthermore, if Page-d promoted careful information seeking as SERP-d does, the participants with Page-d would have spent more time performing tasks and browsing disputed Web pages than with Control (Figures 6 and 7). On the other hand, Figure 8 shows that more participants using Page-d reported non-disputed answers than those using Control. Furthermore, the post questionnaire revealed that some participants said Page-d was useful for filtering out suspicious information (Figure 9). These results indicate that the participants could use suggested disputed topics on Page-d to reduce uncertainty on their final answers for the tasks. Consequently, we consider that the Page-d suggestion works as complementary information to support a judgment on whether browsed information is credible.

Our study has revealed that, even when suggesting the same disputed topics, the timing of suggestion might influence participant search behaviors. Both SERP-d and Page-d can prevent searchers from making the decision which might contain suspicious information. However, SERP-d can motivate searchers to carefully and slowly scrutinize web pages using threat appeal. Page-d is not powerful enough to provoke mental movement towards more careful information seeking. In summary, the results of our study indicate that disputed topic suggestion before visiting web pages can encourage searchers toward careful information seeking more easily than after.

Our study provides insights on search interaction design to enhance user consideration of information credibility in web search. However, there are issues to address in future. The first is the effect of individual variability on disputed topic suggestion. Our study indicates that SERP-d made participants more careful in web search and browsing on average than Page-d and Control. However, we found that SERP-d did not influence some participants' behaviors. One possible reason is related to the participants' prior beliefs or preferences about search topics. For example, White et al. reported that, if searchers have confident belief in topics initially, they are more likely to maintain their belief after a search [25]. Moreover, according to Liao et al., even if people confirm that opposing opinions exist, they will often preferentially select information that supports their prior beliefs [12]. Considering these studies, it is possible that disputed topic suggestion in SERPs does not always influence searchers' search attitude and behavior because they might have strong prior belief or preference. To develop methods that promote careful information seeking, we must study the relationship between prior searcher belief and the effects of disputed topic suggestion.

The second issue is related to the visibility of disputed topics suggestion in SERPs. In our study, we used artificial SERP settings, where web search results with disputed topics appeared more frequently in higher ranked positions; thus, disputed topics attracted more participant attention. However, in reality, commercial search engines order search results using proprietary algorithms. There-

fore, even if disputed topics exist in a list of search results, searchers do not always see them. To enhance searcher engagement in careful search, we must consider other fore-alarming methods easy to implement on search engines like [26], in addition to our disputed topic highlighting method.

6. CONCLUSION AND FUTURE WORK

In this paper, we have studied how disputed topic suggestion influences search behavior and decision making to obtain credible information from the web when *scanning a search results list* and *browsing web pages*. We conducted an online study with 92 participants to evaluate the two styles of disputed topic suggestion. The results show that, even when suggesting the same disputed topic, the timing of suggestion influences participant behaviors. We found that disputed topic suggestion in SERPs encourages people to consider information credibility, prevent them from consuming suspicious information, and make them spend more time searching the web. On the other hand, the results indicate that disputed topic suggestion in web pages does not change people's search behaviors; however, it can help find complementary information to support decision making. Thus, we suggest that focusing on fore-alarming before accessing information is important in the design of support systems to enhance searcher willingness to engage in careful information seeking.

However, several issues require future consideration. The first is the effect of individual variability on disputed topic suggestion. Second, we must examine methods to gather disputed topics from the web and examine methods to implement disputed topic suggestion as fore-alarming into search engines under practical constraints. Furthermore, providing complementary information to resolve disputes is another important issue.

To obtain correct web information and support effective decision making, it is important to strengthen people's credibility judgment process and the development of machine-based credibility judgment systems. We believe that this work will contribute to the promotion of careful information seeking on the web.

7. ACKNOWLEDGMENTS

This work was supported in part by Grants-in-Aid for Scientific Research (#15H01718, #25240050) from MEXT of Japan.

8. REFERENCES

[1] B. T. Adler and L. de Alfaro. A Content-Driven Reputation System for the Wikipedia. In *Proceedings of the 16th International Conference on World Wide Web (WWW 2007)*, pages 261–270, 2007.

[2] S. Akamine, D. Kawahara, Y. Kato, T. Nakagawa, K. Inui, S. Kurohashi, and Y. Kidawara. Wisdom: A web information credibility analysis system. In *Proceedings of the ACL-IJCNLP Software Demonstrations (ACLDemos 2009)*, pages 1–4, 2009.

[3] C. Castillo, M. Mendoza, and B. Poblete. Information Credibility on Twitter. In *Proceedings of the 20th International Conference on World Wide Web (WWW 2011)*, pages 675–684, 2011.

[4] C. L. A. Clarke, E. Agichtein, S. Dumais, and R. W. White. The Influence of Caption Features on Clickthrough Patterns in Web Search. In *Proceedings of the 30th International ACM SIGIR Conference on Research and Development in Information Retrieval*, SIGIR 2007, pages 135–142. ACM, 2007.

[5] N. Diakopoulos and I. Essa. Modulating Video Credibility via Visualization of Quality Evaluations. In *Proceedings of the 4th Workshop on Information Credibility (WICOW 2010)*, pages 75–82. ACM, 2010.

[6] X. L. Dong, E. Gabrilovich, K. Murphy, V. Dang, W. Horn, C. Lugaresi, S. Sun, and W. Zhang. Knowledge-based Trust: Estimating the Trustworthiness of Web Sources. *Proceedings of the VLDB Endowment*, 8(9):938–949, 2015.

[7] R. Ennals, B. Trushkowsky, and J. M. Agosta. Highlighting Disputed Claims on the Web. In *Proceedings of the 19th International Conference on World Wide Web (WWW 2010)*, pages 341–350, 2010.

[8] A. Galland, S. Abiteboul, A. Marian, and P. Senellart. Corroborating Information from Disagreeing Views. In *Proceedings of the 3rd ACM International Conference on Web Search and Data Mining (WSDM 2010)*, pages 131–140. ACM, 2010.

[9] S. Ieong, N. Mishra, E. Sadikov, and L. Zhang. Domain Bias in Web Search. In *Proceedings of the 5th ACM International Conference on Web Search and Data Mining (WSDM 2012)*, pages 413–422. ACM, 2012.

[10] D. Kahneman. A perspective on judgment and choice: mapping bounded rationality. *American psychologist*, 58(9):697, 2003.

[11] C. W. Leong and S. Cucerzan. Supporting Factual Statements with Evidence from the Web. In *Proceedings of the 21st ACM International Conference on Information and Knowledge Management (CIKM 2012)*, pages 1153–1162. ACM, 2012.

[12] Q. V. Liao and W.-T. Fu. Beyond the Filter Bubble: Interactive Effects of Perceived Threat and Topic Involvement on Selective Exposure to Information. In *Proceedings of the 31th ACM SIGCHI Conference on Human Factors in Computing Systems (CHI 2013)*, pages 2359–2368. ACM, 2013.

[13] G. Lindgaard, C. Dudek, D. Sen, L. Sumegi, and P. Noonan. An Exploration of Relations Between Visual Appeal, Trustworthiness and Perceived Usability of Homepages. *ACM Transactions on Computer-Human Interaction*, 18(1):1–30, 2011.

[14] J. Maddock, K. Starbird, H. J. Al-Hassani, D. E. Sandoval, M. Orand, and R. M. Mason. Characterizing Online Rumoring Behavior Using Multi-Dimensional Signatures. In *Proceedings of the 18th ACM Conference on Computer Supported Cooperative Work & Social Computing (CSCW 2015)*, pages 228–241. ACM, 2015.

[15] M. Metzger, A. Flanagin, K. Eyal, D. Lemus, and R. McCann. Credibility for the 21st century: Integrating perspectives on source, message, and media credibility in the contemporary media environment. *Communication yearbook*, 27:293–336, 2003.

[16] M. R. Morris, J. Teevan, and K. Panovich. What Do People Ask Their Social Networks, and Why?: A Survey Study of Status Message Q&A Behavior. In *Proceedings of the the 28th ACM SIGCHI Conference on Human Factors in Computing Systems (CHI 2010)*, pages 1739–1748. ACM, 2010.

[17] S. Nakamura, S. Konishi, A. Jatowt, H. Ohshima, H. Kondo, T. Tezuka, S. Oyama, and K. Tanaka. Trustworthiness Analysis of Web Search Results. In *Proceedings of the 11th European Conference on Research and Advanced Technology for Digital Libraries (ECDL 2007)*, pages 38–49. Springer, 2007.

[18] J. Pasternack and D. Roth. Latent Credibility Analysis. In *Proceedings of the 22nd International Conference on World Wide Web (WWW 2013)*, pages 1009–1020, 2013.

[19] P. Pirolli, E. Wollny, and B. Suh. So You Know You're Getting the Best Possible Information: A Tool that Increases Wikipedia Credibility. In *Proceedings of the 27th ACM SIGCHI Conference on Human Factors in Computing Systems (CHI 2009)*, pages 1505–1508. ACM, 2009.

[20] R. W. Rogers. *Social psyhophysiology*, chapter Cognitive and physiological processes in fear appeals and attitude change: A revised theory of protection motivation, pages 153–176. Guilford Press, 1983.

[21] J. Schwarz and M. Morris. Augmenting Web Pages and Search Results to Support Credibility Assessment. In *Proceedings of the 29th ACM SIGCHI Conference on Human Factors in Computing Systems (CHI 2011)*, pages 1245–1254. ACM, 2011.

[22] E. Sillence, P. Briggs, L. Fishwick, and P. Harris. Trust and Mistrust of Online Health Sites. In *Proceedings of the 22th ACM SIGCHI Conference on Human Factors in Computing Systems (CHI 2004)*, pages 663–670. ACM, 2004.

[23] C. Silverstein, H. Marais, M. Henzinger, and M. Moricz. Analysis of a Very Large Web Search Engine Query Log. *SIGIR Forum*, 33(1):6–12, 1999.

[24] B. Suh, E. H. Chi, A. Kittur, and B. A. Pendleton. Lifting the Veil: Improving Accountability and Social Transparency in Wikipedia with WikiDashBoard. In *Proceeding of the 26th ACM SIGCHI Conference on Human Factors in Computing Systems (CHI 2008)*, pages 1037–1040. ACM, 2008.

[25] R. W. White. Beliefs and biases in web search. In *Proceedings of the 36th International ACM SIGIR Conference on Research and Development in Information Retrieval (SIGIR 2013)*, pages 3–12. ACM, 2013.

[26] Y. Yamamoto. Disputed Sentence Suggestion Towards Credibility-Oriented Web Search. In *Proceedings of the 14th Asia-Pacific international conference on Web Technologies and Applications (APWeb 2012)*, pages 34–45. Springer, 2012.

[27] Y. Yamamoto and K. Tanaka. Enhancing Credibility Judgment of Web Search Results. In *Proceedings of the 29th ACM SIGCHI Conference on Human Factors in Computing Systems (CHI 2011)*, pages 1235–1244. ACM, 2011.

The Role of Comments' Controversy in Large-Scale Online Discussion Forums

Adithya Aggarwal
Schoo of Computing, Informatics & Decision Systems Engineering, Arizona State University, 699 S. Mill Ave., Tempe AZ, USA
aaggar10@asu.edu

Claudia López
Departamento de Informática, Universidad Técnica Federico Santa María, Av. España 1680, Valparaiso, Chile
claudia@inf.utfsm.cl

I-Han Hsiao
School of Computing, Informatics & Decision Systems Engineering, Arizona State University, 699 S. Mill Ave., Tempe AZ, USA
Sharon.Hsiao@asu.edu

ABSTRACT

In this paper, we examine the value of comments in large-scale discussion forums. We survey the relevant literature and employ the key content quality identification features. We then construct comment semantics features and build several regression models to explore the value of comment semantics dynamics. The results reconfirm the usefulness of several essential quality predictors, including time, reputation, length, and editorship. We also found that comment semantics are valuable to shape the answer quality. Specifically, the diversity of comments significantly contributes to the answer quality. In addition, when searching for good quality answers, it is important to look for diversity in the comments, rather than observing local differences (disputable content). Finally, the presence of comments shepherds the community to revise the posts by attracting attentions to the posts and eventually facilitate the editing process.

Keywords
Discussion Forum; Q&A; Programming; Content Controversy; StackOverflow; Constructive Learning

1. INTRODUCTION

Discussion forums have been widely used as a communication medium in and outside classrooms to facilitate learning. These sites have grown steadily over the past few years and have formed sizable repositories of problem solving-solutions. To better support information seeking and learning, a majority of these sites utilize social mechanisms to filter and point out the best solutions/answers instead of providing the set of steps or scaffolds required for learning [1]. In large-scale discussion forums like StackOverflow where solutions are crowd-sourced, the role of social interactions in the form of comments plays a vital role in shaping a post. The research presented in this paper originates from trying to connect the dots between the social interaction features and the post content quality. We investigate the different comment semantic features and employ key quality identification features from relevant literature survey to find the effect they have on the quality of a post in a large-scale discussion forum. Particularly, we focus on how assorted levels of content on StackOverflow can be used to better support scaffolding. Today, data mining techniques have noticeably enhanced the ability to organize and analyze the mass amount of content. For instance, sentiment analysis has been widely explored and applied in mining large-scale social media data. Q&A sites have social features that focus on finding the best answers, however, they emphasize less on highlighting the diverse points of views among the content sea. For instance, unclear questions might tend to raise doubts amongst users leading to the usage of controversial words such as "I'm not sure", "I doubt that", etc; duplicate questions may lead to contentious arguments between experts and novices. On the other hand, a healthy argument between experts commenting on a post could also incorporate controversial phrases; a constructive criticism or a debate leading to editing a post a number of times in order to improve the quality of the post. However, widely-used social mechanisms, such as crowd-sourced evaluation typically ranks all solutions, are useful to point out the best and the worst contents, but they do not necessarily help to discern the gray area. For instance, often times there is more than one "correct" answer, especially for code review questions [2]. Even though the social metrics (votes, acceptance, favorite) point to the correctness of a possible solution, readers have differing backgrounds and varying degrees of previous knowledge which influence which answer is the best for that particular individual. Therefore, these quality indicators may not be universally applied to all users. In the context of learning to program, students can learn by constantly being exposed to similar or different solutions. This enables them to compare and contrast alternatives in order to identify what is important in a problem, distinguish different features of code, and paint a road-map to the problem [3, 4]. Multiple pieces of code can allow a novice to construct patterns and schemas [5], and even erroneous examples may assist learning at various levels [15]. Therefore, in this work, we aim to harness the controversy dynamics along with other comment semantic features in discussion forums to help us explore and understand the quality of a post.

2. LITERATURE REVIEW

Prior research [6] has already classified the many studies on the quality of content into three categories: (1) finding the best answer, (2) ranking all answers, and (3) assessing the quality of the questions. Given our focus on identifying different points of views in the answers can be a valuable learning opportunity, related work that examines the quality of answers (categories 1 and 2) have been the most informative for our purposes. Extensive data mining has been used to identify an answer's ranking, which is given by the votes that the answer has received on the site. Rather than taking a data mining approach to replicate these findings, we aim to extend this line of research by further understanding the impact of the review process, while controlling for other aspects that are known to affect the perceived quality of an answer.

HT '16, July 10-13, 2016, Halifax, NS, Canada
© 2016 ACM. ISBN 978-1-4503-4247-6/16/07...$15.00
DOI: http://dx.doi.org/10.1145/2914586.2914636

There are only a few explored works in opinion mining related to open discussion forums with students' learning. Wen et al. [7] investigated students' opinions towards a course. The researchers introduced subjectivity and sentiment mining based on educational data mining findings, such as boredom was associated with poorer learning. Munezero et al. [8] coded eight derivative human emotions from Plutchik's emotion psychoevolutionary theory [9] to track emotions in a student's learning diaries, which are made available for instructors as a source of informative feedback. In this work, in order to investigate the effects of disputable perspectives among social interactions, we incorporate SentiWordNet [10] to compute the generic language sentiments from discussions, and label controversial semantics with MPQA (Multiple Perspective Question Answering) arguing lexicon [11].

3. METHODOLOGY
3.1 Data
We focus our study on the comments of the posts from StackOverflow. The comments section in SO is utilized when users have something worth saying about the post that could raise a discussion, asking the questioner for clarity or having a procedural point to make about the existing post. We show that the presence of controversial comments under a post strengthens the prediction of post quality (#Votes).

We use the MPQA (Multiple Perspective Question Answering) opinion corpus developed by University of Pittsburgh and adopt the arguing lexicon to investigate the existence of controversial phrases in a comment [11]. The arguing lexicon consists of 17 arguing lexicons of which we detect the presence of 3 strongly controversy lexicons (*doubt, inconsistency,* and *contrast*). Lexicon entries are in the form of regular expression patterns. We perform our analysis on 8038 posts from StackOverflow, 5025 of these are question posts. Java being the most popular of the programming languages, for our analysis we have used posts that have been tagged with 'java' in SO, dated January 01, 2014 to January 10, 2014. We extracted a list of features using StackExchange Data Explorer API from the StackOverflow database. Since our research is centered towards regulating the importance of controversial comments under a post, we divide our data into post level and comment level.

3.2 Feature Engineering
We include StackOverflow content quality detection features based on the literature, including syntactic, user characteristic and social features for both answer and comment levels. To capture the semantics of diverse opinions in comments and answers, we extract both answers' and comments' content semantics and specifically pay attention to their controversy sentiments.

Table 1. Post and comment features

Type	Post Features	Comment Features
Syntactic	Post Length, Type of Post, Post Timestamp	Comment Length, Comment Timestamp
User Characteristics and Social Features	Post Votes, Post Edit Count	Comment Votes, User Reputation
Content Semantic Features	Constructiveness Score [12], Code Percentage, #Unique Users Commenting, #Controversial Comments	Median User Reputation, #Interactions ('@' mentions), Comment Sentiment, Controversy Score, Shannon Entropy

3.3 Descriptive Statistics
Our dataset includes 5,025 questions, 3,013 answers, with total 8,038 posts. Questions and answers had similar constructiveness scores on average, but Questions tend to have more words than answers (83.1 vs. 78.9, p = 0.03) and are edited more often (1.8 vs. 0.7, p < 0.001) on average. The median time of comments is shorter for questions (15 mins), which means that people comment questions quicker than answers (29 mins). A possible explanation can be the most of the comments to questions are clarification type of comments, as a result, they tend to be easier to attend to and result in question askers frequent edits to enhance the content presentation. However, even both answers and questions received comments from 1.9 users on average, users who commented answers provided slightly more comments than those who commented questions (1.6 vs. 1.3 comments per user, *p* < 0.001). In addition, Answers' comments also have larger average entropy than questions' answers. Thus, in this work, we focus on Answers' comments, and how do they affect post quality, if any. One interesting note is that Answers in our dataset often included code, and was provided quickly after a question was posted and had few alternative answers. Overall, 80% of answers included code. The average answer appeared 4.5 minutes after a question is posted on the site. However, the number of alternative answers appeared in a skewed distribution and ranged from 0 to 9, with a mean of 0.8 answers. Contrasting to their comments statistics, it indicates the challenge to provide solutions to programming-related problems.

To further investigate the value of comments to answers, we randomly sample 22,756 comments with post's topic Java in the year 2014. These comments are associated with 8,038 posts. 13,189 comments were related to 5,025 questions and 9,567 comments were associated with 3,013 answers. On average, a question received fewer comments than an answer (2.6 vs 3.2, *p* < 0.001). While 30% of the questions' comments had, at least, one positive vote, only 10% of the answers' votes have positive votes. Nevertheless, the constructiveness score of answers' comments is larger than questions' comments, on average (1.9 vs 1.3, *p* < 0.001). Compared to answers' comments, questions' comments are more positively voted; however, they have a lower score of constructiveness. The mismatch between voting patterns and constructiveness scores again shows that questions comments' can be easier to attend to, but answers' comments may require more cognitive processes (i.e. arguing, contrasting, comparing, etc.) We dig deeper into Answers' comments' semantics. We found that Answers' comments are more controversial and have more entropy than questions' comments. On average, an answer's comment is twice as controversial as a question's comment (0.2 vs. 0.1, *p* < 0.001). Answers' comments are having more distinctive content (higher entropy) than questions' comments (4.2 vs. 3.7, *p* < 0.001). Therefore, even eventually the answers are not accepted, the associated comments left traces of commenters' efforts. Such traces can be valuable resources for readers, for instance, commenters' trial and error experiences.

4. EVALUATION RESULTS
To address our research questions, we conducted regression analyses (first with only post features and then with post and comment features) to model the quality of answers in terms of votes (see Table 2, (1) and (2)) and constructiveness (Table 2, (3) and (4)). We used a linear regression to model the number of votes, which could take negative and positive values. For constructiveness, we conducted logistic regression analyses to

estimate a binary dependent variable that represented a median split of the constructiveness score.

4.1 The Value of Comments

4.1.1 More Heads Might be Better Than One

Regarding the comments, we found that the number of unique users who provide comments is significantly associated with the votes an answer received. The more users comment, the higher the number of votes the answer gets. An increase of one unit in the number of commenters increases the number of votes by 0.295. Additionally, the timing of comments is also significant. The longer the median time of comments, the more votes the answer is expected to get. The effect size of this measure of time is an increase of 0.098 by every second after the answer is provided. This indicates that the amount of people who participate in the discussion of an answer and the speed at which this discussion takes place are strongly related to the attraction and positive perception that the answer will obtain. Such results are in fact aligned with the literature [13,14]. There are other findings that are also aligned with prior research. For instance, we found evidence that the presence of code in the answer and the number of edits of the answer have positive and significant relationships with the number of votes.

4.1.2 Comment Semantics Might Matter to Post Quality: Entropy Better Than Controversy?

To address the comment semantics effects based on each individual's opinions, we evaluate comments' entropy and comments' controversy. We found that the mean entropy of an answer's comments is significantly and positively associated with the answer's votes. A unit of increase in the mean entropy is predicted to increase the number of votes by 0.070 units. Yet, neither the ratio of comments to authors nor the ratio of negative comments to total comments has significant effects. The community would consider more diverse information as good quality and then provide higher ratings, but the more disputable comments would actually indicate the more questionable the contents are. The outcome confirms our hypothesis that controversy can be an index in judging post quality, however, in order to find *good* content, diversity will be a better indicator than controversy. Such finding can be a huge help in auto-assessing fast growing online discussions.

4.1.3 Comments Might Amplify Explanatory Power

We found that the number of unique users who provide comments, their reputation, and the timing of the comments positively relate to the constructiveness of the answer (Table 2, (3) and (4)). Answers that attract more commenters, with higher median reputation and that garner half of the comments in longer periods of time have higher odds to have above median constructiveness. Such finding again confirms literature that good quality content provokes cognitive process is the one involves with the authorship. Among the control variables, the number of editions and the answer length are also significantly related to constructiveness. Longer answers and those with more edits are associated with above median constructiveness. Together the results indicate the characteristics of the comments help to explain the variability of both the number of votes and constructiveness, thus providing support to our main hypothesis that comments could be used as a proxy to find value in answers.

4.1.4 Comments Facilitate Editing Process

We have already found that the comments' semantics are associated with the answers' votes, but not with constructiveness

(Table 2, column (2) & (4)). Such results were initially counterintuitive to our understanding. However, we reason that votes and comments semantics are strongly connected because both of them represent the readers' perceptions of an answer. On the other hand, constructiveness of an answer could only be affected by the comments semantics if the answers are edited as a result of the comments. Therefore, we now turn to assess whether there is a connection between comments and edit count.

Table 3 shows that indeed there is a significant association between the mean entropy of comments and the edit count. The less entropy in the comments, the more the number of edit counts. A unit of increase in the mean entropy of an answer's comments is expected to decrease the count of edits by a factor of 0.577. In plain English, when there is lack of point of views in the comments, answers tend to remain the way it is without editing. Without community shepherds discussions based on the feedback from comments, it is harder to shape answers thought-provoking content.

Table 2. Regression on answers' votes and constructiveness

	(1) Number of votes	(2) Number of votes	(3) Above median constructiveness	(4) Above median constructiveness
Answer length (log)	0.035	-0.165***	1.294***	1.437***
With code	0.236***	0.206***	1.054	1.084
Time to answer the question (log)	-0.006	-0.006	1.044	1.027
Alternative answers	-0.024	-0.017	0.961	0.983
Edit count	0.162***	0.127***	1.399***	1.434***
Number of unique commenters		0.295***		0.819**
Median time of comments (log)		0.098***		1.046**
Median reputation of commenters (log)		-0.000		0.934*
Ratio comments to commenters		-0.027		0.937
Ratio negative comments to comments		0.003		1.034
Mean entropy of comments		0.070**		1.166
Observations	2983	2951	2983	2951
Pseudo R-squared	0.094	0.155	0.046	0.054
Exponentiated coefficients * p<0.05, ** p<0.01, *** p<0.001"				

Table 3. Poisson regression on answers' number of edits

	(1) Answers' edit count	(2) Answer's edit count
Answer length (log)	1.341***	1.120**
With code	2.497***	2.349***
Time to answer the question (log)	1.029	1.033
Alternative answers	1.097***	1.048**
Number of unique commenters		1.238***
Median time of comments (log)		1.056***
Median reputation of commenters (log)		1.040
Ratio comments to commenters		1.145***
Ratio negative comments to		0.931

comments		
Mean entropy of comments		0.577***
Observations	2983	2951
Pseudo R-squared	0.063	0.086
Exponentiated coefficients * p<0.05, ** p<0.01, *** p<0.001"		

4.1.5 Comments Make Answers Become Attractive

Other aspects of an answer's comments are also significant factors on the number of edits. The number of unique commenters, the median time of comments and the ratio of comments to commenters are expected to increase the count of edits. For example, a unit of increase in the number of unique commenters is predicted to increase the number of edits by 1.238 unit. When the ratio of comments to authors increases by one unit, the count of edits is expected to increase by a factor of 1.145. Additionally, the longer it takes for the answer to obtaining half of its comments, the higher the number of edits. We interpret all of these independent variables as attention *attractors*, which represent how attractive the answer is. The more people are involved, the more comments the community can possibly provide and the longer the answer can still receive comments. These are all hints that the answer has attracted attention, and therefore, there is more chance that the answer is further improved through more edits.

4.2 The Effects of Comment Quality

We conducted two regression analyses to assess the comments' quality in terms of votes and constructiveness. Given that only a small proportion of comments had a total count of votes larger than zero, we defined a binary dependent variable to represent whether a comment had positive votes or no. We conducted a logistic regression to model this binary indicator. On the other hand, comment constructiveness was a count variable, therefore, we used a Poisson regression to estimate the effect of the independent variables on the constructiveness score. The results indicate that the larger the entropy score of a comment, the more likely that the comment will have a positive count of votes. A unit of increase in entropy is expected to increase the probability of the comment to have positive votes by a factor of 1.431. However, the controversy score of the comment is not significantly related to the votes. Additionally, longer and earlier comments are more likely to have a positive count of votes. Meanwhile, the pattern of influence of the comments' semantics is the opposite. While entropy does not have a statistically significant relationship with constructiveness, controversy does. More controversial comments are associated with more constructive comments. An increase of a unit in the controversy score is predicted to increase the count of constructiveness score by a factor of 1.036. Together, these results mean that when searching for feedback to improve comments, people are likely to get provoked by controversial content. However, the community tends to cast the votes to appreciate different points of views, but not necessarily opposite points of view.

5. CONCLUSIONS

We investigated comment semantics from StackOverflow site and how does the semantic dynamics affect Answer quality. We not only reconfirm the usefulness of several essential quality predictors, including time, reputation, length, and editorship, we also found the results show that comment semantics increase the model explanatory power and reassure importance of the commenting-editing ecosystem for large-scale programming discussion forums. Although, controversial comments are not significant indicators to post quality, the disputable comments leave traces of commenter's efforts. In the future, more comprehensive features can be considered. Most importantly, we plan to investigate how much students can learn by consuming different comments-supported content and what other semantics structure will affect content quality.

6. REFERENCES

[1] Sande, C.V.D. and Leinhard, G. (2007) Online tutoring in the calculus: Beyond the limit of the limit, education 1(2), 117-160.

[2] Treude, C., Ohad B., and Storey, M.A. "How do programmers ask and answer questions on the web?: Nier track." 33rd International Conference on Software Engineering. IEEE, 2011.

[3] Patitsas, E., M. Craig, and S. Easterbrook, Comparing and contrasting different algorithms leads to increased student learning, in Proceedings of the ninth annual international ACM conference on International computing education research. 2013: San Diego, California, USA. p. 145-152.

[4] Schwartz, D. L., and Bransford, J.D. "A time for telling." *Cognition and instruction* 16.4 (1998): 475-5223.

[5] Margulieux, L. E., Guzdial, M., & Catrambone, R. (2012). Subgoal-labeled instructional material improves performance and transfer in learning to develop mobile applications. In *Proceedings of the ninth annual international conference on International computing education research* (pp. 71-78).

[6] Dalip, D. H., Gonçalves, M. A., Cristo, M., & Calado, P. (2013). Exploiting user feedback to learn to rank answers in q&a forums: a case study with stack overflow. In Proceedings of the 36th international conference on eesearch and development in information retrieval (pp. 543-552).

[7] Wen, M.; Yang, D.; and Rose, C. P. 2014. Sentiment analysis in MOOC discussion forums: What does it tell us? Proceedings of Educational Data Mining.

[8] Munezero, M., Montero, C. S., Mozgovoy, M., & Sutinen, E. (2013, November). Exploiting sentiment analysis to track emotions in students' learning diaries. In Proceedings of the 13th Koli Calling International Conference on Computing Education Research (pp. 145-152). ACM.

[9] Plutchik, R. (1980). A general psychoevolutionary theory of emotion. Theories of emotion, 1, 3-31.

[10] Baccianella, S., Andrea E., and Fabrizio S. "SentiWordNet 3.0: An Enhanced Lexical Resource for Sentiment Analysis and Opinion Mining." LREC. Vol. 10. 2010.

[11] Somasundaran, Swapna, Josef Ruppenhofer, and Janyce Wiebe. "Detecting arguing and sentiment in meetings." Proceedings of the SIGdial Workshop on Discourse and Dialogue. Vol. 6. 2007.

[12] Hsiao, I. H., & Naveed, F. (2015). Identifying learning-inductive content in programming discussion forums. In *Frontiers in Education Conference, 2015.*(pp. 1-8). IEEE.

[13] Anderson, A., Huttenlocher, D., Kleinberg, J., & Leskovec, J. (2012). Discovering value from community activity on focused question answering sites: a case study of stack overflow. In Proceedings of the 18th international conference on Knowledge Discovery and Data mining (pp. 850-858).

[14] Tian, Q., Zhang, P., & Li, B. (2013). Towards Predicting the Best Answers in Community-based Question-Answering Services. In ICWSM.

[15] Tsovaltzi, D., Melis, E., McLaren, B. M., Meyer, A. K., Dietrich, M., & Goguadze, G. (2010). Learning from erroneous examples: when and how do students benefit from them?. In *Sustaining TEL: From Innovation to Learning and Practice* (pp. 357-373).

Cross-system recommendation: User-modelling via Social Media versus Self-Declared Preferences

Sultan Alanazi
School of Computer Science
University of Nottingham
psxsa16
@nottingham.ac.uk

James Goulding
Horizon Institute
University of Nottingham
james.goulding
@nottingham.ac.uk

Derek McAuley
Horizon Institute
University of Nottingham
derek.mcauley
@nottingham.ac.uk

ABSTRACT

It is increasingly rare to encounter a Web service that doesn't engage in some form of automated recommendation, with Collaborative Filtering (CF) techniques being virtually ubiquitous as the means for delivering relevant content. Yet several key issues still remain unresolved, including optimal handling of *cold starts* and how best to maintain *user-privacy* within that context. Recent work has demonstrated a potentially fruitful line of attack in the form of *cross-system user modelling*, which uses features generated from one domain to bootstrap recommendations in another. In this paper we evidence the effectiveness of this approach through direct real-world user feedback, deconstructing a cross-system news recommendation service where user models are generated via social media data. It is shown that even when a relatively naive vector-space approach is used, it is possible to automatically generate user-models that provide statistically superior performance than when items are *explicitly filtered* based on a user's self-declared preferences. Detailed qualitative analysis of why such effects occur indicate that different models are capturing widely different areas within a user's preference space, and that hybrid models represent fertile ground for future research.

1. INTRODUCTION

Recommendation Systems are highly prevalent on the Web, covering fields as diverse as movies, books, music and academic references [17]. At their heart, Collaborative Filtering (CF) techniques have become virtually ubiquitous as a means of identifying and serving relevant content to any given user. While CF is an extensively researched topic area, several key issues remain unresolved. These include: 1. how to ameliorate the problem of *sparsity* within datasets [24]; 2. how to handle the issue of *cold starts* [28], where systems attempt to recommend content to users who have had little or no prior interaction with the system; and 3. how to ensure user privacy given personalization can quickly distil into a task of monitoring and tracking across users.

HT '16, July 10 - 13, 2016, Halifax, NS, Canada

© 2016 Copyright held by the owner/author(s). Publication rights licensed to ACM.
ISBN 978-1-4503-4247-6/16/07...$15.00

DOI: http://dx.doi.org/10.1145/2914586.2914640

Recent researches have proposed a potential solution to these issues in the form of *cross-system* and *cross-domain user modelling* [13, 8]. Here features generated within one system or domain can be used to effectively bootstrap recommendations in another, providing a promising line of attack to handle both sparsity and cold-starts. In this paper, we provide further empirical evidence of the effectiveness of the approach via a focussed study on direct real-world user feedback. This is achieved via implementation of a cross-system news recommendation service, with user model's being automatically generated via social media data (Twitter).

However, in this paper we also ask the question - can a user's interactions with the Web and social media be leveraged in order to produce a cross-system user model that actually out-performs explicit filtering using *self-declared preferences*? And, if so, why? It will be shown that even using a relatively naive vector-space approach, it is possible to automatically generate user-models that provide statistically superior performance than user model's based on *self-declared* preferences. The reasons for these results are qualitatively examined in order to understand why such effects occur, indicating that different models are capturing widely different areas within a user's preference space.

2. BACKGROUND AND MOTIVATION

Recommendation systems have been extensively studied in the research literature, with a multitude of distinct approaches emerging [12, 15, 27]. Collaborative Filtering has proven particularly effective in wide range of applications [23, 10, 5, 14], leveraging the known preferences of a group of users to make recommendations to those whose preferences are only partially observed [25]. A host of mechanisms have been employed to underpin such functionality ranging from Weighted Nearest Neighbor modeling to Bayesian Matrix Completion [18, 22], and with Deep Learning techniques receiving increasing investigation [8]. While CF systems have shown empirical effectiveness in practical settings, several research issues remain, not least the problem of "cold-start" [28, 19, 21]. Cross-Domain Filtering (CDF) has been proposed as a promising solution, bootstrapping recommendations via a user's transactional history in some external system or domain [8]. CDF can be employed when separate item domains exist that share a common set of users [13] or when domains exist that share the same item-set but where 'ratings' are established in different fashions [16]. The field is highly active, with extensions including cross-domain topic modeling [26], cross-domain triadic factorisation [9] and construction of intermediate topic spaces [20].

Despite this promise, CDF does not represent a universal panacea. When applied to CF its assumptions are particularly steep: it requires an extensive user base in both of its domains, as well as sufficient intersection of users and/or items across those domains [7] (further exacerbating well-known sparsity problems that many CF-based systems suffer from [24]). In real-world situations high intersections between user-bases are unlikely - unless situated within niche communities or mass user bases (e.g. Amazon, Netflix, etc.). In addition, transferring user information between such domains generates serious confidentiality and privacy concerns. In this paper, we therefore focus on a Content-Based filtering (CBF) approach, which represents a plausible way to ameliorate many of these issues.

In CBF, recommendations are served by calculating the difference between each item's 'content' (often defined mathematically via some feature set) and some *profile* or model of the user [15]. If such user features can be pre-generated via some cross-domain feature set then not only can cold start be avoided, but a vast intersection of extant users in both domains is no longer required. This combination of CBF and Cross-System approaches already has some precedent [3, 24, 1, 2], and we augment such research by focusing on analysis of direct, real world user-feedback rather than in-sample analysis. Moreover, we investigate whether such an approach can compete with explicitly stated user-preferences - and whether each captures a different, distinct area of the user's preference space.

3. EXPERIMENTAL PLATFORM

An experimental platform was developed to investigate the specific research question: 'can a cross-system user model mined from *social media* generate more accurate recommendations than explicitly stated user preferences?'. If true, this would provide contributing evidence as to the effectiveness of cross-system modelling and the potential value of passive mining of web behaviour. The platform was setup to allow:

- Construction of user-models through: 1. an n-gram vector-space representation derived from social media streams; 2. explicitly defined declaration of categorical user interests; and 3. random parameterization (to serve as a baseline for our testing procedure).

- Application of these models to dynamically rate the relevance of articles supplied to it via any RSS feed.

- Delivery to a user of the most relevant articles based on one of the above models, presenting items via a web interface that allowed for relevance feedback ratings.

As illustrated in Figure 1, functionality is split into 5 *modules*. The **content module** retrieves item sets via external RSS feeds and, using appropriate features, constructs a compressed model for each item (see §3.1). In parallel, the **user modeling module** hosts (potentially multiple) user models for the current participant and, in the case of this research, is also tasked with constructing these models (see §3.2). With this data in place, the **recommendation module** then performs similarity calculations between output items and user models (see §3.3), serving feeds to the **presentation module** for user-evaluation to occur. Once this evaluation is provided, an anonymized log is recorded in the **logging module** ready for post analysis.

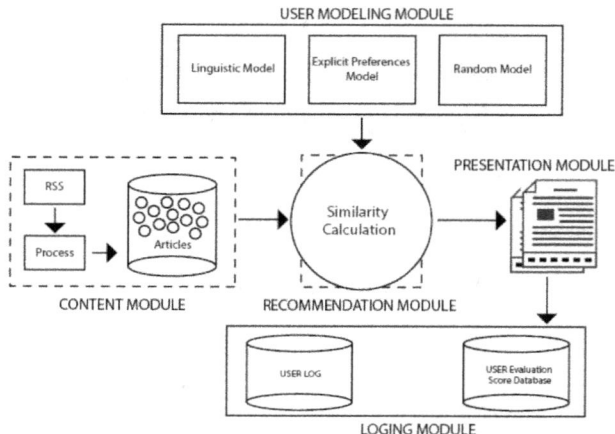

Figure 1: Architecture of Experimental Platform

3.1 Document Modelling

Based as it is on content recommendation, the system currently uses a traditional vector space model (VSM) to represent documents. The content module, first extracts a series of documents from the content source via an RSS feed endpoint transforming each into a corresponding vector space model, $\vec{d}$. For each $\vec{d}$, the VSM iterates through every n-gram it contains, assigning each a weighted importance value, $W_{t,d}$. A range of weighting schemes have been proposed for such this value [4], but we employ the relatively naive *Term Frequency-Inverse Document Frequency* (tf-idf) statistic due to its empirically proven effectiveness [4]. We note that the tf-idf score for any particular n-gram, t, takes: 1. a higher value, if t occurs numerous times within a small number of documents; 2. a low value if t appears fewer times in a document *or* occurs in many documents and 3. a low value, if t occurs in almost all documents. In practical applications the set of features, $\mathcal{F}$, can become extremely large. This leads not only to issues of sparsity and computational efficiency, but also reduce effectiveness of similarity comparisons due to curse of dimensionality. It is therefore desirable to reduce the dimensions of the vector space by removing irrelevant and redundant features [6][1].

3.2 User-Preference Modeling

In order to support comparisons, the experimental system must be able to generate multiple user models for the same individual. While produced via different techniques, the following models are simultaneously constructed for each user when he/she first registers with the system (as represented by the *user-modelling module* in Figure 1):

PASSIVE user-modelling: On registration the user must provide controlled access to an active social media account, which is then mined to generate a linguistic preference model. Users' social media posts are collated, parsed into a bag of words representation (an n-gram frequency model) of their term usage, cleansed and finally encoded as a vector-space model, again using tf-idf.

MANUAL user-modelling: Here user preferences are modelled via presentation of a pre-constructed set of document

---

[1]In practice this was achieved via functionality available in the python scikit-learn libraries (http://scikit-learn.org).

category and sub-category labels, asking the user to rate their level of interest in each (either selected didactically, or generated by parsing the corpus and modelling the k most common topics [26]. In this case data must be actively supplied by the user through a web interface when they first register with the system.

RANDOM user-modelling: In order to provide a baseline, the system generates a random preference-model for each user. This is a VSM containing the same dimensionality as the passive user model, but with tf-idf scores set randomly for each feature in $\mathcal{F}$. Use of this model should therefore produce random recommendation results.

Once models have been established, the documents in dataset $\mathcal{D}$ are ranked according to their relevance to the user (yielding three document rankings).

3.3 Determining Document Relevance

Recommendation occurs when users begin interacting with the system. Participants are presented with a stream of n documents, each in turn and each generated by *one* of the available user models (which model is selected for each recommendation is specified by the testing regime). To achieve this, prior to presentation the recommendation module must generate multiple rankings of all documents in D, one for each user model that may be used during the experiment. For categorical models, documents are ranked according to the number of labels each individual document is tagged with that match the user's explicitly declared categories of interest. For vector space models (i.e. the Passive and Random user-modelling approaches detailed in §3.2), each document, d is ranked by calculating the similarity between its VSM, $\vec{d}$, and the user's preference-model, $\vec{p}$. The relevance score used here is the traditional *cosine similarity* measure:

$$similarity(\vec{d}, \vec{p}) = \frac{\vec{d}.\vec{p}}{||\vec{d}||||\vec{p}||} = \frac{\sum_{i=1}^{|\mathcal{F}|} w_{d,i} w_{p,i}}{\sqrt{\sum_{i=1}^{|\mathcal{F}|} w_{d,i}^2} \sqrt{\sum_{i=1}^{|\mathcal{F}|} w_{p,i}^2}} \quad (1)$$

3.4 Presentation and Logging

When a user interacts with the system, articles are presented to them via a web interface as follows: 1. First one of the system's user-models detailed in §3.2 is selected, the distribution of these selections being stochastic and/or defined by the experimental regime used; 2. For the model selected, the highest recommended document not yet viewed is identified, retrieved via its associated URL and presented to the user with a 7-point Likert scale for relevance evaluation; and 3. The user's assessment rating is then collected and stored in a database for analysis, and the process iterates with a new user-model and a new article presented.

4. EXPERIMENTAL METHOD

In our experiments passive-user models were generated using a user's *Twitter* stream and the *BBC news RSS feed* provided our output documents. First the system's content module retrieved data from the BBC news feed[2] extracting 2180 articles. Each document was transformed into a corresponding VSM, and stored along with category meta data and the source article's URL. Simultaneously explicit category labels were extracted from the feed: *Technology, Sci-*

---

[2]via http://feeds.bbci.co.uk/news/rss.xml

ence, Environment, Entertainment, Arts, Education, Family, Health, Politics, Business, UK, and World.

40 participants from a wide range of backgrounds were registered with the system. Each participant was required to be an active Twitter user and to have posted a minimum of 150 tweets. The maximum number of tweets of any user since signing up to the service was 46,700, the mean was 6479 and the standard deviation 10,332. On registration each user authenticated the system's Twitter application and explicitly declared categorical interests via the web interface (as selected from the tags used by the BBC news feed). This allowed *Manual, Passive* and *Random* Models to then be automatically constructed for each user. In order to construct the passive model, the user's 150 most recent tweets were extracted via the Twitter API[3].

All participants then engaged in a lab-based task experiment where the system presented them with a total of 45 articles[4], whose relevance they were asked to evaluate in sequence. To choose the next article to be presented, the system selected a random user-model from the three available, determined that model's highest ranked unseen document, and presented it to the user along with a Likert evaluation scale. In cases of a tie between a set of documents in any ranking, one was selected at random. Each user was ultimately presented with an equal number of articles for each model. Thus while ranking is deterministic for all models used, each experimental run would still be stochastic in nature in terms of the ordering of articles presented. For each document presented the system recorded the participants *user-id*, the presented article's *document-id* of the article presented, the user's *evaluation score*, and an identifier of the model used to select that article. At the end of this experiment, we were able to test three hypotheses against the 1800 data points produced (40 people × 45 ratings). These hypotheses were: H1. MANUAL vs. RANDOM (i.e. a hypothesis aimed at determining that any sort of filtering is better than simply serving random BBC news articles); H2. PASSIVE vs. RANDOM; and H3. PASSIVE vs MANUAL (i.e. aimed at determining if an implicit filtering approach is superior to one based on explicit statements of preference).

5. EXPERIMENTAL RESULTS

Results of experiments indicated that the PASSIVE model generated the most relevant news item recommendations for users in comparison to both MANUAL and RANDOM models. The mean relevance scores recorded for our baseline model (RANDOM) was 3.81 points. Recommendations generated via automated preferences models (MANUAL) were rated at an average of 4.13 across 600 evaluations. The mean rating of implicit/linguistic filtering model (PASSIVE) was 4.30. In 85% of cases, a user-model improved over the baseline random recommendation. Standard deviation of evaluations was relatively low for all models at 0.912, 0.850 and 0.814 for RANDOM, MANUAL and PASSIVE models respectively. In general, most of the articles selected by the PASSIVE model were scored highest by users - however this was not the case across the board (and in rare cases random selection was favoured). Also of note, was a surprising lack of correlation ($r = 0.05$) between model performance and the number of tweets the participant had posted over

---

[3]https://dev.twitter.com/rest/public

[4]undertaken in 3 rounds for a more palatable experience.

their lifetime. Long term Twitter activity (which we view as a proxy for Twitter experience) did not seem to have any impact on the performance of the PASSIVE model.

5.1 Wilcoxon Signed Ranks Test

A Wilcoxon Signed Ranks Test [11] was run to determine whether there was a statistically significant mean difference between models (full details are provided in Table 1). Participants logged a mean evaluation of 4.13 for MANUAL and 3.81 for RANDOM. Test results produced a value of $p = 0.002$, indicating that the 0.32 increase was statistically significant ($Z = -3.127$, $p = 0.002$). Thus we were able to conclude from hypothesis H1 that the MANUAL model was producing superior performance. Similarly, for hypothesis H2 participants expressed preference for PASSIVE models (4.30) as opposed to the RANDOM baseline (3.81); a statistically significant increase of 0.486 was discovered ($Z = -4.098$, $p = 0.000042$, $p < .05$). Finally, we were also able to show a statistically significant preference for the use of passively mined personal information via the PASSIVE model (4.30) as opposed to the MANUAL filtering (4.13), with an improvement of 0.17 ($Z = -2.045$, $p = 0.041$), $p < .05$.

Table 1: Wilcoxon Signed Ranks Test Statistics

	M - R	P - R	M - P
Z	-3.127	-4.098	-2.045
Asymp. Sig. (2-tailed)	0.002	0.000042	0.041

model R = RANDOM, M = MANUAL, P = PASSIVE

Table 2: Ranking Results

		N	Mean Rank	Sum of Ranks
M - R	Negative Ranks	11	16.14	177.50
	Positive Ranks	29	22.16	642.50
	Ties	0		
	Total	40		
P - R	Negative Ranks	9	8.89	80.00
	Positive Ranks	28	22.25	623.00
	Ties	3		
	Total	40		
M - P	Negative Ranks	14	21.44	262.50
	Positive Ranks	26	18.75	557.50
	Ties	0		
	Total	40		

model R = RANDOM, M = MANUAL, P = PASSIVE

Results indicate that use of passively mined personal information produced the most effective models in our tests, with Table 2 providing a breakdown of how each model compared in terms of inferred user rankings.

6. DISCUSSION AND POST-ANALYSIS

Results correspond to the intuition that generating a user model, whether based on implicitly or explicitly defined preferences, can play an important role in cross-system recommendations. These improvements illustrate the ability of a model that is using just 20,000 *characters*, based on relatively straight-forward VSM techniques and drawn from a completely different domain to obtain positive results. In this section we qualitatively investigate the reasons for this apparent effectiveness - *why* is it producing the results it is?

With the PASSIVE model having produced the highest evaluation scores, we first examined how it considered articles that were recommended by its rivals (in order to shed light on its selections). On average the cosine score it gave its own recommendations was 0.09642, but for MANUAL recommendations it would have given 0.00881 and for RANDOM 0.00155 (for an example of these differences see Figure 2). This means that, as far as the *Twitter generated VSM model* was concerned, those were performing at an order of

magnitude worse than itself. Given that MANUAL achieved statistically significant improvements over RANDOM, we infer from this that the preference information that the PASSIVE model is able to capture via Twitter is wholly *distinct* in nature to that established via an explicit statement of categorical preferences - which strongly suggests that improved recommendations might be achieved by combination of explicitly declared and passively mined preferences.

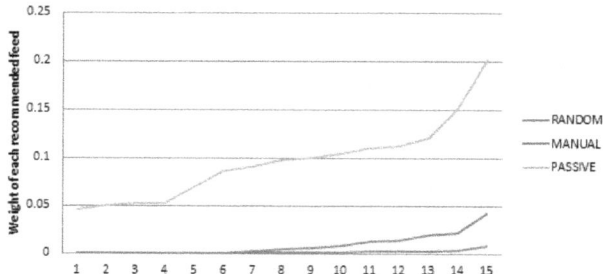

Figure 2: Interpretation of recommendation relevance for all models, based upon the Twitter extracted VSM for *Participant 38* (n.b. articles have been ordered with respect to their cosine value).

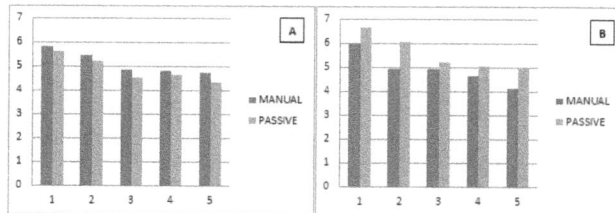

Figure 3: Mean evaluation scores for the [A] Top 5 users favouring MANUAL models and [B] Top 5 users favouring PASSIVE models.

It was noted that there were 5 cases where participants exhibited an overall preference for recommendations made by the MANUAL model. This could be for several reasons: perhaps the labels offered to them during explicit user modeling better expressed their interests than for other participants. It may have been the converse, with their tweets not sufficiently expressing the diversity of their interests. Alternatively it could simply be because their preferences were very focused (e.g. to one category). Closer investigation of the users who most favoured explicitly generated recommendations, however, showed both multiple category selection and ratings statistically indistinguishable from those they gave the PASSIVE model (this proximity is illustrated in Figure 3). From this it seems most likely that these are indeed cases of participants being well matched to the ontology of labels supplied rather than passive models failing them.

This contrasts, however, with the 5 users who most favoured passively generated recommendations, where the difference between that model and their MANUAL evaluations was indeed significant (again see Figure 3). We infer from this that even though, in general, Twitter modelling is giving us different informational value, the information it is producing is still sufficient to overcome anything lost by not incorporating explicitly stated preferences.

Investigation of the articles missed by some models showed that, in particular, the Twitter model could make extremely niche recommendations that cut across broad categories. For example, *Participant 4* declared interest in *Science & Environment*, *Politics* and *Tech* tags, evaluating those MANUAL recommendations at 4.1 (compared to 3.1 for RANDOM). However, a third of his/her PASSIVE model's recommendations did not include these labels - and yet were still awarded an even higher evaluation of 4.5. We infer from this that unlike explicit filtering, which is necessarily bound to some pre-defined ontology of labels, passive filtering was detecting more personalised, specific article recommendations that cut across categories.

For many participants MANUAL preference selection appears consistently too coarse to reflect the subtleties of individual user preferences. *Participant 19* serves as an example of this. He/she was presented with several news articles tagged with the 'UK' label by both PASSIVE and MANUAL models. Yet, those served by the MANUAL model received ratings of only 3.66, compared to 5.50 for those served by the PASSIVE model. This represented a commonly identified theme where a participant was indeed accurately identifying an interest in UK articles, but was unable to specify that it was a specific subset of these that held most interest.

Missing articles due to not manually selecting the superset that a label represented was another common theme. An example of this occurred in *Participant 30*, who highly rated two medical articles recommended by the PASSIVE model (evaluating them both with a score of 6), despite stating no general interest in *health* categorized items. Because this pattern was so frequent, we present some specific examples in closer depth. *Participant 22* stated that items tagged as 'World' (i.e. non-UK) events were not of interest him/her. However, when the PASSIVE model created a VSM via his social media posts, it found several hits to items with the 'World' tag. Two illustrative examples, which the user evaluated as having high relevance to them, were:

news item 1: *"The moment Nepal's earthquake hit my home"*

news item 2: *"The day my generation will talk about for the rest of our lives"*

Investigating the participant's VSM indicated that the similarity was being expressed due to a high tf-idf score for the features 'Nepal' and 'aid', and this was corroborated by the detection of posts in his Twitter timeline expressing empathy for the region following recent natural disasters. A similar situation occurred for a user who indicated a high evaluation for a 'UK' tagged news item (which referenced the UK soccer team, *Chelsea*), despite stating that he no preference for UK specific stories. That article was:

news item 3: *"Why Chelsea won the league, by Alan Shearer"*

Exploration of the participant's VSM initially drew a blank, showing no indication of a high expression for any terms related to *Sport*, *Football* or *Soccer*. However, further investigation identified a tweet on the participant's timeline that referenced "Mourinho" (the coach of the Chelsea Football team at the time of the experiment). This term did indeed have a high tf-idf expression in the document's vector-space model as well as a high activation in the participant's PASSIVE model, consequently resulting in its recommendation. We note that this granularity would be impossible to achieve

via explicitly stated preferences. However, we also noted that for some participants their Twitter hashtags (parsed as n-grams by the PASSIVE model) themselves served as forms of folksonomic tagging and expressions of highly granular categorical interest. An example of this was *Participant 32* who frequently used the hashtags: *#bigdata*, *#datascience*, *#analytics* and *#IoT*. As a result the participant was recommended the following article via the PASSIVE model:

news item 4: *"Why measure feet with iPads?"*

This article discussed how a shoe retailer had introduced tablet devices to automate measure and capturing of invaluable data about their customers' feet. Despite no apparent relevance to any of their other interests, the user assigned the item a score of 6. Because the story was tagged with the label 'Health' it was overlooked by the MANUAL model.

These fine grained investigations drew us to several conclusions concerning the behaviour of the PASSIVE approach, and its divergence from self-declared preferences: 1. Participants did indeed Tweet about things they were interested in reading about, allowing the PASSIVE model to pick up true positives; 2. The dynamic nature of both Social Media posting and News articles meant that collation of data from a constrained time window was appropriate; 3. highly relevant content-based recommendations identified by the PASSIVE model can be easily missed by the MANUAL model if tagged with an over-generalized label; 4. any universal taxonomy for explicit statement of preferences appears unfeasible; 5. while PASSIVE modelling via Twitter produced statistically superior results to MANUAL models, the two approaches appear to be capturing different forms of preference information. From this we concluded not only that a hybrid model would produce improved results, but that generating a user model from numerous combined domains (Web search logs, Twitter posts, Facebook usage, etc.) would like produce even more effective functionality.

7. CONCLUSION

In this paper, we have investigated via direct user-feedback, the effectiveness of a recommendation system based on personal data stream information that combines the advantages of both Cross-System and Content-Based Filtering. A cross-system user model was constructed by mining Twitter data streams, and its performance corroborated via real world user assessments of BBC news recommendations. We showed not only 1. the viability of harnessing linguistic vector-space user models generated from social media data, but also 2. that this automated cross-domain approach can actually be superior to explicit filtering using self-declared preferences. However, post-analysis also indicated that these two approaches were capturing *different* information and there is fertile ground in combining the two mechanisms. While there is much opportunity to improve the complexity of the linguistic model used to represent user preferences, there is equal potential in integrating passive models generated from different data streams (e.g. Facebook, Web Search logs, Product purchase descriptions, etc.), each with its own window into users' interests and preferences.

8. ACKNOWLEDGMENTS

This work was jointly supported by the RCUK Horizon Digital Economy Research Hub grant, EP/G065802/1 and the EPSRC Neodemographics grant, EP/L021080/1.

9. REFERENCES

[1] F. Abel, Q. Gao, G.-J. Houben, and K. Tao. Twitter-based user modeling for news recommendations. In *Proceedings of the Twenty-Third international joint conference on Artificial Intelligence*, pages 2962–2966. AAAI Press, 2013.

[2] F. Abel, E. Herder, G.-J. Houben, N. Henze, and D. Krause. Cross-system user modeling and personalization on the social web. *User Modeling and User-Adapted Interaction*, 23(2):169–209, 2013.

[3] A. Ahmed, A. Das, and A. J. Smola. Scalable hierarchical multitask learning algorithms for conversion optimization in display advertising. In *Proceedings of the 7th ACM International Conference on Web Search and Data Mining*, WSDM '14, pages 153–162, New York, NY, USA, 2014. ACM.

[4] A. Aizawa. An information-theoretic perspective of tf–idf measures. *Information Processing & Management*, 39(1):45–65, 2003.

[5] R. M. Bell and Y. Koren. Improved neighborhood-based collaborative filtering. In *KDD-Cup and Workshop*, pages 7–14. ACM press, 2007.

[6] G. Costa and R. Ortale. Xml document co-clustering via non-negative matrix tri-factorization. In *Tools with Artificial Intelligence (ICTAI), 2014 IEEE 26th International Conference on*, pages 607–614, Nov 2014.

[7] P. Cremonesi and M. Quadrana. Cross-domain recommendations without overlapping data: myth or reality? In *Proceedings of the 8th ACM Conference on Recommender systems*, pages 297–300. ACM, 2014.

[8] A. M. Elkahky, Y. Song, and X. He. A multi-view deep learning approach for cross domain user modeling in recommendation systems. In *Proceedings of the 24th International Conference on World Wide Web*, WWW '15, pages 278–288, Republic and Canton of Geneva, Switzerland, 2015. International World Wide Web Conferences Steering Committee.

[9] L. Hu, J. Cao, G. Xu, L. Cao, Z. Gu, and C. Zhu. Personalized recommendation via cross-domain triadic factorization. In *Proceedings of the 22Nd International Conference on World Wide Web*, WWW '13, pages 595–606, Republic and Canton of Geneva, Switzerland, 2013. International World Wide Web Conferences Steering Committee.

[10] P. Knees, D. Schnitzer, and A. Flexer. Improving neighborhood-based collaborative filtering by reducing hubness. In *Proceedings of International Conference on Multimedia Retrieval*, ICMR '14, pages 161:161–161:168, New York, NY, USA, 2014. ACM.

[11] L. M. LaVange and G. G. Koch. Rank score tests. *Circulation*, 114(23):2528–2533, 2006.

[12] J. Lee, S. Bengio, S. Kim, G. Lebanon, and Y. Singer. Local collaborative ranking. In *Proceedings of the 23rd International Conference on World Wide Web*, WWW '14, pages 85–96, New York, NY, USA, 2014. ACM.

[13] B. Li. Cross-domain collaborative filtering: A brief survey. In *Tools with Artificial Intelligence (ICTAI), 2011 23rd IEEE International Conference on*, pages 1085–1086. IEEE, 2011.

[14] H. Liu, J. Goulding, and T. Brailsford. Towards computation of novel ideas from corpora of scientific text. In *Machine Learning and Knowledge Discovery in Databases*, pages 541–556. Springer, 2015.

[15] Manisha Hiralall. *Recommender systems for e-shops*. Msc dissertation, Vrije Universiteit, 2011.

[16] W. Pan, E. W. Xiang, N. N. Liu, and Q. Yang. Transfer learning in collaborative filtering for sparsity reduction. In *AAAI*, volume 10, pages 230–235, 2010.

[17] D. H. Park, H. K. Kim, I. Y. Choi, and J. K. Kim. A literature review and classification of recommender systems research. *Expert Systems with Applications*, 39:10072–10059, 2012.

[18] J. D. M. Rennie and N. Srebro. Fast maximum margin matrix factorization for collaborative prediction. In *Proceedings of the 22Nd International Conference on Machine Learning*, ICML '05, pages 713–719, New York, NY, USA, 2005. ACM.

[19] Y. Rong, X. Wen, and H. Cheng. A monte carlo algorithm for cold start recommendation. In *Proceedings of the 23rd International Conference on World Wide Web*, WWW '14, pages 327–336, New York, NY, USA, 2014. ACM.

[20] S. D. Roy, T. Mei, W. Zeng, and S. Li. Socialtransfer: cross-domain transfer learning from social streams for media applications. In *Proceedings of the 20th ACM international conference on Multimedia*, pages 649–658. ACM, 2012.

[21] S. Sahebi and P. Brusilovsky. Cross-domain collaborative recommendation in a cold-start context: The impact of user profile size on the quality of recommendation. In *User Modeling, Adaptation, and Personalization*, pages 289–295. Springer, 2013.

[22] R. Salakhutdinov and A. Mnih. Bayesian probabilistic matrix factorization using markov chain monte carlo. In *Proceedings of the 25th International Conference on Machine Learning*, ICML '08, pages 880–887, New York, NY, USA, 2008. ACM.

[23] B. Sarwar, G. Karypis, J. Konstan, and J. Riedl. Item-based collaborative filtering recommendation algorithms. In *Proceedings of the 10th international conference on World Wide Web*, pages 285–295. ACM, 2001.

[24] B. Shapira, L. Rokach, and S. Freilikhman. Facebook single and cross domain data for recommendation systems. *User Modeling and User-Adapted Interaction*, 23(2-3):211–247, 2013.

[25] X. Su and T. M. Khoshgoftaar. A Survey of Collaborative Filtering Techniques. *Artificial Intelligence*, pages 1–19, 2009.

[26] J. Tang, S. Wu, J. Sun, and H. Su. Cross-domain collaboration recommendation. In *Proceedings of the 18th ACM SIGKDD International Conference on Knowledge Discovery and Data Mining*, KDD '12, pages 1285–1293, New York, NY, USA, 2012. ACM.

[27] F. Xia, N. Y. Asabere, A. M. Ahmed, J. Li, and X. Kong. Mobile Multimedia Recommendation in Smart Communities: A Survey, 2013.

[28] D. Zhang, C.-H. Hsu, M. Chen, Q. Chen, N. Xiong, and J. Lloret. Cold-start recommendation using bi-clustering and fusion for large-scale social recommender systems. *Emerging Topics in Computing, IEEE Transactions on*, 2(2):239–250, June 2014.

Identifying Knowledge Anchors
in a Data Graph

Marwan Al-Tawil[1], Vania Dimitrova[1], Dhavalkumar Thakker[2], Brandon Bennett[1]

[1] School of Computing, University of Leeds, UK

[2] School of Electrical Engineering and Computer Science, University of Bradford, UK

{scmata[1], V.G.Dimitrova[1], B.Bennett[1]}@leeds.ac.uk , D.Thakker[2]@bradford.ac.uk

ABSTRACT

The recent growth of the Web of Data has brought to the fore the need to develop intelligent means to support user exploration through big data graphs. To be effective, approaches for data graph exploration should take into account the utility from a user's point of view. We have been investigating *knowledge utility* – how useful the trajectories in a data graph are for expanding users' knowledge. Following the theory for meaningful learning, according to which new knowledge is developed starting from familiar entities (anchors) and expanding to new and unfamiliar entities, we propose here an approach to identify knowledge anchors in a data graph. Our approach is underpinned by the Cognitive Science notion of basic level objects in domain taxonomies. Several metrics for extracting knowledge anchors in a data graph, and the corresponding algorithms, are presented. The metrics performance is examined, and a hybridization approach that combines the strengths of each metric is proposed.

Keywords

Data graphs; exploratory search; knowledge utility; basic level objects.

1. INTRODUCTION

Data graphs (in the form of RDF Linked Data) have become widely available on the Web and are being used in a myriad of applications [1, 2, 17]. Gradually, data graphs are also being exposed to users, taking advantage of the exploration of the rich knowledge encoded in the graph. In many cases, users exploring data graphs will have no (or limited) familiarity with the specific domain and little (or no) awareness of the encoded knowledge in the graph. In other words, the *users' cognitive structures* about the domain may not match the *semantic structure of the data graph*. This can hinder graph exploration, as the users may not be able to identify which paths are most useful, leading to confusion, high cognitive load, and frustration.

Our research deals with supporting navigation in data graphs through intelligent nudging, directing people to trajectories with high utility. Specifically, we consider *knowledge utility* – how useful a trajectory in a graph is to expand one's knowledge in the domain. Our earlier research has shown that while exploring data

HT '16, July 10-13, 2016, Halifax, NS, Canada
© 2016 ACM. ISBN 978-1-4503-4247-6/16/07...$15.00
DOI: http://dx.doi.org/10.1145/2914586.2914637

graphs in unfamiliar (or partially familiar) domains, users *serendipitously* learn new things [5, 15]. To make the serendipitous learning 'more likely', we seek to identify 'good' trajectories which are helpful for expanding one's knowledge.

It is critical to identify anchoring entities in the data graph that serve as knowledge bridges to learn new concepts. Such anchors can also be used to facilitate adaptation and personalization [29]. Our earlier observations, in a controlled user study investigating nudging strategies for exploration [15], have suggested that paths which start with familiar and highly inclusive entities and bring something new are likely to have good knowledge utility. This directed us to adopt the subsumption theory for meaningful learning [6], where familiar and inclusive entities are used as knowledge anchors to subsume new knowledge into users' cognitive structure. Hence, the key challenge is:

How to develop automatic ways to identify data graph entities that provide knowledge anchors for navigation paths.

We utilize the Cognitive Science notion of basic level objects[1] [7], to develop algorithms for identifying *knowledge anchors in a data graph* (KA_{DG}). These anchors will refer to the most inclusive categories at which objects are easily identified; and hence can provide good anchors for knowledge exploration. We will present two groups of metrics for identifying KA_{DG} together with algorithms for applying these metrics:

- *distinctiveness metrics* which identify differentiated categories whose attributes are shared amongst the category members and not associated to members of other categories; and
- *homogeneity metrics* which identify basic categories whose members share many attributes together.

The main contribution of the research presented in this paper is:

- Formal description and implementation of metrics and the corresponding algorithms for identifying KA_{DG}.
- Analysis of the performance of the algorithms using a benchmarking set of knowledge anchors identified by humans.

2. RELATED WORK

The growth of data graphs, including Linked Data, has opened a new avenue of research in developing computational models to facilitate data exploration by layman users. One of the key challenges in supporting exploration over data graphs is ensuring that the interaction brings some benefit (utility) for the user [12, 19]. Our work focuses on knowledge expansion.

---

[1] The term "basic level objects" has been used in Cognitive Science. Other developments, e.g. Formal Concept Analysts, call them "concepts.

Earlier research on exploration through data graphs examines different ways to provide intelligent support for users' navigation. Personalized exploration based on user interests has been presented in [23]. Extracting semantic patterns from linked data sources to improve diversity in recommendation results to users has been proposed in [18, 24]. The concept of utility of statement has been presented in [13] to rank RDF statements. A related strand of research focuses on improving search efficiency by considering user interests [8, 9, 17] or diversifying user's exploration paths with recommendations based on the navigation history [10]. There is also a wealth of research in developing semantic data browsers, that lay out exploration paths using relationships in the underpinning ontologies [3, 4, 21, 34]. A survey of semantic data browsers is provided in [12].

We add to this research stream by opening a new avenue with the introduction of the concept of '*knowledge utility*' of exploration paths. Our work has broad implication for maximizing the learning effect for the users navigating through data graphs that often come from heterogeneous sources. We follow the subsumption theory for meaningful learning [6], according to which to incorporate new knowledge, the most familiar and inclusive entities in the user's cognition can be used as *knowledge anchors* for introducing new knowledge. Anchors in data graphs are similar to notion of basic level objects in domain taxonomies. It states that category objects in a taxonomy are structured such that there is a level of abstraction at which most basic level categories selections are made. We operationalize this notion for automating the search for knowledge anchors in data graphs.

The technical approaches that are most relevant to the research presented in this paper refer to the adoption of basic level objects in ontology summarization [11, 24, 27] and in Formal Concept Analysis (FCA) [14, 25, and 26]. Ontology summarization has been seen as an important technology to help ontology engineers quickly make sense of an ontology, in order to understand, reuse and build new ontologies [28]. Measures for ranking and re-ranking using centrality, distance, similarity and coherence have been used to generate good explanations. The notion of relevance has been used in [27] to produce graph summaries. The closest work to the context in this paper is the summarization approach presented in [11], which highlighted the value of cognitive science (natural categories) for identifying key concepts in an ontology to aid ontology engineers to better understand the ontology and quickly judge it suitability.

Formal Concept Analysis is a method for analysis of object-attribute data tables [14]. The psychological approaches to basic level objects have been formally defined for selecting important formal concepts in a concept lattice by considering the cohesion of a formal concept [25]. More recently, the work in [26] has reviewed and formalized the main existing psychological approaches to basic level concepts. The approaches utilized the validity of formal concepts to produce informative concepts capable of reducing the user's overload.

These works on ontology summarization and FCA utilize basic level objects with the aim of identifying key concepts in an ontology to help experts to examine and reengineer the ontology. In our work, we apply the notion of basic level objects in a data graph to identify *concepts which are likely to be familiar to users who are not domain experts*. Further, we are unique in our use for these concepts to support users' exploration in order to expand her domain knowledge. This brings forth various research challenges, including: dealing with larger number of entities, from 100s of entities in a typical ontology versus millions of entities in a typical data graph, and the need to exploit large number of data instances available in the data graphs compared to schematic ontologies. Our work is the first of its kind in utilizing Rosch's seminal cognitive science work [7] in the context of data exploration of data graphs. The formal framework that maps Rosch's definition of basic level objects and cue validity to data graphs is the key contribution of the work presented in this paper.

3. BASIC LEVEL OBJECTS IN COGNITIVE SCIENCE

The notion of basic level objects was introduced in Cognitive Science research illustrating that domain taxonomies include category objects which are at the basic level of abstraction [7, 20]. These category objects are commonly used in our daily life and people are usually able to recognize them quickly. For example, considering the Music domain, most people are likely to recognize objects in the category Guitar (*basic level*). However, layman users who are not experts in the music domain are unlikely to be able to recognize objects from the category Resonator Guitar (*subordinate level)* and may consider such objects as equivalent to their parent Guitar (closest basic level) rather than String Instrument (*superordinate level*).

Basic level categories "carry the most information, possess the highest category cue validity, and are, thus, the most differentiated from one another" [7]. Crucial for identifying basic level categories is calculating *cue validity*: "the validity of a given cue x as a predictor of a given category y (the conditional probability of y/x) increases as the frequency with which cue x is associated with category y increases and decreases as the frequency with which cue x is associated with categories other than y increases" [7]. Consequently, to identify basic level categories in a domain taxonomy, we will explore two avenues:

Distinctiveness (highest cue validity) identifies most differentiated category objects. A differentiated category object has most (or all) of its cues (i.e. attributes) linked to the category members (i.e. subclasses) only, and not linked to other category objects in the taxonomy. Each entity that is linked through a relationship to members of the category will have a single validity value used as a predictor of the distinctiveness of the category object. The aggregation of all validity values will indicate the distinctiveness of the category object.

Homogeneity (highest commonality between category members) identifies category objects whose members have high similarity values. The higher the similarity between category members, the more likely it is that the category object is at the basic level of abstraction. This is complementary to the distinctiveness feature. A category object with high cue validity will usually have high number of entities common to its members.

4. ALGORITHMS FOR IDENTIFYING KNOWLEDGE ANCHORS

4.1 Preliminaries

Linked Data graphs are built using traditional Web standards (e.g. Uniform Resource Identifiers (URIs) and HTTP) and use a common data graph model - the Resource Descriptive Framework (RDF). RDF describes entities (vertices) and attributes (edges) in the data graph, represented as RDF statements. Each statement is a triple of the form <*Subject - Predicate - Object*> [22]. The

Subject and *Predicate* denote entities in the graph. An *Object* is either a URI or a string. Each *Predicate* URI denotes a directed attribute which has a *Subject* as a source and an *Object* as a target. Formally, we define a data graph as:

Definition 1 [Data graph] A Data Graph DG is a labeled directed graph $DG = \langle V, E, P \rangle$, depicting a set of RDF triples where:

- $V = \{v_1, v_2, ..., v_n\}$ is a finite set of vertices.
- $E = \{e, e_2, ..., e_m\}$ is a finite set of edge types, where $e_1 = $ `rdfs:subClassOf` is the subsumption relationship, and $e_2, ..., e_n$ can correspond to any other semantic relationships.
- $P = \{p, p_2, ..., p_k\}$ where each p_i is a proposition in the form of a triple $\langle v_s, e_i, v_o \rangle$ with $v_s, v_o \in V$, where v_s is the *Subject* (source) and v_o is the *Object*(target); and $e_i \in E$ is the edge type.

Using the subsumption relationship `rdfs:subClassOf` and following its transitivity, for each entity $v \in V$ we can derive the entities v' that are subclasses of v, we denote this as $v' \subseteq v$.

The entities set V in the data graph is divided into the following:
Category entities: $C \subseteq V$ is the set of all entities that have at least one subclass and at least one superclass, other than the abstract domain entity d which is the superclass for all entities.

Leaf entities: $L \subseteq V$ is a set of entities that have no subclasses.

Figure 1 shows entities extracted from a data graph in the Music domain starting from the abstract domain entity `Instrument`.

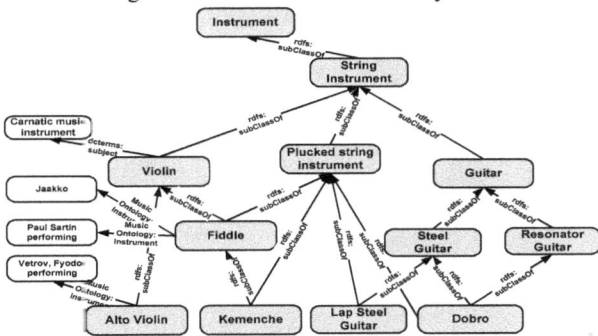

Figure 1. Extract from the MusicPinta data graph [5] showing category and leaf entities (in shaded shapes) and relationships. Hierarchical relationships are subsumption `rdfs:subClassOf` and `dcterms:subject` that links an entity to its DBpedia category. `MusicOntology:instrument` a the domain-specific relationship that links a musical instrument to a performance.

Definition 2 [Normal Graph] A normal graph is a data graph where no entity is *both* a category entity and a leaf entity (in other words, every category entity has *at least one subclass*). We assume that we are always dealing with normal graphs. Our algorithms may not give sensible results for non-normal graphs.

Definition 3 [Hierarchical relationships E_H] Hierarchical relationships are the edge types $\{e_1, e_2, ..\} \in E_H$ of the data graph that denote category membership between the *Subject* and *Object* entities in the corresponding triples. E_H always includes the subsumption relationship `rdfs:subclassOf` but may also contain other relationships showing membership inclusion (e.g., `dcterms:subject` as shown in Figure 1).

Definition 4 [Domain-specific relationships E_D] Domain specific relationships are the edge types other than the hierarchical relationships, i.e. $E = E_H \cup E_D$ (e.g., Figure 1 shows the relationship `MusicOntology:instrument`).

4.2 Algorithms for Identifying KA_{DG}

Any entity $v \in V$ in a data graph DG, except the abstract domain entity d and the set of leaf entities L, i.e. $v \in \{C\}$, could potentially be identified as a knowledge anchor in DG. The set of all knowledge anchors in DG is denoted as KA_{DG}. We follow the distinctiveness and homogeneity approaches described in Section 3 to define metrics and corresponding algorithms for discovering KA_{DG} in a given data graph DG. The definitions follow the formal concept analysis approach in [26], and adapt the suggested metrics in the context of finding knowledge anchors in a data graph. In addition, we describe algorithms for identifying KA_{DG}.

4.2.1 Distinctiveness Metrics
This group of algorithms aims to identify the most differentiated basic categories whose attributes are shared amongst the category members but are not associated to members of other categories.

Attribute Validity (AV)
The attribute validity definition here corresponds to the cue validity definition in [7] and adapts the formula from [26]. We use 'attribute validity' to indicate the association with data graphs - 'cues' in data graphs are attributes of the entities and are represented as relationships in terms of triples.

The attribute validity value of an entity $v \in \{C\}$ is calculated with regard to a relationship type e, as the aggregation of the attribute validity values for all entities v'_e linked to subclasses $v' : v' \subseteq v$. In other words, the validity of each v'_e acts as a predictor for the validity of v. The attribute validity value of v'_e *increases*, as the number of relationships of type e between v'_e and the *subclasses* $v' : v' \subseteq v$ increases; whereas the attribute validity value of v'_e *decreases* as the number of relationships of type e between v'_e and *all entities* in the data graph increases.

We define the set of vertices $W(v,e)$ related as *Subjects* to the subclasses $v' : v' \subseteq v$, via relationship of type e:

$$W(v,e) = \{ v'_e : \exists v' [v' \subseteq v \wedge \langle v'_e, e, v' \rangle \in P] \} \quad (1)$$

The following formula defines the attribute validity metric for a given entity v with regard to a relationship type e.

$$AV(v,e) = \sum_{v'_e \in W(v,e)} \frac{|\{\langle v'_e, e, v' \rangle : v' \subseteq v\}|}{|\{\langle v'_e, e, v_a \rangle : v_a \in V\}|} \quad (2)$$

For example (see Figure 1), the attribute validity value for `Guitar` will aggregate attribute validity values of its members, one of which is `Dobro`. The attribute validity value for `Dobro` with regard to the `rdfs:subclassOf` relationship type and the given category entity `Guitar` equals the number of `rdfs:subclassOf` relationships between `Dobro` and the subclasses of `Guitar` (2 relationships), divided by the number of `rdfs:subclassOf` relationships between `Dobro` and all entities in the data graph (3 relationships).

Category-Attribute Collocation (CAC):

This approach was used in [33] to improve the cue validity metric by adding the so called category-feature collocation measure which takes into account the frequency of the attribute within the members of the category. This gives preference to 'good' categories that have many attributes shared by their members. In our case, a good category will be an entity $v \in \{C\}$ with high number of relationships of type e between v'_e and the subclasses $v' : v' \subseteq v$, relative to the number of its subclasses. The following formula defines the category-attribute collocation metric for a given entity v with regard to a relationship type e.

$$CAC(v,e) = \sum_{v'_e \in W(v,e)} \frac{|\{\langle v'_e, e, v' \rangle : v' \subseteq v\}|}{|\{\langle v'_e, e, v_a \rangle : v_a \in V\}|} \cdot \frac{|\{\langle v'_e, e, v' \rangle : v' \subseteq v\}|}{|V|} \quad (3)$$

For example (see Figure 1), the category entity `Violin` has three performances (attributes) linked to its subclasses `Fiddle` and `Alto Violin` via `MusicOntology:instrument`. This will add a weight of 2/3 to the AV of `Violin`.

Category Utility (CU):

This approach was presented in [30] as an alternative metric for obtaining categories at the basic level. The metric takes into account that a category is useful if it can improve the ability to predict the attributes for members of the category, i.e. a good category will have many attributes shared by its members (as mentioned in the category-attribute collocation metric). At the same time, it should possess 'unique' attributes that are not related to many other categories (efficiency of category recognition). We adapt the formula in [26] for a data graph:

$$CU(v,e) = \frac{|V'|}{|V|} \sum_{v'_e \in W(v,e)} \left(\frac{|\{\langle v'_e, e, v' \rangle : v' \subseteq v\}|}{|V'|} \right)^2 - \left(\frac{|\{\langle v'_e, e, v_a \rangle : v_a \in V\}|}{|V|} \right)^2 (4)$$

For example (see Figure 1), considering again Violin. In addition to the proportion of performances divided by number of subclasses for Violin, the category utility will also include the proportion of all performances linking Violin (3 in this case) over the total number of entities in the graph (12).

The algorithm for calculating the metrics is given in Algorithm I.

Algorithm I: Distinctiveness Metrics

Input: $DG = \langle V, E, P \rangle, e \in E$

1.   **for all** $v \in \{C\}$ **do**
2. $V' :=$ the set of all $v' : v' \subseteq v$
3.   **for all** $v'_e : \exists \langle v'_e, e, v' \rangle$ **do**
4. $N_e :=$ set of all $\langle v'_e, e, v' \rangle : v' \in V'$
5. $M_e :=$ set of all $\langle v'_e, e, v_a \rangle : v_a \in V$
6. $AV_{v'_e} := |N_e|/|M_e|$
7. $CAC_{v'_e} := (|N_e|/|M_e|) \cdot (|N_e|/|V'|)$
8. $CU_{v'_e} := (|N_e|/|V'|)^2 - (|M_e|/|V|)^2$
9. $AV_v := AV_v + AV_{v'_e}$
10. $CAC_v := CAC_v + CAC_{v'_e}$
11. $CU_v := CU_v + CU_{v'_e}$
12.   **end for**
13. $CU_v := \frac{|V'|}{|V|} \cdot CU_v$
14.   **end for**

Output: AV_v, CAC_v, CU_v for all $v \in \{C\}$

The algorithm takes a data graph and a relationship type (hierarchical or domain-specific relationship) as input and returns values for the three distinctiveness metrics for each entity $v \in \{C\}$.

For an entity v, all subclasses are retrieved using the subsumption relationship (line 2). Then, for each entity v'_e linked to one or more subclass entities v' via triples $\langle v'_e, e, v' \rangle$ (line 3), several steps are conducted: retrieving all triples with *Subject* v'_e and *Object* any subclass v' (line 4); retrieving all triples with *Subject* v'_e and *Object* any graph entity v (line 5); applying the formulas for calculating the AV, CAC, and CU metrics for v'_e (lines 6-8); and aggregating values for v'_e to the overall values for v (lines 9-11).

4.2.2 Homogeneity Metrics

As outlined in Section 3, knowledge anchors will be *more homogeneous* because their members will be similar to each other. We utilize three set-based similarity metrics: Common Neighbours (*CN*), Jaccard (*Jac*), and Cosine (*Cos*) [31, 32]. For example (see Figure 1), consider the entity `Guitar` and the hierarchical relationship `rdfs:subClassOf`. `Guitar` has two subclasses which share one common entity (`Dobro`) and have all together two entities (`Dobro` and `Lap Steel Guitar`). The Jaccard similarity for `Guitar` will be 1/2.

The algorithm for calculating the metrics is given in Algorithm II.

Algorithm II: Homogeneity Metrics

Input: $DG = \langle V, E, P \rangle, e \in E$

1.   **for all** $v \in \{C\}$ **do**
2. $V' :=$ the set of all $v' : v' \subseteq v$
3.   **for all** $(v', v'') : v' \in V' \wedge v'' \in V'$ **do**
4. $V'_e := \{v'_e : \exists \langle v'_e, e, v' \rangle\}$
5. $V''_e := \{v''_e : \exists \langle v''_e, e, v'' \rangle\}$
6. $I := V'_e \cap V''_e$
7. $U := V'_e \cup V''_e$
8. $CN_{v',v''} := |I|$
9. $Jac_{v',v''} := |I|/|U|$
10. $Cos_{v',v''} := |I|/(\sqrt{|V'_e|} \cdot \sqrt{|V''_e|})$
11. $CN_v = CN_v + CN_{v',v''}$
12. $Jac_v = Jac_v + Jac_{v',v''}$
13. $Cos_v = Cos_v + Cos_{v',v''}$
14.   **end for**
15. $CN_v = CN_v /(|V'| \cdot (|V'|-1)/2)$
16. $Jac_v = Jac_v /(|V'| \cdot (|V'|-1)/2)$
17. $Cos_v = Cos_v /(|V'| \cdot (|V'|-1)/2)$
18.   **end for**

Output: CN_v, Jac_v, Cos_v for all $v \in \{C\}$

The algorithm takes a data graph and a relationship type (hierarchical or domain-specific relationship) as input and returns values for the three homogeneity metrics for each entity $v \in \{C\}$.

For an entity v, all subclasses are retrieved using the subsumption relationship (line 2). For each pair of subclass entities v' and v'' (line 3), several steps are conducted: retrieving all entities linked via triples with v' and v'' (lines 4-5); calculating their intersection and union (lines 6-7); applying the formulas for calculating the similarity metrics *CN*, *Jac*, and *Cos* (lines 8-10); and aggregating these values to the overall values for v (lines 11-13); and normalizing the aggregated values (lines 15-17).

Each KA_{DG} metric was implemented by running SPARQL queries over the MusicPinta data graph [5] stored in a triple store. This implementation allowed examining the performance of the KA_{DG} metrics over a specific data graph, as presented next.

5. EXPERIMENTAL STUDY

In order to evaluate the KA_{DG} metrics, we compared the outputs of the implementation of the two algorithms over the MusicPinta data graph versus a benchmarking set of basic level objects from the categories in the data graph, as identified by humans. Ten online surveys[2] were run adopting two strategies.

- **Strategy1 – leaf instruments.** Eight surveys presented the 256 leaf entities: each survey showed 32 MusicPinta leaf entities and 8 additional images minimizing bias.
- **Strategy2 – category instruments.** Two surveys presented the 103 category entities: each survey showed 54 category entities plus 14 images minimizing bias.

The image allocation in surveys was random. Every survey had four respondents from the study participants. Each participant was allocated *only to one survey*. Each image was shown for 10 seconds on the participant's screen and he/she was asked to type the name of the given object (for Strategy1) or the category of objects (in Strategy2) as quickly as possible. Following Cognitive Science studies to identify basic objects, we extracted the benchmarking lists of knowledge anchors using accuracy and frequency [16]. Two benchmarking sets of KA_{DG} were obtained:

Set1 [resulting from Strategy1]. We consider accurate naming of a category entity (parent) when a leaf entity is seen.
Set2 [resulting from Strategy 2]. We consider naming a category entity with its exact name, or its superclass (parent), or its subclass (member). Entities with frequency equal or above two (i.e. named by two different users) were identified as KA_{DG}. From the two strategies, two groups of benchmarking sets are identified:

StrongAnchors [intersection of *Set1* and *Set2*] = {Accordion, Bell, Bouzouki, Clarinet, Drum, Flute, Guitar, Harmonica, Harp, Saxophone, String instrument, Trumpet, Violin, Xylophone}.
WeakAnchors [union of *Set1* and *Set2*] = {Accordion, Banjo, Bell, Bouzouki, Cello, Clarinet, Drum, Electric piano, Flute, Gong, Guitar, Harmonica, Harp, Lute, Lyre, Organ, Recorder, Saxophone, String Instrument, Trombone, Trumpet, Tuba, Violin, Xylophone}.

6. EXPERIMENTAL RESULTS

The two benchmarking sets – *StrongAnchors* and *WeakAnchors* - are used to examine the performance of the KA_{DG} metrics. For each KA_{DG} metric, we aggregate (using union) the KA_{DG} entities identified using the two hierarchical relationships (rdfs:subclassOf and dcterms:subject). Since the three homogeneity metrics returned the same values, we choose one metric when reporting the results, namely *Jaccard similarity*[3]. A cut-off threshold point for the result lists with potential KA_{DG} entities was identified by normalizing the output values from each metric and taking the mean value for the *60th percentile* of the

lists. Each KA_{DG} metric (the three distinctiveness metrics and the Jaccard metric), was applied over both families of relationships – hierarchical and domain-specific. Precision and Recall values were calculated using the two benchmarking sets.

The precision values were poor (ranging from 0.16 to 0.26 for *StrongAnchors* and from 0.21 to 0.35 for the *WeakAnchors*). Recall values for the *StrongAnchors* were better (ranging from 0.46 to 0.77), while for the *WeakAnchors* recall values were very mixed (ranging from 0.18 to 0.73). Inspecting the False Positive (FP) entities, we noticed two main reasons for the poor precision.

Firstly, the algorithms were selecting entities with a low number of subclasses (e.g. Zurna). To take into account the number of subclasses for the entities, we multiply the metrics values by SN_v:

$$SN_v = 1 - (1/|\{v' : v' \subseteq v\}|) \qquad (5)$$

Secondly, the algorithms returned FP entities which had long label names (e.g. Plucked string-instrument). We adopt a name simplicity approach which is based on the data graph: it filters out all entities whose name length is higher than the *weighted median* for the length of labels of all entities. For the MusicPinta data graph, the weighted median is 1.2. Precision results were improved noticeably (lowest value 0.36 to highest value 0.62), especially for the WeakAnchors set. Our baseline is calculated using all entities whose name length is less than weighted median (0.25 for WeakAnchors and 0.41 for StrogAnchors). Further analysis of FP and FN indicated that the algorithms had different performance on the different taxonomical levels, which is formulated in two heuristics for hybridization:

Heuristic 1: *Use hierarchical Jaccard metric for the most specific categories in the graph.*
Heuristic 2: *Take majority voting for other taxonomical levels.*

Applying these heuristics improved precision values (lowest value 0.48 to highest value 0.65), especially for the *WeakAnchors* set.

7. CONCLUSION

Exploration of data is becoming a key daily life activity. The success of data graphs to support exploration brings forth the challenge of building systematic approaches to aid user exploration with the aim of knowledge expansion. We build on research acknowledging that data exploration should take into account knowledge utility of the exploration paths. This emphasizes the importance of identifying anchoring entities in a data graph that serve as knowledge bridges to learn new concepts.

In this paper, we utilize Rosch's seminal work in cognitive science, which defines basic level objects in domain taxonomies, adapting it for data graph exploration. We present a formal framework that maps Rosch's definitions of basic level objects and cue validity to data graphs. We develop two groups of metrics for identifying knowledge anchors in a data graph together with algorithms for applying these metrics. The performance of the metrics is examined using two benchmarking sets, and a hybridization approach is proposed. The results shown that using the hierarchical Jaccard metric for the most specific categories in the graph and considering majority voting of results for all taxonomical levels, brings out the best results in the algorithms.

The presented research has many potential applications to support users data exploration. Our approach can be also applied to ontology summarization where the knowledge anchors from the data graph allows capturing a lay person's view of the domain.

---

[2] The study was conducted with Qualtrics (www.qualtrics.com).

[3] The Jaccard similarity metric is widely used, and was used in identifying basic formal concepts in the context of formal concept analysis [25].

The knowledge anchors can be also used to solve the key problem of 'cold start' in personalization and adaptation. The immediate future work is to apply the metrics in another domain (e.g. data graph with career options which will be used to generate career paths). In the long run, we aim to utilize the metrics to generate navigation paths using subsumption strategies for meaningful learning while taking into account user's domain familiarity.

8. REFERENCES

[1] Schraefel, MC. What does it look like, really? Imagining how citizens might effectively, usefully and easily find, explore, query and re-present open/linked data. In *Proc. ISWC 2010*.

[2] Waitelonis, J., Knuth, M., Wolf, L., Hercher, J. and Sack, H. The Path is the Destination-Enabling a New Search Paradigm with Linked Data. *In LD in the Future Internet @ Future Internet Assembly, 2010*.

[3] Popov, I.O., Schraefel, M., Hall, W., Shadbolt, N. Connecting the Dots: A Multi-pivot approach to data exploration. In ISWC, 2011.

[4] Thellmann, K., Galkin, M., Orlandi, F., and Auer, S. LinkDaViz – Automatic Binding of Linked Data to Visualizations. In ISWC, 2015.

[5] Thakker, D., Dimitrova, V., Lau, L., Yang-Turner, F. & Despotakis, D. Assisting User Browsing over Linked Data: Requirements Elicitation with a User Study. *In ICWE 2013*

[6] Ausubel, D. A Subsumption Theory of Meaningful Verbal Learning and Retention. In Journal of General Psychology. Volume 66, Issue 2, 1962, pp. 213-224.

[7] Rosch, E., Mervis, C. B., Gray, W. D., Johnson, D. M., &Boyes-Braem, P. Basic objects in natural categories. Cognitive Psychology, 1976, 8, 382-439.

[8] Sah, M. & Wade, V. Personalized Concept-based Search and Exploration on the Web of Data using Results Categorization. In ESWC 2013.

[9] Rossel,O. Implemention of a "search and browse" scenario for the LinkedData. In IESD, 2014.

[10] Vocht1, et, al. A Visual Exploration Workflow as Enablerfor the Exploitation of Linked Open Data. In IESD, 2014.

[11] Peroni, S., Motta, E., d'Aquin, M. Identifying key concepts in an ontology through the integration of cognitive principles with statistical and topological measures. In ASWC, 2008.

[12] Marie, N., Gandon, F. Survey of linked data based exploration. In IESD@ISWC2014.

[13] Dean, M., Basu, P., Carterette, B., Partridge, C. and Hendler, J. What to Send First? A Study of Utility in the Semantic Web. In (LHD+SemQuant), 2012, @ ISWC2012..

[14] Wille, R. Formal Concept Analysis as Mathematical Theory of Concepts and Concept Hierarchies. In Formal Concept Analysis: Foundations and Applications, Springer 2005.

[15] Al-Tawil, M., Thakker, D. and Dimitrova, V. Nudging to Expand User's Domain Knowledge while Exploring Linked Data. In (IESD), 2014, @ ISWC2014.

[16] Tanaka, J., & Taylor, M. Object Categories and Expertise: Is the Basic Level in the Eye of the Beholder? Cognitive Psychology, 1991, 23, pp 457-482.

[17] Marie, N., Corby, O., Gandon, F. and Ribiere, M. Composite interests' exploration thanks to on-the-fly linked data spreading activation. In Hypertext 2013.

[18] Maccatrozzo , V., Aroyo , L., Robert , R. Crowdsourced Evaluation of Semantic Patterns for Recommen-dations. In UMAP 2013. LBR.

[19] Nunes, T., Schwabe, D. Exploration of Semi-Structured Data Sources. In (IESD), 2014, @ ISWC2014.

[20] Rosen, E. Principles of categorization. In E. Rosch & B. B. Lloyd (Eds.), 1978. Cognition and categorization. pp. 27-48.

[21] Thakker, D., Despotakis, D., Dimitrova, V., Lau, L., Brna, P. (2012). Taming digital traces for informal learning: A semantic-driven approach. In Proceedings of EC-TEL 2012.

[22] Bizer, C., Heath, T., and Berners-Lee, T. Linked Data - the story so far. International Journal on Semantic Web and Information Systems, 5, (3), pp 1-22.

[23] Ruotsalo, T., et al. Supporting Exploratory Search Tasks with Interactive User Modeling. In ASIST, 2013.

[24] Zhang, X., Cheng, G. and Qu, Y. Ontology Summarization Based on RDF Sentence Graph. In WWW, 2007.

[25] Belohlavek, R., Trnecka, M. Basic level of concepts in formal concept analysis. In ICFCA, 2012, pp 28-44.

[26] Belohlavek, R., Trnecka, M. Basic Level in Formal Concept Analysis: Interesting Concepts and Psychological Ramifications. In IJCAI 2013.

[27] Troullinou, G., Kondylakis, H., Daskalaki , E., Plexousakis , D. RDF Digest: Efficient Summarization of RDF/S KBs. In ESWC, 2015.

[28] Li, N., Motta, E. Evaluations of user-driven ontology summarization. In EKAW 2010. pp 544-553.

[29] Al-Tawil, M., Dimitrova, V., Thakker, D. Using Basic Level Concepts in a Linked Data Graph to Detect User's Domain Familiarity. In UMAP2015, Dublin, Ireland.

[30] Corter, J. E., Gluck, M. A. Explaining basic categories: Feature predictability and information. Psychological Bulletin, 111(2):291–303, 1992.

[31] David Liben-Nowell and Jon Kleinberg. The link-prediction problem for social networks. In Journal of the American Society for Information Science and Technology, 2007.

[32] U Kang, et al. Axiomatic Analysis of Co-occurrence Similarity Functions. Microsoft Research, WA, USA, 2012

[33] Jones, G. V. Identifyingbasic categories. Psychological Bulletin, 94:423–428, 1983.

[34] Heim, P., Ertl, T., Ziegler, J. Facet graphs: complex semantic querying made easy. In Proceedings of ESWC2010, Berlin, Heidelberg, pp. 288-302.

The Effect of Synonym Substitution on Search Results

Michael Antunovic
School of ITMS
Mawson Lakes Campus
University of South Australia
michael.antunovic@mymail.unisa.edu.au

Ivan Lee
School of ITMS
Mawson Lakes Campus
University of South Australia
Ivan.Lee@unisa.edu.au

Helen Ashman
School of ITMS
Mawson Lakes Campus
University of South Australia
Helen.Ashman@unisa.edu.au

ABSTRACT

Synonyms or other semantic associations can be used in web search in query substitution to improve or augment the query to retrieve more relevant search results. The value of substitution depends on how well the synonyms preserve semantic meaning, as any attrition in meaning can result in semantic drift of query results. Many synonyms are not synonyms in the traditional, thesaurus sense, but are semantic associations discovered automatically from online data, with the risk of semantic drift in substitution. This discovery of synonyms or other semantic associations arises from different methods applied over web search logs, and in this paper we review the candidate synonym pairs of words or phrases generated from three different methods applied over the same web search logs. The suitability of the candidate synonym pairs for the purpose of query substitution is evaluated in an experiment where 68 subjects assessed the search results generated by both the original query and the substituted query. It was found that two of the discovery methods returned significantly worse results with the substitution than were returned by the original query for the majority of queries, with only around 20-22% of substituted queries generating either improved or equally-relevant results. The third method however returned a very similar level of superior results as the original query, and saw over 71% of substituted queries generating either improved or equally-relevant results. These results indicate that even when candidate synonym pairs are confirmed as being semantically associated using other methods, they still may not be suitable for query substitution, depending on the method of synonym discovery.

Categories and Subject Descriptors

H.3.3 [Information Storage and Retrieval]: Information Search and Retrieval – Search process, Selection process.
H.5.4 [Information Storage and Retrieval]: Hypertext/ Hypermedia – User issues

Keywords

synonym discovery; Web search; query substitution

HT '16, July 10-13, 2016, Halifax, NS, Canada
© 2016 ACM. ISBN 978-1-4503-4247-6/16/07...$15.00
DOI: http://dx.doi.org/10.1145/2914586.2914635

1. INTRODUCTION

The semantic associations of hypertext are represented in links, with many of those links being calculated or discovered without the need for human intervention. The trail of users' interactions with search engines is a promising source of semantic associations, and methods that analyse this source can discover semantic associations between entities and concepts that do not appear in traditional dictionaries or thesauri.

We previously looked at three different methods for finding semantic associations from logs of searches, and compared the accuracy and type of semantic associations generated by each of the three methods [1]. The three methods were:

1. the analysis of queries submitted to the search engine, in particular where queries are reformulated;

2. the analysis of clickthrough data, where a user click is interpreted as affirming the result's relevance; and

3. the analysis of coselection data (where two or more clicks are made by the same user in the same search task).

It was found that the most reliable methods were the click-based (2 and 3 above) but that the query analysis method (1 above) generated far more potential semantic associations, although with a much higher error rate.

The things being semantically associated in the prior work were words or phrases from real searches. So the semantic associations could also be considered as synonyms. This indicated the potential for reformulating and/or extending users' queries with synonymous terms. The importance of query suggestion in improving web search is growing, with many search engines implementing some form of suggestion either through entire query phrases, predictive text input, or spelling and grammatical corrections. However, reissuing query terms without prompting the user is generally limited to spelling corrections confirmed by external dictionary sources [2]. The implementation of such query substitution needs further investigation from user studies to confirm various methods of sourcing substitute queries. Despite numerous studies looking at query suggestion, few implement user evaluations to confirm substituted query relevance, mostly using statistical measures to gauge relevance of suggested queries.

A number of synonym candidates were previously confirmed as semantic associations [1] and in this paper they are now assessed for their suitability for direct substitution in queries. Synonyms from all three of the methods used for discovering semantic associations were evaluated, from which we selected only those pairs that were confirmed as being semantically associated by the previous work.

2. RELATED WORK

2.1 Discovery of synonyms in search logs

Research on the semantics of synonyms is predominantly related to their discovery in web log data, sometimes as a side observation to another goal, such as word sense disambiguation [3]. More recent work concerns the discovery of entity synonyms [4] [5] [6] to help bridge the gap between user intent and search engines. Chakrabarti et al. [4] created a framework to discover entity synonyms, based on a similarity measure that analyses the lexical composition of queries in click logs with the benefit that external resources are not required, and is more scalable than competing approaches.

Cheng et al. [5] used web search logs to discover entity synonyms with string matching for less-popular queries, and click data for popular queries. They recommended against using click data to discover entity relationships due to variance in query length of entity queries and direction substitution of these terms for data matching of entity names and titles. For the difference in query length across users, as the increasing number of search sessions are validated by clicks, so is the variance in queries used to locate them. This approach required considerable noise filtering through whitelist creation and maintenance.

Chaudhuri et al. [7] used web documents to perform string-matching techniques with more detail of common knowledge items that may manifest in web logs as a result of user wisdom. They highlighted the difficulty in referencing an external source for entity-synonym matching in string-based tokenisation and investigated document-based *IDTokenSet* to improve synonym generation. This however involves the lookup and referencing for each and every query to multiple documents in the retrieval and processing of caption text and document content.

Wei [8] looked at the discovery of synonyms taking into account the context in which they occur, later implemented in Wei et al. [9]. They included some consideration for user intent that was also undertaken by Li et al. [10], where the noise of differing user intents is one of the issues in datasets that can return less-than-ideal query substitutions.

2.2 Query expansion vs substitution

A key use of synonymous terms applied to web search is for the expansion or substitution of user queries to enhance the relevance of the query, or to provide a broader range of results.

Jones et al. [11] replaced the parts of a query or an entire query with candidate suggestions based on their point-wise mutual information approach, leading to segmentation of terms for candidate substitution. This gives quality substitutions where pattern-matching is high, but for where term overlap is low, the potential for useful synonymous queries is missed.

Guo et al. [12] proposed a discriminative model that resulted in increased performance. This approaches faces the drawback of requiring sufficiently-labelled data, as well as the lack of scalability. The work incorporated various forms of query refinement prior to substitution, such as correction of spelling that in some instances appeared to do so incorrectly. They also combined a number of parameters to develop their model according to lexical features such as word frequency, order and composition, but did not use clicks for candidate refinements.

Another interesting method of query substitution is one that takes long queries and conducts trimming operations to provide shorter queries containing the same terms [13]. This may be useful for discovering synonyms but is also likely to return lower success rates and user satisfaction, a consideration for their future work. The authors argue that query size reduction eliminates noise, but may introduce more ambiguity [14].

Query expansion is similar to query substitution in that a new query is submitted to the search engine. However an expanded query can retain the terms from the original query and add new ones, whereas in query substitution the entire query or significant keywords are replaced. Query expansion techniques are generally split into two main types, Interactive Query Expansion (IQE) which relies on user input and selection for expansion, and Automatic Query Expansion (AQE) which performs expansion without input from the user, based on predefined settings from the system. With more user control comes a greater requirement to make discriminating decisions based only on words, but early research has indicated this is a powerful and adaptive solution [15]. Kanaan et al. [16] compared IQE to AQE for Arabic text, giving results as high as 86.4% precision for IQE. Recent works focus more on AQE, with a comprehensive survey of literature and analysis of methods and practice and corresponding challenges by Carpiento et al. [17]. They review numerous AQE approaches, ranging from analysis of linguistics to web and search log analysis. These include leveraging relevance feedback from external resources such as Wikipedia for AQE [18] and using clustering for query expansion using relevance feedback [13].

Cui et al. [19] used query expansion based on matching query terms to document terms comparing global with local analysis techniques that separate the analysis of clicked resources by many users from the explicit relevance judgements provided by the user. Based on prior work [20], they assumed query terms have a high probability of relevance to terms in the clicked document. The method fared better than early competing context analysis methods in validating query-to-document relations.

Lu et al. [21] applied query expansion with synonyms referenced from a domain-specific TREC collection in biomedical search with great success. For shorter and gene-specific queries in particular, there is the greatest potential for improvement as the medical domain allows for substitution of known keywords regardless of query length.

The most closely-related work into the application of synonyms in web search is the study by Wei et al. [9] who investigated the discovery of synonyms across three different methods and compared them both statistically using Discounted Cumulative Gain (DCG) and with human evaluators. The three methods compared candidate synonymised queries from firstly, a traditional thesaurus-based approach which does not take into account context, a second approach that utilised co-clicks from a large, real-world search engine web log, and a third approach which used the external resource of WordNet for the syn-sets provided in the popular ontology database. The DCG analysis was only applied to the thesaurus-based synonym candidates and not to the two other methods. The other two methods were evaluated by user experience impact, in that they measured the click-through rate of a system implementing the synonyms via query expansion of a real-world search engine. In both cases, there was marked improvement of 2% for CTR and -11.4% abandon rate. However, it was unclear what users were asked to do in the evaluation and how it was conducted, and by what parameters these rates were calculated. Also, the three methods were not analysed consistently, with the baseline only evaluated by DCG and not evaluated for relevance by the same users that used the query expansion candidates in a search engine.

3. EXPERIMENTAL DESIGN

3.1 Data sources

The candidate synonym pairs used in this experiment were discovered in prior work [22]. Six years' of student interactions with search engines was logged, including students' clicked results and reformulations of queries. From this was generated three classes of candidate synonym pairs as follows:

- Query reformulation candidates: when a user submits a reformulated query, the substituted words or phrases are considered to be semantically associated with the words or phrases used in the prior query but displaced in the reformulated query;
- Agglomerative synonym candidates: clicked results are aggregated according to what queries they were returned for, so when the aggregates overlap significantly, the query terms that generated the aggregates are considered to be semantically associated;
- Coselection synonym candidates: like the agglomerative method, clicked results are clustered according to what queries they were returned for, and when the clusters overlap significantly, the query terms that generated the aggregates are considered to be semantically associated. The major difference is that clicked results are grouped according to a similarity measure that ensures clusters can only be formed when results are both clicked by the same user in the same search session, a constraint not used in the agglomerative, single-click discovery method.

In all three cases, the same web log data was used, as it contained all click information as well as reformulations.

The only other collection of data for the experiment was in the capture of search results to serve in the online survey, so as to ensure that any ranking updates would not affect the consistency of returned results presented to different evaluators.

3.2 User interface design

The evaluators' task was to review a number of web search result pages, with the original query term shown, the substituted query hidden, and the results presented in two columns. One column showed the results for the original query, while the other column showed results for the substituted query which was a synonym of the initial query. The evaluators were asked to select the most relevant column of results for the query shown.

The search result evaluation system was designed to take into account the fact that the user needs to see both search result sets concurrently in order to make a relevance judgement based on the query presented. The second query term (the candidate substitute) was hidden so as to eliminate any possible bias in making the judgement, to ensure that only the search results were evaluated, and not the queries themselves. Since scanning both columns horizontally will occur more often than a top-down scan of a single column [23], it is likely that users will check at least the top results of a two-column presentation and select the most appropriate results to the search terms.

The hypertext links of results were made non-functional to discourage clicking and to ensure users made relevance judgments based entirely on the caption text presented. Only the top 10 search results were collected and used for each query in the query pairs evaluated, since the majority of users do not click beyond the first page of search results [24].

3.3 Controls

The primary control implemented in the rating system was to hide the second query of the pair, so as to ensure the user would judge the result sets for their suitability for the original query. The order of presentation of results to assess was randomised.

The evaluators were not aware of the three different discovery methods providing the query pairs, and an equal number of candidate synonym pairs from each method was used for the queries. A set of control query pairs was generated randomly from the same set of queries used in the original data, which were known to be semantically unrelated from the prior work [1]

3.4 Rating system

The online survey gave the rater five options: *left column more relevant*; *right column more relevant*; *equal relevance*; *neither column relevant*; and *undecided*. Evaluators were asked to decide which of the two columns or results presented was most relevant to the query shown. The left column presented the results of the original, initial query, while the right column showed the results from the substituted query, although the evaluators were not aware of this at the time. The *neither column* relevant choice was included for completeness but was never chosen, since the results always included at least one column of query-specific results determined by the search engine. To assess the reliability of ratings between evaluators, the Fleiss-Kappa inter-ranker agreement measure was used [25] to determine if ratings were statistically significant.

4. RESULTS

To test the online survey system and gain an idea of how long it would take the evaluators, the entire set of 772 candidate synonym pairs generated previously [1] were evaluated by two test users. Of the original 831 candidate synonym pairs 59 were omitted due to generating fewer than 10 search results.

Rating all 772 evaluations took each test user about 4 hours. To reduce this to a more manageable 20-30 minutes, the number of candidate synonym pairs was set to 100. The proportion of queries across the classes of candidate synonym pairs, including the control pairs, was revised, ensuring that a minimum of 15 and a maximum of 30 candidate synonym pairs was selected from each class, including the control set.

In total, 68 evaluators from the University of South Australia completed all evaluations. Two evaluators failed the controls, with one evaluator merely clicking at random while the other repeatedly clicked the same rating for the entire set of evaluations, and these two were omitted from the survey. A further 4 evaluators failed to complete the full set of evaluations. Although the survey only required evaluators to have familiarity with use of a search engine, the source data used to generate the candidate synonym pairs meant that the general demographic of the evaluators matched the topic areas of the source data.

4.1 Query reformulation

In the prior work [1], candidate synonym pairs generated by the query reformulation method were the least likely to be genuine semantic associations, with over 16% of pairs found to be completely unrelated, and only 24.9% decided to be "equivalent", with the remaining 59% being either "associated" or "super/sub concept". So it might be anticipated that a significant proportion of the substituted queries would be rated poorly compared to the original queries. The results confirmed this. The majority of ratings agreed that the initial query was most relevant. Table 1 summarises the findings.

rating	percentage
initial query most relevant	64.8
query substitution most relevant	10.8
equally relevant	10.8
undecided	13.5

Table 1. Evaluator rating distribution for candidate synonym pairs generated by query reformulation. The "neither relevant" choice was not selected by evaluators.

It seems many of the substitutes had an element of semantic drift, when the substituted term was semantically associated with the initial term, but different enough to take the query results off-topic. As the whole point of query reformulation is to refine the intent of the original query, this represents a drift in user intent. The results here are evidence of this intent drift.

There were some successful substitutions, ranked as being equally-relevant or more relevant than the initial query, including *how to model an angel in wax* returning more relevant results than *3ds max wing tutorial*, and *combined physical data link is wrong* more relevant than *combined physical data link*. However nearly 65% of candidate synonym pairs were not suitable for substitution.

4.2 Agglomerative

The candidate synonym pairs generated by the agglomerative method were found in prior work [1] to be unrelated only 6.4% of the time, with a strong showing of 43.6% being "equivalent", and 50% being either "associated" or "super/sub concept".

The good semantic association between candidate synonym pairs did not translate into successful query substitutes. The substitution failed to either match or improve on the initial query 70.5% of the time, performing worse than the query reformulation method in this respect. However the substitute query did improve or at least match the initial query 23.4% of the time. Table 2 summarises the findings.

rating	percentage
initial query most relevant	70.5
query substitution most relevant	11.7
equally relevant	11.7
undecided	5.8

Table 2. Evaluator rating distribution for candidate synonym pairs generated by the agglomerative method. The "neither relevant" choice was not selected by evaluators.

It seems that candidate synonym pairs derived from the agglomerative method suffer enough semantic drift to render the substitution in a query unhelpful. It also indicates that even with semantically-equivalent phrases, substitution may not work, because with 43.6% of candidate synonym pairs confirmed as "equivalent" in the prior work [1], one would expect a similar level of equal relevance in substituting one query for another, but the equal or better relevance in substitution was just under half of the semantic equivalence rate, at 23.4%.

There were some successes however. In two cases the substituted query was rated as returning better results than the original query, with *desk help jobs url.uk* and *IT help desk jobs* being one. The other successful substitution was *error foster*

linux maya node parent ref unknown and *2008 constraint error linux maya parent*, where the shorter, less-specific query was rated as returning more relevant results.

For queries ranked as being equally relevant, some examples include *mac on screenshot* and *a grab on powermac screen*. The next example was *fuel prices* and *petrol price*, showing synonymity between *fuel* and *petrol*.

In general, candidate synonym pairs generated by the agglomerative method were poor query substitutes, despite the substituted terms being established as semantically associated.

4.3 Coselection

The candidate synonym pairs generated by the coselection method had the low rate of 2.07% of candidate synonym pairs being found to be unrelated in the prior work [1], this being the lowest of all three methods. The method would be expected to have the highest relevance due to this, and because it has been shown to filter ambiguity out of otherwise associated pairs [22].

The coselection method results stand in contrast to the other two methods. The number of failed substitutions was very much lower than the other two methods, with only 19% of initial queries giving more relevant results than the substituted queries, compared to 70.5% and 64.8% for the other two methods. Also 71.3% of the substituted queries were equally-relevant or more relevant than the original. 14.2% of substituted queries were better than the initial query, a small improvement on the agglomerative and query reformulation methods. This shows a high level of semantic association between candidate synonyms in each pair. Table 3 summarises the findings.

rating	percentage
initial query most relevant	19.0
query substitution most relevant	14.2
equally relevant	57.1
undecided	9.5

Table 3. Evaluator rating distribution for candidate synonym pairs generated by the coselection method. The "neither relevant" choice was not selected by evaluators.

Some examples of candidate synonym pairs where the substitution was rated more relevant than the original query include a plural, *google video* and *google videos*, and an IS-A relationship, *perstejn* and *castle pernstejn*. Amongst the equally-relevant pairs was *css validator* and *validation w3c*. Another example is the candidate synonym pair *sdl documentation* and *sdl wiki*, which imply that *documentation* and *wiki* are synonymous as well, which would not have been recognised as synonymous pre-web. Another example of entity synonyms is *softimage tutorials* and *tutorials xsi*, where *xsi* and *softimage* have a company-product relationship, and the main product of the company is synonymous with the company name.

An equally-relevant candidate synonym pair was *rarlab* and *winrar*, where the company producing the compression software is synonymous with their product. The query *snow white and the seven dwarfs* returned equally-relevant results to *snow white*, indicating keywords that did not affect the relevance of results. In another example, *cg society* was equally relevant to *cg networks*, where *society* and *networks* were synonymous in the context of computer graphics. This type of synonym would not have been identified pre-web and is one that has been generated from user searches and creation of relationships that extend beyond the traditional form of synonym.

5. DISCUSSION

5.1 Synonyms in query substitution

We now ask why did candidate synonym pairs from two of the discovery methods fail to give good results in the query substitution scenario? Why did the agglomerative method perform so poorly when its discovered synonym pairs had been found to have had the highest rate of equal relevance [1]?

Clearly the question being asked in the prior experiment was quite different. In the prior experiment, the human evaluators were being asked what sort of semantic relationship existed between the two candidate synonyms. There was no interpretation of which was the 'proper' query that the other query had to match, merely whether they were semantically related. So *apple ipad* and *apple* would have been seen to be related, although so too would *apple* and *braeburn*. Likewise misspellings such as *jaguar* and *jagaur* would be seen to be mutually relevant. This paper however has a dominant, 'proper' query against which the substituted query was being judged, and in some cases, the substitution could represent semantic drift. For example, a search on *apple ipad* would not necessarily be better-answered by a search on *apple* alone, especially if the user was looking for information on the iPad specifically. Conversely, a user wanting information on *apple* as a technology provider more generally might find the more specific results from *apple ipad* not suitable for their information need.

Another possible problem with query substitutions is ambiguity of the initial query. While *apple* is obviously related to *apple ipad*, it is also related to *braeburn* in a different context. While it might be suitable to substitute the ambiguous term *apple* for *apple ipad*, it would lead to very poor results for the less-dominant meaning of *apple* represented in *braeburn*. The term *apple* generates generates a top ten set of technology-specific results which has no overlap with the search for *braeburn*. Even substituting longer queries does not always address the ambiguity problem, with for example *apple early mcintosh* yielding a top ten of results solely about the variety of fruit, while *apple early macintosh* yields a top ten of results solely about the history of the desktop computers, so any spelling-based query substitution would fail to impress the user.

The ambiguity problem is most prevalent in the agglomerative discovery method, as it uses transitivity to associate terms that might not be genuinely related [22]. For example, the agglomerative method might observe that *apple ipad* is semantically related to *apple*, and that *apple* is semantically related to *braeburn*, and would wrongly conclude that *apple ipad* is also semantically related to *braeburn*. This is where the coselection discovery method works better, as it only associates two terms when the same user clicks on the same results. A user clicking on pages for *apple ipad* results is unlikely to also click on pages for *braeburn* so the semantic association between them would never be formed. Similarly, the query reformulation method does not generate false semantic associations around ambiguity since the user reformulating the query is continuing the same search session. With both the query reformulation and coselection discovery methods, there is continuity represented in the data which assumes that the user is staying 'on-topic'. In contrast, the agglomerative method does not observe any continuity in sessions and does not detect when the topic has changed or arises from different users making different searches.

So the expectation that even confirmed synonyms can be substituted is very much dependent on the synonym discovery method. The evidence here indicates that the only the coselection method can be relied on for query substitution, and candidate synonym pairs from the coselection method would be successful in 71.3% of cases in generating results of at least equal relevance to that of the substituted query. The agglomerative and query reformulation methods would score significantly worse, as Table 4 attests:

method	original query equal or better	substitute query equal or better
query reformulation	75.6	21.4
agglomerative	82.2	23.4
coselection	76.1	71.3

Table 4. proportions of equal or better results for initial query versus substituted query for the three methods.

This suggests that as far as query substitution is concerned, there is little benefit in substituting in synonyms from any of the three synonym discovery methods, as the results sets are mostly less relevant than just using the original query.

The low relevance of the substituted queries may be in part because in all three discovery methods, a significant proportion of the notionally-equivalent synonyms arose from minor edits such as spelling corrections or pluralisations [1]. However we saw above that some apparent misspellings are not necessarily wrong (at least in the context of search) as *mcintosh* and *macintosh* radically affect the outcome of a search on *apple early*. Even where the spelling does appear to be incorrect, search engines still index pages with the alternative spelling. So for example, the queries *jagaur* and *jaguar* both return the same Wikipedia page[1]. However there are also results returned from the misspelled query *jagaur* that are of low relevance compared to the correctly-spelled *jaguar*, the latter returning results about the brand of car, while *jagaur* returns a number of results where the misspelled string actually appears in the linked page. Clearly the search engine is giving the user the choice to either persist with what appears to be a misspelled query or to correct their query. However if a search engine substituted amended spelling in a query, it could lead to low-relevance results, even if the substitution had been confirmed as a genuine spelling error.

6. CONCLUSION

It seems that the different types of apparent synonyms will greatly affect the suitability of synonym substitution from the three synonym discovery methods assessed. Without knowing what sort of semantic relation is represented in the candidate synonym pair, or if one of the terms is ambiguous, it is difficult to predict the outcome of synonym substitution.

This does lead to a number of future research opportunities, in particular to work out which types of semantic relation will contribute to synonym substitution in web search and which are not helpful. This line of future research will not only be of use for the three synonym discovery methods assessed here, but for all synonyms, as they all fall into various categories such as super- or sub-concept, associated, minor edits, ambiguous, as well as fully-equivalent synonyms.

---

[1] On 15/02/2016, https://en.wikipedia.org/wiki/Jaguar_Cars, using the StartPage search engine.

7. REFERENCES

[1] Michael Antunovic, Glyn Caon, Mark Truran, and Helen Ashman. Discovering semantic associations from web search interactions. In HT '13: Proceedings of the 24th ACM conference on Hypertext and hypermedia. ACM, New York, USA, May 2013.

[2] S Cucerzan and E Brill. Spelling correction as an iterative process that exploits the collective knowledge of web users. In Proceedings of EMNLP 2004, pages 293–300, July 2004.

[3] Mirella Lapata and Frank Keller. An Information Retrieval Approach to Sense Ranking. In Human Language Technology Conference of the North American Chapter of the Association of Computational Linguistics, pages 348–355, 2007.

[4] Kaushik Chakrabarti, Surajit Chaudhuri, Tao Cheng, and Dong Xin. A Framework for Robust Discovery of Entity Synonyms. In Proceedings of the 18th ACM SIGKDD International Conference on Knowledge Discovery and Data Mining, pages 1384–1392, NY, USA, 2012. ACM.

[5] Tao Cheng, Hady W. Lauw, and Stelios Paparizos. Entity Synonyms for Structured Web Search. IEEE Transactions on Knowledge and Data Engineering, 24(10):1862–1875, October 2012.

[6] Hamid Mousavi, Shi Gao, and Carlo Zaniolo. Discovering Attribute and Entity Synonyms for Knowledge Integration and Semantic Web Search. In Proceedings of the 3rd International Workshop on Semantic Search Over the Web, pages 2:1–2:4, NY, USA, 2013. ACM.

[7] Surajit Chaudhuri, Venkatesh Ganti, and Dong Xin. Exploiting web search to generate synonyms for entities. WWW, pages 151–160, 2009.

[8] Xing Wei. Context sensitive synonym discovery for web search queries. CIKM'09, January 2009.

[9] Xing Wei, Fuchun Peng, Huishin Tseng, Yumao Lu, Xuerui Wang, and Benoit Dumoulin. Search with Synonyms: Problems and Solutions. In Proceedings of the 23rd International Conference on Computational Linguistics: Posters, pages 1318–1326, Stroudsburg, PA, USA, 2010. Association for Computational Linguistics.

[10] Yanen Li, Bo-June Paul Hsu, and ChengXiang Zhai. Unsupervised identification of synonymous query intent templates for attribute intents. In Proceedings of the 22nd ACM international conference on information & knowledge management, pages 2029–2038, NY, USA, 2013. ACM.

[11] Rosie Jones, Benjamin Rey, Omid Madani, and Wiley Greiner. Generating query substitutions. In WWW '06: Proceedings of the 15th international conference on World Wide Web. ACM, May 2006.

[12] Jiafeng Guo, Gu Xu, Xueqi Cheng, and Hang Li. Named Entity Recognition in Query. In Proceedings of the 32Nd International ACM SIGIR Conference on Research and Development in Information Retrieval, pages 267–274, NY, USA, 2009. ACM.

[13] Yan Chen and Yan-Qing Zhang. A Query Substitution-Search Result Refinement Approach for Long Query Web Searches. In Proceedings of the 2009 IEEE/WIC/ACM International Joint Conference on Web Intelligence and Intelligent Agent Technology - Volume 01, pages 245–251, Washington, DC, USA, 2009. IEEE Computer Society.

[14] Bernard J Jansen, Amanda Spink, Judy Bateman, and Tefko Saracevic. Real Life Information Retrieval: A Study of User Queries on the Web. ACM SIGIR Forum, 32(1):5–17, April 1998.

[15] I Ruthven. Re-examining the potential effectiveness of interactive query expansion. In Reexamining the potential effectiveness of interactive query expansion, pages 213–220, 2003.

[16] Ghassan Kanaan, R Al-Shalabi, Sameh Ghwanmeh, and B Bani-Ismail. Interactive and automatic query expansion: A comparative study with an application on Arabic. Amer. J. Appl. Sciences, 5(11):1433–1436, 2008.

[17] Claudio Carpineto and Giovanni Romano. A Survey of Automatic Query Expansion in Information Retrieval. ACM Computing Surveys, 44(1):1–50, January 2012.

[18] W S Wong, R W P Luk, H V Leong, K S Ho, and D L Lee. Re-examining the Effects of Adding Relevance Information in a Relevance Feedback Environment. Inf. Process. Manage., 44(3):1086–1116, May 2008.

[19] Hang Cui, Ji-Rong Wen, Jian-Yun Nie, and Wei-Ying Ma. Probabilistic query expansion using query logs. In WWW '02: Proceedings of the 11th international conference on World Wide Web. ACM, May 2002.

[20] Ji-Rong Wen, Jian-Yun Nie, and Hong-Jiang Zhang. Clustering User Queries of a Search Engine. In Proceedings of the 10th International Conference on World Wide Web, pages 162–168, NY, USA, 2001. ACM.

[21] Yue Lu, Hui Fang, and ChengXiang Zhai. An Empirical Study of Gene Synonym Query Expansion in Biomedical Information Retrieval. Inf. Retr., 12(1):51–68, February 2009.

[22] Helen Ashman, Michael Antunovic, Satit Chaprasit, Gavin Smith, and Mark Truran. Implicit association via crowd-sourced coselection. In HT '11: Proceedings of the 22nd ACM conference on Hypertext and hypermedia. ACM, June 2011.

[23] Joseph H Goldberg, Mark J Stimson, Marion Lewenstein, Neil Scott, and Anna M Wichansky. Eye Tracking in Web Search Tasks: Design Implications. In Proceedings of the 2002 Symposium on Eye Tracking Research and Applications, pages 51–58, NY, USA, 2002. ACM.

[24] Ryen W White and Dan Morris. Investigating the Querying and Browsing Behavior of Advanced Search Engine Users. In Proceedings of the 30th Annual International ACM SIGIR Conference on Research and Development in Information Retrieval, pages 255–262, NY, USA, 2007. ACM.

[25] Joseph L Fleiss and Jacob Cohen. The equivalence of weighted kappa and the intraclass correlation coefficient as measures of reliability. Educational and psychological measurement, 1973.

Storyspace 3

Mark Bernstein
Eastgate Systems, Inc.
134 Main Street
Watertown MA 02472 USA
+1 (617) 924-0044
bernstein@eastgate.com

ABSTRACT
Storyspace was introduced in one of the first papers presented at the first ACM Workshop of Hypertext, and gave rise to a number of significant hypertexts, both fiction and nonfiction. A new implementation of Storyspace for contemporary computing environments is clearly desirable. This has been undertaken, with modest resources and in a short time frame. A number of surprising new facilities, many of them originally proposed in contrast or opposition to Storyspace, can be supported without altering or complicating the underlying Storyspace node and link model.

Keywords
Storyspace, hypertext, hypermedia, literature, fiction, education, design, implementation, support, history of computing, maps, links.

1.INTRODUCTION
We seldom discuss the design and implementation of hypertext systems anymore. This was once the core concern of this conference, but few new systems have a been described in these Proceedings in recent years [25][2][27].

Over time, the constraints and design forces on hypertext systems have changed. Yet *afternoon* is still the same, and we still want to read *afternoon* [29]. Our interests are not those of the bibliographer, the book collector, or the media archaeologist: we simply want to read about (or teach our students about) the fellow who wants to say that he may have seen his son die this morning. We prefer convenience, but are willing to take a certain amount of trouble. We prefer economy, but are willing accept a measure of expense. We want the experience to conform to the author's expectation (intention here is a suspect quality), but of course we need not mimic every incidental detail, shortcut and flaw.

Though Storyspace was perhaps the smallest of the first-generation hypertext systems, its implementation demanded substantial resources. Development was funded in part by a grant from the Markle Foundation, with support from Broderbund software, the University of North Carolina, Jackson (Michigan) Community College, as well as the Roger Schank's Artificial Intelligence lab at Yale, where Storyspace authors Michael Joyce and Jay David Bolter were visiting fellows in successive years. Writing of Storyspace 1, like other first-generation hypertext systems, was a substantial undertaking [3].

2.STORYSPACE
Resources on this scale are not readily available for developing hypertext systems today. This has long been the case; Janet Murray once remarked that Storyspace's shortcomings reflected the dearth of resources available to humanities computing. More recently, novelist Paul La Farge attributed the failure of previous efforts to create sustained narrative in hypertext fiction to Storyspace's impoverished visual design[40].

Still, we have learned a great deal about hypertext systems since 1987. Software development tools and methodologies have advanced substantially. What had once required many hands and many dollars had now to be reproduced as a part-time summer project by a single hand.

Storyspace 1 [7] [28] [30] is a stand-alone, monolithic hypertext writing and reading environment, one chiefly intended for reading and writing hypertext narrative. From the start, it offered a versatile visual map of node-link hypertexts organized with a hierarchical backbone, the capability of multiple perspectives and views, and directional dynamic links whose behavior could depend on the reader's trajectory through the hypertext. Storyspace hypertexts were widely reviewed, admired and reviled, and many continue to be taught and studied[9].

Over the years, Storyspace has been reimplemented for new computing environments. Storyspace 1 was written, in Pascal, for Macintosh System 5. Reimplementations by this author include Storyspace for Windows (in C), Storyspace 2 (in C++ for Metrowerks PowerPlant and OS X), and now Storyspace 3 (in Objective C++ for the Macintosh Cocoa framework using the Hereford foundation from Tinderbox).

3.IMPLEMENTATION
New hypertext systems are pleasant and interesting tools for study and research. Because they are new, they are small: changes can be made and tested quickly. Because they are small, changes have limited scope. Rapid iteration permits freer experimentation. Moreover, even where resources are ample, the temporal constraints of contemporary research impose important limitations on experiments that involve mature systems. The timescales of the summer internship, the master's thesis, and of the doctoral

dissertation impose stern and unyielding restrictions. The more time we spend waiting for the compiler, the less time we have for creative research.

Mature hypertext systems like Storyspace present a significant challenge to agile research because everything, naturally, depends on the hypertext and its nodes.

3.1. Recompiling The World

Three of the oldest classes in Storyspace 2 – the first object-oriented implementation – are Hypertext, Link, and Node. Over time, these classes naturally acquired new functionality and responsibilities. As Storyspace and its foundation gained new facilities, moreover, almost all these facilities relied on Node and Hypertext. A text pane obtains the text it is to view from the Node, the Map View obtains the title of each item from its Node, the pasteboard manager copies a representation of the Node to the clipboard when the user selects Copy from the Edit menu. Everyone needs to use Node, and Node needs to provide convenience functions to everyone.

As a result, changes to the interface of Node or Hypertext require recompiling everything else. This is a small penalty for a small system, but over time the penalty grows. Testing such large and monolithic classes is difficult, development slows, and the prospect of improving core classes grows unpleasant. This unpleasantness may sometimes be tolerable in an industrial environment, but it is inimical to experimentation. Besides, we have better uses for graduate students than waiting for the compiler.

The classic prescription for large and monolithic objects, of course, is to decompose them into a cluster of small objects, each with a single responsibility [34]. Unfortunately, such decompositions proved difficult to find – and because every step along the way again requires recompiling the world, the work is exceedingly slow and costly. The classic refactoring prescriptions – encapsulating instance variables, splitting the object along implementation seams, sprouting classes – are frustrated by the regularity and flexibility of the underlying attribute-value store. Each step in each refactoring is likely to require recompiling everything.

To restore the system's malleability, we introduced a family of new classes, NodeFacades and HypertextFacades, each of which owns only a single instance variable – the underlying Node or Hypertext. These facades provide small and focused slices of functionality; for example, NodeLinks provides access to links associated with a specific node, NodeIndexer provides an API to support tf-idf similarity searches, and NodeDeleter provides access to methods for deleting Nodes. Initially, these classes are simple facades, forwarding calls to Node or Hypertext. Client classes can now use one or more facades in place of using Hypertext or Node, and so the dependency graph is gradually decoupled. Because the Facade objects simply wrap a pointer, they can be created and thrown away at will. No changes need to be made to Node or Hypertext, and so this work can proceed quickly.

In time, some methods in the underlying classes were seldom or never used without the intermediacy of the Facade. Here, functionality could be refactored from the underlying class to the Facade, and the underlying class can now use the Facade. This refactoring is invariant with respect to the underlying class's interface, and so it once again avoids recompilation. The progressive refactoring can continue until the base classes are

extensively hollowed out until they serve as Value Objects with a plethora of trivial helper methods.

I mention this refactoring because it is likely to impact any compiled hypertext system with significant age or complexity. It bears some resemblance to familiar idioms – pImpl, proxy, interface object – but it seems to have been seldom discussed in the monograph literature[23][31][22][24] and might prove broadly useful in hypertext research.

4. GUARD FIELDS

4.1. The Storyspace Guard Field

The distinctive feature of Storyspace is its dynamic link, a unidirectional link that can be activated or deactivated by a *guard field*. The guard field is a simply boolean expression whose terms may include the word clicked or the names of previously-visited notes enclosed in quotation marks. The guard field

$$("A" \& (!"B")) \mid Anne$$

is satisfied if the reader has read the note "A" but not the note "B", or if the reader has clicked on the word "Anne". Guard fields proved invaluable for breaking cycles[5], a central anxiety of early hypertext research [18][11].

The original design of guard fields proved effective in terms of hypertext rhetoric was well of engineering. The notation is concise, a consideration that mattered greatly when storage and memory alike amounted to a few hundred kilobytes. The original formulation lends itself readily to parsing by recursive descent; fast and reliable guard field interpreters were never a source of concern. The underlying mechanism, which simply disables unwanted links, is easy for new writers to understand.

Yet the original formulation was not without disadvantages. The syntax was always hard to teach. The rest of Storyspace could be explained in one class session – a session in which, in the early years, many students had their first encounter with a computer – but guard fields needed a second session to themselves. While isolated guard fields are easy enough to test, moreover, the entire hypertext network becomes, with guard fields, a distributed program describing an elaborate finite state machine. The lack of visualization and debugging tools, and the distribution of the implicit state machine over thousands of links, makes editing a challenge; we know the conditions that the author imposed for this particular link, but may have no idea why those conditions were desirable or how following this link changes the state of other links. Some reasonable constraints – for example, that a link may be followed *n* times but not more – are difficult or impossible to express with guard fields. Other constraints that can be concisely stated in the story domain – *you cannot end Act I without establishing that there's a gun in the drawer* – must be enforced by multiple guard fields on many different links, and while these may not be particularly difficult for experienced writers to compose, understanding their purpose and intent can be a challenge to editors and critics who are asked to deduce the domain constraint from this distributed array of predicates.

4.2. Extending The Guard Field

The terseness of the original notation, so valuable in an era when memory capacity was scarce, has always baffled novices. Simple syntactic sugar can greatly clarify the notation:

Old: $("A" \& (!"B")) \mid Anne$

New: $(visited(A) \& unvisited(B)) \mid clicked(Anne)$

The new notation is less esoteric and more readable. We can now cope with notes that have the same name; the guard field

visited(/Biographies/Washington)

is satisfied only after visiting the note named "Washington" that is located in the container, "Biographies." A common guard field

unvisited()

is satisfied when the link's destination has not previously been visited in this reading.

Since Storyspace 3 is built on the attribute-value store developed to support Tinderbox, we may easily extend guard fields to refer to generalized predicates. For example, if we use the note /Amy to keep track of the current state of the character named "Amy", then the guard field

$Cash(/Amy)>100

is satisfied if Amy has plenty of money, and the guard field

$Location(/Amy)!="Paris"

is satisfied if Amy is in London or Athens.

Storyspace 3 supports traditional guard field syntax as well by wrapping it in a new boolean function:

guard(*legacy guard-expression*)

Adding the wrapper when importing legacy documents is trivial, and in this way existing Storyspace hypertexts continue to operate as they always have while writers are offered a variety of new notational opportunities.

5. ASSERTIONS AND REQUIREMENTS

The Storyspace tradition of hypertext fiction has conducted a long dialogue with the separate tradition of instrumental *interactive fiction* growing originally from Crowther and Woods' *Adventure* [16] [35] [37]. As a rule, interactive fictions use links to vary what takes place in the narrative world, while hyperfiction more frequently uses links to vary the way underlying events are described: interactive fiction generally focuses on *story* while hyperfiction has predominantly focused on *plot* [10]. Storyspace accepts (and helped create) this framing in its use of guard fields that enable or disable individual links, thus determining whether a node or *writing space* can be seen now, or if access to it must be deferred. Exceptions to these inclinations abound, but the differing emphases on plot and story, *suzjet* and *fabula*, cannot be mistaken.

It is interesting to note in passing that the concerns of adaptive hypertext [20] are more closely allied with those of interactive fiction than with hyperfiction. In interactiuve fiction, we test whether the reader has acquired the Golden Key to decide whether or not they may pass to the second level of the adventure; in adaptive hypertext, we test whether the student has mastered arrays before they can proceed to study stacks and queues. In each case, we want to preclude access to a lexia until specified preconditions have been satisfied.

In conventional Storyspace hypertexts these preconditions must be checked on every link to the restricted writing space. This is certainly possible, but it is not always convenient, and the requirement is easy to overlook when revising the hypertext. Storyspace 3 augments guard fields with an additional predicate, **$Requirements**, for each writing space. If a note has requirements, they must be met before any incoming link can be traversed. Typical requirements are very much like guard fields: the requirement

unvisited(this)

asserts that this writing space can only appear once in any reading. We may also, as in guard fields, interrogate state variables the writer has chosen to use. A note with the requirement

$Cash(/Amy)>100 | $Cash(/May)>100

can be read if Amy or May have plenty of money.

Note that if a writing space has no requirements, link behavior is unchanged from Storyspace 1. Since no writing spaces created with Storyspace 1 have any requirements, Storyspace 3 performs them without change and without a separate legacy or compatibility mode.

When a link is successfully traversed, Storyspace 3 records that the note has been visited and increments the note's counter, **$Visits.** In addition, the note may have an $OnVisit action that asserts changes to the document state. For example, the action

$Cash(/Amy)=$Cash(/Amy)-50

reduces Amy's cash balance, and

$Score(/ArrayQuiz)=$Score(/ArrayQuiz)+1

gives the student-reader credit for a correct answer.

6. EAGER LINKS

A number of early hypertext formalisms envisioned a multi-pane or multi-window collage of panes in which specified transitions might occurs as soon as their preconditions were met[42]. Tim Oren's GUIDES, for example, embodied animated characters who could, through gesture or expression, indicate willingness to discuss a topic raised in the text [39], and the generalization of this formalism to encompass arguments among the guides themselves was readily foreseen. "Conversations With Friends" [4] distinguishes between *eager* links, which would lead a character to speak up immediately when their preconditions were satisfied, and *timid* links, which would simply lead the character to seek attention.

Storyspace 3 extends the $Requirements mechanism by providing *shark* links. If a note's requirements are satisfied, Storyspace additionally checks to see if any shark links lead away from the note. If an outbound shark link exists and if it can be followed – if its guard field and its destination's $Requirements are satisfied – then the shark link is followed immediately.

Just as $Requirements simplify guard fields by allowing the writer to refactor terms shared by all a note's inbound links, shark links provide convenient exception handling. Suppose that a character is to board a steamship, and that it is necessary that we actually see them purchasing a ticket. If they already have purchased a ticket, they may proceed on board. If the reader's trajectory has no yet encompassed a scene in which the character obtains a ticket, a shark link may interpolate here a trip to the ticket office. The same effect could be obtained with multiple guarded links, but at the cost of added complexity.

7. SCULPTURAL HYPERTEXT

Sculptural hypertext [36][6] was originally proposed as a radical, exotic alternative to familiar note-and-link hypertext. Storyspace 3 incorporates a flexible sculptural hypertext mechanism within the familiar formalism of Storyspace.

Storyspace hypertexts offer both text links – links anchored to text spans – and *plain links,* which are notionally anchored to the writing space as a whole. Plain links for each note are kept in an ordered list. If a reader clicks on a word not otherwise linked, or if she presses the [Return] key, Storyspace follows the highest-priority plain link which has a satisfied guard field. Only if there are no satisfied plain links does Storyspace require an explicit selection.

In Storyspace 3, we can go even further. If the reader has not clicked on a text link, and if no basic links are found, we next examine the value of the *current deck,* a list of string tokens. If the current deck is empty (as it is in all Storyspace 1 documents), Storyspace 3 waits for an explicit selection. If the current deck is not empty, however, Storyspace 3 gathers a pool of all notes for which

- the note's $Deck has a term in common with the *current deck*

- the note's $Requirements are satisfied.

- the note is unvisited or, if no eligible note is unvisited, the note has not been visited more than any other eligible note.

If more than one such note is found, one note is chosen at random from the eligible set, and that note becomes the destination.

Though sculptural hypertext has not yet proven to be of great interest to hypertext research, it has become a staple of literary games – particularly through Failbetter's *Fallen London* [1] and more broadly through narrativist games like Morningstar's *Fiasco* or Czege's *My Life With Master* (see [33]).

8. GENERALIZED STRETCHTEXT

When hypertext systems were more often discussed and their design more energetically debated, stretchtext – epitomized by Peter J. Brown's Guide [13] – was generally viewed as inherently in opposition to node-link hypertext like Storyspace. Despite the enthusiasm in early hypertext research for formalism [26], the formal properties of complex stretchtext networks were never thoroughly elucidated, and a late effort to reconcile stretchtext with more familiar paradigms [10] attracted scant notice.

After a long quiescence, however, interest in stretchtext has increased among the vernacular literary games and IF communities[21]. *Pry,* a novella by Danny Cannizzaro and Samantha Gorman, is a stretchtext fiction that reflects concepts originally proposed in Fluid[43], and a pattern library of Stretchtext idioms found in TWINE fiction is in preparation [14].

Though Storyspace 3 strives to avoid modes, combining all its extensions in a single formalism, one modality cannot be avoided. The Storyspace reader clicks to follow links, but the writer and editor must be allowed to click to select and revise text. Storyspace 3 leverages this long-extant and seemingly-inescapable modal behavior to support generalized stretchtext through macro expansion.

When writing, we may insert placeholders that can be interpreted by the performance engine. For example, the placeholder

^include(/sayings/Cicero)

will be replaced, in the reader's view, by the text of the note Cicero in the container "sayings". Similarly,

^replace(anchor,note,*action*)

will embed a link with the specified anchor, If the link is clicked, the anchor text will be replaced by the contents of the designated

note, and an optional action may be performed in order to record a change of state.

9.REPRESENTATION
9.1.Document Representation
The central issue confronting the original Storyspace document format was speed of loading and saving documents. Storyspace originally ran on 6mHz 68000 processors equipped with a slow 800K floppy disk drive. Data transfer alone required most of the resources of the computer, and hence it was vital that additional processing be minimized. Even then, performance was barely adequate; Stuart Moulthrop's *Victory Garden* [38], a hypertext of 986 lexia, 2804 links, and 96,000 words, originally required five minutes to load[1]. In addition, the limit imposed by 800K disk capacity place a premium on compactness.

These design forces led Storyspace 1 to adopt a file format which was little more than a flattened representation of structs as they appeared in memory. These were segregated into file chapters, beginning with an introductory header struct that listed offsets to each chapter – the collection of node descriptors, the collection of link descriptors, the text heap, and so forth. Pointers were replaced by fixed element IDs but little additional processing was required in order to read or write the document file.

This file representation proved satisfactory for many years, and continues to be supported. Its weakness, however, lay in its fragility. If a file was damaged by software error or media defect, recovery was not much easier than manually reconstructing the memory image of the running program. In particular, if any of the offsets recorded in the header were incorrect, the entire file would be rendered unreadable.[7]

The passage of time and operation of Moore's Law transformed the design forces that impact the document's external representation. Processors are orders of magnitude faster, and even laptop and tablet computers make additional processors available for compute-bound tasks. We no longer labor to squeeze a novel onto a floppy disk when even a mobile phone can easily store a library of tens of thousands of books. Storyspace 3 thus follows Tinderbox in adopting Tinderbox's XML representation for its files[8]. XML is not notably compact – *Victory Garden,* for example, grows from 800K to 40 Mb – but this file size (and its 2s load time) are negligible concerns.

9.2.Internal Representation
Performance concerns also mandated that Storyspace 1 represent its nodes and links as static frames with fixed offsets so that access to any facet of any node required no more than simple pointer arithmetic. In consequence, a number of Storyspace facilities were constrained to use fixed buffers; note titles, for example, were originally limited to 32 bytes. (In addition to the constraints imposed by performance, it should be kept in mind that no general-purpose language besides LISP at that time possessed what would today be regarded as even a rudimentary string library.)

In addition, implicit considerations of the personal computing environment led to plausible design assumptions that, with the

---

[1] These performance concerns were by no means unique to Storyspace. Students using Intermedia for their coursework habitually brought a book to the computer lab, the better to pass the delays imposed by database latency[41].

passage of time, became obsolete and even risible. The Macintosh screen had a fixed height of 342 pixels, sufficient to display perhaps 30 lines of rendered type in a space of just under five inches (12cm). Scrolling a few screenfuls of text was a reasonable compromise, though some early writers preferred to avoid scrolling entirely, but the notionally-infinite plane in which all Macintosh images were rendered was limited in practice to 32,767 pixels. That amounted to nearly 100 screens of text, which seemed both amply in principle and approaching the capacity of contemporary scroll bars to control. In time, both screens and documents became larger; ultimately, the size of the graphic plane became a real constraint on the Storyspace outline view, which could only display a few thousand writing spaces. This was of little concern, of course, when 1000-node hypertexts were at the outer bound of feasibility, but the constraint persisted into the 21st century. Here, too, a reimplementation removes difficulties that the quirks of early systems arbitrarily imposed.

Modern processors and programming environments present Storyspace with far different constraints. Hypertext nodes are represented as attribute-value stores with prototype inheritance. Almost no caching or performance optimization is required to obtain adequate performance.

10. CONCLUSION

A single summer's development campaign by a single developer – a developer who could not in this time be relieved of other commitments – sufficed to reimplement Storyspace for OS X *El Capitan*. Much has been written about preservation and archeology of digital literature (see [32] [17]), and this effort concretely improves the accessibility of a number of hypertexts about which much has been written. Additional benefits of the reimplementation include greatly improved typography and enactment and improved accessibility for readers with visual or motor impairment.

A variety of new facilities have been added to Storyspace, providing support for interactive fiction, sculptural hypertext, and generalized stretchtext without introducing additional operating modes or affecting the simplicity of the underlying link model [19].

The success of a writing tool depends on the success of the work written with its aid. That success was clear, in the end, for the original Storyspace. Though this is the 27th ACM Hypertext Conference, we arguably write fewer significant hypertexts today than we wrote at the time of the tenth. "Where again," I might ask, "are the hypertexts?" Hypertext broadly, and hypertext fiction specifically, were for some years the target of a reaction against the commercial internet[15], against corporate publishing [12], or against postmodernism. Those battles have been lost and won: perhaps it is time we once more picked up our virtual pens.

11. ACKNOWLEDGMENTS

I am grateful to many correspondents for assistance on topics addressed in this paper, including Jay David Bolter, Michael Joyce, Matt Kirschenbaum, George P. Landow, Stacey Mason, Janet Murray, and Emily Short. Brent Simmons and Lee Hasiuk provided welcome technical advice during implementation. Mark Anderson provided many useful corrections and suggestions for *Getting Started With Hypertext Narrative,* on which this paper is largely based.

12. REFERENCES

[1] Alexis Kennedy, E. "Fallen London".

[2] Atzenbeck, C., Bernstein, M., Al-Shafey, M. A., and Mason, S. 2013. "TouchStory: Combining Hyperfiction and Multitouch Proceedings of the 24th ACM Conference on Hypertext and Social Media". *HT '13*. 189-195.

[3] Barret, B. 2012 *Memory Machines: the evolution of hypertext*. Anthem Press.

[4] Bernstein, M. 1995 *Conversations With Friends: Hypertexts With Characters*. In Hypermedia Design, S. Fraïse, F. Garzotto, T. Isakowitz, J. Nanard, and M. Nanard, eds. Springer.

[5] Bernstein, M. 1998. "Patterns of Hypertext". *Hypertext '98*. 21-29.

[6] Bernstein, M. 2001. "Card Shark and Thespis: exotic tools for hypertext narrative". *Hypertext 2001: Proceedings of the 12th ACM Conference on Hypertext and Hypermedia*. 41-50.

[7] Bernstein, M. 2002. "Storyspace 1". *Proceedings of the 13th ACM Hypertext Conference*. 172-181.

[8] Bernstein, M. 2003. "Collage, composites, construction". *Proceedings of the fourteenth ACM conference on Hypertext and hypermedia*. 122-123.

[9] Bernstein, M. 2010. "Criticism". *Proceedings of the 21st ACM conference on Hypertext and hypermedia*. 235-244.

[10] Bernstein, M. 2009. "On Hypertext Narrative". *ACM Hypertext 2009*.

[11] Bernstein, M., Joyce, M., and Levine, D. B. 1992. "Contours of Constructive Hypertext". *European Conference on Hypermedia Technology*. 161.

[12] Birkerts, S. 1994 *The Gutenberg Elegies*. Faber and Faber.

[13] Brown, P. 1991. "Higher Level Hypertext Facilities: Procedures With Arguments". *Hypermedia*. 3, 2, 91-100.

[14] Dias, B. 2016. "A Garden of Devices in Dynamic Prose". *in preparation*.

[15] Carr, N. G. 2010 *The shallows : what the Internet is doing to our brains*. W.W. Norton.

[16] Crowther, W. and Woods, D. 1976. "Adventure".

[17] Grigar, D. and Moulthrop, S. A. "Pathfinders".

[18] DeYoung, L. 1990. "Linking Considered Harmful". *ECHT'90 - Hypertext: Concepts, Systems and Applications*. 238-249.

[19] E. James Whitehead, J. 2002. "Uniform Comparison of Data Models Using Containment Modeling". *Hypertext '02*. 182-191.

[20] E. Knutov, P. De Bra, and Pechenizkiy, M. 2009. "AH 12 years later: a comprehensive survey of adaptive hypermedia methods and techniques". *New Review of Hypermedia and Multimedia*. 15, 5-38.

[21] Short, E. 2016. "Set, check, or gate? A problem in personality stats".

[22] Feathers, M. C. 2005 *Working effectively with legacy code*. Prentice Hall Professional Technical Reference.

[23] Fowler, M. 1999 *Refactoring*. Addison-Wesley.

[24] Freeman, S. and Pryce, N. 2010 *Growing object-oriented software, guided by tests*. Addison Wesley.

[25] Gaffney, C., Conlan, O., and Wade, V. 2014. "The AMAS Authoring Tool 2.0: A UX Evaluation Proceedings of the 25th ACM Conference on Hypertext and Social Media". *HT '14*. 224-230.

[26] Halasz, F. and Schwartz, M. 1994. "The Dexter Hypertext Reference Model". *Communications of the ACM*. 37, 2, 30-39.

[27] Hargood, C., Davies, R., Millard, D. E., Taylor, M. R., and Brooker, S. 2012. "Exploring (the Poetics of) Strange (and Fractal) Hypertexts Proceedings of the 23rd ACM

Conference on Hypertext and Social Media". *HT '12*. 181-186.

[28] Bolter, J. D. and Joyce, M. 1987. "Hypertext and Creative Writing". *Hypertext '87*. 41-50.

[29] Joyce, M. 1990. "afternoon, a story".

[30] Joyce, M. 1988. "Siren Shapes: Exploratory and Constructive Hypertext". *Academic Computing*. 11 ff.

[31] Kerievsky, J. 2005 *Refactoring to patterns*. Addison-Wesley.

[32] Kirschenbaum, M. G. 2008 *Mechanisms : new media and the forensic imagination*. MIT Press.

[33] Bernstein, M. 2016 *Getting Started With Hypertext Narrative*. Eastgate Systems, Inc.

[34] Martin, R. C. 2009 *Clean code : a handbook of agile software craftsmanship*. Prentice Hall.

[35] Merrit Kopas, E. 2015 *Videogames For Humans*. Instar Books.

[36] Millard, D. E., Hargood, C., Jewell, M. O., and Weal, M. J. 2013. "Canyons, Deltas and Plains: Towards a Unified Sculptural Model of Location-based Hypertext Proceedings of the 24th ACM Conference on Hypertext and Social Media". *HT '13*. 109-118.

[37] Montfort, N. 2003 *Twisty little passages : an approach to interactive fiction*. MIT Press.

[38] Moulthrop, S. 1991 *Victory Garden*. Eastgate Systems, Inc.

[39] Oren, T., Solomon, G., Kreitman, K., and Don, A. 1990 *Guides: Characterizing the Interface*. In The Art of Human Computer Interface Design, B. Laurel, ed. Addison Wesley.

[40] Farge, P. L. 2008. "Luminous Airplanes".

[41] Smith, K. E. and Zdonik, S. B. 1987. "Intermedia: A case Study of the Differences Between Relational and Object-Oriented Database Systems". *OOPSLA 87*. 22(12), 12, 452-165.

[42] Stotts, P. D. and Furuta, R. 1989. "Petri-net based hypertext: Document structure with browsing semantics". *ACM Transactions on Office Information Systems*. 7, 1, 3-29.

[43] Zellweger, P. T., Mangen, A., and Newman, P. 2002. "Reading and Writing Fluid Hypertexts". *Hypertext 2002*. 45-54.

Classical Hypermedia Virtues on the Web with Webstrates

Niels Olof Bouvin
Department of Computer Science
Aarhus University, Denmark
bouvin@cs.au.dk

Clemens Nylandsted Klokmose
Center for Advanced Visualization & Interaction
Aarhus University, Denmark
clemens@cavi.au.dk

ABSTRACT

We show and analyze herein how Webstrates can augment the Web from a classical hypermedia perspective. Webstrates turns the DOM of Web pages into persistent and collaborative objects. We demonstrate how this can be applied to realize bidirectional links, shared collaborative annotations, and in-browser authorship and development.

Categories and Subject Descriptors

H.4.5 [**Hypertext/Hypermedia**]: Architectures

Keywords

Web; hypermedia; collaboration; dynamic documents

Introduction

The vision of hypermedia was to create a richly intertwingled world of words, ideas, and concepts; an all-encompassing collection of documents and works readily available for the information worker to peruse, structure, correlate, add to, and amend using powerful tools and abstractions [15, 23, 36].

What we have ended up with is both less and far more. The modern Web *is* all-encompassing in scope, and available to a high and growing percentage of the world's population. On the Web, we find incredibly rich collections of human knowledge, vast social networks connecting billions, commercial as well as public ventures that have upended business as usual, and communities, small and large, around any topic you might care to mention. The Web has shaped the way software is being built, deployed, and used. A modern developer is faced with a bewilderingly rich range of choices in technologies, platforms, frameworks, and concepts.

Yet all is not as well as it might be. The Web still does not offer the level of hypermedia structuring mechanisms once considered standard for a hypermedia system (e.g., bidirectional links). The original vision of the Web [10] included the notion of a collaborative inter-creative space where authorship and consumption were equal. While that can be

HT '16, July 10-13, 2016, Halifax, NS, Canada

© 2016 ACM. ISBN 978-1-4503-4247-6/16/07...$15.00

DOI: http://dx.doi.org/10.1145/2914586.2914622

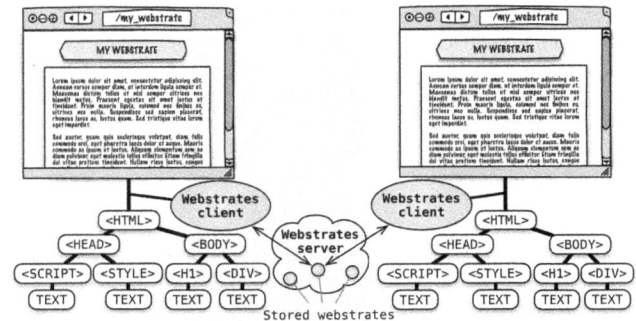

Figure 1: Webstrates persist and synchronize through operational transformations any changes to the Document Object Model of pages, called Webstrates, served from the Webstrates server to all clients of the same webstrate (from [32]).

found in the form of, e.g., wikis and Web-based productivity suites such as Google Docs, these are usually either limited in functionality, or closed proprietary platforms.

Earlier attempts have been made to rectify some of the shortcomings of the Web, such as augmenting the hypermedia functionality available [13]. Invariantly, these attempts have not been successful in gaining widespread use.

The system Webstrates [32] demonstrate how a relatively simple change to the workings of the Web can provide users with a collaborative and, crucially, user extensible platform for the creation, editing, and structuring of documents *and* applications, limited only by the modern Web browser.

Webstrates makes the Document Object Model (DOM), which is the runtime in-memory representation of Web pages, a persisted and collaborative object. Client-side changes to the DOM are persisted to the server and synchronized to all other clients of the same page using operational transform [22] (Figure 1). Webstrates is presented as a prototype realization of a software vision, *shareable dynamic media*, that builds upon Alan Kay's seminal software vision but where collaboration among users and distribution across heterogeneous devices are emphasized. The authors demonstrate in [32] from a UI systems perspective how Webstrates can enable software malleability and personalization, collaboration with personalized interfaces, remote user interface extension at run-time, and orchestration of complex distributed and collaborative user interactions.

We review herein historical hypermedia, and based on this, analyze the modern Web, and present examples of how the extension to the Web brought forth by Webstrates can realize principles from classical hypermedia on the Web.

Classical Hypermedia Systems

Hypermedia as a discipline is quite old. We describe in this section select aspects of the systems that predate the Web, which has become largely lost, and some of which we would like to see reintroduced into common usage.

The original vision for hypermedia [15] had the knowledge worker working alone, reading, annotating, and linking documents, and occasionally sharing documents and trails with others, or purchasing trails pre-authored by *trail blazers*. As hypermedia moved from theoretical construct to actuality, Engelbart and his lab [24] led the way in demonstrating NLS/Augment, that, among many other groundbreaking achievements, featured collaborative authoring and linking of structured documents across multiple remote computers.

Much later, systems such as Intermedia [34] would demonstrate the possiblities of a collaborative hypermedia system that supported a rich set of media types and associated editors, as well as disjunct "webs" of hypermedia structures over a corpus of documents. Separating documents and hypermedia structures became a cornerstone of the Dexter model [30], and the foundations of open hypermedia, inspired in part by the observation of Meyrowitz [35] that lack of widespread hypermedia adoption could be attributed to the closed nature of the systems—all required their own environments and editors, rather than those applications commonly used. The open hypermedia community addressed this through a class of hypermedia systems [9, 18, 25, 27] that could almost seamlessly integrate with existing tools, and by doing so, allowed their users to link documents across third-party applications.

While the various open hypermedia initiatives showed that hypermedia integration was viable, the approach was both labour-intensive (making third-party applications work with a hypermedia service is hard) and fragile (a new version of an applications could break functionality; links, etc., required the hypermedia service to be present). One way to ensure robustness is to have control over editors as well as hypermedia functionality, and while this, by definition, has been the case for all monolithic hypermedia systems, one of the more remarkable was NoteCards [31]. NoteCards is a significant hypermedia system, not least because it was built in the, for the time highly advanced, InterLisp software development environment, which enabled its developers at Xerox PARC to easily extend it. Thus, NoteCards became a testbed for many different structuring mechanisms, such as graphical structure browsers, guided tours, and tabletops [40]. Having a fertile and highly interactive development platform, where developers and researchers could easily extend functionality, made this possible. A contemporaneous system was Hyper-Card [26], and if NoteCards represents one of the cutting edge research systems of its day, then HyperCard was the everyman hypermedia authoring tool available to all owners of Mac computers. While neither its hypermedia functionality nor its flexibility was as rich as NoteCards, it provided its users with an easily accessible development model, which made the creation of a plethora of HyperCard stacks possible. HyperCard demonstrated that if tools are available and easily used, then users can and will become creators and developers, not only of hypertexts, but of interactive programs.

The Web as Hypermedia

Whether the Web qualifies as a hypermedia system may once have been a matter of debate [38], but it is today the dominant paradigm for information exchange. While Berners-Lee's original graphical browser [10], was a browser and an editor both, the dominant paradigm became the Mosaic browser and all its heirs, which focused solely on browsing. Rather than a vision of global editability [20], it became mainly a vehicle for consumption. Web authoring became largely the domain of specialists. If readers were permitted to contribute, it was in closely delineated spaces, filling and submitting forms. With enough freedom and community dedication, very rich sites, e.g., Wikipedia, could be built.

The modern Web browser remains largely a tool for browsing, but it has gained notable functionality over the years, e.g., access to developer tools for inspection, debugging, and manipulation of Web pages. Even so, most Web development still takes place outside the browser, working with editors and servers. As shall be seen below, we believe that this need no longer be the case, and by focusing on developing *for* the browser *in* the browser (and by the people), it is possible to once again shift the way we have come to use computers.

The original hypertext pioneers had bold visions of what hypertext might entail in collecting and correlating all human knowledge, and in doing so augmenting the human mind. What they, and perhaps none, could have foreseen were the uses a system as flexible and global as the Web could be put to. Today, the Web has gone beyond "simply" hypermedia to encompass not only most of human knowledge, but also a large part of humanity's economic transactions, and a not inconsiderable part of its social and political life. Its very ubiquity, across all modern mobile and desktop platforms, makes it an ideal platform to build new types of software.

The Web supports basic inline unidirectional linking between documents, where earlier hypermedia systems often supported far richer structures, such as external bidirectional n-ary links, first-class composites, external annotations, or hierarchical structures, sometimes even collaboratively created. The lacklustre hypermedia functionality of the Web prompted the development of a special class of Web augmenting hypermedia systems [12, 14, 16, 17, 21, 29], where users could add links and other external structures to existing Web pages. Sharing the weaknesses of other open hypermedia systems, none of these systems gained any widespread use. The Web community, too, attempted generating meta-layers of meaning through XLink [17, 19] and the many initiatives collectively known as the Semantic Web [11, 33]. Both relied on either browser functionality that never materialised, or communities of use that, outside of specialist fields, never grew to a sizeable part of the Web.

However, with the advent of the modern Web browser, there is no longer any need for either integration with outside applications (as with open hypermedia) or waiting for the general adoption of new Web standards (as with the Semantic Web). Everything needed to create a high functioning hypermedia system is present in the average desktop or mobile device.

The Dexter model [30] formally recognized hypermedia structures as first class objects, and not just attributes of selections. By separating documents, anchors, and the structures referencing the anchors, one can create an extensible and collaborative environment for editing, sharing, annotating, and structuring media in its many forms. As we demonstrate below, the modern Web browser has the infrastructure to handle all this, enabling a far richer hypermedia experience than the conventional Web support.

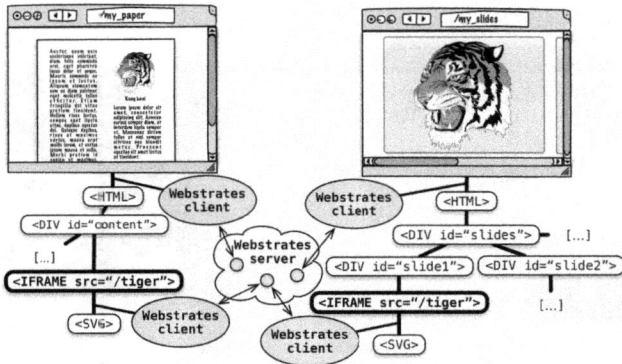

Figure 2: A figure webstrate is transcluded using the `iframe` node in both a paper webstrate and a slideshow webstrate (reprinted from [32] with permission).

Webstrates

Webstrates is a DOM-centric Web architecture that makes the DOM of any page, called a webstrate, served from the Webstrates server a collaborative and persistent object. Any changes to the DOM of a webstrate are persisted on the server and synchronized to all other clients of the same webstrate. including changes to any inlined JavaScript or CSS. Consistency between clients is ensured through operational transformations [22]. Webstrates does not introduce a new framework or API, but instead relies on the standardized API of and interaction with the DOM, but with with a new set of rules of engagement.

Klokmose et al. [32] demonstrate a number of uses for Webstrates focusing on enabling software malleability and personalization, collaboration through personalized interfaces, remote user interface extension at run-time, and orchestration of complex distributed and collaborative user interactions. These examples leverage *transclusions* [37] of one webstrate in another. The Web supports transclusion through the `iframe` tag, where one Web page can be embedded in another by reference. When transcluder and transcludee are served from the same domain, the JavaScript runtime of the two pages can interact. Thus, JavaScript from the outer page can manipulate the DOM of the inner and vice versa.

Transclusion can allow a document webstrate to be transcluded into an application-like webstrate that provides tools for editing the document. This mechanism can allow two or more users in real-time to collaborate on authoring a paper through personal text-editors that are functionally as well as visually different, and the authors can, at run-time, share tools and extend their respective user interfaces. A text-editor webstrate can be transcluded into a developer webstrate and thereby allow live modification of a running user interface (of another user). Transclusion in Webstrates is illustrated in Figure 2 where a figure webstrate is both transcluded in a paper webstrate and a slideshow webstrate. Changes to the figure webstrate will be reflected in both the paper and slideshow.

Development and authoring in webstrates happen *inside* the browser; either directly through the developer tools of the browser, or through webstrates built for development as, e.g., the code editor mentioned above. Thus, the distinction between development and use or browsing and authorship becomes a phenomenon of use.

Reference implementation

The reference implementation of Webstrates [8] consists of a NodeJS [3] server and a transparent JavaScript client. Synchronization and consistent concurrent editing of the DOM are implemented using operational transformations [22] through the ShareJS [6] library, and webstrates are persisted in a MongoDB [2] database as JsonML [1] documents. When a Web page is loaded from the Webstrates server, the Webstrates JavaScript client is statically served to the client browser. The client asynchronously loads the data of the given webstrate in JsonML from the server based on the resource name in the URL, and populates the DOM of the page. The client observes local changes to the DOM using the MutationObserver DOM API [7] and subscribes to changes from other clients of the same page through a web socket connection to the server (see Figure 1). Observed mutations to the DOM are translated to JSON operations on the JsonML representation of the DOM. These operations consist of an absolute path into the JSON document, an action (e.g., insertion in a list or deletion in a string) and a value (e.g., the element to be inserted or the substring to be deleted). As the browser guarantees that the DOM can be serialized to well-formed HTML, our JsonML representation will always be well-formed as well.

The reference implementation includes a basic authentication mechanism using external providers (e.g., GitHub), and webstrates can be annotated with access rights (read-write, read, no access) as an attribute on the root `HTML` node of the DOM. A new webstrate is created by requesting a new resource name. Due to the reliance of transclusion through iframes, the current implementation of Webstrates is centralized, as modern browsers restrict crossing iframe boundaries when pages are served from different domains. This is something that can be overcome technically, but which also opens up for a number of security challenges.

The reference implementation provides a simple HTTP API for creating new webstrates using other (versions) of webstrates as prototypes. Duplicating a webstrate can also be achieved by copying the HTML serialized DOM of a webstrate into another using the developer tools of the browser, as all state and behavior are stored in the DOM.

Demonstrators

We present below two demonstrators that illustrate how rich hypermedia functionality can be realized in Webstrates. Both demonstrators are simple yet usable pieces of software that each required little more than a work day to implement. While there are many other kinds of hypermedia structures that we could have chosen as our test cases (e.g., guided tours [40] or fluid annotations [41]), linking and annotating form the basis on which many other mechanisms can be built.

Web article archive with bidirectional links

The first demonstrator is a Web article archive, where a user can collect articles, take notes, and create bidirectional links between the articles and the notes. Figure 3 shows a user researching interviews with Ted Nelson.

The Web archive consists of three types of webstrates: an archive webstrate (the top level webstrate), a set of article webstrates, and a webstrate for storing an external bidirectional link collection. The user can paste in a URL to a Web page (Figure 3b top), upon which it will

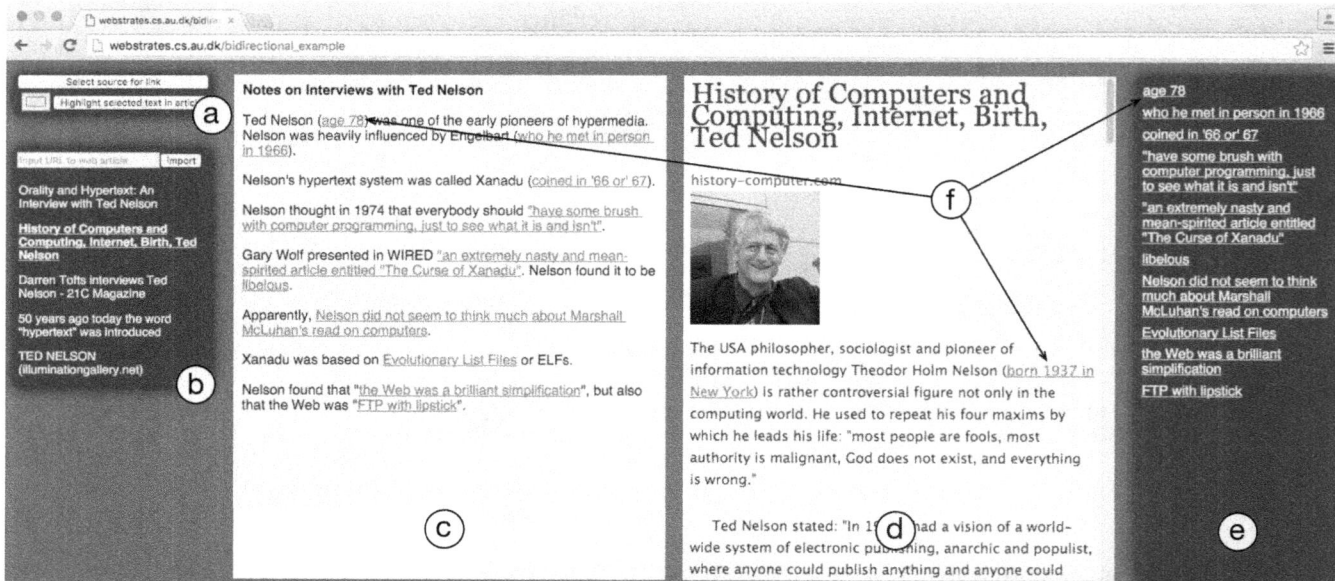

Figure 3: A simple Web article archive implemented with Webstrates, and with bidirectional links between notes and articles. a) Toolbar for creating links and highlighting text. b) Archive of Web articles. New articles are added using the form in the top. c) Notes. d) Article view. e) Collection of bidirectional links stored in a transcluded webstrate. f) The two anchors of a bidirectional link and the link in the external link structure.

Figure 4: A PDF being annotated by two users, one on an iPad. Their individual annotation layers can be toggled using the controls in the top left corner.

be processed into clean easily readable HTML (using the Readability [5] API) and stored in a new webstrate. A link to the article webstrate is added to the DOM of the archive webstrate (Figure 3b). Clicking on an article link will translude it in an `iframe` in the archive webstrate (Figure 3d). The notes (Figure 3c) are a `div` element in the archive webstrate that is editable through the `contentEditable` attribute. To create a link, the user makes a selection in the notes, presses the "select source for link" button (Figure 3a), makes a selection in an article, and presses the same button now labelled "select target for link". An anchor element with a unique ID is added to both the notes and the article (of the form `<a id='anchorId'>text</a>`), and a bidirectional link node is added to an external link webstrate that is transcluded in an `iframe` (Figure 3e-f). The bidirectional link has the form `<bilink anchor1='url:anchorId' anchor2='url:anchorId'>text</bilink>`. An anchor in the notes or articles is only visualized as links (red and underlined) if the anchor is part of a bidirectional link in the link collection. Clicking a link in the notes will open the linked article and highlight the anchor. Clicking a link in an article will scroll the notes to the given anchor and highlight it. Clicking a link in the list of bidirectional links will highlight the link in both notes and article.

This demonstrator shows that it is straightforward to implement bidirectional links with an external link structure on top of the Webstrates platform. We leverage that changes to the DOM are persisted, so storing a link, the HTML for an article, or a note is just a matter of manipulating the DOM, and does not require any explicit interaction with, or development of, a backend server. Here, we use inlined anchors. This works well for a single user application, but if articles and notes were shared between users, each applying their own external link structures, documents could become polluted with anchors, leading to conflicts with overlapping anchors (forbidden in HTML), and requiring the users to have write permission to the linked webstrates. Alternatively, external, computable location specifications [28] could be used. This could be implemented by storing a DOM query expressed as a JavaScript function in the bidirectional link instead of an explicit anchor reference, not unlike [39]. A third more robust option would be to extend Webstrates with unique DOM node IDs, and link directly to nodes or sets of nodes.

This demonstrator is designed for a single user, but could easily be extended to support external link collections shared between users similar to how it is done with annotations in the next demonstrator. The implementation of this demonstrator contains ~240 lines of JavaScript (excluding libraries).

Shared PDF annotations

The second demonstrator is a collaborative PDF annotation tool. Figure 4 features the first page of [30] displaying annotations of two users, C (blue) and B (red). This demonstrator consists of three types of webstrates: a PDF data webstrate, two PDF viewer webstrates, and two annotation webstrates. The data webstrate contains the raw data of a PDF as a base64 encoded string directly in the DOM. The PDF viewer webstrates transclude the data webstrate and render the PDF on a `canvas` element using PDF.js [4]. The viewer webstrate is personal and identifies the given user and stores their preferences (e.g., annotation color). The PDF is annotated using a pen (here an Apple Pencil on an iPad Pro) or a mouse. Annotations are stored in separate webstrates transcluded into the viewer and rendered on top of the PDF. Thus, annotations can be shared between users. Figure 4 shows user C's PDF viewer, where user B's annotations has been transcluded in as well and can be toggled on and off using the top left controls. The PDF viewer observes changes to annotations (using the MutationObserver DOM API), so user C will see any new annotations B may make in real-time. Changing page is done by updating a page number attribute in the DOM of the view. This is done through JavaScript using the keyboard on a desktop computer and with gestures on a tablet. Thus, page browsing will be synchronized between all devices with the same viewer open.

This demonstrator shows how external annotation layers can be created using Webstrates and transclusion, and how Webstrates can facilitate collaboration. It also shows how non Web-native media like a PDF can be integrated using modern Web standards. The implementation of this demonstrator contains ~400 lines of JavaScript code (excluding libraries).

Discussion

We believe Webstrates has the potential to be a vehicle to bring the roots of hypermedia (back) into the Web. With the two demonstrators above we show how external link structures (in the vein of the Dexter Reference Model) and annotation layers can be realized as hypermedia documents themselves; documents that can be shared and collaboratively edited. Webstrates breaks with the tradition of Web development happening offline on static files. Webstrates is *document centric* and makes the DOM a first class citizen of a hypermedia system, just as earlier hypermedia systems elevated the link and the anchor. This is in contrast to the current trend in Web frameworks where the DOM is used primarily as an ephemeral view in a traditional Model-View-Controller application architecture. Development of Webstrates currently requires experience in Web development and a certain proficiency in using the developer tools of the browser, but we can easily imagine webstrates developed for end-user authorship akin to HyperCard and beyond. Webstrates is yet an immature platform, but it has demonstrated significant potential; not necessarily to support the Web as a heavy-weight application platform to create software for millions, but instead as a platform for user expression and *personal* media. Limitations and challenges of implementing Webstrates include (but are not limited to) dealing with large amounts of data exceeding what can be stored in the DOM (and held in memory of the browser), overcoming the restrictions of transclusion using `iframes` while at the same time keeping user data safe, some performance and synchronization issues (as raised in [32]), and providing a distribution platform for users to share and collaborate on webstrates.

Conclusion

The Web grew to its current popularity partly because of its simplicity, but lost in the process much that had been commonplace for hypermedia systems. Now the Web and its tools have evolved to a stage, where the common browser can become the platform for changing the way we work with information, alone or together. We have demonstrated that principles of classical hypermedia systems can be reinvigorated on the Web by rethinking the serving foundation of the Web, and in doing so we have made these principles available across both desktop and mobile devices.

We invite the interested to experiment with the reference implementation of Webstrates [8], and to explore the possibilities of what can be achieved once you realize that a synchronised DOM forms a strong foundation for collaborative hypermedia on the Web.

Acknowledgement

This work was funded by ParticipatoryIT, AU, Denmark.

References

[1] JsonML. http://jsonml.org/.

[2] MongoDB. http://mongodb.org/.

[3] Node.js. http://nodejs.org/.

[4] PDF.js. http://mozilla.github.io/pdf.js/.

[5] Readability. https://readability.com.

[6] ShareJS. http://github.com/share/ShareJS/.

[7] W3C DOM4. http://www.w3.org/TR/domcore/.

[8] Webstrates. http://github.com/cklokmose/Webstrates.

[9] K. M. Anderson, R. N. Taylor, and E. J. Whitehead Jr. Chimera: Hypertext for heterogeneous software environments. In *Proc. 1994 Euro. Hypertext Conf.*, pages 97–107. ACM, Sept. 1994.

[10] T. Berners-Lee, R. Cailliau, J.-F. Groff, and B. Pollerman. World-Wide Web: The information universe. *Electronic Networking: Research, Applications and Policy*, 1(2), 1992.

[11] T. Berners-Lee, J. Hendler, and O. Lassila. The semantic web. *Scientific American*, 284(5):28+, 2001.

[12] N. O. Bouvin. Unifying strategies for Web augmentation. In *Proc. 10th Hypertext Conf.*, pages 91–100, Darmstadt, Germany, Feb. 1999. ACM Press.

[13] N. O. Bouvin. Augmenting the Web through open hypermedia. *The New Review of Hypermedia and Multimedia*, 8:3–26, 2002.

[14] N. O. Bouvin, P. T. Zellweger, K. Grønbæk, and J. D. Mackinlay. Fluid annotations through open hypermedia: Using and extending emerging Web standards. In *Proc. WWW2002 Conf.*, pages 160–171, Honolulu, USA, May 2002. W3C. .

[15] V. Bush. As we may think. *The Atlantic Monthly*, 176 (1):101–108, July 1945.

[16] L. A. Carr, W. Hall, and S. Hitchcock. Link services or link agents? In *Proc. 9th Hypertext Conf.*, pages 113–122, Pittsburgh, PA, USA, June 1998. ACM Press.

[17] B. G. Christensen, F. A. Hansen, and N. O. Bouvin. Xspect: bridging open hypermedia and XLink. In *Proceedings of the 12th International World Wide Web Conference*, pages 490–499, Budapest, Hungary, May 2003. W3C, ACM Press. .

[18] H. C. Davis, D. E. Millard, S. Reich, N. O. Bouvin, K. Grønbæk, K. M. Anderson, U. K. Wiil, P. J. Nürnberg, and L. Sloth. Interoperability between hypermedia systems: The standardisation work of the OHSWG. In *Proc. 10th Hypertext Conf.*, pages 201–202, Darmstadt, Germany, Feb. 1999. ACM Press.

[19] S. DeRose, E. Maler, D. Orchard, and B. Trafford (editors). XML Linking Language (XLink). W3C Recommendation 27 June 2001, W3C, June 2001. http://www.w3.org/TR/xlink/.

[20] A. Di Iorio and F. Vitali. From the writable web to global editability. In *Proc. 16th Hypertext Conf.*, pages 35–45, New York, NY, USA, 2005. ACM.

[21] O. Díaz, C. Arellano, and M. Azanza. A language for end-user web augmentation: Caring for producers and consumers alike. *ACM Trans. Web*, 7(2):9:1–9:51, May 2013.

[22] C. A. Ellis and S. J. Gibbs. Concurrency control in groupware systems. In *ACM Sigmod Record*, volume 18, pages 399–407. ACM, 1989.

[23] D. Engelbart. A conceptual framework for the augmentation of man's intellect. In P. Howerton, editor, *Vistas in Information Handling*, volume 1, pages 1–29. Spartan Books, Washington DC, USA, 1963.

[24] D. C. Engelbart and W. K. English. A research center for augmenting human intellect. In *Proceedings of the December 9-11, 1968, Fall Joint Computer Conference, Part I*, AFIPS '68 (Fall, part I), pages 395–410, New York, NY, USA, 1968. ACM.

[25] A. M. Fountain, W. Hall, I. Heath, and H. C. Davis. Microcosm: An open model for hypermedia with dynamic linking. In *Proc. Euro. Hypertext Conf.*, 1990.

[26] D. Goodman. *Complete HyperCard 2.0 Handbook*. Random House Inc., 1990.

[27] K. Grønbæk and R. H. Trigg. Design issues for a Dexter based hypermedia system. *CACM*, 37(2):40–49, Feb. 1994.

[28] K. Grønbæk and R. H. Trigg. Toward a Dexter based model for open hypermedia: Unifying embedded references and link objects. In *Proc. 7th Hypertext Conf.*, pages 149–160, Bethesda, MD, USA, Mar. 1996.

[29] K. Grønbæk, N. O. Bouvin, and L. Sloth. Designing Dexter based hypermedia services for the World Wide Web. In *Proc. 8th Hypertext Conf.*, pages 146–156, Southampton, UK, Apr. 1997. ACM Press.

[30] F. G. Halasz and M. D. Schwartz. The Dexter hypertext reference model. *CACM*, 37(2):30–39, Feb. 1994.

[31] F. G. Halasz, T. P. Moran, and R. H. Trigg. NoteCards in a nutshell. In *Proceedings of ACM Conference on Human Factors in Computing Systems and Graphics Interface*, pages 45–52, Toronto, Canada, Apr. 1987.

[32] C. N. Klokmose, J. R. Eagan, S. Baader, W. Mackay, and M. Beaudouin-Lafon. Webstrates: Shareable dynamic media. In *Proc. UIST 2015*, pages 280–290, New York, NY, USA, 2015. ACM. .

[33] C. C. Marshall and F. M. Shipman. Which semantic web? In *Proc. 14th Hypertext Conf.*, pages 57–66, Nottingham, UK, Aug. 2003. ACM Press. .

[34] N. K. Meyrowitz. Intermedia: The architecture and construction of an object-oriented hypermedia system and applications framework. In *OOPSLA 1986 Proc.*, 1986.

[35] N. K. Meyrowitz. The missing link: Why we're all doing hypertext wrong. In E. Barrett, editor, *The Society of Text: Hypertext, Hypermedia and the Social Construction of Information*, pages 107–114. MIT Press, Cambridge, USA, 1989.

[36] T. H. Nelson. *Computer Lib/Dream Machines*. Mindful Press, 1974.

[37] T. H. Nelson. The heart of connection: hypermedia unified by transclusion. *CACM*, 38(8):31–34, 1995.

[38] P. J. Nürnberg and H. Ashman. What was the question? reconciling open hypermedia and world wide web research. In *Proc. 10th Hypertext Conf.*, pages 83–90, Darmstadt, Germany, Feb. 1999. ACM Press.

[39] T. A. Phelps and R. Wilensky. Robust intra-document locations. In *Proc. WWW2000 Conf.*, pages 105–118, Amsterdam, Holland, May 2000. W3C.

[40] R. H. Trigg. Guided tours and tabletops: tools for communicating in a hypertext environment. In *Proc. CSCW 1998 Conf.*, pages 216–226, 1988. .

[41] P. T. Zellweger, N. O. Bouvin, H. Jehøj, and J. D. Mackinlay. Fluid annotations in an open world. In *Proc. 12th Hypertext Conf.*, pages 9–18, Århus, Denmark, Aug. 2001.

ALAT: Finally an Easy To Use Adaptation Authoring Tool

Paul De Bra, Natalia Stash,
Wouter Boereboom, Celine Chen
Dept. of Math. and Computer Science
Eindhoven University of Technology (TU/e)
Eindhoven, the Netherlands
{p.m.e.d.bra, n.v.stash}@tue.nl,
{w.boereboom, j.chenyuexu}@gmail.com

Joris Den Ouden, Martijn Kunstman,
John Oostrum, Egon Verbakel
de Roode Kikker
Eindhoven, the Netherlands
{j.den.ouden, m.kunstman, j.oostrum,
e.verbakel}@deroodekikker.nl

ABSTRACT

Research papers about adaptive hypermedia systems, frameworks or applications tend to focus on the end-result: how the applications are used by end-users, how adaptation improves user satisfaction, learning, etc. What they do not describe is how difficult and labor-intensive the creation of the applications can be. In this paper we present ALAT, a new authoring tool for the Generic Adaptation Language and Engine GALE, developed at the TU/e. ALAT is specifically designed in close collaboration with an educational software company to ensure that specifying the desired adaptation can be done by non-technical authors. This is achieved by combining a simple responsive authoring-interface with underlying templates that help generate the adaptation code for GALE.

CCS Concepts

•**Information systems** → **Web applications; Web interfaces;**
•**Human-centered computing** → **Interactive systems and tools;**
Interaction design; Systems and tools for interaction design;

Keywords

authoring, adaptive hypermedia, interface design, usability

1. INTRODUCTION

Adaptive hypermedia [1, 14] nowadays comes in two flavors: *expert-driven* and *data-driven*. Everyone is experiencing automatic personalization on many web-based services (like YouTube, Facebook, Amazon, etc.). This is all realized through data-driven adaptation. In special-purpose applications, such as an on-line course text that is offered as hypermedia (through a website), an expert, skilled author or pedagogical designer needs to define adaptation rules, not purely based on content and navigation paths followed by (other) users, but based on insight as to which navigation or *learning* order between learning objects or concepts makes sense. In some cases this is not universal advice but depends on personal traits such as a *cognitive* or *learning style*.

Special purpose systems have been created for adaptive learning, Interbook [2] being one of the oldest but still best known ex-

amples. An author would create an annotated Word file: a course text with delineated sections, each associated with *outcome concepts* you learn about when studying the section and *background concepts* that are "prerequisites" for studying that section. A compiler would then turn this into an adaptive website. The possible forms of adaptation were all hardcoded in the system. Authoring was easy but the adaptation possibilities limited.

At the other extreme general purpose systems have been created, like AHA! [6] and its successor GALE [17, 16]. In AHA! and even more in GALE nothing is hardcoded. The user modeling and adaptation are defined using the GALE adaptation language GAM that allows arbitrary Java code to be used in the rules. Creating content (e. g. learning material) is completely separate from defining the adaptation and can be done using any HTML authoring tool. In line with other adaptive hypermedia research papers, when we published reference [17] we emphasized what GALE was capable of and ignored the authoring process. The (adaptive!) thesis [16] describes the adaptation authoring *language* but no easy to use tools for "generating" adaptation in this language.

In Section 2 we briefly review different authoring approaches and interfaces that were created for adaptive hypermedia, including the GRAPPLE authoring tool GAT [7] we helped to create. We highlight good ideas and problematic ones in different authoring tools. Section 3 briefly recalls the adaptation functionality of GALE to illustrate the challenge to make that functionality available to non-technical authors. Section 4 describes the new authoring tool ALAT. The aim of this description is to show how most of the adaptation power of GALE can be made usable to non-technical authors through the new authoring tool.

2. ADAPTIVE HYPERMEDIA AUTHORING

When the first adaptive course at the TU/e [3] was turned into the more generic adaptive system AHA! adding adaptation rules became difficult. An authoring tool was created that completely separated the creation of *content* from that of *conceptual structure*. This separation has become the standard way of authoring in all other authoring tools we refer to in this section (and in many more). As AHA! and later also GALE just serve "pages" like a Web server (and in fact as a Web server extension) we can allow users to use whichever is their favorite Web page creation tool.

The *Graph Author* for AHA! was first described in [5]. A snapshot of this interface is shown in Figure 1. The figure shows two panes: the left pane shows part of a hierarchy of *concepts*, also called a *domain model*. The right pane shows all "pedagogical rules" in what we call the *adaptation model*. The adaptation rules that implement the behavior are drawn from a template. The design of such templates is left to an expert. Authors just "draw arrows". When the domain and adaptation models become much larger than

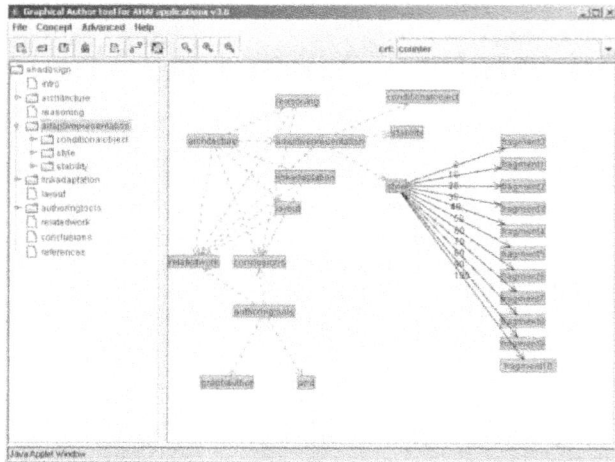

Figure 1: The Graph Author (tool for AHA!).

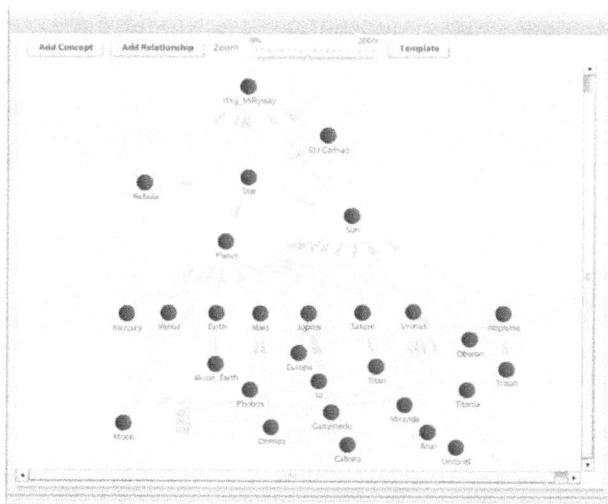

Figure 2: The Domain Tool in GAT.

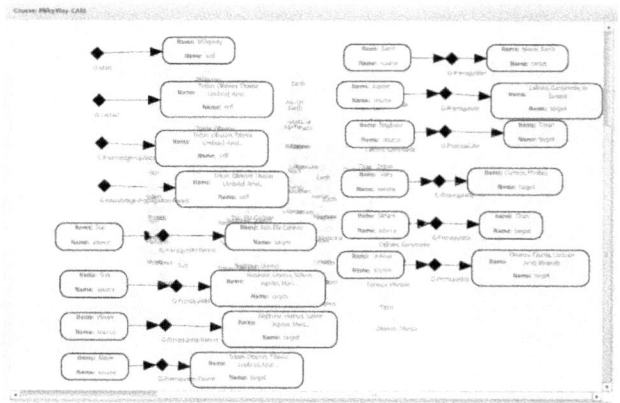

Figure 3: The Course Tool in GAT.

in the figure the accordion menu keeps the domain model readable whereas the graph representing the adaptation model will become cluttered and unreadable.

In the European research project GRAPPLE[1] GALE [16, 17] was created as successor to AHA! and a corresponding graphical authoring tool GAT [7] was created as well. The GAT tool consists of three parts: a *domain tool*, a *pedagogical relationship tool* and a *course tool*. Figure 2 shows the graph part of the domain tool and Figure 3 shows the graph part of the course tool.

The Domain Tool[2] in GAT allows for labeled binary relations between concepts. The domain model can thus become a richly interconnected collection of concepts, much like a *domain-specific ontology*. It can be much richer than the purely hierarchical domain model shown by the GraphAuthor tool in figure 1. At the same time the graph presentation (instead of an accordion menu) quickly becomes cluttered and unreadable as the domain model grows.

For the adaptive part of an application GAT uses the Course

Tool[3] (initial design ideas described in [13]), shown in figure 3. It uses a very compact graphical representation for a collection of adaptation rules that would make for a huge graph in the GraphAuthor, but it does not make it easy to see which incoming and outgoing pedagogical relations (like prerequisites) each concept has.

During a course on adaptive hypermedia students were given a choice of using GAT to develop a GALE application or using the underlying adaptation language GAM directly. Students using GAT were generally less happy than students using GAM. Still, when in the next run of this course we asked students to only use GAM and evaluate it, writing the adaptation rules was found to be the most technically challenging part of authoring [15]. Hence the need for a new authoring tool described in this paper.

Our experience mirrors what we find about authoring tools created in other projects. The creators of ACTSim [11] made the creation of adaptive educational soft skill simulations easy by creating a limited special-purpose tool. Still, they too use a graph presentation that becomes harder to view as the models become larger.

WOTAN [9] combines an indented list hierarchy (or accordion menu) with an interface representing the current project in a directed graph. To some extent that corresponds to the domain and adaptation model representation in the Graph Author. The graph presentation uses automated layout and clustering of groups of nodes to prevent visual clutter. WOTAN also "cheats" in its indented list view: concepts can have multiple parents and therefore appear multiple times in the indented list.

We also looked into MOT 3.0 [8] that is based on the five-layer LAOS framework [4] and offers an editor that is essentially a text editor for writing adaptation rules, at least as difficult to use as the GAT *pedagogical relationship tool* for writing adaptation rule templates.

Finally we also considered AMAS [12] that focuses on ease of authoring and usability by non-experts. Subsequent designs, described by Gaffney, Conlan and Wade in [10] focused on the user experience and led to a graph-based interface that again appears to work well on small examples but we question whether it would be usable with large graphs.

The investigation into these different authoring environments has taught us that an interface for displaying and editing a *concept hierarchy* appears to work well and scales well with growing applications, and that displaying a graph of relations between concepts always leads to visual clutter with larger models.

---

[1]See http://grapple.win.tue.nl/ for a description and deliverables.
[2]The Domain Tool was mainly developed by Giunti Labs.

[3]The Course Tool was mainly developed at the University of Warwick.

3. GALE ADAPTATION FUNCTIONALITY

ALAT has been designed together with an educational company (developing a platform for on-line courses mostly for grade school) and the interface design therefore has to be suitable for authors of such learning material. But ALAT is also, and perhaps even first and foremost a new authoring tool *for GALE* [16]. This means that it tries to enable authors to use as much as possible of the user modeling and adaptation functionality GALE offers, but without requiring any technical skills.

Rather than explain GALE's functionality using GALE's own adaptation language (GAM) described in [16, 17] we use the blueprint format used by ALAT. In GALE an application (or course) consists of *concepts*. Each concept has a number of (named) *properties* that have a fixed value and (named) *attributes* that have a value that is computed through rules. Typical use of these attributes (of which the names and meaning can be chosen arbitrarily) includes:

- a Boolean attribute *suitability* to check that all *prerequisites* for the concept are satisfied.

- an integer attribute *visited* to count how many times the user has visited the concept.

- a real (Double) attribute *knowledge* to keep track of the user's knowledge of the concept.

In GALE the attribute values can be updated when certain events occur (like the user visiting a concept) or can be computed from the values of other attributes (and possibly properties).

Finally, concepts can also have relationships between them. In GALE there are two predefined relationships:

- When concept A *extends* concept B it inherits all the properties and attributes (from B). We can define one "generic" concept with properties and attributes and then have all other concepts extend it.

- Through the *parent* relationships we build a *hierarchy* of concepts. GALE also offers *views* to present (parts of) the concept hierarchy as a navigation menu (for instance as an accordion menu).

In ALAT we use concept *blueprints* (templates) that define a structure common to *all concepts* of an application and that define some *special concept types* with additional structure for those. A course can contain concepts to be studied and concepts that represent tests for instance. The author selects a type for each new concept and does not need to know anything about the code that defines the behavior of concepts of that type. The selection list (in ALAT) that is offered to authors to choose a concept type is generated from the blueprint and can thus be different for different applications (or application areas) for which ALAT is used as authoring too. Below we show an (incomplete) example blueprint template. As you can see the blueprints are written using JSON syntax.

```
{
  "defaultAttributes":[
    {
      "name":"suitability",
      "type":"Boolean",
      "value":"true"
    },
    {
      "name":"knowledge",
      "type":"Double",
      "value":"0",
      "operator":"AVG"
```

```
    },
    ...
  ],
  "conceptTypes":[
    {
      "name":"text-topic",
      "default_attributes":[
        {
          "name":"info",
          "type":"String",
          "value":"This is an information concept!"
        },
        ...
      ],
      "default_rules":[
        "visited",
        "knowledge_update",
        ...
      ]
    }
  ]
}
```

The "default_rules" refer to what is defined in a different blueprint for which we show a small (incomplete) example:

```
{
  "def_att_rules":[
    {
      "name":"hasprerequisite",
      "type":"binary",
      "target":"suitability",
      "tooltip":
        "Target concept must be learned
        before source is recommended.",
      "code":"${%target%#knowledge} > 0.8",
      "operator":"and"
    }
  ],
  "persistent_att_rules":[
    {
      "name":"visited",
      "type":"unary",
      "properties":[
        {
          "name":"visited",
          "type":"Integer",
          "defval":""
        }
      ],
      "tooltip":"stores number of concept
              visits in 'visited'",
      "code":"#[visited]:Integer event +
      'if (${#suitability}) { ${#visited}++;}'"
    }
  ],
  "def_relations":[
    {
      "name":"rotatesAround",
      "tooltip":"source concept rotates
              around the target object."
    }
  ]
}
```

The blueprint contains three parts:

- The first part (def_att_rules) corresponds to attributes whose value is computed (whenever needed). For these attributes their *value* is not stored permanently but the *code* to compute that value is stored. The concept's attribute for which the value is computed is "suitability" (called the "target" attribute). The code fragment computes the suitability by check-

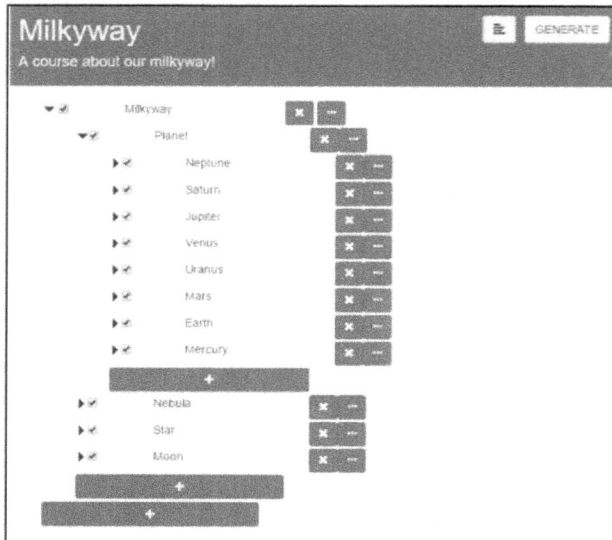

Figure 4: Hierarchical presentation in ALAT.

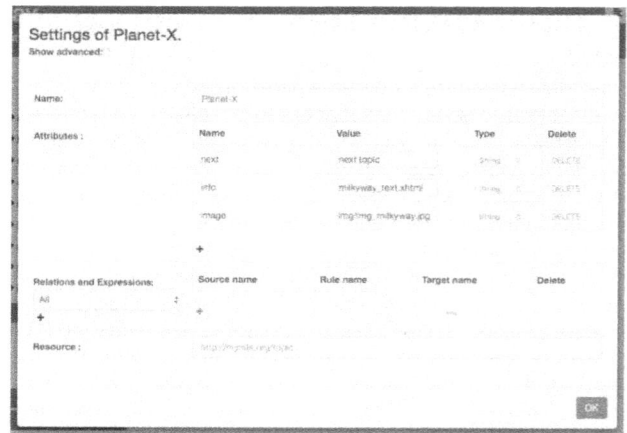

Figure 5: Concept Details in ALAT.

ing whether the knowledge (attribute value) of the target concept is greater than 0.8. So if concept A has concept B as a prerequisite then the suitability of A depends on the knowledge of B being greater than 0.8. If A has several prerequisites these pieces of code are combined using the logical "and" operator to form the complete code for A's suitability.

- The second part (persistent_att_rules) defines how an event triggers an update to some attribute value. That value is stored permanently. The example defines a rule called "visited" which defines the updates for an attribute that is also called "visited". The code fragment increments the visited attribute when the concept is visited while being suitable. The event code for an attribute is actually a piece of Java code. Several rules can contribute to the code, and each piece of code is added to the event code. Hence the "event +" part which indicates that the code is concatenated (as a string) to the already existing event code.

- The third part (def_relations) just defines relations that have no associated behavior. They can be used in code fragments for attributes or other relations and for generating adaptation in the (page) presentation. The "rotatesAround" relation between *planet* and *star* can be used in generating part of the page describing what a star or a planet is.

When using ALAT the "adaptation model" is assembled from the small code fragments shown in the blueprint. This "assembly" does not provide the complete adaptation power of GALE but offers the same power that GAT did. In all the examples of GALE applications we have seen so far, some of which are mentioned in [15], the code that was hand-written in GAM could all have been produced by ALAT in a relatively straightforward way.

4. ALAT: THE NEW GALE AUTHORING TOOL

ALAT is the result of many brainstorming sessions, followed by mockup design by a professional designer, followed by many iterations of coding, testing and refining. As the look and feel of the

final tool still stays quite close to the earlier mockup design we illustrate ALAT using screen shots from the actual tool only. The tool not only completely hides the technical details you saw in section 3 but even does not require any knowledge of these details. The blueprints contain *tooltips* that are shown in ALAT and that should be written in a language the non-technical author understands.

4.1 Creating and Navigating the Concept Hierarchy

Because of what we learned in section 2 ALAT does not use a graph-like domain or adaptation model presentation but shows a hierarchical domain structure through an accordion menu. There is a "flat" and a "hierarchical" view. We only show the hierarchical one, in figure 4. At each level that is shown there is a blue bar with + button to add a concept at the corresponding level, an X button to delete (a concept or complete sub-hierarchy) and three dots to access concept details.

From De Roode Kikker we learned that in school a teacher may wish to offer only part of a course (purchased from a publisher) to his students. For this purpose ALAT places a checkbox in front of each concept. When the teacher unchecks some boxes these concepts (and the whole subtree below them, if applicable) will automatically not appear in the course and all associated adaptation rules will not be included in the generated adaptation model.

4.2 Editing Concept Details

When an author adds a concept a small dialog box appears to enter the concept name and type. The "conceptTypes" from the blueprint determines the possible choices for the type. The concept details dialog that follows is shown in figure 5 in which a newly Milkyway concept named "Planet-X" is shown. Comparing this dialog box to the first blueprint from section 3 it is clear that most information is hidden. The attributes and rules that are common to *all* concepts are hidden. Only the attributes that are added for the chosen concept type are shown. In the Milkyway example from [17] these are "next", "info" and "image".

In figure 6 we show the concept details for the concept "Earth" in which the author has added attributes and relationships. The dialog box contains four different parts:

- Name: Each concept must have a name that is unique within the course. That name is given when the concept is created but it can be changed later through this dialog box (as long as it stays unique).

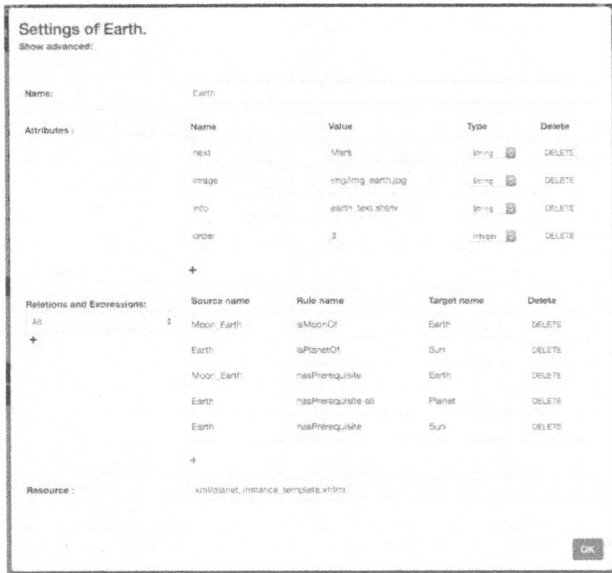

Figure 6: Concept Details for "Earth" in ALAT.

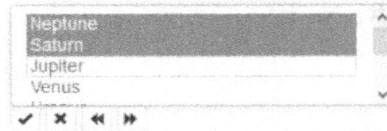

Figure 7: Dialog box to select concepts for a relation in ALAT.

- Attributes: The attributes that are common to all concepts are *not* shown. The attributes "next", "info" and "image" follow from the Milkyway concept type and the attribute "order" was added by the author through this interface. The hidden standard attributes can be made visible by ticking the "show advanced" checkbox. Unlike the additional attributes the standard ones cannot be deleted as doing so would break standard adaptation rules associated with them.

- Relations and Expressions: again, the standard ones coming from the blueprint are not shown unless the "show advanced" checkbox is ticked. They would include "visited" and "knowledge update" for instance. In adaptive courses a concept may have some *prerequisites*, and in our example the concept Earth has two prerequisites: Planet and Sun. We not only show some prerequisites but also added some more relationships (isMoonOf and isPlanetOf). Binary relations have a *source* and *target* concept and are shown in the Concept Details window for *both* concepts. We see for instance that Moon_Earth has Earth as a prerequisite and that Moon_Earth has an isMoonOf relationship with Earth. When adding a relationship it is selected from the list (that shows All in the figure). This list is determined by the second blueprint we showed in section 3 and can be extended with new relationships (that then cannot have associated code). Relationships are always created for the source concept. The dialog box shown in figure 7 is used to select target concepts. You can select multiple concepts and ALAT will create a relation for each of them.

- Resource: this final element is the name of the file to be used for the page. The resources can come from any website and need not reside on the server on which the adaptation model is stored.

The authoring process for the domain and adaptation model of an application/course ends with a simple press of the "generate" button. ALAT generates a file called "concepts.gam" in the main directory for the course.

5. DISCUSSION AND FUTURE WORK

Designing authoring interfaces for adaptive (educational) hypermedia has been a process of trial and error throughout the past two decades, not only for the TU/e research group but as section 2 has shown also for other researchers. It has also not been widely published about. Publications concentrate on the end-user experience, not on the process of designing or creating the applications or frameworks.

In the design of ALAT we have worked closely with an educational software company. This has confirmed that it is essential to make an authoring interface very simple. So we opted for showing a concept hierarchy, hiding all adaptation-related details from the authors (through blueprints), yet allowing experts to add features (attributes, relations, adaptation rules) if desired. The interface is guided by the blueprints in deciding what to show in selection boxes and which attributes and relations to provide. The ability to "deselect" parts of an application was also an explicit wish from teachers using courses that have been prepared (sold) by a publisher.

While we are confident that ALAT is much easier to use than any authoring interface we created in the past we still need to run extensive evaluations. An authoring experiment is planned in the second quarter of 2016, not in time for this paper but for a future publication.

We also plan on adding an interface for a graph visualization tool so that the graph of relationships between concepts can be shown. But based on our previous experience we intend to use that graphical interface as "read-only", not as an editor.

The attentive reader may have noticed that in this paper we have only considered adaptation based on what the individual user has done. Group adaptation, or collaborative filtering, has not been considered. This is not a limitation of the authoring interface ALAT per se but is a restriction built into GALE. Although GALE can (and does) include the user's identity in its data model, as what is called an "entity" and can handle groups as entities and can have adaptation rules that update the "user model" for such a group entity GALE currently has a deliberate limitation that an entity cannot access the user model of another entity. This guarantees that every user model is kept private. Only when GALE gains a controlled way to access group entities can we consider making group adaptation available in the authoring process as well. We are looking forward to our experiments with different author- and user-groups to find out which desires for this and possible other future extensions pop up.

Readers who like to experience ALAT first hand and experiment can visit http://gale.win.tue.nl/ALAT and register. The tool allows you to create new adaptive applications, while keeping the (pages) on your own server.

6. ACKNOWLEDGMENTS

This research is partly funded by the City of Eindhoven in the "Adaptive Learning" project. Additional funding came from the Eindhoven University of Technology and from De Roode Kikker.

7. REFERENCES

[1] P. Brusilovsky. Adaptive hypermedia. *User Modeling and User-Adapted Interaction*, 11(1-2):87–110, 2001.

[2] P. Brusilovsky, J. Eklund, and E. Schwarz. Web-based education for all: a tool for development adaptive courseware. *Computer Networks and ISDN Systems*, 30(1-7):291 – 300, 1998. Proceedings of the Seventh International World Wide Web Conference.

[3] L. Calvi and P. De Bra. Proficiency-adapted information browsing and filtering in hypermedia educational systems. *User Modeling and User-Adapted Interaction*, 7(4):257–277, 1997.

[4] A. Cristea and A. De Mooij. Laos: Layered www ahs authoring model and their corresponding algebraic operators. In *The Twelfth International World Wide Web Conference, Alternate Track on Education*, 2003.

[5] P. De Bra, A. Aerts, B. Berden, B. de Lange, B. Rousseau, T. Santic, D. Smits, and N. Stash. Aha! the adaptive hypermedia architecture. In *Proceedings of the fourteenth ACM conference on Hypertext*, pages 81–84. ACM, 2003.

[6] P. De Bra, D. Smits, and N. Stash. The design of aha! In *Proceedings of the seventeenth ACM conference on Hypertext*, page 133. ACM, 2006, adaptive version at http://aha.win.tue.nl/ahadesign/.

[7] P. De Bra, D. Smits, K. van der Sluijs, A. Cristea, and M. Hendrix. Grapple: Personalization and adaptation in learning management systems. In *Proceedings of the ED-MEDIA World Conference on Educational Multimedia and Hypermedia*, pages 3029–3038. AACE, 2010.

[8] J. Foss and A. Cristea. The next generation authoring adaptive hypermedia: Using and evaluating the mot3. 0 and peal tools. In *Proceedings of the twentyfirst ACM conference on Hypertext*, pages 83–92. ACM, 2010.

[9] M. Freire and P. Rodriguez. Comparing graphs and trees for adaptive hypermedia authoring. In *Proceedings Third International Workshop on Authoring of Adaptive and Adaptable Educational Hypermedia (A3EH; in conjunction with AIED)*, pages 4–12, 2005.

[10] C. Gaffney, O. Conlan, and V. Wade. The amas authoring tool 2.0: A ux evaluation. In *Proceedings of the twentyfifth ACM Conference on Hypertext and Social Media*, pages 224–230. ACM, 2014.

[11] C. Gaffney, D. Dagger, and V. Wade. Authoring and delivering personalised simulations-an innovative approach to adaptive elearning for soft skills. *Journal of Universal Computer Science*, 16(19):2780–2800, 2010.

[12] C. Hampson, O. Conlan, and V. Wade. Challenges in locating content and services for adaptive elearning courses. In *Eleventh IEEE International Conference on Advanced Learning Technologies (ICALT)*, pages 157–159. IEEE, 2011.

[13] M. Hendrix, P. De Bra, M. Pechenizkiy, D. Smits, and A. Cristea. Defining adaptation in a generic multi layer model: Cam: The grapple conceptual adaptation model. In *Third European Conference on Technology Enhanced Learning (EC-TEL)*, pages 132–143. Springer LNCS 5192, 2008.

[14] E. Knutov, P. De Bra, and M. Pechenizkiy. Ah 12 years later: a comprehensive survey of adaptive hypermedia methods and techniques. *New Review of Hypermedia and Multimedia*, 15(1):5–38, 2009.

[15] V. Ramos, P. De Bra, and d. Smits. Gale extensibility evaluation : a qualitative approach. In *World Conference on E-Learning in Corporate, Government, Healthcare and Hither Education (E-Learn)*, pages 296–305, 2013.

[16] D. Smits. *Towards a Generic Distributed Adaptive Hypermedia Environment*. PhD thesis, Eindhoven University of Technology, adaptive version on http://gale.win.tue.nl/thesis/, ISBN 978-90-386-3115-8, 2012.

[17] D. Smits and P. De Bra. Gale: a highly extensible adaptive hypermedia engine. In *Proceedings of the twentysecond ACM conference on Hypertext*, pages 63–72. ACM, 2011.

Mining Interaction Patterns in the Design of Web Applications for Improving User Experience

Vassiliki Gkantouna
University of Patras
gkantoun@ceid.upatras.gr

Athanasios Tsakalidis
University of Patras
tsak@ceid.upatras.gr

Giannis Tzimas
Technological Educational Institute of
Western Greece
tzimas@teimes.gr

ABSTRACT

The key success factor for modern web applications is their acceptance by the end-users which heavily depends on the quality of the user experience that they offer to them. Users require applications designed in such a way that it enables them to learn the supported functionalities easily, so that they can quickly find the information that they are looking for. Therefore, the usability and the overall design quality of an application can determine its success or failure. In this paper, we analyze the conceptual model of CMS-based web applications in terms of the incorporated design fragments that support the various user interaction processes. We consider these fragments as recurrent interaction patterns occurring in the application model, consisting of a configuration of front-end interface components that interrelate each other and interact with the user to achieve certain functionality. We have developed a methodology that automatically extracts the conceptual model of a web application and subsequently performs a pattern-based analysis of the model in order to identify the occurrences of all the recurrent interaction patterns. Finally, we calculate evaluation metrics revealing whether these patterns are used consistently throughout the application design. By utilizing these patterns, developers can produce more consistent and predictable designs, improving the ease of use of web applications.

Keywords

Design Evaluation; Design Patterns; Interaction Patterns; CMS; Design Quality; Web Applications

1. INTRODUCTION

Modern web applications are progressively becoming more and more complex in order to support sophisticated functionalities and integrate advanced business logic. To assist developers facing the intrinsic complexity of web application development, a plethora of Model-Driven Web Engineering approaches [1] has proposed the use of web design patterns ([2], [11]) for producing successful designs. They provide designers with proven solutions to recurring design problems that can be reused in different contexts where the correspondence problem arises. At the same time, the adoption of design patterns can also improve both the usability and the quality of an application since their use enforces a coherent design style and makes it easier for the end-users to recognize typical patterns of user interactions (i.e. interaction patterns). Despite the fact that

there are catalogues of available web design patterns ([21], [22]), developers have difficulties to apply them consistently throughout the design model of an application, often resulting in pattern variants which can cause serious design inconsistencies and disorientation of user's perception about the system. This highlights the need for tools supporting developers inspect the design of web applications in terms of consistency and usability, even at the conceptual level, in order to discover potential design problems in the way they support the various user interaction processes, as it is crucial for the quality of user experience.

Towards this end, we analyze and evaluate the conceptual model of web applications in terms of the incorporated design fragments that support the various user interaction processes within an application's context. At the conceptual level, we consider these fragments as recurrent interaction patterns occurring in the application model, consisting of a configuration of front-end interface components that interrelate each other and interact with the user to achieve certain behavior or functionality. To be able to inspect the consistent use of these patterns, we also consider pattern variants. More specifically, we consider that an interaction pattern consists of a core specification, i.e., an invariant composition of front-end design elements that characterizes the pattern and by a number of pattern variants which extend the core specification with all the valid modalities in which the pattern composition can start (starting variants) or terminate (termination variants). We have developed a methodology that automatically extracts the conceptual model of a web application and subsequently performs a pattern-based analysis of the model in order to identify the occurrences of all the incorporated recurrent patterns. To verify that the identified patterns actually define user interaction processes for performing certain functionality, we additionally inspect their occurrences to examine whether the recurrence of the design elements at the hypertext design goes with a recurrence at the data level i.e. the content they deliver to the end-users. This is done by utilizing a semantic similarity measurement technique. Finally, we calculate evaluation metrics revealing whether these patterns are used consistently throughout the application design. We argue that the identified patterns can benefit both sides of the user interaction, the software developers and the end-users. By utilizing the patterns, developers can produce more consistent and predictable designs improving the ease of use of an application.

In order to automate the process of analyzing the design of a web application, we narrowed down the methodology's scope to the domain of Content Management Systems (CMSs), since they provide a common base of source code which can be systematically processed for obtaining the automated extraction of the application's conceptual model. The proposed methodology is accompanied by a tool support available in [5], allowing developers to apply the methodology on websites developed by using the Joomla! [13] and Drupal [8] CMS platforms. Due to space limitations, in this work we present the methodology for the case of

HT '16, July 10-13, 2016, Halifax, NS, Canada
© 2016 ACM. ISBN 978-1-4503-4247-6/16/07...$15.00
DOI: http://dx.doi.org/10.1145/2914586.2914631

Joomla!-based websites. The remaining of this paper is organized as follows: Section 2 provides an overview of the related work and discusses the contribution of this work. Section 3 presents in detail the methodology for analyzing and evaluating the conceptual model of a Web application in terms of interaction patterns, while section 4 discusses conclusions and future work.

2. RELATED WORK AND CONTRIBUTION

Our primary goal in this work is to inspect the design of web applications in terms of the design fragments (i.e. recurrent patterns) that allow users to interact with the application for performing certain task. We consider two main types of interaction patterns: (i) the one which results from applying well-known design patterns for handling common interaction design problems and (ii) the other which has emerged as a result of the design decisions made by developers for adopting specific reusable design structures to support the various ways in which users can interact with the system (i.e., user interaction processes) for performing certain tasks within the application context. The latter type can result in either effective reusable design solutions consistently used into the application model for supporting predictable user behavior and making the application easy to use, or in problematic design cases causing inconsistencies that introduce unpredictability and make users find the interaction with the system an ineffective process.

The concept of interaction patterns appears in the field of Human Computer Interaction. In [16], [18], [19] and [20], there is a variety of UI patterns specifications which have derived from analyzing and reviewing the UIs of a large number of successful web applications. Related to UI patterns are the web interaction design patterns that provide solutions to recurring interaction problems of web applications users. Specific Web UI patterns can be found in [6], [12], [14] and [22]. Although the research on detecting software design patterns is mature, the research on the automated detection of design patterns in the conceptual model of an application is very limited. In [9], authors present the Web Quality Analyzer which analyzes the conceptual schema of WebML-based web applications and identifies the occurrences of a predefined set of WebML design patterns, allowing designers to automatically monitor the application's design consistency. In [10], authors present an approach for supporting the automatic identification of web interaction design patterns in a Web application. The approach is based on reverse engineering techniques which search the code of a website's pages for detecting a set of predefined features that characterize a pattern.

The key difference of our approach is that there is no limitation to focus strictly on the detection of predefined interaction patterns in the design of an application. On the contrary, we provide a methodology for supporting the automated detection of all the recurrent design structures occurring within the conceptual model for supporting the various user interaction processes. Such structures may be a well-known design pattern or they can also be reusable design compositions (effective or not) used by the developers to accomplish certain functionality. In this way, we can detect even patterns which may be hidden in a particular instantiation of a design problem, making it hard even for experienced designers to recognize them and come up with reusable design examples. These patterns can probably lead to: (i) the identification of new interaction design patterns for handling common interaction problems in the CMS domain which can be used as building blocks in future designs, offering a high quality user experience, or (ii) they can even stand as anti-patterns in case they are evaluated to cause serious design inconsistencies. To the best of our knowledge, this is the first effort to provide a mechanism for supporting the automated identification of interaction design patterns and anti-patterns for the CMS domain and for promoting the pattern-based CMS design and development.

3. METHODOLOGY

In this section, we present the methodology for automatically mining and evaluating the incorporated interaction patterns in the conceptual model of a web application. First, we extract the conceptual model of the application, at hypertext level, in the form of a directed graph which is then submitted to a pattern-based analysis with the aim of (i) identifying the occurrences of all the recurrent patterns lying within it, (ii) verifying which of them support a user interaction process for implementing certain functionality and (iii) calculate a set of evaluation metrics to assess if the identified patterns are used consistently throughout the application model. In order to explain the concepts and illustrate the potential of the proposed methodology, in what follows, we refer to various instances of a real website, called the AtticaBank[1], which has been developed on the Joomla! CMS platform.

3.1 Extracting the Conceptual Model

At the hypertext level, the conceptual model of a web application specifies its composition and navigation. The composition of a website defines which pages compose its hypertext and their internal organization in terms of design elements for publishing content and allowing users to interact with the system. The navigation defines the different ways in which the various design elements and pages can be connected through links to specify the allowed navigation paths, the selections offered to the end-users as well as the sequence of pages presented to them when they interact with the content displayed in a page. In other words, the conceptual model of a Web application specifies the organization of its front-end interfaces in terms of pages, made of design elements which are linked to support the user's navigation and interaction. Thus, the main task for automatically extracting the conceptual model of a website is to identify the organization of the front-end design elements that compose the hypertext of its HTML pages. In the context of a Joomla!-based website, such design elements are called components and modules. A page is composed by one component specifying the organization of content in its main part, and by a set

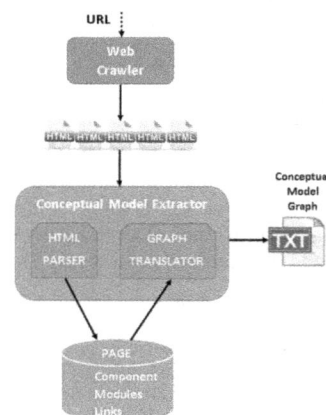

Figure 1. The conceptual model extraction process.

---

[1] Available at http://www.atticabank.gr/en/

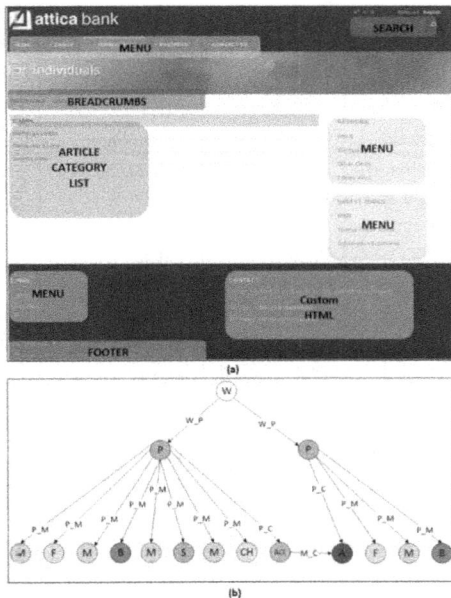

Figure 2. (a) The organization of a page in terms of Joomla! design elements (component and modules). (b) The equivalent graph representation of the page's hypertext.

of modules specifying the organization of content in its peripheral positions. There is a variety of components and modules categories, each one containing various types for interacting with the system and supporting alternative ways of arranging the content delivered to the end-users. The content that they publish is extracted from the tables of the website's underlying database. To specify the hypertext organization for all the pages of a website, we have developed a set of tools as depicted in Figure 1.

By given the URL of a Joomla!-based website, the Web Crawler crawls its pages which are then parsed by the Conceptual Model Extractor to identify their organization as a set of components and modules. In the HTML code of a page, components and modules can be found as <div> elements having an HTML class attribute value (i.e. <div class="value">) which specifies its style i.e. the exact type of the component-module it represents (available in [5]). Thus, by parsing the HTML code of a page and locating the occurrences of these characteristic values within it, we can recover the page's organization as a set of Joomla! design elements. The identified components and modules within a page are stored in the "Page" repository along with additional information about the incoming and outgoing links of the page. For example, Figure 2(a) presents the Joomla! design elements identified for the "Loans" page of the AtticaBank website. As we can see, the page consists of the "Article Category List" component which displays a list with the articles of the "Loans" category and a set of modules such as menus, footer, etc. Once this is done for all the pages of the website, we manage to capture its composition and navigation, i.e. to capture its conceptual model. Then, we employ the Graph Translator which represents the recovered model as a directed graph. An example can be found in Figure 2(b) which presents an instance of the conceptual model graph for the AtticaBank website (root node W), consisting of two connected pages. The left page node (P) represents the equivalent graph representation of the "Loans" page depicted in Figure 2(a). By selecting one of the available list items (i.e. the various loans types) published by the ACL node of the left page node the user can navigate to the right page node consisting of an A (Article) component which publishes information for the

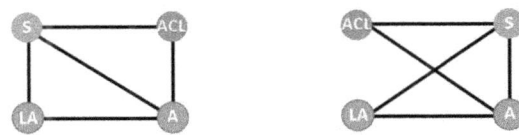

Figure 3. An example of two isomorphic subgraphs. A stands for the Article, ACL for the Article Category List, LA for the Latest Articles and S for the Search box.

selected loan type. Finally, the tool produces a TXT file as an output, containing the graph representation of the conceptual model, which is going to be the input for the graph mining algorithm of the next phase.

3.2 Identification of the Recurrent Interaction Patterns

After the extraction of the application's conceptual model, the next step is to inspect and analyze it in terms of the recurrent patterns (i.e., design fragments) that support user interaction processes for achieving certain tasks. These interaction patterns are configurations of Joomla! components and modules which when located in a particular layout may serve a certain application purpose. To this end, we perform a pattern-based analysis of the recovered model aiming to identify and evaluate the occurrences of all the incorporated recurrent interaction patterns.

To identify these patterns (their core specifications along with their starting and termination variants), we have used an approach which is based on the subgraph isomorphism problem. The latter is synopsized to finding whether the isomorphic image of a subgraph exists in a larger graph. An example of two isomorphic subgraphs (having components and modules on the nodes) is depicted in Figure 3. As we can see, despite the different configuration of nodes in the two subgraphs, the edges connecting the nodes of the same color/label remain the same. Table 1 contains some sequences of the nodes that are connected in the subgraphs of Figure 3. By observing these sequences, one can notice that they actually reveal the recurrent patterns within a graph, both their core specifications and their starting and termination variants. Clearly, the identification of the isomorphic subgraphs within a graph is an alternative way to obtain the identification of the incorporated recurrent patterns. Based on this, we have employed a graph mining algorithm which identifies the occurrences of all the recurrent patterns lying in the conceptual model, by locating all the isomorphic subgraphs within its equivalent graph representation. Then, in order to verify that the identified recurrent patterns are actually interaction patterns, i.e. they define a user interaction process for performing a certain functionality, we additionally inspect their occurrences to examine whether the recurrence of the design elements occurring at the hypertext design goes with a recurrence in the content-data they deliver to the end-users. To achieve this, we have used a semantic similarity measurement

Table 1. The sequences of the connected nodes.

Starting Variant	Pattern's Core Specification			Ending Variant
	S	ACL	A	
	S	ACL	A	S
LA	S	ACL	A	
	ACL	S	LA	
A	ACL	S	LA	
	ACL	S	LA	A

221

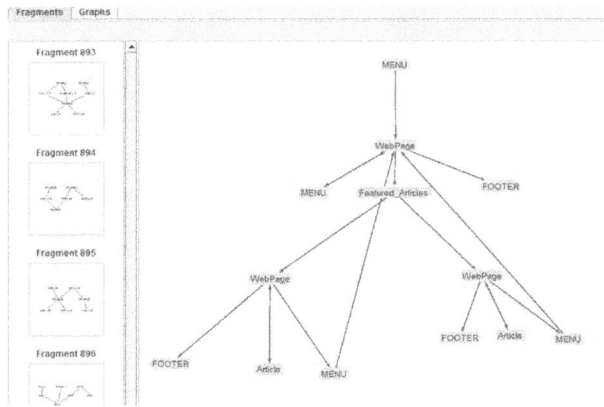

Figure 4. A recurrent subgraph detected in the conceptual model of the AtticaBank website.

technique among the patterns occurrences. The following subsections present the aforementioned tasks in detail.

3.2.1 Mining the Recurrent Patterns

In order to identify the recurrent patterns within the conceptual model graph G, we apply the gSpan algorithm [23] on the graph for detecting the isomorphic subgraphs images. To apply the gSpan, we use the Parsemis project [15] which supports an implementation of the algorithm within a graphical environment for visualizing the identified frequent subgraphs. When looking for the occurrences of a subgraph in G, gSpan encounters except for its identical occurrences, its isomorphic images too. In this way, the graph G is analyzed in terms of its frequent subgraphs (representing recurrent patterns). An example can be found in Figure 4 which presents an identified subgraph-pattern for the AtticaBank website. The subgraph consists of a composition of Joomla! design elements (components and modules) involving three different pages of the website. The Parsemis tool provides the identified subgraphs in a TXT file containing the configuration of the Joomla! design elements that compose each subgraph as well as their occurrences in the graph. Then, we process this file in a way similar with the one presented in the example of Table 1 (based on the sequences of the connected nodes in the subgraphs) and identify the core specifications and the starting and ending variants of each identified pattern.

3.2.2 Interaction Patterns Selection

In this task, we inspect the occurrences of the identified recurrent patterns to examine whether the recurrence of the design elements at the hypertext design goes with a recurrence in the content-data they deliver to the end-users. The content published by the various components and modules is extracted from the tables of the website's database. Thus, to examine if there is a coexisting recurrence at the data level, we have to examine from which tables of the database the Joomla! components and modules (that make up a pattern) extract content. If the corresponding components and modules in a pattern's occurrences publish content from the same data tables, then there is a high possibility of identifying a reusable interaction pattern for implementing a certain task.

However, we assume that we do not have access to the database of the website under study. Based on this, we attempt to examine if there is a recurrence at the data level, by computing the semantic closeness of the content published by the pattern's corresponding Joomla! design elements among its occurrences. The rationale behind this is that the contents of the pages that come from the same database's table usually have a very close semantic relation. To

Table 2. Measuring semantic similarity among occurrences.

PATTERN	MENU [Module]	CATEGORY LIST [Component]	CATEGORY LIST [Component]	ARTICLE [Component]
Occ.1	Individuals Top Menu	Individuals Deposits Categories Page	Individuals Deposits Time Accounts Category Page	Individuals SingleTerm Deposits Details
Occ.2	Business Top Menu	Business Deposits Categories Page	Business Deposits Time Accounts Category Page	Business SingleTerm Deposits Details
SemSim Score		72%	100%	100%
AverageSemSimScore Occ1.-Occ.2				90%
Occ. 3	Individuals Top Menu	Individuals Loans Categories Page	Individuals Mortgage Loans Category Page	Individuals Housing Mortgage Loan Details
SemSim Score		30%	30%	20%
AverageSemSimScore Occ1.-Occ.3				27%

compute the semantic closeness of the published content between two occurrences of a pattern, we have defined two metrics, the "SemSimScore" and the "AverageSemSimScore". On the grounds that the main content of a page, published by components, is indicative of the page's semantics, the "SemSimScore" metric addresses the semantic similarity measurement of the content published by the Joomla! components occurring in a pattern. Then, the "AverageSemSimScore" computes the average value of the individual "SemSimScore" values between the pattern occurrences. To compute the "SemSimScore" metric, we have used the methodology proposed in [17] for WordNet-based semantic similarity measurement. In Table 2, we can see an example of a pattern supporting the user's navigation among the various categories of an object type. To verify that the pattern is actually used in the AtticaBank website, we inspect its occurrences to examine if there is also a recurrence at the content that the pattern's components deliver to the end-users. In Table 2, we can see three occurrences of the pattern Occ.1, Occ.2 and Occ.3. In Occ.1, all the categories and the subcategories of the deposits for Individuals customers are displayed. In Occ.2, the same happens except for the fact that it is intended for Business customers. By comparing the semantic similarity of the content published by the pattern's corresponding components for these two occurrences, they have an AverageSemSimScore of 90% which means that they are semantically very close. Occ.3 refers to the case of displaying all the categories and the subcategories of the loans for Individuals customers. In the same way, we can compute the AverageSemSimScore for Occ.1 and Occ.3 which is 27%, implying that these occurrences are not semantically close. This is actually expected, since their only common base is that they refer to the customer of type Individuals, the rest of the content displayed on them is irrelevant. By using the AverageSemSimScore metric, we can obtain a safe estimation about the recurrence at the data level among the occurrences of the identified patterns. We compute the AverageSemSimScore metric for all the occurrences of the identified patterns (core specification and variants) and we select

Table 3. The measurement scale for the SPM metric.

SPM range	Measurement scale value
$0 \leq SPM < 0.2$	Insufficient
$0.2 \leq SPM < 0.4$	Weak
$0.4 \leq SPM < 0.6$	Discrete
$0.6 \leq SPM < 0.8$	Good
$0.8 \leq SPM \leq 1$	Optimum

Table 4. Pattern variants.

	MENU	CATEGORY LIST	CATEGORY LIST	ARTICLE
VAR. 1	[Module]	[Component]	[Component]	[Component]
Occ. 1	Individuals Top Menu	Individuals Deposits Categories Page	Individuals Deposits Time Accounts Category Page	Individuals Single Term Deposits Details
VAR. 2	BANNER [Module]	CATEGORY LIST [Component]	CATEGORY LIST [Component]	ARTICLE [Component]
Occ. 4	Home Page Banner	Individuals Deposits Categories Page	Individuals Deposits Time Accounts Category Page	Individuals Single Term Deposits Details

and store in a "Interaction Patterns Repository" only the ones having an AverageSemSimScore over 70%.

3.3 Evaluation of Interaction Pattern Variants Consistent Use

In this final step, we focus on evaluating the consistent use of the identified interaction patterns for determining their impact on the overall application's quality. Patterns which are consistently used throughout the conceptual model of an application enhance the ease of use of the application, since they facilitate users identify typical sequences of interactions with the system for performing common tasks. This results in foreseeable navigation behavior, enhancing the quality of the user experience. On the other hand, patterns which are not use consistently cause design inconsistencies and make the user feel disoriented. To this end, we calculate some metrics to evaluate whether the patterns stored in the "Interaction Patterns Repository" are used consistently throughout the conceptual model. In [9], authors have introduced a methodology for evaluating the consistent application of predefined WebML design patterns within the conceptual schema of a WebML-based applications. We utilize this methodology in order to introduce metrics computing the consistent application of an interaction pattern's variants throughout the application model. Assuming a pattern can have N starting and M termination variants, we have defined two metrics that compute the statistical variance of the occurrences of the N starting and the M termination variants of the pattern, normalized according to the best-case variance. These metrics are called Start-Point Metric (SPM) and End-Point Metric (EPM) respectively. SPM is defined as (EPM is defined in an analogous way):

$$SPM = \sigma^2 / \sigma_{BC}^2 \qquad (1)$$

σ^2 is the statistical variance of the N starting variants occurrences which is calculated according to the formula (2):

$$\sigma^2 = \frac{1}{N} \sum_{i=0}^{N} \left(p_i - \frac{1}{N} \right)^2 \qquad (2)$$

where p_i is the percentage of occurrences for the i-th pattern variant. σ_{BC}^2 is instead the best case variance and it is calculated by the formula (2) assuming that only one variant has been coherently used throughout the application. The last step in the metrics definition is the creation of a measurement scale (Table 3) which defines a mapping between the numerical results obtained through the calculus method and a set of (predefined) meaningful and discrete values, expressing a consistency level. We compute these metrics for all the occurrences of all the interaction patterns' starting and ending variants and store the results in the "Results Repository", which are also provided in a TXT file ("Results"). For example, in Table 4, we consider the core specification of an interaction pattern for allowing users browse the hierarchy of Deposits categories and subcategories. In Table 4, there are two occurrences of the two starting variants of the pattern. In fact, in these occurrences, the pattern variants perform the same functiona-

lity, except for the fact that they differ on the starting point they provide to users for browsing the hierarchy of categories. The value of the SPM metric for the first variant is about 0.68 ('Good') since it is a typical way for browsing the hierarchy of categories for various object types whereas the value for the second variant is 0.39 ('Weak') due to the fact that it has a limited number of occurrences. By observing the low value of the second variant on the "Results" file, developers can inspect the identified occurrences of the variant on the AtticaBank website in order to verify if it is actually a design inconsistency. It is worth noting that in some cases it could happen that detected inconsistencies can be caused by conscious design choices in order to respond to specific application constraints. This is just a simple example of showing how the proposed methodology can be used to assist the design process and support designer to improve the quality of a website by highlighting design fragments that need to be inspected in order to make interaction with the application an easy and effortless process.

4. CONCLUSIONS AND FUTURE WORK

In this paper, we have illustrated a model-driven approach for mining interaction patterns in the conceptual model of websites built on the Joomla! CMS. To achieve this, we provide an automated way for extracting the conceptual model of a website which is then submitted to a pattern-based analysis for the identification of all the interaction patterns lying within it. Finally, the identified patterns variants are evaluated towards their consistent use throughout the application. Most of the work presented here can be applied also to web applications built by using other CMSs with slight straightforward modifications. By applying the methodology on a website, developers can gain important information regarding its design quality and particularly about the various design fragments that allow the users to interact with it for performing certain task. On one side, the methodology can detect effective reusable design solutions consistently used throughout the application for supporting predictable user navigation behavior in order to perform certain task. Such reusable solutions can be used as building blocks for producing predictable future designs. They also facilitate the discovery of new interaction design patterns for the CMS domain. On the other side, the methodology can also detect recurrent design constructs indicating design inconsistencies making the user feel disoriented.

In the future, we plan to apply the methodology to a very large number of domain-specific websites for populating a central interaction patterns repository. In this way, it is possible to come up with useful design guidelines for building successful Joomla!-based websites.

5. REFERENCES

[1] Aragón, G., Escalona, M. J., Lang, M., Hilera, J. R., 2013. An Analysis of Model-Driven Web Engineering Methodologies, In International Journal of Innovative Computing, Information and Control, Vol. 9, no. 1, pp. 413-436.

[2] Bernstein, M., 1998. Patterns of Hypertext. In Hypertext 98 - Proceedings of the Ninth ACM Conference on Hypertext and Hypermedia, Pittsburgh, PA, USA, June 20-24, 1998, pp. 21-29.

[3] Brambilla, M., Mauri, A., 2012. Model-Driven Development of Social Network Enabled Applications with WebML and Social Primitives, In Grossniklaus, M., Wimmer, M., (Eds.), Current Trends in Web Engineering, LNCS, Springer, Berlin, 2012, Vol. 7703, pp. 41-55.

[4] Ceri S., Fraternali P., Bongio A., 2000. Web Modeling Language (WebML): a Modeling Language for Designing Web Sites. In the Proceedings of WWW Conference. Amsterdam, NL, May 2000, pp. 137-157.

[5] CMS Patterns, (2015) Available at: http://alkistis.ceid.upatras.gr/research/modeling/patterns/ (Accessed: 22 February 2016).

[6] D.K. van Duyne, J.A. Landay, J. Hong, 2002. The design of sites, Addison-Wesley, Boston, US.

[7] Díaz, P., Rosson, M.B., Aedo, I., Carroll, J.M., 2009. Web design patterns: Investigating user goals and browsing strategies. In: Pipek, V., Rosson, M.B., de Ruyter, B., Wulf, V. (eds.) IS-EUD 2009. LNCS, vol. 5435, pp. 186–204. Springer, Heidelberg.

[8] Drupal CMS (2015). Available at: https://www.drupal.org/ (Accessed: 22 February 2016).

[9] Fraternali, P., Matera, M., Maurino A., 2002. WQA: an XSL Framework for Analyzing the Quality of Web Applications. In the Proceedings of the 2nd International Workshop on Web-Oriented Software Technologies – IWWOST'02. Malaga, Spain, June 10–14, 2002, pp. 46–61.

[10] G.A. Lucca, A.R. Fasolino, and P. Tramontana, 2005. Recovering interaction design patterns in web applications, Proceedings of the Ninth European Conference on Software Maintenance and Reengineering, March 2005, pp. 366-374.

[11] Gamma, E., Helm, R., Johnson, R., Vlissides, J., 1995. Design Patterns: Elements of Reusable Object-Oriented Software, Addison-Wesley Longman Publishing Co., Inc., Boston, MA.

[12] Graham, 2003. A pattern language for Web Usability, Addison-Wesley, Boston, US.

[13] Joomla! CMS (2015). Available at: http://www.joomla.org/ (Accessed: 22 February 2016).

[14] M. van Welie, G. C. van der Veer, 2003. Pattern Languages in Interaction Design: Structure and Organization, Proceedings of Ninth International Conference on Human-Computer Interaction, Interact 2003, Zürich, Switzerland, pp. 527-534.

[15] Philippsen, M., 2011. ParSeMiS - the Parallel and Sequential Mining Suite. Available at: https://www2.cs.fau.de/EN/research/zold/ParSeMiS/index.html (Accessed: 22 February 2016).

[16] Scott, B., Neil, T., 2009. Designing Web Interfaces: Principles and Patterns for Rich Interactions. O'Reilly, Sebastopol.

[17] Simpson, T., Dao, T., 2010. WordNet-based semantic similarity measurement. Available at: http://www.codeproject.com/Articles/11835/WordNet-based-semantic-similarity-measurement (Accessed: 22 February 2016).

[18] Tidwell, J. 2006. Designing Interfaces. O'Reilly, Sebastopol.

[19] Toxboe, A., 2010. Pattern library. Available at: http://ui-patterns.com (Accessed: 22 February 2016).

[20] Valverde, F., Pastor, O., 2008. Applying interaction patterns: Towards a model-driven approach for rich internet applications development. In Proceedings of the International Workshop on Web Oriented Software Technology (IWWOST). CEUR Workshop. CEUR-WS.org, RWTH Aachen, 13–18.

[21] Website patterns (2015). Available at: http://c2.com/cgi/wiki?HypermediaDesignPatternsRepository (Accessed: 22 February 2016).

[22] Welie, M. v. (2008): Interaction Design Patterns. Available at http://www.welie.com/patterns/ (Accessed: 22 February 2016).

[23] Yan, X., Han, J., 2002. gSpan: Graph-based substructure pattern mining. In ICDM '02, page 721, Washington,DC, USA, 2002. IEEE Computer Society

Issue-Focused Documentaries versus Other Films: Rating and Type Prediction based on User-Authored Reviews

Ming Jiang
GSLIS – The iSchool at Illinois
University of Illinois at Urbana-Champaign
{mjiang17@illinois.edu}

Jana Diesner
GSLIS – The iSchool at Illinois
University of Illinois at Urbana-Champaign
{jdiesner@illinois.edu}

ABSTRACT

User-authored reviews offer a window into micro-level engagement with issue-focused documentary films, which is a critical yet insufficiently understood topic in media impact assessment. Based on our data, features, and supervised learning method, we find that ratings of non-documentary (feature film) reviews can be predicted with higher accuracy (73.67%, F1 score) than ratings of documentary reviews (68.05%). We also constructed a classifier that separates reviews of documentaries from reviews of feature films with an accuracy of 71.32%. However, as our goal with this paper is not to improve the accuracy of predicting the rating and type or genre of film reviews, but to advance our understanding of the perception of documentaries in comparison to feature films, we also identified commonalities and differences between these two types of films as well as between low versus high ratings. We find that in contrast to reviews of feature films, comments on documentaries are shorter but composed of longer sentences, are less emotional, contain less positive and more negative terms, are lexically more concise, and are more focused on verbs than on nouns and adjectives. Compared to low-rated reviews, comments with a high rating are shorter, are more emotional and contain more positive than negative sentiment, and have less question marks and more exclamation points. Overall, this work contributes to advancing our understanding of the impact of different types of information products on individual information consumers.

Keywords

Rating prediction; Type prediction; Documentary films; Social impact

1. INTRODUCTION

The impact of media and information products on individuals and small groups has traditionally been measured by surveying people pre and post media exposure [6; 29]. Such surveys as well as in-depth focus group discussions can lead to a deep understanding of a problem domain and people's perception of it, but this process

HT '16, July 10-13, 2016, Halifax, NS, Canada
© 2016 ACM. ISBN 978-1-4503-4247-6/16/07...$15.00
DOI: http://dx.doi.org/10.1145/2914586.2914638.

limits scalability [2; 11]. Additionally, peoples' thoughts about information they have consumed can be measured by examining user-authored comments, which can be published on customer review sites, among other sources [19]. Unlike classic interviews with individual information consumers, online reviews can become part of the public discourse about a film or an issue. Analyzing digital reviews eliminates classic issues with surveys, such as answers biased by social desirability, and enables the consideration of large amounts of data over long periods of time. Data mining and Natural Language Processing (NLP) techniques make this approach scalable [5; 19].

In this paper, we focus on a specific subset of media products, namely documentary films, and analyze them in contrast to other types of films. Researchers and practitioners in the field of media impact assessment have defined various sets of impact goals, which often include an increase in public awareness about an issue (other goals are, for example, changes in consumer attitude and behavior, corporate policy, and political action) [3; 12]. Analyzing film reviews offers one way to study a certain subset of the public opinion about a documentary on the micro (i.e., individual) level. We argue that understanding this type of individual engagement contributes to our knowledge about the social impact of documentaries.

Review analysis is a classic subject of study in social computing. Prior work has resulted in knowledge and models for predicting the rating, helpfulness, and sentiment of reviews (details in the Background section) [21; 31; 32]. This work typically does not differentiate between sub-genres of film, but rather uses randomly drawn samples of films from across genres, which is an appropriate solution for results meant to generalize to all types of film. We build upon and extend this prior research in order to a) develop a better understanding of the perception of issue-focused documentaries as a specific genre, and b) identify differences in the ratings and underlying text characteristics of the reviews of documentaries versus other films. Our solution to this task is explained in the Methods section. The findings are presented in the Results section and interpreted in the Discussion section.

We focus on documentaries that address issues of inequality and social justice. These films are often produced as a vehicle to induce change on the individual, group and, ultimately, societal level [6; 7; 18; 22; 30]. The intent of impact co-exists with classic goals of film production, mainly compelling storytelling and appealing cinematography [33]. As stated by a major funder of documentaries, "these stories inspire imaginations, disrupt stereotypes, and help transform attitudes that perpetuate injustice" [15]. However, our understanding of the (aggregated) perception of documentaries is underdeveloped. The research presented in this paper aims to help to fill this gap. As documentaries are meant to inspire engagement with the public, we are not concerned with improving the accuracy of predicting ratings of films based on reviews, but rather we aim to improve the understanding of differences in the reflection on documentaries versus other films. In summary, in this paper, we use NLP techniques to find answers to the following questions:

1. How does the predictability of ratings of documentaries compare to the predictability of ratings of other types of films?

2. If differences exist, what features of the content of publicly available, user-contributed reviews of films account for these differences?

2. BACKGROUND

The majority of existing work on review mining can be divided into four research areas: First, predicting review helpfulness, which typically is based on explicit votes made by users [17; 19; 21; 26]. Second, rating prediction, with the goal of anticipating user preferences, and third, sentiment analysis, which aims at identifying the features of a product that users like or don't like [8; 10; 28; 38; 39]. Studies on the latter two topics can be further divided into building a) binary classifiers [8; 10; 38], or b) multi-class predictors [30; 32]. Fourth, review summarization, which is meant to identify the gist of information from a set of reviews [23; 26]. All of the abovementioned techniques take the content of the reviews into account, and at least the first three groups may also leverage additional meta-data, such as time stamps and information about the user and the reviewed product.

Our paper falls into the first category, i.e., rating prediction. Scholars have repeatedly confirmed the following features as being helpful for this task: 1) Bag of words, which represents lexical characteristics, 2) parts of speech (POS) tags, which capture shallow syntactic information, and 3) deep syntax information from parse tree, which are useful e.g., to handle negation detection [22; 35]. Prevalent themes identified via topic modeling have also been used as a feature [27]. Finally, features of reviews of other products about which the reviewer of a target product has also written a comment can be considered, e.g., to calibrate a specific rating within a user's profile of rating patterns [28]. Prior work has also identified suitable prediction algorithms or models. Most scholars either use ranking algorithms or apply classification models. For ranking a set of reviews, regression models have emerged as a proper solution [30]. For classification tasks, SVMs [16], Naïve Bayes [31], and Neural Networks [36] have consistently resulted in comparatively highly accurate performance. Overall, most prior rating prediction studies have achieved accuracy rates (F1) of 40% to 85%; average values seem to be around 75% [1; 9; 24; 25; 31; 32].

For the domain of film, we observe a lack of work on the relationship between genre and rating. In this paper, we focus on measuring different features that are appropriate for predicting ratings of documentary reviews, and contrast our findings to results based on other types of films.

3. DATA

We selected documentaries that address different dimensions of inequality and social justice, e.g., economic, political, and cultural issues. The sample is partially based on films which we have considered in our prior related work on social impact assessment of documentaries [13]. We then searched for feature films that address similar topics, have a similar amount of reviews, and have

Table 1. Dataset statistics

Type of film	Number of reviews	Rating distribution (average and standard deviation)		
		5&4 star (high)	3 star (medium)	1&2 star (low)
Documentaries	8,090	87.45% ↓ 7.22%	5.30% ↓ 3.20%	7.25% ↓ 5.52%
Non-documentaries	8,261	82.55% ↓ 8.64%	7.73% ↓ 3.74%	9.73% ↓ 5.46%

a similar distribution of rating values. In our sample, non-documentaries tend to receive more reviews than documentaries. To keep the amount of reviews on both types of films similar, we considered a smaller set of non-documentaries. We collected reviews on 20 issue-focused documentaries (N=8,090) and 11 other films (N=8,261) from Amazon.com (with their permission). The other films fall into the following genres (a single film can be in multiple categories): drama (7), comedy (4), romance (2), cartoon (2), and science fiction (1). In this paper, we also refer to the films that are not documentaries as "feature films", and acknowledge that this might be an overly general classification or genre. Table 1 provides a summary of the dataset.

4. METHOD

Each review is user-rated on a 5-point scale. We consolidated the ratings as follows: a) high ratings, which include all 5 and 4 star reviews; b) medium ratings (3 stars); and c) low ratings (1 and 2 stars). As medium ratings are neither clearly high nor low, and also form the smallest portion of the sample, we disregarded them for further analysis. This implies that we ultimately construct two binary classifiers (one per type or genre of film) for high versus low ratings.

We removed overly short reviews that mainly consisted of stop words. In order to construct a sample that has a similar number of instances of high and low rated reviews for learning, we used the number of low ratings per type (smaller set) as the upper bound for the number of reviews considered per prediction category. We randomly sampled an equally sized corpus of reviews with a high rating from the same films. This process resulted in a total sample size for learning of N=1,000 for documentaries and 1,668 for non-documentaries.

4.1 Feature Selection

All features are extracted from the content of the reviews. Our feature selection is guided by prior work as well as our close reading of a small sample of the reviews. We consider four types of features: meta-data of the texts, text content, regular expressions, and syntax. We use the Stanford NLP toolkit to parse the data and calculate the values specified below [34].

We hypothesize that the text characteristics of the reviews for different genres might differ for two reasons: First, documentaries are a more specifically defined genre than feature films, which might suggest a tighter distribution of unigrams in documentary reviews. Second, these types of film might evoke different styles of engagement, which might be reflected in peoples' writing.

4.1.1 Text Meta-data
We consider the average length of both reviews and of the sentences per review.

4.1.2 Lexical Features
Four content features are considered: salient terms, informativeness, token level sentiment, and transition words. In

order to identify the salient terms, we select the top 250 unigrams per film according to their TF*IDF scores as calculated in Eq1, and normalize the scores by article length (see Eq2).

$$\ !\ !\ !\ !"\#(!\ !!)\ !\ !"(!\ !!)\ !!\ !!"\#\left(!\ !\ \frac{!}{!"(!)}\right)\ !!!!!!!!!!!!!!!\ !\ !\ /$$

$$!!!!\ !_{!}\ "\#\$\ \%\&()*(!\ !!)\ !\ \frac{!"!!\ !!\ !}{\sum_{!\ !_{!!}}!"!!\ !!\ !}\ !!!!!!!!!!!!!!!!!!!!!\ !\ !$$

where ! represents the corpus per film, ! is any term appearing in !, d is any review in the collection, ! is the total number of reviews per film, and !"!! ! is the number of reviews that contain term !. Terms are not syntactically disambiguated for this step.

We also calculate information entropy as it represents the informativeness of a review (Eq3) [38]. Review entropy is computed based on the amount of information that each w carries, which is determined by the w's normalized weight in the review d and corpus C (See Eq4). For this project, we conducted several experiments with different values of !, and decided to set ! to 0.3.

$$!!!!!!!!!!!!!!!\ (!)\ !\ !\sum_{!\ !!}[!\ !(!)\ !"\#_{!}\ !(!)]\ !!!!!!!!!!!!!!!!!(!)$$

$$!(!)\ !\ \blacksquare!\ \frac{!"!!"\#!\ !!\ !}{\sum_{!\ !_{!!}}\ !"!!"\#!\ !!\ !}\ !\ (!\ !\ !)\ !\ \frac{!"!!"\#!\ !!\ !}{\sum_{!\ !_{!!}}\ !"!!"\#!\ !!\ !}\ !!!!(4)$$

For sentiment identification and quantification, we follow the example of prior studies that use previously constructed and validated dictionaries for this purpose, and chose to use a widely adopted subjectivity lexicon [39]. Terms were syntactically disambiguated for this step. As part of the sentiment analysis, we account for negations by using rule-based negation detection (see Table 2) that relies on deep parsing (as provided by the Stanford NLP Parser).

Finally, we consider transition words [4]. We calculate a) the number of unique transition words per text, and b) the ratio of logical relationships (see Eq5), including addition, introduction, emphasis, conflict/concession, causal, condition, time, and conclusion.

$$!!!!!!!!!!!\ "\#\%(!"_{!})\ !\ \frac{\sum_{!"\ !!\ !_{!}}\ !"!!"\ !!\ !}{\sum_{!\ !!_{!}}\sum_{!\ "!!"_{!}}\ !"\ !!!\ !!!\ !}\ !!!!!!!!!!!!!!!!!!!!\ !\ !$$

where $!"_{!}$ represents the $!!!$ logical relationship, and !" is any transition word that belongs to the category of $!"_{!}$.

Table 2. Rule-based negation detection

Direct negation rules	Indirect negation rules
neg(VB/JJ, not)	neg(w, not) + amod(w, JJ) => not JJ
	neg(w, not) + xcomp(JJ, w) => not JJ
	neg(w, not) + admod(RB, w) => not RB

4.1.3 Regular Expression
We calculate the ratio of question marks and exclamation points per review (also by using the Stanford NLP Parser).

4.1.4 Syntax Features
We identify the POS per word and parse tree constituents per sentence. For each review, we calculate a) the number of unique POS tags, and b) the ratio of nouns (i.e., NN, NNS, NNP & NNPS), verbs (i.e., VB, VBD, VBG, VBN, VBP & VBZ), adjectives (i.e., JJ, JJR & JJS), and adverbs (i.e., RB, RBR & RBS).

4.2 Learning and Evaluation
Following the example of prior studies, we use a SVM with a radial kernel for learning. The classifier was implemented using the R package e1071 [14]. For our experiments, we conducted 10-fold cross validations, and report the averaged results. For assessing prediction accuracy, we use the standard metrics of precision, recall, and the F1 score.

5. RESULTS

5.1 Classification Performance
Based on our data, features, and learning method, we find that ratings of non-documentaries can be predicted with higher accuracy (73.67%, F1 score) than ratings of documentaries (68.05%) (Table 3). This difference could be due to differences in the sample size per type of film (larger for non-documentaries), or could mean that high versus low-rated reviews are more distinct for feature films than for documentaries. Our accuracy rates for rating prediction of feature films are a little lower than in prior work (about 75%, see Background section for details), while no point of comparison exists specifically for documentaries.

Especially for feature films, precision is higher than recall when

Table 3. Accuracy of rating prediction per type of film (average and standard deviation)*

Used Features	Recall		Precision		F1	
	Docu	Non-Docu	Docu	Non-Docu	Docu	Non-Docu
Review length (RL)	78.19%	68.15%	59.48%	66.02%	67.43%	66.87%
Avg. sentence length	48.25%	49.76%	61.43%	65.31%	53.64%	56.32%
Unigram	70.29%	63.78%	61.54%	65.96%	65.13%	64.64%
Entropy	70.13%	63.31%	61.70%	65.46%	65.52%	64.30%
Sentiment%	69.42%	66.27%	63.41%	76.48%	65.98%	70.95%
Transition words	60.99%	54.39%	61.76%	67.67%	61.00%	60.01%
Question mark% (Q)	**91.99%**	**93.47%**	55.86%	55.44%	69.44%	69.54%
Exclamation mark%	19.92%	13.89%	**74.93%**	78.64%	31.25%	23.58%
POS	61.52%	60.52%	64.51%	70.46%	62.78%	64.97%
Num_Sentiment+Negative% (Senti_N)	74.11%	59.36%	65.93%	78.72%	69.41%	67.55%
Num_Sentiment +Positive% (Senti_P)	77.67%	70.57%	60.83%	70.39%	67.91%	70.18%
Senti_N+Q+RL	75.05%	60.10%	66.12%	**79.05%**	**69.91%**	68.08%
Senti_P+Q+RL	78.99%	72.65%	62.26%	71.87%	69.39%	72.04%
All	**68.16%**	**71.84%**	**68.82%**	**75.86%**	**68.05%**	**73.67%**

* highest value per column marked in bold

Recall	Precision	F1
72.19% ! 0.013	70.50% ! 0.019	71.32% ! 0.013

* using all texts and features

using all features (Table 3). Our model is more likely to predict a truly high rating as a low rating than vice versa, which means low ratings are easier to recognize, while high ratings are more ambiguous.

The ratio of question marks is the strongest individual feature with respect to recall for both types of film (91.99% for documentary reviews, 93.47% for feature films reviews). For precision, the strongest feature for documentary reviews is the ratio of exclamation points (74.93%), and for feature films, it is a combination of the amount of words with a negative sentiment, the ratio of question marks, and review length (79.05%).

For combining multiple features for learning, the F1 values suggest that the number of negative sentiment terms plus the ratio of question marks plus review length is the best feature set for classifying documentary reviews, while for non-documentary reviews, combining all features results in the highest accuracy rates. We also find negative sentiment to be more indicative of documentary reviews, and positive sentiment to be a better predictor for non-documentary reviews. At least two explanations seem plausible, but require further testing for confirmation. First, documentary reviews might be written by a more critical audience. Second, and independent of the reviewers' perception and style, documentary reviews might address or represent the severity of given social justice issues.

Instead of building two binary classifiers, the prediction task solved in this paper can also be approached as a 4-label classification problem (high versus low-rated reviews of documentaries versus other films). Using the same sample of documentaries as for the previous task, and an equally sized sample of non-documentary reviews, we tested this approach by using all introduced features, and achieved an overall F1 score of 44.55%, which is considerably lower than the accuracy obtained with the prior approach.

Finally, we trained a binary classifier that aims to tell apart reviews of documentaries versus other films (Table 4). Using the full set of reviews and features, we obtained an accuracy rate of 71.32% (F1) for distinguishing reviews per type, regardless of the rating. This finding suggests that reviews per genre have distinct characteristics, which are analyzed in more detail in the next section.

5.2 Feature Analysis

In this section, we analyze the differences between the set of documentaries reviews versus feature film reviews based on the entire corpus.

5.2.1 Feature Comparison by Rating

Most of the findings in this section are shown in Table 5. In our sample, high-rated reviews are considerably shorter than low-rated reviews. This might indicate that agreement or excitement get expressed with brevity, while disagreement or disappointment are associated with more detailed explanations.

Low-rated reviews contain more question marks and less exclamation points than high-rated reviews. This suggests that people raise more questions in critical or negative reviews, and emphasize their opinion more in positive reviews.

Table 5. Feature comparison by rating group

Selected Feature	4&5 stars (high)		1&2 stars (low)	
	Docu	Non-Docu	Docu	Non-Docu
Review length	76	78	145	140
Sentiment%	12.82%	13.88%	10.57%	10.22%
Positive %	41.15%	56.84%	30.02%	33.31%
Negative %	22.11%	16.02%	37.76%	37.31%
Conflict%	8.13%	9.51%	12.00%	15.13%
Emphasis%	12.88%	10.05%	8.80%	10.17%
Question mark%	1.65%	1.38%	5.68%	4.95%
Exclamation mark%	13.59%	14.52%	5.08%	6.14%

As one might expect, higher ratings correlate with more positive and less negative sentiment, and also with higher emotionality. The gap between the ratio of positive to negative words decreases with decreasing ratings.

5.2.2 Feature Comparison by Type of Film

Most of the findings in this section are represented in Table 6. On average, non-documentary reviews are longer, but composed of shorter sentences than documentary reviews. This could indicate that feature film reviews are easier to write. Also, documentary reviews have a slightly higher entropy than feature film reviews.

Across types of film, in total, reviews contain more positive than negative terms (Table 6). This finding suggests a general level of courtesy and politeness among laymen film reviewers. Compared to documentaries, comments on non-documentaries have a slightly higher ratio of sentiment words, a considerably larger ratio of positive terms, and a lower portion of negative terms. These findings indicate that reviews of feature films are more emotional and enthusiastic. A possible explanation for this effect

Table 6. Feature comparison by type of film

Feature Type	Feature	Docu	Non-Docu
Text meta-data	Review length (in words)	82.6310	91.4873
	Avg. sentence length	14.0075	12.6440
Regular expressions	Question mark%	1.98%	1.90%
	Exclamation mark%	12.53%	12.75%
Sentiment	Sentiwords%	12.60%	13.23%
	Positive%	40.18%	53.33%
	Negative%	23.45%	19.23%
POS	# Unique POS tags	14.6671	13.7680
	NN%	24.38%	26.42%
	VB%	18.42%	15.58%
	JJ%	11.20%	14.11%
	RB%	6.24%	6.22%
Transition words	Unique transition words%	6.85%	6.94%
	Addition%	43.79%	40.02%
	Introduction%	0.77%	0.60%
	Emphasis%	12.49%	9.80%
	Conflict%	8.93%	11.01%
	Causal%	5.64%	6.07%
	Condition%	4.11%	3.22%
	Time%	5.40%	5.12%
	Conclusion%	0.18%	0.20%
Unigram	Top unigram 1	0.0112	0.0108
	Top unigram 2	0.0179	0.0100
	Top unigram 3	0.0173	0.0181
	Top unigram 4	0.0212	0.0141
	Top unigram 5	0.0118	0.0119
Information quantity	Entropy	1.7525	1.7387

Table 7. Example for top 20 unigrams*

Fed Up (Docu)	sugar, food, *movie, documentary,* people, *film, watch,* fat, health, *great,* industry, foods, eat, *good,* government, eye, eating, *informative,* obesity, children
War Horse (Non-Docu)	horse, *film,* war, *joey, spielberg, story,* horses, *great, good,* albert, love, *movies, scenes, watch, time,* family, *loved,* boy, animal, man

* words not central to key topic of film in italics

might be the way in which similar topics are presented in documentaries versus feature films.

With respect to syntax, people use comparatively more nouns and adjectives in non-documentary reviews, and more verbs in documentary reviews. This might suggest that non-documentary reviews are more about objects or social entities and their modifiers (e.g., great film!), while documentary reviews might focus more on activities. More analyses are needed to test this assumption, but the latter finding is a desirable outcome for impact creators.

Finally, the unigram analysis shows a stronger focus tendency in documentary reviews. This finding might reflect the fact that the themes addressed in documentaries and/or their reviews are more focused on specific topic, while individual feature films might cover a broader scope of topics. To illustrate this point, we provide an example: We show the top 20 unigrams (based on TF*IDF) from two randomly selected films in Table 7. This comparison reveals that more than half of the unigrams occurring in reviews on *Fed Up* (a documentary) focus on junk food and associated health issues (about 13 of the terms), which is the main issue of the film. For *War Horse* (a non-documentary), the top unigrams represent several topics, including the actual theme of the film (about 8 of the 20 terms, including "horse", "war", "horses"), the leading actor ("joey"), the director ("spielberg"), and other themes.

6. CONCLUSION AND DISCUSSION

We have built two binary classifiers that predict high versus low ratings of reviews of issue-focused documentaries versus other films with 68.05% and 73.67% accuracy (F1), respectively. We also constructed a classifier that separates reviews of documentaries from reviews of feature films with an accuracy of 71.32%. However, as our goal with this paper is not to improve rating and type prediction accuracy, but to advance our understanding of the perception of documentaries in comparison to feature films, we also identified commonalities and differences between these two genres as well as between low versus high ratings in general: In contrast to reviews of feature films, comments on documentaries are shorter but composed of longer sentences, are less emotional, contain less positive and more negative terms, are lexically more concise, and are more focused on verbs than nouns and adjectives. Compared to low-rated reviews, comments with a high rating are shorter, are more emotional and contain more positive than negative sentiment, and have less question marks and more exclamation points.

Our work has several limitations. First, by aggregating all reviews per film, we gain only a general sense of the users' opinions and engagement with a film. Time slicing the reviews would allow for analyzing changes in the perception of a film over time. Second, we apply a very coarse definition of feature films. Our work could be improved by further splitting feature films into more precise genres. Third, most reviews on Amazon are authored by laymen.

We have started to complement this work by also considering reviews from expert critics, which are typically published in traditional print media.

ACKNOWLEDGMENTS
This work is supported by the FORD Foundation, JustFilms division, grant 0155-0370. We thank Amazon.com for giving us permission to collect and use customer review data from their site. We thank Chieh-Li Chin and Rezvaneh Rezapour from the iSchool at UIUC for their help with and advice about this paper.

7. REFERENCES

[1] Adomavicius, G. and Kwon, Y., 2007. New recommendation techniques for multicriteria rating systems. *Intelligent Systems, IEEE 22*, 3, 48-55.

[2] Bernard, H.R., 2012. *Social Research Methods: Qualitative and Quantitative Approaches.* Sage.

[3] Britdoc, *The end of the line. A social impact evaluation.* http://animatingdemocracy.org/resource/end-line-social-impact-evaluation.

[4] Campbell, G.M., Buckhoff, M., and Dowell, J.A., Transition Words. https://msu.edu/~jdowell/135/transw.html.

[5] Chaovalit, P. and Zhou, L., 2005. Movie review mining: A comparison between supervised and unsupervised classification approaches. In *Proceedings of the 38th Annual Hawaii International Conference on System Sciences, (HICSS'05).* IEEE, 112c.

[6] Chattoo, C.B., 2014. *Assessing the Social Impact of Issue-Focused Documentaries: Research Methods and Future Considerations.* Center for Media and Social Impact, School of Communication at American University.

[7] Clark, J. and Abrash, B., 2011. *Social Justice Documentary: Designing for Impact.* Center for Social Media, School of Communication at American University http://www.centerforsocialmedia.org/designing-impact.

[8] Cui, H., Mittal, V., and Datar, M., 2006. Comparative experiments on sentiment classification for online product reviews. In *Proceedings of the 21st International Conference on Artificial intelligence, (AAAI'06).* 1265-1270.

[9] De Albornoz, J.C., Plaza, L., Gervás, P., and Díaz, A., 2011. A Joint Model of Feature Mining and Sentiment Analysis for Product Review Rating. In *Advances in Information Retrieval.* Springer, Berlin Heidelberg, 55-66.

[10] Devitt, A. and Ahmad, K., 2007. Sentiment polarity identification in financial news: A cohesion-based approach. In *Proceedings of the 45th Annual Meeting of the Association of Computational Linguistics, (ACL'07).* Association of Computational Linguistics, 25-27.

[11] Diesner, J., Kim, J., and Pak, S., 2014. Computational impact assessment of social justice documentaries. *Metrics for Measuring Publishing Value: Alternative and Otherwise 17*, 3.

[12] Diesner, J. and Rezapour, R., 2015. Social Computing for Impact Assessment of Social Change Projects. In *Proceedings of the International Conference on Social Computing, Behavioral-Cultural Modeling, and Prediction, (SBP'15).* Springer, 34-43.

[13] Diesner, J., Rezapour, R., and Jiang, M., 2016. Assessing public awareness of social justice documentary films based

on news coverage versus social media. In *Proceedings of the iConference*.

[14] Dimitriadou, E., Hornik, K., Leisch, F., Meyer, D., and Weingessel, A., 2011. Misc functions of the department of statistics (e1071), TU Wien. In *R package 1*, Version: 1-6.

[15] Ford Foundation, Just Films. http://www.fordfoundation.org/work/our-grants/justfilms.

[16] Ganu, G., Elhadad, N., and Marian, A., 2009. Beyond the stars: improving rating predictions using review text content. In *Proceedings of the 12th International Workshop on the Web and Databases, (WebDB'09)*. 1-6.

[17] Green, D. and Patel, M., 2013. *Deepening Engagement for Lasting Impact: A Framework for Masuring Media Performance and Results*. John S. and James L. Knight Foundation and Bill & Melinda Gates Foundation.

[18] Hong, Y., Lu, J., Yao, J., Zhu, Q., and Zhou, G., 2012. What reviews are satisfactory: novel features for automatic helpfulness voting. In *Proceedings of the 35th International ACM Conference on Research and Development in Information Retrieval, (SIGIR'12)*. ACM, 495-504.

[19] Hu, M. and Liu, B., 2004. Mining and summarizing customer reviews. In *Proceedings of the 10th ACM International Conference on Knowledge Discovery and Data Mining, (KDD'04)*. ACM, 168-177.

[20] Kim, S.-M., Pantel, P., Chklovski, T., and Pennacchiotti, M., 2006. Automatically assessing review helpfulness. In *Proceedings of the Conference on Empirical Methods in Natural Language Processing, (EMNLP'06)*. Association for Computational Linguistics, 423-430.

[21] Knight Foundation, 2011. *Impact: A Guide to Evaluating Community Information Projects*. http://www.knightfoundation.org/publications/impact-practical-guide-evaluating-community-inform.

[22] Li, S., Zhang, H., Xu, W., Chen, G., and Guo, J., 2010. Exploiting combined multi-level model for document sentiment analysis. In *Proceedings of the 20th International Conference on Pattern Recognition, (ICPR'10)*. IEEE, 4141-4144.

[23] Liu, C.-L., Hsaio, W.-H., Lee, C.-H., Lu, G.-C., and Jou, E., 2012. Movie rating and review summarization in mobile environment. *IEEE Transactions on Systems, Man, and Cybernetics, Part C: Applications and Reviews*. 42, 3, 397-407.

[24] Liu, J. and Seneff, S., 2009. Review sentiment scoring via a parse-and-paraphrase paradigm. In *Proceedings of the Conference on Empirical Methods in Natural Language Processing, (EMNLP'09)*. Association for Computational Linguistics, 161-169.

[25] Liu, Y., Huang, X., An, A., and Yu, X., 2008. Modeling and predicting the helpfulness of online reviews. In *Proceedings of the 8th IEEE International Conference on Data Mining, (ICDM'08)*. 443-452.

[26] Ly, D.K., Sugiyama, K., Lin, Z., and Kan, M.-Y., 2011. Product review summarization from a deeper perspective. In *Proceedings of the 11th Annual International ACM/IEEE Joint Conference on Digital Libraries, (JCDL'11)*. ACM, 311-314.

[27] Mcauley, J. and Leskovec, J., 2013. Hidden factors and hidden topics: understanding rating dimensions with review text. In *Proceedings of the 7th ACM Conference on Recommender Systems, (RecSys'13)*. ACM, 165-172.

[28] Mukherjee, S., Basu, G., and Joshi, S., 2013. Incorporating author preference in sentiment rating prediction of reviews. In *Proceedings of the 22nd International Conference on World Wide Web, (WWW'13)*. ACM, 47-48.

[29] Napoli, P., 2014. *Measuring Media Impact: An Overview of the Field*. Media Impact Project, USC Annenberg Norman Lear Center.

[30] Pang, B. and Lee, L., 2005. Seeing stars: Exploiting class relationships for sentiment categorization with respect to rating scales. In *Proceedings of the 43rd Annual Meeting on Association for Computational Linguistics, (ACL'05)*. Association for Computational Linguistics, 115-124.

[31] Pang, B., Lee, L., and Vaithyanathan, S., 2002. Thumbs up?: sentiment classification using machine learning techniques. In *Proceedings of the Conference on Empirical Methods in Natural Language Processing-Volume 10, (EMNLP'02)*. Association for Computational Linguistics, 79-86.

[32] Qu, L., Ifrim, G., and Weikum, G., 2010. The bag-of-opinions method for review rating prediction from sparse text patterns. In *Proceedings of the 23rd International Conference on Computational Linguistics, (COLING'10)*. Association for Computational Linguistics, 913-921.

[33] Rose, F., 2012. *The Art of Immersion: How the Digital Generation Is Remaking Hollywood, Madison Avenue, and the Way We Tell Stories*. W.W. Norton & Company, New York, NY.

[34] Socher, R., Bauer, J., Manning, C.D., and Ng, A.Y., 2013. Parsing with compositional vector grammars. In *Proceedings of the 51st Annual Meeting of the Association for Computational Linguistics, (ACL'13)*. Association for Computational Linguistics, 455-465.

[35] Taboada, M., Brooke, J., Tofiloski, M., Voll, K., and Stede, M., 2011. Lexicon-based methods for sentiment analysis. *Computational Linguistics*. 37, 2, 267-307.

[36] Tang, D., Qin, B., Liu, T., and Yang, Y., 2015. User modeling with neural network for review rating prediction. In *Proceedings of the 24th International Joint Conference on Artificial Intelligence, (IJCAT'15)*. 1340-1346.

[37] Turney, P.D., 2002. Thumbs up or thumbs down?: semantic orientation applied to unsupervised classification of reviews. In *Proceedings of the 40th Annual Meeting on Association for Computational Linguistics, (ACL'02)*. Association for Computational Linguistics, 417-417.

[38] Weaver, W. and Shannon, C.E., 1949. *The Mathematical Theory of Communication*. University of Illinois Press, Urbana, Illinois.

[39] Wilson, T., Wiebe, J., and Hoffmann, P., 2005. Recognizing contextual polarity in phrase-level sentiment analysis. In *Proceedings of the Conference on Human Language Technology and Empirical Methods in Natural Language Processing, (HLT'05)*. Association for Computational Linguistics, 347-354.

Approximate Contagion Model of Common Knowledge on Facebook

Gizem Korkmaz
Virginia Tech
gkorkmaz@vbi.vt.edu

Chris J. Kuhlman
Virginia Tech
ckuhlman@vbi.vt.edu

S. S. Ravi
University at Albany—SUNY
sravi@albany.edu

Fernando Vega-Redondo
Bocconi University
fernando.vega@unibocconi.it

ABSTRACT

Computational modeling of information exchange over social media is important for understanding coordination in online environments. Many contagion dynamics models that have been used to model Twitter, Facebook, and blog information transmission are polynomial-time computable, and hence can be efficiently simulated on networked populations. Game-theoretic models of collective action (i.e., coordination problems that require common knowledge among agents), however, have dynamics that are controlled in part by specific network structures such as cliques and bicliques. Contagion dynamics with these models cannot be efficiently computed because finding all bicliques in a graph, for example, is an NF-hard problem. We investigate a recent model of common knowledge dynamics that represents information spread on Facebook—in which the biclique is the characterizing structure—and convert the model into an efficiently computable one by using an approximation. We demonstrate this through experiments on seven different graphs for a total of 168 sets of conditions, including a 4-order of magnitude span in dynamics parameter values. Our approach speeds computations in two ways: (i) it obviates the need to find all bicliques in a social network, which is a very time-consuming task (computations can take 30 to 120 hours or more of wall clock time), and (ii) it reduces the time of simulation computations, in some cases by well over an order of magnitude. Our method also enables evaluation of much larger networks that are being mined from social media.

Categories and Subject Descriptors

I.6.4 [**Simulation and Modeling**]: Model Validation and Analysis; I.6.3 [**Simulation and Modeling**]: Applications; J.4 [**Social and Behavioral Sciences**]: Sociology

Keywords

contagion processes, modeling, simulation, common knowledge, coordination, approximate models

1. INTRODUCTION

1.1 Background, Motivation, Related Work

Computational modeling of information exchange over social media is important for understanding online coordination. The existing models that study information diffusion on (online) social networks of agents (vertices) mainly focus on 2-state contagion dynamics, where state 0 (resp., 1) means an agent does not (resp., does) possess a contagion. Some examples of contagions are information [12], rumors [12], fear [7], and social unrest [8]. A small sample of these models includes threshold models [9, 4, 23], independent cascade and linear threshold models [13], stochastic models [18], and others [12, 19] to model information spread on Twitter [18, 17, 8], Facebook [20], and blogs [10]. Another class of models is SIR- (susceptible-infectious-recovered) and SIS-based models, including multi-contagion variants that have been used for generalized contagions [6] and web browser use [3]. All of these models are pure influence models in the sense that an agent in state 0 changes to state 1 based on the number, θ, of its neighbors that are already in state 1 (θ is an agent's *threshold*). Moreover, the models are efficiently computable so that simulations of contagion spread using these models can be performed in polynomial time; e.g., [15].

Another class of contagion studies is based on dynamic game-theoretic models of collective action (e.g., Chwe [5], Korkmaz et al. [14]). These are coordination problems, in which each agent makes a decision, with the potential to achieve mutual benefits only if her decision is consistent with those of others. Based on these models, agents in state 0 may change state simultaneously when none of them are currently in state 1. This collective behavior requires that not only agents know about each other (e.g., their thresholds) but also this information is *common knowledge* (CK). The contagion dynamics in these models depend on specific network structures such as cliques [5].

In this paper, we focus on the model proposed in [14], herein called CKF, for collective action through *C*ommon *K*nowledge on *F*acebook. Among other mechanisms, it models the unique aspect of Facebook communication where users can post information on their own or their friends' *walls* (or *timelines*). For example, if agent v_a posts a message on agent v_b's timeline, then v_b's friend v_c can also read the post. Hence, this model captures friend-of-friend communication. (The relevant parts of the model are overviewed in Section 2).

It is demonstrated in [14] that the characterizing network structure for achieving CK among a set of agents in a communication network is the biclique (a complete bipartite graph). The problem is that computing all vertex-maximal bicliques in a network is an NP-hard problem [1]. An important practical result is that identifying all bicliques in a network using a serial code can take a wall clock time of 120 hours or more on high performance computing nodes (Intel Sandy Bridge processors), even for networks with a few tens of thousands of vertices. This is a required step for computing contagion dynamics on networks, meaning that computing network dynamics with the CKF model is NP-hard. The upshot is that contagion spreading can be studied only on relatively small networks, while graph-based data sets with a million vertices are becoming more common [17].

In this paper, we present an approach that retains only one particular type of biclique, resulting in polynomial time computations for network dynamics and obviates the need for preprocessing computations of bicliques.

1.2 Contributions of This Work

First, our proposed solution is to utilize only those bicliques that form star subgraphs, which are efficiently computed, and use these as CK sets. Hence, we ignore a large number of bicliques in a network (as will be seen). Second, we identify a stylized class of networks, with particular structures, for which our approach does not perform well in computing contagion dynamics in the worst case. We also present data on bicliques illustrating that our approximation ignores hundreds of thousands of bicliques in some cases, so these CK sets are ignored in dynamics computations. The point is that it is not obvious a priori that our approach will be effective. Third, we provide simulation data for contagion dynamics on seven networks, ranging from mined social network data to stylized networks, demonstrating that our approximate approach yields very good results on practical networks. These networks have wide ranges in properties (e.g., the numbers of bicliques in graphs range over 5 orders of magnitude and thresholds for the study of dynamics range over 4 orders of magnitude, among other variables). Fourth, we demonstrate the time savings in computing bicliques (which can be over 100 hours) *and* in computing network contagion dynamics through simulation (where we demonstrate a speedup of a factor of 50 or 70 in some cases). Fifth, our approach provides a way to study larger networks in practice.

We emphasize that our focus here is primarily on social network structures, which are very often "heavy-tailed" in degree distribution. That is, social networks often have a smaller group of vertices with high connectivity, similar to those with scale-free or power law degree distributions.

2. CKF CONTAGION MODEL AND EXAMPLE DYNAMICS

The model of common knowledge on Facebook (CKF) considers agents who have private information about their information triple (ID$_i$, x_i, θ_i). Here, ID$_i \in \mathbb{N}$ is the identifier, $x_i \in \{0, 1\}$ is the state, and $\theta_i \in \mathbb{N}$ is the threshold of

agent v_i. The interaction between the agents is represented by a communication network in which a link between two agents means that they share their ID's, states and thresholds on each others' *wall/timeline*. This information is also observable by friends-of-friends. Agents who are connected such that they form a biclique (additional edges may be present among agents and have no effect) know their own information triple (ID$_i$, x_i, θ_i), and those of every other agent in the biclique. Further, each agent v_i knows that the other agents know v_i's triple, and so on [14]. This is the *common knowledge*, which facilitates coordination among agents, producing collective state changes and contagion spread [14, 21].

We address the computation of contagion spread that is governed by biclique subgraphs in networks, because this is the network structure that gives rise to common knowledge [14]. Three $K_{4,4}$-bicliques with different threshold assignments (listed next to the vertices) are given in Figure 1 to illustrate contagion dynamics. Each of these networks represents a set of 8 agents (vertices) who share common knowledge of ID's, states, and thresholds. Each vertex $v_j \in V[K_{4,4}]$ knows (v_i, x_i, θ_i) for all $v_i \in V[K_{4,4}]$, where $V[K_{4,4}]$ is the set of vertices in a $K_{4,4}$ biclique. We assume that all vertices v_j in each example are originally in state 0; i.e., $x_j = 0 \; \forall v_j$, the inactive state.

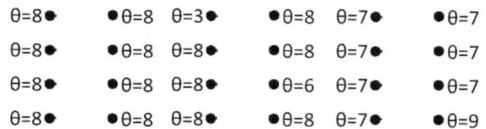

Figure 1: Three $K_{4,4}$-bicliques with 8 agents. Each of the three bicliques has threshold assignments to vertices as shown. In the left and center bicliques, all vertices change state from 0 to 1. In the right $K_{4,4}$, the 7 vertices with $\theta = 7$ change to state 1, but the lower right vertex with $\theta = 9$ remains in state 0.

In the first (left) example, each vertex has threshold 8, meaning each vertex requires 8 vertices to be in state 1 (counting itself), in order to change to state 1. Since each vertex knows the states and thresholds of all other vertices in the biclique, and each vertex v_j knows that all other vertices know that v_j knows their states, and so, recursively, each v_j reasons that all vertices have their threshold condition satisfied and will change to 1. Hence, all 8 vertices change state, even though none of the vertices were originally in state 1. This is how contagion can result from knowledge and coordination among vertices that share common knowledge.

The middle $K_{4,4}$ of Figure 1 has the difference that now two vertices have thresholds $\theta < 8$. Since there are 8 vertices sharing common knowledge, the same logic as above applies, and all 8 vertices will transition from state 0 to 1 simultaneously.

The last (right) $K_{4,4}$ has one vertex with $\theta = 9$; the remaining vertices have $\theta = 7$. The vertex with $\theta = 9$ will not change state to 1 because it requires a total of nine vertices, but there are only eight in this common knowledge set. However, the remaining seven vertices have $\theta = 7$ and hence will transition to state 1, owing to common knowledge. Thus, this example shows that within a CK set, a subset of vertices may change state.

Another parameter in the model is the *participation probability*, p_p, which is the probability that an agent will be online and participating in the contagion process at each time step. If an agent is not participating, it does not contribute to the contagion dynamics (so that its data triple is not used), but since the person's Facebook wall still exists, the node and its incident edges are still part of CK sets.

Note that the CKF model does not require seed nodes (initially assigned state 1) in order for contagion diffusion to take place, unlike many other models [9, 4, 23, 13, 18] (unless $\theta = 0$ in these other models).

Bicliques play an important role in the dynamics of the model and they are the source of the computational issue. Hence we focus on this aspect of it. Other aspects of the model can be found in [14].

3. RESULTS: APPROXIMATE COMMON KNOWLEDGE MODEL OF FACEBOOK

The CKF model is not efficiently implementable because it requires identification of all node-maximal bicliques (CK sets) in a graph, which is an NP-hard problem [1]. Here we propose an approach to make the model efficiently implementable by considering only those bicliques that are stars as an approximation to capture the dynamics of the CKF model. We are motivated here by social networks, which typically possess scale-free or exponential degree distributions, and hence there are nodes in these graphs with high degree and, consequently, star-shaped bicliques with many nodes. However, the approximate model works with other network structures, as we show below. We use the following definitions throughout:

- *Star biclique*: A biclique in which one bipartite set has one vertex. Each node in the graph with n vertices is the center vertex of a star, and hence there are n stars.

- *Non-star biclique*: A biclique in which the size of each partite set is at least 2. These are node-maximal distinct bicliques. An example is $K_{4,4}$ in Figure 1.

First, we address the impact of computing all (both star and non-star) bicliques in a network. Then a toy network example is provided to illustrate that the proposed approximation can be poor in generating the same results as the full model, in the worst case. Next we provide evidence from structural analysis of the networks that indicates that our approach ignores many bicliques of appreciable size. Finally, we provide simulation data in comparing the full and approximate CKF models for a wide range of networks and structures, including over 4 orders of magnitude in thresholds, and 12 participation probabilities. These data illustrate that the approximate model, in fact, captures the dynamics of the full model very well. We also quantify the significant time savings that the approximate model provides.

3.1 Illustrations of Computational Impacts

Non-star bicliques were computed on several networks, some of which are used herein. Other networks (such as ca-hepth from the SNAP library [16]) could not be used because enumerating non-star bicliques were stopped after 120 hours of compute time. Computing these bicliques on the Enron network of Table 1 required 62 hours using a serial algorithm. These computations were run on dual-socket Intel Sandy Bridge (Dell C6220) E5-2670 2.60GHz 8-core processors with 64GB 1600MHz DDR3 RAM.

3.2 An Example Illustrating Worst Case Performance of the Approximate Model

Consider the graph in Figure 2, which is a collection of eight $K_{4,4}$ subgraphs connected in a circle configuration. If all vertices have threshold 8, then since each $K_{4,4}$-biclique has 8 vertices, the nodes in each biclique will change to state 1 in one time step. However, if instead only stars are considered as CK sets, then there will be no diffusion since the maximum sized star has 6 vertices. Hence, the approximate (star biclique) model can be arbitrarily poor in computing the number of nodes in state 1. We note that this example requires a particular structure (collections of subgraphs that are precisely bicliques with no additional edges) that is not often representative of social networks (as described above), and a particular threshold.

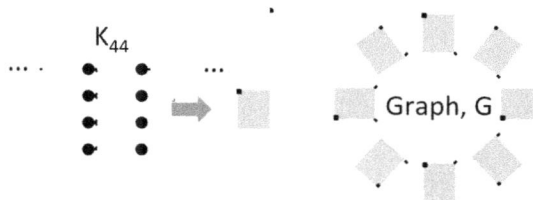

Figure 2: Graph of 8 connected $K_{4,4}$-bicliques in a ring fashion. If all vertices have threshold $\theta = 8$, then the full CKF model produces a cascade, but the reduced model using only star bicliques produces no diffusion.

3.3 Data Illustrating the Number of Bicliques Ignored in the Approximate Model

Table 1 contains the networks of this study, separated into real (i.e., mined) and scale-free (SF) stylized networks. FB is a Facebook user network [22], AH is a school of youth interactions [11], P2PG is a peer-to-peer network, and Enron is an Enron email network [16]. The remaining (SF) networks were generated by a standard preferential attachment method [2].

Table 1: Characteristics of social networks analyzed. Here, n and m are the numbers of vertices and edges, respectively; d_{ave} and d_{max} are the average and maximum degrees; n_{bc} is the number of non-star bicliques, and n_{CK} is the number of distinct CK sets generated on these bicliques, respectively.

Net	n	m	d_{ave}	d_{max}	n_{bc}	n_{CK}
FB	43,953	182,384	8.30	223	614,504	258,668
AH	2,448	5,277	4.31	10	10,388	1,496
P2PG	10,876	39,940	7.34	101	11,332	5,663
Enron	33,696	180,811	10.7	1,383	789,099,550	50,467,699
SF-1	4,956	45,031	18.2	269	84,599,732	41,695,882
SF-2	4,974	44,886	18.0	262	99,054,962	48,734,344
SF-3	4,941	44,973	18.2	263	130,892,216	64,363,550

The number of non-star bicliques, n_{bc}, is greater than the number of distinct maximal CK sets based on the non-star bicliques, n_{CK}. For example, ten vertices may form the following four non-star bicliques: $K_{2,8}$, $K_{3,7}$, $K_{4,6}$, $K_{5,5}$. In fact, there are $\sum_{j=2}^{5} \binom{10}{j} = 627$ distinct non-star bicliques on 10 vertices. However, each of these bicliques reduces to a single CK set that is composed of the same set of ten vertices.

We have $n_{CK} \gg n$ for most of the networks, indicating that there are many more non-star bicliques than the number of star bicliques, n, in the graph. Hence the *number* of bicliques that we ignore in the approximate model is large. Next, we look at the *sizes* of these bicliques.

Figure 3 shows how the frequencies of CK set sizes vary when generated from star and non-star bicliques. Hence, the full model utilizes *all* of these bicliques. In these plots, we observe that there are many non-star bicliques of large sizes, and hence it is not clear that ignoring these bicliques will preserve the contagion dynamics of the full model. In particular, note that in Figure 3(a), there are 10^3 to 10^7 bicliques with sizes ranging from 10 to 70, which are being ignored in the approximate (star biclique) model. Similar observations are relevant for at least the Enron and FB networks of Figure 3(b).

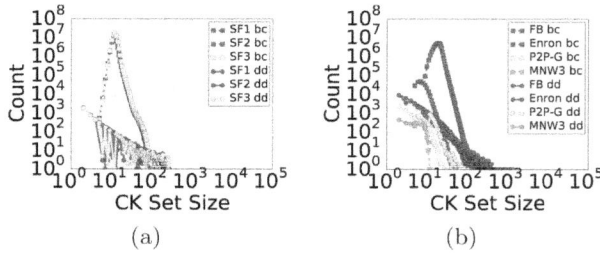

(a)   (b)

Figure 3: Frequency of common knowledge (CK) set sizes based on (*dd*)-star bicliques (circles), and (*bc*)-non-star bicliques (squares). (a) Three SF graphs. (b) Four real networks.

3.4 Experimental Comparison Of Approximate and Full Common Knowledge Models of Facebook

We exercise the two models—the approximate (star biclique) model and the full model—for all of the networks in Table 1. The only difference between the two models is the approximation by including only star bicliques in the approximate model, versus *all* bicliques in the full model; otherwise the models are *identical*. For each (model, network) pair, we run one simulation (each consisting of 50 runs of the contagion process) that contains each of the (θ, p_p) pairs given in Table 2, for a total of 168 sets of conditions. The p_p values differ for θ_l and θ_h; θ_h was selected because it is the maximum threshold for which diffusion will occur in the full CKF model. In the subsequent plots, each curve represents the time-pointwise average of the contagion size over the 50 runs. The solid curves represent the full (original) model, where all CK sets from all bicliques (including stars) are utilized, and dashed curves represent the approximate model where only stars are used for CK sets. As we will see, the solid and dashed curves overlap on the plots, indicating very good agreement of results between the models. This is the case for *all* 168 sets of conditions; not only those plotted here.

Figure 4 contains data for the FB network. Figures 4(a) and 4(c) contain *Epi* curves; that is, the number of vertices newly converting to state 1 at each time, up to 30 time units. Figures 4(b) and 4(d) contain the corresponding *Cum* curves; that is, the cumulative number of vertices in state 1 at each time, up to 30 time units. The first two plots corre-

Table 2: Simulation matrix for each network in Table 1. Each vertex is assigned the same threshold and same participation probability in a simulation.

Threshold	Participation Probabilities
$\theta_l = d_{ave}$	0.01, 0.05, 0.1, 0.2, 0.3, 0.4
$\theta_h = d_{max} + 1$	0.99, 0.995, 0.997, 0.999, 0.9999, 1.0

spond to $\theta_l = 9$ and the latter two correspond to $\theta_h = 224$. For each of θ_l and θ_h, the different color curves in each plot correspond to different participation probabilities, per Table 2. The highest participation probability corresponds to gray and the minimum one corresponds to blue, for each of θ_l and θ_h. Since the ordinate value on the Cum curve is the corresponding area under the Epi curve, one would expect the differences to be more gradually varying in the Cum curves. In fact, this is not the case: both sets of curves show excellent agreement between the two models, over all test parameter values for θ and p_p.

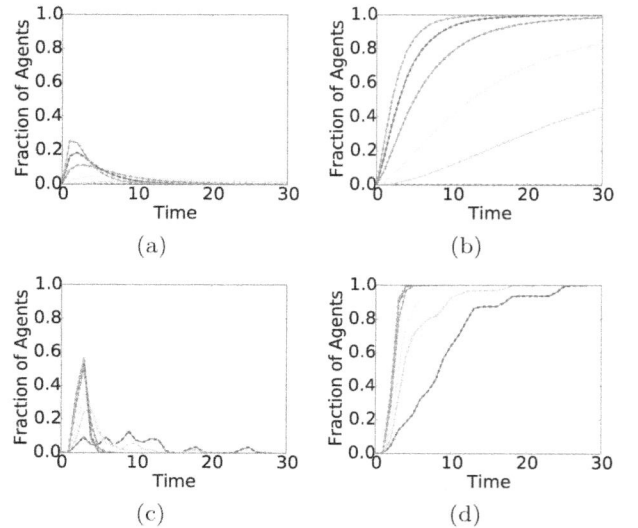

(a)   (b)

(c)   (d)

Figure 4: Fraction of agents in state 1 as a function of time for the star (dashed) and full (solid) models for network FB. (a) Epi, $\theta_l = 9$. (b) Cum, $\theta_l = 9$. (c) Epi, $\theta_h = 224$. (d) Cum, $\theta_h = 224$. The data indicate excellent agreement between the full and approximate CKF models.

Although the Epi curves are harder to match between models and hence provide a better comparison (because they are the derivatives of the Cum curves), we show the Cum curves because they are easier to inspect visually; the Epi curves for the remaining networks show the excellent agreement indicated in Figure 4.

Figure 5 shows one set of Cum curves for each of four networks: Figure 5(a) Enron, $\theta_h = 1384$; Figure 5(b) AH, $\theta_l = 4$; Figure 5(c) P2PG, $\theta_h = 102$; and Figure 5(d) SF1, $\theta_l = 18$. Note that in this plot alone, data over four orders of magnitude in threshold are presented. Again, the agreement between the full CKF model (solid curves) and the star-only biclique CKF model (dashed curves) is excellent.

The data for Enron (Figure 5(a)) show a stair-step pattern for $p_p = 0.999$. This is because the dynamics are very sensitive to p_p for high thresholds. Because $\theta_h = d_{max} + 1$, all agents (vertices) of the subgraph centered at the vertex with degree d_{max} must be participating before vertices start to change to state 1. This is why the p_p values for θ_h are so large in Table 2.

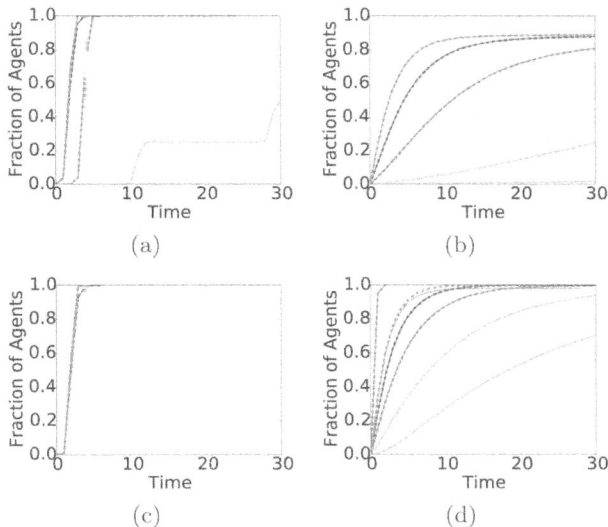

Figure 5: Fraction of agents in state 1 as a function of time for the star (dashed) and full (solid) models for different networks, thresholds, and participation probabilities. (a) Enron, $\theta_h = 1384$. (b) AH, $\theta_l = 4$. (c) P2PG, $\theta_h = 102$. (d) SF1, $\theta_l = 18$. Data over four orders of magnitude in threshold are presented. The data indicate excellent agreement between the full and approximate CKF models.

Our preliminary analysis suggests that the star-only model is a good approximation for the full model because every vertex v_i is part of at least $d_i + 1$ bicliques, where d_i is the degree of v_i. That is, v_i is a member of the CK sets that are produced from stars centered at v_i itself and each of v_i's distance-1 neighbors. It is nonetheless still surprising that the bicliques that are not stars do not alter the dynamics to some readily observable level.

3.5 Timing Data

The execution times were recorded for all runs of all simulations. For a specific set of conditions, a simulation of the full model takes time t_{full} to complete the 50 diffusion instances. The corresponding time for the star-only biclique model is t_{star}. The ratio t_{full}/t_{star} of compute times for the full model to the approximate model were compiled and averaged. Figure 6 shows these data for each of the data-driven networks. As the number of CK sets, n_{CK}, increases, the ratio of computational time increases because these lists of bicliques must be traversed to determine whether vertices change state in the full model. The star-only biclique computations reduce simulation times from about a factor of 2 to a factor greater than 70. This is on top of the time savings achieved by not having to compute all bicliques, which can be over 100 hours of wall clock time.

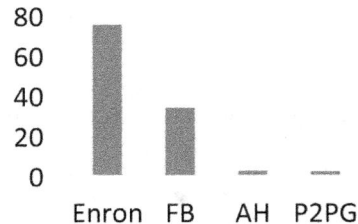

Figure 6: The average ratio of t_{full}/t_{star} for each of the four real networks. These data illustrate that the simulations—not counting the time to compute bicliques—with all bicliques (full model) take much longer than those that utilize star-only bicliques. Hence, the approximate model saves on computation time in addition to the time to identify bicliques.

4. CONCLUSIONS

Modeling and simulation of information spread on social networks enables understanding of the dynamics of coordination and collective action in online environments. Generating results in a timely fashion, in turn, requires computationally efficient implementations of model dynamics. We focus on a unique CKF model of Facebook interaction through timelines. In this model, the biclique network structure characterizes CK [14], but identifying all node-maximal bicliques—which is required for CKF contagion dynamics—is an NP-hard problem [1]. We demonstrate through experiments that it can take 120 or more hours to compute all bicliques of a network, even for relatively small graphs of tens of thousands of vertices. We introduce an approximation into the model, which is to consider only bicliques that have star structures. This makes the simulation process computationally efficient. The results from the approximate and full CKF models are in a very good agreement, thus justifying the use of the approximate model. This obviates the need to compute all bicliques, and we show that it can also reduce the time to compute contagion dynamics in simulations by up to a factor of 70 in these experiments. These results are generated on seven networks with different n, m, d_{ave}, d_{max}, and different network structures, whose numbers of biclique-based CK sets range over 5 orders of magnitude, using thresholds θ that range over 4 orders of magnitude. Future work includes using mean square error or some variant of it to quantify differences between the full and approximate model results.

5. ACKNOWLEDGMENTS

We thank the anonymous reviewers for their useful comments and suggestions. We thank our external collaborators and members of the Network Dynamics and Simulation Science Laboratory (NDSSL). This work was partially supported by DTRA Grant HDTRA1-11-1-0016, DTRA CNIMS Contract HDTRA1-11-D-0016-0001, and NSF NetSE Grant CNS-1011769.

6. REFERENCES

[1] G. Alexe, S. Alexe, Y. Crama, S. Foldes, P. L. Hammer, and B. Simeone. Consensus algorithms for

the generation of all maximal bicliques. *DAM*, 145:11–21, 2004.

[2] A. Barabasi and R. Albert. Emergence of scaling in random networks. *Nature*, 286:509–512, 1999.

[3] A. Beutel, B. A. Prakash, R. Rosenfeld, and C. Faloutsos. Interacting viruses in networks: Can both survive? In *Proceedings of the 18th ACM SIGKDD International Conference on Knowledge Discovery and Data Mining*, pages 426–434, 2012.

[4] D. Centola and M. Macy. Complex Contagions and the Weakness of Long Ties. *Am. J. Soc.*, 113(3):702–734, 2007.

[5] M. S.-Y. Chwe. Structure and strategy in collective action. *Am. J. of Soc.*, 105:128–156, 1999.

[6] P. S. Dodds and D. J. Watts. A generalized model of social and biological contagion. *J. of Theo. Bio.*, 232(4):587–604, 2005.

[7] J. M. Epstein, J. Parker, D. Cummings, and R. A. Hammond. Coupled contagion dynamics of fear and disease: Mathematical and computational explorations. *PLoS ONE*, 3:e3955–1–e3955–11, 2008.

[8] S. Gonzalez-Bailon, J. Borge-Holthoefer, A. Rivero, and Y. Moreno. The dynamics of protest recruitment through an online network. *Nature Scientific Reports*, pages 1–7, 2011.

[9] M. Granovetter. Threshold Models of Collective Behavior. *Am. J. of Soc.*, 83(6):1420–1443, 1978.

[10] D. Gruhl, R. Guha, D. Liben-Nowell, and A. Tomkins. Information diffusion through blogspace. In *Proc. of the 13th International World Wide Web Conference (WWW 2004)*, pages 491–501, 2004.

[11] K. M. Harris. The National Longitudinal Study of Adolescent Health (Add Health), Waves III, 2008. Carolina Population Center, UNC.

[12] K. Kawachi, M. Seki, H. Yoshida, Y. Otake, K. Warashina, and H. Ueda. A rumor transmission model with various contact interactions. *Journal of Theoretical Biology*, 253:55–60, 2008.

[13] D. Kempe, J. Kleinberg, and E. Tardos. Maximizing the spread of influence through a social network. In *KDD*, pages 137–146, 2003.

[14] G. Korkmaz, C. J. Kuhlman, A. Marathe, M. V. Marathe, and F. Vega-Redondo. Collective action through common knowledge using a Facebook model. In *Thirteen International Conference on Autonomous Agents and Multiagent Systems (AAMAS)*, 2014.

[15] C. J. Kuhlman, V. A. Kumar, M. V. Marathe, S. S. Ravi, and D. J. Rosenkrantz. Inhibiting diffusion of complex contagions in social networks: Theoretical and experimental results. *Journal Data Mining and Knowledge Discovery*, 2014.

[16] J. Leskovec and A. Krevl. SNAP Datasets: Stanford large network dataset collection. http://snap.stanford.edu/data, Jun 2014.

[17] S. Myers and J. Leskovec. Clash of the contagions: Cooperation and competition in information diffusion. In *2012 IEEE 12th International Conference on Data Mining (ICDM)*, pages 539–548, 2012.

[18] D. Romero, B. Meeder, and J. Kleinberg. Differences in the mechanics of information diffusion. In *WWW*, 2011.

[19] D. Siegel. Social networks and collective action. *American Journal of Political Science*, 53:122–138, 2009.

[20] E. Sun, I. Rosenn, C. A. Marlow, and T. M. Lento. Gesundheit! modeling contagion through facebook news feed. In *(ICWSM 2009)*, 2009.

[21] K. A. Thomas, P. DeScioli, O. S. Haque, and S. Pinker. The psychology of coordination and common knowledge. *Journal of Personality and Social Psychology*, 107:657–676, 2014.

[22] B. Viswanath, A. Mislove, M. Cha, and K. P. Gummadi. On the evolution of user interaction in Facebook. In *(WOSN'09)*, August 2009.

[23] D. Watts. A simple model of global cascades on random networks. *PNAS*, 99(9):5766–5771, 2002.

The Influence of Frequency, Recency and Semantic Context on the Reuse of Tags in Social Tagging Systems

Dominik Kowald
Know-Center
Graz University of Technology
Graz, Austria
dkowald@know-center.at

Elisabeth Lex
Knowledge Technologies Institute
Graz University of Technology
Graz, Austria
elisabeth.lex@tugraz.at

ABSTRACT

In this paper, we study factors that influence tag reuse behavior in social tagging systems. Our work is guided by the activation equation of the cognitive model ACT-R, which states that the usefulness of information in human memory depends on the three factors usage frequency, recency and semantic context. It is our aim to shed light on the influence of these factors on tag reuse. In our experiments, we utilize six datasets from the social tagging systems Flickr, CiteULike, BibSonomy, Delicious, LastFM and MovieLens, covering a range of various tagging settings. Our results confirm that frequency, recency and semantic context positively influence the reuse probability of tags. However, the extent to which each factor individually influences tag reuse strongly depends on the *type of folksonomy* present in a social tagging system. Our work can serve as guideline for researchers and developers of tag-based recommender systems when designing algorithms for social tagging environments.

Keywords

social tagging; tag reuse; tag prediction; tag recommendation; frequency; recency; semantic context; ACT-R; BLL

1. INTRODUCTION

With the advent of the Web 2.0, social tagging has become an essential tool to collaboratively annotate content with freely chosen *tags* (i.e., keywords). The result of a social tagging process is a network connecting users, content resources and tags, which is referred to as *folksonomy* [9]. Since tags can be used to search for, browse and share content, they facilitate discovery and navigation in the Social Web [13]. Many social networks such as Medium, Twitter, Instagram and Facebook have adopted tagging in the form of hashtags as well [22].

Therefore, previous work has proposed tag recommendation algorithms with the aim to assist users in finding descriptive tags [4] and to control the shared tag vocabulary

HT '16, July 10–13, 2016, Halifax, Nova Scotia, Canada.
© 2016 ACM. ISBN 978-1-4503-4247-6/16/07. . . $15.00
DOI: http://dx.doi.org/10.1145/2914586.2914617

[28]. In this respect, recent research has shown that a substantial amount of tag assignments can be explained by analyzing the information access in human memory [6, 24, 23], which is mainly influenced by past usage frequency, recency and the current semantic context [2, 1].

Even though there is already a large body of research available, which proposes algorithms for recommending tags [11, 20, 10, 18, 29, 21], none of these approaches incorporate all three aforementioned factors. For example, FolkRank [10] solely utilizes tag frequency and the current semantic context, whereas GIRP [29] solely builds on tag frequency and recency. Typically these methods have been evaluated as integrated models and thus, it remains unclear to what extent the individual factors of the approaches contribute to the final algorithmic performance.

The present work: Factors that influence tag reuse.
In this work, we study factors that potentially influence the tag reuse behavior in social tagging systems (see also related work such as [8, 3, 7]). Specifically, we analyze the influence of frequency, recency and semantic context on the reuse of tags. Hence, it is our goal to better understand to what extent these factors can be exploited to predict the reuse of tags given a specific *folksonomy type*. This should lead to a guideline for designing and implementing tag prediction algorithms for given environments.

To that end, we integrate and extend our previous work on tag recommender systems [17, 14, 27], where we adapted the activation equation from the cognitive architecture ACT-R [1] to develop a model termed BLL_{AC}. This model enables the prediction of future tag assignments for a user u by modeling the usefulness of a piece of information i – in our case, a tag – in u's memory based on three factors: (i) how *frequent* i was used by u in the past, (ii) how *recent* (i.e., the time since the last usage) i was used by u in the past, and (iii) how useful i is for u in the current *semantic context*.

This is achieved by the two components of the activation equation: First, the base-level learning component (BLL), which integrates the factors of frequency and recency via a power function for reflecting the time-dependent decay of tag reuse [2] and second, the associated component (AC), which models the current semantic context as the similarity of tag i to tags already associated with the currently tagged resource r. However, since BLL_{AC} utilizes the three factors, (i) frequency, (ii) recency, and (iii) semantic context, as an integrated model, it is still unclear to what extent these factors individually contribute to the efficacy of the model. Besides, we assume that the influence of these factors on predicting tag reuse depends on the folksonomy type, i.e., *narrow* (e.g., Flickr), *mixed*[1] (e.g., BibSonomy) or *broad* (e.g., MovieLens) [9], of the given social tagging system. This leads to the following two research questions:

- *RQ1:* How are the factors of frequency, recency and semantic context influencing a tag's probability of being reused in social tagging systems?

- *RQ2:* Can the factors of frequency, recency and semantic context be exploited to efficiently predict a user's tag reuse given a specific folksonomy type?

Methods and findings. In order to address *RQ1*, we conducted an empirical study on six social tagging datasets (i.e., Flickr, CiteULike, BibSonomy, Delicious, LastFM and MovieLens), in which we analyzed the influence of the three factors frequency, recency and semantic context on the reuse probability of tags (see Section 2). Next, to answer *RQ2*, we carried out a prediction study on the same datasets, in which we not only compared algorithms that reflect these factors individually but also approaches that combine these factors or incorporate social influences, e.g., by suggesting related tags of other users (see Section 3). We find that frequency, recency and semantic context positively influence the reuse probability of tags in all systems (*RQ1*) and that the efficacy of these factors for predicting a user's tags depends on the folksonomy type of the given system (*RQ2*).

Significance of this work. To the best of our knowledge, this is the first study of its kind, which analyzes the reuse of tags to provide a transparent overview of the factors that influence the prediction of tags and, at the same time, relates these factors to the folksonomy type of the given system. Our findings may serve as a guideline for researchers and developers of tag-based recommender systems with regard to choosing the right prediction and recommendation methods for given social tagging environments.

2. EMPIRICAL STUDY

In this section, we present the datasets, methodology and results of our empirical study carried out to address *RQ1*.

2.1 Datasets

For the sake of this study, we turn to publicly available, real-world datasets gathered from the six social tagging systems Flickr[2], CiteULike[3], BibSonomy[4], Delicious[2], LastFM[5] and MovieLens[5]. To make our results comparable and to ensure reproducibility, we utilize the exact same dataset samples that were used in the study of [16]. A major advantage of these dataset samples is that they were created without any *p*-core pruning technique to ensure an unbiased evaluation [5]. Additionally, these datasets represent social tagging systems of various domains (i.e., images, Web links, references, music and movies), and differ in size and narrowness degree. The narrowness degree is defined as the average number of posts per resource, which allows to distinguish between narrow (Flickr), mixed (CiteULike, BibSonomy, De-

---

[1]With *mixed* folksonomies, we denote folksonomies that cannot strictly be categorized into the narrow or broad setting.
[2]https://www.uni-koblenz.de/FB4/Institutes/IFI/AGStaab/Research/DataSets/PINTSExperimentsDataSets
[3]http://www.citeulike.org/faq/data.adp
[4]http://www.kde.cs.uni-kassel.de/bibsonomy/dumps
[5]http://grouplens.org/datasets/

Dataset	$|U|$	$|R|$	$|T|$	$|P|$	$|P|/|R|$
Flickr	9,590	856,755	125,119	856,755	1.000
CiteULike	18,474	811,175	273,883	900,794	1.110
BibSonomy	10,179	683,478	201,254	772,108	1.129
Delicious	15,980	963,741	184,012	1,447,267	1.501
LastFM	1,892	12,522	9,748	71,062	5.674
MovieLens	4,009	7,601	15,238	55,484	7.299

Table 1: Statistics of our datasets. Here, $|U|$ is the number of users, $|R|$ is the number of resources, $|T|$ is the number of distinct tags, $|P|$ is the number of posts and $|P|/|R|$ is the degree of narrowness.

licious) and broad (LastFM, MovieLens) folksonomies [9]. The final statistics of our datasets are shown in Table 1.

2.2 Methodology

In order to analyze the tag reuse behavior of users, we split our datasets into training and test sets via an evaluation protocol, which persists the chronological order of the data. Thus, for each user u, we sorted his/her n posts by time, allocated the nth (i.e., the most recent) post to the test set and the first $n-1$ posts to the training set [16, 11].

Next, in order to quantify the influence of frequency, recency and semantic context on the reuse of tags, we compared the tag assignments of the first $n-1$ posts in the training set (i.e., reflecting the past) of user u with the tag assignments of u's n^{th} post in the test set (i.e., reflecting the future). More specifically, for each tag i of u, we counted the number of times i was used by u in the training set (i.e., the frequency value) and determined if i was also reused by u in the test set (i.e., the reuse probability of i by u). This procedure was repeated for the tags of each user $u \in U$. Finally, to obtain a statistically reliable value, we pooled together all tags with the same frequency value and calculated the mean reuse probability of these tags based on the individual ones.

We followed a similar procedure to study the influence of recency and semantic context. In the case of tag recency, we calculated the days elapsed since the last use of i by u. In the case of the semantic context, we determined the tag co-occurrence value between i and the tags already assigned to the currently tagged resource r (i.e., the second component of the activation equation). Then, as in the case of tag frequency, we pooled together the tags with the same recency or semantic context values and calculated the mean reuse probability based on the individual ones for both factors.

2.3 Results

In Figure 1, we plotted the mean tag reuse probability over (i) tag frequency, (ii) tag recency (in days), and (iii) tag similarity with the current semantic context on a log-log scale for our six datasets. We also provided the k (i.e., the slope) and R^2 (i.e., the determination coefficient) estimates of the linear regression on the data. Specifically, we use the sign of k to determine how tag reuse is influenced by the factors and R^2 to check if the data follows a power function. Across all six datasets, we can make three main observations:

1. The *more frequently* a tag was used in the past ($k > 0$), the higher its reuse probability is.

2. The *more recently* a tag was used in the past ($k < 0$), the higher its reuse probability is.

3. The *more similar* a tag is to tags in the *current semantic context* ($k > 0$), the higher its reuse probability is.

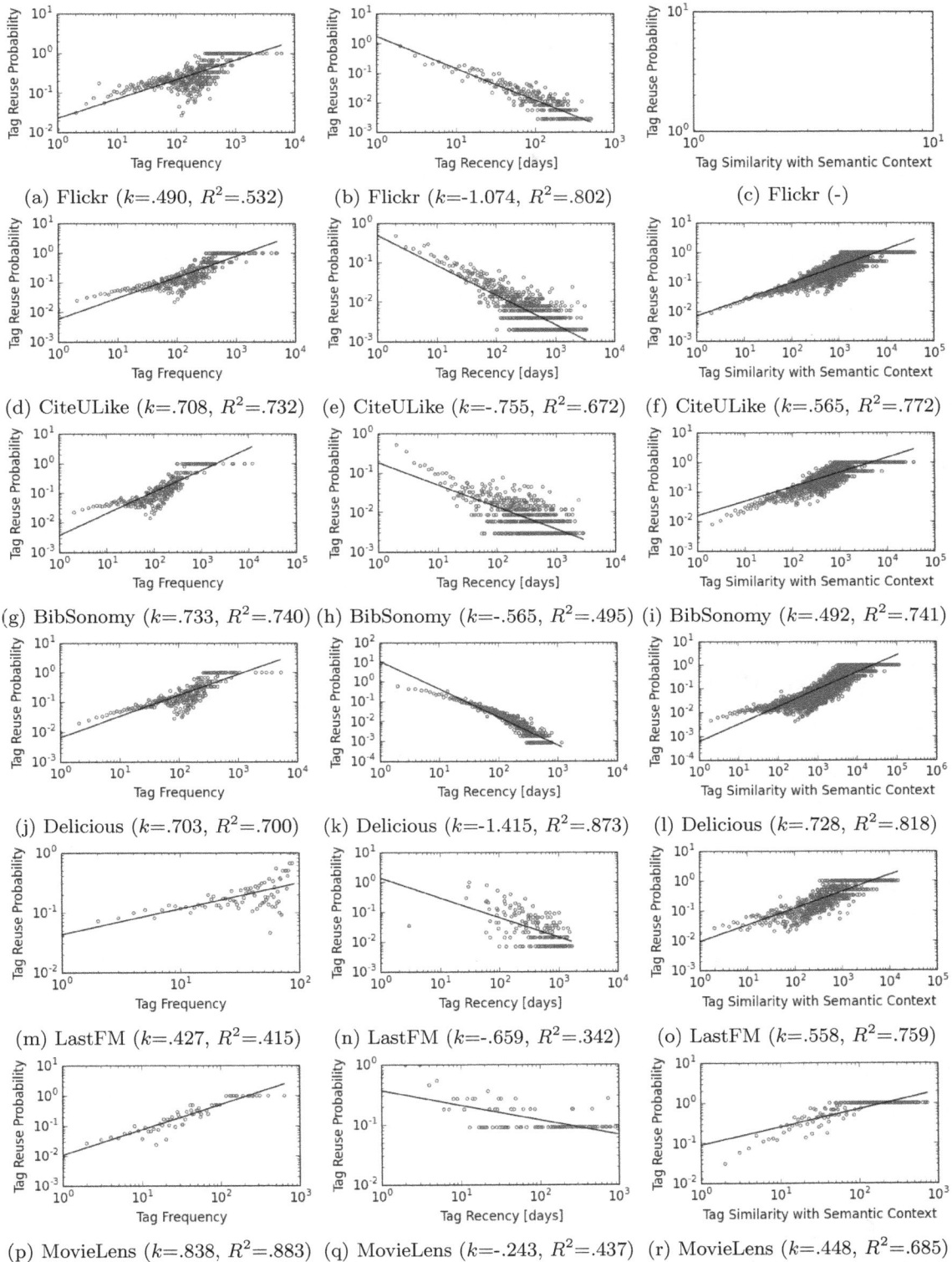

Figure 1: The influence of frequency, recency and semantic context on tag reuse in six social tagging systems (*RQ1*). Clearly, all three factors positively influence a tag's probability of being reused: Slope $k > 0$ for frequency, $k < 0$ for recency and $k > 0$ for semantic context. Furthermore, the generally high R^2 estimates of the linear regression indicate that large amounts of the data can be explained by a power function. *Please note* that there is no semantic context in Flickr since users solely tag their own resources in this system.

Folksonomy type	Dataset	Metric	Individual factors			Combination			Social	
			Frequency	Recency	SemCon	GIRP	BLL	BLL_{AC}	FR	PITF
Narrow	Flickr	F_1@5	.371	.464	-	.455	**.470**	.470	.365	.350
		nDCG@10	.569	.702	-	.686	**.711**	.711	.561	.535
Mixed	CiteULike	F_1@5	.231	.236	.041	.243	.254	**.259**	.250	.178
		nDCG@10	.367	.385	.069	.394	.413	**.422**	.392	.294
	BibSonomy	F_1@5	.253	.252	.063	.262	.269	**.280**	.279	.215
		nDCG@10	.371	.368	.090	.386	.396	**.409**	.408	.327
	Delicious	F_1@5	.173	.179	.108	.190	.203	**.243**	.196	.199
		nDCG@10	.267	.287	.158	.298	.318	**.374**	.292	.302
Broad	LastFM	F_1@5	.193	.189	.202	.198	.202	.251	.270	**.276**
		nDCG@10	.292	.293	.302	.303	.313	.375	.399	**.414**
	MovieLens	F_1@5	.077	.076	.077	.077	.079	.086	.153	**.156**
		nDCG@10	.177	.183	.176	.177	.187	.203	.319	**.324**

Table 2: Prediction accuracy results of algorithms that (i) reflect the individual factors of frequency, recency and semantic context, (ii) combine these factors, and (iii) utilize social influences ($RQ2$). We see not only that all three individual factors can be exploited to efficiently predict a user's tags but also that the efficacy of the algorithms depends on the folksonomy type (i.e., narrow, mixed, broad) of the given system.

As such, all three factors (i.e., frequency, recency and semantic context) have a positive influence on a tag's probability of being reused. Furthermore, the generally high R^2 estimates in the log-log scaled plots indicate that large amounts of the data can be explained by a power function, as also indicated by the first component of the activation equation [2]. Thus, the first research question of our work ($RQ1$) can be answered affirmatively. In order to better understand the (individual) influence of each of the factors for predicting tags given a specific folksonomy type ($RQ2$), we conducted a prediction study described in the next section.

3. PREDICTION STUDY

In this section, we present the algorithms, methodology and results of our prediction study, which was conducted to address our second research question ($RQ2$). Specifically, we want to establish to what extent the factors of frequency, recency and semantic context can be exploited individually to efficiently predict a user's tag reuse given a specific folksonomy type of a social tagging system.

3.1 Algorithms

In terms of the compared algorithms, we utilize approaches that reflect the three factors individually, approaches that combine these factors and approaches that incorporate social influences (e.g., via related tags of other users).

Individual factors. To account for tag frequency, we utilize the Most Popular Tags (MP_u) approach, which ranks the tags of a user based on their usage frequency [11]. To predict tags solely based on tag recency, we rank the tags of a user by the timestamp of their last usage. Since the third factor of interest, the semantic context $SemCon$, is represented by the second component of the activation equation, we recommend the tags that highly co-occurred with tags already assigned to the currently tagged resource [14].

Combination of factors. We utilize three algorithms based on combinations of the factors, which enables us to analyze if the performance of the individual factors can be improved when they are combined in the form of hybrid approaches. The first one, $GIRP$ [29], integrates frequency and recency using an approach that models the effect of time (i.e., recency) via an exponential function. The second one, BLL [17], implements the first component of the activation equation and models the effect of time via a power function as suggested by [2]. The third algorithm in this respect, BLL_{AC} [14], is the full implementation of the model, accounting for all three factors (frequency, recency and semantic context).

Social influences. To compare these methods that aim to predict a user's individual tag reuse with approaches that also integrate social influences [25], we incorporate two well-known algorithms from tag recommender research in our study. The first one, FolkRank (FR) [10], is an extension of Google's PageRank approach to iteratively rank the entities in folksonomies. The second one, Pairwise Interaction Tensor Factorization ($PITF$) [21], is based on factorization machines and has become one of the most successful methods for recommending tags. For both algorithms, we use the same parameter settings as in [16] (i.e., we set the preference vector weighting d for FR to .7 and the dimension of factorization λ for PITF to 256).

3.2 Methodology

We conducted our prediction study on the same datasets and training/test set splits as in our empirical study (see Section 2.2). This allowed us to train the algorithms based on the posts in the training set and compare the top-10 tags that an algorithm predicted for user u and resource r of a post in the test set with the set of relevant tags in this test set post [11, 12]. Based on that, we computed two prediction accuracy metrics known from research on information retrieval and recommender systems. Specifically, we report the F1-score (F_1@5) for the top-5 predicted tags[6] and the ranking-aware metric Normalized Discounted Cumulative Gain (nDCG@10) for the top-10 predicted tags [19].

To ensure the reproducibility of our results, we conducted this study via the open-source tag recommender evaluation and benchmarking framework $TagRec$ [15, 26], which can be freely downloaded from GitHub[7] for scientific purposes.

3.3 Results

In Table 2, we present the results of our prediction study indicated by the F_1@5 and nDCG@10 metrics. Across all six datasets and both metrics, we observe three patterns of results based on the folksonomy type of the tagging systems.

---

[6]F_1@5 was also used as the main metric in PKDD'09: http://www.kde.cs.uni-kassel.de/ws/dc09/evaluation
[7]https://github.com/learning-layers/TagRec/

Narrow. In the narrow folksonomy Flickr, the semantic context has no influence since users are solely tagging their own images. The results show that frequency and especially recency can be exploited to efficiently predict a user's tag reuse in this narrow setting. Furthermore, these factors even outperform FR and PITF, the two algorithms that also utilize social influences by means of other users' tags. When combining frequency and recency, we see that the accuracy of the strong recency factor can only be slightly improved in the case of BLL, which models the time component via a power function, and even decreases in the case of GIRP, which builds on an exponential temporal decay function.

Mixed. For the mixed folksonomies CiteULike, BibSonomy and Delicious, we observe a good performance for the factors of frequency and recency, and an average one for the semantic context. Additionally, the results suggest that a combination of all three factors in the form of BLL_{AC} provides the highest accuracy estimates and outperforms FR and PITF. Again, BLL (and thus, the power function) is apparently better suited to combine frequency and recency than GIRP (and thus, the exponential function).

Broad. Interestingly, the algorithms in the broad folksonomies LastFM and MovieLens had a completely different behavior. In these datasets, since there are a lot of tags assigned by other users to the currently tagged resource, the semantic context is a much more important factor for predicting tags than in the narrow and mixed settings. Similarly to the narrow case, the combination of the factors only slightly improves the accuracy of the individual factors. Due to a high number of average posts per resource (5.674 for LastFM and 7.299 for MovieLens – see Table 1), FR and PITF, which utilize related tags of other users as well, provide the best results in the broad setting.

Summary. Our results are summarized in Table 3. Overall, they confirm that the factors of frequency, recency and semantic context can be exploited to efficiently predict a user's tag reuse. Which factor to consider, however, strongly depends on the folksonomy type of the given social tagging system. As such, the second research question of our work ($RQ2$) can also be answered affirmatively.

4. CONCLUSION AND FUTURE WORK

In this paper, we analyzed the influence of frequency, recency and semantic context on the reuse of tags in social tagging systems. To that end, we conducted an empirical study and a prediction study on datasets gathered from the six social tagging systems Flickr, CiteULike, BibSonomy, Delicious, LastFM and MovieLens. The empirical study aimed to answer our first research question of this work ($RQ1$) and determine how the factors of frequency, recency and semantic context influence a tag's probability of being reused. The three main findings of this analysis are: (i) the *more frequently* a tag was used in the past, the higher its reuse probability is, (ii) the *more recently* a tag was used in the past, the higher its reuse probability is, and (iii) the *more similar* a tag is to tags in the *current semantic context*, the higher its reuse probability is. This confirms that all three factors (i.e., frequency, recency and semantic context) have a positive influence on a tag's probability of being reused.

Our prediction study was designed to determine to what extent these three factors can be exploited to efficiently

Folksonomy type	Frequency	Recency	SemCon	Comb	Social
Narrow	+/-	+	-	+/-	-
Mixed	+	+	+/-	+	+/-
Broad	+/-	+/-	+	+/-	+

Table 3: Summary of our prediction accuracy results showing the performance of the algorithms based on the given folksonomy type. *Please note* that "+" indicates a good performance, "+/-" indicates an average performance and "-" indicates a poor performance of a factor/an approach in a specific setting.

predict a user's tag reuse given a specific folksonomy type ($RQ2$). With that regard, we applied not only algorithms that reflect these three factors individually (*Frequency*, *Recency* and *SemCon*) but also algorithms that combine these factors (*GIRP*, *BLL* and BLL_{AC}) and incorporate social influences, i.e., related tags of other users (*FR* and *PITF*). We observed three patterns of results based on the folksonomy type of the datasets, which are summarized in Table 3. In the narrow case, the factor of recency is the most important one, whereas in the mixed case all three factors highly contribute to the prediction accuracy and thus, the combination of these factors (*Comb*) provides the best results. Finally, in case of the broad folksonomies, the semantic context becomes a much more important factor than in the other two settings. Furthermore, the best results in this setting are obtained for PITF, which utilizes social influences (*Social*), such as related tags of other users, as well.

Overall, our results show that frequency, recency and semantic context positively influence the reuse probability of tags in all six datasets ($RQ1$) and that the efficacy of these factors in terms of predicting a user's tags depends on the folksonomy type of the given social tagging system ($RQ2$). Additionally, with our findings summarized in Table 3, we provide a transparent overview of the factors that influence the prediction of tags based on the given folksonomy type. We believe that our findings may be a guideline for researchers and developers in the area of tag-based recommender systems, helping them to choose the correct prediction method for a given social tagging environment.

Limitations and future work. One limitation of this study is that it is mainly focused on the factors that influence the *individual* reuse of tags. Thus, for future work, we would like to extend this by also analyzing the influence of the reuse (i.e., imitation) of other users' tags [28] and study how this *social influence* effects tag predictions. Furthermore, we plan to expand our model of the *semantic context*, since to date, we have analyzed it solely based on the tags that were already assigned to the currently tagged resource. In this respect, we want to incorporate other resource-dependent information, such as the resource title or content, as well.

Finally, we plan to enhance our guideline with results for other types of social systems that utilize the concept of tags. To that end, we would like to determine the influence of frequency, recency and semantic context in systems that incorporate *hashtags* (e.g., Twitter, Facebook and Instagram). At the same time, this would allow us to verify that our findings can be generalized to various types of tags.

Acknowledgments. The authors would like to thank Paul Seitlinger, Tobias Ley, Ilire Hasani-Mavriqi and Emanuel Lacic for valuable comments on this paper. This work is funded by the Know-Center and the EU-IP Learning Layers.

5. REFERENCES

[1] J. R. Anderson, D. Bothell, M. D. Byrne, S. Douglass, C. Lebiere, and Y. Qin. An integrated theory of the mind. *Psychological review*, 111(4):1036, 2004.

[2] J. R. Anderson and L. J. Schooler. Reflections of the environment in memory. *Psychological science*, 2(6):396–408, 1991.

[3] C. Cattuto, V. Loreto, and L. Pietronero. Semiotic dynamics and collaborative tagging. *Proceedings of the National Academy of Sciences*, 104(5):1461–1464, 2007.

[4] K. Dellschaft and S. Staab. Measuring the influence of tag recommenders on the indexing quality in tagging systems. In *Proc. of HT'12*, pages 73–82. ACM, 2012.

[5] S. Doerfel and R. Jäschke. An analysis of tag-recommender evaluation procedures. In *Proc. of RecSys'13*, pages 343–346. ACM, 2013.

[6] W.-T. Fu. The microstructures of social tagging: a rational model. In *Proc. of CSCW'08*, pages 229–238. ACM, 2008.

[7] W.-T. Fu, T. Kannampallil, R. Kang, and J. He. Semantic imitation in social tagging. *ACM Transactions on Computer-Human Interaction (TOCHI)*, 17(3):12, 2010.

[8] S. A. Golder and B. A. Huberman. Usage patterns of collaborative tagging systems. *Journal of information science*, 32(2):198–208, 2006.

[9] D. Helic, C. Körner, M. Granitzer, M. Strohmaier, and C. Trattner. Navigational efficiency of broad vs. narrow folksonomies. In *Proc. of HT'12*, pages 63–72. ACM, 2012.

[10] A. Hotho, R. Jäschke, C. Schmitz, G. Stumme, and K.-D. Althoff. Folkrank: A ranking algorithm for folksonomies. In *LWA*, volume 1, pages 111–114, 2006.

[11] R. Jäschke, L. Marinho, A. Hotho, L. Schmidt-Thieme, and G. Stumme. Tag recommendations in folksonomies. In *Knowledge Discovery in Databases: PKDD 2007*, pages 506–514. Springer, 2007.

[12] R. Jäschke, L. Marinho, A. Hotho, L. Schmidt-Thieme, and G. Stumme. Tag recommendations in social bookmarking systems. *Ai Communications*, 21(4):231–247, 2008.

[13] C. Körner, D. Benz, A. Hotho, M. Strohmaier, and G. Stumme. Stop thinking, start tagging: tag semantics emerge from collaborative verbosity. In *Proc. of WWW'10*, pages 521–530. ACM, 2010.

[14] D. Kowald, S. Kopeinik, P. Seitlinger, T. Ley, D. Albert, and C. Trattner. Refining frequency-based tag reuse predictions by means of time and semantic context. In *Mining, Modeling, and Recommending'Things' in Social Media*, pages 55–74. Springer, 2015.

[15] D. Kowald, E. Lacic, and C. Trattner. Tagrec: towards a standardized tag recommender benchmarking framework. In *Proc. of HT'14*, pages 305–307. ACM, 2014.

[16] D. Kowald and E. Lex. Evaluating tag recommender algorithms in real-world folksonomies: A comparative study. In *Proc. of RecSys'15*, RecSys '15, pages 265–268, New York, NY, USA, 2015. ACM.

[17] D. Kowald, P. Seitlinger, C. Trattner, and T. Ley.

Long time no see: The probability of reusing tags as a function of frequency and recency. In *Proc. of WWW'14 companion*, pages 463–468. International World Wide Web Conferences Steering Committee, 2014.

[18] R. Krestel, P. Fankhauser, and W. Nejdl. Latent dirichlet allocation for tag recommendation. In *Proc. of RecSys'09*, pages 61–68. ACM, 2009.

[19] M. Lipczak. *Hybrid tag recommendation in collaborative tagging systems*. PhD thesis, Dalhousie University Halifax, 2012.

[20] L. B. Marinho and L. Schmidt-Thieme. Collaborative tag recommendations. In *Data Analysis, Machine Learning and Applications*, pages 533–540. Springer, 2008.

[21] S. Rendle and L. Schmidt-Thieme. Pairwise interaction tensor factorization for personalized tag recommendation. In *Proc. of WSDM'10*, pages 81–90. ACM, 2010.

[22] D. M. Romero, B. Meeder, and J. Kleinberg. Differences in the mechanics of information diffusion across topics: idioms, political hashtags, and complex contagion on twitter. In *Proc. of WWW'11*, pages 695–704. ACM, 2011.

[23] P. Seitlinger and T. Ley. Implicit imitation in social tagging: familiarity and semantic reconstruction. In *Proc. of CHI'12*, pages 1631–1640. ACM, 2012.

[24] P. Seitlinger, T. Ley, and D. Albert. Verbatim and semantic imitation in indexing resources on the web: A fuzzy-trace account of social tagging. *Applied Cognitive Psychology*, 2014.

[25] H. Steck. Item popularity and recommendation accuracy. In *Proc. of RecSys'11*, pages 125–132. ACM, 2011.

[26] C. Trattner, D. Kowald, and E. Lacic. Tagrec: towards a toolkit for reproducible evaluation and development of tag-based recommender algorithms. *ACM SIGWEB Newsletter*, Winter, 2015.

[27] C. Trattner, D. Kowald, P. Seitlinger, T. Ley, and S. Kopeinik. Modeling activation processes in human memory to predict the use of tags in social bookmarking systems. *The Journal of Web Science*, 2(1):1–18, 2016.

[28] C. Wagner, P. Singer, M. Strohmaier, and B. A. Huberman. Semantic stability in social tagging streams. In *Proc. of WWW'14*, pages 735–746. ACM, 2014.

[29] L. Zhang, J. Tang, and M. Zhang. Integrating temporal usage pattern into personalized tag prediction. In *Web Technologies and Applications*. Springer, 2012.

Understanding and Predicting Online Food Recipe Production Patterns

Tomasz Kusmierczyk
NTNU, Trondheim, Norway
tomaszku@idi.ntnu.no

Christoph Trattner
Know-Center, Graz, Austria
ctrattner@know-center.at

Kjetil Nørvåg
NTNU, Trondheim, Norway
noervaag@idi.ntnu.no

ABSTRACT

Studying online food patterns has recently become an active field of research. While there are a growing body of studies that investigate how online food in consumed, little effort has been devoted yet to understand how online food recipes are being created. To contribute to this lack of knowledge in the area, we present in this paper the results of a large-scale study that aims at understanding how historical, social and temporal factors impact on the online food creation process. Several experiments reveal the extent to which various factors are useful in predicting future recipe production.

Keywords

online food recipes; creational patterns; recipe creation; ingredient usage; predictive modeling; food recommender systems

1. INTRODUCTION

Investigating online user patterns does not only help us in understanding and learning about what people want and need but also how to improve user experiences. In the context of food, and in particular nutrition research, a huge body of literature exists that tries to understand how we consume or produce food in our daily lives. Previous studies were typically performed offline in a survey-based format and were capturing only a small fraction of a population, failing to elicit data objectively. Recent innovations in research follow a more pragmatic way by mining patterns users leave behind in the World Wide Web. The main advantage of such a method is that behavior can be computed without the direct involvement of the user. As such, it allows to learn user behavior or the behavior of a whole population fast, objective and on a large scale.

Problem Statement. While current research in this area is mostly devoted to understand how people consume food online, i.e. how people search, view or rate recipes in online food community forums and how this, e.g., correlates to real-life health related issues, little attention has yet been devoted yet to understand online food production patterns. To the best of our knowledge, *no other work has yet been devoted to the problem of understanding and predicting online food production patterns such as type of recipe being created or ingredients used.*

HT '16, July 10-13, 2016, Halifax, NS, Canada

© 2016 ACM. ISBN 978-1-4503-4247-6/16/07. . . $15.00

DOI: http://dx.doi.org/10.1145/2914586.2914632

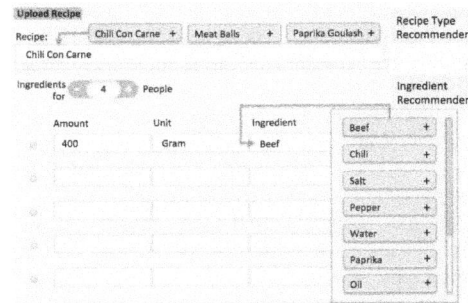

Figure 1: Example of a recommender system that tries to support the user in the food production process in an online food community.

The main goal of this research is to (i) *shed light on online food production patterns*, (ii) *the predictability of these patterns*, and in particular (iii) *the impact of information consumption as well as historical, social and temporal factors*. The two production patterns we are interested in investigating in this paper are (i) *type of recipe being created* by a user in an online food community system and (ii) the *types of ingredients being used*.

Application. The topic of this paper not only enables us to understand, how online food communities evolve and how this might impact our health, but could also help in the design of food recommender systems that could support people in the food production process. Currently, this process is a time-consuming task, and as shown in many other domains such a system would help the user not only to perform this kind of task more efficiently but could also increase the user experience or increase the quality of the content being created. Figure 1 shows how such a system could look like, aiming at predicting and recommending the type of recipe the user is likely going to create, as well as the ingredients used to create the recipe.

Research Questions. To drive our research, we have identified two research questions. The first one is on understanding the factors and their corresponding correlations with the online food creation process while the second one is on the usefulness of these correlations in a prediction task. In particular, the questions are as follows:

- **RQ1.** To what extent do historical, social and temporal factors have an impact on the online food production patterns such as type of recipe being created and ingredients used?

- **RQ2.** To what extent are these factors useful to predict online food recipe production?

Table 1: Basic statistics of the dataset.

#users	199k	#ingredients	1,483	#recipes	406k
#publishing	18k	#food types	2,523	#ratings	7,795k
#rating	19k	#categories	246		

2. RELATED WORK

Studying online food patterns is a relatively new topic of research and only a few related studies exist so far in this context.

From the consumption side, the most prominent work is the study of West et al. [18]. In their work, they analyzed seasonal trends and correlation between heart diseases and online food consumption using website log files from allrecipes.com.[1] Similar studies exploiting online recipe ratings were performed by Said and Bellogin [13], by Abbar et al. in the context of Twitter [1], and recently by De Choudhury and Sharman [5] in the context of Instagram. Another recent study in this context is the work of Wagner et al. [17], who investigated the dynamics of online food consumption in an European food community platform based on data from log files.

The most popular work in this strand of research in the area of recommender systems was done by Berkovsky and Freyne [3, 7], who were the first to study online food recipe consumption patterns and preferences, with the purpose of building systems for recommending recipes. Another relevant work is the experiments of Teng et al. [14] where they try to induce a number of features to train a statistical model that is able to recommend recipes to users. Recent studies also worth mention here are the works of Trevisiol et al. [16], Ge et al. [9], and Elsweiler & Harvey [6], who studied intelligent meal planning and health-aware food recommender systems. Finally, there is the study of Rokicki et al. [12] proposing an interesting approach to recommend healthy recipes to diabetes patients.

As mentioned in the introduction, from the producer side, very little research has been performed yet. Apart from our own preliminary research on temporality in online food recipe production [10, 11, 15], to the best of our knowledge, the only other related work is the one by Ahn et al. [2], who mined and analyzed three different online food community platforms, in order to unveil patterns in recipe creation across different food cultures.

3. DATASET

Our work relies on a dataset obtained from the German online food community website kochbar.de[2]. The basic statistics of the dataset are presented in the Table 1.

The dataset contains more than 400 thousand recipes from the years 2008-2014, and recipes are labeled with 246 categories such as 'Desserts' or 'Christmas'. Additionally, for each recipe, metadata covering information about ingredients, publication time and title is provided. In the initial dataset, ingredients were lists of arbitrary strings provided as free-form text by the users, and several standard pre-processing steps such as filtering, name translation and unification were performed in order to clean the data.

Furthermore, based on the recipe titles, we mined the types of recipes that we denote further in the paper as "food types". We identified those as titles appearing at least 5 times, i.e., if some title, for example 'apple pie', appears for 5 or more recipes we assume that it represents a common food type. Then, using substring inclusion, we matched all recipe titles to extracted types. For exam-

---

[1] http://allrecipes.com
[2] http://kochbar.de

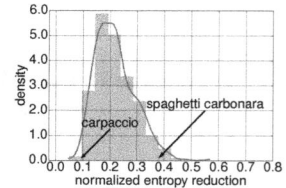

Figure 2: Distribution of reduction in ingredients entropy when food type is known.

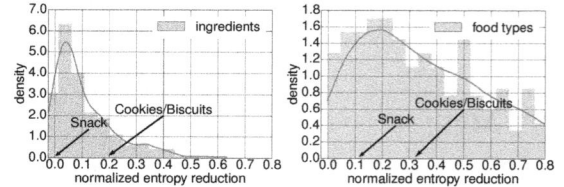

Figure 3: Distributions of reduction in entropies of ingredients and food types when category is known.

ple, 'Magic *Apple Pie* by Mrs Schultz' was identified as a special variant of '*apple pie*'.

The second important entity in our dataset, next to a recipe, is the user. The almost 200k users established 195k friendship relations. 18 thousand users were active publishers that uploaded at least one recipe and around 19 thousand were actively rating recipes, providing in total 7 million ratings. Most of the ratings (99.1%) are 5-star ratings, so in our analysis we ignore the value and just consider the fact of the rating itself.

4. UNDERSTANDING ONLINE FOOD PRODUCTION PATTERNS

In this section, we study the extent to which particular factors have an impact on the online food production process (RQ1).

4.1 Food Types vs. Ingredients

In our study we are analyzing both food types and ingredients, and the initial expectation was that some ingredients should be more typical for particular food types than for the others. However, the quantitative evaluation shows this is not the case, i.e., in most cases we are not able to say to what extent there is a correlation between a particular pair of food type and ingredient.

Figure 2 provides a deeper insight into quantitative dependencies between food types and ingredients. As a measure for evaluating the discriminative power of food type we use the normalized entropy reduction (horizontal axis) $\frac{H(X)-H_{type}(X)}{H(X)}$, where $H(X)$ is the entropy of ingredients measured over all recipes and $H_{type}(X)$ is the entropy measured only over recipes of the particular type. Two illustrative examples are 'spaghetti carbonara' that determines well both set of ingredients and their frequencies distribution (entropy is reduced by almost 40%.), while on the other hand, 'carpaccio' is a very general type and not helpful for ingredients prediction (entropy is reduced only by 10%). The average reduction over all recipes is 22%.

4.2 Categories vs. Types and Ingredients

Users tend to have their own sets of favorite categories, and in order to validate the extent to which the preference towards some categories can be useful in a prediction task, we measured how well categories determine ingredients and food types. The result-

Figure 4: Similarities (measured over ingredients and food types) between recipes uploaded and rated by users.

ing plots are shown in Figure 3, where the horizontal axis represents normalized entropy reduction, in this case: $\frac{H(X) - H_{category}(X)}{H(X)}$, where $H(X)$ is the entropy measured over all recipes and $H_{category}(X)$ is the entropy measured only over recipes from the particular category. The value is highest for the most discriminative categories, indicating that they are also the best for predicting other items.

Average reduction over all recipes for ingredients entropy (first plot) is equal to 11%. For food types (second plot) entropy distribution is more flat and skewed towards high values, e.g., the mean is 40%. However some categories are more discriminative than the others, for example 'Cookies/Biscuits' vs. 'Snack'.

4.3 Production vs. Consumption

Before investigating online food production patterns in more detail, we wanted to understand better differences between online food consumption (recipe rating behavior) and production (recipe creation behavior).

Figure 4 provides insights into the relations between recipes consumed (rated) and produced (uploaded) by users. The horizontal axis measures the average cosine similarity between recipes published by the user u: $x(u) = avg_{r,r' \in U_u} sim(r, r')$. The vertical axis measures the average cosine similarity between recipes published and rated by the user u: $y(u) = avg_{r \in U_u, r' \in R_u} sim(r, r')$. U_u is the set of uploads by u and R_u the set of ratings by u.

We observe that users upload and rate in different ways, i.e., similarities along horizontal and vertical axes have different values and distributions. Users under the equal similarity line $y = x$ (with higher similarities within uploaded recipes than between uploaded and rated recipes) follow their own publishing style. Users above the line (with higher similarity between uploads and ratings) have publishing styles strongly influenced by information acquired from ratings.

When similarity is measured over common ingredients, for approximately 32% of the users their uploads are significantly less similar to other uploads than to ratings. For them ratings seem to be a better predictor than historical uploads. Only for 11% the opposite is true. For the rest 57%, the observed differences between similarities were not found statistically significant, i.e., t-test with $\alpha = 0.001$ was not able to reject the hypothesis that $x(u) = y(u)$.

For food types we find similar patterns as for ingredients. In the first group, where uploads to ratings similarities dominate, we observed 48% of the users. For 51% we did not observe statistically significant (according to t-test) differences. Only for less than 1% of the users similarities between uploads dominate over uploads to ratings similarities.

4.4 Historical Factors

Historical information is in many cases a very useful source of information for predicting the future. Henceforth, we were interested in investigating how useful user's historical uploads can be in future content prediction.

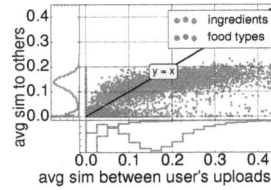

Figure 5: Similarities (measured over ingredients and food types) between user's own recipes and to other users' uploads.

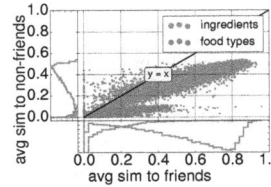

Figure 6: Similarities to user friends in comparison to non-friends.

Figure 5 presents a comparison of recipes from a single user to other users' recipes, and show mean cosine similarities measured over ingredients and food types. Each user is represented by single data point (one for ingredients and one for food types) and characterized by two values: mean similarity between recipes he uploaded (horizontal axis) and mean similarity to recipes uploaded by the other users (vertical axis).

The plots are biased towards the horizontal axis, i.e., towards high similarities between single user's recipes. However, our observations indicate that historical factors might be useful for the prediction of future user production only to some extent. For 41% of users (for ingredients) and 6% of users (for food types), the mean similarity between their uploads is higher than to uploads by others. For 42% (for ingredients) and 93% (for food types), we were not able to distinguish between single user's uploads and uploads by the other users (t-test was not able to reject means equality hypothesis). Finally, we found a group of users that behave in the opposite of expected way, i.e., they avoid repeating themselves and their uploads resemble more what others produce.

4.5 Social Factors

Social factors have been found to be a very useful source of information in many prediction tasks. In the context of online food communities, social connections are expressed by explicit friendship relations.

Figure 6 compares the mean cosine similarity of users to their friends (horizontal coordinate) and to other people that they are not connected to (vertical coordinate). The difference to previous plots where similarity is measured on recipe level should be noted. Here we focus on users' general preferences, i.e., all recipes from a user are merged together and similarities are averaged over users and not over recipes.

We also observe that from social connections such as friendship we can obtain useful information about user's preferences and biases. For example, approximately 95% of the users prefer the same items (items/food types) as their friends, while the opposite is true for only 5%.

4.6 Temporal Factors

People in their daily lives follow regular patterns that are related to time. For example, we behave differently on working days than during weekends. These periodic factors can also influence online food production patterns.

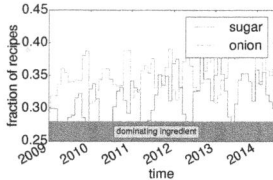

Figure 7: Uploading popularity plot of two sample ingredients. Typically, one of the items (blue one) is dominating, however, due to the shift in temporal patterns the other (red one) seasonally becomes more popular.

In this study, we focus on the popularity of various ingredients and food types, and find that most of them follow seasonal and weekly trends. We noticed that some items are used in recipes more often in some periods than in the others. Our findings also confirm the hypothesis that these changes are significant enough to change relative popularities of different items. For example, Figure 7 presents a sample situation where seasonality determines ingredients usage (sugar vs. onion) and relative popularity.

5. PREDICTING ONLINE FOOD PRODUCTION PATTERNS

While the previous section focused on understanding the impact of various factors in the online food recipe creation process, the focus of this section is the predictability of this process (RQ2). The two problems we are trying to tackle now are the following: (1) *Given a target user u, what type of recipe r is he going to produce?* (2) *Given a target user u, which of the available ingredients i is he going to use?* The second problem we study in two settings: without recipe type given and in a context-aware setting when recipe type is already known (extracted from the recipe title entered by the user).

In addition to set of users $u \in \mathscr{U}$, the set of recipes $r \in \mathscr{R}$, the set of types of recipes $t \in \mathscr{T}$, ingredients $i \in \mathscr{I}$, and categories $c \in \mathscr{C}$ we consider influential factors, such as temporal context T (seasonal and weekly trends), friendship F. The task is then to propose a scoring function $S(u,e)$ (where $e \in \{t,i\}$) that assigns a preference score (predicts ranking) for candidate recipe type t or ingredient i for user u.

5.1 Evaluation Protocol

The evaluation protocol we follow in this paper is the one usually used in order to evaluate predictive models and recommender system offline in a time-based manner [4].

We split the dataset in training and test samples according to the time line, employing the leave-one-out strategy. Hence, the training set contains all the recipes published by user apart from the last published (this one is put into the test set). In our evaluation, we considered only users who have at least one recipe produced. Users who have uploaded exactly one recipe were considered as cold-start users (their only recipe was moved to the test set). In order to determine the quality of our predictors we used the $nDCG@k$ measure ($k = 3$ for food types and $k = 10$ for ingredients used).

5.2 Predictors

Historical Predictors. The first proposed scoring function, based on findings from Section 4.4, depends on the popularity of the item e (either ingredient i or type t) in historically uploaded recipes and is defined as following:

$$\text{MPU}(u,e) = \sum_{r \in U_u} [e \in r]$$

where [*condition*] takes 1 if *condition* is true and 0 otherwise and the expression $e \in r$ means that e (either ingredient, food type or category) is assigned to the recipe r. U_u is the set of recipes uploaded by the user u in the past.

Similarly, relying on findings from Section 4.3 where we showed that uploads often strongly correlate with ratings, we can define:

$$\text{MPU-R}(u,e) = \sum_{r \in R_u} [e \in r]$$

where R_u is the set of recipes rated by the user u in the past.

For some users the historical data may be very sparse. Hence, it might be better to smooth the scores by incorporating the information from recipes of other users that are somehow related, for example through common categories (Sections 4.2 and 4.4). The predictor that measures the popularity of the item e in categories used by the user u is defined as following:

$$\text{C}(u,e) = \sum_{c \in \mathscr{C}} w(u,c) \cdot \left(\sum_{r \in \mathscr{R}} [c \in r \wedge e \in r] \right)$$

where $w(u,c) = \sum_{r \in U_u} [c \in r]$ measures the popularity of category c in user u's recipes. The second part weights the popularity of the item e in recipes from the category.

Food types and ingredients are strongly correlated (Section 4.1). When the set $T \subset \mathscr{T}$ (typically of size of only one or two) of types assigned to the recipe is known (extracted from the recipe title already typed by the user) the above scoring function can be adjusted in the following way:

$$\text{C}[T](u,i) = \sum_{t \in T, c \in \mathscr{C}} w(t)w(u,c) \cdot \left(\sum_{r \in \mathscr{R}} [c \in r \wedge i \in r \wedge t \in r] \right)$$

where $w(t)$ if the relative weight of a type t. We define $w(t) = \frac{1}{\sum_{r \in \mathscr{R}} [t \in r]}$ to give a higher importance to less popular and more specific types.

Similar to the case of uploads, we define a set of predictors that reflect the popularity in recipes rated by the user u: respectively C-R and C-R[T] where U_u is replaced with R_u in the formulas.

Social Predictors. In Section 4.5 we have shown that social factors have a strong impact on food production. Hence, we propose to exploit friendship relations in the following scoring function:

$$\text{F}(u,e) = \sum_{f \in F_u} \sum_{r \in U_f} [e \in r]$$

where F_u is the set of direct friends of the user u. Assuming context (set of types T) to be known above scoring function is adjusted in the following way:

$$\text{F}[T](u,i) = \sum_{t \in T} \sum_{f \in F_u} \sum_{r \in U_f} w(t) \cdot [i \in r \wedge t \in r]$$

By replacing U_u with R_u in the above formulas we get the scoring functions over ratings instead of uploads, respectively F-R and F-R[T].

Temporal Predictors. Temporal impact on the online food production process was observed (Section 4.6) on both seasonal and weekly (to a lesser extent) level implying two variants of the time-dependent scoring function:

$$\text{T}[time](u,e) = \sum_{u' \in \mathscr{U}} \sum_{r' \in U_{u'}} [tm(r') = tm(u) \wedge e \in r']$$

where *time* can be either a month or a week day and $tm(.)$ is a function that returns respectively month or week day of the web site access or recipe upload.

Similarly, we can also consider temporal factors for ratings T-R[*time*] and with the context known T[*time*, *T*](u,i).

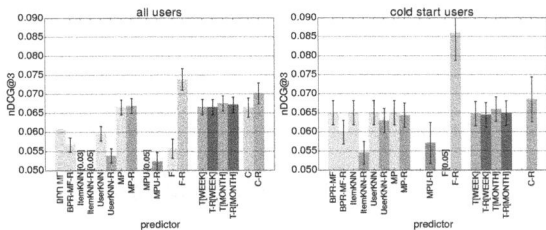

Figure 8: Food types prediction quality (means and standard errors) for cold start and all users. Colors are used to mark different groups of methods.

5.3 Baseline Methods

For the first baseline we used a non-personalized scoring function, the so-called *most popular* approach:

$$\mathrm{MP}(u,e) = \sum_{r \in \mathcal{R}} [e \in r]$$

Additionally, we introduced *the most popular based on ratings* score:

$$\mathrm{MP\text{-}R}(u,e) = \sum_{u \in \mathcal{U}} \sum_{r \in R_u} [e \in r]$$

Similar to above, we also define context-aware baselines MP[T] and MP-R[T] which measure popularity when family type is known.

Apart from these naive methods, we also compare to state-of-the-art methods from the literature, namely BPR-MF, ItemKNN, and UserKNN (only applicable in context-blind case) in two variants. The first variant relies on uploads and the second (suffix R, e.g, BPR-MF-R) on ratings. We used the popular implementations from *MyMediaLite* library with the default settings [8].

5.4 Results and Discussion

Food Type Prediction. Figure 8 summarizes the results of our food types prediction experiment, considering all users and only cold-start users. As shown, the prediction of food types is a hard task and henceforth the obtained values on both plots are low, and baselines achieve relatively high scores and few approaches overpower them. One predictor, namely F-R (popularity in ratings by user friends), performs significantly better than the others. The strength of the method is especially notable on the second plot (for cold start users). The second best results are obtained via C-R (popularity in often rated categories). Time-based functions perform no better than baselines. The worst among our approaches are MPU and MPU-R that rely entirely on user's previous uploads and ratings, suggesting that one of the key factors influencing results quality is the data sparsity, e.g., just by regularizing with categorical information we can improve from one of the worst approaches (MPU-R) to almost the best one (C-R).

Ingredient Prediction. Figure 9 summarizes the results of the ingredients prediction experiment in two cases: (a) recipe type is unknown and in (b) recipe type is given. What is notable is that when context (recipe type) is included, the prediction is much easier, resulting in higher values ($nDCG@10 \sim 0.7$). Furthermore, we observe that rating-based predictors perform remarkably better than those based on uploads. Similarly, as previously observed, we note that the best prediction quality is obtained for scoring functions based on social factors such as friendship (F-R and F-R[T]) and for the methods that exploit categories to overcome data deficiency (C-R and C-R[T]). On the other hand, we hypothesize that

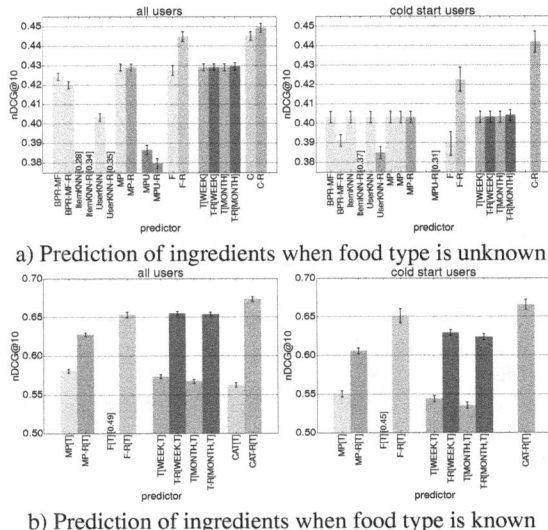

a) Prediction of ingredients when food type is unknown

b) Prediction of ingredients when food type is known

Figure 9: Ingredients prediction quality (means and standard errors) for cold start and all users.

due to the lack of sufficient evidence, recommenders such as MPU and MPU-R, as well as popular methods such as UserKNN and ItemKNN, perform poorly. Time-based methods perform better than these baselines but their prediction quality depends on food type information availability.

6. CONCLUSIONS

In this paper, we extended our understanding on the factors that have an impact on the users in their content creation process in online food communities. We approached this by conducting several analytical and predictive experiments on a large-scale dataset obtained from one of the largest online food community platforms available on the Web, namely *kochbar.de*. As our empirical analysis reveals, factors such as user history, social relations and temporality have indeed a significant impact on how recipes are created and why certain types of recipes and ingredients are being used by the user. In particular, our findings were as follows:

- Information consumption often correlates with future information production.

- Food types, ingredients and categories show strong correlations.

- Only some fraction of users follow their own styles and have strong preferences towards ingredients, food types and categories.

- There are strong correlations between social factors such as friendship and content being produced.

- Ingredients and food type popularities are season-dependent influencing their relative prevalence.

- It is easier to predict ingredients than exact food type.

- Approaches relying on social factors and applying ratings and categorical information are the most useful to predict future production.

7. REFERENCES

[1] S. Abbar, Y. Mejova, and I. Weber. You tweet what you eat: Studying food consumption through twitter. In *Proc. of CHI'15*, 2015.

[2] Y.-Y. Ahn, S. E. Ahnert, J. P. Bagrow, and A.-L. Barabási. Flavor network and the principles of food pairing. *Scientific reports*, 1, 2011.

[3] S. Berkovsky and J. Freyne. Group-based recipe recommendations: Analysis of data aggregation strategies. In *Proc. of RecSys '10*, pages 111–118, 2010.

[4] P. G. Campos, F. Díez, and I. Cantador. Time-aware recommender systems: A comprehensive survey and analysis of existing evaluation protocols. *UMUAI*, 24(1-2):67–119, 2014.

[5] M. De Choudhury and S. S. Sharma. Characterizing dietary choices, nutrition, and language in food deserts via social media. In *Proc. of CSCW '16*, 2016.

[6] D. Elsweiler and M. Harvey. Towards automatic meal plan recommendations for balanced nutrition. In *Proc. of RecSys '15*, pages 313–316, 2015.

[7] J. Freyne and S. Berkovsky. Intelligent food planning: Personalized recipe recommendation. In *Proc. of IUI '10*, pages 321–324, 2010.

[8] Z. Gantner, S. Rendle, C. Freudenthaler, and L. Schmidt-Thieme. MyMediaLite: a free recommender system library. In *Proc. of RecSys '11*, pages 305–308, 2011.

[9] M. Ge, F. Ricci, and D. Massimo. Health-aware food recommender system. In *Proc. of RecSys '15*, pages 333–334, 2015.

[10] T. Kusmierczyk, C. Trattner, and K. Nørvåg. Temporal patterns in online food innovation. In *Proc. of WWW '15 Companion*, pages 1345–1350, 2015.

[11] T. Kusmierczyk, C. Trattner, and K. Nørvåg. Temporality in online food recipe consumption and production. In *Proc. of WWW'15*, 2015.

[12] M. Rokicki, E. Herder, and E. Demidova. What's on my plate: Towards recommending recipe variations for diabetes patients. In *Posters, Demos, Late-breaking Results and Workshop Proc. of UMAP'15*, 2015.

[13] A. Said and A. Bellogín. You are what you eat! tracking health through recipe interactions. In *Proc. of RSWeb'14*, 2014.

[14] C.-Y. Teng, Y.-R. Lin, and L. A. Adamic. Recipe recommendation using ingredient networks. In *Proc. of WebSci'12*, 2012.

[15] C. Trattner, T. Kusmierczyk, and K. Nørvåg. FOODWEB - studying food consumption and production patterns on the web. *ERCIM News*, 2016(104), 2016.

[16] M. Trevisiol, L. Chiarandini, and R. A. Baeza-Yates. Buon appetito: recommending personalized menus. In *Proc. of HT'14*, pages 327–329, 2014.

[17] C. Wagner, P. Singer, and M. Strohmaier. The nature and evolution of online food preferences. *EPJ Data Science*, 3(1):1–22, 2014.

[18] R. West, R. W. White, and E. Horvitz. From cookies to cooks: Insights on dietary patterns via analysis of web usage logs. In *Proc. of WWW'13*, 2013.

High Enough? Explaining and Predicting Traveler Satisfaction Using Airline Reviews

Emanuel Lacic
KTI
Graz University of Technology
Graz, Austria
elacic@know-center.at

Dominik Kowald
Know-Center
Graz University of Technology
Graz, Austria
dkowald@know-center.at

Elisabeth Lex
KTI
Graz University of Technology
Graz, Austria
elisabeth.lex@tugraz.at

ABSTRACT

Air travel is one of the most frequently used means of transportation in our every-day life. Thus, it is not surprising that an increasing number of travelers share their experiences with airlines and airports in form of online reviews on the Web. In this work, we thrive to explain and uncover the features of airline reviews that contribute most to traveler satisfaction. To that end, we examine reviews crawled from the Skytrax air travel review portal. Skytrax provides four review categories to review airports, lounges, airlines and seats. Each review category consists of several five-star ratings as well as free-text review content. In this paper, we conduct a comprehensive feature study and we find that not only five-star rating information such as airport queuing time and lounge comfort highly correlate with traveler satisfaction but also inferred features in the form of the review text sentiment. Based on our findings, we create classifiers to predict traveler satisfaction using the best performing rating features. Our results reveal that given our methodology, traveler satisfaction can be predicted with high accuracy. Additionally, we find that training a model on the sentiment of the review text provides a competitive alternative when no five-star rating information is available. We believe that our work is of interest for researchers in the area of modeling and predicting user satisfaction based on available review data on the Web.

Keywords

traveler satisfaction; airline reviews; skytrax; user satisfaction prediction; feature analysis; sentiment analysis; clustering analysis

1. INTRODUCTION

In the last decades, air travel has become one of the most frequently used means of transportation. The International Air Transport Association (IATA) expects traveler numbers to reach 7.3 billion by 2034, representing a 4.1% average annual growth in demand for air connectivity [1]. At the same time, an increasing number of airlines is competing for market shares, which raises the need to attract customers while balancing costs and services.

---

[1] http://www.iata.org/pressroom/pr/Pages/2014-10-16-01.aspx

HT '16, July 10-13, 2016, Halifax, NS, Canada

© 2016 ACM. ISBN 978-1-4503-4247-6/16/07. . . $15.00

DOI: http://dx.doi.org/10.1145/2914586.2914629

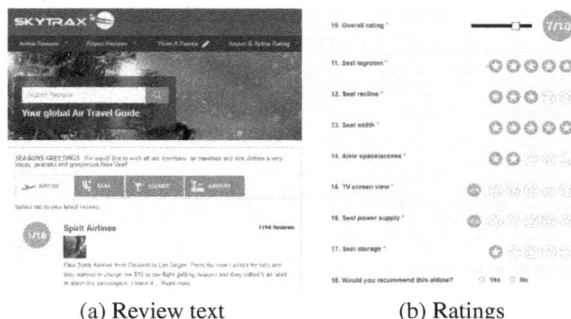

(a) Review text (b) Ratings

Figure 1: The Skytrax airline (a) review and (b) rating portal. Within each of the four review categories, users state their traveler satisfaction via several rating features, a review text, an overall rating and a binary signal indicated by the *Would you recommend this airline/airport?* checkbox.

A growing number of customers (i.e., travelers) share their experiences and viewpoints on airlines and airports in form of online reviews in order to help others to better judge airline and airport quality. Such reviews may consist of free-text reviews combined with ratings (e.g., by means of 5-star ratings). As a consequence, a vast amount of airline review data is available on the Web, which is not only of interest for the airline industry but also for researchers working on analyzing the impact of the factors/features contributing to user satisfaction [2, 3, 4].

In this paper, we present work-in-progress on a recently started project that aims at explaining and predicting traveler satisfaction using airline review data. Specifically, it is our goal to identify critical features that contribute to air travel satisfaction based on rating and textual reviews. Our idea is to exploit these features in order to predict whether a traveler is satisfied with her airline/airport choice based on the given ratings and/or textual review. This is summed up in the following two research questions that guide our work:

RQ1: Which airline review features are most indicative for traveler satisfaction?

RQ2: To what extent can we predict traveler satisfaction using the available rating and inferred sentiment of airline reviews?

Explaining traveler satisfaction. To better explain how the features contribute to traveler satisfaction, and thus, to address *RQ1*, we exploit real-world airline review data, which was crawled from the Skytrax portal. As shown in Figure 1, in Skytrax users can (a) enter review text and (b) rate various services. Moreover, the user can state her final traveler satisfaction not only using an overall rating between 1 and 10 but also using a checkbox to indicate if she would recommend this airline or airport to other travelers. In terms of rating features, we explore features derived from four different review categories, namely airport, lounge, airline and seat reviews. In terms of inferred features, we extract and make use of the review text sentiment (see Section 3).

To identify which review features are most indicative for traveler satisfaction, we conduct a feature analysis in which we correlate rating and the inferred sentiment with the overall rating given by the user. We find that airport *queuing* time, lounge *comfort*, airline *cabin staff* quality and seat *legroom* space are factors that highly impact the overall traveler satisfaction. We also find that the sentiment of the review content is a good indicator to determine whether a traveler was satisfied with the travel. Additionally, we perform clustering and cluster labelling of the textual content in order to identify topics, which are discussed in the reviews. In the long run, this may help to extend the rating schema. For example, if many users discuss the topic "immigration" in their textual review, the rating portal could introduce a novel rating feature, which enables users to rate the quality of the immigration service.

Predicting traveler satisfaction. We utilize the available rating information as well as the sentiment of the textual reviews as features for our prediction study (*RQ2*). We formulate the prediction task as a binary classification problem of the final traveler satisfaction signal indicated by the *Would you recommend this airline/airport?* checkbox (see Figure 1).

We find strong performance in predicting the traveler satisfaction using the individual rating features. By using a combination of the best performing rating features, we demonstrate that the prediction accuracy can even be increased. Additionally, we show that a classifier, which solely uses the sentiment of the review text, provides a competitive performance in terms of prediction accuracy. This could especially be beneficial in cases where rating features are missing. In terms of metrics, we report the prediction accuracy by means of the F1-score and AUC (i.e., area under ROC curve).

Significance of this work. With this study, we aim at explaining which airline review features have the most impact on predicting traveler satisfaction. Our findings can provide guidance for stakeholders in the airline industry, as well as for researchers, who study online review data to better understand what is important to travellers and what impacts user satisfaction.

2. RELATED WORK

Since Heskett et al. [8] established a relationship between traveler satisfaction and profitability, research on the airline service quality has become an important issue for the airline industry. As a consequence, the authors of [14] claim that it is crucial to continuously collect and evaluate data about traveler satisfaction and how it relates to the provided service quality in order to be competitive in the airline industry. However, most work that conduct research in airline service quality rely on gathered offline data coming from on-site questionnaires [17, 11], airline submissions [18] or in-depth interviews [19].

Nowadays, online reviews are getting more popular and as a consequence, there is the opportunity to leverage them as a rich and powerful source of information. In fact, there is a lot of valuable hidden information available in online reviews [12]. As such, Web sites like the already mentioned Skytrax portal, AirlineRatings [2] and TripAdvisor [3] are important for the airline industry to study how service quality is perceived by the travelers. Furthermore, this

[2]http://http://www.airlineratings.com/
[3]http://www.tripadvisor.com

Review categories	Airports	Lounges	Airlines	Seats
# Users	11,834	1,598	29,645	1,147
# Reviews	17,721	2,264	41,396	1,258
Traveler Satisfaction	22.12%	36.04%	53.38%	36.41%

Table 1: Statistics of the Skytrax dataset showing how many reviews were given by the users in the four categories. Additionally, we report the traveler satisfaction in the categories as the relative number of reviews that were indicated as airlines or airports that would be recommended to other travelers.

data may be a valuable source for researchers that aim at better understanding the factors that contribute to user satisfaction.

One recent work going into that direction is the one described in [20], in which the authors mined review data about airlines' in-flight services from the Skytrax portal. By grouping travelers via feature-based and clustering-based modelling, the authors showed that inferences can be captured to explain how travelers evaluate in-flight services. Another recent work of Yao et al. [21] presented a research framework to extract and explore information on a user's opinion about airline service features from a large static corpus of online review texts.

In our work, we perform a comprehensive feature analysis using rating features and inferred sentiment from airport, lounge, airline and seat reviews in order to explain which features actually contribute to traveler satisfaction. Moreover, we show how these features can be utilized to predict traveler satisfaction. Our methods and results provide practical insights on how to build upon work like [21] in order to predict traveler satisfaction using online airline reviews.

3. AIRLINE REVIEW DATA

Within the air travel industry, the London-based company Skytrax has established itself as a leader in conducting air travel research. Skytrax provides international audits and airport rankings and gives traveler-based satisfaction awards in its yearly *World Airport Awards* and *World Airline Awards*. Their airport and airline review Web portal has positioned itself as one of the most popular independent review sites within the air travel industry. In this work, we incorporate a recent publicly made available airline review dataset [4] scraped from Skytrax's Web portal. This dataset contains not only rating features and textual content of airline reviews but also features that indicate the final traveler satisfaction (see Figure 1).

Rating features. The rating data gathered from Skytrax is divided into four different review categories: (1) airport, (2) lounge, (3) airline, and (4) seat reviews. Each review category has 7 - 8 individual rating features that map the perceived quality of a specific service. The individual rating features are based on a 5-star scale and are accompanied by an additional overall rating on a 1 - 10 scale. Table 1 shows the statistics of the dataset and reveals that most reviews are targeted at airports and airlines, and less at specific seats or lounges.

Inferred features. The posted review text can also contain valuable information about the perceived service quality and satisfaction of a traveler [12]. To that end, we manually enriched the available dataset by inferring the sentiment from the review text. Based on recent research, which compared several sentiment analysis tools [16], we used the AlchemyAPI [5] for this task. For each review, the API was called using the textual content and the re-

[4]https://github.com/quankiquanki/skytrax-reviews-dataset
[5]http://www.alchemyapi.com/

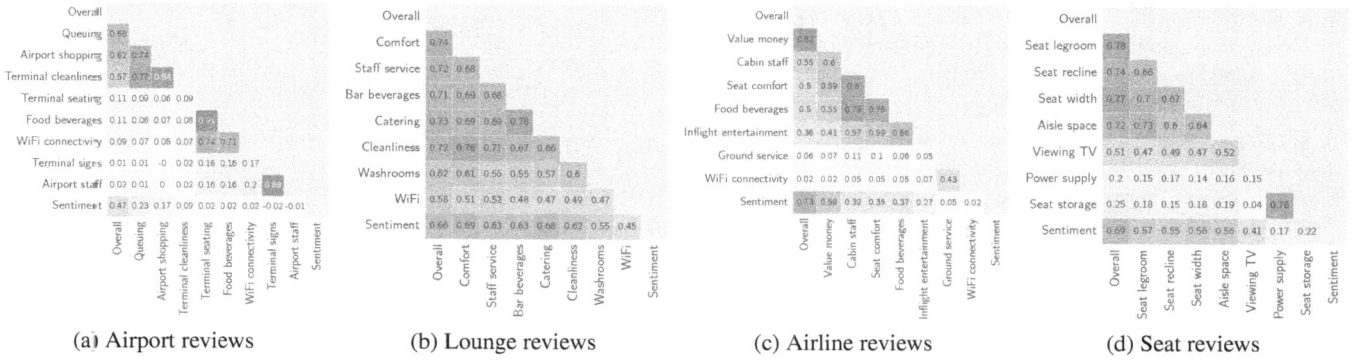

(a) Airport reviews   (b) Lounge reviews   (c) Airline reviews   (d) Seat reviews

Figure 2: Pearson correlation of the airline review features with the overall rating given by the users. Aside from rating and review sentiment, each review category features an overall rating, which indicates traveler satisfaction (*RQ1*). *Note:* all correlations values higher than .02 have a p-value < .001.

turned value, denoting if the sentiment is positive or negative, was added to the review data. As we will show in this paper, the sentiment of the review text further helps in explaining and predicting traveler satisfaction and is especially useful when rating features are missing.

Traveler satisfaction. We use the overall rating to evaluate how the different review features influence the traveler's satisfaction. Furthermore, in order to make a final decision on how a traveler was satisfied with an airline or airport, we utilize the binary signal represented as the *Would you recommend this airline/airport?* checkbox of Skytrax. As such, Table 1 also shows how travelers are satisfied based on the four review categories. For example, airport reviews mostly resulted in a negative traveler satisfaction, whereas airline reviews almost contain the same amount of satisfactory and unsatisfactory experiences.

4. EXPLAINING TRAVELER SATISFACTION

In this section, we aim to answer the first research question of our work (*RQ1*) and determine the review features that contribute the most to traveler satisfaction.

4.1 Methodology

As already outlined in Section 3, each review category reveals an overall rating, which states how a user perceived an airport, lounge, airline or seat during the travel. For example, the *Dalaman* airport, located in south-west Turkey, received the worst overall rating with a mean of 2.17. On the contrary, the best rated airport is the *Singapore's Changi* airport with an average overall rating of 7.09. With respect to airlines, *Bangkok Airways* was the best rated one with a mean overall rating of 7.99, whereas *Air Canada Rouge* is the worst rated airline with a mean of 2.54.

In order to determine which features actually influence these overall scores, we conduct a feature analysis in which we correlate the rating and inferred features (i.e., the sentiment) with the overall rating given by the user. To explore the influences of these features, we use the Pearson's product-moment correlation coefficient [10]. In this respect, we further correlate the ratings of the features among each other because we believe that knowing how features influence not only the overall rating but also the rating of other features, helps us in even better understanding the factors that contribute to traveler satisfaction.

In addition to the correlation analysis of rating and inferred features, we further incorporate the textual content of online airline

reviews. Our aim is to uncover additional features that could be introduced to the rating schema. To that end, we perform clustering and cluster labeling of the review content in order to identify topics, which are discussed in reviews. In contrast to [20], we do not cluster the content with the commonly used k-means approach but rather using Suffix Tree Clustering (STC) [22], an approach that focuses on the problem of cluster labeling. We justify our choice since this clustering technique merges base clusters with high textual overlaps and was shown to outperform group average agglomerative hierarchical clustering, k-means, buckshot, fractionation and single-pass algorithms [22, 15].

4.2 Results

Figure 2 shows the results of our feature correlation analysis on rating and inferred (i.e., sentiment) features based on the four categories.

Airport reviews. In airport reviews, the *overall rating* mostly correlates with ratings assigned to *queuing*, *airport shopping* and *terminal cleanliness*. Looking at the review text, we hypothesize that this is usually caused by short or long queuing times, the availability or quality of airport shopping and how dirty or worn out the airport facilities (e.g., toilets, restaurant, passages, etc.) are. A mild correlation with the sentiment of the review text can also be found. One interesting observation is that there is a relationship between the traveler satisfaction of *terminal seats* and the offered *foods and beverages* as well as available *WIFI connectivity*. It can also be observed that the *airport staff* and *terminal signs* ratings correlate. By looking again in the review text, we think that staff politeness and professionalism, in combination with experiencing issues with signs (e.g., unclear, contradictory, etc.), plays a mayor role in that relationship.

Lounge reviews. Compared to airport reviews, the overall satisfaction within lounge reviews highly correlates with most rating features. The top four features are the perceived *lounge comfort*, available *catering* services, *staff service* quality and the area *cleanliness*. A probably expected observation is that the perceived *catering* quality is mostly in relation with the availability of *beverages*. An interesting finding in lounge reviews is that the sentiment not only correlates with the overall traveler satisfaction but also with the various rating features that denote specific services provided in lounges.

Airline reviews. The top associated rating feature in airline reviews is *value-for-money*. We also find that satisfaction in respect to *seat comfort*, as well as the availability of *food and beverages* is related to how a traveler perceives the *cabin staff*. The extracted sentiment from the review text mostly correlates with the *overall rating*, being here the second best correlating feature and as such a strong signal for traveler satisfaction.

Seat reviews. With respect to the overall satisfaction of a traveler's seat, the best correlating features are *legroom*, *width*, *recline* and *aisle space*. The correlation of these distinctive features suggests that for a traveler, the available personal space is key. Another interesting observation is that how a traveler is satisfied with the available *seat storage* is highly associated with the availability and satisfaction of a *power supply*. The review sentiment, similar as in the case of lounge and airline reviews, is again a strong indicator for the traveler satisfaction denoted by the overall rating.

Extracting review topics. With respect to clustering and cluster labelling, in Figure 3, we report a snapshot of our preliminary results using the Suffix Tree Clustering (STC) approach. By utilizing STC, additional textual features (i.e., cluster labels) can be extracted from the review content. For example, we see in Figure 3 that travelers write about *boarding time* when experiencing negative traveler satisfaction, which in turn results into a negative review about the specific airline. On the contrary, travelers seem to be satisfied with airports when, for example, a smooth *immigration* is ensured and when *gates* are labeled well and easy to reach. Consequently, existing rating schemes could be extended with such cluster labels if they reflect recurring points of discussion in textual reviews.

5. PREDICTING TRAVELER SATISFACTION

In this section, we aim to address our second research question (*RQ2*) in order to determine the features that can be exploited to predict the final traveler satisfaction. Therefore, we formulate the prediction task as a binary classification problem. Given that reviews are marked as either *positive* or *negative* traveler satisfaction by means of the *Would you recommend this airline/airport?* checkbox of Skytrax, we aim to predict this outcome using the available rating and inferred features.

5.1 Methodology

We performed our experiments using several standard classification algorithms (e.g., NaiveBayes, C4.5, Random Forest, CART, etc. [1, 23]) provided by the popular machine learning tool WEKA [6]. In this work, however, we report the results of the Hoeffding Tree.

Introduced by Domigos and Hulten [5], the Hoeffding Tree algorithm is an incremental decision tree learner for large data streams. The tree itself tracks only attribute statistics in its leafs and uses it to grow and make classification decisions for incoming data. When sufficient statistics have accumulated at each leaf, a node-splitting approach determines whether a node-split should happen and the leaf be replaced with a new decision node. We chose this algorithm due to its practical advantage for real-time data mining [9].

In order to evaluate the classification performance, we sorted the reviews of the four categories in chronological order and used the 20% most recent reviews for testing and the rest for training. Next, using each of the four training sets, we examined whether the final user satisfaction of a target review from the corresponding test set could be predicted. With this procedure, we aim to simulate a real-world environment in which future reviewing behavior should be predicted based on past reviews. To determine the best performing

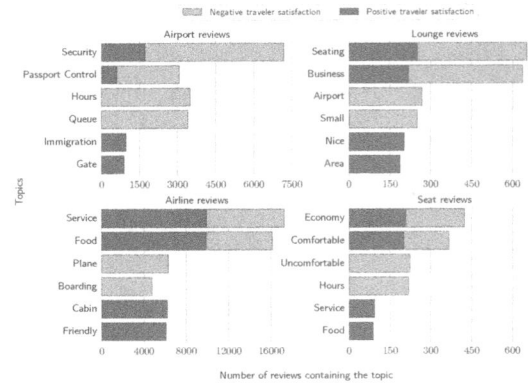

Figure 3: Snapshot of our preliminary clustering and cluster labeling analysis of the review content using the Suffix Tree Clustering (STC) approach. The extracted topics are grouped by having a positive or negative traveler satisfaction denoted by the *Would you recommend this airline/airport?* checkbox of Skytrax.

features for traveler satisfaction prediction, we trained and evaluated the classification model in the following three settings.

Firstly, for each single rating feature, we created a separate classifier and evaluated its performance. Secondly, we used a combination of features that highly correlate with the traveler satisfaction while having a low inter-correlation [7] (e.g., *overall* rating, *queuing* rating and *airport shopping* rating in case of airport reviews). Thirdly, we trained a model solely based on the inferred review text sentiment. In order to finally quantify the prediction performance, we used a set of well-known information retrieval metrics. In particular, we report the prediction accuracy by means of the F1-score (F1) and Area Under the ROC curve (AUC) [13].

5.2 Results

In this section, we present a discussion on runtime considerations, as well as our prediction results of the Hoeffding Tree algorithm for the individual rating features, the combination of rating features and the review text sentiment.

Runtime considerations. When training and testing the different classification approaches, we achieved the best accuracy performance using the Hoeffding Tree algorithm. Moreover, we found a maximum model training runtime of 0.06 seconds for this classifier in case of the rating feature combination for airline reviews. This clearly underpins our choice for the Hoeffding Tree classifier since runtime is crucial when freshly mined online review data should be instantly incorporated in the classification model. In other words, the Hoeffding Tree can build a competitive model in reasonable time and it enables incremental data updates without re-training the model. This is crucial for real-time data mining applications [9].

Individual rating features. Our prediction results based on the review categories are shown in Table 2. In general, we find strong accuracy performance in predicting the traveler satisfaction using the overall rating feature (e.g., F1 = 0.939 for seat reviews). Furthermore, the performance of rating features that have shown a high correlation with the overall rating (see *RQ1*) also perform reasonably well in terms of satisfaction prediction. For example, using the *value-for-money* feature (F1 = 0.863) in airline reviews provides higher prediction accuracy than using the overall rating (F1 = 0.838).

Airport reviews		
Feature	F1	AUC
Overall	0.963	0.948
Queuing	0.869	0.875
Airport shopping	0.859	0.876
Terminal cleanliness	0.828	0.814
Terminal seating	0.791	0.534
Food beverages	0.792	0.530
WiFi connectivity	0.774	0.519
Terminal signs	0.800	0.502
Airport staff	0.678	0.499
Combination	**0.967**	**0.976**
Airport Sentiment	0.719	0.715
Lounge reviews		
Feature	F1	AUC
Overall	0.834	0.878
Comfort	0.762	0.839
Staff service	0.768	0.819
Bar beverages	0.783	0.838
Catering	0.783	0.829
Cleanliness	0.773	0.817
Washrooms	0.750	0.826
WiFi	0.743	0.795
Combination	**0.837**	**0.884**
Lounge Sentiment	0.773	0.822
Airline reviews		
Feature	F1	AUC
Overall	0.838	0.971
Value money	**0.863**	0.940
Cabin staff	0.794	0.884
Seat comfort	0.750	0.843
Food beverages	0.741	0.827
Inflight entertainment	0.693	0.754
Ground service	0.622	0.533
WiFi connectivity	0.615	0.509
Combination	0.842	**0.975**
Airline Sentiment	0.839	0.896
Seat reviews		
Feature	F1	AUC
Overall	**0.939**	**0.985**
Seat legroom	0.872	0.919
Seat width	0.847	0.890
Aisle space	0.840	0.895
Seat recline	0.802	0.855
Viewing TV	0.730	0.759
Seat storage	0.711	0.576
Power supply	0.647	0.529
Combination	0.925	0.984
Seat Sentiment	0.812	0.849

Table 2: Classification results using the Hoeffding Tree algorithm for each of the four review categories. The accuracy performance of each single rating feature is reported, as well as the performance when the rating features are combined. Additionally, we report the accuracy, which is achieved by only using review text sentiment as the sole feature. All results are reported by means of the F1-score and AUC (RQ2).

This finding indicates that travelers perceive the received value for the spent money as the strongest influence on their final satisfaction with a flight. In contrast, we observe that features with a weak correlation to the overall rating also reach low AUC estimates below 0.6, which is only slightly above random guessing.

Combination of rating features. Overall, the combination of rating features results in strong prediction results with respect to F1-score and AUC. The best performance is achieved with airport and

lounge reviews. While being the second best performing feature in airline and seat reviews, the prediction accuracy is still high and does not differ that much from the best performing feature. In case of airport, lounge and airline reviews the feature combination even shows the best AUC performance.

Review text sentiment. Compared to other rating features, review text sentiment is a competitive feature when predicting traveler satisfaction. For example, we can observe that for airline reviews, the sentiment is the third best performing feature (F1 = 0.839), outperforming even the overall rating. Especially in cases where rating features are missing, such a performance is highly beneficial.

6. CONCLUSION AND FUTURE WORK

In this paper, we discuss how online reviews can be an important source of information to explain (*RQ1*) and predict (*RQ2*) traveler satisfaction. We utilized data crawled from the Skytrax portal in order to show that rating features such as airport *queuing* time, lounge *comfort*, airline *cabin staff* quality and seat *legroom* size highly contribute to the overall traveler satisfaction. Moreover, we found a strong correlation between review text sentiment and the final traveler satisfaction (*RQ1*). Based on these findings, we trained several classifiers and we report the results of the Hoeffding Tree algorithm, which not only provides strong accuracy performance but also a competitive runtime. The algorithm is especially suited for real-world settings, where the goal is to continuously mine and predict traveler satisfaction using online reviews. As such, our proposed methods and findings of this work should be of interest for researchers in the area of modeling and predicting user satisfaction based on review data on the Web. To sum up, we found not only that traveler satisfaction can indeed be predicted with high accuracy but also that inferred features such as the extracted sentiment bear great potential in explaining and predicting traveler satisfaction (*RQ2*).

Limitations and future work. In our opinion, a limitation of this work is the lack of a direct comparison with other incremental classifiers such as Incremental Tree Induction (i.e., ITI, the successor of ID5R) or FlexDT (Flexible Decision Tree based on fuzzy logic). As such, we plan to conduct an extensive comparison between different incremental classifiers when mining and predicting user satisfaction using online reviews. Moreover, we aim to continue our preliminary investigations of extracting review topics presented in Figure 3 by further analyzing the textual content of online airline reviews. In this respect, we plan to extend the topic extraction process conducted on the review text with additional approaches like TextRank (i.e., one of the most well-known graph-based approaches for keyphrase extraction) and Topical PageRank (runs TextRank multiple times for topics induced by a Latent Dirichlet Allocation from the text). Therefore, it is not only our intend to uncover additional features that help in explaining traveler satisfaction but also to integrate them in the process of predicting traveler satisfaction. With respect to our prediction study, we plan to incorporate further approaches known from research on recommender systems such as Collaborative Filtering or Matrix Factorization.

Acknowledgments. The authors would like to thank Dieter Theiler and Simone Kopeinik for valuable comments on this work. This work is supported by the Know-Center and the EU funded project Learning Layers (FP7, Grant Agreement 318209). The Know-Center is funded within the Austrian COMET Program - Competence Centers for Excellent Technologies - under the auspices of the Austrian Ministry of Transport, Innovation and Technology, the Austrian Ministry of Economics and Labor and by the State of Styria. COMET is managed by the Austrian Research Promotion Agency (FFG).

7. REFERENCES

[1] L. Breiman, J. Friedman, C. J. Stone, and R. A. Olshen. *Classification and regression trees.* CRC press, 1984.

[2] P. Chatterjee. Online reviews: do consumers use them? *Advances in Consumer Research*, 2001.

[3] P.-Y. Chen, S.-y. Wu, and J. Yoon. The impact of online recommendations and consumer feedback on sales. *ICIS 2004 Proceedings*, page 58, 2004.

[4] Y. Chen, S. Fay, and Q. Wang. Marketing implications of online consumer product reviews. *Business Week*, 7150:1–36, 2003.

[5] P. Domingos and G. Hulten. Mining high-speed data streams. In *Proceedings of the sixth ACM SIGKDD international conference on Knowledge discovery and data mining*, pages 71–80. ACM, 2000.

[6] M. Hall, E. Frank, G. Holmes, B. Pfahringer, P. Reutemann, and I. H. Witten. The weka data mining software: an update. *ACM SIGKDD explorations newsletter*, 11(1):10–18, 2009.

[7] M. A. Hall. *Correlation-based feature selection for machine learning.* PhD thesis, The University of Waikato, 1999.

[8] J. L. Heskett, L. Schlesinger, et al. Putting the service-profit chain to work. *Harvard business review*, 72(2):164–174, 1994.

[9] G. Hulten, L. Spencer, and P. Domingos. Mining time-changing data streams. In *Proceedings of the seventh ACM SIGKDD international conference on Knowledge discovery and data mining*, pages 97–106. ACM, 2001.

[10] J. Lee Rodgers and W. A. Nicewander. Thirteen ways to look at the correlation coefficient. *The American Statistician*, 42(1):59–66, 1988.

[11] J. J. Liou and G.-H. Tzeng. A dominance-based rough set approach to customer behavior in the airline market. *Information Sciences*, 180(11):2230–2238, 2010.

[12] B. Pang and L. Lee. Opinion mining and sentiment analysis. *Foundations and trends in information retrieval*, 2(1-2):1–135, 2008.

[13] D. M. W. Powers. Evaluation: from precision, recall and f-measure to roc, informedness, markedness and correlation. *International Journal of Machine Learning Technology*, 2011.

[14] G. C. Saha and Theingi. Service quality, satisfaction, and behavioural intentions: A study of low-cost airline carriers in thailand. *Managing Service Quality: An International Journal*, 19(3):350–372, 2009.

[15] S. Sambasivam and N. Theodosopoulos. Advanced data clustering methods of mining web documents. *Issues in Informing Science and Information Technology*, 3:563–579, 2006.

[16] J. Serrano-Guerrero, J. A. Olivas, F. P. Romero, and E. Herrera-Viedma. Sentiment analysis: A review and comparative analysis of web services. *Information Sciences*, 311:18–38, 2015.

[17] N. M. Suki. Passenger satisfaction with airline service quality in malaysia: A structural equation modeling approach. *Research in Transportation Business & Management*, 10:26–32, 2014.

[18] S. Tiernan, D. L. Rhoades, and B. Waguespack Jr. Airline service quality: Exploratory analysis of consumer perceptions and operational performance in the usa and eu. *Managing Service Quality: An International Journal*, 18(3):212–224, 2008.

[19] I. Vlachos and Z. Lin. Drivers of airline loyalty: Evidence from the business travelers in china. *Transportation Research Part E: Logistics and Transportation Review*, 71:1–17, 2014.

[20] I. Yakut, T. Turkoglu, and F. Yakut. Understanding customers' evaluations through mining airline reviews. *International Journal of Data Mining & Knowledge Management Process*, 2015.

[21] B. Yao, H. Yuan, Y. Qian, and L. Li. On exploring airline service features from massive online review. In *Proceedings of the 12th International Conference on Service Systems and Service Management (ICSSSM)*, pages 1–6. IEEE, 2015.

[22] O. Zamir and O. Etzioni. Web document clustering: A feasibility demonstration. In *Proceedings of the 21st annual international ACM SIGIR conference on Research and development in information retrieval*, pages 46–54, 1998.

[23] Y. Zhao and Y. Zhang. Comparison of decision tree methods for finding active objects. *Advances in Space Research*, 41(12):1955–1959, 2008.

Using Online Controlled Experiments to Examine Authority Effects on User Behavior in Email Campaigns

Kwan Hui Lim[*†], Ee-Peng Lim[†], Binyan Jiang[#‡], and Palakorn Achananuparp[†]
[*]The University of Melbourne, Australia, and [†]Singapore Management University, Singapore
[#]Hong Kong Polytechnic University, Hong Kong, and [‡]Carnegie Mellon University, USA
limk2@student.unimelb.edu.au, {eplim,palakorna}@smu.edu.sg, binyanj@andrew.cmu.edu

ABSTRACT

Authority users often play important roles in a social system. They are expected to write good reviews at product review sites; provide high quality answers in question answering systems; and share interesting content in social networks. In the context of marketing and advertising, knowing how users react to emails and messages from authority senders is important, given the prevalence of email in our everyday life. Using a real-life academic event, we designed and conducted an online controlled experiment to determine how email senders of different types of authority (department head, event organizer and a general email account) affect the range of response behavior of recipients, which includes opening the email, browsing the event website, and registering for the event. In addition, we proposed a systematic approach to analyze the user response behavior to email campaigns from the time the user receives the email till he/she browses the website in a seamless manner.

Keywords: Online Controlled Experiments, A/B Testing, Behavioral Analysis, Authority, Email, Marketing

1. INTRODUCTION

Email is an important communication media, used by more than 2.58 billion users worldwide, who collectively generated more than $13.6 billion in revenue [24]. In particular, individuals and organizations frequently use email for personal communication and internal coordination, respectively [19]. Many organizations use email not only for internal communications, but also in their marketing campaigns due to the prevalence of email and its low cost. From the perspective of an organization, email campaigns provide a good return on investment as "for every $1 spent, $44.25 is the average return on email marketing investment" [25].

Fig. 1 outlines the typical workflow of an event promotion campaign, which starts with the broadcasting of emails and ends with the user performing a specific action, e.g., register for an event or buy a product. There are however multiple

HT '16, July 10-13, 2016, Halifax, NS, Canada
© 2016 ACM. ISBN 978-1-4503-4247-6/16/07. . . $15.00
DOI: http://dx.doi.org/10.1145/2914586.2914619

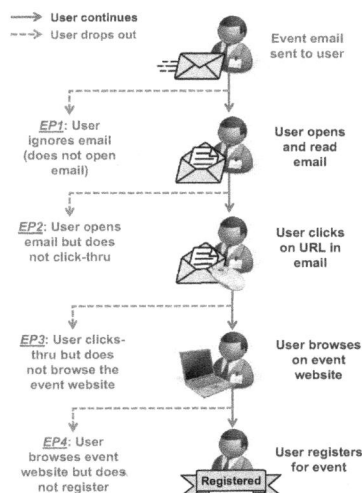

Figure 1: Typical Email Campaign Flowchart

exit points (EP) in the series of user actions, i.e., EP1-4 in Fig. 1. The user may possibly give up before achieving the desired end goal of registering for the event. To maximize the effectiveness of such campaigns, it is of utmost importance to understand the churn of users at each of these exit points so as to improve the design of future campaigns.

There is a large body of literature on the different factors that affect how likely a user will respond to an email [6, 17, 16, 23, 10]. Research has shown that authority is a key influence in people's decision making process [14, 8]. In this research, we investigate the effects of two different authority status of senders: *superior* and *domain expert*, on user behaviors in email campaigns. The first type of authority refers to someone who is a *superior* in the organization hierarchy. The second type of authority refers to someone who is a *domain expert* with knowledge and experience not easily found among others. Conducting online experiments on users in a real world setting (as opposed to a laboratory environment) adds further complexity to this research, in the form of business processes imposed by the event organizer. The event and users are real and any experiments should not undermine the success of the event itself. Hence, cross-platform individual level behavior analysis, and organic experiment setting are the unique considerations in our work.

Research Objectives. In this online controlled experiment, we are interested in investigating the outcome of email campaigns and how it could be influenced by the authority status of email senders. An email campaign typically advertises a particular event, product or service with the goal of motivating the user to comply with the marketing messages, e.g., register for the particular event or purchase/adopt the product/service. We measure the outcomes of cross platform email campaigns in terms of: (i) the open rate and click-through rate of emails; (ii) user activities on the event website; and (iii) registration rate of the event.

Contributions. Our main contributions are as follows:

- We propose a systematic approach to analyze email campaigns, with a focus on better understanding the potential exit points of users. (Fig. 1 and Sect. 4)

- We design a series of experiments to determine the effects of email senders' authority status on their recipients' behaviors in opening the email, browsing the event website, and registering for the event. (Sect. 3)

- We derive our key findings from the experiments, and show that the emails from superiors are highly effective in prompting users to react to the email and subsequently register for the event. (Sect. 4)

- We develop a multi-platform online experimentation system that facilitates the experimenters to seamlessly conduct an online controlled experiment over email and website. (Fig. 2 and Sect. 3.2)

2. RELATED WORK

There exists a large body of email-related studies that cover email response behavior [28], email mailbox management [29, 11, 27, 13, 12], email activity prediction [9, 22, 19, 5], and social network based email functions [30, 18]. Among these works, we are most interested in those related to email campaigns, in particular campaigns that involve elements of a controlled experiment. For example, [15] studied authority senders in the form of university professors and college students. Their experiment involved sending email requests (using the professor's email and college student's email) to a group of university students and random email addresses to complete an online survey. Similarly, [4] used the email accounts of a university's Department of Transportation and Survey Center to send out email invitations for an online survey related to transportation issues. In contrast, [26] studied how authority logos and trust messages affect a user's attitude towards online purchases using credit cards. They sent out messages with different authority logos (VeriSign, an international brand, and TWCA, a Taiwan-based domestic brand). Similarly, [7] studied the influence of sender and advertiser trust on user response in viral email advertising. They sent out viral marketing emails using trusted and less trusted email senders, where the emails contain content regarding trusted and less trusted advertisers.

As far as we are aware, there has been no prior work that concurrently study the authority effect of both the *superior* and *domain expert* on the entire spectrum of user response data (from email open to event registration), within the context of a real-life event (an academic workshop). While these earlier works highlight various interesting findings, our proposed research differs in the following ways: (i) instead of using an hypothetical scenario, our controlled experiment is conducted alongside a real-life event (i.e., an academic workshop), with the additional challenge of an experimental design that does not undermine the success of the event itself; (ii) instead of examining only a specific subset of aggregated data (e.g., only email click-through rate and time), we examine the entire spectrum of user response data (i.e., email

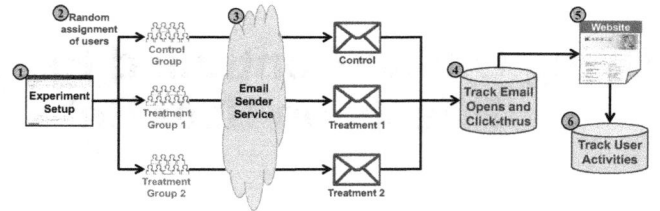

Figure 2: Multi-platform Online Experimentation System in Support of Experiment Design

open rate/time, email click-through rate/time, website visit, event registration, etc), thus providing a fine-grained analysis into user behavior from start to end; and (iii) instead of examining only a single type of authority, we concurrently examine the effects of both types of authority: *superior* and *domain expert*, within the same real-life event.

3. EXPERIMENTAL DESIGN

Our experiment was based on a two-day academic workshop that was attended by more than 150 participants, mainly from universities, research institutes and industry. This workshop was co-organized by three universities and included presentations by multiple speakers in the general area of data mining. Our experiment participants comprise 730 users, who belong to various departments from three large universities. The occupations of these users range from undergraduate and postgraduate students to university staff, representing the various occupations and hierarchical levels within a typical university.

3.1 Overview of Experiment

For this experiment, we define three types of email senders, namely: (i) general (non-personal) account; (ii) department superior; and (iii) event organizer. The general account is the email account of the organization hosting the event, while the latter two are the personal email accounts of Head of Departments (HOD) and event organizer, who represent the *superior* and *domain expert* authority respectively. Correspondingly, we want to identify three groups of users:

- Control Group (CGroup): Users who receive the event emails from a general account.

- Treatment Group 1 (TGroup1): Users who receive the event emails from their HODs.

- Treatment Group 2 (TGroup2): Users who receive the event emails from the event organizer.

For TGroup1, the HOD is the *superior* of the department that TGroup1 users currently belong to. For TGroup2, the event organizer acts as the *domain expert* in the area of data mining (the workshop topic) but otherwise have a minimal working relationship with TGroup2 users. CGroup reflects the mode of operation currently used by most organizations, i.e., they use a general organization email account to advertise their organization's promotions, events and newsletters. In contrast, TGroup1 and TGroup2 represents the different type of authority figures with TGroup1 receiving emails from a *superior* (department head) while TGroup2 receives emails from a *domain expert* (event organizer). Table 1 shows the breakdown of users in their respective experiment groups.[1]

---

[1] Due to technical problems, we were unable to properly track the emails sent to some users in TGroup1. These users were excluded to maintain the accuracy of our experiments.

Table 1: User Breakdown of Experimental Groups

Group	Uni. A Dept.	A1	Uni. B B1	B2	B3	Uni. C C1	C2	Total
TGroup1	97	33	-	23	-	-		*153*
TGroup2	98	35	76	24	30	25		*288*
CGroup	97	35	78	24	30	25		*289*
Total	*292*	*103*	*154*	*60*	*50*	*72*		*730*

All users are uniquely identified by their email addresses and our experiment involves first sending emails to these 730 users, followed by tracking and collecting their activities on both the email (opens and click-throughs) and website (clicks and mouse-overs on page elements) platforms. In particular we study the difference in user activities between users in CGroup (*general account*) and those in TGroup1 (*department head*) or TGroup2 (*event organizer*), by examining whether there are differences in terms of: (i) email open rate (Sect. 4.1); (ii) distribution of email open times (Sect. 4.2); (iii) email click-through rate (Sect. 4.3); (iv) distribution of email click-through times (Sect. 4.4); (v) probability of active users on the event website (Sect. 4.5); and (vi) probability of user registration (Sect. 4.6).

3.2 Multi-platform Online Experimentation System

To study user behavior across the different stages of an email campaign, we need to design a multi-platform online experimentation system that can automate and track such an experiment across both email and website platforms. Fig. 2 illustrates our proposed experimentation system, which comprises the following features:

1. Configure various parameters (e.g., user groups, email accounts, website URL) of the online experiment.

2. Allocate users to control and treatment groups based on random assignment.

3. Send emails to users in each group using a particular type of sender account, i.e., department head, event organizer, or general account.

4. Track user activities on the emails, namely email opens and user clicks on a link in the email, which then directs users to the event page.

5. If the user clicks-through to the event website, continue to track his/her activities on the website, i.e., clicks and mouse-overs on the various page elements.

6. Analyze the collected data of user activities on both email and website platforms.

While there exist applications for monitoring email campaigns and website visits [1, 2, 3], these applications monitor emails and websites independently, instead of as an integrated application. Even with integration, they only report activities at an aggregated level and do not provide analysis at the individual user level. These fine-grained user activities allow us to better understand why users leave at each exit point. More importantly, we would require a system that is able to conduct an integrated controlled experiment on both email and website and thereafter track the user activities as they traverse across these two platforms. Thus, we designed and developed a multi-platform online experimentation system that integrates with and extends our existing website experimentation platform, the **L**iving **A**nalytic**S** **E**xpe**R**imentations system [21, 20]. This system enables us to easily conduct experiments to study user behavior across

the different stages of an email campaign. In addition, our proposed system automates and manages the main steps of this experiment, which we describe next.

3.3 Formatting and Sending of Emails

Our experimentation system facilitates the sending of emails to users in the three experimental groups. Before an email is sent, the system makes two main modifications to the email, namely: (i) it converts all URLs into a unique link that enables us to track when it is clicked; and (ii) it inserts into the email a tracking pixel that allows us to determine when the email is opened. In addition, we are able to track the user who has opened an email or clicked on an email link, and the time when this action was performed. From an experimenter's point-of-view, this is akin to the broadcasting of an email and requires no additional workload on the experimenter apart from defining the experimental user groups and type of emails to send to each group.

We control for email content and design by using the same template for sending to the three experimental groups. At the top of this email template, the following text is added "FYI, you may be interested in this workshop. Best regards, [Sender Name]". In addition, all emails are sent at approximately the same time to control for the effects of day and time on the three experimental groups. The main difference is the type of sender account and signing-off name that is used, i.e., HOD, event organizer or general account. This experiment design allows us to best evaluate the authority effects of email senders without the influence of the email content design and email delivery time.

3.4 Tracking of User Activities

As mentioned in the previous section, our system modifies each email before sending it out, and each reformatted link is unique to each user for a particular experiment. Once this link is clicked, it makes a web service call to our system that records the link which was clicked, the user who clicked it and the time of link clicking. Similarly, when the email is opened, the embedded tracking pixel makes a similar web service call to our system that records the user who opened this email and the time of email opening. To protect the privacy of users, the replies of users to the senders are directed to the true senders instead of our experimentation system.

One key functionality of our proposed system is its ability to automatically track users' activities across multiple platforms, without the need for any intervention by the experimenter. If a user clicks on the email link to visit the event website, our system establishes a "handshaking" process, which establishes the email recipient as the website visitor. This "handshaking" is facilitated by the unique link created by our system during the email sending stage, which then enables us to uniquely identify this user by his/her email address as the user browses the website. Thereafter, we will be able to track and monitor the user's activities (mouse clicks and mouse-overs) on the website. The tracking of user's activities on both the email and website is automatically performed by our experimentation system, without needing the experimenter to develop any specific tracking program for the emails and websites.

4. USER BEHAVIOR ON EMAIL / WEBSITE

As illustrated in Fig. 1, there are four main exit points in a typical campaign where a user might possibly leave without

Table 2: Summary of Emails Sent, Opened and Clicked-through, and Active and Registered Users.

	Emails Sent	Emails Opened	Clicked-through	Active Users	Registered Users
TGroup1	153	61	22	14	6
TGroup2	288	88	20	14	6
CGroup	289	76	12	9	1

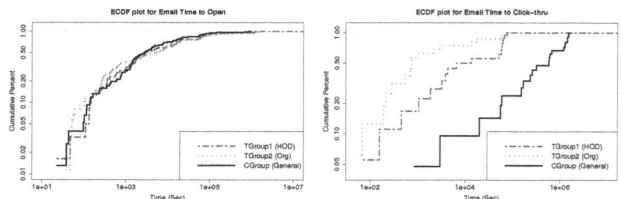

Figure 3: Time to Email Open (left) and Click-thru (right)

achieving the end goal. We will now examine each exit point sequentially to determine if the authority status of email senders affect the user outflow at each exit point.

4.1 Authority Effect on Email Open Rate

The first exit point we examine is when a user receives an email but ignores it completely, i.e., does not even open the email as illustrated in EP1 of Fig. 1. Thus, we are interested to see if the email sender affects the email open rates. TGroup1, TGroup2 and CGroup show an email open rate of 0.399, 0.306 and 0.263 respectively. One main observation is that TGroup1 outperforms CGroup by more than 51% in terms of email open rate, while TGroup2 manages a 15.8% improvement over the latter. This result indicates that the authority effect of the *superior* (HOD) has the greatest influence on email open rate, followed by that of the *domain expert* (event organizer), then the general account.

After examining the differences between the email open rates, we now determine if the differences are statistically significant. Using our collected data (Table 2), we conduct a two-sided Fisher's Exact Test to determine if there is any significant difference for the following null hypotheses:

- H_{A0}: The *email open rate* of *CGroup (general account)* is equal to that of *TGroup1 (department head)*.

- H_{B0}: The *email open rate* of *CGroup (general account)* is equal to that of *TGroup2 (event organizer)*.

The resulting p-values are 0.0048 and 0.2691 for H_{A0} and H_{B0} respectively. At significance level $\alpha = 0.01$, we reject H_{A0} and fail to reject H_{B0}. There is moderate evidence to suggest that emails sent by the HODs are more likely to be opened by its recipients compared to emails from a general account. However, there is insufficient evidence to suggest that emails sent by the event organizer are statistically more effective than those sent by a general account.

4.2 Authority Effect on Email Open Time

In addition to the email open rate, we also investigate if users take less time to open emails from the HOD (TGroup1) or event organizer (TGroup2) compared to that from a general account (CGroup). Fig. 3 shows an Empirical Cumulative Distribution Function (ECDF) plot of the time taken by a user before he/she opens the email. The results show no observable difference among TGroup1, TGroup2 and CGroup in terms of the time taken to open the email.

To further support our observation that there is no difference in email open times, we test for statistical differences in the email open times by conducting a Two-sample Kolmogorov-Smirnov test on the following null hypotheses:

- H_{C0}: Distribution of *email open times* of *CGroup (general acct.)* is equal to that of *TGroup1 (dept. head)*.

- H_{D0}: Distribution of *email open times* of *CGroup (general acct.)* is equal to that of *TGroup2 (event org.)*.

The resulting p-values are 0.7724 and 0.3034 for H_{C0} and H_{D0} respectively. At significance level $\alpha = 0.01$, we fail to reject H_{C0} and H_{D0}. Thus, there is insufficient evidence to show that emails sent by the HODs or event organizer are opened by its recipients in a different amount of time, compared to that sent by the general account.

This lack of difference in email open times could be explained by the mailbox checking routines of users. Users are likely to check their mailbox only at specific time intervals and upon checking their mailbox, they will look at the email preview (including sender name/address) before deciding whether to open the email. Thus, users in a group are unlikely to open an email faster than users in other groups as they would not have checked their emails. However, once they have checked their mailbox, users in TGroup1 and TGroup2 are more likely to proceed to open and read the email, as discussed previously in Sect. 4.1.

4.3 Authority Effect on Email Click Rate

After a user opens an email, the next possible exit point is when he/she simply closes the email after reading it, without clicking through to visit the event website, i.e., EP2 of Fig. 1. We now investigate if the authority status of email sender is effective in influencing the recipient to visit the event website. Our experiment shows that the email click-through rate of TGroup1, TGroup2 and CGroup are 0.144, 0.069 and 0.042 respectively. One main observation is that TGroup1 offered the best improvement with an increased email click-through rate of almost 3.5 times that of CGroup, while TGroup2 offered an improvement of 67% over CGroup. This result indicates that there is an authority effect on email click-through rates, with the authority type of *superior* (HOD) being most effective, followed by the *domain expert*, then the general email account.

Similar to the previous sections, we now determine if the differences in email click-through rate are statistically significant. Using Table 2, we conduct a two-sided Fisher's Exact Test on the following null hypotheses:

- H_{E0}: The *email click-through rate* of *CGroup (general acct.)* is equal to that of *TGroup1 (dept. head)*.

- H_{F0}: The *email click-through rate* of *CGroup (general acct.)* is equal to that of *TGroup2 (event org.)*.

We obtained p-values of 0.0002 for H_{E0} and 0.1506 for H_{F0}. At significance level $\alpha = 0.01$, we reject H_{E0} and fail to reject H_{F0}. There is strong evidence to suggest that emails sent by HODs are more effective than those sent by the general account, in attracting the recipients' attention to the extent that these recipients are interested in visiting the event website to find out more. There is insufficient evidence to suggest the same for emails sent by the event organizer.

4.4 Authority Effect on Email Click Time

In addition to the email click-through rate, we also investigate if the email sender affects the amount of time taken by the recipient before he/she clicks through the email. Specifically, we are interested to see if a user takes a shorter time to click-through an email from the HOD (TGroup1) or event organizer (TGroup2) compared to that from a general account (CGroup). Fig. 3 shows that users who received emails from either their HOD (TGroup1) or the event organizer (TGroup2) are more likely to click-through in a shorter amount of time, compared to those received from the general account (CGroup). This result further reinforces our hypothesis that users receiving emails from their HODs and the event organizer are more likely to react to it and in a shorter time, compared to emails from a general account.

Having determined that authority status does affect email click-through time, we now examine if the difference is statistically significant by conducting a Two-sample Kolmogorov-Smirnov test on the following null hypotheses:

- H_{G0}: Distribution of *email click-through times* of *CGroup (general acct.)* is equal to *TGroup1 (dept. head)*.
- H_{H0}: Distribution of *email click-through times* of *CGroup (general acct.)* is equal to *TGroup2 (event org.)*.

The resulting p-values are <0.0001 for both H_{G0} and H_{H0}. At significance level $\alpha = 0.01$, we reject H_{G0} and H_{H0}. There is strong evidence to indicate that emails sent by the HODs or event organizer causes its recipient to click-through in a different amount of time, compared to emails sent by the general account.

4.5 Authority Effect on Website Activity

Even after receiving the email and clicking through, a user might simply visit the event website but leave without browsing any content, i.e., EP3 of Fig. 1. Thus, we now examine if the authority status of email sender is able to influence the recipients' behavior even on the event website. For this purpose, we define an active user as one who has interacted with any element on the event website, i.e., a mouse-click or mouse-over. Our experiment shows that the proportion of active users in TGroup1, TGroup2 and CGroup are 0.092, 0.049 and 0.031 respectively. This result once again shows the authority effect on user behavior in email campaigns, particularly that the authority type of *superior* (HOD) are almost two times more effective than the *domain expert* authority (event organizer). Both types of authority are also shown to be more effective than our control group without any authority (the general email account).

We now determine if the differences in website activity are statistically significant and use Table 2 to conduct a two-sided Fisher's Exact Test on the following null hypotheses:

- H_{I0}: Probability of *active users on the website* in *CGroup (general acct.)* is equal to *TGroup1 (dept. head)*.
- H_{J0}: Probability of *active users on the website* in *CGroup (general acct.)* is equal to *TGroup2 (event org.)*.

The resulting p-value are 0.0115 for H_{I0} and 0.2971 for H_{J0}. At significance level $\alpha = 0.05$, we reject H_{I0} and fail to reject H_{J0}. The significant difference in H_{I0} indicates that emails sent by the HODs effectively cause its recipient to be more active on the event website, compared to that sent by the general account. One significant improvement is that users in TGroup1 (9.2% active) are almost three times more likely to be active than users in CGroup (3.1% active), in terms of their browsing activities on the event website. While we do not observe any significant difference in H_{B0}, we notice that 4.9% of users in TGroup2 are active on the event website compared to only 3.1% of users in CGroup.

4.6 Authority Effect on Event Registration

The main goal of any email campaign is not only to entice users to read the email but ultimately to perform some specific action, such as registering for an event. We now further investigate if the authority status of email sender affects the conversion rate of users, i.e., do they register for the event or leave without registering, as shown in EP4 of Fig. 1. The registration rates of users in TGroup1, TGroup2, and CGroup are 0.039, 0.021 and 0.003 respectively, indicating that the authority types of *superior* (HOD) and *domain expert* (event organizer) are approximately eleven and six times more effective than that without authority, in terms of influencing users to register for the workshop.

Once again, we want to determine if the differences in event registration rates are statistically significant. Using Table 2, we conduct a two-sided Fisher's Exact Test on the following null hypotheses:

- H_{K0}: Probability of *event registration* in *CGroup (general acct.)* is equal to that of *TGroup1 (dept. head)*.
- H_{L0}: Probability of *event registration* in *CGroup (general acct.)* is equal to that of *TGroup2 (event org.)*.

We obtained p-values of 0.0080 and 0.0684 for H_{K0} and H_{L0} respectively. At significance level $\alpha = 0.01$, we reject H_{K0} and fail to reject H_{L0}. There is strong evidence to indicate a significant difference in H_{K0}, which shows that emails sent by HODs are more effective in getting users to register for the event, compared to emails sent by a general account. In particular, we observe a substantial and significant improvement of more than 11 times more converted users in TGroup1 (3.9% registration) compared to that of CGroup (0.3% registration). While we fail to reject H_{L0}, there is mild evidence (at significance level $\alpha = 0.1$) to suggest that emails sent by the event organizer (TGroup2) are six times more effective than emails sent by a general account (CGroup), in terms of converting users to register for the event.

5. CONCLUSION

In this paper, we designed and conducted an email campaign experiment to evaluate the authority effect of different types of email sender on user behavior in both email and website. We also proposed a systematic approach to analyze such email campaigns and discussed the four exit points where potential users might leave before completing a desired action or end-goal, such as registering for an event or purchasing an item. Other than experiment design, we developed a multi-platform experimentation system that manages and automates the key stages of controlled experiments, from user grouping randomization to data collection of user responses across multiple platforms, i.e., from emails to websites. Our findings show that the authority status of an email sender has a significant effect on the user response and emails sent by their department heads are the most effective in terms of: (i) email open rate; (ii) email click-through rate; (iii) email click-through time; (iv) proportion of active website users; and (v) event registration rate.

Acknowledgments. This research is supported by the Singapore National Research Foundation under its International Research Centre @ Singapore Funding Initiative and administered by the IDM Programme Office, Media Development Authority (MDA). The authors thank Feida Zhu, Adrian Vu, Agus Trisnajaya Kwee and the reviewers for their useful comments.

6. REFERENCES

[1] Customer.io, 2014. http://customer.io/.

[2] Google analytics, 2014. http://www.google.com/analytics.

[3] Mailchimp, 2014. http://mailchimp.com/.

[4] S. Boulianne, C. A. Klofstad, and D. Basson. Sponsor prominence and responses patterns to an online survey. *International Journal of Public Opinion Research*, 23(1):79–87, 2011.

[5] D. D. Castro, Z. Karnin, L. Lewin-Eytan, and Y. Maarek. You've got mail, and here is what you could do with it!: Analyzing and predicting actions on email messages. In *Proceedings of the Ninth ACM International Conference on Web Search and Data Mining (WSDM'16)*, pages 307–316, 2016.

[6] L. Chittenden and R. Rettie. An evaluation of e-mail marketing and factors affecting response. *Journal of Targeting, Measurement and Analysis for Marketing*, 11(3):203–217, 2003.

[7] S. Cho, J. Huh, and R. J. Faber. The influence of sender trust and advertiser trust on multistage effects of viral advertising. *Journal of Advertising*, 43(1):100–114, 2014.

[8] R. B. Cialdini. *Influence: Science and Practice*. Allyn & Bacon, 2001.

[9] L. A. Dabbish, R. E. Kraut, S. Fussell, and S. Kiesler. Understanding email use: Predicting action on a message. In *Proc. of CHI'09*, pages 691–700, 2009.

[10] W. Fan and Z. Yan. Factors affecting response rates of the web survey: A systematic review. *Computers in Human Behavior*, 26(2):132–139, 2010.

[11] D. Fisher, A. J. Brush, E. Gleave, and M. A. Smith. Revisiting whittaker & sidner's "email overload" ten years later. In *Proceedings of the 20th conference on Computer supported cooperative work (CSCW'06)*, pages 309–312, 2006.

[12] M. Grbovic, G. Halawi, Z. Karnin, and Y. Maarek. How many folders do you really need?: Classifying email into a handful of categories. In *Proceedings of the 23rd ACM International Conference on Conference on Information and Knowledge Management (CIKM'14)*, pages 869–878, 2014.

[13] C. Grevet, D. Choi, D. Kumar, and E. Gilbert. Overload is overloaded: email in the age of gmail. In *Proceedings of the SIGCHI Conference on Human Factors in Computing Systems (CHI'14)*, pages 793–802, 2014.

[14] R. Guadagno and R. B. Cialdini. Online persuasion and compliance: Social influence on the internet and beyond. *The social net: Human behavior in cyberspace*, pages 91–113, 2005.

[15] N. Guéguen and C. Jacob. Solicitation by e-mail and solicitor's status: A field study of social influence on the web. *CyberPsychology & Behavior*, 5(4):377–383, 2002.

[16] R. Janke. Effects of mentioning the incentive prize in the email subject line on survey response. *Evidence Based Library and Information Practice*, 9(1), 2014.

[17] M. D. Kaplowitz, F. Lupi, M. P. Couper, and L. Thorp. The effect of invitation design on web survey response rates. *Social Science Computer Review*, 30(3):339–349, 2012.

[18] T. Karagiannis and M. Vojnovic. Behavioral profiles for advanced email features. In *Proceedings of the 18th international conference on World wide web (WWW'09)*, pages 711–720, 2009.

[19] F. Kooti, L. M. Aiello, M. Grbovic, K. Lerman, and A. Mantrach. Evolution of conversations in the age of email overload. In *Proceedings of the 24th International Conference on World Wide Web (WWW'15)*, pages 603–613, 2015.

[20] K. H. Lim, B. Jiang, E.-P. Lim, and P. Achananuparp. Do you know the speaker? An online experiment with authority messages on event websites. In *Proceedings of the 23rd International Conference on World Wide Web Companion (WWW'14)*, pages 1247–1252, 2014.

[21] K. H. Lim, E.-P. Lim, P. Achananuparp, A. Vu, A. T. Kwee, and F. Zhu. LASER: A Living AnalyticS ExpeRimentation system for large-scale online controlled experiments. In *Proceedings of the 23rd International Conference on World Wide Web Companion (WWW'14)*, pages 71–74, 2014.

[22] B.-W. On, E.-P. Lim, J. Jiang, and L.-N. Teow. Engagingness and responsiveness behavior models on the enron email network and its application to email reply order prediction. In *The Influence of Technology on Social Network Analysis and Mining*, volume 6 of *LNCS*, pages 227–253. Springer Vienna, 2013.

[23] J. E. Phelps, R. Lewis, L. Mobilio, D. Perry, and N. Raman. Viral marketing or electronic word-of-mouth advertising: Examining consumer responses and motivations to pass along email. *Journal of Advertising Research*, 44(4):333–348, 2004.

[24] Radicati Group, Inc. Email statistics report 2015-2019, 2015. http://www.radicati.com/wp/wp-content/uploads/2015/07/Email-Market-2015-2019-Executive-Summary.pdf.

[25] Salesforce.com. 25 mind blowing email marketing stats, 2013. https://www.salesforce.com/blog/2013/07/email-marketing-stats.html.

[26] W. Shu and C. Y. Cheng. How to improve consumer attitudes toward using credit cards online: An experimental study. *Electronic Commerce Research and Applications*, 11(4):335–345, 2012.

[27] J. C. Tang, T. Matthews, J. Cerruti, S. Dill, E. Wilcox, J. Schoudt, and H. Badenes. Global differences in attributes of email usage. In *Proceedings of the 2009 International Workshop on Intercultural Collaboration (IWIC'09)*, pages 239–258, 2009.

[28] J. R. Tyler and J. C. Tang. When can i expect an email response? a study of rhythms in email usage. In *Proceedings of the Eighth European Conference on Computer Supported Cooperative Work (ECSCW'03)*, pages 239–258, 2003.

[29] S. Whittaker and C. Sidner. Email overload: Exploring personal information management of email. In *Proceedings of the SIGCHI conference on Human factors in computing systems (CHI'09)*, pages 276–283, 2009.

[30] S. Yoo, Y. Yang, F. Lin, and I.-C. Moon. Mining social networks for personalized email prioritization. In *Proceedings of the 15th ACM SIGKDD international conference on Knowledge discovery and data mining (KDD'09)*, pages 967–976, 2009.

What Happens Offline Stays Offline? Examining Sustainability of A Hybrid Social System

Rosta Farzan
School of Information
Sciences
University of Pittsburgh
rfarzan@pitt.edu

Di Lu
School of Information
Sciences
University of Pittsburgh
dil16@pitt.edu

Yu-Ru Lin
School of Information
Sciences
University of Pittsburgh
yurulin@pitt.edu

ABSTRACT

The emergence of social Web has gone beyond connecting people and documents online to further connecting people, places, and artifacts both online and offline. A variety of online platforms with the specific goal of supporting offline connections have been attracting the attention of practitioners and users of social Web systems. Such hybrid platforms have been shown to contribute to online and offline prosperity of connections and engagements of people. In this work, we present a study of hybrid social Web systems in terms of factors contributing to their sustainability. Our results suggests that emphasis on online interactions and online representation of offline activities can lead to higher level of sustainability. Based on our results, we provide a set of design guidelines to address the challenges of sustaining user activities in hybrid social Web systems.

CCS Concepts

•Human-centered computing → Collaborative and social computing theory, concepts and paradigms; Empirical studies in collaborative and social computing; *Human computer interaction (HCI); Empirical studies in HCI;* •Information systems → *Web applications;*

Keywords

Hybrid communities; Sustainability; Online and offline traces; Archival study; Meetup

1. INTRODUCTION

Since the introduction of the concept of Hypertext and World Wide Web in the early 60s, the Web has gone through an enormous growth in connecting beyond documents and well into connecting people and documents together. The Web as "Social hypertext" [8] has become pervasive in the modern society. The emerging model of the social Web goes beyond connecting people together to further connecting

HT '16, July 10-13, 2016, Halifax, NS, Canada

© 2016 ACM. ISBN 978-1-4503-4247-6/16/07. . . $15.00

DOI: http://dx.doi.org/10.1145/2914586.2914625

people, places, and artifacts with navigation and communication patterns that span online and offline worlds. Online applications with explicit goals of promoting offline connections have been thriving. The hybrid and intertwined online-offline nature of the emerging Web is an important feature that can indeed contribute to significant positive outcomes such as community development [11, 12], citizen engagement in political and social movements [13, 14, 29], and marketing, and business promotions. Further, the offline interactions can give strength to the online sense of community and help thrive the online communities. The popularity of online-offline hybrid platforms has been increasing as evidenced by a significant proliferation of commercial and non-commercial examples such as neighborhood-oriented social networks that are designed to connect individuals and their neighbors online (e.g. Nextdoor[1]) or location-based social networks that have added the dimension of location into social networking services (e.g. Yelp[2], or Foursquare [3]). However, little research efforts have been focused on understanding how hybrid social Web systems utilize both the virtual and physical connections and how their distinct challenges and opportunities influence their sustainability [26].

The concept of hybrid social Web systems was first described by [29] as a "hybrid people and technology-based phenomenon as an electronic-to-face community" which takes advantage of technological features such as searching among a large number of people with similar interests as well as advantages of face-to-face offline connections such as developing strong interpersonal connections with a small group of people. Meetup.com, as a typical example, aims to revitalize local communities and help people to organize and discover local events of interests [1]. In a hybrid application, like Meetup.com, people with similar interests use online technologies to find each other and organize themselves, so that they can get together as a group or "meet up" offline. We argue that, a sustainable hybrid Web system not only requires individuals to actively participate in the two worlds to reinforce, complement, synergies, and reciprocate online-offline interactions [25]. The benefits of the hybrid Web system diminishes if any aspects of these weakens. If individuals only participate in online discussions and do not attend the offline events, the system would not succeed with their main goals. At the same time, it is argued that if individuals do not return to the online platform and continue their interactions through other mediums such as text messages or

---

[1]https://nextdoor.com/
[2]https://www.yelp.com/
[3]https://foursquare.com/

private emails, there will not be opportunities for growth of the community [26]. However, the awareness about and the impact of the interplay between online and offline interactions have often been overlooked. While online connections and interactions are quite visible, online-offline connections are usually latent to users on hybrid Web systems. What happens offline is often invisible to the online communities. Further, the online interactions are often not situated within the offline gatherings and are disconnected from the face-to-face interactions. In this work, we aim to examine the challenge of sustainability in the hybrid social Web systems. The goal of our current work is to quantitatively study how awareness of users' activities online and offline play a role in the sustainability of hybrid social Web systems. We focus on Meetup.com and use it as an exemplary platform to study our research questions of sustainability in hybrid platforms.

2. RELATED WORK

2.1 Sustainability in online communities

Online communities that rely on user-generated content often face challenges to attract enough members to produce content in high quantity and quality [4]. Ensuring individuals have both the opportunity and the motivation to participate and contribute is the key to the ability to attract new members, retain existing members, and facilitate content generation [24, 20, 5, 17]. Kim [16] identified four critical elements of a sustainable online community to help members build attachment with the group as well as with the other members. The representation of prior online activities has shown to positively influence participation from both newcomers and existing members [3, 18, 22]. Millen and Patterson [22] conducted a field study in a geography-based online community suggesting that channeling mechanisms which encourages members to observe the general activities of the community is an effective feature to stimulate members' engagement. It has been also argued that observing contribution and feedback from the existing members in the community are important incentives for motivating newcomers to participate [18, 3]. This is an unsurprising phenomena supported by various social theories such as social presence, social influence and diffusion of innovation [10, 6]. According to social presence theory [10], offline interactions increase the social presence of community members and help them understand, trust, and identify with one another. Thus, the offline interactions of online communities were proposed as an effective factors to strengthen solidarity and intimacy among community members, and as a result, encourage them to be more active in contributing content online[17, 30]. To this end, the results from a field survey of 77 online communities associated with neighborhood communities suggested that offline interaction was significantly related to members' online activities in terms of posting messages [20]. Their survey analysis revealed that online and offline communication among communities' members are critical for the systems to have an impact on community involvement; however, there was very little awareness about those offline activities in the online platform.

2.2 Hybrid social Web systems

Many social Web systems, even if they have been designed for mainly online connections among geographically distributed individuals, attempt to enrich the interactions among their members by organizing offline meetings among members who share the same geographic location or by organizing regular events that bring their members together offline [15, 21]. In a study of online relationship building within Internet newsgroups, Park and Floyd showed that a large number of individuals supplement the online interaction through other mediums such as phone calls, and face-to-face interactions. They posited that for many, there is no clear line between online and offline activities [23]. The intertwined nature of online-offline interactions leads to four types of relationships between individuals: reinforcement, complementarity, synergy, and reciprocity [25]. Reinforcement happens when online or offline interactions amplifies the other types of interaction. Complementarity happens when possibilities of both online and offline interaction allows distinctive aspects of each forms of interactions to compensate for weaknesses of the other form. Synergy happens when, as a result of both online and offline interactions, outcomes beyond the absolute sum of both interactions can be achieved. Reciprocity represent the mutual interdependence of online-offline interactions. These relationships can lead to outcomes such as the promotion of a stronger sense of community, facilitation of collaboration through increased awareness of members in the community, extension of online encounters into richer relationships by deepening interactions with social signals, and the socialization of newcomers into the community [21].

The importance and occurrence of offline interactions in conjunction with online communications have been acknowledged by a number of studies [2, 28, 15, 19, 9]. A few studies have attempted to assess and quantify the impact of offline gatherings on online participation. While there is strong evidence in support of supplementing online interactions with offline gatherings, there is also evidence that highlights the challenges arising as a result of offline connections. In some cases, offline connections can lead to weakening of the online interactions as a result of creating stronger clicks among those who can meet offline, or by shifting the interactions offline thereby reducing online interactions [26]. It has been argued that offline gatherings can promote stronger bonds that lead to stronger bonding social capital, but this is accomplished at the expense of decreasing weak ties and bridging social capital [27].

3. MEETUP.COM

Meetup (http://Meetup.com/) is one of the most popular online communities that allow users to form and join online local groups with common interests, and to organize local events. As of November 2015, there are about 23 million users in Meetup, and about 531,000 meet-ups a month on average are organized by 218,217 groups in 180 different countries [1]. While Meetup provides the online space for a group of people, the major goal of Meetup is to facilitate offline group meeting, in which people connect through "events" in both online platform and offline meetings. According to the main topics and types of events, Meetup groups are classified into different categories, varying from outdoor adventure to fine arts and culture. Each Meetup event is a hybrid event happening both online and offline.

Meetup provides multiple means for groups to bring out information about the offline gatherings in the online space. Each Meetup group has a dedicated page presenting all the group information including their group description, memberships, events information, and recent activities. Two specific parts of this page include information about the offline happenings: the "What's new" panel and "Past events" section. In the "What's new" panel , the thumbnails of the three most recent photos uploaded in the group are presented, followed by the news feeds about the recent online activities. The "past events" section shows the recent past events with basic information including event name, time, description abstract, number of members who RSVPed as attending, and the number of available photos. An individual event page is allocated for each event, which shows all the information about the event. By clicking the photos thumbnails, one can access the photo page, where the details of the photos such as who have uploaded the photo, the time it has been uploaded, and comments associated with the photo are displayed. Similar to other online groups, Meetup supports online interactions by allowing members to communicate in a thread-based message board as well as send messages to the group mailing list. Members can also post comments for each event on individual event pages or for each photo on the individual photo pages. In addition, comments can also be "liked' by other members. The recent online activities such as new joins, comments and RSVPs are also shown in the "What's new" panel in the home page.

4. RESEARCH HYPOTHESES

We define the sustainability of hybrid social Web systems as *the capability of attracting people attending offline activities as well as participating on the online platform.* Informed by prior research in online communities, we identify two components as main indicators of sustainability in hybrid social Webs systems: (1) Traces of online activities that can be observed through actions such as online comments, online messages, online ratings and feedback; (2) Traces of offline activities represented online that can be observed through the content of online discussions referring to offline events or pictures of the offline events. Furthermore, we argue that the measure of sustainability should take into account the hybrid nature of the community; i.e. not just online or offline participation. In fact, such a measure exists within hybrid platforms such as Meetup.com. On Meetup, individuals interested in attending an event RSVP on the site whether they are attending or not. This RSVPs information not only signals the level of offline participation, but also provides an indication of offline participation in the online environment as opposed to, for example, the host asking for text or private email messages from those interested to attend. Therefore, we define a measure such as the online RSVP of offline attendance as a hybrid measure of sustainability.

We hypothesize that indication of stronger online and offline traces of activities play an important role in sustainability of hybrid social Web systems as the awareness of those activities help users learn, understand, trust, and identify with the community [10, 6]. Within the context of Meetup.com, we have formulated the following hypotheses:

- H1 Indication of stronger online traces represented as higher number of comments left by users will lead to higher level of interest in future events.

- H2: Representation of offline activities in the online platform in the form of photos will lead to higher level of interest in future events.

Furthermore, we argue that for highly active groups, representation of online and offline presence can be even more effective because (1) the representation of online and offline activities is more positive since it highlight strong social presence as a result of high level of activities; (2) the large number of events causes the users to experience an instance of information overload (in this case of event overload) which leads to users desiring more cues to make decisions about which events to attend. Therefore, we formulate the following two hypotheses in relation to the interaction between group activity level, online interactions, and online representation of offline activities.

- H3: Compared to groups with low level of activities, indication of stronger online traces will lead to significantly higher level of interest in the future events for groups with high level of activities.

- H4: Compared to groups with low level of activities, presence of photos from prior events will lead to significantly higher level of interest in the future events for groups with high level of activities.

5. RESEARCH METHODOLOGY

5.1 Data Collection

Meetup provides an API to collect data about Meetup users and events organized through the platform. The data includes information about events, groups, users, and RSVPs. Events data contains information about venue, date, organizers, and description of the events. Users data includes residential location, hometown, and users' topics of interests. RSVPs data are associated with each event and provide information about individuals who have indicated attending the event. Additionally, the Meetup API provides information about comments posted in association to each event as well as pictures posted after each event. Utilizing the Meetup API, we collected data for 119 active public Meetup groups, in 29 categories, in the city of Pittsburgh, PA. We define active Meetup groups as those organized at least two events per month. We collected the events data for each of the groups within a year, from October 1, 2014 to September 30, 2015.

We defined number of comments associated with each event as measure of traces of online activity and pictures posted for each event as the measure of online representation of traces of offline activities. We noted that for some categories of groups, events' pictures might be a biased feature. For example, the Meetup groups on photography has an outlier high number of pictures; on the other hand, for groups dedicated to activities such as writing, the context does not involve picture taking. We excluded 29 groups from 11 categories, which resulted in our final dataset including 12,007 events from 90 Meetup groups in 18 categories. Similar to the general trend of data on social Web systems, all of our variables follow a skewed distribution; i.e. there are a large number of groups with small number of events and members, and small number of groups with very large number of events and members. Similarly, there are large number of events with small number of comments.

5.2 Statistical Analysis

To examine whether and how online interactions and the online representation of offline activities affect the sustain-

263

ability of Meetup groups, we conducted regression analyses. We considered the number of RSVPs (plus wait-listed members) as the hybrid outcome measure of sustainability. Since the outcome measure is a count data with high skewness (Skewness = 4.66, Kurtosis = 35.37), we modeled the data using Negative Binomial distribution. In Meetup, the same hosts and same groups often organize multiple events and multiple groups can belong to the same category. So we defined the model as a repeated measure with the event nested within host, group, and category.

We used the number of comments to measure users' online interactions and the number of photos to measure the online representation of offline activities. Our data is a correlational data. To account for that and to be able to study what causes sustainability of the groups, we conducted lagged longitudinal analysis; i.e. for each event in our dataset happening in time T+1, we calculated the independent variables in time T by aggregating number of comments and photos in time T prior to the current event happening. We defined time T as four weeks prior to the time of the current event since in distribution of intervals between the events 99% of the data lies below 28 days; that leads to only 1% of our events with missing data in our analyses, since those events do not have any meetings happening four weeks prior to their happening [4]. The number of photos of prior events is highly skewed and more than 70% of the events do not have any photos from their prior events in the past four weeks. To account for the skewness, we discretized the number of photos to a binary variable; i.e. whether or not there was any photos posted for the events in the prior four-week time period. In our analysis, we control for number of people attending in events in time T by including the average number of RSVPs for the events in the prior four weeks. Furthermore, we controlled for the group tenure and activity level of the group. We classified groups to high or low activity level, if they had higher or fewer than median (equal to 20) events organized in the prior four weeks respectively.

6. RESULTS

Table 1 presents the results of the regression analysis. Our results shows that both online traces and the representation of offline activities in Meetup groups are significantly associated with the level of members' interest in future events. Keeping all other variables constant, one more prior comment relates to 1.4% more people indicating interest in attending a new event. Moreover, any photos posted for prior events has a positive effect on the popularity of the future events. Compared to events with no photos posted, presence of any photos for events in the past four weeks will result in 37% more people expressing their interest to attend the future events (Estimated average of attendance: with photos=4.59, without photos=3.34). The result of our regression analysis confirm both hypotheses H1 and H2.

To assess hypotheses H3 and H4, on whether the online and offline traces have distinct impact on high versus low activity groups, we added the interaction terms of activity level with indication of online and offline activities into the previous regression model. The plots of the interactions effects are presented in Figure 1. As shown in Figure 1a, prior comments influence the high activity groups differently than the

---

[4]that includes the events happening at the start of our data collection

Parameters	Coef.	SE	Wald χ^2	Sig.
Photos vs. no photos	1.374	.023	119.71	<.001
prior # of Comments	1.014	.003	31.475	<.001
High vs. low activity	.774	.024	115.448	<.001
prior # of attendees	1.129	.002	3780.643	<.001
Group Tenure	1.302	.039	46.923	<.001

Table 1: Results of the Negative Binomial Regression Analysis

low activity groups (coef=1.23, SE=.012,Wald χ^2=327.529, sig. <.001). While the predicted number of RSVPs for events increases as the average number of comments in prior events increases for both high and low activity groups, the slope of change for the high activity groups is significantly larger than of the low activity groups. Similarly, Figure 1b suggests that the effect of presence of prior photos are also significantly different for the high activity groups versus the low activity groups. For the low activity groups, having prior photos will merely result in an increase of 0.5 in the average number of RSVPs of a new event, compared to no prior photos presented; however, the high activity groups are more significantly influenced by the presence of photos for prior events. The average number of RSVPs increases by 1.8 for the high activity groups as a result of the presence of any photos for the prior events. Therefore, our hypotheses H3 and H4 are both confirmed.

In addition, all of the control variables in the model are significantly related to the number of RSVPs for a new event. The activity level of the group in the past is negatively associated with expressing interests in a new event. An event will attract 23% less people if it is organized by a group that was highly active in the past, compared to the events organized by groups with low activity level (Estimated mean of attendance: high activity=3.44, low activity=4.45). The group tenure is positively related to the number of RSVPs for a new event; i.e. older groups will attract more attendees. Also, expectedly, there is a positive relationship between the average number of RSVPs for events in the past four weeks and the number of people expressing interests for a new event.

7. DISCUSSION AND FUTURE WORK

In this paper, we explored the possible influential factors that affect the sustainability of hybrid social Web systems. We defined their sustainability as the capability of attracting people attending offline meetings as well as keep participating on the online platform. Using the Meetup groups as an exemplary hybrid platform, we investigated the approaches used to present the online representation of offline activities as well as the online interactions on the platform. We found that Meetup provided several mechanisms such as the discussion board, group email-list, commenting and photo uploading of events to support members' online interactions as well as present offline activities of the group; however, the level of awareness about what happens offline is somewhat limited in the current platform. Although the photos can be utilized as an artifact representing what has happened offline in the online platform, we observed a very low incidence of photos being posted across the Meetup groups.

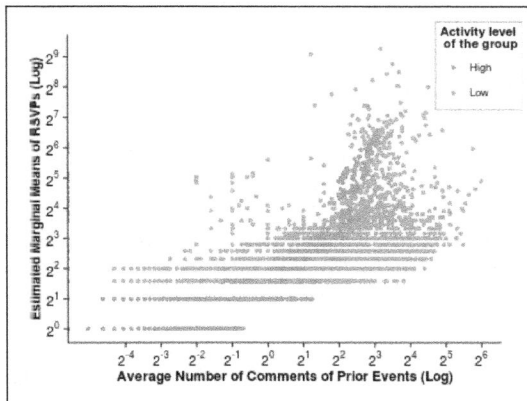

(a) The interaction effect of prior online activities (comments) and the activity level of the group

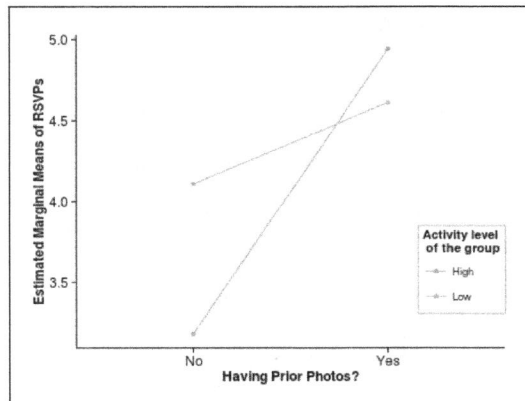

(b) The interaction effect of the representation of prior offline activities (photos) and the activity level of the group

Figure 1: The Plot of Interaction Effects

Moreover, taking pictures and posting them is sensitive to the context of the nature of the offline activities. In some categories of groups (e.g., language/ethnic identity, writing, education, learning, etc.), the contexts of the events do not stimulate picture taking and posting.

Further, we examined whether and how the online interactions and the online representation of offline activities of previous events on Meetup relate with the number of people expressing interest in participating in the future events. Our results showed that both factors positively relate to the sustainability of the Meetup events. That is, presenting the prior online and offline activities in the online platform seems to be an effective mechanism to sustain hybrid social Web systems. This finding confirms prior research in online communities on positive impact of social presence; i.e. representation of presence of others serves an encouraging factors engaging users in the desired activity. Our results provide design guidelines for designers of hybrid social Web systems to (1) provide support for online interactions, encourage such interactions, and make them visible to members of the community; (2) foster stronger representation of traces of offline activities in the online platform.

Our results also suggested that these factors can be particularly important for groups with higher level of activities. To sustain their activities as high as it has already been achieved, it is essential to provide awareness about such activities. Both factors of the previous online participation and the online representation of offline activities have a larger positive impact on the sustainability of the hybrid groups with higher level of activities. We also found that the large amount of past events is negatively associated with member' participation in the hybrid communities. These two results together may indicate a sense of competition between events, if there are a large number of them available. This can be specifically a challenge for hybrid social Web systems that rely on limited offline user population. While theoretically, an individual can participate in many online activities simultaneously, they can only be present in one offline event at any point of time; therefore, each event is competing with other events in attracting the time of the individual members. Increase number of events can specifically increase this competition and lead into starvation of participants for a larger

number of events. Similarly, large number of events can lead to a sense of information overload for the users, overwhelming their decision-making capabilities with too much information [7]. This brings up an important design decisions for hybrid social Web systems to optimize the number of events leading to highest level of sustainability.

While the present work provides the first attempt to model sustainability in hybrid social Web systems, our investigation is not comprehensive. Especially, we plan to further study the sustainability of these hybrid systems by distinguishing factors contributing to the attraction of new members versus retention of existing members in both online and offline context. We also acknowledge that our current work adopted a strictly quantitative approach in studying the effect of comments and photos on the sustainability of the groups. However, both the content of the comments and the photos can be very informative in understanding of intertwined natured of the hybrid social Web systems. As our future work, we plan to enrich our statistical analysis with content analysis of comments and photos as well as interviews with Meetup users.

Moreover, to generalize our results, a more comprehensive study needs to be conducted in the context of various different hybrid social Web systems with consideration of other potential indication of traces of offline activities than just photos. In addition, even with our attempt of conducting lagged regression analysis, the current study is a correlational study and there can be hidden factors that contributed to both dependent and independent variables in our analyses. Further research, especially in the form of randomized controlled experiment, is required to confirm the causal relationships between the potential factors - members' online participation and the online representation of offline activities in the online platform - and the sustainability of hybrid social Web systems.

Nevertheless, the current work makes an important initial effort to conceptualize the sustainability in hybrid social Web systems. It sheds a light towards a more effective design for hybrid social Web systems by highlighting promising results on the importance of online interactions and online representation of offline activities.

8. REFERENCES

[1] About meetup. http://meetup.com/about. [Online; accessed November-2015].

[2] S. Angelopoulos and Y. Merali. Bridging the divide between virtual and embodied spaces: Exploring the effect of offline interactions on the sociability of participants of topic-specific online communities. In *System Sciences (HICSS), 2015 48th Hawaii International Conference on*, pages 1994–2002. IEEE, 2015.

[3] M. Burke, C. Marlow, and T. Lento. Feed me: motivating newcomer contribution in social network sites. In *Proceedings of the SIGCHI conference on human factors in computing systems*, pages 945–954. ACM, 2009.

[4] B. S. Butler. Membership size, communication activity, and sustainability: A resource-based model of online social structures. *Information systems research*, 12(4):346–362, 2001.

[5] C. M. Cheung and M. K. Lee. Understanding the sustainability of a virtual community: model development and empirical test. *Journal of Information Science*, 2009.

[6] R. B. Cialdini. Influence: The psychology of persuasion. *New York: Morrow*, 1993.

[7] M. J. Eppler and J. Mengis. The concept of information overload: A review of literature from organization science, accounting, marketing, mis, and related disciplines. *The information society*, 20(5):325–344, 2004.

[8] T. Erickson. The world-wide-web as social hypertext. *Communications of the ACM*, 39(1):15–17, 1996.

[9] E. Ganglbauer, G. Fitzpatrick, Ö. Subasi, and F. Güldenpfennig. Think globally, act locally: a case study of a free food sharing community and social networking. In *Proceedings of the 17th ACM conference on Computer supported cooperative work & social computing*, pages 911–921. ACM, 2014.

[10] C. N. Gunawardena. Social presence theory and implications for interaction and collaborative learning in computer conferences. *International journal of educational telecommunications*, 1(2):147–166, 1995.

[11] K. Hampton and B. Wellman. Neighboring in netville: How the internet supports community and social capital in a wired suburb. *city and community*, 2(4):277–311, 2003.

[12] K. N. Hampton. Neighborhoods in the network society the e-neighbors study. *Information, Communication & Society*, 10(5):714–748, 2007.

[13] N. Hara. Internet use for political mobilization: Voices of participants. *First Monday*, 13(7), 2008.

[14] N. Hara and Z. Estrada. Analyzing the mobilization of grassroots activities via the internet: a case study. *Journal of Information Science*, 31(6):503–514, 2005.

[15] L. Jin, D. Robey, and M.-C. Boudreau. The nature of hybrid community: An exploratory study of open source software user groups. *The Journal of Community Informatics*, 11(1), 2015.

[16] A. J. Kim. *Community building on the web: Secret strategies for successful online communities.* Addison-Wesley Longman Publishing Co., Inc., 2000.

[17] J. Koh, Y.-G. Kim, B. Butler, and G.-W. Bock. Encouraging participation in virtual communities. *Commun. ACM*, 50(2):68–73, Feb. 2007.

[18] C. Lampe and E. Johnston. Follow the (slash) dot: effects of feedback on new members in an online community. In *Proceedings of the 2005 international ACM SIGGROUP conference on Supporting group work*, pages 11–20. ACM, 2005.

[19] H.-F. Lin. The role of online and offline features in sustaining virtual communities: an empirical study. *Internet Research*, 17(2):119–138, 2007.

[20] C. Lopez. Modeling sustainability of participatory information systems for urban communities: A mixed-method approach, January 2016.

[21] W. McCully, C. Lampe, C. Sarkar, A. Velasquez, and A. Sreevinasan. Online and offline interactions in online communities. In *Proceedings of the 7th international symposium on wikis and open collaboration*, pages 39–48. ACM, 2011.

[22] D. R. Millen and J. F. Patterson. Stimulating social engagement in a community network. In *Proceedings of the 2002 ACM conference on Computer supported cooperative work*, pages 306–313. ACM, 2002.

[23] M. R. Parks and K. Floyd. Making friends in cyberspace. *Journal of Computer-Mediated Communication*, 1(4):0–0, 1996.

[24] C. Ridings and M. Wasko. Online discussion group sustainability: Investigating the interplay between structural dynamics and social dynamics over time. *Journal of the Association for Information Systems*, 11(2):95, 2010.

[25] D. Robey, K. S. Schwaig, and L. Jin. Intertwining material and virtual work. *Information and organization*, 13(2):111–129, 2003.

[26] L. F. Sessions. How offline gatherings affect online communities: When virtual community members 'meetup'. *Information, Communication & Society*, 13(3):375–395, 2010.

[27] C. Shen and C. Cage. Exodus to the real world? assessing the impact of offline meetups on community participation and social capital. *New Media & Society*, page 1461444813504275, 2013.

[28] D. Tewksbury. Online-offline knowledge sharing in the occupy movement: Howtooccupy. org and discursive communities of practice. *American Communication Journal*, 15(1):11–23, 2013.

[29] B. D. Weinberg and C. B. Williams. The 2004 us presidential campaign: Impact of hybrid offline and online âĂŸmeetupâĂŹcommunities. *Direct, Data and Digital Marketing Practice*, 8(1):46–57, 2006.

[30] R. L. Williams and J. Cothrel. Four smart ways to run online communities. *MIT Sloan Management Review*, 41(4):81, 2000.

Development of Failure Detection System for Network Control using Collective Intelligence of Social Networking Service in Large-Scale Disasters

Chihiro Maru
Ochanomizu University
Bunkyo, Tokyo, Japan
chihiro@ogl.is.ocha.ac.jp

Miki Enoki
IBM Research - Tokyo
Chuo, Tokyo, Japan
enomiki@jp.ibm.com

Akihiro Nakao
University of Tokyo
Bunkyo, Tokyo, Japan
nakao@iii.u-tokyo.ac.jp

Shu Yamamoto
University of Tokyo
Bunkyo, Tokyo, Japan
shu@iii.u-tokyo.ac.jp

Saneyasu Yamaguchi
Kogakuin Univirsity
Shinjuku, Tokyo, Japan
sane@cc.kogakuin.ac.jp

Masato Oguchi
Ochanomizu University
Bunkyo, Tokyo, Japan
oguchi@is.ocha.ac.jp

ABSTRACT

When the Great East Japan Earthquake occurred in 2011, it was difficult to immediately grasp all telecommunications network conditions using only information from network monitoring devices because the damage was considerably heavy and a severe congestion control state occurred. Moreover, at the time of the earthquake, telephone and e-mail services could not be used in many cases, although social networking services (SNSs) were still available. In an emergency, such as an earthquake, users proactively convey information on telecommunications network conditions through SNSs. Therefore, the collective intelligence of SNSs is suitable as a means of information detection complementary to conventional observation through network monitoring devices. In this paper, we propose a network failure detection system that detects telephony failures with a high degree of accuracy by using the collective intelligence of Twitter, one of the most widely used SNSs. We also show that network control can be performed automatically and autonomically using information on telecommunications network conditions detected with our system.

Keywords

Twitter, SNSs, Collective Intelligence, Failure Detection, Telephony Failures, Network Control, DPN

1. INTRODUCTION

Large-scale disasters, such as earthquakes, often cause telephony failures because base stations and network facilities become damaged and many users try to access the telecommunications network at the same time. In such emergencies, it is important that communications via telephone and e-mail services be available. Usually, network conditions can only be grasped using network monitoring devices. However, when the Great East Japan Earthquake [1] occurred in 2011, it was difficult to immediately grasp all telecommunications network conditions using only information from network monitoring devices because the damage was considerably heavy and a severe congestion control state occurred [2].

Conventionally, telecommunications network conditions are monitored using information from inside a network, using only network monitoring devices [3]. To solve the above-mentioned problem, we propose a network failure detection system using information from outside a network that is complementary to network monitoring devices.

In subsequent research on the Great East Japan Earthquake [4], survey participants responded that they were able to use social networking services (SNSs). Such services are also advantageous in that they can obtain information from users in real time. In an emergency, such as an earthquake, users proactively convey information about telecommunications network conditions through SNSs. For example, Twitter can be used to obtain information on the locations and causes of telephony failures and on the degree of impact to users, which cannot be obtained using only network monitoring devices. Therefore, the collective intelligence of SNSs is suitable as a means of information detection complementary to conventional observation using network monitoring devices. The objective of this study was to achieve automatic and autonomic network control by using collective intelligence analyzed from Twitter [5], one of the most widely used SNSs. This system is targeted to network managers who need to automatically detect telephony failures during emergencies.

Twitter accessibility is an issue when Internet services are down. However, if wireless LAN access is not available, other services such as 3G networks and LTE networks may be used. Moreover, people in areas where failures have not occurred can provide information on telephony failures.

The contributions of this work are summarized as follows.

1. By designing and prototyping an SNS-based network failure detection system, we can detect telephony failures with a high degree of accuracy and prioritize locations for network recovery.

HT '16, July 10-13, 2016, Halifax, NS, Canada

© 2016 ACM. ISBN 978-1-4503-4247-6/16/07... $15.00

DOI: http://dx.doi.org/10.1145/2914586.2914620

2. By integrating our SNS-based network failure detection system into a network control system, we can automatically and autonomously perform network control using the collective intelligence of SNSs.

The remainder of this paper is organized as follows. In Section 2, we introduce related research studies and give an overview of our proposed system in Section 3. In Section 4, we discuss the determination of initial keywords and a candidate data detection method. In Section 5, we discuss the location classification method and degree of significance calculation in Section 6. In Section 7, we give an overview of our network control system using information detected with our network failure detection system. We conclude the paper in Section 8 with a brief summary and discuss future research directions.

2. RELATED WORK

There are a number of methods for detecting detailed information by analyzing the data from SNSs when large events occur [6–18]. Mizuno et al. [18] introduced a system to detect disaster situations using the content of tweets and location information posted by users during a disaster. This study is similar to ours in that it was focused on detecting not only the occurrence of an event but also secondary damage caused by it for managers. However, our study differs from these previous ones because we particularly focused on the detection of network failures and automatic network control using detected information.

Conventionally, network control is performed using information detected using network monitoring devices [3]. The ITU-T Focus Group on Disaster Relief Systems [3] detects network failures with a monitoring system using a wireless sensor network in emergencies and automatically notifies network managers when an event level exceeds the warning level. On the other hand, our study is unique in that we focused on performing network control using the collective intelligence of SNSs. Our study complements the fact that it is difficult to grasp network conditions for users by correctly using conventional methods. Qiu et al. [19] reported that users posted messages on Twitter before they called a customer service center if they experienced network failures. This shows that using Twitter is effective in detecting network failures. Takeshita et al. [20–22] had a similar motivation to ours in that they used tweets related to network performance issues to oversee network operation. Our study differs from these previous ones in that they only performed failure detection during normal periods. We focused on natural disasters and the results from a system that performs network control on the basis of detected information.

3. OVERVIEW OF PROPOSED SYSTEM

An overview of our proposed network failure detection system is given in Figure 1.

The process flow of the proposed system is as follows.

(1) Determine initial keywords about telephone failures by detecting failure expressions using a bootstrap method and collect tweets containing the keywords.

(2) Classify the tweets of (1) in accordance with location information into each location group.

(3) Calculate characteristic words with the data set of (2) and add tweets containing the words to the data set of (2).

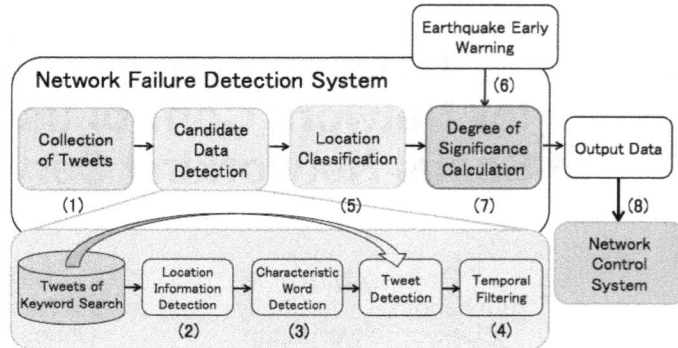

Figure 1: Network failures detection system

(4) Consider the post time of each tweet and apply temporal filtering to cut irrelevant tweets.

(5) Classify location from tweets detected using the candidate data detection method as to whether the failure occurred at this or another location.

(6) Analyze external information, such as earthquake early warning, and obtain the time, position, and strength of the earthquake.

(7) Calculate the degree of significance for network recovery.

(8) Perform network control automatically and autonomically using information on telecommunications network conditions detected with our system.

It is important that telephony failures be detected immediately. For real-time processing, we collect tweets every minute and use tweets in the last 60 minutes as potential tweets for failure detection. The proposed system outputs failure information for each detected location and updates the analysis results within one minute.

With this system, detailed information about the situation of a telecommunications network for users can be acquired. It is then possible to control traffic on the basis of contents in accordance with the information.

4. DETAILS OF DATA DETECTION METHOD OF PROPOSED SYSTEM

In this chapter, we discuss the determination of initial keywords and the candidate data detection method of our proposed system. Then, we discuss an evaluation experiment.

We used the corpus of tweets in Japanese from the Great East Japan Earthquake because our system is targeted for large-scale disasters. Table 1 lists the details of the corpus. This corpus includes various types of tweets in addition to those about telephony failures.

Table 1: Corpus of tweets from Great East Japan Earthquake

Date	2011/03/11
Number of Tweets	8,815,519

4.1 Determination of Initial Keywords

To determine the initial keywords that are set in the keyword search of our system, we perform the detection of failure expressions using a bootstrap method [23]. Figure 2 shows the flow of the detection of failure expressions using a bootstrap method.

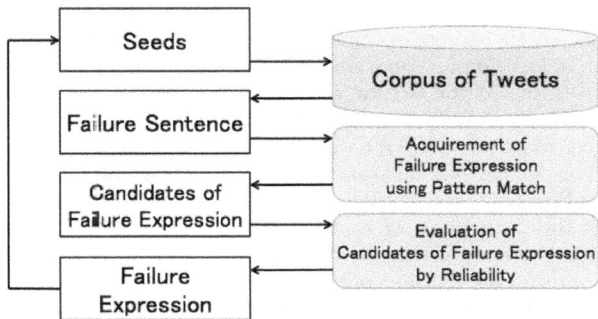

Figure 2: Detection of Failure Expression using a bootstrap method

First, we give initial seeds to the corpus of tweets from the Great East Japan Earthquake and collect tweets containing the seeds. All the tweets of the corpus contain the word "telephone". We then define the detected tweets as failure sentences. In this study, the words "congestion", "wrong", and "out of order" in Japanese were set to the initial seeds to obtain tweets about telephone problems. Next, we acquired the failure expression candidates using pattern match. This means that the combinations of verbal imperfective forms and negative auxiliary verbs are acquired from the failure sentences using the pattern match of a part of speech. Next, we score the reliability of detected failure expression candidates, because once low-precision results are obtained, the rate will continue to fall. The reliability of failure expression candidates is calculated as follows. When the set of failure sentences that contain a *candidate* that is a failure expression is S, the distance between the word "telephone" and the *candidate* in a sentence is $distance(s)$.

$$score(candidate) = \sum_{s \in S} \frac{1}{distance(s)} \qquad (1)$$

This formula is based on the assumption that a word that appears many times in failure sentences and emerges close to the word "telephone" is likely to have a relation to failures. Then, the top N% of *candidate* is defined as failure expressions. These expressions are given to the corpus as new seeds, and the same procedure is repeated. The failure expressions obtained by repeating this procedure a certain number of times are defined as initial keywords for our system.

4.2 Candidate Data Detection Method

In this section, we give an overview of the candidate data detection method of our system.

4.2.1 Keyword Search

We set the obtained initial keywords using a Search API [24] to collect tweets regarding telephony failures.

4.2.2 Location Information Detection

Various tweets can be associated with location. For example, Twitter users may register their location on their profile, and sometimes they geotag a tweet. We conducted a morphological analysis of tweets and their registered geotagged locations by using MeCab [25], which separates sentences into a set of words. Latitude and longitude details of geotags were converted into city names using the Yahoo! reverseGeoCoder API [26]. We then classified the tweets of the keyword search in accordance with the detected location information into each location group.

4.2.3 Characteristic Words Detection

To collect tweets that do not contain the same location but refer to the same failure, we detected characteristic words in the tweets. We then collected tweets that contained such words and not other location information and added them to the tweets for each piece of location information.

4.2.4 Temporal Filtering

In each piece of location information, there are a number of tweets that were unrelated to telephony failures. Therefore, we considered the timestamps of tweets and discarded tweets that were unrelated. Twitter users tend to simultaneously post similar tweets when large-scale disasters occur, and in this study, we considered this feature and determined a certain time threshold to eliminate tweets. To determine this threshold, we examined the time variations of the number of tweets that referred to telephony failures and generalized them. Figure 3 shows the time variation of the number of tweets that referred to telephony failures during an earthquake in Nagano on November 22, 2014. The green bars show the number of tweets and the red line shows the cumulative frequency value.

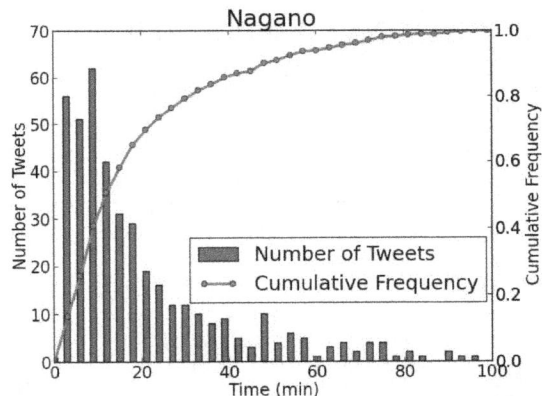

Figure 3: Time variations of tweets that refer to telephony failures

We considered cumulative frequency because the number of samples was small. The time variation of cumulative frequency is similar to the cumulative distribution function of an exponential distribution. This trend is also the same for earthquakes that occurred in Hokkaido and Ibaraki in 2014. Therefore, we fit each time variation of a cumulative frequency to the cumulative distribution function of exponential distributions so that we could determine a certain threshold to discard tweets. This cumulative distribution function is defined as

$$f(x) = 1 - e^{-\lambda x} \qquad (2)$$

Figure 4 shows the results of fitting earthquakes in Hokkaido, Ibaraki, and Nagano.

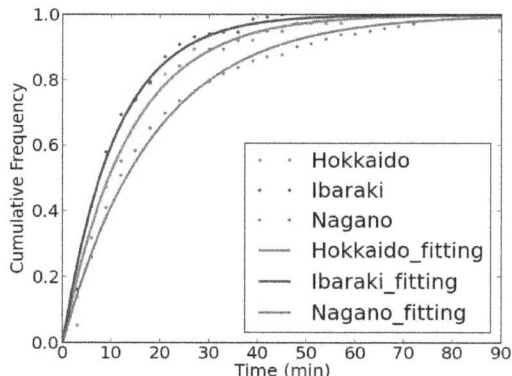

Figure 4: Results of fitting cumulative distribution functions of exponential distribution

The results showed that time variations of cumulative frequencies can be fitted to the cumulative distribution functions of an exponential distribution in all cases. Since this is an exponential distribution, we can detect 80% of the events in 60 minutes. Hence, for real-time processing, we collect tweets every minute and use tweets in the last 60 minutes as potential tweets for failure detection.

5. LOCATION CLASSIFICATION METHOD

We judged the contents of the tweets detected using the candidate data detection method to filter out tweets reporting telephony failures. When our system detects telephone problems, we want to classify whether users could not make a call to the detected location or users could not call from the detected location. Figure 5 shows examples of tweets that were detected using the candidate data detection method.

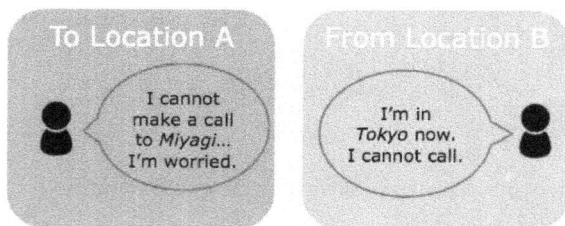

Figure 5: Examples of tweets detected using candidate data detection method

The left tweet shows that the user could not make a call to the detected location (Miyagi), while the right tweet shows that the user could not call from the detected location (Tokyo). Therefore, these tweets are different types and must be distinguished from each other.

We chose tweets not in Location B but in Location A because a failure was likely to occur in Location A. It was possible to filter out tweets with information on location associated with failures in this way. To distinguish between these tweets, we developed a method that uses machine learning.

5.1 Machine Learning Filter Method

First, we used the candidate data detection method and collected the tweets obtained from keyword search for each item of location information. For each detected location, we then classified the tweets into those of Location A or other tweets. To classify, we created a classifier using a support vector machine (SVM); SVM-light [27] with a default linear kernel. In the classification with machine learning, we used only Bag of Words (BoW) and rules as features. The BoW uses the occurrence of each word in a tweet as a feature, which is commonly used. We defined subjects of BoW as all parts of speech and only nouns, verbs, and adjectives. When rules are added as features, the subject of BoW are only nouns, verbs, and adjectives. The rules are:

1. words in the person or family dictionary are in the tweet
2. cannot make a call to (the detected location) is in the tweet

The person or family dictionary includes words related to people, e.g., mother, son, and sister. We selected these rules because tweets of Location A often satisfied any one of these rules.

5.2 Experiments and Results

We used tweets detected using the candidate data detection method from the corpus of tweets from the Great East Japan Earthquake as a training set. The set was made up of 1,746 tweets of Location A and 858 other tweets. We used leave-one-out cross validation as an assay method. Table 2 lists the results of the machine learning filter method.

Table 2: Evaluation of machine learning filter method

Method	Precision [%]	Recall [%]	F-value [%]
Subject of BoW is all parts of speech	80.76	96.85	88.08
Subjects of BoW are nouns, verbs, and adjectives	84.84	97.37	90.67
Rules are added as features	86.06	98.62	91.91

When the subjects of BoW are only nouns, verbs, and adjectives, the F-value increases compared with all parts of speech. This is because words that appear many times but do not affect the classification are eliminated. Moreover, adding the rules as features can increase the F-value, which suggests that adding rules is effective. Therefore, we were able to show that our proposed system performed well in terms of location classification.

6. DEGREE OF SIGNIFICANCE CALCULATION OF LOCATION INFORMATION

During the Great East Japan Earthquake, it was difficult to efficiently manage area recovery such as determining recovery priorities for networks and systems. To prioritize locations, we calculated the degree of significance, which has three indicators.

1. Tweet Rate of Telephony Failure
2. Seismic Intensity
3. Tweet Increasing Rate

For indicator 1, we obtained the ratio of tweets with information on location associated with telephony failures to tweets classified into each location group using the results from the location classification method discussed in Section 5. For indicator 2, we predicted seismic intensity in the detected locations using external information such as earthquake early warnings issued by the Japan Meteorological Agency. For indicator 3, we examined the rate of increase in tweets in emergencies compared with those during normal periods. We prioritized locations using these indicators. The degree of significance is calculated as follows.

1. For each indicator, the highest value among detected locations is set to 1, and values of other detected locations are normalized on the basis of the highest one.
2. For each locations, the average of the three normalized values is calculated.

Figure 6 shows time variations of the number of tweets in each prefecture during the earthquake, and Figure 7 shows the results of the degree of significance in each prefecture during the earthquake. The numbers in Figure 7 show recovery priorities.

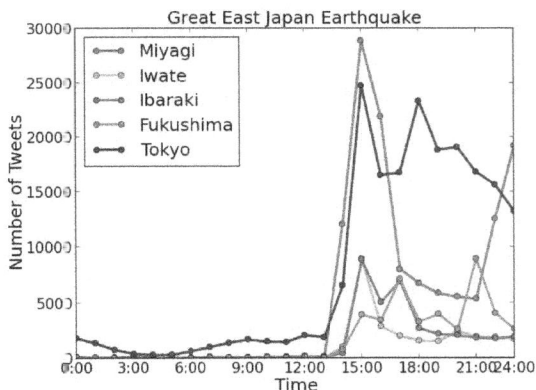

Figure 6: Time variations of number of tweets in each prefecture during Great East Japan Earthquake

As shown in Figure 6, the number of tweets in all areas increased rapidly. The number of tweets in Miyagi Prefecture, the seismic center of the earthquake, was large. However, the number of tweets in Tokyo Prefecture was also large, which should always be so because Tokyo is the principal city in Japan. Therefore, it is difficult to prioritize locations only from the number of tweets from this graph. On the other hand, as shown in Figure 7, the degree of significance in Tokyo Prefecture was smaller than in other locations. Therefore, locations with many tweets do not necessarily have high priorities. Locations with extensive dam-

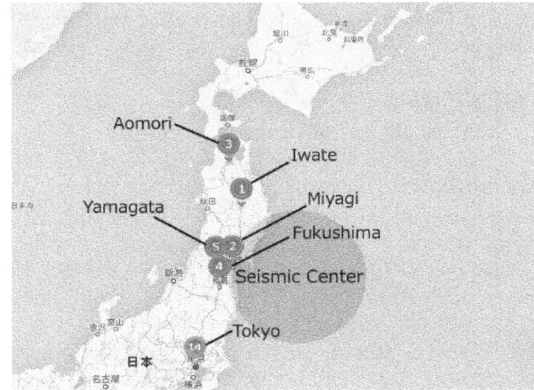

Figure 7: Degree of significance in each prefecture during Great East Japan Earthquake

age, such as Miyagi and Iwate Prefectures, were highly prioritized. Therefore, we can prioritize locations by calculating the degree of significance using the three indicators.

7. NETWORK CONTROL SYSTEM BASED ON SNS ANALYSIS

We constructed a network control system to automatically and autonomically optimize network traffic using information on telecommunications network conditions detected with our proposed system. We developed our control system on a network system called FLARE [28] to perform route control. We also implemented our network control system on a wide-area network testbed called Japan Gigabit Network eXtreme (JGN-X) [29]. The details of our network control system were described in our other papers.

8. CONCLUSIONS

We proposed a system for performing automatic and autonomic network control on the basis of the collective intelligence of an SNS.

We first designed and prototyped our SNS-based network failure detection system. We then evaluated our system using data from the Great East Japan Earthquake. As a result, our system could detect telephony failures with a high degree of accuracy and correctly extract the locations of failures and availability of telephone connections. Moreover, we calculated the degree of significance of each location for network recovery. As a result, we confirmed that locations with extensive damages, such as Miyagi and Iwate Prefectures, were highly prioritized. Hence, by using these results, we can determine recovery priorities in emergencies.

Next, we integrated our SNS-based network failure detection system into a network control system. That is to say, we constructed a network control system using information on network conditions detected with our system.

For future work, we aim toward information detection for detecting more detailed situations for users and connects to enable control through SNS analysis.

9. ACKNOWLEDGMENTS

This work is partially supported by the Strategic Information and Communications R&D Promotion Programme

(SCOPE) and Core Research for Evolutionary Science and Technology (CREST).

10. REFERENCES

[1] "Great East Japan Earthquake - Wikipedia, March 2011", https://en.wikipedia.org/wiki/2011_Tohoku_earthquake_and_tsunami

[2] K. Kagawa, Y. Kuno, H. Tamura, H. Takada, M. Furutani, and N. Minamikata, "Improvement of Credibility for Operation System in the Case of Large Disaster," NTT DOCOMO technical journal, vol.20, no.4, pp.26-36, 2013.

[3] ITU-T Forcus Group on Disaster Relief Systems, "Monitoring Systems for Outside Plant Facilities," ITU-T Recommendations, no.L.81, pp.1-10, 2009.

[4] A. Acar, and Y. Muraki, "Twitter for Crisis Communication: Lessons Learned from Japan's Tsunami Disaster," International Journal of Web Based Communities, vol.7, no.3, pp.392-402, 2011.

[5] "Twitter," http://twitter.com/

[6] T. Sakaki, M. Okazaki, and Y. Matsuo, "Earthquake Shakes Twitter Users: Real-Time Event Detection by Social Sensors," Proceedings of the 19th International Conference on World Wide Web, pp.851-860, 2010.

[7] National Institute for Land and Infrastructure Management, "A Study on Method for Detection of Disaster Outbreak by Means of Social Media Analysis," https://www.kantei.go.jp/jp/singi/it2/senmon_bunka/bousai/dai5/siryou5.pdf, 2014.

[8] S. Saito, Y. Ikawa, and H. Suzuki, "Early Detection of Disasters with Contextual Information on Twitter," Technical Report of IEICE, vol.114, no.81, pp.7-12, 2014.

[9] A. Sadilek, H. Kautz, and V. Silenzio, "Predicting Disease Transmission from Geo-Tagged Micro-Blog Data," Proceeding of the 26th AAAI Conference on Artificial Intelligence, pp.136-142, 2012.

[10] P. Metaxas, E. Mustafaraj, and D. Gayo-Avello, "How(not) to Predict Elections," Privacy, Security, Risk and Trust and 2011 IEEE Third International Conference on Social Computing, pp.165-171, 2011.

[11] S. Verma, S. Vieweg, W. Corvey, L. Palen, J. Martin, M. Palmer, A. Schram, and K. Anderson, "Natural Language Processing to the Rescue?: Extracting "Situational Awareness" Tweets During Mass Emergency," ICWSM, 2011.

[12] K. Rudra, S. Ghosh, N. Ganguly, P. Goyal, and S. Ghosh, "Extracting Situational Information from Microblogs during Disaster Events: a Classification-Summarization Approach," Proceedings of the 24th ACM International on Conference on Information and Knowledge Management, pp.583-592, 2015.

[13] S. Panem, M. Gupta, and V. Varma, "Structured Information Extraction from Natural Disaster Events on Twitter," Proceedings of the 5th ACM International Workshop on Web-scale Knowledge Representation Retrieval&Reasoning, pp.1-8, 2014.

[14] I. Varga, M. Sano, K. Torisawa, C. Hashimoto, K. Ohtake, T. Kawai, J. Oh, and S. Saeger, "Aid is Out There: Looking for Help from Tweets during a Large Scale Disaster," ACL, pp.1619-1629, 2013.

[15] T. Sakaki, T. Yanagihara, K. Nawa, and Y. Matsuo, "Driving Information Extraction from Twitter," The IEICE Transactions on Information and Systems, vol.J98-D, no.6, pp.1019-1032, 2015.

[16] M. Cameron, R. Power, B. Robinson, and J. Yin, "Emergency Situation Awareness from Twitter for Crisis Management," Proceedings of the 21st International Conference Companion on World Wide Web, pp.695-698, 2012.

[17] Y. Qu, C. Huang, P. Zhang, and J. Zhang, "Microblogging after a Major Disaster in China: a Case Study of the 2010 Yushu Earthquake," Proceedings of the ACM 2011 Conference on Computer Supported Cooperative Work, pp.25-34, 2011.

[18] J. Mizuno, J. Goto, K. Ohtake, T. Kawada, K. Torizawa, J. Kloetzer, M. Tanaka, C. Hashimoto, and A. Okumura, "Performance Evaluation of Disaster Information Analysis System DISAANA and its Question Answer Mode," IPSJ Consumer Device&System (CDS), vol.2015-CDS-14, no.14, pp.1-13, 2015.

[19] T. Qiu, J. Feng, Z. Ge, J. Wang, J. Xu, and J. Yates, "Listen to Me if You can: Tracking User Experience of Mobile Network on Social Media," Proceedings of the 10th ACM SIGCOMM Conference on Internet Measurement, pp.288-293, 2010.

[20] K. Takeshita, M. Yokota, K. Nishimatsu, and Haruhisa Hasegawa, "Proposal of the Network Failure Information Acquisition Method from Social Network Services," IEICE Society Conference 2012, B-7-35, 2012.

[21] K.Takeshita, M.Yokota, K. Nishimatsu, and H. Hasegawa, "Evaluation of the Network Failure Information Acquisition System from Social Network Services," Proceedings of the 2013 IEICE General Conference, B-7-44, 2013.

[22] K. Takeshita, M. Yokota, and K. Nishimatsu, "Early Network Failure Detection System by Analyzing Twitter Data," IFIP/IEEE International Symposium on, pp.279-286, 2015.

[23] K. Kurihara, K. Shimada, "Bug sentence extraction from Twitter using the bootstrap method," Natural Language Processing 2015, pp.341-344, 2015.

[24] "Twitter Serch API," https://dev.twitter.com/rest/public/search

[25] "MeCab," http://mecab.sourceforge.net/

[26] "Yahoo! reverseGeoCoder API," http://developer.yahoo.co.jp/webapi/map/openlocalplatform/v1/reversegeocoder.html

[27] T. Joachims, "Making Large Scale SVM Learning Practical," 1999.

[28] A. Nakao, "Software-Defined Data Plane Enhancing SDN and NFV," Special Section on Quality of Diversifying Communication Networks and Services, IEICE Transactions on Communications, vol.E98-B, no.1, pp.12-19, 2015.

[29] "JGN-X," http://www.jgn.nict.go.jp/english/

Analyzing the Perceptions of Change in a Distributed Collection of Web Documents

Luis Meneses, Sampath Jayarathna, Richard Furuta and Frank Shipman

Center for the Study of Digital Libraries and Department of Computer Science and Engineering
Texas A&M University
College Station, TX 77843-3112 USA
(ldmm, sampath, furuta, shipman)@cse.tamu.edu

ABSTRACT

It is not unusual for documents on the Web to degrade and suffer from problems associated with unexpected change. In an analysis of the Association for Computing Machinery conference list, we found that categorizing the degree of change affecting digital documents over time is a difficult task. More specifically, we found that categorizing this degree of change is not a binary problem where documents are either unchanged or they have changed so dramatically that they do not fit within the scope of the collection. It is in part, a characterization of the intent of the change. In this paper, we present a case study that compares change detection methods based on machine learning algorithms against the assessment made by human subjects in a user study. Consequently, this paper will focus on two research questions. First, how can we categorize the various degrees of change that documents endure? And second, how did our automatic detection methods fare against the human assessment of change in the ACM conference list?

Categories and Subject Descriptors

H.3.7 [**Information Storage and Retrieval**]: Digital Libraries – *collection, systems issues, user issues.*

General Terms

Management, Design, Reliability, Experimentation, Verification.

Keywords

Web resource management, distributed collections, web change classification.

1. INTRODUCTION

Imagine a library filled with books that have missing pages. It might seem as overly exaggerated, but that metaphor can depict the state of digital collections that have been affected by unexpected change. It is not unusual for digital documents to have problems associated with the persistence of links, especially when dealing with references to external resources. External resources on the Web are highly volatile and prone to exhibit unexpected change as cases of "broken links" [1] or "linkrot" [2]. Therefore, our work has been motivated to mitigate the impact of unexpected change in documents stored in decentralized collections [3].

We have found that electronic resources can change, both intentionally and unintentionally, because of different factors and circumstances. More so, Web documents are not static resources and a certain degree of change is expected from them [4]. Our current efforts continue long-standing study of the problems that surface when managing distributed collections and curating missing resources [5-7].

Distributed collections of Web documents that are hosted in institutional repositories operate under the assumption that they are more resilient and able to withstand change. Distributed collections are different from traditional collections in that the curator does not possess the documents. Without possession of the documents, the curator cannot control how they change. By definition, a digital repository must include procedures and tools for curating, organizing, storing, and retrieving the documents and media contained in the collection. Surprisingly, we have found these features – which are often found in digital collections with emphasis in long-term storage – do not fully preserve the referenced documents and make them impervious to change. For example, as of February 2016 the Association for Computing Machinery Digital Library has 19 unique links referencing the different sites of the Hypertext conference series and 10 of them report errors or point to the wrong content. Figure 1 shows a screenshot of http://www.ht00.org – which now displays information about banking and investments.

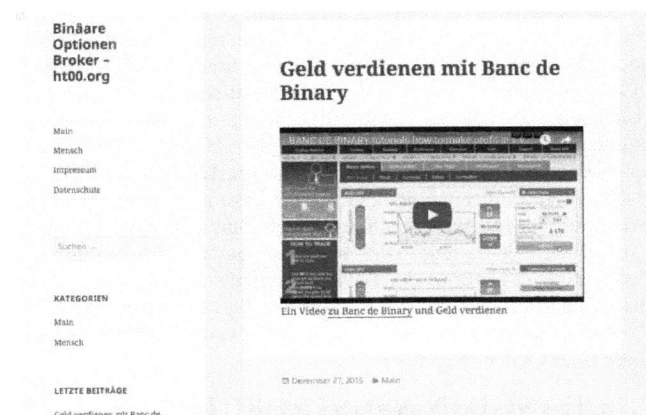

Figure 1: Screenshot of http://www.ht00.org. Accessed on 2/19/2016.

In this paper, we present a case study that compares change detection methods based on machine learning algorithms against the assessment made by human subjects in a user study. More so, our study aims to quantify and analyze the perceptions and reactions of users when they come across documents that have been affected by unexpected change. Consequently, this paper will focus on two research questions. First, how can we categorize the various degrees of change that documents endure? And second, how did our automatic detection methods fare against the human assessment of change that we found in the ACM conference list? This point becomes increasingly interesting when we take into account that the resources found in a digital collection are often curated and maintained by experts with affiliations to professionally managed institutions.

2. PREVIOUS WORK

Previous work on finding missing resources is based around the premise that documents and information are not lost but simply misplaced [8] as a consequence of the lack of integrity in the Web [9, 10]. Other studies have also focused on finding the longevity of documents in the Web [11] and in distributed collections [12, 13].

Phelps and Wilensky pioneered the use of lexical signatures to locate missing content in the Web [14]. They claimed that if a Web request returned a 404 error, querying a search engine with a five–term lexical signature could retrieve the missing content. Park et al. used Phelps and Wilensky's previous research to perform an evaluation of nine lexical signature generators that incorporate term frequency measures [15]. Additionally, Klein and Nelson have extracted lexical signatures from titles and backlinks to find missing Web resources [16].

Dalal et al. used a different method to find appropriate replacements for missing resources from the Web that belonged to a collection in Walden's Paths [17]. Their approach was based on a two–step process. First, metadata was extracted when the path was created thus preserving the author's intent and vision. Second, the extracted metadata was used to find pages when they cannot be retrieved. In the specific case of collections such as Walden's Paths, each node in a path is destined to make a contribution towards the overall concept and the continuity in the narration. Therefore, finding replacements becomes a critical factor to maintain the integrity of the collections and preserve their semantic meaning.

On the other hand, previous work on link persistence has focused on characterizing the availability of resources over time. Nelson and Allen measured the persistence and availability of documents in a digital library [18]. Koehler found that specialized document collections – such as legal, educational and some scientific citations – tend to stabilize over time [19]. However, citations in some domains have higher rates of failure [20]. McCown et al. also explored other factors that might cause a resource to fail by examining its age, path depth, top-level domain and file extension [21]. Here we extend this body of work by examining a distributed collection of Web documents as a part of an institutional digital library, describe the types of issues found in the collection, and examine the potential to automatically identify these issues when they arise.

3. CHANGE IN A DISTRUBUTED COLLECTIONS

To conduct our experiment we needed a document corpus. For this purpose, we harvested the metadata for the conference proceedings found in the Association for Computing Machinery Digital Library. While the ACM Digital Library stores and maintains the "Full text of every article ever published by ACM" and bibliographic citations from major publishers in computing, it includes the links to the actual conference sites as distributed

resources that are hosted externally and therefore more prone to be affected by unexpected change.

3.1 A Distributed Collection within an Institutional Digital Library

The ACM maintains a list of the conference proceedings (http://dl.acm.org/proceedings.cfm), which we retrieved on 9/27/2014 and used as our starting point. Then we followed each hyperlink to a metadata page that displayed basic information for each corresponding conference and workshop, which in turn allowed us to extract the external URLs. As a result of this procedure, we were able to extract 6086 URLs – out of which 2001 were unique. Additionally, we also stored the metadata associated with each retrieved page. This metadata included the anchor text, URL requested, URL retrieved, HTTP headers and response code. Approximately 75% of the page requests resulted in a response code indicating success (200), which means that no problems were found when trying to fulfill the request. The remaining pages were mostly divided among page not found (404) responses and timeouts.

We then proceeded to inspect and categorize the 1492 pages that were retrieved with a 200 HTTP response code. We categorized these pages into three categories by evaluating the relationship between the anchor text and the corresponding retrieved page. As a result of this categorization, we found that 917 pages were "clearly correct" and 531 were incorrect. Additionally, we were unable to evaluate 44 pages because their contents didn't provide us enough information to make an accurate assessment. These pages could have been placed into the "incorrect" category, but we decided to use an additional category to make our experiment as transparent as possible.

3.2 Categorization of the Types of Change

The 531 pages that were reported by the HTTP server as being correctly retrieved but were clearly not the original contents were then analyzed in an effort to understand how conference sites degrade over time. The coding scheme evolved through examination of the particular collection rather than using a pre-defined classification scheme.

In the end, nine categories were used to classify the "incorrect" pages, which we list in (approximate) order of severity. These nine groups provide insight regarding the different stages that conference pages go through until they are ultimately abandoned:

1. **Kind of correct:** (197 entries) Pages that contain related content, but they do not fully match the semantic concept encapsulated in the anchor text. When taking into account conference proceedings, these pages often link to a different year in the conference series. For example, Anchor text "Conference X 2006" references the Conference X 2009 site.

2. **University/institution pages:** (36 entries) This case surfaces when a site has been taken down, but the server configuration redirects the user to its parent institution. In cases dealing with conference sites, servers would usually redirect the user to the website of the University that hosted the conference or to a related professional organization.

3. **Directory listings pages:** (18 entries) Pages displaying a listing of files or a "Hello World" page. Probably caused by an error in the server configuration. Here the original content looks to still be available but the new web server does not recognize homepage.html as a default page to view for this URL.

4. **Blank pages:** (141 entries) pages that returned no content.

5. **Failed redirects:** (30 entries)

6. **Error pages:** (17 entries) Pages that specifically state that an error has occurred.

7. **Pages in a different language:** (32 entries) Pages that didn't match the language found in the anchor text. Most of these pages were in a language different than English.

8. **Domain for sale pages:** (17 entries) Pages that indicated that the domain name registration has lapsed and it is being sold by a registrar, or taken over by a third party in order to profit from the sale.

9. **Deceiving pages:** (43 entries) Pages that have been taken over by a third party. The content displayed in these pages is totally unrelated to the original purpose of the site. We believe that these pages were not created to deceive users, but as an attempt to manipulate the PageRank algorithm [22]. Figure 2 shows a screenshot corresponding to the IDC 2004 site that displays an example of this case.

Many of these links still lead to information related to the original purpose but clearly not to the originally intended materials. There are a number of categories that result when no content is available depending on how the servers are configured – blank pages, failed redirects, some directory listings, error pages, and university/institutional pages. The remaining pages are perhaps the most problematic, when the web address has been taken over and is either for sale or being used for other purposes.

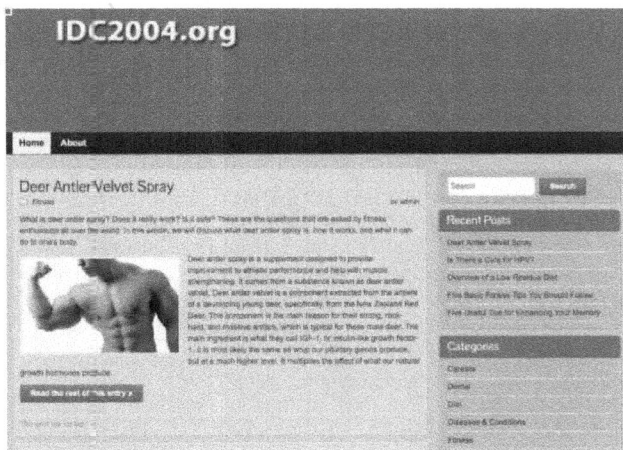

Figure 2: Screenshot of the IDC 2004 site showing an example of a "Deceiving Page". Accessed at http://www.idc2004.org on 9/27/2014

4. CLASSIFICATION FEATURES

To develop classifiers for the types of issues identified in Section 3, we explored the potential for a variety of features to help discriminate between the categories observed. In particular, we consider features computed based on the contents and links returned by the initial request (the *base node*) and the contents and links returned by traversing the links in the base node. As we wanted to limit the number of HTTP requests required, this analysis did not examine the potential of the broader network topology to facilitate classification.

We included twelve link-based features. These features are divided into topology features, content-type features, anchor-text features, and child node features. Most of the link-based features were computed for the base node and are based on the number of out-links in that page. In addition we calculated some of the features for child nodes that are the valid out-links in these base-nodes.

The content of resources is generally highly indicative of their purpose. Eight quantitative measures related to the content of the resources were included as features for developing classifiers. These features are divided into image features and text-content features.

The text associated with resources is the most obvious feature for determining the topics. While a deep understanding of the domain of conference web sites could have been used to develop a domain-oriented expectation model (e.g., a discussion of content submission, organizing committees, schedule, keynotes, travel, and hotels), we instead focused on generating quantitative measures based on the text content that could be potentially valuable across domains.

In particular, we generated topic models to examine the similarity among the metadata and the contents of the base node and the metadata and the contents of the child nodes. We used Latent Dirichlet Allocation (LDA) to model the content of the text [23] and the KL-divergence similarity measure to compare them [24].

5. RESULTS

Results from examining the conference web site collection include examining the trends found in the collection, the generation of a test collection for exploring the potential to automatically classify resources based on the types of issues found in Section 3.2, and a comparison of the performance of different classifiers when provided the features in Section 4.

5.1 Classification Algorithms

We performed our binary and category classification with 71 algorithms that are implemented in the Weka toolkit [25]. We report the best classification results based on the F-measures from the following classifiers: K*, Decorate, Random Committee, Rotation Forest, Bagging, Boosting (e.g., LogitBoost) and decisions trees (e.g., Random Forest). The algorithmic details of these classifiers are beyond the scope of this paper and interested readers are referred to [25, 26].

To finalize the topic model, we initially explored how varying the number of topics in the LDA model affected classifier performance. As part of these experiments we varied the number of topics K between 5 and 25. The F-measure of seven classifiers when given the 20 features from Section 4 to classify the incorrect and unsure categories varied between 0.54 to 0.64. After training and testing the category classification data and performing this evaluation, we found that the best performing classifiers exhibit their best performance with 5 topics (K=5). Therefore, we used 5 topics for the remainder of our experiments involving the training and testing datasets and the analysis of the classifier results.

The results of our experiments for the "clearly correct", "incorrect" and "unsure" categories as a binary classification problem, and the performance metrics for the 7 most effective classifiers from our evaluation are presented in Table 1. The majority of our classifiers performed consistently with an F-measure of 0.63; Random Forest was the best performer for the binary classification. Decorate and Random Committee both exhibit a slightly higher F-measure for "correct" category, but Random Forest offers a substantially better F-measure for the "not correct" category.

Two categories of pages in our "incorrect/unsure" dataset, the "unsure" and "different language" groups, are the result of our inability to classify the contents returned for a resource as being either correct or incorrect. Although we originally grouped these two categories into the same "not correct" group, it is possible that some of these pages might contain valid or "correct" pages. The results displayed in Table 2 show the performance of the classifiers when just the "different language" and "unsure" categories were removed from the training/testing corpus.

Table 1: Binary classification (correct, not correct) combining all incorrect categories into single category.

	Precision		Recall		F-Measure	
	C	N	C	N	C	N
Decorate	0.635	0.637	0.641	0.632	0.638	0.635
RandomCommittee	0.606	0.632	0.672	0.562	0.637	0.595
RotationForest	0.626	0.629	0.632	0.623	0.629	0.626
RandomForest	0.643	0.653	0.664	0.632	0.635	0.642
K*	0.633	0.631	0.629	0.635	0.631	0.633
Bagging	0.628	0.633	0.641	0.62	0.634	0.627
LogitBoost	0.61	0.617	0.629	0.597	0.619	0.607

Table 2: Classification of only the "incorrect" categories by removing the "pages in a different language" and "unsure" categories

	Precision	Recall	F-Measure
Decorate	0.824	0.833	0.824
RandomCommittee	0.759	0.781	0.765
RotationForest	0.82	0.826	0.813
RandomForest	0.798	0.807	0.793
K*	0.767	0.785	0.767
Bagging	0.778	0.781	0.758
LogitBoost	0.79	0.8	0.784

6. EVALUATION

One of the main difficulties of the type of our study is finding a way to compare the results obtained using machine learning algorithms against the assessment made by humans. For this purpose, we carried out a user study where human subjects were asked to analyze the contents of Web documents and assess if these documents belonged to a specific collection.

The user study was administered through the Web using a Django [27] backend. In the user study, participants were asked to go over fifty randomly selected documents (25 correct and 25 incorrect) from the ACM corpus that we described in section 3. More specifically, participants were shown a screenshot of the Web document along with its corresponding anchor text – which was extracted form the ACM Digital Library – and a brief questionnaire that was aimed towards identifying the degradation of a document and its possible causes. In the end, we collected data from 62 participants – mostly upper-level Computer Science undergraduates – and assessed the validity of 2875 pages.

Interestingly, the study participants did not have difficulties identifying documents in the correct category. However, this was not the case in the other categories. Table 3 shows a summary of the user responses for the document classification. Documents in the correct category were correctly identified in 71% of the cases, but users were not able correctly identify the documents that were incorrect. Surprisingly, documents in the "error page" category were incorrect identified in 98% of the cases. Similar scenarios occurred with documents were it was evident that the documents are incorrect, such as in the "domain for sale" and "hello world" categories. The identification did marginally improve in less evident cases, for example in the "deceiving", "kind of correct" and "not correct" categories. Our analysis indicates that the language of the text and explicit error codes did not influence the user responses. On the other hand, layout, presentation and content of the documents were significant factors in the classification. We also analyzed the amount of time users took to classify documents, but we could not find any statistical evidence that would shed insights to support their choices and decisions.

At this point, the question that remains to be answered is whether the classification algorithms perform better than the human subjects. The answer to this question is two-fold: we believe that the algorithms performed more consistently. However, human subjects were able to identify pages in the correct category slightly better than the algorithms, but failed when asked to identify pages in the incorrect categories. On the other hand, the machine learning algorithms outperformed human subjects when identifying pages in the incorrect categories. Table 4 shows a comparison between the classification by humans and the algorithms. The difference in performance is significant, which for us is a clear indication that managing the effects of unexpected changes in collections of Web documents is a more serious problem than we had originally anticipated.

Table 3: User responses for the document classification in the user study by categories. Shaded: Correct – Not Shaded: Incorrect

	Correct	Error	Deceiving	Hello World	Kind of Correct	Not Correct	Domain for Sale	University
Very Much	456	54	99	54	242	56	59	59
Somewhat	567	5	32	7	299	80	5	37
Undecided	74	0	10	7	45	17	3	10
Not Really	178	0	21	0	75	13	5	14
Not At All	163	1	29	4	63	13	6	13
Total	1438	60	191	72	724	179	78	133
Correctly Identified %	0.71	0.02	0.31	0.15	0.25	0.24	0.18	0.28
Incorrectly Identified %	0.29	0.98	0.69	0.85	0.75	0.76	0.82	0.72

Table 4: Comparison between the classifications made by human subjects and the classification algorithms.

Classification	Human Subjects		Algorithms	
	Correct	Incorrect	Correct	Incorrect
Precision	0.71	0.24	0.64	0.65
Recall	0.48	0.46	0.66	0.63
F-measure	0.58	0.32	0.65	0.64

7. DISCUSSION

The analysis of the conference website links within the ACM Digital Library shows that institutional archives are not immune to some of the challenges of distributed collection management – which include unexpected changes within the contents of its documents. Knowing when changes to a resource require human attention is not a simple problem. Only once such an assessment has been made can we apply techniques to recover or replace a broken resource.

As we have stated before, some of our findings align with previous work. We coincide that upon our initial assessment, 404 HTTP errors were more prevalent in our corpus. However, upon further inspection we found that 36% of the pages that were supposed to be correct as reported by their HTTP response code were actually incorrect. For us this is a clear indication that the correctness of a web page is relative and that there is a growing need for methods to categorize and locate likely problematic resources that might require the attention of collection managers.

As the categorization of changes to the collection shows, determining the degree of change affecting a digital collection over time is a difficult task. A web resource may gradually degrade from being correct to one that is still of some use by providing access to related information or information about the institution to contact for more information. Changes in web servers, directory structures, etc. may cause requests to still result in a successful 200 code from the server yet provide no information to the requestor. A number of these categories were purposely left out of the evaluation of the classification algorithms as these cases can be handled by previous work. More specifically, detecting "blank pages", "failed redirects", "directory listings", "domain for sale" and "error pages" are handled with previous work on identifying Soft 404 error pages [6, 28].

Being able to distinguish between the "kind of correct" and "deceiving" pages is important to collection managers. A contribution of our research is detecting when documents change unexpectedly and fall into more problematic categories such as "kind of correct" and "deceiving pages".

This last point lead us to investigate and inquiry: Why are the documents in the "deceiving pages" category created? Although the pages in this category are very diverse in content and presentation, they do share two characteristics. First, the number of links that point to other pages within the site is much greater than the number of out-links. On average, pages in the "deceiving" category had 66 links, which is more than twice the average in the "correct" and "kind of correct" categories (20 and 27 links respectively). And second, the domain names that host these pages once belonged to a reputable institution for number of years (i.e., a conference series) before being abandoned. Consequently, these abandoned domain names have value – not necessarily due to current network traffic but in the perception of their authority/validity. We could hypothesize that these pages are created to manipulate PageRank scores by utilizing a large number of links from a page that once had a high PageRank, but

have been taken over by a third party. This problem becomes increasingly interesting when we consider that the cost of creating a web page is small and that some search engines (most notably Google) do not share the overall rankings for their indexed sites, which can lead some parties to abuse these malicious techniques. Examining the variation of other features across categories of change may provide additional insight into the motivations and characterizations of change.

Another potential source of information for identifying the severity of change is web archival services. We explored use of such archives but chose to leave them out of the current approach. In the specific case of the ACM conference list, some conference sites were not crawled at all. Thus, archival services would have provide us with an incomplete index that would not have allowed us to fully answer the research questions for this paper. Additionally, irregular crawling intervals and data embargoes can reduce the value of information from such archives for timely identification of change.

Our research is on investigating methods to detect unexpected changes in Web documents within a collection. However, the degree of change that we are focusing on falls within a specific range: not as subtle as a few terms substitutions in the body of a Web page and not to cause servers to report errors explicitly. Our analysis focused on the instances that fall between these two extreme cases, which makes their detection more difficult and require the assistance of a classification system and detection framework such as the one that we have described in this paper.

It was not surprising for us that the documents in the "correct" category were more consistently identified during the user study. However, now that data collection phase of the study is over and its results are analyzed, we believe that the premises we established were influential towards its outcome. In this study, subjects were operating under the assumption that they were identifying and categorizing conference websites. Therefore, we hypothesize that the nature of these sites – being institutional and backed up by professional and academic organizations – might have led the subjects to believe that the documents were in the "correct" category despite showing explicit symptoms of change. This effect could potentially explain the incorrect classification of some of the documents the "incorrect categories"; most notably the ones in the "domain for sale", "hello world" and other categories that displayed explicit error codes and content in different languages – which were clear indications of their incorrectness.

There is a wide range of follow-on work related to the classification problem explored here. We limited our approach to features that could be computed quickly with a minimal number of HTTP requests per collection resource. A pragmatic direction of future work is to develop a software package that combines approaches for determining when HTTP error-codes are likely temporary or permanent, recognizing Soft 404 responses, detecting Web spam, and categorizing the remaining changed pages as described here.

8. ACKNOWLEDGMENTS

This work was supported in part by National Science Foundation grants DUE–0840715 and DUE–1044212.

9. REFERENCES

[1] M. Kobayashi and K. Takeda, "Information retrieval on the web," *ACM Computing Surveys,* vol. 32, pp. 144-173, 2000.

[2] M. K. Taylor and D. Hudson, "" Linkrot" and the Usefulness of Web Site Bibliographies," *Reference & User Services Quarterly,* pp. 273-277, 2000.

[3] P. Logasa Bogen, D. Pogue, F. Poursardar, Y. Li, R. Furuta, and F. Shipman, "WPv4: a re-imagined Walden's paths to support diverse user communities," in *Proceedings of the 11th annual International ACM/IEEE Joint Conference on Digital Libraries*, Ottawa, Ontario, Canada, 2011, pp. 419-420.

[4] P. L. Bogen, R. Furuta, and F. Shipman, "A quantitative evaluation of techniques for detection of abnormal change events in blogs," presented at the Proceedings of the 12th ACM/IEEE-CS joint conference on Digital Libraries, Washington, DC, USA, 2012.

[5] L. Francisco-Revilla, F. Shipman, R. Furuta, U. Karadkar, and A. Arora, "Managing change on the web," in *Proceedings of the 1st ACM/IEEE-CS Joint Conference on Digital Libraries*, Roanoke, Virginia, United States, 2001.

[6] L. Meneses, R. Furuta, and F. M. Shipman, "Identifying "Soft 404" Error Pages: Analyzing the Lexical Signatures of Documents in Distributed Collections," in *Proceedings of Theory and Practice of Digital Libraries 2012*, Paphos, Cyprus, 2012.

[7] L. Meneses, H. Barthwal, S. Singh, R. Furuta, and F. Shipman, "Restoring Semantically Incomplete Document Collections Using Lexical Signatures," in *Research and Advanced Technology for Digital Libraries*. vol. 8092, T. Aalberg, C. Papatheodorou, M. Dobreva, G. Tsakonas, and C. Farrugia, Eds., ed: Springer Berlin Heidelberg, 2013, pp. 321-332.

[8] R. Baeza-Yates, I. Pereira, and N. Ziviani, "Genealogical trees on the web: a search engine user perspective," in *Proceedings of the 17th international conference on World Wide Web*, Beijing, China, 2008.

[9] H. Ashman, "Electronic document addressing: dealing with change," *ACM Computing Surveys,* vol. 32, pp. 201-212, 2000.

[10] H. C. Davis, "Hypertext link integrity," *ACM Computing Surveys,* vol. 31, p. 28, 1999.

[11] B. Kahle, "Preserving the Internet," *Scientific American,* vol. 276, pp. 82-83, March 1997 1997.

[12] W. Koehler, "Web page change and persistence---a four-year longitudinal study," *Journal of the American Society for Information Science and Technology,* vol. 53, pp. 162-171, 2002.

[13] D. Spinellis, "The decay and failures of web references," *Communications of the ACM,* vol. 46, pp. 71-77, 2003.

[14] T. A. Phelps and R. Wilensky, "Robust Hyperlinks Cost Just Five Words Each," University of California at Berkeley2000.

[15] S.-T. Park, D. M. Pennock, C. L. Giles, and R. Krovetz, "Analysis of lexical signatures for improving information persistence on the World Wide Web," *Transactions on Information Systems,* vol. 22, pp. 540-572, 2004.

[16] M. Klein, J. Ware, and M. L. Nelson, "Rediscovering missing web pages using link neighborhood lexical signatures," in *Proceedings of the 11th annual international ACM/IEEE Joint Conference on Digital libraries*, Ottawa, Ontario, Canada, 2011.

[17] Z. Dalal, S. Dash, P. Dave, L. Francisco-Revilla, R. Furuta, U. Karadkar*, et al.*, "Managing distributed collections: evaluating web page changes, movement, and replacement," in *Proceedings of the 4th ACM/IEEE-CS Joint Conference on Digital Libraries*, Tuscon, AZ, USA, 2004, pp. 160-168.

[18] M. Nelson and D. Allen. (2002, January 2002) Object Persistence and Availability in Digital Libraries. *D-Lib Magazine.*

[19] W. Koehler, "A longitudinal study of Web pages continued: a consideration of document persistence," *Information Research,* vol. 9, 2004.

[20] D. H. L. Goh and P. K. Ng, "Link decay in leading information science journals," *Journal of the American Society for Information Science and Technology,* vol. 58, pp. 15-24, 2007.

[21] F. McCown, S. Chan, M. L. Nelson, and J. Bollen, "The availability and persistence of web references in D-Lib Magazine," *arXiv preprint cs/0511077,* 2005.

[22] L. Page, S. Brin, R. Motwani, and T. Winograd, "The PageRank citation ranking: Bringing order to the web," Stanford University1999.

[23] D. M. Blei, A. Y. Ng, and M. I. Jordan, "Latent dirichlet allocation," *the Journal of machine Learning research,* vol. 3, pp. 993-1022, 2003.

[24] C. M. Bishop, *Pattern recognition and machine learning* vol. 1: springer New York, 2006.

[25] I. H. Witten and E. Frank, *Data Mining: Practical machine learning tools and techniques*: Morgan Kaufmann, 2005.

[26] M. Hall, E. Frank, G. Holmes, B. Pfahringer, P. Reutemann, and I. H. Witten, "The WEKA data mining software: an update," *ACM SIGKDD explorations newsletter,* vol. 11, pp. 10-18, 2009.

[27] (2/20/2016). *The Web framework for perfectionists with deadlines | Django.* Available: https://djangoproject.com

[28] Z. Bar-Yossef, A. Z. Broder, R. Kumar, and A. Tomkins, "Sic transit gloria telae: towards an understanding of the web's decay," in *Proceedings of the 13th international conference on World Wide Web*, New York, NY, USA, 2004.

There is Something Beyond the Twitter Network

Andrzej Pacuk
Institute of Informatics,
University of Warsaw, Poland
apacuk@mimuw.edu.pl

Piotr Sankowski
Institute of Informatics,
University of Warsaw, Poland
sank@mimuw.edu.pl

Karol Węgrzycki
Institute of Informatics,
University of Warsaw, Poland
k.wegrzycki@mimuw.edu.pl

Piotr Wygocki
Institute of Informatics,
University of Warsaw, Poland
wygos@mimuw.edu.pl

ABSTRACT

How information spreads through a social network? Can we assume, that the information is spread only through a given social network graph? What is the correct way to compare the models of information flow? These are the basic questions we address in this work.

We focus on meticulous comparison of various, well-known models of rumor propagation in the social network. We introduce the model incorporating mass media and effects of absent nodes. In this model the information appears spontaneously in the graph. Using the most conservative metric, we showed that the distribution of cascades sizes generated by this model fits the real data much better than the previously considered models.

CCS Concepts

•Computing methodologies → Simulation evaluation; •Information systems → Content analysis and feature selection; •Applied computing → Sociology;

Keywords

Social networks;Social Network Analysis;Information Diffusion;Cascades Size Distribution;Twitter

1. INTRODUCTION

Sociology, empirical investigation, critical analysis, social policy, political science and market analysis—it is just the beginning of the long list of research areas focused on the information diffusion. Today, when more and more communication can be tracked and logged, those fields of research can benefit from the analysis of the social networks. The research on the information diffusion can be applied to maximize the influence [12] and virality of the rumor, enhancing recommender systems or improving routing algorithms [8].

HT '16, July 10 - 13, 2016, Halifax, NS, Canada

© 2016 Copyright held by the owner/author(s). Publication rights licensed to ACM.
ISBN 978-1-4503-4247-6/16/07...$15.00

DOI: http://dx.doi.org/10.1145/2914586.2914623

Current, state-of-the-art models of the information diffusion do not correctly predict the distribution of cascades sizes [7] (the cascade size is the number of nodes sharing a given information). Application of these models in the aforementioned areas can lead to a hardware overload, non-optimal recommendations erroneous predictions about influence. In this work we claim that, the main problem is the fact that the information does not diffuse only in the known social network. Namely, there is something beyond the easily observable relations. Our analysis on the Twitter network has showed that the information spreads not only by the known connections of acquaintance. To model the information diffusion one needs to incorporate effects of inoculating a rumor by absent nodes, different social networks, mass media or a word of mouth. All effects might be responsible for spawning the rumor by nodes that are not connected in social network. We introduce the *multi-source* α^k model, that can be expressed as an extension to the standard *compound Poisson process*. This model incorporates the spontaneous rumor inoculation in the simple information diffusion model. The application of such well based method allows us to tune the cascade size distribution to a real data with almost no cost in the time complexity.

The contribution of this work is to propose a simple, replicable metric and an anonymised dataset to provide the measurable comparison between information diffusion models. Moreover, we provide the efficient source code to evaluate basic models [18]. Finally, we claim that the Kolmogorov-Smirnov (K-S) test should be used to collate distributions of information cascades sizes. Based on that test, we showed that the effects of mass media are substantial to model the information diffusion.

1.1 Related Work

The dynamics of an information flow in social networks has been studied by numerous researchers (see e.g., [7, 19, 14]).

Originally, the epidemiology and the solid-state physic areas suggested different models such as SIR (susceptible infectious recovered) or SIS (susceptible infectious susceptible). These models had been employed to predict dynamics of information spread. However, all of these models assume that everyone in the population is in the contact with everyone else [2], which is unrealistic in the large social network.

The classical example of a modified spreading process has been considered in [1] by adding the effect of *stifler*. *Stiflers* never spread the information, even if they were exposed to it multiple times. Nevertheless, *stiflers* can actively convert spreaders or susceptible nodes into *stiflers*. Nevertheless, it is unclear who would act as a *stifler* in the fast news propagating network like Twitter or Digg.

Leskovec et al. [15] proposed the cascade generation model and simulated it on the dataset of blog links. Their model assumed that every connection in the information propagation graph is equally important and used a single parameter that measures infectiousness of an average rumor. Then, they acknowledge a simple improvements in their model of the cascade generation. Most notably, they noted that exponential decrease of the infectiousness can also be considered to model the information spread.

Collaterally, researchers have analyzed properties of the social network graph [9, 1] and the distribution of the cascades sizes (or rumor popularities) [10]. Today, it is well known, that cascades sizes follow a heavy tail distribution [14] but due to the lack of appropriate data it is still unclear, whether it follows the power-law (Pareto) or the lognormal distribution.

Since then, computer scientists noticed that the state-of-the-art rumor propagation models do not predict such distribution. Steeg et al. [19] observed that information propagates onto an entire graph too often and Cui et al. [7] showed an evident phase transition for middle sized rumors. However, those observations lack the systematized metric to compare predictions with the real cascade size distribution. In this work we claim that K-S test is the most conservative benchmark for testing these features. Moreover, we propose that every experiment ought to be meticulously tested to avoid misinterpretations.

2. MODELING INFORMATION CASCADES

2.1 Comparison Metric and Evaluation

Since heavy tailed distribution of cascade sizes had been observed, there has been some attempts to readjust the diffusion models to the real data [7, 19]. Unfortunately, none of them has proposed an adequate metric to measure this distribution.

It is tempting to propose a metric that would somehow punish errors on a tail of distribution (in contrary to exponential distribution, the large events do happen more often in the power-law distribution). Another naive idea is to assume that the power-law distribution is linear on a log-log plot and use the linear regression to fit it. Unfortunately, Clauset et al. [6] claim that both of those methods have serious problems with variation and many distributions might be misclasified by these metrics.

The method of analyzing a power-law distributed data should [6] involve goodness-of-fit test. The most commonly used is Kolmogorov-Smirnov test (K-S test):

$$\sup_x |X(x) - Y(x)|,$$

which computes the maximal difference between cumulative distribution functions (CDF) of a real and predicted distributions ($X(x)$ is the CDF of a predicted data and $Y(x)$ the CDF of a real data). Recently, Bild et al. [3] showed that using the aforementioned methods, the lifetime of a tweet does not follow the Pareto distribution but in fact it is the type-II discrete Weibull distribution.

Introducing models with multiple parameters may lead to

the serious overfitting. When one introduces a flexible model like ICM [11], one needs to carefully analyze the model to avoid overfitting. It might be tempting to use machine learning approach based on the large number of features. This might result in a better fit to the real distribution of cascades sizes. On the other hand, the reasoning based on this approach can be hard. In this paper, we focus on the models that describe the fundamental mechanisms of the information diffusion.

The analysed models are trained using grid search. We chose the parameters, so the empirical error of K-S test is smaller than 0.001.

2.2 Dataset Description

We analyzed the set of over 500 million tweets, extracted from 10% sample of Twitter tweets collected from May 19 to May 30 2013. In our dataset, each tweet beside the content of the tweet contained hashtags list, user id and if existed ids of the mentioned users, retweeted user id and id of the user this tweet was a reply to.

Based on that, we generated the graph of retweets: the vertices in graph are user ids that occurred in our dataset. If there exists a tweet with user A retweeting, replying or mentioning user B, then we add an edge from vertex A to B. The graph of retweets contained 71 million vertices and 230 million edges.

The popularity of the hashtag is the number of users that had used it. Recall, that our goal is to analyze the information diffusion on social network. Hence, we have focused merely on fresh hashtags: we keep hashtags that did not occur during the first day of our sample. The specific day used as the first day for new hashtags should not influence the results of the tests, because the majority of the cascades last less than few days [13]. Finally, we obtained 7.7 million of distinct, fresh hashtags. Based on these hashtags, we generated popularity distribution, that will be used to compare models of information diffusion.

The graph of retweets strongly depends on the number of gathered events. Be aware that the parameters of the presented algorithms depend on the specific retweet graph. The parameters for graph produced from all events from a given month will be probably different. For example, in the introduced models, the probability that an individual will retweet decreases with the density of the graph. On the other hand, we need general models independent from the instance of the network. A standard approach to avoid overfitting is to divide the set of tweets into two independent subsets: the training set used for tuning parameters and the test set used for the validation. We divided the set of the retweets into two sets each containing half of the available, consecutive, full days. We evaluated model α, model α^k and multi-source α^k on both training and test sets. The grid search shows that the optimal parameters for training and test set are identical. The K-S test values for both sets are identical up to 0.001 error. Overall ranking of the models is not changed. Hence, our analysis is not prone to overfitting. To achieve better precision, through the rest of the work, we use the graph based on all events.

To promote the study on information diffusion we share our dataset with other researchers [17]. We have removed unnecessary parameters and anonymized our dataset according to the Twitter rules regarding public sharing.

2.3 The Graph of Retweets versus the Follower-Followee Graph

There is another choice of information dissemination graph, namely, the follower-followee graph. Bild et al. [3] claim, that people are more selective in what they say, rather than whom they listen. Moreover, Bild et al. [3] assert that the graph of retweets may encode the true interest among the users better than follower-followee graph. Since the cascades consist of interactions, the graph of retweets seems to be a better choice than the follower-followee graph. Note that follower-followee relationship is perturbed by a Twitter recommendation system. Altogether, we believe that the graph of retweets describes the relationships between the users much better than the follower-followee graph. Moreover, the current retweet graph can be obtained by using the Twitter API [20]. Unfortunately the up-to-date, follower-followee graph is currently unavailable.

2.4 Cascade Generation Model

The *cascade generation model* (CGM) introduced by [15] uses constant α, which is the probability that the information is passed from a user to its follower.

According to [15] the cascade is generated in the following steps:

1. Uniformly at random pick a starting point of the cascade and add it to the set of *newly informed* nodes.

2. Every *newly informed* node, for each of his direct neighbors makes a separate decision to inform the neighbor with the probability α.

3. Let *newly informed* be the set of nodes that have been informed for the first time in step 2 and add them to the generated cascade.

4. Add all *newly informed* nodes to the generated cascade.

5. Repeat steps 2 to 4 until *newly informed* set is empty.

In CGM regime all nodes have an identical impact ($\alpha = $ const). The final graph of the information spread is called a cascade.

2.5 Model Alpha

CGM is modeling communication with all connected nodes independently. That is, in the step 2, newly informed node might potentially pass the information only to some subset of its acquaintances. However, Twitter is a microblogging platform where messages posted by a user are instantly received by all of its followers. Then, each follower may share these messages with his followers by replying, retweeting or mentioning.

We propose the *model* α which resembles the CGM, but is better suited for the schemes of communication in the Twitter network. The single cascade of *model* α is generated as follows

1. Uniformly at random pick a starting point of the cascade and add it to the set of the *newly informed* nodes.

2. Every *newly informed* node independently with the probability α becomes a *spreader* and then informs all their direct neighbors.

3. Let *newly informed* be the new set of nodes that have been informed for the first time in step 2.

4. Add all new *spreading* nodes to the generated cascade.

5. Repeat the steps 2 to 4 until the *newly informed* set is empty.

Indeed, the *model* α differs from CGM:

- The main difference is in the point 2., where in the *model* α the newly informed node makes a single decision: either to inform all of his followers or to inform none of them.

- In the CGM nodes might had multiple chances to become a spreader (after receiving an information from each of the followed nodes). However, in the model α, each of the informed nodes has just one chance to become a spreader: only after being informed for the first time.

- The final cascade size is the total number of spreaders, whereas in CGM it is the number of informed nodes.

2.5.1 Experimental Results

We simulated model α on the graph of retweets. We used *grid search* algorithm with step 0.0001 to tune parameter α. Subsequently, for every α we ran 10 million simulations to generate the cascades size distribution. Then we computed K-S test for each distribution. The best K-S test 0.0447 was achieved for $\alpha = 0.0884$. Our experiments show that roughly 4% of cascades in this model are larger than 10 000. On the other hand, in the real data, the large cascades constitute 0.01% of all cascades. This amount of the large cascades is the main reason for such low K-S test result of the model α. Hence, we need a model in which the number of extremely large cascades is heavily reduced.

2.6 Exponential Model

Twitter rumors have a limited lifetime. The information obeys the effect: the further from source, the lower the virality of the information. *Model* α^k will simulate that process by decreasing the infectiousness of the information after each round. The only difference from *model* α is decreasing probability of becoming a spreader:

- In the first round each neighbor of a initial vertex is informed and then with probability α becomes the spreader.

- During the round no. k each previously, not informed neighbor of the new spreaders from the round $k - 1$ is informed and subsequently, with probability α^k becomes a spreader.

2.6.1 Experimental Simulations of Exponential Model

Once again, we conducted simulations on Twitter retweets graph. We used *grid search* algorithm with step 0.0001 to tune parameter α. For each α we performed 10 million simulations and then we computed K-S test on each distribution versus real distribution. For $\alpha = 0.1357$ we obtained the best K-S test value 0.0207 which is roughly the half of the value of model α. The K-S test value is mostly affected by the probabilities of a few smallest cascades sizes. Namely, in *model* α^k 74.2% of cascades have size 1, versus 76.2% in the real data.

2.7 Multi-source Exponential Model

The exact structure of the connections between all people in the world is unknown. It can be modeled by the graph of followers [4] or the graph of retweets [7], which can successfully approximate the real connections. Because of existence of mass media, absent nodes or communications through channels unavailable for researchers such as telephones, private conversations or emails, sometimes the information emerges somehow randomly in the new source nodes.

We have a graph with extremely many nodes n. Moreover, probability p that a randomly selected node will spread the information it was not informed of, through our network is ridiculously low. Hence, the number of spreaders that get to known the information from a different source can be modeled by the Binomial distribution:

$$X \sim \mathrm{B}(n, p).$$

However, by the law of rare events, this can be approximated by Poisson distribution:

$$X \sim \mathrm{Pois}(np).$$

Of course here, we assume that we do not consider globally known rumors, where probability p is not that low (e.g., the information concerning a soccer match TV transmission, where Twitter users share the exceptional achievements through a social network).

We can model the information diffusion as follows:

- Randomly choose the first node that will be informed.

- Propagate the information using the *model* α^k from the previous section.

- Until there are new, informed nodes, in each round randomly choose $X \sim \mathrm{Pois}(\lambda)$ new source nodes and propagate information from those nodes by *model* α^k.

This model has one additional parameter λ which is interpreted as the expected number of nodes randomly informed in each round. Leskovec et al. [15] show that, the single-sourced cascades very rarely collide with each other. Hence, if one assumes that all cascades are disjoint, then the final rumor size can be approximated by the sum of the cascades sizes. Procedure MULTISOURCEALPHAEXP(α, λ) (see Algorithm 1) computes the size of random rumor, where:

- RANDOMALPHAEXPCASCADE(α) returns properties (the total size and the number of rounds) of a random cascade generated by *model* α^k.

- RANDOMPOISSON(λ) gives a random integer from $\mathrm{Pois}(\lambda)$.

The distribution of cascade properties (pairs of the total size and the number of rounds) generated by the *model* α^k can be precomputed. So choosing the random cascades will take $O(1)$ time. Hence, the time complexity of Algorithm 1 is $O(t(\lambda + 1))$, where t is the expected number of rounds. However, for sufficiently large values of λ the algorithm may not stop.

Now, the results of multi-source α^k model can be reformulated as:

$$X_0 + Y(t) = X_0 + \sum_{i=1}^{N(t)} X_i = \sum_{i=0}^{N(t)} X_i,$$

Algorithm 1 Model multi-source α^k

procedure MULTISOURCEALPHAEXP(α, λ)
  (size, rounds) ← RANDOMALPHAEXPCASCADE(α)
  for curr_round ← 1 to rounds **do**
    for i ← 1 to RANDOMPOISSON(λ) **do**
      (s, r) ← RANDOMALPHAEXPCASCADE(α)
      size ← size + s
      rounds ← max(rounds, curr_round + r)
    end for
  end for
  return size
end procedure

---

where:

- t is a total number of rounds in a single simulation.

- Cascades sizes $X_i : i \geq 0$ are independent random variables from a distribution generated by *model* α^k.

- $N(t) \sim \mathrm{Pois}(t\lambda)$ is a *Poisson process* with rate λ.

Such definition of $Y(t)$ is called *compound Poisson process*. Because we always start with the initial cascade, *multi-source model* α^k is a simple extension of this process.

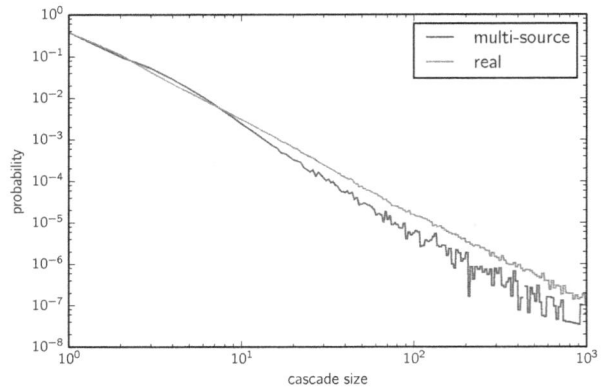

Figure 1: The cascade sizes distribution for multi source α^k. The data was bucketized into buckets of logarithmic size to reduce variance (as suggested in [16])

2.7.1 Experimental Simulations

Based on the Algorithm 1, we simulated *multi-source model* α^k on the Twitter retweets graph. We conducted an effective *grid search* algorithm over parameters α and λ with step size 0.0001. For each pair of parameters we run 10 million simulations to obtain a cascade size distribution. Finally, for them, we computed K-S test. The minimal value of K-S test 0.0116 was obtained for $\alpha = 0.1215$ and $\lambda = 0.1850$. The K-S test value is roughly the half of the value for model α^k. The results for $\lambda = 0.0$ are the same as the results of model α^k, since $\lambda = 0.0$ implies that we generate only a single source of an information.

On Figure 1 one can see the comparison of the real distribution of cascades sizes and the distribution generated by multi-source model α^k for the best pair of parameters α and λ.

3. DISCUSSION AND FUTURE WORK

The observation that rumor popularity follows the power-law enables researchers to precisely model the information diffusion in the social network. Here, we showed that simple, one parameter models are insufficient. These models produce cascades either extremely large or small. That phenomenon is known as the *phase transition* [7]. Gradually decreasing infectiousness of the information over time prevents this problem and results in more accurate predictions.

Our main contribution is that the rumor can spread through a different, unknown media. We proposed to model it by informing random nodes in the network. This improvement significantly boost the estimated distribution of cascade size. Finally, it demonstrates that the underlaying network of the social interactions is much more complex than just the graph of retweets and the study on the new ways of estimating it needs more attention.

Based on the observations made by Leskovec et al. [15] regarding the cascade collisions, we proposed the method based on the *compound Poisson process*. This enables us to produce accurate multi-sourced cascades with a very little cost. Moreover, this technique significantly lowered the simulation time.

We present the final results and comparison of these models in Table 1. On Figure 2 we have shown the comparison between the CDFs computed for different models. Recall, that the K-S test responds to the maximal difference of the CDFs. The best K-S test value is obtained for the multi-source α^k model. In order to speed up simulation of model α, we have truncated simulations of 4% of largest cascades. Cutting off these cascades does not change the final K-S test results, because in the real cascade size distribution the probability that the size of a cascade is larger than $1\,000$ is less than 0.001.

Table 1: The K-S test comparison of the discussed models with the real cascade size distribution (log-log scale).

Model	K-S test
Model α	0.0447
Model α^k	0.0207
Model multi-source α^k	0.0116

To obtain even more accurate results, one would need to incorporate more complex effects, for example:

- Geographically close nodes might be informed through an unknown social network. Close nodes should be informed with higher probability than distant [21].

- The probability of randomly informing a node may decrease in time because the information may become obsolete [7].

- The evolution of the social network structure within time [5].

As mentioned in Section 2.2, the probability of spreading the information (i.e., parameter α in the model α) decreases

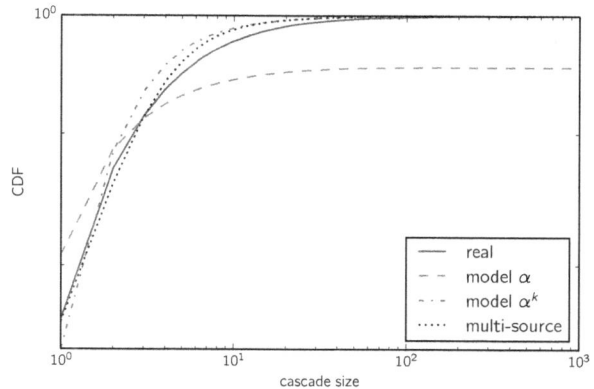

Figure 2: The comparison of CDFs for the discussed models.

with the size of the graph of retweets. It would be very interesting to investigate the dependence between the model parameters and the density of the graph of retweets. Moreover, it would be interesting to study the growth rate of the graph of retweets.

We have published the gathered data [17] and the efficient source code for simulating the basic models [18].

4. ACKNOWLEDGMENTS

This work was supported by ERC StG project PAAl-POC 680912 and FET project MULTIPLEX 317532. We would also want to thank Stefano Leonardi for sharing the data and Rafał Latała for meaningful discussions.

5. REFERENCES

[1] M. Barthelemy, A. Barrat, and A. Vespignani. The role of geography and traffic in the structure of complex networks. *Advances in Complex Systems*, 10(1):5–28, 2007.

[2] N. Bayley. The mathematical theory of epidemics. *Griffin, London*, 1975.

[3] D. R. Bild, Y. Liu, R. P. Dick, Z. M. Mao, and D. S. Wallach. Aggregate characterization of user behavior in twitter and analysis of the retweet graph. *ACM Trans. Internet Techn.*, 15(1):4:1–4:24, 2015.

[4] P. Brach, A. Epasto, A. Panconesi, and P. Sankowski. Spreading rumours without the network. In A. Sala, A. Goel, and K. P. Gummadi, editors, *Proceedings of the second ACM conference on Online social networks, COSN 2014, Dublin, Ireland, October 1-2, 2014*, pages 107–118. ACM, 2014.

[5] C. Brandt and J. Leskovec. Status and friendship: mechanisms of social network evolution. In C. Chung, A. Z. Broder, K. Shim, and T. Suel, editors, *23rd International World Wide Web Conference, WWW '14, Seoul, Republic of Korea, April 7-11, 2014, Companion Volume*, pages 229–230. ACM, 2014.

[6] A. Clauset, C. R. Shalizi, and M. E. J. Newman. Power-law distributions in empirical data. *SIAM Review*, 51(4):661–703, 2009.

[7] B. Cui, S. J. Yang, and C. Homan. Non-independent cascade formation: Temporal and spatial effects. In J. Li, X. S. Wang, M. N. Garofalakis, I. Soboroff, T. Suel, and M. Wang, editors, *Proceedings of the 23rd ACM International Conference on Conference on Information and Knowledge Management, CIKM 2014, Shanghai, China, November 3-7, 2014*, pages 1923–1926. ACM, 2014.

[8] A. Gaba, S. Voulgaris, K. Iwanicki, and M. van Steen. Revisiting gossip-based ad-hoc routing. In *WiMAN 2012: Proceedings of the 6th International Workshop on Wireless Mesh and Ad Hoc Networks*, Munich, Germany, July 2012. IEEE.

[9] R. Ghosh and B. A. Huberman. Ultrametricity of information cascades. *CoRR*, abs/1310.2619, 2013.

[10] J. L. Iribarren and E. Moro. Branching dynamics of viral information spreading. *CoRR*, abs/1110.1884, 2011.

[11] D. Kempe, J. Kleinberg, and E. Tardos. Maximizing the spread of influence through a social network. In *Proceedings of the Ninth ACM SIGKDD International Conference on Knowledge Discovery and Data Mining*, KDD '03, pages 137–146, New York, NY, USA, 2003. ACM.

[12] D. Kempe, J. M. Kleinberg, and É. Tardos. Maximizing the spread of influence through a social network. In L. Getoor, T. E. Senator, P. M. Domingos, and C. Faloutsos, editors, *Proceedings of the Ninth ACM SIGKDD International Conference on Knowledge Discovery and Data Mining, Washington, DC, USA, August 24 - 27, 2003*, pages 137–146. ACM, 2003.

[13] H. Kwak, C. Lee, H. Park, and S. Moon. What is twitter, a social network or a news media? In *Proceedings of the 19th International Conference on World Wide Web*, WWW '10, pages 591–600, New York, NY, USA, 2010. ACM.

[14] K. Lerman and R. Ghosh. Information contagion: An empirical study of the spread of news on digg and twitter social networks. In W. W. Cohen and S. Gosling, editors, *Proceedings of the Fourth International Conference on Weblogs and Social Media, ICWSM 2010, Washington, DC, USA, May 23-26, 2010*. The AAAI Press, 2010.

[15] J. Leskovec, M. McGlohon, C. Faloutsos, N. S. Glance, and M. Hurst. Patterns of cascading behavior in large blog graphs. In *Proceedings of the Seventh SIAM International Conference on Data Mining, April 26-28, 2007, Minneapolis, Minnesota, USA*, pages 551–556. SIAM, 2007.

[16] S. Milojevic. Power law distributions in information science: Making the case for logarithmic binning. *JASIST*, 61(12):2417–2425, 2010.

[17] A. Pacuk, K. Wegrzycki, and P. Wygocki. Retweet graph. http://social-networks.mimuw.edu.pl/data/, 2016.

[18] A. Pacuk, K. Wegrzycki, and P. Wygocki. Rumor spreading. https://github.com/approx-uw/rumor_spreading/, 2016.

[19] G. V. Steeg, R. Ghosh, and K. Lerman. What stops social epidemics? In L. A. Adamic, R. A. Baeza-Yates, and S. Counts, editors, *Proceedings of the Fifth International Conference on Weblogs and Social Media, Barcelona, Catalonia, Spain, July 17-21, 2011*. The AAAI Press, 2011.

[20] twitter.com. Twitter api. https://dev.twitter.com/rest/public, 2016.

[21] R. West, R. W. White, and E. Horvitz. Here and there: goals, activities, and predictions about location from geotagged queries. In G. J. F. Jones, P. Sheridan, D. Kelly, M. de Rijke, and T. Sakai, editors, *The 36th International ACM SIGIR conference on research and development in Information Retrieval, SIGIR '13, Dublin, Ireland - July 28 - August 01, 2013*, pages 817–820. ACM, 2013.

Exploring Maintenance Practices in Crowd-Mapping

Giovanni Quattrone
Dept. of Computer Science
University College London, UK
g.quattrone@cs.ucl.ac.uk

Martin Dittus
Dept. of Computer Science
University College London, UK
martin.dittus.11@ucl.ac.uk

Licia Capra
Dept. of Computer Science
University College London, UK
l.capra@ucl.ac.uk

ABSTRACT

Crowd-mapping is a form of collaborative work that empowers users to gather and share geographic knowledge. OpenStreetMap is one of the most successful examples of such paradigm, where the goal of building a global map of the world is collectively performed by over 2M contributors. Despite geographic information being intrinsically evolving, little research has so far gone into analysing maintenance practices in these domains. In this paper, we perform a preliminary exploration to quantitatively capture maintenance dynamics in geographic crowd-sourced datasets, in terms of: the extent to which different maintenance actions are taking place, the type of spatial information that is being maintained, and who engages in these practices. We apply this method to 117 countries in OSM, over one year of mapping activity. Our findings reveal that, although maintenance practices vary substantially from country to country in terms of how widespread they are, strong commonalities exist in terms of what metadata is being maintained and by whom.

Keywords

Maintenance work; collaboration practices; OpenStreetMap; crowd-sourcing; volunteered geographic information

1. INTRODUCTION

Crowd-sourcing has become a successful paradigm for knowledge gathering, where a crowd is mobilised to collect and maintain large repositories of information [11, 3]. The most successful example to date of this paradigm is Wikipedia, with its online community of editors that voluntarily contribute to build and maintain the whole body of knowledge. Another type of knowledge where crowd-sourcing has been widely applied is that of volunteered geographic information, with citizens becoming surveyors, in council-monitoring applications like FixMyStreet;[1] local reporters, as powered by Ushaidi's Crowdmap;[2] and cartographers, in geo-wikis like

[1] http //www.fixmystreet.com/

[2] http //www.ushahidi.com/products/crowdmap

HT '16, July 10-13, 2016, Halifax, NS, Canada

© 2016 ACM. ISBN 978-1-4503-4247-6/16/07... $15.00

DOI: http://dx.doi.org/10.1145/2914586.2914621

Cyclopath[3] and OpenStreetMap.[4] It is the latter type of knowledge that we are interested in this paper.

Research has developed methods to quantitatively analyse the accuracy [2, 5, 6, 7, 8, 9, 17], coverage [27, 8, 18], growth [25], and bias [27, 12, 8, 24] of volunteered geographic information. These methods have mainly been applied to OpenStreetMap, making this dataset probably the most widely and deeply investigated geographic information repository to date. However, there is currently a gap in terms of methods to quantitatively capture *maintenance practices* in geographic crowd-sourcing communities like OpenStreetMap. Geographic information is naturally volatile and always evolving (e.g., where a grocery store is today, a coffee shop might be tomorrow); indeed, companies like Google spend several billions of dollars each year just to maintain their proprietary maps up-to-date and to improve their accuracy.[5] Yet little is known about maintenance practices of geographic crowd-sourced information: whether maintenance takes place at all and, if so, about what, and by whom.

In order to analyse maintenance practices in spatial crowd-sourced datasets, we have developed a method that quantitatively captures: *(i)* the different types of maintenance actions that take place (i.e., enrichment vs. correction vs. removal of existing information), and how widespread they are; *(ii)* what type of spatial objects (e.g., schools, hospitals, restaurants) are being maintained; and *(iii)* who is mostly engaged in maintenance practices. We have applied this method to OpenStreetMap, analysing one year of mapping activity in 117 different countries. Our findings reveal that maintenance practices vary substantially from country to country, both in terms of their adoption and in terms of the type of spatial objects that are being maintained. However, there are strong commonalities in terms of the metadata that is being maintained and who engages in maintenance practice. Based on these quantitative findings we elaborate on the implications of relevance to those interested in crowd-sourcing spatial information.

2. RELATED WORK

Maintenance practices have been extensively studied in online self-organised communities, most especially Wikipedia. In this domain, researchers often refer to collaborative practices, rather than maintenance ones, intended as the editing activity performed by different editors on the same Wikipedia article, for example to update its content or to improve its quality.

In Wikipedia, collaboration has been studied from two main different perspectives: *(i)* the information that is being maintained;

[3] http://cyclopath.org/

[4] http://www.openstreetmap.org/

[5] http://www.wired.com/2014/12/google-maps-ground-truth

and *(ii)* who performs this practice. We review some of the works in each of these themes next.

What information is being maintained. Kaltenbrunner and Laniado analysed the evolution over time of maintenance practices on different topics in Wikipedia [13]. They found that Wikipedia is the most up-to-date encyclopaedia ever seen, and that maintenance is often triggered by external events, with ongoing events being often edited and discussed on Wikipedia nearly in real-time. On the other hand, articles about historical or scientific facts (i.e., those that are not on people's minds) may take years to reach similar levels of user attention.

Who engages in collaboration practices. A study conducted by Laniado and Tasso [15] described the evolution of the user collaboration network in Wikipedia. They found that there exists a nucleus of very active contributors, who seem to spread over the whole wiki, and who interact preferentially with inexperienced users. Other studies that focused on users and their collaborative practices found that the top Wikipedia editors are those who are more involved in article maintenance, revising already existing articles, using quality assurance systems, and invoking community norms [10, 23].

Maintenance/collaboration practices is an active research area also for volunteered geographic information (VGI); however, in this context, current research is mainly investigating how to design tools to facilitate collaboration practices in crisis mapping [1, 4, 14] and little research has gone into analysing these practices more generally. As we shift our attention from encyclopaedic knowledge to spatial knowledge, different collaboration practices may be adopted. In fact, geographic repositories differ from classic encyclopaedic ones in two fundamental ways: *space* and *time*. Specifically, geographic content has an intrinsic spatial dimension, and there is a relationship between the location of a contributor and the type of knowledge that she can offer. Furthermore, compared to the body of knowledge that repositories like Wikipedia maintain, most geographic content is intrinsically volatile and continuously evolving, as a result of natural processes, such as urbanisation. As the nature of content varies, so might the corresponding editing practices. Indeed, a study conducted a few years ago by Mashhadi et al. [19] showed that some properties that typically hold in encyclopaedic type of crowd-sourcing repositories like Wikipedia, do not hold in geographic ones such as OpenStreetMap; for example, it was found that, in the former, the quality of an article depends on how much editing experience its contributors had in the past, while no relationship was found between quality of the map and editing experience of mappers in OSM.

In this paper, we aim to cover this gap, by proposing a method to quantitatively capture maintenance practices in spatial crowd-sourced datasets. Before presenting the method itself, and reporting on the results obtained, we first briefly illustrate the dataset we chose for analysis, provide a working definition of maintenance over such dataset, and spell out the research questions our method aims to answer.

3. DATASET

We chose to apply our method to OpenStreetMap (hereafter OSM), as this is to date the most successful example of spatial crowd-sourced dataset, having been running since 2004, and comprising the largest (and most geographically widespread) user and content base. Furthermore, OSM has been subject to extensive research, so that we can relate our findings to previous studies.

The OSM dataset is freely available to download[6] and contains the history from 2006 of all edits (over 2.7 billions) performed by

---

[6]http://www.geofabrik.de/data/download.html

all users (over 2 millions) on all spatial objects. In OSM jargon, spatial objects can be one of three types: *nodes*, *ways*, and *relations*. Nodes are single geo-spatial points and typically represent Points-of-Interest (POIs); ways mostly represent roads (as well as streams, railway lines, and the like); finally, relations are used for grouping other objects together, based on logical (and usually local) relationships (e.g., bus routes).

We filter the data in a number of ways before we begin our analysis. Specifically, we restricted our attention to edits of POIs only, i.e., specific point locations described in OSM by latitude/longitude coordinates, plus a variety of attributes (or tags). By focusing on this subset of OSM objects (instead of ways and relations), we aim to capture the actions of a wide range of contributors, from casual mappers to highly-engaged ones; indeed, as Mooney and Corcoran describe: "*Editing or adding tags to objects in OSM is technically one of the simplest operations which contributors can perform as there is very good support in all of the software and web-based editors for this edit action*" [20]. In OSM, a POI edit is represented as a tuple:

$$\langle uid, changeset, tstamp, ver, lat, lon, taglist \rangle$$

where uid identifies the user who performed this edit; $changeset$ denotes the editing session within which this edit was performed; $tstamp$ is the timestamp of when this edit took place; ver is a sequential value indicating the edit version of this POI (i.e., $ver = 1$ indicates the POI has just been created, while $ver > 1$ indicates the current edit is an update (i.e., maintenance) of an already existing POI); lat and lon denote the geographic coordinates of the POI. Finally, $taglist$ contains an arbitrary list of attribute-value pairs that further describe the POI; examples of such attributes are 'name' (e.g., 'Hollywood Cafe'), 'amenity type' (used to distinguish between different categories of POIs, such as 'restaurant', 'pubs', 'school'), address details, opening hours, accessibility considerations, and so on. For the purpose of this study, we consider POIs to be all OSM nodes that have either a *name* or an *amenity* tag at any point in the relevant period.[7] Finally, we ignored the tag *created_by*, as this is added automatically by editing software and does not reflect user intent.

The second pruning step we performed was time-based. We wanted to avoid the initial phase of OSM, when almost all contributions are creations of new objects, with little to no maintenance work taking place. We thus extracted all POI edits from January 1st to December 31st 2014.

From the above dataset, we make an attempt to identify contributions by human editors, while discarding automated contributions representing bulk data imports. In some regions, a significant portion of OSM contributions are automated imports of public domain map data sets, often produced by national mapping organisations or derived from historic map data.[8] While such data can play an important role in filling gaps on the map, it was not produced by the OSM community of volunteer contributors, and is not representative of human maintenance practices, which is the subject of this study. Imports are not explicitly marked as such in the OSM dataset; we thus needed heuristics to identify them. We applied the same approach used in [24], and marked as imports those edits which came from a single user, in very large quantities (i.e., more than one thousand edits), in a short period of time (i.e., less than one hour), and that were spread over a large geographic area (i.e., in the scale of a whole city).

The final part of this pruning process is to select the geographical

---

[7]http://wiki.openstreetmap.org/wiki/Map_Features
[8]http://wiki.openstreetmap.org/wiki/Import

areas of the world to analyse. We chose to study maintenance practices at country level. From the above sample, we discard countries with too little OSM editing activity to be meaningfully analysed (i.e., countries with less than one thousand contributions during the period of study). We ended up with a dataset having around 3.4M edits, of 2.7M POIs, done by 80k users, over the 117 countries highlighted in Figure 1.

Figure 1: Map of the 117 Countries Under Analysis

4. FORMS OF MAINTENANCE

In order to quantitatively analyse maintenance of OSM information (and, more specifically, OSM POIs), we first need to automatically identify edits, in the OSM edit history, that are representative of such practice. We simply classify as maintenance actions all edits with $ver > 1$. Preliminary analysis shows that the time interval between two consecutive edits ($ver = n$ and $ver = n + 1$) is one week or longer for 90% of such edits, and that different users perform them.

We then distinguish three different forms of information maintenance, based on the type of *action* that took place since the POI previous version:

- *Add*, maintenance work where at least one new tag has been added to an existing POI (e.g., the tag 'opening_hours', along with its associated value, has been added to a restaurant already mapped in OSM).

- *Update*, maintenance work where the value of at least one of the already existing tags associated with a POI has been updated (e.g., the value of the tag 'amenity' has been changed from 'restaurant' to 'cafe', for a POI previously added to OSM).

- *Remove*, maintenance work where at least one tag has been deleted from an existing POI (e.g., the tag 'is_in', along with its associated value, has been removed from a POI present in OSM).

Note that the same edit may belong to different action classes (e.g., a single edit can both add a tag and update another). In our study, we will analyse them separately, as the drivers behind such actions can be quite different, and might thus result in different practices. In fact, intuitively, an add action can be seen as a sign of the user intent to *enrich* existing information, and it might be spurred by the emergence of novel location based services that require semantically richer POI information (e.g., opening hours, webpage). Conversely, an update action can be seen as a sign of the user intent to *correct* existing information; this may be the case for POIs that were last edited a long time ago, and thus now contain stale information (e.g., different business name or type), or the

case for POIs whose name contains spelling mistakes. Finally, a remove action can be seen as a sign of the user intent to *polish* existing information; this may be the case for POIs that contain some deprecated tags.

5. RESEARCH QUESTIONS

In this work, we aim to explore the following research questions:

RQ1 (Spread) – How widespread is maintenance work? We begin our exploration by looking at the extent to which such practice is currently taking place across the 117 countries under exam.

RQ2 (What) – What information is being maintained? We then look more specifically at the type of information that is being maintained, to elicit POI information that is commonly maintained across all countries, if any, as well as potential regional differences.

RQ3 (Who) – Who is engaged in information maintenance? We finally shift our attention to the users performing maintenance edits, to understand whether this practice is evenly shared among editors, or whether it is undertaken by a select few.

To answer these questions we defined new metrics and conducted a large-scale quantitative analysis of maintenance practices of over 80k OSM mappers spread across 117 different countries.

6. METRICS AND RESULTS

RQ1 – How widespread is maintenance?

For each country under exam, we compute a *Maintenance Ratio* (MR), defined as the proportion of maintenance work that took place there, relative to the total number of edits (i.e., covering both creation and maintenance of POIs), for the period of study. Formally, let OSM_e be the set of OSM edits for a given country, and $OSM_m \subseteq OSM_e$ the set of OSM edits devoted to maintaining existing POIs. Then $MR = \frac{|OSM_m|}{|OSM_e|}$, $MR \in [0, 1]$. Intuitively, the closer this metric is to 1, the higher the proportion of maintenance work in that country (in 2014); vice versa, values close to zero indicate that almost all OSM editing activity is devoted to the creation of new POIs.

Table 1 shows the computed MR values in the 117 countries under exam, divided in quartiles. Maintenance practices vary widely: in a quarter of the analysed countries, maintenance is almost as frequent as the creation of new POIs ($MR > 0.42$), while there is another quarter of countries where maintenance is a much less widespread practice ($MR < 0.23$). There are also a few countries (e.g., Malawi, Mozambique, and Togo) where MR is almost zero, meaning that, in these countries, crowd workers are almost completely focused on the addition of new POIs, rather than in the maintenance of existing ones.

Min	1st Qu.	Median	3rd Qu.	Max.	Freq. Distr
0.02	0.23	0.33	0.42	0.77	

Table 1: Summary Statistics of Maintenance Ratio in the 117 Analysed Countries

To visualise where maintenance practices are taking place and to what extent, we report in Figure 2 a heatmap of MR values in the 117 analysed countries. Note that maintenance ratio is high

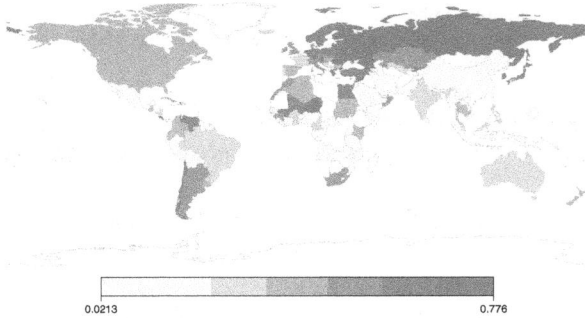

Figure 2: Maintenance Ratio in all Analysed Countries

	Min	1st Qu.	Median	3rd Qu.	Max.	Freq. Distr
AA^{add}	0.14	0.42	0.52	0.59	0.88	
AA^{update}	0.07	0.24	0.32	0.38	0.75	
AA^{remove}	0.03	0.08	0.11	0.18	0.47	

Table 2: Summary Statistics of Action Adoption in the 117 Analysed Countries, divided by Adds, Updates, Removes

both in countries with a long-standing OSM history (e.g., United Kingdom, Germany), and in countries where OSM activity started much later (e.g., Niger, Paraguay). Conversely, we find low values of MR in countries that joined OSM relatively recently (e.g., Peru, Angola), but also in countries that have had intense OSM activity for many years (e.g., France).

This result is somewhat surprising, as one might hypothesise that maintenance is a direct consequence of map maturity; that is, crowd workers first concentrate on adding information to a near empty map, and only later, as the map becomes richer and denser of information, crowd work starts to move towards maintaining what is already there. This phenomenon does hold, but only to a certain extent: we computed the number of OSM POIs mapped in a country, normalised by the area of the country, as proxy of OSM map maturity; we then computed the Spearman correlation [21] between such proxy and MR. As expected, we did obtain a positive correlation ($\rho = 0.39$, p-value < 0.001), meaning that maintenance practices are more widespread in countries where OSM map maturity is higher. However, the strength of the correlation is not very high. We hypothesise that a variety of local factors may play an important role in the rapid uptake of maintenance practice; for example, initiatives like the Humanitarian OpenStreetMap Team (HOT) may have fostered maintenance activities in countries with lower-than-average map maturity, in order to rapidly update the map following a natural disaster [22]. Also, rapid urbanisation in some regions may have caused faster than usual changes in the physical world, with consequent maintenance activity taking place on the digital map.

As different underlying phenomena may trigger maintenance work, we were interested in observing possibly different forms of maintenance (i.e., add, update or removal tags), when such practice does take place. To this purpose, we define a new metric, *Action Adoption* AA^{act} as the number of maintenance edits of type $act \in \{add, update, remove\}$ over the total number of maintenance edits that occurred in a country. Formally, let OSM_m be the set of OSM edits devoted to maintaining existing POIs, then $AA^{act} = \frac{|OSM_m^{act}|}{|OSM_m|}$, where $OSM_m^{act} \subseteq OSM_m$ is the set of OSM edits of action act over the initial set OSM_m. $AA^{act} \in [0, 1]$; a value of such metric close to 1 means that almost all maintenance edits are of action act, and vice versa.

Table 2 illustrates quartiles of the Action Adoption AA^{act} metric, $act \in \{add, update, remove\}$, binned over the 117 analysed countries. Results across all quartiles show that the add action (i.e., enriching existing information) is the most common one, usually more common than the update and remove actions combined (i.e.,

correcting existing information); furthermore, when correcting existing information, it is usually the case of updating an existing tag, rather than removing any. While this is the most common way of performing maintenance across the countries under exam, we also observe a big variance of the AA^{act} metric between the first and fourth quartiles, in each row (action) of Table 2 (i.e., AA^{add} ranges from 0.14 to 0.88, AA^{update} ranges from 0.07 to 0.75, and $AA^{removal}$ from 0.03 to 0.47). This suggests that there exist countries that do not follow the previously mentioned pattern. Indeed, we performed a manual investigation of some such cases and found that, for example, in Haiti, Turkey, and Niger the removal of tags is the most frequent maintenance practice performed; in Oman, Costa Rica and Azerbaijan, the updating of tags values is most frequent action instead.

RQ2 – What information is being maintained?

To understand if different types of POIs call for different levels of maintenance, we grouped POIs in each country according to their amenity type (e.g., restaurant, school, hospital, etc.). For each POI type, we then computed the corresponding Maintenance Ratio (MR) metric. We found a very skewed distribution in each country, with a minority of POI types (less than 10% of all types) being frequently maintained, and several hundreds of POI types receiving near zero maintenance instead. We then looked more closely into the frequently maintained ones, to see if there were commonalities among the analysed countries. Surprisingly, we found almost no overlap, with each country having a distinct set of POI types it maintains. For example, in the Netherlands, the most maintained POI types are 'restaurant', 'cafe' and 'place_of_worship', while in Russia the most maintained ones are 'clinic', 'dentist' and 'public_building'. Although we do not know the cause, this result signals that different countries maintain distinct types of spatial information.

We then moved our attention from the types of spatial objects that are being maintained, to the set of *tags* that are being maintained, regardless of the POI type they refer to. To this purpose, we define *Tag Adoption* $TA_t^{act} = \frac{adoption_t^{act}}{|OSM_m^{act}|}$ as the ratio of the number of times tag t has been used for a certain action ($adoption_t^{act}$) over the total number of times action act occurred ($|OSM_m^{act}|$). $TA_t^{act} \in [0, 1]$; high values of TA_t^{act} indicate that tag t has been frequently used when act took place (e.g., tag 'addr:street' has been frequently used during an 'add' maintenance practice), and vice versa.

We computed Tag Adoption TA_t^{act} in each of the 117 countries under exams, for different maintenance actions $act \in \{add, update, remove\}$. We also computed this metric for the 'creation' action (i.e., when a POI is added to the map for the first time), to serve as a baseline. As for the case of POI types, in each country and for each action, we found a very skewed distribution, with only a minority of tags (less than 5%) being frequently edited. However, contrary to what we found for POI types, when zooming into this group of frequently edited tags, we found significant overlaps across countries. Table 3 reports both the name of the tags most frequently edited, and the number of countries in which such tags appeared in the list of the 5% most edited ones; the table further

Creation		Maintenance	
Adding a tag		Adding a tag	
Tag	# Countries	Tag	# Countries
name	117	name	108
amentiy	114	addr:street	44
place	78	addr:city	43
shop	64	wikipedia	31
addr:street	42	addr:housenumber	29
source	38	name:en	27
addr:city	31	addr:postcode	26
highway	22	source	24
addr:housenumber	21	operator	24
natural	16	name:ru	24

Maintenance			
Updating a tag		Removing a tag	
Tag	# Countries	Tag	# Countries
name	117	name	79
place	106	amenity	70
amenity	78	source	28
opening_hours	52	fixme	27
wikipedia	45	highway	26
shop	39	place	24
addr:street	31	building	21
source	30	note	18
name:en	27	is_in	16
website	24	wikipedia:en	16

Table 3: Top Ten Globally Adopted Tags for Each Action

NumEdts		ActDays	
Class	# Users	Class	# Users
(0,1]	25,235	(0,1]	50,177
(1,10]	36,295	(1,5]	20,442
(10,100]	15,335	(5,10]	4,074
(100,1k]	3,927	(10,100]	6,100
(1k,10k]	606	(100,1k]	605

Table 4: Summary Statistics of Classes of Users

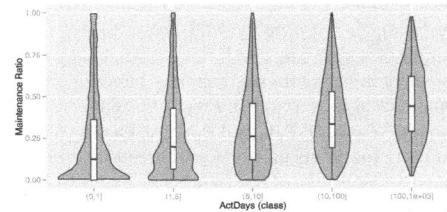

Figure 3: ActDays Vs. Maintenance Ratio

distinguishes between a creation edit (top left of Table 3) and the three different types of maintenance edits (add, update, remove). For readability, only the top ten most globally adopted tags for each action are reported.

Although we cannot be sure of the rationale for these tags to be globally maintained, we can draw some interesting observations. As an example, let us consider the *addition* of tags – which, as seen before, is by far the most frequently performed maintenance practice worldwide. Aside from adding names to POIs that did not have one before, this practice seems to focus on address details (e.g, 'addr:street', 'addr:city', 'addr:housenumber', 'addr:postcode'). This corroborates the intuition that information maintenance is often subject to external drivers, such as the integration of location-based services over the base map,[9] which do require address information to operate effectively.

RQ3 – Who engages in information maintenance?

We finally move our attention from what information is being maintained to who takes charge of performing maintenance work. Previous studies of OSM have shown that there exists a small set of highly engaged (expert) users who are responsible for the majority of the mapping [24]; we wanted to investigate whether the very same users were also those taking charge of maintenance work. One might expect this to be the case for various reasons, ranging from motivation (i.e., the same drivers that make them map extensively may also drive them to maintain extensively), to knowledge (e.g., having previously contributed a lot of information, they might know what information is most stale and in need of updates), to skills (e.g., updating existing information may require users to have acquired a certain skill-set first, as was observed in other crowd sourcing communities like Wikipedia [16, 23, 26]).

To do so, we first grouped users within each country into five different classes of engagement (or expertise). We measured user's engagement using two alternative proxies: *(i) NumEdts*, that is their total number of OSM edits; and *(ii) ActDays*, that is the number of days during which they performed OSM editing activity.

---

[9]https://blog.openstreetmap.org/2015/02/16/routing-on-openstreetmap-org/

Summary statistics of the number of users per each class, across all countries, are reported in Table 4.

We computed the Maintenance Ratio (MR) metric defined before, but on a per user basis rather than on a per country basis. Figure 3 shows the quartiles (in yellow) and the frequency distributions (in green) of MR for each class of users according to the metric $ActDays$. Similar results were obtained when we grouped users according to the metric $NumEdts$. These results show that the more experienced the users are, the more effort they devote to maintaining existing POIs compared to the effort they spend to edit new ones.

7. CONCLUSION

In this paper, we have proposed a method to quantify maintenance work carried out in knowledge production communities, where knowledge has a distinct spatial nature, and where it naturally evolves over time. We have applied our method and metrics to OpenStreetMap in particular, one of the most successful examples of geographic crowd-sourced datasets. Our study of maintenance of OpenStreetMap POIs across 117 countries has revealed that such practice varies substantially from country to country, both in terms of its adoption, and in terms of the type of POIs that are being maintained. It has also revealed that, while the POI types that are being maintained differ, the tags that are being added/updated/removed are common across many countries. Our study also revealed that some maintenance actions, such as the addition of new tags to existing spatial objects, are more frequent than other actions, such as the updating or the removal of tags. At the moment, these maintenance actions are prevalently done by highly active users.

From a theoretical perspective, this work has presented a method to make visible the otherwise hidden maintenance practices of self-organised communities of practice interested in gathering and maintaining geographic knowledge. We have applied this method to a specific community and data type (OpenStreetMap and its POIs). However, we believe the same method can be used to study other data types within OpenStreetMap (e.g., ways and relations), as well as other crowd-mapping platforms, such as CrowdMap and FixMyStreet, for comparative studies. The method can also be reapplied to the same community and data type over time, in order to capture changes in behaviour, for example, as might be induced by major updates of the tools offered to support this practice.

8. REFERENCES

[1] J. Anderson, R. Soden, K. M. Anderson, M. Kogan, and L. Palen. EPIC-OSM: A Software Framework for OpenStreetMap Data Analytics. In *2016 49th Hawaii International Conference on System Sciences (HICSS)*, pages 5468–5477. IEEE, 2016.

[2] J. Arsanjani, C. Barron, M. Bakillah, and M. Helbich. Assessing the Quality of OpenStreetMap Contributors together with their Contributions. In *Proc. of AGILE*, 2013.

[3] D. Brabham. *Crowdsourcing*. MIT Press, 2013.

[4] M. Dittus, G. Quattrone, and L. Capra. Analysing volunteer engagement in humanitarian mapping: building contributor communities at large scale. In *Proc. of CSCW*. ACM, 2016.

[5] H. Fana, A. Zipfa, Q. Fub, and P. Neisa. Quality assessment for building footprints data on OpenStreetMap. *International Journal of Geographical Information Science (IJGIS)*, 28(4):700âĂŞ–719, 2014.

[6] J. Girres and G. Touya. Quality assessment of the French OpenStreetMap dataset. *Transactions in GIS*, 14(4):435–459, 2010.

[7] M. Goodchild. Citizens as Sensors: the World of Volunteered Geography. *GeoJournal*, 69(4):211–221, 2007.

[8] M. Haklay. How good is volunteered geographical information? A comparative study of OpenStreetMap and Ordnance Survey datasets. *Environment and Planning B: Planning and Design*, 37(4):682–703, 2010.

[9] M. Haklay, S. Basiouka, V. Antoniou, and A. Ather. How Many Volunteers Does it Take to Map an Area Well? The Validity of Linus Law to Volunteered Geographic Information. *The Cartographic Journal*, 47(4):315–322, 2010.

[10] A. Halfaker, R. Geiger, J. Morgan, and J. Riedl. The Rise and Decline of an Open Collaboration System: How Wikipedia's reaction to sudden popularity is causing its decline. *American Behavioral Scientist*, 57(5):664–688, 2013.

[11] J. Howe. The Rise of Crowdsourcing. *Wired*, 2006.

[12] K. Ishida. Geographical Bias on Social Media and Geo-local Contents System with Mobile Devices. In *Proc. of HICSS*, pages 1790–1796, 2012.

[13] A. Kaltenbrunner and D. Laniado. There is no deadline: time evolution of wikipedia discussions. In *Proceedings of the Eighth Annual International Symposium on Wikis and Open Collaboration*, page 6. ACM, 2012.

[14] M. Kogan, J. Anderson, R. Soden, K. M. Anderson, and L. Palen. Collaboration in OpenStreetMap: A Network Analysis of Two Humanitarian Events. In *Proc. of CHI*, 2016.

[15] D. Laniado and R. Tasso. Co-authorship 2.0: Patterns of collaboration in wikipedia. In *Proceedings of the 22nd ACM conference on Hypertext and hypermedia*, pages 201–210. ACM, 2011.

[16] J. Liu and S. Ram. Who does what: Collaboration patterns in the wikipedia and their impact on article quality. *ACM Transactions on Management Information Systems (TMIS)*, 2(2):11, 2011.

[17] I. Ludwig, A. Voss, and M. Krause-Traudes. A Comparison of the Street Networks of Navteq and OSM in Germany. *Advancing Geoinformation Science for a Changing World*, 1(2):65–84, 2011.

[18] A. Mashhadi, G. Quattrone, and L. Capra. Putting ubiquitous crowd-sourcing into context. In *Proceedings of the 2013 conference on Computer supported cooperative work*, pages 611–622. ACM, 2013.

[19] A. Mashhadi, G. Quattrone, L. Capra, and P. Mooney. On the accuracy of urban crowd-sourcing for maintaining large-scale geospatial databases. In *Proceedings of the Eighth Annual International Symposium on Wikis and Open Collaboration*, page 15. ACM, 2012.

[20] P. Mooney and P. Corcoran. Analysis of Interaction and Co-editing Patterns amongst OpenStreetMap Contributors. *Transactions in GIS 2013*, 2013.

[21] J. Myers and A. Well. *Research Design and Statistical Analysis (2nd ed.)*. Routledge, 2003.

[22] L. Palen, R. Soden, T. J. Anderson, and M. Barrenechea. Success & scale in a data-producing organization: The socio-technical evolution of openstreetmap in response to humanitarian events. In *Proceedings of the 33rd annual ACM conference on human factors in computing systems*, pages 4113–4122. ACM, 2015.

[23] K. Panciera, A. Halfaker, and L. Terveen. Wikipedians are born, not made: a study of power editors on wikipedia. In *Proceedings of the ACM 2009 international conference on Supporting group work*, pages 51–60. ACM, 2009.

[24] G. Quattrone, L. Capra, and P. De Meo. There's no such thing as the perfect map: Quantifying bias in spatial crowd-sourcing datasets. In *Proceedings of the 18th ACM Conference on Computer Supported Cooperative Work & Social Computing*, pages 1021–1032. ACM, 2015.

[25] G. Quattrone, A. Mashhadi, D. Quercia, C. Smith-Clarke, and L. Capra. Modelling growth of urban crowd-sourced information. In *Proceedings of the 7th ACM international conference on Web search and data mining*, pages 563–572. ACM, 2014.

[26] D. M. Wilkinson and B. A. Huberman. Assessing the value of coooperation in wikipedia. *arXiv preprint cs/0702140*, 2007.

[27] D. Zielstra and A. Zipf. A Comparative Study of Proprietary Geodata and Volunteered Geographic Information for Germany. In *Proc. of AGILE*, 2010.

Classification of Twitter Accounts into Targeting Accounts and Non-Targeting Accounts[*]

Hikaru Takemura[†]
Graduate School of Informatics
Kyoto University
Sakyo, Kyoto 606-8501 Japan
takemura@dl.kuis.kyoto-u.ac.jp

Keishi Tajima
Graduate School of Informatics
Kyoto University
Sakyo, Kyoto 606-8501 Japan
tajima@i.kyoto-u.ac.jp

ABSTRACT

In this paper, we propose a method for classifying Twitter accounts into *non-targeting accounts*, which post messages to the general public, and *targeting accounts*, which post messages to specific people. For example, an account posting general news information is a non-targeting account, while an account posting announcements to members of a specific organization is a targeting account. An account posting information on very specific minor topic, and an account used for communication with friends, are also targeting accounts. Our method finds some properties that are common to most followers of a given account, and calculate how much a user set with such a consistency deviates from a random sample from the given universe of users (e.g., the set of all Twitter users in some country). If it largely deviates, the account is a targeting account. We use two types of properties of followers: (1) terms in their metadata and (2) their followees. The result of our experiment shows that one of our methods, which computes two scores based on these two types of properties and combines them using SVM, achieves the accuracy 0.944, and outperforms the baselines.

Keywords

microblog; social network; target users; user intention; target specificity; target diversity

1. INTRODUCTION

Twitter is the most popular microblogging service of today. In Twitter, accounts can *follow* (i.e., subscribe) other accounts. In this paper, we call those who follow some account *followers* of the account, and we call those followed by some account *followeEs* of the account.

Twitter is used for various purposes. News companies use it for disseminating latest news to the general public, while some organizations use it to post announcements to their members. It is also used for communication with friends, and there are also accounts used for public discussion on specific topics with anyone interested in the topics.

Among the four examples above, only news companies are targeting the general public, and accounts in the other three examples are targeting specific people. We call the former type of accounts *non-targeting accounts*, and call the latter type of accounts *targeting accounts*. Accounts in the second and third examples are targeting accounts because they target concrete already-known people: members of the organizations and friends of the owners. On the other hand, the accounts in the fourth example do not have particular people in their minds, but they target people that are interested in some specific topics. In other words, targets in the second and third examples are extensionally specified, while targets in the fourth example are specified only intentionally. Another example of accounts targeting any users that are interested in a specific topic is @ACMHT, which is targeting people interested in ACM Hypertext Conference.

Of course, the meaning of "the general public" depends on the context. For example, we explained that news media accounts target the general public, but even news media accounts usually target people in some specific countries. Therefore, if we regard the set of all Twitter users in the world as the general public, they are targeting very specific people. However, when we focus only on Twitter users in some specific country, news media accounts in that country are targeting the general public. As shown in this example, the distinction of targeting accounts and non-targeting accounts depends on what user set is regarded as the universe. We assume that the universe is specified appropriately by the users who want the classification result depending on their purpose of the classification. It may be the set of all active Twitter accounts in some country, and it may be the set of all accounts within a given distance from a focused account in the Twitter network.

In this paper, we propose a method for classifying Twitter accounts into targeting accounts and non-targeting accounts based on how specific their target audiences are. We assume that the current set of followers of an account is a sample set of the target audience intended by it, and approximate how specific the intended target is by measuring how unusually consistent the current follower set is. We find properties that are common to most of the followers, and calculate how much a user set with such a consistency deviates from a random sample from the given universe of Twitter users.

[*]This work was supported by JSPS Kakenhi 26540163.

[†]Currently at FOLIO, Inc.

HT '16, July 10 - 13, 2016, Halifax, NS, Canada

© 2016 Copyright held by the owner/author(s). Publication rights licensed to ACM.
ISBN 978-1-4503-4247-6/16/07...$15.00

DOI: http://dx.doi.org/10.1145/2914586.2914639

If it largely deviates, i.e., if most of the current followers unusually have some properties in common, we determine that the account is targeting some specific kind of people. Otherwise, the account is non-targeting account.

We developed several variations of our method, which use two types of properties of followers: (1) terms in their metadata and (2) their followeEs. We conducted an experiment on a data set created by randomly sampling Twitter accounts, and manually classifying them into targeting and non-targeting accounts. One of our methods that combines two scores computed from the two types of properties above achieved the accuracy 0.944.

Our classification method has several applications. Information on distinctive properties of the target audience intended by an account is useful for recommendation of accounts to follow [4, 3, 12, 16, 2, 8, 6, 1]. If a candidate account is a non-targeting account, the similarity between its current followers and the target user of the recommendation is not important. Even when a candidate is a targeting account, if its followers have only one property in common, only that property is important for the recommendation.

Our method is also useful when we evaluate the quality (not popularity) of Twitter accounts because we should not simply compare the number of followers of non-targeting accounts and those of accounts targeting very specific people.

Our method can also be used in tweet search systems. When users submit a query "iPhone 6s" to a tweet search system, they may want public news about it, may want technical information about it, or may want to know how ordinary users are talking about it. In such a case, we can classify messages by classifying their authors with our method.

2. RELATED WORK

There have been many studies on the classification of Twitter users based on their purpose of using Twitter. Java et al. [7] analyzed the topological and geographical structure of Twitter's follow network and found that there are three types of accounts in Twitter: information sources, information seekers, and friends. Kwak et al. [9] also reported that Twitter is used both as a social network service and as a media for disseminating or gathering information. Wu et al. [14] proposed a method for classifying Twitter users into elite users (celebrities, media, organizations, blogs) and ordinary users. They use the information on "lists" (a function of Twitter for classifying one's followeEs). These studies distinguish information disseminating/gathering users and communication users. On the other hand, we classify information disseminating users further into targeting users and non-targeting users.

Yan et al. [15] proposed a method for classifying Twitter users into open accounts and closed accounts. Their classification is similar to but not the same as ours. In their definition, open accounts disseminate information to the general public, while closed accounts tweet to a certain accounts for communication. Their classification includes two factors: unidirectional information dissemination or bidirectional communication, and targeting the general pubic or specific people. In our definition, however, these two factors are orthogonal. For example, an account posting announcements directed to students of an university is disseminating information unidirectionally to specific people. We classify such an account as a targeting account, but they classify organizations posting announcements as open accounts [15].

In our previous papers [11, 10], we proposed a method of classifying follow links based on the purpose of the followers. We proposed three axes for classifying follow links, and one of the axes corresponds to classification based on whether the followeE can be replaced with another account posting similar information or not. If the follower is simply interested in information in the tweets, the followeE can be replaced with another account posting similar information, but if the follower is interested in the followeE user itself, it cannot be replaced with any other account even if it posts very similar information. This classification is related to whether the follower has a specific user in his mind. In the papers [11] and [10], however, we focused on the intention of the followers, while in this paper we focus on the intention of the opposite side, i.e., the intention of users who post messages. In addition, in our previous papers, we classify follow links while in this paper we classify accounts.

There is also research on estimating influential power of Twitter accounts [13, 5]. Influential power is related to the size of the audience but our target-specificity reflects the diversity of the audience. For example, a popular sports news company must have greater influential power than a minor general news company, but is more target-specific.

To the best of our knowledge, there has been no research on measuring target specificity of Web pages. Target specificity of Web pages is harder to estimate than that of Twitter accounts because we cannot know the detailed profiles of visitors of each Web page, while we can know various information on the followers of a Twitter account.

3. OUR CLASSIFICATION METHOD

As explained before, we measure target specificity of an account by finding some unusually common properties of its followers, and measuring how much a user set with such a consistency deviates from a random sample from the given universe of users. In this section, we explain the details.

3.1 Measuring Unusual Consistency of Sets

We first explain our basic strategy for measuring unusual consistency of a set of followers. Notice that high target specificity in our definition does not imply that the followers are similar to each other in all respects. For example, most followers of an account of a local news company must have one common property, the area of residence, but these followers must include all kinds of people, who are dissimilar to each other in the other aspects. In our definition, this account of a local news company has high target specificity.

Figure 1 (a) shows a case where most followers have a common property A. If A is not so common in the whole universe, this set has high specificity. On the other hand, Figure 1 (b) shows a case where no property is common to more than half of the followers, but all the followers are covered by only two properties A and B. If A and B are not so common in the whole universe, this follower set should also be regarded as a very specific audience.

Following this intuition, we define $c(S)$, *unusual consistency* of a set S, based on how well S is covered by a small number of unusual properties. For every property X found in S, we compute $S_X = \{e \in S | e \text{ has the property } X\}$. For each S_X, we also compute its score $s(S_X, S)$ representing how unusual it is for S to include a subset that is as consistent as S_X. The details of $s(S_X, S)$ will be explained later, but $s(S_X, S)$ becomes large when S_X is large and X

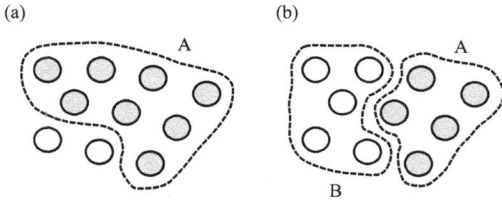

Figure 1: Two cases of sets with high specificity.

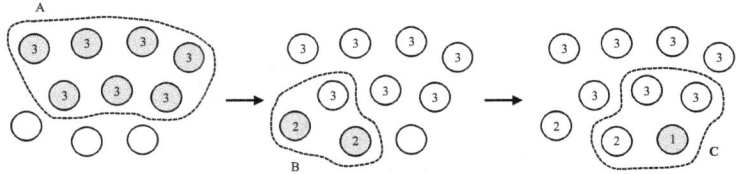

Figure 2: Computation of $c(S)$.

is rare in S. We then compute the score of each $e \in S$ by $\max(\{s(S_X, S) \mid e \in S_X\})$. Finally, $c(S)$ is defined by the average score of all elements of S.

Figure 2 shows an example of the computation of $c(S)$. Let elements of S have three properties A, B, C, and let $s(S_A, S) = 3$, $s(S_B, S) = 2$, $s(S_C, S) = 1$. We assign 3 to all elements that has A, assign 2 to all elements that has B but not A, and assign 1 to all elements that has C but not A nor B. We then compute the average of the scores of the elements, and obtain $c(S) = (3 * 7 + 2 * 2 + 1 * 1)/10 = 2.6$.

This strategy gives S a high value of $c(S)$ as long as many elements in S have at least one common property which is rare in the universe. In the example in Figure 2, one element has both properties A and B. Even if we remove the property B from this element, $c(S)$ does not change as long as that element has A. On the other hand, if we remove A from this element, the score $c(S)$ becomes smaller. In other words, for each $e \in S$, only one property X with the highest score $s(S_X, S)$ is used for the computation of $c(S)$.

3.2 Two Ways to Define $s(S_X, S)$

We compared two ways to define $s(S_X, S)$, which are denoted by $s_1(S_X, S)$ and $s_2(S_X, S)$. $s_1(S_X, S)$ is defined based on $P(S_X, |S|)$, the probability that a set of the size $|S|$ randomly sampled from the universe includes a subset that is as consistent as S_X. The lower $P(S_X, |S|)$ is, the higher score we give to S_X. We first define $P(S_X, n)$ as below:

$$P(S_X, n) = \sum_{x=|S_X|}^{n} \binom{n}{x} p^x (1-p)^{n-x} \quad \text{where} \quad p = \frac{|U_X|}{|U|}$$

where U is the given universe of elements (in our case the universe of users), and U_X is the set of all elements in U that have the property X. We then define $s_1(S_X, S)$ as follows:

$$s_1(S_X, S) = \begin{cases} \frac{|S_X|}{|S|} \log_2(2 - P(S_X, |S|)) & \text{if } \frac{|S_X|}{|S|} > \theta, \\ 0 & \text{otherwise.} \end{cases}$$

We include the factor $|S_X|/|S|$ so that S_X which is too small compared with S would not obtain a high score even if X is extremely rare in U. In addition, if $|S_X|/|S|$ is smaller than (or equal to) a threshold θ, we let $s_1(S_X, S)$ be 0.

On the other hand, we define $s_2(S_X, S)$ by using the difference between the cover ratio of X in S (i.e., in the follower set) and in the universe. If the former is large and the latter is small, S has unusual consistency. Following this intuition, we define $s_2(S_X, S)$ by the formula below:

$$s_2(S_X, S) = \max(\{\frac{|S_X|}{|S|} - \frac{|U_X|}{|U|}, 0\}).$$

Notice that $s_2(S_X, S)$ does not also have a large value unless $|S_X|/|S|$ is large even if X is extremely rare in U.

3.3 Two Types of Properties of Followers

Next, we explain what properties of followers we use. According to our observation of Twitter accounts, there are two main factors that cause the target-specificity. One is *user specificity*. Some accounts post messages directed to specific already-known users. The other is *topic specificity*. Some accounts post messages on a very specific topic only to users who are interested in that topic. These two factors correspond to the two kinds of target specificity explained in Section 1: extensionally specified target and intentionally specified target. There are also accounts that have both user specificity and topic specificity.

Followers of a user-specific account belong to the same community, and often have the same terms in their profiles or location information, e.g., names of organizations or geographic areas. Followers of a topic-specific account share the same interests, and also often have the same terms describing their interests in their profiles.

Similarly, users belonging to the same community often have common followeEs, e.g., another member of the community. Users sharing the same interests also often have common followeEs, e.g., some popular accounts related to their common interests.

Based on these observations, we use two types of properties of followers: (1) noun phrases in their profiles or location information, and (2) their followeEs.

Given accounts to classify, we first compute $c(S)$ of the follower set S of each account in two ways: only using their common terms, and only using their common followeEs. We normalize these two scores so that they have the same average and variance. Let $c_t(S)$ and $c_f(S)$ be the two normalized scores. We then compared the following four methods of classifying the accounts based on these two scores:

1. compare $\max(\{c_t(S), c_f(S)\})$ with a threshold,
2. compare their sum $c_t(S) + c_f(S)$ with a threshold,
3. construct a SVM by using the two scores, and
4. construct a decision tree by using the two scores.

For the former two methods, we determined the best threshold for our data set.

4. EXPERIMENTS AND DISCUSSION

In this Section, we explain the results of our experiments.

4.1 Data Set

We created a data set by randomly generating 64bit user IDs and downloading the Twitter user data with the IDs (ignoring non-existent ones) until we obtain 1,000 Twitter accounts whose timezone is Japan, with at least one follower, and with at least one tweet. We hired six experienced Twitter users as assessors, assigned three of them to each account, and asked them to classify the accounts into: (A) accounts posting messages to general public of Twitter users in Japan and (B) the others. Among 1,000 accounts, 77 were labeled as unassessable (e.g., not in Japanese language) by one or more assessors. Among the remaining 923 accounts, 705 (A:33 + B:672, 76.4%) accounts were classified into the same category by all three assigned assessors. As a simple analysis, let us assume that there is a correct classification, and each assessor classify each account into a correct category in the probability P. Because three assessors agreed on 705/923 accounts, we have $P^3 + (1-P)^3 = 705/923$, which suggests $P \approx 0.914$. If so, the classification agreed by two or three assessors is correct in 97.9% cases because $\frac{P^3+3P^2(1-P)}{P^3+3P^2(1-P)+3P(1-P)^2+(1-P)^3} = \frac{P^3+3P^2(1-P)}{1} \approx 0.979$. This suggests that the classification agreed by two or more assessors is reliable enough. Based on this analysis, we simply take the majority of three assessors, and we classified 93 and 830 accounts into (A) and (B), respectively.

For 830 accounts classified into (B) by the majority, we also asked whether it has (B_1) user-specificity, (B_2) topic-specificity, or (B_3) both, in order to see how our method behaves on data in these sub-categories. In this additional classification of (B), the following number of accounts were classified into the same sub-category (B_i) by three assessors, and two or more assessors, respectively:

by 3:   (B_1) 132, (B_2) 202, (B_3) 2   total: 336,
by 2 or 3: (B_1) 375, (B_2) 320, (B_3) 30   total: 725.

As a similar analysis, let us assume that each assessor classify each account into the correct category in a probability P, while misclassifying it into each of the two wrong categories in the probability $(1-P)/2$. Because three assessors agreed on 336/830 accounts, $P^3 + 2*((1-P)/2)^3 = 336/830$, i.e., $P \approx 0.736$. Unfortunately, this number is not as good as that for the main classification, 0.914, but we again take the majority (and exclude 105 accounts that were classified into B_1, B_2, B_3 by the three assessors). This classification is not as reliable as the main classification into (A) and (B), but we use this additional classification of (B) only for an auxiliary analysis, which will be explained later.

We then randomly selected 90, 30, 30, 30 accounts from those classified into A, B_1, B_2, B_3, respectively, as the data set for the experiment. The ratio of the four categories in the data set is important because it affects the accuracy of the classification methods. The appropriate ratio of them depends on the target application because we should use the ratio expected in the input in the target application. Our main target application is a system that recommends Twitter accounts to follow. In such a system, non-targeting accounts posting information to the general public are more likely to be recommendation candidates although the ratio of non-targeting accounts in the whole Twitter universe is low as shown above. Because it is difficult to presume a specific ratio in the expected input to our method, we simply assumed 1:1 for non-targeting v.s. targeting accounts, and 1:1:1 for three kinds of targeting accounts.

We used these 90+30+30+30=180 accounts as the data set. Table 1 shows statistics on the accounts in each category: the mean and the standard deviation of the numbers of followers, followeEs, and tweets. Non-targeting accounts have more followers and followeEs than targeting accounts in average, but the standard deviation is also large. On the other hand, all categories have similar number of tweets.

For each of these 180 accounts, we collected its at most

Table 1: Basic Statistics on the Data Set

	follower		followeE		tweet	
	μ	σ	μ	σ	μ	σ
(A)	475,679	535,894	11,274	37,906	9,763	14,607
(B_1)	573	1,389	598	1,545	8,829	29,505
(B_2)	58,142	171,784	3,353	7,218	9,992	23,572
(B_3)	82,942	262,161	1,568	3,594	5,677	6,600

Table 2: Accuracy with One Type of Properties

property	$s_1(S_X, S)$			$s_2(S_X, S)$
	$\theta = 0.01$	$\theta = 0.03$	$\theta = 0.05$	
terms	**0.861**	0.850	0,839	0.850
followeEs	0.828	0.828	0.817	**0.833**

1,000 followers. For each of these followers, we collected noun phrases in its profile and location information (stop words removed), and also collected its at most 1,000 followeEs. As the universe U, we used the set of all active Twitter accounts whose timezone is Japan, and when computing $|U|$, we assumed that the ratio of active users in Twitter universe is 0.01.

4.2 Baseline Methods

We compared our methods with two baseline methods:

- **follower**: classification based on the comparison of the numbers of followers with a threshold, and

- **SVM**: a binary SVM whose features are the maximum cover ratio of common nouns in profiles or location information of followers, and that of common followeEs.

4.3 Experimental Results

We first show the accuracy of our method with either only common terms or only common followeEs in Table 2. We tested both $s_1(S_X, S)$ ($\theta = 0.01, 0.03, 0.05$) and $s_2(S_X, S)$, and we used the best classification threshold in each case.

A bold number shows the best accuracy in each row. The accuracy of these 8 variations are close to each other. The method only with common terms achieved the highest accuracy 0.861 when we used $s_1(S_X, S)$ with $\theta = 0.01$. It correctly classified 155/180 accounts, and the breakdown of the 25 misclassified accounts is: (A) 8, (B_1) 0, (B_2) 9, (B_3) 8. The method only with common followeEs achieved the highest accuracy 0.833 with $s_2(S_X, S)$. It correctly classified 150/180 accounts, and the breakdown of the 30 misclassified accounts is: (A) 6, (B_1) 3, (B_2) 12, (B_3) 9. These results suggest that our methods works better for user-specificity than for topic-specificity. We can also see that $s_1(S_X, S)$ shows slightly higher accuracy with the smaller θ. This suggests that even rare properties in the follower set can be useful for characterizing the target audience.

Figure 3 shows the distribution of the two scores of targeting and non-targeting accounts. The X-axis represents scores based on common terms and the Y-axis represents scores based on common followeEs. The score based on common terms are computed by $s_1(S_X, S)$ with $\theta = 0.01$, and the score based on common followeEs are computed by $s_2(S_X, S)$, i.e., by the best method in each case. When we use common terms, scores of most non-targeting accounts are very low, with the average 0.004 and the maximum 0.067,

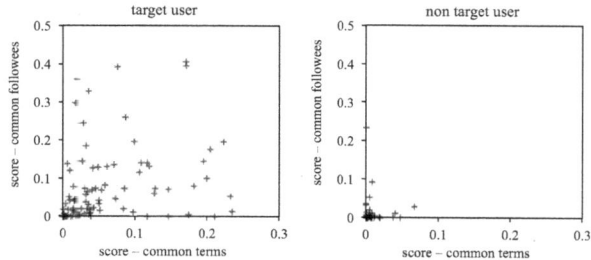

Figure 3: A scatter diagram of two scores (based on common terms and based on common followeEs) for targeting accounts and non-targeting accounts.

Table 3: Accuracy with Both Types of Properties

Proposed Methods				Baselines	
max	sum	SVM	decision tree	follower	SVM
0.856	0.872	**0.944**	0.906	0.878	0.828

while those of most targeting accounts are high, with the average 0.065. The best classification threshold is 0.009. We can see a similar trend in the scores based on common followeEs, and the best classification thresholds is 0.012.

Figure 3 shows that two scores of targeting accounts have only weak positive correlation. This suggests that we can improve the classification by using both scores.

Table 3 shows the accuracy of our four methods that combine the both scores (see Section 3.3). It also shows the accuracy of the two baselines. We used $s_1(S_X, S)$ with $\theta = 0.01$ for common terms, and $s_2(S_X, S)$ for common followeEs. For SVMs, we used LIBSVM[1] with the Gaussian kernel. For decision trees, we used scikit-learn[2]. The simple follower method achieves high accuracy 0.878, but two of our methods achieve even higher accuracy 0.944 and 0.906. The SVM based on our scores outperforms the SVM based on simple cover ratios of the most common properties.

Table 4 shows the results for two targeting accounts and two non-targeting accounts. @MCstaff_Fukuoka, which posts information on a concert hall in Fukuoka, is a targeting account while @tenkijp, which posts weather information in Japan, is non-targeting account because we regard the set of Twitter accounts in Japan as the universe. Table 4 shows noticeable terms and followeEs common to their followers, their $|S_X|/|S|$, $|U_X|/|U|$, $s(S_X, S)$, and the final $c(S)$.

Common terms and common followeEs extracted from the followers of @MCstaff_Fukuoka are all related to the topic of the account. Hakata is a city in Fukuoka, @fukuoka_yokane is an account by a CD shop in Fukuoka, and @f_sunpalace is another account posting information on the same concert hall. These terms and followeEs appear more frequently in the followers than in the universe, so their $s(S_X, S)$ are high. As a result, $c(S)$ of this account is high.

This example also suggests that even when some accounts have no geographical information in metadata, we can sometimes find a common followeE, such as @fukuoka_yokane, related to their geographical areas. The data for another targeting account, @Jars0830, shows similar statistics.

Common terms extracted from the followers of @tenkijp,

[1]http://www.csie.ntu.edu.tw/~cjlin/libsvm/
[2]http://scikit-learn.org/stable/modules/tree.html

Table 4: Details of Results for Some Accounts

account	term/followeE	$|S_X|/|S|$	$|U_X|/|U|$	$s(S_X,S)$	$c(S)$
@MCstaff_Fukuoka	Fukuoka	0.563	0.047	0.390	
	music	0.114	0.096	0.076	0.235
	Hakata	0.095	0.003	0.076	
	@fukuoka_yokane	0.069	0.023	0.046	
	@f_sunpalace	0.063	0.023	0.040	0.010
	@mbc_o2_eiji	0.059	0.028	0.031	
@Jars0830	Arashi	0.439	0.039	0.304	
	participation	0.190	0.026	0.131	0.233
	line	0.130	0.045	0.090	
	@Yamnos5	0.249	0.004	0.246	
	@ars_762	0.109	0.072	0.037	0.067
	@nino_xoxo_	0.070	0.033	0.037	
@tenkijp	Tokyo	0.033	0.196	0	
	hobby	0.022	0.095	9.3e-16	2.5e-5
	music	0.021	0.096	1.2e-15	
	@tenkijp_jishin	0.421	10.4	0	
	@Kantei_Saigai	0.358	14.8	0	0
	@bouei_saigai	0.277	6.31	0	
@masason	fan	0.059	0.676	2.6e-17	
	Tokyo	0.027	0.196	0	1.2e-12
	music	0.024	0.096	1.3e-15	
	@shigeruishiba	0.050	0.939	0	
	@WSJJapan	0.066	3.56	0	0
	@HeizoTakenaka	0.05	3.62	0	

i.e., Tokyo, hobby, and music, are not rare words. The word Tokyo appears more frequently in the universe than in the followers, so its $s(S_X, S)$ is low. $s(S_X, S)$ of "music" was high for @MCstaff_Fukuoka, but $s(S_X, S)$ of "music" for @tenkijp is low because it appears less frequently in the followers than in the universe. Similarly, common followeEs are popular accounts. @tenkijp_jishin posts earthquake information, and @Kantei_Saigai is an account owned by the government posting disaster information. These followeEs have high values for $|S_X|/|S|$, but they also have high values for $|U_X|/|U|$, so their scores $s(S_X, S)$ are low, and as a result, $c(S)$ of this account is low. The data for another non-targeting account, @masason, showed similar statistics.

5. CONCLUSION

In this paper, we proposed a method for classifying Twitter accounts into targeting ones and non-targeting ones. Our method approximates how specific the target audience of a given account is by measuring how much the current follower set is deviating from a random sample from the given universe of the users. We use two types of properties of followers, common terms in metadata and common followeEs. We tested four ways to combine two scores computed from these two types of properties, and the method that uses SVM achieved the highest classification accuracy, 0.944.

One problem in our evaluation is that we excluded 105 accounts for which three assessors did not agree on the classification into B_1, B_2, B_3 (but two or three of them agreed on the classification into B). This may have removed some accounts for which the classification is especially difficult. This is a serious issue common to many classification problems whose classification criteria is inherently subjective.

An important remaining work is to incorporate our method in some application, e.g., a Twitter user recommendation system, and to show that it really improves its quality.

6. REFERENCES

[1] M. Armentano, D. Godoy, and A. Amandi. Topology-based recommendation of users in micro-blogging communities. *J. Comput. Sci. Technol.*, 27(3):624–634, 2012.

[2] M. G. Armentano, D. Godoy, and A. A. Amandi. Followee recommendation based on text analysis of micro-blogging activity. *Inf. Syst.*, 38(8), Nov. 2013.

[3] L. Backstrom and J. Leskovec. Supervised random walks: predicting and recommending links in social networks. In *Proc. of WSDM*, pages 635–644, 2011.

[4] X. Cai, M. Bain, A. Krzywicki, W. Wobcke, Y. S. Kim, P. Compton, and A. Mahidadia. Learning collaborative filtering and its application to people to people recommendation in social networks. In *Proc. of ICDM*, pages 743–748, 2010.

[5] M. Cha, H. Haddadi, F. Benevenuto, and P. K. Gummadi. Measuring user influence in Twitter: The million follower fallacy. In *Proc. of AAAI ICWSM*, pages 10–17, 2010.

[6] J. Hannon, M. Bennett, and B. Smyth. Recommending twitter users to follow using content and collaborative filtering approaches. In *Proc. of RecSys*, pages 199–206, 2010.

[7] A. Java, X. Song, T. Finin, and B. Tseng. Why we Twitter: Understanding microblogging usage and communities. *Proc. of KDD*, pages 56–65, 2007.

[8] Y. Kim and K. Shim. Twilite: A recommendation system for twitter using a probabilistic model based on latent dirichlet allocation. *Inf. Syst.*, 42:59–77, Jun. 2014.

[9] H. Kwak, C. Lee, H. Park, and S. Moon. What is twitter, a social network or a news media? In *Proc. of WWW*, pages 591–600, 2010.

[10] H. Takemura, A. Tanaka, and K. Tajima. Classification of Twitter follow links based on the followers' intention. In *Proc. of ACM Symposium on Applied Computing*, pages 1174–1180, Apr. 2015.

[11] A. Tanaka, H. Takemura, and K. Tajima. Why you follow: A classification scheme for Twitter follow links. In *Proc. of ACM Hypertext*, pages 324–326, Sep. 2014.

[12] S. Wan, Y. Lan, J. Guo, C. Fan, and X. Cheng. Informational friend recommendation in social media. In *Proc. of SIGIR*, pages 1045–1048, 2013.

[13] J. Weng, E.-P. Lim, J. Jiang, and Q. He. TwitterRank: Finding topic-sensitive influential twitterers. In *Proc. of WSDM*, pages 261–270, 2010.

[14] S. Wu, J. M. Hofman, W. A. Mason, and D. J. Watts. Who says what to whom on twitter. In *Proc. of WWW*, pages 705–714, 2011.

[15] L. Yan, Q. Ma, and M. Yoshikawa. Classifying Twitter users based on user profile and followers distribution. In *Proc. of DEXA*, pages 396–403. Springer, 2013.

[16] G. Zhao, M. L. Lee, W. Hsu, W. Chen, and H. Hu. Community-based user recommendation in uni-directional social networks. In *Proc. of CIKM*, pages 189–198, 2013.

A Fuzzy-Based Personalized Recommender System for Local Businesses

Chun-Hua Tsai
School of Information Sciences
University of Pittsburgh
135 N Bellefield Ave, Pittsburgh, PA 15213
cht77@pitt.edu

ABSTRACT

On-line reviewing systems have become prevalent in our society. User-provided reviews of local businesses have provided rich information in terms of users' preferences regarding businesses and their interactions in reviewing systems; however, little is known about how the reviewing behaviors of users can benefit businesses in terms of suggesting potential collaboration opportunities. In the current study, we aim to build a recommendation system for businesses to provide suggestions for business collaboration. Based on historical data from Yelp that shows two businesses being reviewed by the same users within a same season, we were able to identify businesses that might attract the same customers in the future, and hence provide them with a collaboration suggestion. Our results suggest that the evidence—two businesses sharing reviews from same users—can provide recommendations for businesses to pursue future collaborative marketing opportunities.

Categories and Subject Descriptors

I.5.2 [**Computing Methodologies**]: Design Methodology—*classification, feature selection, recommender system*

Keywords

Fuzzy Logic, Reviewing Network, Recommender System

1. INTRODUCTION

The effect of agglomeration economies is always an interesting research question for urban economic studies. Agglomeration economics is defined as businesses that benefit from their location, shared histories, or workers found near each other [3]. As a result, businesses can share commercial interests, due to economic scale and network effects. Hence, complementary and substitute businesses tend to cluster near each other. For example, the gas stations may locate themselves close to supermarket to attract drivers to refill their cars and perform grocery shopping in the same area.

HT '16, July 10–13, 2016, Halifax, Nova Scotia, Canada.
© 2016 ACM. ISBN 978-1-4503-4247-6/16/07...$15.00
DOI: http://dx.doi.org/10.1145/2914586.2914641

Alternately, similar restaurants may open in the same areas to attract customers with the same tastes. Through city urbanization, these clusters usually gather naturally over a long term, but local businesses can benefit more if we can distinguish potential collaboration opportunities in advance. This turns the task of suggesting collaboration among local businesses into an interesting research problem.

Online reviewing systems like Yelp have become popular destinations in our information society, where people can search for and review businesses, as well as interact with friends. The rich data from these systems provides plenty of opportunities to provide meaningful personalized recommendation results, based on users' historical data. Different approaches have arisen to study personalized recommender systems like these, such as those that are based on user interests [11], social factors [5] and heterogeneous networks [16] to help users browse, search, and explore the system, given their own preference of information. However, little attention has been paid to the recommendations from the business side. As a crowd-sourced local business review and social networking site [9], Yelp provides users with options to share reviews on businesses. These shared reviews allow us understand the latent relationships among different businesses. If two businesses receive overlapping reviews from the same group of users, we can infer that they share the same targeted consumer groups. This provides a different angle to observe and analyze the economic behavior that occurs between businesses.

In this study, we build a review network among businesses, based on user reviews on Yelp. The goal of this study is to predict the likelihood that two businesses will attract the same user's review in the future. The key to fulfilling such a prediction task is the predictor selection [14]. This study further considers various prediction features, including geographical distance, reviewing network, the fuzzy-businesses vector, and content similarity. The experimental result supports the effectiveness of the proposed features, as the prediction model is improved by 31% in AUC value. Based on the result, we aim to build a recommendation system for businesses on Yelp that is dedicated to making suggestions for businesses that share the same target consumers. The system will allow local businesses to easily reach out for potential collaboration opportunities.

The remainder of this paper is divided into six sections. We firstly review the related work of recommender system in section 2. In section 3, we describe the dataset and its preprocessing procedures. In section 4, we discuss the approach of feature selection and experiment setting. The experimental result and prototype system will be shown in section 5. Finally, we summarize our findings and future research directions.

2. RELATED WORKS

A recommender system is used to process, digest, and provide users with meaningful personalized suggestions. One line of research focuses on developing personalized recommendation systems. For instance, [5, 8] have tried to build recommender systems based on the social network of Yelp and user profile information. [5] proposes a unified and personalized recommendation model that is based on probabilistic matrix factorization to explore three social factors in the Yelp network: personal interest, interpersonal interest similarities, and interpersonal interests as a whole. [8] uses the side information of users, based on a set of sparse linear methods, to improve the performance of conventional recommender systems. In the meantime, [13] has adopted a global search approach to collect external data to obtain a people-collaboration recommender system in conference.

The variant information can be combined into heterogeneous networks for recommendation tasks. [16] builds an attribute-rich heterogeneous information network of Yelp reviews and combines various related information from the network with user feedback to provide high-quality recommendations for users. While much prior research has focused on providing recommendations for users based on their similar interests in businesses, social structure, or participation in reviewing systems, little attention has been paid to the relationships between businesses. However, understanding relationships between businesses and further developing a recommendation system for businesses could be beneficial in many different domains, especially in collaborative marketing and location-based recommendations.

Precise user modeling is the key to providing meaningful recommendation results. However, in a real-world recommender system, user preferences are usually vague or may be incomplete. For example, the preference of a movie might be represented as a rating (1-5 stars) and a genre (scary, action, and so forth). As a result, it is challenging to combine the two features into user modeling. The study of [17] proposed the fuzzy-set theoretic method (FTM), which offered a series of methods to manage non-stochastic uncertainty. This approach defined the representational method, aggregation method, and similarity measures for a content-based recommender system. Fuzzy logic is widely used in [10, 18, 15] for recommender systems.

3. DATA

We adopted the Yelp Dataset Challenge dataset[1]. This dataset contains 61,184 businesses and 12 million reviews from 10 cities across 4 countries. The type of businesses included is diverse, and includes restaurants, bars, clubs, and many others. The dataset also includes business metadata, such as geo-location, categories, open hours, and other attributions. We filtered out the businesses who shared fewer than 2 reviews with any other businesses. Based on this criteria, we obtained a shared review network with 24,593 nodes and 2.17 million edges. Each edge is included with comment text from users.

---

[1] http://www.yelp.com/dataset_challenge

We conducted a preliminary exploration of shared review networks within the dataset. Figure 1(a) shows the scatter plots of geographic distance and user comment overlap. In this plot, we can observe the relationship of comment overlap over geographic distances. Unsurprisingly, businesses that are close together seem to share more reviews. The distribution follows the power law, which means the businesses share reviews in a near distance. However, note the second spike, around 190 to 300 miles. It is interesting that a group of users tend to comment on the same stores over a long distance (exceeding normal urban territory). When further exploring these data points, we find that most of the reviews land in Las Vegas and Phoenix area (See Figure 1(b)). This pattern indicates review behavior across two popular tourist cities. This pattern also implies that people travel between these cities and write a review on Yelp, even from a long distance. These results support the cycle of agglomeration economies over either a short or long distance.

4. APPROACH

4.1 Problem

We focus on the link prediction problem for a shared review network among businesses with Yelp reviews. We define the review network as G = (V, E), in which each edge $e = (u, v) \in E$ is an interaction between stores u and v at a particular time, t. Here, the interaction is defined as a connection in terms of sequential user reviews. We can construct a shared review network, based on user review information. Our goal is to predict future reviews at $t' > t$. In other word, the goal is to find a review link that will be formed at a future time t', based on data observed at time t. We can treat this as a binary classification problem to distinguish the positive/negative links at the future time t'.

4.2 Baseline

The content-based approach has been widely used in many different recommender systems [13, 11, 15, 18, 17]. In this study, we adopt the content similarity of Yelp reviews as a baseline. For each business, we aggregate all its reviews into a long text, called comment text. The similarity between two businesses will be represented by the degree of their comment text similarity, which can be calculated with a vector space model (VSM) [12].

The VSM is an algebraic model for representing text documents as vectors. Each document is presented by a high-dimensional vector in the space of words, where each entry corresponds to a different word, and entry value is the number where that word appears in the document. Using VSM, we could obtain a term-document matrix. However, not all terms (or words) are equally important; for example, 'as' is less important than 'aspect' in context. We want to put less discriminatory power on the term in the collection that occurs more frequently. Therefore, we have adopted a classic VSM, which is known as a term frequency-inverse document frequency (TF-IDF) model. The weighting for document d is d is $V_d = [w_{1,d}, w_{2,d}, ..., w_{N,d}]^T$, where $w_{t,d} = tf_{t,d} \cdot \log \frac{|D|}{|d' \in D | t \in d'|}$ and $tf_{t,d}$ is the term frequency of term t in document d. $\log \frac{|D|}{|d' \in D | t \in d'|}$ is the inverse document frequency. $|D|$ is the total number of the document set; $|d' \in D | t \in d'|$ is the number of documents containing the term t.

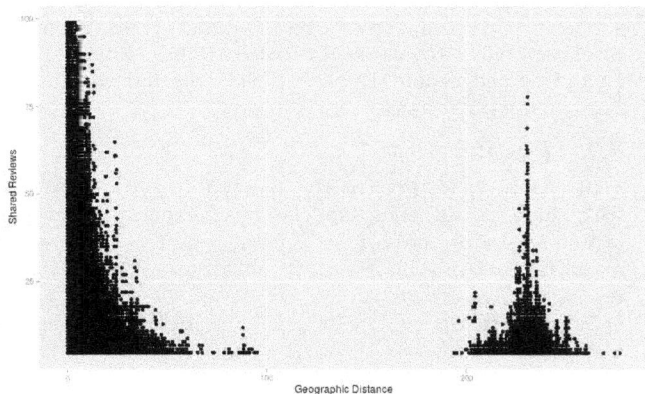

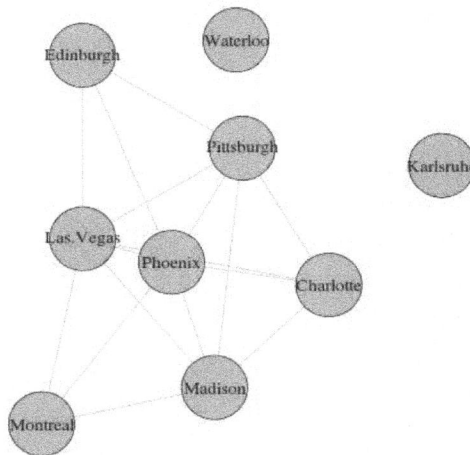

Figure 1: (a) Scatter plots of geographic distance and user comment overlap of all Yelp datasets. This distribution shows the two spikes through geographic distances between businesses. The distance within 100 miles follows the power law distribution; namely, that the closer businesses share more customer reviews. The distance of between 190 to 260 miles show a normal distribution that two or more cities shared a review over a long distance; (b) shared review network between 10 cities within the Yelp dataset. The cities that shared more reviews will generally be close to each other. For instance, Las Vegas and Phoenix shared more reviews between each other, while Karlsruhe and Waterloo have limited shared reviews with other cities farther away.

The specific steps that we used to adpot VSM on businesses' comment text are shown as below: 1) Stopwords (such as a, about, an, are, etc.) were removed, because they help construct sentences but do not represent any specific context of reviews. We also did a word-stemming to remove the suffix of each word. For example, 'eat' and 'eating' could be substituted by the single term 'eat'. The remaining words were used to create a term frequency matrix. Second, the comment text of each business could be presented by a high-dimensional vector in our word space. Each entry corresponds to a different word, and entry value is the frequency of that word repeating in this comment text. Third, we used TF-IDF to calculate the re-weighted term frequency vector for each business. Finally, the similarity of comment text between the two businesses is calculated by the Euclidean distance of their vectors.

4.3 Fuzzy Business Vector

The similarity of two businesses can be obtained from shared characteristics [4]. There are various attributes to describe a business, with which we can construct a high-dimensional space to hold all businesses, and each business can be represented as a vector. Given the hypothesis that similar businesses share more similar descriptions than different businesses, similar attributes can be extracted from similar businesses, and will give a short Euclidean distance for these two business vectors. Based on the Yelp data set, selected attributes are: business category, review count, business star, open hours, and an attribute combo, which includes WIFI, parking, credit card acceptance, and other attributes of the business. The same weights are given to all dimensions.

For dimensions with numerical values (like review count), we can simply use their numerical values to calculate the Eu-

clidean distance. On the other hand, to calculate two businesses' Euclidean distance in a categorical dimension, like business categories, we adopt an FLM (fuzzy set theoretic method) [17] as a way to represent the business vector similarity between two businesses. FLM is characterized by its membership function, which is defined as $u_a(x) : x \in X \to [0, 1]$, where X is a domain space. We use two businesses' attribution intersection divided by attribution union, which can be defined as $Sim_{BusinessVector} = \frac{A \cup B - A \cap B}{A \cup B}$, where A and B are the business attribution value sets.

4.4 Review Network

Finding the right features is the key for the prediction model. For link prediction, it is necessary to extract the features that represent some properties between two paired nodes in a network. In Yelp, users can review their comments of the visited businesses. In previous studies [13, 11, 15, 18, 17], the network is defined as a user's social network or coauthorship network. In this paper, the goal is to recommend potential collaboration opportunities for local businesses. Hence, the review network is built by shared reviews. For example, if 2 users have reviewed businesses A and B at the same time, then we define a link between A and B with weight equal to 2. Based on this network, we consider 4 classic network proximity features as predictors [6].

1) Common Neighbors (CN): The CN [7] of two stores x and y is computed as $Sim_{CN}(x, y) = \Gamma(x) \cap \Gamma(y)$, where $\Gamma()$ indicates the set of neighbors of the given stores x and y. Here we define the set of neighbors as all stores with shared comments observed at t.

2) Jaccard Coefficient (JC): The JC [2] measures similarity between finite neighbor sets. Here we defined neigh-

bor sets as a shared review at time t. For any two given stores, it is the intersection of their shared review divided by the union of their shared review. It is computed as $Sim_{JC} = \|\Gamma(x) \cap \Gamma(y)\| / \|\Gamma(x) \cup \Gamma(y)\|$, where x or y is the given business and $\Gamma(\cdot)$ represents the shared reviews they have.

3) Adamic/Adar (AA): The AA [1] is a typical local network similarity measurement that considers a weighted parameter between network nodes. The weighted parameter w is defined as $w_{x,y} = \frac{1}{log(z)}$, where z is the shared neighbors between businesses x and y. We then extend the function to $Sim_{AA}(x,y) = \sum \gamma(x) \cap \gamma(y) \cdot w_{x,y}$, where we sum the shared reviews between businesses x, y and multiply by the weight w.

4) Geographic Distance (GD) [14]: The GD is used to measure the actual geographic distance between two businesses. We used the Haversine formula to compute the geographic distance between two points on earth, based on longitude and latitude data. Then the formula can be defined as:

$$Sim_{GD}(x,y) = 2r\ arcsin*$$

$$(\sqrt{haversin(\phi_y - \phi_x) + \frac{cos(\phi_x)cos(\phi_y)}{haversin(\lambda_y \lambda_x)}})$$

where r is the radius of the sphere, ϕ_x and ϕ_y are the latitude of businesses x and y, and λ_x and λ_y are the longitude of businesses x and y.

5. EXPERIMENT

5.1 Design

Let B_t be the set of businesses who shared reviews in year t, and $B_{t'}$ be the set of businesses who shared at least two reviews in year $t' = [t+1]$. To predict a shared review link, we divide B_t into two non-overlapping partitions. The first partition is selected as the training data set and the later partition as the testing dataset. We use $B_{t'}$ as a ground truth to generate the positive and negative link. The positive link is established among the businesses that have at least two shared reviews in $B_{t'}$ and the negative link is established among those who have no shared reviews record in $B_{t'}$.

We divide the whole dataset into 4 seasonal partitions from 2013 to 2014. We will predict the shared review link in t' years, based on the feature information in time t. We also limited the ego network to 4 hops, because this covers the most possible review links. However, the positive and negative links are unbalanced; the negative links are much greater than the positive links. Hence, we randomly choose 1:1 positive and negative links to represent the performance of our proposed model. All the performance measures will be reported by the averaged values of 10-fold cross-validation.

We adopt logistic regression as a classifier in this experiment. The classifier performance is measured by F-Score and AUC as merits to evaluate the model performance. First, the F-Score is calculated by the harmonic mean of precision and recall, for which the formula is $F_1 = 2 * \frac{precision*recall}{precision+recall}$. Second, the area under the curve (AUC) that is the merit of the classifier will rank a randomly chosen positive instance than a negative instance. A higher AUC value means a higher accuracy rate of the classification model. We divide

the proposed features into three classification models: 1) content-based baseline; 2) network-based baseline; and 3) a hybrid model. The content-based model is considered to have two features: a fuzzy business vector(BV) and content similarity(CS). The network-based model includes common neighbors (CN), the Jaccard coefficient (JC), Adamic/Adar (AA) and geographic distance (GD). The hybrid model is combined with the two models above.

5.2 Results

In Figure 2, we present the seasonal experiment results with three classification models. Similar performance patterns are shown across four different quarters. There is a major performance improvement between the content-based model and the hybrid model. In detail, the hybrid model is better than the content-based model by 16-17% and the network-based models by 11-15% in its F-score. Moreover, the hybrid model is better than the content-based model by 31-33% and the network-based models by 4-5% in AUC. The hybrid model outperforms the other two models and supports the effectiveness of this prediction model.

Hence, this result helps to predict potential collaborative opportunities between businesses, based on empirical data. Our experiment proves that the business can predict future review links, based on the hybrid model. The best case is shown on quarter 2 with 86% AUC value. This evidence indicates that the classifier is both effective and useful. This finding suggests a further analysis of the economic behavior from a different angle and to further design a local business recommender system. In other words, the hybrid features are effective to fulfill a recommender system for the local businesses that shared the same group of user reviews. This finding may help local businesses to discover potential collaborative opportunities and benefit from common commercial interests.

5.3 Prototype of Recommendation System

Figure 3 shows the demo recommendation system based on the proposed prediction model. We ranked the recommendation result list, based on predicting their likelihood, and plotted them in a map layout. In our demo system, we bundled a Google Map service to provide an AJAX-style user interface. The recommendation result can be used to discover potential commercial opportunities between businesses. For example, a local restaurant might find a link with a nearby nightclub, supermarket, or dessert shop. The businesses may initiate collaboration through the system suggestions. Moreover, in a map view, the business can explore collaborative opportunities by scaling the geographic distance, to find collaborative opportunities across cities. For ecample, note the potential for business collaboration between Las Vegas and Phoenix. Some of the businesses may actually link through the same group of customers. Based on this recommender system, businesses can discover a hidden value, even over a long distance.

6. DISCUSSION

In the current study, we propose an effective methodology to predict the likelihood that any two businesses attract the same group of target reviews by using historical Yelp data. We build a review network that connects two businesses if they received reviews from the same users, and further present a prediction model that integrates networks,

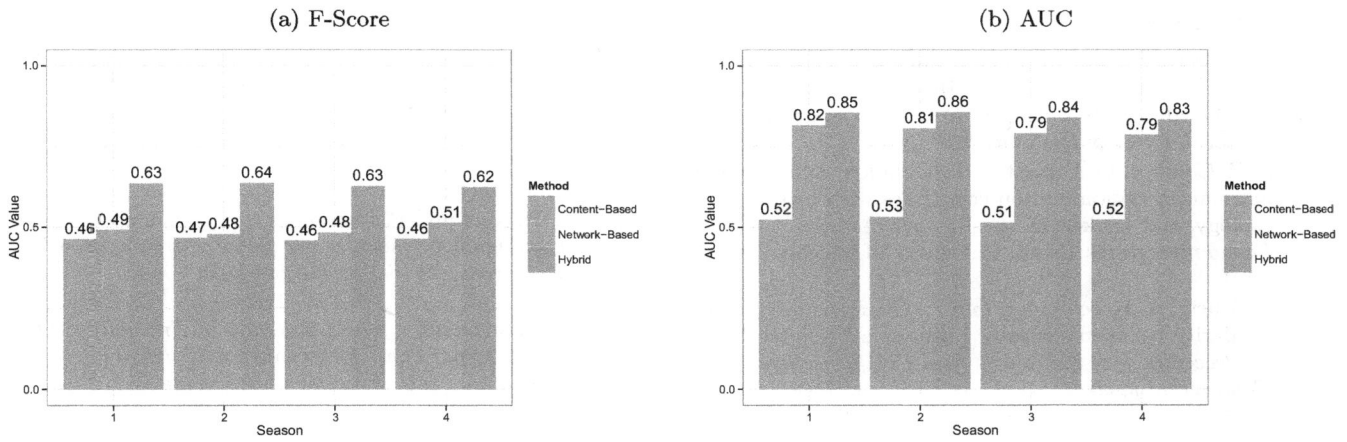

(a) F-Score   (b) AUC

Figure 2: (a) The experiment result of F-Score: in all seasons, the performance of Hybrid model is better than content-based and network-based models by 11%; (b) The experiment result of AUC: in all seasons, the performance of Hybrid model is better than content-based model by 31% and network-based model by 4%.

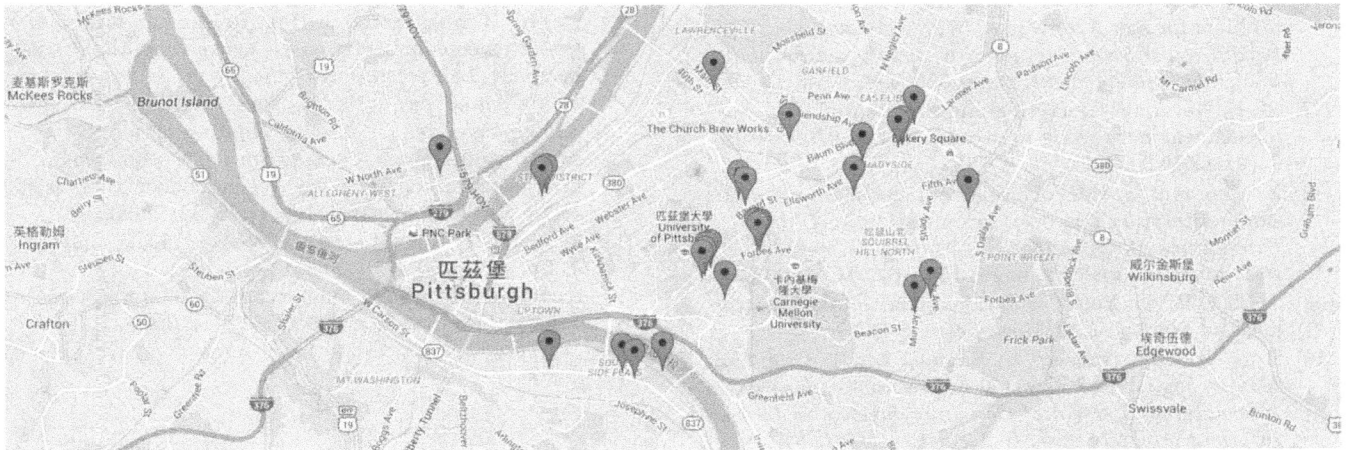

Figure 3: A location-based view of the recommendation result for a local business in Pittsburgh. This result provides the information of potential collaborative opportunities to the local business.

fuzzy business vectors, and content similarity features. Our experimental results suggest that the model performs relatively well in predicting future links between businesses. The best case is outperforming the baseline model by 33%. Furthermore, our prediction model can be used as a core model in a business recommendation system that can generate a list of businesses that will potentially attract the same target customers to each business.

The major contributions of this study are: 1) to the best of our knowledge, this is the first work to build a review network for local businesses to enable collaborative prediction and recommendation. We use user-centric community data to analyze the economic and business value. Second, our proposed prediction features largely outperform the baseline model by 33%. This finding indicates the need to further build up a recommender system for local businesses. Finally, we provide a beta version of a location-based recommender system that local businesses can use to explore the distance-free potential collaborative opportunities, and

that may realize a benefit through shared commercial interests.

We acknowledge the current work also has some limitations. Although we present the prototype of business recommendation system using the prediction model, the performance of the recommendation system needs to be further evaluated. In this case, we do not have a baseline to compare our system with, so we plan to conduct a user study to evaluate the overall usefulness and satisfaction of the recommendation results. Also, in the current study, we built the review network based only on the binary variable that a same user comments on both businesses, but that does not consider the variance of shared reviews. It is possible that the positive or negative relationship in the shared-comments network can also contribute to the prediction task. Hence, further investigation into the different ways of building review networks is needed to improve the prediction model. Beyond that, understanding the geographic difference in consuming patterns and mining the costumer shopping sequence are also some future directions for our research.

7. REFERENCES

[1] L. A. Adamic and E. Adar. Friends and neighbors on the web. *Social networks*, 25(3):211–230, 2003.

[2] G. Chowdhury. *Introduction to modern information retrieval.* Facet publishing, 2010.

[3] P.-P. Combes, G. Duranton, L. Gobillon, and S. Roux. Estimating agglomeration economies with history, geology, and worker effects. In *Agglomeration Economics*, pages 15–66. University of Chicago Press, 2010.

[4] M. Ehrig, A. Koschmider, and A. Oberweis. Measuring similarity between semantic business process models. In *Proceedings of the fourth Asia-Pacific conference on Comceptual modelling-Volume 67*, pages 71–80. Australian Computer Society, Inc., 2007.

[5] H. Feng and X. Qian. Recommendation via user's personality and social contextual. In *Proceedings of the 22nd ACM international conference on Conference on information & knowledge management*, pages 1521–1524. ACM, 2013.

[6] D. Liben-Nowell and J. Kleinberg. The link prediction problem for social networks. In *Proceedings of the twelfth international conference on Information and knowledge management*, pages 556–559. ACM, 2003.

[7] M. E. Newman. Clustering and preferential attachment in growing networks. *Physical Review E*, 64(2):025102, 2001.

[8] X. Ning and G. Karypis. Sparse linear methods with side information for top-n recommendations. In *Proceedings of the sixth ACM conference on Recommender systems*, pages 155–162. ACM, 2012.

[9] J. M. O'Brien. Yelp's ambitious plan to take over the local ad market. *CNNMoney.com*, 2, 2007.

[10] B. Ojokoh, M. Omisore, O. Samuel, and T. Ogunniyi. A fuzzy logic based personalized recommender system. *International Journal of Computer Science and Information Technology & Security (IJCSITS)*, 2:1008–1015, 2012.

[11] X. Qian, H. Feng, G. Zhao, and T. Mei. Personalized recommendation combining user interest and social circle. *Knowledge and Data Engineering, IEEE Transactions on*, 26(7):1763–1777, 2014.

[12] G. Salton, A. Wong, and C.-S. Yang. A vector space model for automatic indexing. *Communications of the ACM*, 18(11):613–620, 1975.

[13] C.-H. Tsai and P. Brusilovsky. A personalized people recommender system using global search approach. *iConference 2016 Proceedings*, 2016.

[14] C.-H. Tsai and Y.-R. Lin. Tracing and predicting collaboration for junior scholars. In *Proceedings of the 25th International Conference on World Wide Web Companion*. International World Wide Web Conferences Steering Committee, 2016.

[15] S. K. Verma, N. Mittal, and B. Agarwal. Hybrid recommender system based on fuzzy clustering and collaborative filtering. In *2013 4th International Conference on Computer and Communication Technology (ICCCT)*, 2013.

[16] X. Yu, X. Ren, Y. Sun, B. Sturt, U. Khandelwal, Q. Gu, B. Norick, and J. Han. Recommendation in heterogeneous information networks with implicit user feedback. In *Proceedings of the 7th ACM conference on Recommender systems*, pages 347–350. ACM, 2013.

[17] A. Zenebe and A. F. Norcio. Representation, similarity measures and aggregation methods using fuzzy sets for content-based recommender systems. *Fuzzy Sets and Systems*, 160(1):76–94, 2009.

[18] Z. Zhang, H. Lin, K. Liu, D. Wu, G. Zhang, and J. Lu. A hybrid fuzzy-based personalized recommender system for telecom products/services. *Information Sciences*, 235:117–129, 2013.

Search Tactics of Images' Textual Descriptions

Yi-Ling Lin
Department of Information
Management,
National Sun Yat-Sen University
Kaohsiung, 80424,Taiwan
yllin@mis.nsysu.edu.tw

Wen-Lin Lan
Department of Information
Management,
National Sun Yat-Sen University
Kaohsiung, 80424, Taiwan
m044020040@student.nsysu.edu.tw

Ren-Yi Hong
Department of Information
Management,
National Sun Yat-Sen University
Kaohsiung, 80424, Taiwan
m034020023@student.nsysu.edu.tw

I-Han(Sharon) Hsiao
School of Computing, Informatics &
Decision Systems Engineering,
Arizona State University
Tempe, 85281 AZ, USA
Sharon.Hsiao@asu.edu

ABSTRACT

The images' textual descriptions from experts and the general public, subject headings and social tags, are provided to facilitate image search process. Search tactics represents a series of search choices and actions with the textual descriptions provided on the systems during the search process. However, integration of different textual descriptions for image finding have rarely been investigated. This study investigates how two types of textual descriptions in relation to subject headings and social tags affect user' search tactics. Thirty-six participants were recruited for this study. Multiple methods were employed to collect data, including questionnaires, interviews, and eye-tracking analysis. Eliciting participants' viewing behaviors, this study benefits our understanding of different search tactics of users and provide adaptive mechanisms to fulfill their search needs. The results of this study provided four guidelines for practitioners when designing adaptive image search interface to fulfill users search tactics.

Keywords

Web search; information retrieval; user behavior; user studies; eye tracking.

1. INTRODUCTION

With more and more digital image sharing online and various content of images, obtaining useful textual descriptions of images to facilitate image finding becomes increasingly more challenging. Nowadays, finding an image mainly relies on Web-based keyword search approach and the classical metadata-based approach. Web-based keyword search is based on textual indices to identify the image resource; whereas metadata-based approach relies on textual metadata provided by professionals. To effectively find images online for different users' needs, we need various textual descriptions to distinguish images. Among a variety of textual descriptions, subject headings and social tags, represent textual descriptions from experts' and novices' perspectives. Although many researchers have explored the value [5, 12, 15, 20] and the integration solutions [8, 16, 22] for enhancing item's accessibility, rare studies have examined users' search behaviors with the textual

HT'16, July 10–13, 2016, Halifax, Nova Scotia, Canada.
Copyright 2016 ACM. ISBN 978-1-4503-4247-6/16/07 …$15.00.
DOI: http://dx.doi.org/10.1145/2914586.2914626

descriptions, subject headings and social tags, when the search system provides them differently.

To know about users' search behaviors with textual descriptions of images, this study investigates whether and how different textual descriptions affect user' search tactics on image finding. Search tactics in the Web environment shows dynamic interactions between users and the search system. A search tactic is usually considered a basic unit of analysis of the information searching process. During the process, users usually apply different types of search tactics such as moving forward and back through hyperlinks, query formulations and reformulation, and scanning search results, to achieve their search goals [1, 17, 19]. Since everyone has different background and preferences for using different textual descriptions, one might execute several preferred search tactics to perform particular search behaviors within a task. Although traditional logs can provide some ideas about what queries users typed in and what text descriptions users clicked to find image items, it is still hard to claim that how different textual descriptions influence users to make different search tactics especially when an integration of different textual descriptions is provided.

Beyond traditional self-reported or log data, eye-tracking methodologies enrich the dataset by recording users' real-time eye movements. This helps in understanding how users proceed on their search for their various needs and informs different aspects of users' search behavior. Which of the textual descriptions could provide users a picture of the image corpus? Which could provide users an idea to make queries? Which could give users a broad view to initiate the search at the beginning of the search task? Which could guide the user to find his/her desired images? The questions might be able to be answered by the data acquired from the eye-tracking devices.

Therefore, this study investigates how the participants have consumed or perceived the textual descriptions in relation to subject headings and social tags during their search process by using an eye tracker, which can lead us to gain more insights into how textual descriptions from the experts or novices affect the selection of search tactics while finding images.

2. RELATED WORK

A search tactic might contain a series of search behaviors that are performed to accomplish a search objective. Research regarding search tactics has been focused on two directions: identification of search tactics and discovery of search tactic patterns [3, 4, 13, 14].

Apart from the research on search tactics or tactic patterns, some studies examined the effect of various factors that influence the selection of search tactics. Aula and her colleagues [1] investigated whether experienced Web users have specific search strategies to perform their search, while Wildemuth [21] explored the effect of domain knowledge on search behaviors. Other factors, such as task types [7, 13], and search processes [18, 24] were examined the effect on search tactics. Xie and Joo [23] had an overall investigation on different factors in relation to task, user-perceived knowledge, search process and system on search tactic selection. This study investigated whether images' textual descriptions influence the selection of search tactics.

3. METHODOLOGY

This study analyzes the questionnaires and the viewing behaviors on subject headings and social tags obtained by the eye-tracking device in order to determine the relationship between textual descriptions and the selection of search tactics behind queries, clicks, the type of tasks, and the type of interfaces.

3.1 Subjects

Thirty-six participants with normal vision took part in the experiment for monetary compensation. Sixteen of them were males and the mean age was 22.86 years (SD= 1.032). Eleven of them are not in computer science related major. Twenty-two subjects reported using computers for more than five hours a day. For the easiness rating of using common computer tools with the Likert scale (1 not easy at all -5 very easy), four subjects gave a rating of 3, seventeen gave a rating of 4 and fifteen gave a rating of 5.

3.2 Apparatus

A Tobii X2-60 eye tracker was used to display the stimulus at the resolution of 1440X900 pixels and to record participants' eye movements. This eye tracker is a revolutionary small and versatile 60 Hz eye tracking research system. The participants viewed the experimental system at a distance of about 50 cm. The experiment was conducted in a private laboratory with a constant ambient light. The related definitions are necessary to follow the analysis and to understand the results presented in the upcoming subsections.

- AOI. This acronym stands for Area of Interest, and it corresponds to well-defined regions in the interface where the user looked at while performing the task.
- Fixation. A fixation is a moment where the eye is motionless (Ehmke & Wilson, 2007) and encoding info (Poole & Ball, 2010).
- Saccade. Eye movements occurred between fixations (Poole & Ball, 2010).

3.3 Materials

3.3.1 Collection

The materials consisted of a collection of images crawled from Flickr. This image collection is uploaded to Flickr by the Library of Congress[1] prior to January 2013. It contains 15,194 images that are identified by the "Library of Congress" tag. Around 83% of images (12,541) have more than one tag. Overall, there are 1,216,318 tags provided by the Library of Congress and Flickr's users, among which 12,896 are unique tags. The maximum number of tags per image was 73 close to Flickr's 75 limit. Since the images belong to the Library of Congress collection, they also have assigned subject headings. We were able to retrieve subject

headings for 6,923 images, which in total have 27,232 subject headings (of which 1,596 are unique). We further identified 5,281 images with both subject headings and social tags, and used these images to create the materials for our experiment.

3.3.2 Tasks

The exploratory search scenario simulated a complicated situation where a user has a broader information need that requires multiple searches interwoven with browsing and analysis of the retrieved information [10, 11]. To support this scenario, we designed three exploratory search tasks according to the specific content of this collection (One sample task is shown in table 1).

Table 1. Sample of the search task and description.

Sample task detail
Please find 12 photos, which are related to baseball between 1880 and 1920. These photos should comply with the following conditions.
-Six of them are related to different baseball teams.
-Two of them should include trainers(coaches) in the photos.
-Two of them should include spectators in the photos.
-Two are related to MLB World Series in distinct years.

3.3.3 Dual-Perspective Navigation Framework

To examine two types of textual descriptions in relation to subject headings and social tags for image search tactics, we applied an experimental interface with two textual descriptions, called Dual-Perspective Navigation Framework [9], with two single description interfaces. DPNF is a combination of the traditional faceted browsing and tag-cloud interface. It integrates subject headings and social tags at the same interface to provide multiple accesses points for users, and to support cross-navigation between subject headings and social tags as shown in Figure 1. A controlled user study has proven that DPNF is more efficient than single descriptor interfaces, subject heading-only and tag-only interfaces. Participants spent significantly less time, fewer interface interactions, and less back tracking to complete an exploratory task without an extra workload. In addition, participants were more satisfied with DPNF interface than with the others. In this study, we investigated how the participants have consumed different textual descriptions during their search process, particularly when different textual descriptions are provided at the same time. Thus, DPNF is the platform where we can observe users' search behaviors with both subject headings and social tags.

3.4 Procedure

The study was organized as a within-subject experiment for approximately an hour. Over the experiment, each subject had to perform the required tasks on three interfaces, the subject-only interface, tag-only interface, and DPNF interface (the detail of the interfaces can refer to [9]). Since the goal of this study is to investigate how users perceive or use subject headings and tags with their search tactics, we decided to test the integration of both features, subject headings and tags, on the DPNF interface at the end of the experiment. In addition, the order of search tasks was rotated using the Latin square design.

The overall procedure was as follows: First, we informed the recruited participants about the objectives of the study and obtained

---

[1] http://www.flickr.com/photos/library_of_congress/

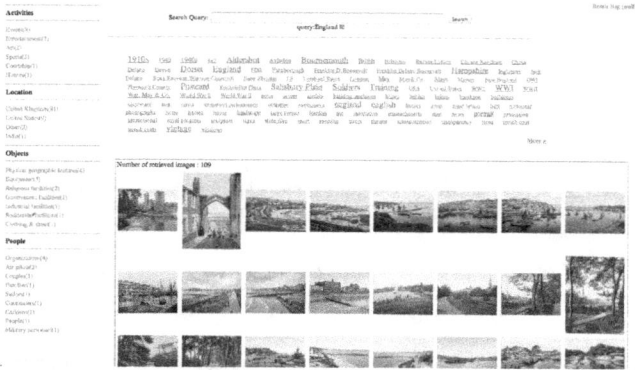

Figure 1. A screenshot of the DPNF interface

their consent (~5 minutes). Then each participant completed a short background survey (~2 minutes). Before performing the official tasks, each participant was given sufficient time to learn to use the features of the targeted interface with a detailed explanation of the different requirements of each search task (~5 minutes per interface). At the beginning of each official task, the participant was given 5 minutes to read the given task and then started their performance on the tested interface without time limitation. A 5-minute break was issued after each interface test. A post questionnaire with questions about the features, subject headings and social tags, was presented upon completion of the first two assigned tasks with both single perspective interfaces (~ 5 minutes). This post questionnaire focuses on comparing users' perceptions with subject headings and social tags in terms of their search tactics. After the participant completed work with all three interfaces, he or she was asked to fill in the *post-experiment* questionnaire that focuses on comparing the three search interfaces in terms of the participant's preference, perception, etc. This survey was followed by a structured interview. The experiment took approximately 60 minutes to complete.

4. RESULTS

4.1 Eye-Tracking Data Analysis

In this study, we analyze eye-gaze data from only the DPNF interface. In the eye-tracking analysis, we defined six AOIs including the AOI of tag cloud (denoted in T), the AOI of task (A), the AOI of search bar (Q), the AOI subject heading (H), the AOI of result (R) and the AOI of detail (D). The sample screenshot of AOIs on the DPNF interface is shown in Figure 2. Whenever the participants clicked any image from the result AOI, the system would direct the participant to the page that shows the detailed information of the clicked image. In this section, we collapsed the successive fixations within an AOI to do our sequence pattern analysis. For example, if a participant's eyes had two fixations in the AOI of the tag cloud and then moved his eyes to the result AOI to check three images, his/her original sequence would be TTRRR (expanded sequence) and the collapsed sequence would be TR.

To investigate the frequent saccade patterns, we employ PexSPAM [6], which extends the fast SPAM algorithm [2] with gap and regular expression constraints. By incorporating with regular expression constraints, PexSPAM allows us to focus the comparison between groups on patterns of interest in an exploratory discovery. Given a sequence S = s1, s2, s3....sn, the support of a pattern P is the proportion of sequences of S which contains P as a sub-sequence at least once. In our work, we set the minimum support in 5% to exclude patterns lower than that. We also set the minimum sequence length to 2 and the gap to 0. In our work, we only consider the sequences with at least one attempt. We

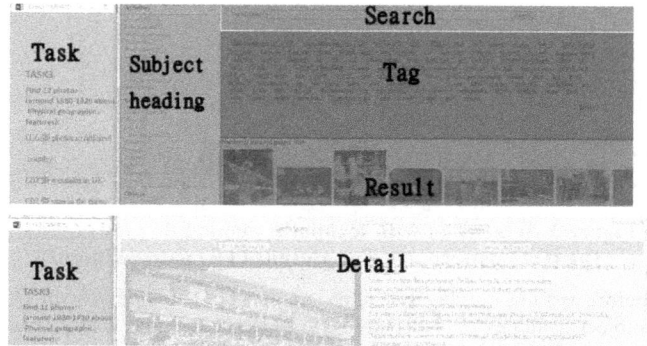

Figure 2. AOIs of the DPNF interface on the result page (top), detail page (bottom)

Table 2. Top 10 patterns ordered by support

Rank	Pattern	Support	Rank	Pattern	Support
1	RD	0.472	6	TH	0.214
2	RT	0.381	7	TRT	0.183
3	TR	0.367	8	AT	0.168
4	TRD	0.295	9	HR	0.143
5	HT	0.221	10	TA	0.141

discover 76 common patterns. The top 10 patterns and the corresponding support can be found in Table 2.

Most of the participants would examine the images in the result area before getting into the detailed image page (Table 2). Among top 10 patterns, we could find that the participants fixated on the tag cloud area more than the subject heading area. Seven out of top ten patterns are involved with the fixations on the tag cloud area. The participants checked tags before and after examining the image result set (i.e. RT, TR, TRD, TRT), which might indicate that the participants thought the tags could lead them to the images they wanted. We also found that the participants fixated tags before and after the task description (AT and TA) showing that tags might be direct to represent their search needs for the task. In spite of tags, the participants also checked subject headings before examining the images (i.e. HR). When we checked the longer sequence of patterns, we found that HTR is more popular than THR. This might indicate that the participants might tend to apply subject headings first to narrow down the search set before applying tags to get to the specific results. This might also imply that subject headings are good to narrow down the search set and tags are easier to use to find a specific item. Although HTR is popular in our patterns, the patterns with TR are still more frequently used than HTR patterns.

Table 3. Patterns with Q ordered by support

Rank	Pattern	Support	Rank	Pattern	Support
1	TQ	0.125	6	AQ	0.046
2	QT	0.122	7	QTQ	0.044
3	TQT	0.085	8	QH	0.044
4	QTR	0.059	9	QTH	0.042
5	QR	0.046	10	TQTR	0.040

We also explored the relationship between search queries and tags, and between search queries and subject headings (Table 3). We can see that the participants fixated tags before and after search query area (i.e. TQ, QT, TQT, QTR, QR, and QTQ in Figure 3.) more frequently than subject headings (i.e. QH and QTH). Tags seem to give the participants more hints to issue queries and give the participants more directly overview of the results after issuing a query. Besides, we found that subject headings were not fixated

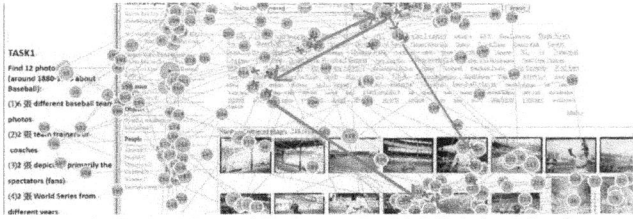

Figure 3. Screenshot with scanpaths highlighting the Query-Tag (QT) pattern and Tag-Results (TR) pattern in red

before issuing a query but after. At the top 10 patterns with Q, subject headings only occurred after Q (i.e. QH and QTH). The reason might be that subject headings are not as specific as tags are, and subject headings could only give the participants a big overview of the result set. Therefore, after issuing queries, the participants attempted to check if their search direction is correct by examining the subject headings.

Moreover, we split the search sequence into two parts to see how different the patterns change along the search (Table 4). For example, if a sequence has 10 fixated AOIs (e.g. TRATRDHTRD), the initial partition will be the first to the fifth fixated AOIs (i.e. TRATR), and the secondary part will be the sixth to the tenth (i.e. DHTRD). We found that the participants tried to check tags and subject headings more frequently at the initial part than at the secondary part. After searching for a while, they tended to use or check tags to find their target images (the patterns with H still occurred at the end but with the lower rank).

Table 4. Patterns in the initial and secondary sequences

Initial part of a sequence			Secondary part of a sequence	
Rank	Pattern	Support	Pattern	Support
1	TR	0.485	RD	0.504
2	RD	0.444	RT	0.374
3	RT	0.42	TR	0.341
4	HT	0.314	TRD	0.287
5	TH	0.308	RTRD	0.216

To be more clearly about how the participants adopt subject headings and tags at the initial part of their search, we further examine the 'sequence to the first two images' (Table 5). We found that subject headings got more fixations at this very beginning stage of the search (i.e. TH, HT, HA, AH, and HR). This result indicates that subject headings might provide better search direction when the search result set is big. The participants might feel that subject headings are useful to narrow down a big data set and bring them to a sub result set which is closer to what they were finding.

Table 5. Patterns at the sequence to the first two images

Rank	Pattern	Support	Rank	Pattern	Support
1	TH	0.641	6	HA	0.538
2	HT	0.615	7	AH	0.513
3	AT	0.59	8	TA	0.513
4	TR	0.59	9	RA	0.436
5	RT	0.564	10	HR	0.436

In addition, we also checked whether people with computer related background (IT users) have any different search behaviors from people without computer related background (non-IT users). From their top patterns, there are no big difference between them. However, we noticed that IT users had HR pattern with higher support 0.162 comparing to non-IT users with only 0.0105.

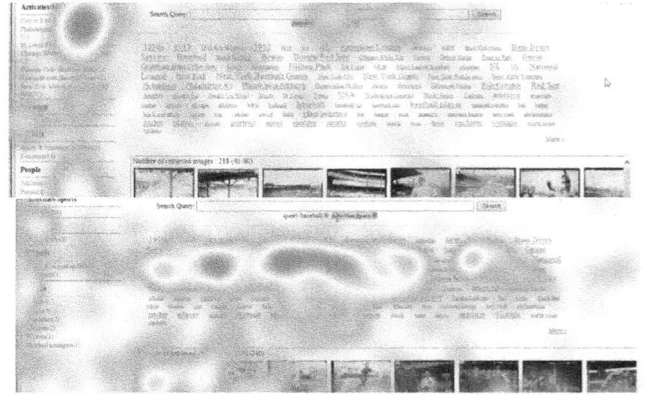

Figure 4. Heap maps of IT (top) and non-IT users (bottom)

The sample heat maps in Figure 4 can show that IT users had more attention on subject headings and non-IT users had more attention on tags. Besides, non-IT users also had more RD patterns than IT users. This might illustrate that IT users are more likely to explore or use system features than non-IT users. System features might be easier for IT users to adopt to support their search.

4.2 Subjective Data Analysis

We conducted two kinds of questionnaires: 1) The post questionnaire after performing tasks with the two single perspective interfaces was issued to understand users' perceptions of two textual descriptions in relation to the reasons to select search tactics including search efficiency, friendly guide, idea to generate queries, overview of the corpus, easy to learn, and search effectiveness. 2) The post-experiment questionnaire was issued at the end of the experiment to understand users' preference among three interfaces.

At the post questionnaire, participants were asked to evaluate several Likert–type (1-5) questions. The Mann-Whitney U test (controlling for Type 1 error across tests by using a Bonferroni correction) was conducted to evaluate differences among the two baseline interfaces (subject heading-only and tag-only interfaces) on median change in users' ratings. Table 6 shows the median of users' ratings for each question in the survey.

Table 6. Response (median) of the post questionnaire

Questions\Interfaces (*=significant at p < .05 and **=significant at p < .001)	Subject Heading	Social Tag
1. How efficient to find a target image under a search status? (p < .05)	5*	4*
2. How efficient to provide a guide of a search direction? (p < .001)	5**	3**
3. How useful to provide an idea to generate queries?	4	4
4. How effective to filter search results after a clicking? (p < .05)	5*	4*
5. How easy to learn to support a search?	5	4
6. How often to use query search?	2	4
7. How often to apply the textual description? (p < .05)	4*	3*

Another source of user feedback was a questionnaire administered after the entire study. At that point of the study, users had gained practical experience with all three types of interfaces. A Kruskal-Wallis test was conducted to evaluate differences among the three interfaces on median change in users' ratings (Table 7).

Table 7. Response (median) of the post experiment questionnaire questions

Questions	Subject Heading	Social Tag	DPN F
1. How efficient to improve search performance?	4*	3*	5*
2. How much do you prefer to use the interface?	4**	2**	5**
3. How complete information does the interface provide?	4*	2*	4*
4. How satisfied with this interface?	4**	2**	4**

We also asked the participants to give some comments on why using different textual descriptions. From the comments of the 36 participants, we organized several reasons for utilizing the tag cloud and subject heading facets.

Reasons for utilizing tags in the tag cloud on the DPNF interface:

1) **Neither subject headings nor queries could help to find the target items (10 out of the 36 participants).** The majority of the participants considered using the tag cloud because they couldn't get enough search support after using subject headings or issuing queries.

2) **Tags are clear and direct to support image finding (7/36).** Seven participants found the tag cloud are clear and direct to give them searching direction.

3) **Tags are more detailed which can help me to narrow down the search results (6/36).** Six participants used the tag cloud to help them narrow their search results when the result set is relatively small retrieved by some search criteria earlier.

4) **Tags provide more information about years** (5/36). Five users found the tag cloud very useful for searching years.

5) **Didn't use tags at all** (4/36).

6) **Other** (have no idea how to issue a suitable query) (4/36).

Reasons to apply subject headings in the subject heading facets on the DPNF interface:

1) **Neither tags nor queries could help me to find the target items** (3/36).

2) **Subject headings are clear and with important keywords to lead me to find items** (5/36).

3) **Subject headings are more structured which can help me to narrow down the search results** (14/36). Fourteen of the participants made use of subject heading when searching with high number of results in the result set especially at the beginning of the search.

4) **Subject headings provide more information about special topics or criteria,** such as countries form the location facet, and players from the people facet (4/36). Four participants found specific topics useful in the subjects.

5) **Subject headings are created by professionals so they should be better to begin with for assisting the search** (9/36). Nine of the participants considered using it at the beginning of the searching task since it was designed by the experts and should be useful to narrow down a search.

6) **Other** (1/36).

5. SUMMARY AND CONCLUSIONS

To sum up our eye-tracking data results and subjective data analysis, we organize our findings into the four search tactics. In practice, the findings of this study provide some guidelines for interface designers to fulfill users need for their different search tactics.

Search tactics 1: Identifying search leads to get start

According to the patterns found in the sequence to the first two images, except checking on the task description (A), our participants started their search task by fixating either tags (T) or subject headings (H) to identify their search leads. Some participants demonstrated that subject headings are created by professionals so the subject headings should be better to begin with for assisting the search, and they are clear and with important keywords to lead the participants to find items; some participants appealed that tags are clear and direct to support image finding.

Search tactics 2: Accessing forward and backward

In terms of accessing forward and backward among hyperlinks with subject headings and tags, our participants tended to start with subject headings first and then tags, which is consistent with the subjective data from the questionnaire. Subject headings gave our participants broad ideas about the context and helped them to narrow down the search results. Then they tended to apply tags more frequently since tags are more specific to what they were looking for. Among the patterns with only subject headings (H) and tags (T), the pattern HT is with higher support than TH. When the participants' search is closer to the target results, our participants applied tags to get to the specific sub set of results more frequently than applied subject headings.

Search tactics 3: Evaluating individual item

When a participant gets into the detailed page of a specific image, we think she/he is evaluating whether the individual item fulfill her/his needs. We discovered that the patterns with T have higher support than with H. Given the comments of our participants; we learned that tags are more detailed for our participants and provide fine-grained information such as years so the participants can use them to locate the items more easily.

Search tactics 4: Evaluating search results

We studied the patterns ending with R to see how our participants move their fixations from different AOIs to the result AOI (R). We found that our participants used T to R more frequently. Although they also used H to R, they didn't use H to go forward and backward R such as HRHRHR. However, the situation occurred with T, such as TRT and TRTR. We noticed that our participants likes to fixate T before R even after they fixated H(i.e. HTR). These findings are consistent with the comments from our participants. Tags are clear and direct to support our participants find the images and help them narrow search results when the result set is relatively small retrieved by earlier search criteria.

The findings can give practitioners guidelines in designing any adaptive interfaces for image finding base on users' search tactics. First of all, for users with different backgrounds, an effective system should provide different textual descriptions to lead their initial search. Secondly, it might be useful to provide subject headings earlier than tags since the subject headings give most of users a broad view of the image context. Thirdly, when users seek more details of the images, providing sufficient tags might be important. Tags are usually more specific to the target image, which can guide users a narrower view of their search results. Lastly, when users are evaluating their results, tags at the same window of the results may guide users to reevaluate their search results.

The study still has several limitations. Currently, we only analyzed the eye tracking data and subjective data with a very basic method. We still need statistics analyses to prove the significant different usages between subject headings and social tags. In addition, it will be useful to combine several kinds of data analyses including logs, eye-tracking data, and subjective data across different interfaces to discover more insights of the future work.

6. ACKNOWLEDGEMENTS

This work was sponsored by Sayling Wen Cultural & Educational Foundation, Service Science Society of Taiwan and MOST 103-2410-H-110 -009 to the first author.

7. REFERENCES

[1] Aula, A. et al. 2005. Information search and re-access strategies of experienced web users. *Proceedings of the 14th international conference on World Wide Web - WWW '05* (2005), 583.

[2] Ayres, J. et al. 2002. Sequential pattern mining using a bitmap representation. *Proceedings of the eighth ACM SIGKDD international conference on Knowledge discovery and data mining* (2002), 429–435.

[3] Bates, M.J. 1979. Information search tactics. *Journal of the American Society for Information Science*. 30, 4 (1979), 205–214.

[4] Fidel, R. 1985. Moves in online searching. *Online Review*. 9, 1 (1985), 61–74.

[5] Hayman, S. and Lothian, N. 2007. Taxonomy directed fikjsibinues integrating user tagging and controlled vocabularies for Australian education networks. *World Library and Information Congress: 73rd IFLA General Conference and Council*. August (2007), 1–27.

[6] Ho, J. et al. 2005. Sequential pattern mining with constraints on large protein databases. *Proceedings of the 12th International Conference on Management of Data (COMAD)* (2005), 89–100.

[7] Kim, K. and Allen, B. 2002. Cognitive and task influences on Web searching behaviors. *Journal of American Society for Information Sceince*. 53, 2 (2002), 109–119.

[8] Koraljka, G. et al. 2014. Enhancing social tagging with automated keywords from the Dewey Decimal Classification. *Journal of Documentation*. 70, 5 (2014), 801–828.

[9] Lin, Y. et al. 2016. Finding Cultural Heritage Images through a Dual-Perspective Navigation Framework. *Information Processing & Management*. (2016).

[10] Lin, Y. et al. 2010. Imagesieve: Exploratory search of museum archives with named entity-based faceted browsing. *Proceedings of the American Society for Information Science and Technology*. 47, 1 (Nov. 2010), 1–10.

[11] Marchionini, G. 2006. Exploratory search: From finding to understanding. *Communications of the ACM*. 49, 4 (Apr. 2006), 41–46.

[12] Rolla, P.J. 2009. User tags versus subject headings: can user-supplied data improve subject access to library collections? *Library Resources & Techinical Services*. 53, 3 (2009), 174.

[13] Shiri, A.A. and Revie, C. 2003. The effects of topic complexity and familiarity on cognitive and physical moves in a thesaurus-enhanced search environment. *Journal of Information Sceince*. 29, 6 (2003), 517–526.

[14] Shute, S.J. and Smith, P.J. 1993. Knowledge-based search tactics. *Information Processing & Management*. 29, 1 (1993), 29–45.

[15] Steele, T. 2009. The new cooperative cataloging. *Library Hi Tech*. 27, 1 (Jun. 2009), 68–77.

[16] Syn, S.Y. and Spring, M.B. 2013. Finding subject terms for classificatory metadata from user-generated social tags. *Journal of the American Society for Information Science and Technology*. 64, 5 (2013), 964–980.

[17] Thatcher, A. 2006. Information-seeking behaviours and cognitive search strategies in different search tasks on the WWW. *International Journal of Industrial Ergonomics*. 36, 12 (2006), 1055–1068.

[18] Vakkari, P. et al. 2003. Changes of search terms and tactics while writing a research proposal: A longitudinal case study. *Information Processing & Management*. 39, 3 (2003), 445–463.

[19] Wang, P. et al. 2000. Users' interaction with World Wide Web resources: An exploratory study using a holistic approach. *Information processing & management*. 36, 2 (2000), 229–251.

[20] Weller, K. 2007. Folksonomies and ontologies: two new players in indexing and knowledge representation Folksonomies. *Online Information* (2007), 108–115.

[21] Wildemuth, B.M. 2004. The effects of domain knolwedge on search tactic formulation. *Journal of American Society for Information Sceince and Technology*. 55, (2004), 246–258.

[22] Wu, D. et al. 2012. Comparing social tags with subject headings on annotating books: A study comparing the information science domain in English and Chinese. *Journal of Information Science*. 39, 2 (Oct. 2012), 169–187.

[23] Xie, I. and Joo, S. 2012. Factors affecting the selection of search tactics: Tasks, knowledge, process, and systems. *Information Processing & Management*. 48, (2012), 254–270.

[24] Xie, I. and Joo, S. 2010. Transitions in search tactics during the Web-based search process. *Journal of American Society for Information Sceince and Technology*. 61, 11 (2010), 2188–2205.

Human vs. Automated Text Analysis: Estimating Positive and Negative Affect

Kathryn Schaefer Ziemer
Biocomplexity Institute of Virginia Tech
900 N. Glebe Rd
Arlington, VA
ziemer@vbi.vt.edu

Gizem Korkmaz
Biocomplexity Institute of Virginia Tech
900 N. Glebe Rd
Arlington, VA
gkorkmaz@vbi.vt.edu

ABSTRACT

Automated text analysis (ATA) has been a widely used tool for determining the sentiment of writing samples. However, it is unclear how ATA compares to human ratings of text when estimating affect. There are costs and benefits associated with each method, and comparing the two approaches will help determine which one provides the most useful and accurate results. This study uses 279 journal entries from individuals with chronic pain in order to estimate the positive and negative affect scores reported directly by participants. We use Lasso to select the features that are most predictive of affect. Our results indicate that the model combining human coders and ATA accounts for the most variance in self-reported positive affect scores, resulting in adjusted $R^2 = 0.36$. For negative affect scores, we obtain a lower adjusted $R^2 = 0.30$ with the combined model, however, ATA results in significantly higher adjusted $R^2 = 0.27$ compared to the model using only human coders, $R^2 = 0.14$. This suggests that utilizing human coders may be the most beneficial when the focus is on positive affect, but automated text analysis may be sufficient when studying negative affect.

Categories and Subject Descriptors

J.4 [**Computer Applications**]: Social and Behavioral Sciences; I.2.7 [**Natural Language Processing**]: Text analysis

Keywords

automated text analysis; human coding; expressive writing; feature selection; Lasso; LIWC; sentiment analysis

1. INTRODUCTION

1.1 Background and Motivation

Emotion drives people's attitudes and behaviors, making it an important construct that applies to a number of different contexts, including education, marketing, mental and physical health, and politics [1, 2, 12, 14]. In this paper, we focus on affect, which is defined as self-reported emotions that last between a few minutes and hours [5]. In the social sciences, affect has traditionally been measured using self-report scales, which ask participants to rate how intensely they feel different emotions [27]. Since it is not always possible to obtain self-report measures of emotions, narratives and text-based information have become an alternative way to determine affect.

Much research has been conducted using sentiment analysis to interpret text-based information on the web, especially on social media [11, 18, 19]. In sentiment analysis and other types of automated text analysis, human coders often serve as the ground truth for validation and training [3, 24]. However, self-reported information provides a direct measure of affect as compared to human ratings, which infer affect. Moreover, it is important to understand how automated text analysis and human coders compare when estimating an individual's self-reported affect as there are costs and benefits to each method, and a combination of the two methods may in fact produce the best results. While human coders can understand complex language structure and the underlying meaning of the text, this method is also time-consuming, expensive, and can suffer from low interrater agreement. Alternatively, automated text analysis tools provide a more cost-effective and efficient way of analyzing writing, but are limited in the interpretation of word meaning [23]. Moreover, many of the current approaches to sentiment analysis only focus on positive and negative words, but other types of words may be equally important in estimating affect [11].

This study compares human coders with automated text analysis in estimating affect. We utilize the Linguistic Inquiry Word Count (LIWC) program [22], the most commonly used automatic text analysis tool in social sciences. In addition, we use the Lasso method to select the features from LIWC categories that are most predictive of affect.

1.2 Related Work

In the social sciences, the LIWC has been most frequently used with expressive writing narratives [23]. Expressive writing is a form of journaling where individuals write about their thoughts and feelings regarding a difficult situation or a trauma [20]. Research has found that this type of writing produces small, but significant improvements in reported health, psychological well-being, physiological functioning, and general functioning [13]. Writing about positive topics has been found to produce similar benefits [7].

HT '16, July 10-13, 2016, Halifax, NS, Canada

© 2016 ACM. ISBN 978-1-4503-4247-6/16/07. . . $15.00

DOI: http://dx.doi.org/10.1145/2914586.2914634

Expressive writing research has utilized the LIWC to examine the association between word usage and outcomes. In this regard, findings have been mixed. In some studies, negative and positive emotion words correlate in the expected direction with positive and negative affect, whereas in other studies emotion words do not appear to be associated with affect [26, 15, 4]. Research on emotion suggests that positive and negative emotions are not opposite ends of a single spectrum, but represent two separate dimensions [27]. As such, affect represents a complex construct that may not be captured completely by use of emotion words.

While the LIWC has been used to estimate affect, research has not explored whether LIWC or human coders serve as a better estimator. This study aims to compare these methods using the narratives of individuals with chronic pain who participated in an online expressive writing intervention. Expressive writing was used for this analysis since it is the most frequently used narrative with the LIWC. Moreover, positive and negative affect were included as separate outcome measures since they represent separate dimensions.

2. DATA

2.1 Expressive Writing Intervention

The narratives for the present study were obtained from a pilot positive expressive writing intervention. Participants were recruited from online chronic pain forums and were randomized to either a self-compassion writing condition or a self-efficacy writing condition. The self-compassion writing intervention encouraged participants to think and write about what a compassionate friend would say to them. The self-efficacy writing intervention encouraged participants to write about their successful experiences in managing their pain. Participants wrote for 20 minutes on either a self-compassion topic or a self-efficacy topic once a week for three consecutive weeks.

Figure 1 illustrates a snapshot of the wordcloud of the participant essays. In the figure, the minimum frequency is chosen as 100. We generated wordclouds for self-efficacy and self-compassion writing conditions. The word frequencies (and wordclouds) for both conditions were similar.

After each writing session, they completed the Positive and Negative Affect Schedule (PANAS) short form, a measure of positive and negative affective levels [27, 16]. The measure includes five positive emotions (alert, inspired, excited, enthusiastic, and determined) and five negative emotions (afraid, upset, nervous distressed, and scared). Confirmatory factor analyses have supported a two-factor structure of positive affect and negative affect for the PANAS [9, 17]. Participants rate how intensely they currently feel each emotion on a 5-point scale (1=very slightly or not at all, 5=extremely). Items of the five positive emotions are summed to create the positive affect (PA) scale and items of the five negative emotions are summed to create the negative affect (NA) scale. Total scores range from 5 to 25 for the PA and NA, where higher scores indicate higher positive and negative affect, respectively. The PANAS has been used with a multitude of clinical and healthy populations, including chronic pain samples [10]. In the present study, Cronbach's alphas were high for both the positive (.85-.89) and negative (.87-.91) subscales across the three writing sessions. In the present study, the PANAS NA and PA were used as the outcome measures of negative affect and positive affect.

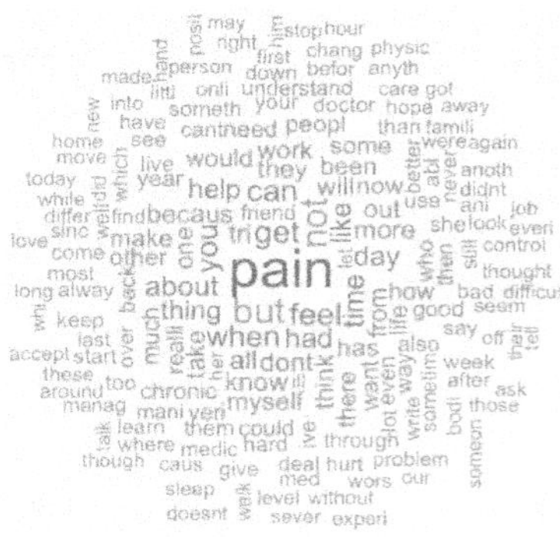

Figure 1: Wordcloud of the participant essays. The most frequent words include pain, feel, try, time, help, etc.

2.2 Participants

Ninety-three participants with chronic pain completed the writing intervention. Most participants had been living with pain for over eight years (63.4%) and used medication for pain (95.7%). Across the entire sample, the average age of participants was 49.6 years (SD=11.0; range=19-74). The majority of participants were white (93.5%), female (86.0%), living in the U.S. (92.4%), unemployed (62.4%), married (65.6%), and had at least a college degree (58.0%).

2.3 Human Coders

The essays were coded by two psychology graduate student judges who were blind to the assigned writing condition. They independently coded the emotional tone of each essay (1=mostly negative, 2=mixed negative and positive, 3=mostly positive) using previously agreed upon definitions for each category. Essays were coded based on the overall tone of the writing, where the mostly negative category indicated that the majority of the writing (i.e., over half) expressed negative viewpoints, the mostly positive category indicated that the majority of the writing expressed positive viewpoints, and the mixed category indicated that both negative and positive viewpoints were expressed in approximately equal proportion. In order to train the judges, five essays were randomly selected using a random number generator and the judges coded the essays together and discussed their rationale for their ratings. All essays that had disagreements were discussed until consensus was reached. The Kappa coefficient, which measures the inter-rater agreement [8], was 0.83 prior to consensus, indicating a high level of agreement.

2.4 Software

The Linguistic Inquiry and Word Count (LIWC) [21] software (version 2007) was used to analyze the content of the writing. The LIWC utilizes a semantic dictionary to calculate the percentage of words that fall within 70 different word categories. The LIWC 2007 dictionary is composed of 4,500 words and word stems [21] and each word or word-stem is grouped into one or more word categories. For example, the word "cried" is in five word categories (sadness, negative emotion, overall affect, verb, and past tense verb).

The word categories represent linguistic and psychological processes. The dictionary and LIWC categories were established through multiple steps that involved collecting dictionaries words, using experts and judges to recommend inclusion/exclusion of words in each category, and psychometrically evaluating the LIWC program using different types of text files [21]. The validity and reliability of the LIWC has continued to be established across a number of different contexts, languages, and populations [3, 6, 15, 23].

3. METHODS

We are interested in finding which features are good estimators of affect. For the data under consideration, we used $n = 279$ observations $p = 70$ features from the LIWC categories. However, it is unlikely that all these features are good signals of both positive and negative affect. Therefore, feature selection methods were used to reduce the dimensionality of our data.

3.1 Regression with Lasso regularization

We employed Least Absolute Shrinkage and Selection Operator (Lasso) regression for feature selection [25]. Lasso is a penalized likelihood method for model estimation that performs simultaneous variable selection and coefficient estimation to produce a parsimonious list of predictors. Lasso is a constrained version of ordinary least squares (OLS) regression (Lasso minimizes the sum of squared errors, but with an added constraint on the sum of the absolute values of the coefficients), and it computes a sparse regression estimate vector, β^*, by solving the following optimization problem:

$$\beta^* = \operatorname{argmin}_\beta \|\mathbf{Y} - \mathbf{X}\beta\|_2^2 + \lambda\|\beta\|_1$$

where $\mathbf{X} \in \mathbb{R}^{n \times (p+1)}$ is a *feature matrix* (e.g., LIWC categories), $\mathbf{Y}$ is the vector of continuous response variables (i.e., affect scores), and $\beta \in \mathbb{R}^{p+1}$ is a vector of coefficients to be estimated (p features and one intercept term). $\lambda \geq 0$ is the regularization or shrinkage parameter, since it controls the penalty on the L1-norm of β's; high values of the parameter encourage sparser models by reducing many of the coefficients to zero and hence the Lasso method can perform the variable selection procedure.

We used the glmnet package in R (version 3.1.2), and implemented Lasso with 10-fold cross-validation in order to choose the optimal regularization parameter. We conducted four regressions with Lasso penalty to estimate: (i) positive affect using LIWC categories, (ii) negative affect using LIWC categories, (iii) positive affect using LIWC categories and human ratings, and (iv) negative affect using LIWC categories and human ratings. Moreover, we controlled for the writing conditions of self-efficacy and self-compassion by including writing condition as a dummy variable.

3.2 Linear Regression with Lasso-selected Features

Since the accurate estimates of model uncertainty are not straightforward from Lasso, the subset of features that are selected by Lasso were used in a second linear regression without the penalty, λ. Linear regression was used instead of classifiers or artifical neural networks because our response variable was continuous (rather than categorical). We report the resulting coefficients (including the standard errors), and the adjusted R^2 as the measure for goodness-of-fit.

4. RESULTS

4.1 Preliminary Analyses

We first conducted preliminary analyses as a benchmark using only LIWC positive and negative word categories since these are the categories most commonly used for sentiment analysis to determine affect. Separate linear regression models were conducted using the PANAS positive and PANAS negative affect scores as the outcome variables and the number of positive and negative emotion words (LIWC) as the independent variables. We used linear regression without Lasso penalty because the number of features is 1 in each regression. For positive affect, only the number of negative words was significant ($\beta = -0.35$, $p = 0.05$). For negative affect, the number of positive emotion words was significant ($\beta = -0.57$, $p < 0.01$), whereas the number of negative words was not. This suggests that the number of emotion words are more associated with the opposite affect and have an inverse relationship. This also provides additional evidence that positive and negative affect are not opposite ends of the same dimension, but are two separate dimensions. Together, positive and negative emotion words accounted for a very small amount of the variance for positive affect ($R^2 = 0.02$) and negative affect ($R^2 = 0.04$).

4.2 Estimating Affect with Human Coders

Separate linear regression models were estimated for positive and negative affect using the coder ratings as the predictor. Similar to the previous analyses, we used linear regression without Lasso penalty. Results indicate that the ratings were significantly associated with both positive ($\beta = 2.74$, $p < 0.001$) and negative affect ($\beta = -2.09$, $p < 0.001$). Essays rated as more positive were associated with a more positive affect and a lower negative affect. Moreover, the ratings accounted for a fairly large amount of variance in positive affect ($R^2 = 0.23$) and negative affect ($R^2 = 0.14$). This indicates that the ratings of human coders are better estimators of affect than the number of positive and negative words. However, many other types of words are included in the writing that may be useful for estimating affect. Therefore, in the next step of the analyses, we explored whether including additional LIWC categories increased the validity.

4.3 Estimating Affect with LIWC

4.3.1 Positive Affect

For positive affect, the Lasso method selected 16 LIWC categories (see Table 1). Many of the LIWC categories chosen have face validity in terms of their relation to positive affect (e.g., positive emotion, achievement). The use of question marks, tentative, negations, and sadness words suggest uncertainty and negativity, which are inversely associated with positive affect. Note that writing condition was not selected as an important feature for estimating positive affect. This indicates that there was not a significant difference between the writing conditions in estimating affect.

The LIWC word categories selected by Lasso were used as explanatory variables in a linear regression with the PANAS positive affect scores as the outcome. The model produced an R^2 of 0.24, which indicates that the Lasso selected variables accounted for 24% of the variance in positive affect (see Table 1). A greater number of words in the categories of death, see, and first person singular pronouns were significantly associated with a more positive affect. In addition, having a higher word count (i.e., longer essays) was also a significant indicator of a more positive affect. Conversely, a greater number of words in the categories of negations, social processes, and sadness were significant. The positive association with death and the negative association with social processes may initially appear puzzling. It could be that the individuals able to write about death were at peace with the idea. In addition, many of the participants wrote about social isolation and negative interactions with doctors, friends, and family members, which would indicate that social process words were associated with a less positive experience.

In order to compare the estimation of the Lasso selected LIWC categories with the full LIWC model, we also ran a linear regression with all 70 of the LIWC categories as the independent variables. This model produced an R^2 of .20, indicating that all of the LIWC categories combined accounted for 20% of the variance in positive affect. The Lasso selected LIWC categories accounted for a greater amount of the variance in positive affect than the entire collection of LIWC categories. Moreover, the Lasso selected LIWC categories accounted for more variance than the human coders' ratings ($R^2 = 0.23$).

Table 1: Estimating Positive Emotion Using Lasso Selected LIWC Categories

Category	Examples	Estimate	SE
Intercept		11.41***	3.022
Word count		0.002*	0.001
Words per sentence		-0.007	0.004
Question marks		-1.97	1.075
First person singular pronouns	I, me, mine	0.30*	0.120
Common verbs	walk, went, see	-0.20	0.166
Present tense	is, does, hear	-0.02	0.127
Negations	no, not, never	-0.86**	0.298
Social processes	talk, they, child	-0.23*	0.108
Positive emotion	love, nice, sweet	0.35	0.208
Sadness	crying, grief, sad	-1.66***	0.477
Tentative	maybe, perhaps, guess	-0.19	0.195
Certainty	always, never	a 0.79	0.403
See	view, saw, seen	2.27**	0.722
Space	down, in, thin	0.18	0.204
Achievement	earn, hero, win	0.38	0.244
Death	bury, coffin, kill	7.27***	1.813

* $p < 0.05$; ** $p < 0.01$; *** $p < 0.001$

4.3.2 Negative Affect

For negative affect, Lasso selected 14 LIWC categories (see Table 2). Once again, many of the LIWC categories chosen have face validity in terms of their relation to negative affect. Writing condition was again not selected as an important variable for estimating negative affect. It should also be noted that different LIWC categories were chosen to estimate negative affect as compared to positive affect, which provides additional evidence for the separate dimensions of negative and positive affect.

The second regression model that used Lasso-selected LIWC categories produced an R^2 of 0.27, which indicates that the Lasso selected features accounted for 27% of the variance in negative affect (see Table 2). A greater number of question marks, anxiety words, sexual words, and home words were associated with higher negative affect, whereas a greater number of dictionary words and positive emotions indicated lower negative affect. Using more home words may be associated with a higher negative affect because of problems with loved ones. As indicated above, many individuals with chronic pain wrote about negative experiences with family members and not being able to physically leave their home

which would explain its association with negative affect. In addition, some participants described how chronic pain has interfered in their sexual functioning, which would explain the positive association between sexual words and negative affect. Finally, the use of question marks may indicate uncertainty, which can create anxiety and increase negative affect.

The linear regression that uses all 70 of the LIWC categories as the independent variables were compared to the Lasso method. This model produced an R^2 of .28, indicating that all of the LIWC variables combined accounted for 28% of the variance in negative affect. The Lasso selected LIWC categories accounted for a comparable amount of the variance in negative affect than the entire collection of LIWC categories. Moreover, the Lasso selected LIWC categories accounted for more variance than the human coders' ratings ($R^2 = 0.14$).

Table 2: Estimating Negative Emotion Using Lasso Selected LIWC Categories

Categories	Examples	Estimate	SE
Intercept		39.23***	7.353
Words per sentence		0.01	0.004
Question marks		2.93**	1.023
Unique words		0.05	0.036
Dictionary words		-0.35**	0.109
Function words	a, it, them	-0.02	0.102
Positive emotion	love, nice, sweet	-0.46*	0.193
Anxiety	worried, fearful, nervous	1.21**	0.458
Anger	hate, kill, annoy	0.89	0.599
Sadness	crying, grief, sad	0.59	0.475
Causation	because, effect, hence	-0.59	0.302
Inhibition	block, constrain, stop	-0.62	0.422
Sexual	love, horny	3.20*	1.263
Home	family	1.41**	0.499
Filler	Blah, I mean, you know	1.21	0.715

* $p < 0.05$; ** $p < 0.01$; *** $p < 0.001$

4.4 Combining LIWC and Human Coders

In the previous analyses, LIWC was compared to human coders in estimating affect. However, there may be benefits of combining the two approaches to utilize the strengths of each method. For this next stage of analysis, we included human coders' ratings in addition to the LIWC categories in Lasso regression. We performed two regressions to estimate positive and negative affect.

4.4.1 Positive Affect

For positive affect, the Lasso method selected 19 LIWC categories as well as the human coders' ratings (see Table 3). Many of the LIWC categories were the same as those chosen in the previous analysis when human coders' ratings were not included. Several categories were added, including dictionary words, numbers, friends, discrepancy, cognitive processes, body, and religion. These categories seem to indicate specific cognitive mechanisms (e.g., discrepancy, cognitive processes) or topics (e.g., body and religion). A few categories that were selected before were not selected this time, including positive emotion, question marks, common verbs, and words per sentence. The fact that positive emotion was not chosen indicates that human coders' ratings were perhaps a stronger choice in estimating positive affect than the use of positive emotion words.

The categories selected by Lasso were used as predictors in a linear regression with the PANAS positive affect scores as the outcome. A greater number of words in the categories of death, discrepancy, certainty, and first person singular pronouns significantly estimated a more positive affect. In addition, coders' ratings significantly estimated positive affect. Conversely, a greater number of dictionary words and words in the categories of religion and sadness significantly estimated a less positive affect. The model produced an R^2 of 0.36, which indicates that LIWC combined with human coders' ratings accounted for 36% of the variance in positive affect (see Table 3). As indicated in Figure 2, this is much higher than the R^2 of the LIWC variables alone (0.24) or the coders alone (0.23) and suggests that substantial benefit can be obtained from using both human coders and automated text processing for estimating affect.

Table 3: Estimating Positive Emotion Using Human Coders and LIWC Categories

Variables	Examples	Estimate	SE
Intercept		15.77*	6.374
Word count		0.001	0.001
Dictionary		-0.14*	0.072
First person singular pronouns	I, me, mine	0.35**	0.112
Present tense	is, does, hear	0.001	0.095
Negations	no, not, never	-0.49	0.288
Numbers	second, thousand	0.13	0.305
Social processes	talk, they, child	-0.11	0.112
Friends	buddy, friend, neighbor	-0.74	1.079
Sadness	crying, grief, sad	-1.10*	0.465
Cognitive processes	cause, know, ought	-0.11	0.111
Discrepancy	should, would, could	0.71*	0.309
Tentative	maybe, perhaps, guess	-0.14	0.215
Certainty	always, never	0.85*	0.387
See	view, saw, seen	1.06	0.677
Body	cheek, hands, spit	0.39	0.299
Space	down, in, thin	0.30	0.189
Achievement	earn, hero, win	0.29	0.245
Religion	alter, church, mosque	-1.22*	0.610
Death	bury, coffin, kill	7.27***	1.813
Human Coders	negative, mixed, positive	2.44***	0.319

$* \ p < 0.05; \quad ** \ p < 0.01; \quad *** \ p < 0.001$

4.4.2 Negative Affect

For negative affect, Lasso selected 11 LIWC categories in addition to the human coders' ratings (see Table 3). Several categories that were selected before were not selected this time, including inhibition, sadness, and positive emotion. The fact that these words were not chosen indicates that human coders' ratings captured the combined effect that these words had on negative affect.

Similar to the previous analyses, a second linear regression with Lasso-selected features and the PANAS negative affect scores was estimated. As in the previous analysis, coders' ratings significantly estimated negative affect, where essays rated as negative estimated a negative affect. Moreover, a greater number of words in the categories of anxiety, sexual, and home significantly estimated a more negative affect. A greater number of words per sentence, and question marks also estimated a more negative affect. Conversely, a greater number of dictionary words significantly estimated a less negative affect. The model produced an R^2 of 0.30, which indicates that the LIWC combined with human coders' ratings accounted for 30% of the variance in negative affect (see Table 3). This is slightly higher than the R^2 of the LIWC variables alone (0.28) and much higher than for coders alone (0.14) (see Figure 2). This suggests that although including the coders' ratings explained some additional variance, coders did not have a large impact above and beyond LIWC in estimating negative affect.

Table 4: Estimating Negative Emotion Using Human Coders and LIWC Categories

Variables	Examples	Estimate	SE
Intercept		41.00***	7.180
Words per sentence		0.01*	0.003
Question marks		2.36*	1.001
Unique words		0.03	0.035
Dictionary words		-0.33**	0.105
Function words	a, it, them	-0.02	0.097
Anxiety	worried, fearful, nervous	1.23**	0.446
Anger	hate, kill, annoy	0.55	0.590
Causation	because, effect, hence	-0.56	0.286
Sexual	love, horny	2.81*	1.216
Home	family	1.15*	0.478
Filler	blah, I mean, you know	0.98	0.702
Human Coders	negative, mixed, positive	-1.41***	0.295

$* \ p < 0.05; \quad ** \ p < 0.01; \quad *** \ p < 0.001$

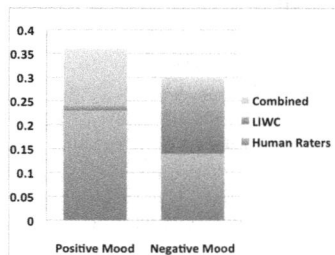

Figure 2: Adjusted R-squared (cumulative) for the three models: (i) human raters only, (ii) LIWC only, and (iii) combined models. The combined model accounted for the most variance in positive affect and only slightly more variance in negative affect as compared to LIWC alone.

5. CONCLUSIONS AND FUTURE WORK

This study compared three models for estimating direct measures of positive and negative affect: 1) human ratings alone, 2) automated text categories alone, and 3) combined human ratings and automated text categories. For positive affect, the combined model accounted for more variance than the human ratings alone or LIWC categories alone. Therefore, human ratings and automated text analysis appear to provide different, but complementary information about positive affect and, when combined, provide the most powerful model for estimating positive affect. For negative affect, the LIWC alone accounted for more variance than human ratings alone and the combined model did not add much improvement. Therefore, automated text analysis performs better than human coders when estimating negative affect. While human ratings and ATA each have costs and benefits, the type of method, or combination of methods, that is best depends on what is being estimated.

Future work will involve adding personal characteristics (e.g., age, gender, personality traits) as potential predictors of affect. Additional methods should also be explored for combining human ratings with LIWC categories. We are aware that LIWC has limitations (e.g., does not include modifiers/negations). Therefore, we plan to develop our own algorithms that account for the combination of words (e.g., n-grams) rather than single words. Finally, other outcome variables beside affect should be explored, such as measures of depression, and life satisfaction.

6. REFERENCES

[1] I. Ajzen. The theory of planned behavior. *Organizational behavior and human decision processes*, 50(2):179–211, 1991.

[2] I. Ajzen. Nature and operation of attitudes. *Annual review of psychology*, 52(1):27–58, 2001.

[3] G. W. Alpers, A. J. Winzelberg, C. Classen, H. Roberts, P. Dev, C. Koopman, and C. B. Taylor. Evaluation of computerized text analysis in an internet breast cancer support group. *Computers in Human Behavior*, 21(2):361–376, 2005.

[4] J. Alvarez-Conrad, L. A. Zoellner, and E. B. Foa. Linguistic predictors of trauma pathology and physical health. *Applied Cognitive Psychology*, 15(7):S159–S170, 2001.

[5] K. Bakhtiyari, M. Taghavi, and H. Husain. Hybrid affective computingâĂŤkeyboard, mouse and touch screen: from review to experiment. *Neural Computing and Applications*, 26(6):1277–1296, 2015.

[6] E. O. Bantum and J. E. Owen. Evaluating the validity of computerized content analysis programs for identification of emotional expression in cancer narratives. *Psychological assessment*, 21(1):79, 2009.

[7] C. M. Burton and L. A. King. The health benefits of writing about intensely positive experiences. *Journal of research in personality*, 38(2):150–163, 2004.

[8] J. Cohen. A coefficient of agreement for nominal scales. *Educational and psychological measurement*, 20(1), 1960.

[9] J. R. Crawford and J. D. Henry. The positive and negative affect schedule (panas): Construct validity, measurement properties and normative data in a large non-clinical sample. *British Journal of Clinical Psychology*, 43(3):245–265, 2004.

[10] M. C. Davis, A. J. Zautra, and J. W. Reich. Vulnerability to stress among women in chronic pain from fibromyalgia and osteoarthritis davis et al. stress vulnerability. *Annals of Behavioral Medicine*, 23(3):215–226, 2001.

[11] R. Feldman. Techniques and applications for sentiment analysis. *Communications of the ACM*, 56(4):82–89, 2013.

[12] M. Fishbein and I. Ajzen. *Belief, attitude, intention and behavior: An introduction to theory and research.* 1975.

[13] J. Frattaroli. Experimental disclosure and its moderators: a meta-analysis. *Psychological bulletin*, 132(6):823, 2006.

[14] B. L. Fredrickson. The role of positive emotions in positive psychology: The broaden-and-build theory of positive emotions. *American psychologist*, 56(3):218, 2001.

[15] J. H. Kahn, R. M. Tobin, A. E. Massey, and J. A. Anderson. Measuring emotional expression with the linguistic inquiry and word count. *The American journal of psychology*, pages 263–286, 2007.

[16] K. Kercher. Assessing subjective well-being in the old-old the panas as a measure of orthogonal dimensions of positive and negative affect. *Research on Aging*, 14(2):131–168, 1992.

[17] A. Mackinnon, A. F. Jorm, H. Christensen, A. E. Korten, P. A. Jacomb, and B. Rodgers. A short form of the positive and negative affect schedule: Evaluation of factorial validity and invariance across demographic variables in a community sample. *Personality and Individual differences*, 27(3):405–416, 1999.

[18] S. Mishra, J. Diesner, J. Byrne, and E. Surbeck. Sentiment analysis with incremental human-in-the-loop learning and lexical resource customization. In *Proceedings of the 26th ACM Conference on Hypertext & Social Media*, pages 323–325. ACM, 2015.

[19] A. Ortigosa, J. M. Martín, and R. M. Carro. Sentiment analysis in facebook and its application to e-learning. *Computers in Human Behavior*, 31:527–541, 2014.

[20] J. W. Pennebaker and S. K. Beall. Confronting a traumatic event: toward an understanding of inhibition and disease. *Journal of abnormal psychology*, 95(3):274, 1986.

[21] J. W. Pennebaker, C. K. Chung, M. Ireland, A. Gonzales, and R. J. Booth. The development and psychometric properties of liwc2007. *UT Faculty/Researcher Works*, 2007.

[22] J. W. Pennebaker, M. E. Francis, and R. J. Booth. Linguistic inquiry and word count: Liwc 2001. *Mahway: Lawrence Erlbaum Associates*, 71:2001, 2001.

[23] Y. R. Tausczik and J. W. Pennebaker. The psychological meaning of words: Liwc and computerized text analysis methods. *Journal of language and social psychology*, 29(1):24–54, 2010.

[24] M. Thelwall, K. Buckley, G. Paltoglou, D. Cai, and A. Kappas. Sentiment strength detection in short informal text. *Journal of the American Society for Information Science and Technology*, 61(12):2544–2558, 2010.

[25] R. Tibshirani. Regression shrinkage and selection via the lasso. *Journal of the Royal Statistical Society. Series B (Methodological)*, pages 267–288, 1996.

[26] W. Tov, K. L. Ng, H. Lin, and L. Qiu. Detecting well-being via computerized content analysis of brief diary entries. *Psychological assessment*, 25(4):1069, 2013.

[27] D. Watson, L. A. Clark, and A. Tellegen. Development and validation of brief measures of positive and negative affect: the panas scales. *Journal of personality and social psychology*, 54(6):1063, 1988.

Framework for Sentiment Analysis of Arabic Text

Latifah Almuqren
Department of Computer Science,
Warwick University,
Coventry, UK.
L.Almuqren@warwick.ac.uk

Alexandra I. Cristea
Department of Computer Science,
Warwick University,
Coventry, UK
A.I.Cristea@warwick.ac.uk

ABSTRACT
This paper analyses *challenges*, and provides a *model* and a *framework* for mining Arabic tweets to measure *customer satisfaction* toward telecom companies in Saudi Arabia, to predict the ratio of *customer churn* and overcome the specific challenges with the semantic sentiment analysis of Arabic text.

Keywords
Semantic Sentiment Analysis (SSA), Arabic, Twitter, Sentiment

1.   INTRODUCTION
Enhancing customer satisfaction is a popular topic in marketing. Customer satisfaction is attained by examining customer expectations toward the products of a company [5]. *Customer churn* is defined in the telecom field as transferring from one company to another [3]. Traditionally, *customer satisfaction* has been measured through customer interviews and questionnaires, but these cannot measure customer satisfaction in real time [9].

Twitter is a widely popular messaging service categorised as a micro-blogging website [23]. By mining these tweets, a database of emotions can be created, to analyse the sentiments and related subjective contexts of micro-blogging conversations.

The Arabic language is quite challenging for SSA interpretation [10], due to the variety of forms in Arabic language, such as Modern Standard Arabic (MSA) and the informal language, or colloquial Arabic, and the structure of the language, such as the direction of writing from right to left.

However, *customer satisfaction* based on real time methods for Saudi Arabian companies is an understudied area. Thus, this study examines microblogging site mining techniques for the purpose of capturing user satisfaction toward telecom companies in Saudi Arabia, and how to use data for recommendations to companies.

In the current paper, we focus on investigating three questions:
RQ1. What are the variables influencing customer satisfaction and affect customer churn?
RQ2. What social media data mining techniques are appropriate for capturing customer satisfaction toward telecom companies in Saudi Arabia from microblogging sites?
RQ3. What are the challenges for SSA tools for Arabic tweets?
The remainder of the paper is structured as follows. Section 2 presents our customer satisfaction model and related work. Section 3 explains our suggested research framework. Section 4 summarizes the challenges in Arabic Semantic Sentiment Analysis (SSA). Finally, Section 5 provides conclusions and future work.

2. NEW MODEL AND RELATED WORK
From a literature analysis of 50 papers on predictions of customer satisfaction based on Twitter, and of Twitter analysis for Arabic text, we have created a customer satisfaction model containing all variables that link Twitter and user satisfaction (Figure 1). Unlike the Kano Model, measuring customer's satisfaction per product features [22], our model focuses on customer satisfaction and churn, overall. Additionally, our model doesn't concentrate on the environmental causes, unlike [11].

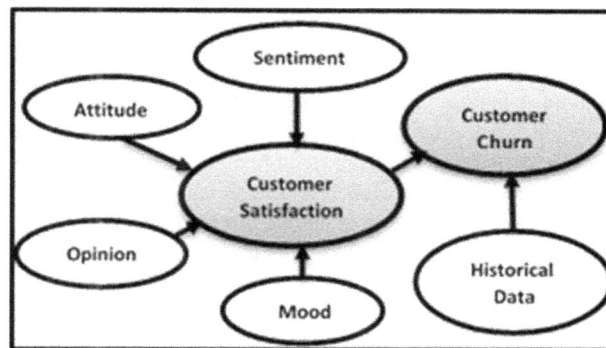

Figure 1: Our customer satisfaction model

Mood
Bollen et al. [7] examined the influence of public mood on the closing value of the Dow Jones Industrial Average (DJIA), by estimating 6 emotions. Results show that not all changes in the public mood lead to DJIA value shifts, but a 'calm' mood could predict DJIA values.

Opinion, Attitude and Sentiment
Salampasis et al. [21] analysed consumers' behaviour about food products, using their micro blogging messages (i.e., tweets) to monitor and analyse consumer opinion, attitude and sentiments expressed in shared posts and comments. Results showed that the success of branding required monitoring sentiments for a long period of time, because these sentiments do not change quickly.

Semantic Sentiment Analysis
Our study plans to use Semantic Sentiment Analysis (SSA) of Arabic tweets to measure customer satisfaction. Collines et al. [8] measured public transport rider satisfaction toward transit system services using the riders' tweets on Twitter. They used a Sentiment Strength Detection Algorithm (SentiStrength), to detect rider sentiments in real time.

Mostafa [16] analysed 3,516 tweets to measure consumer sentiment toward brands such as Nokia, T-Mobile, IBM, and DHL, using a predefined lexicon. Results indicated a generally positive consumer sentiment toward several famous brands.

Historical Data
Many studies have focused on using historical data, using data mining to create a prediction model [12]. Also, Kampakis &

Adamides [13] predicted the score of football matches using Twitter mining and historical data, with a high accuracy of 75%.

3. USER SATISFACTION FRAMEWORK

Based on previous studies of Twitter mining, as well as on the lack of tools and annotated corpuses for Arabic, we suggest a new study with the following phases (Figure 2). The customer satisfaction model is based solely on customer sentiment, measured from Twitter, via Semantic Sentiment Analysis (SSA). This represents the link between the model and the framework.

1. **Data Collection:** Build a corpus of Arabic SSA messages from the Twitter semantic (search) API [1,9,18, 19] for six months, with Arabic native speakers to annotate the collected real time tweets that mention telecom companies, to monitor the latest sentiment of telecom customer continuously and add annotations.

2. **Building an In-Domain Arabic Lexicon**: Use a corpus-based approach to build the lexicon, using all data from the same domain. The classified tokens (breaking Arabic expressions down into smaller tokens) and lemmas (each word reduced to a citation form) may be used as seeds for an automated machine learning algorithm, after weighing term-frequency (to judge and include the additional words from the *Saudi dialectal Arabic* (SDA)), and then finalise the lists of positive, negative and neutral words [1,14]. A lexicon seed comprises a list of words from the SDA having identical semantic, lexical and semantic-lexical relationships for positive, negative and neutral emotions [2, 15]. A seed is constructed from frequently used words in Twitter and never used words in Twitter (via expansion algorithms) [15].

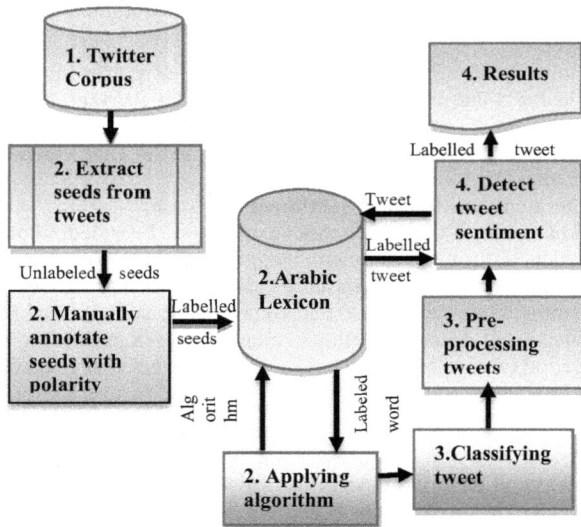

Figure 2: The User Satisfaction Capturing Framework

3. **Pre-Processing Tweets:** Normalize and tokenize all tweets. Tokens are stemmed via a revised n-gram approach [13].

4. **SSA**: Detect customer satisfaction using SSA for each tweet, applying classifiers with proven high accuracy for Arabic text: Support Vector Machines, KNN, Naïve Byes [2, 3, 9].

4. CHALLENGES AND SOLUTIONS

Most SSA tools are for English. These need a lot of adjustment to function with Arabic. To develop SSA tools for Arabic text requires an understanding of the unique Arabic internal structure, nature, terms and linguistic rules, plus dialectical and colloquial differences in different Arabic regions. Each form has its own syntax and vocabulary, which makes building an Arabic lexicon difficult [4]. Additionally, different words may have the same meaning in different dialects. For example, "a lot" in the Moroccan dialect is (باهي), but it is (صافي) in Libyan [17].

Arabic script properties also pose challenges, such as:

- **Diacritization:** A word may have different meanings, based on the small diacritical marks above or under letters. For example (شعر) could mean "hair" with a small diacritical mark above its first letter, or it could mean "poem" with a small diacritical mark below that letter [17].

- **Negation:** In English, negative words often use a prefix, such as un- or im-, etc. (e.g., impossible vs. possible). In Arabic, however, a negative word is preceded by a separate term. For example, *unhelpful* (غير مفيد) vs. *helpful* (مفيد). This causes a problem, as the sentence-level classifier treats the negation as two separate words. Azmi & Alzanin solved this problem by joining the words in a pre-processing phase [6].

- **Spelling Errors:** Mixing up small dialectical marks and long vowels leads to errors: e.g., *you* (انتي) should be spelled (انت).

Azmi & Alzanin and Saif et al. [6, 20] proposed a revised n-gram to correct misspelled words and improve classification. If they couldn't find a word in a vocabulary table, they searched for similarities in that table. If two words were at least 70% similar, they counted them as referring to the same notion, such as the terms *succccess* (نجااح) and *success* (نجاح) (Figure 3).

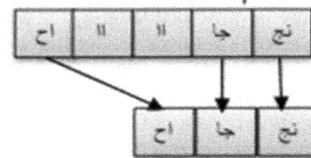

Figure 3: A revised n-gram approach

5. CONCLUSIONS

Due to increasing global competition, companies are more eager than ever to understand *customer sentiments*, to be better able to improve customer care and avoid losing customers to their competition. This research provides a *customer satisfaction model* to compute *customer churn* (answering research question RQ1), as well as a *framework to capture user satisfaction* toward telecom companies (answering research question RQ2) and examines some *challenges and their potential solutions* in using SSA for Arabic text, due to the unique nature of Arabic (answering research question RQ3). To meet the challenges related to Arabic script properties, this study proposes solutions in the pre-processing stage, such as normalization, revised n-gram or contextual rules. These solutions are expected to greatly enhance classifier accuracy. Additional research in this area should be conducted using these suggested approaches. Finally, this study highlights the importance of moving away from an English-only approach to SSA and lexicon building, pointing to the exciting new avenues opened by other rich languages and their respective cultures.

6. REFERENCES

[1] Abdulla, N., Majdalawi, R., Mohammed, S., Al-Ayyoub, M. and Al-Kabi, M. 2014. Automatic lexicon construction for Arabic sentiment analysis. *In Proceedings of the Future Internet of Things and Cloud (FiCloud)*, (Barcelona,Spain, 2014). IEEE , 547-552. DOI= 10.1109/FiCloud.2014.95

[2] Abdul-Mageed,M., Kübler, S. and Diab, M. 2014. SAMAR: A system for subjectivity and sentiment analysis of Arabic social media. *Computer Speech and Language.* 28, 1 (January. 2014),20-37.

[3] Ahmed, S., Pasquier, M. and Qadah, G. 2013. Key issues in conducting sentiment analysis on Arabic social media text. *In 9th International Conference on Innovations in Information Technolog (IIT)*, (Abu Dhabi, UAE, March 17-19, 2013). IEEE, 72-77. DOI= 10.1109/Innovations.2013.6544396

[4] Albraheem, L. and Al-Khalifa, H. S. 2012. Exploring the problems of sentiment analysis in informal Arabic. In Proceedings of iiWAS, (Bali,Indonesia, December, 2012). IIWAS '12, ACM, New York, NY, 415-418. DOI= 10.1145/2428736.2428813

[5] Athanassopoulos, A. D. and Iliakopoulos, A. 2003. Modeling customer satisfaction in telecommunications: Assessing the effects of multiple transaction points on the perceived overall performance of the provider. *Production and Operations Management.* 12, 2 (June. 2003) 224-245.

[6] Azmi, A. M. and Alzanin, S. M. 2014. Aara'–a system for mining the polarity of Saudi public opinion through e-newspaper comments *Journal of Information Science.*40, 3 (March. 2014), 398-410. DOI= 10.1177/0165551514524675

[7] Bollen, J., Mao, H. and Zeng, X. 2011. Twitter mood predicts the stock market. *Journal of Computational Science.* 2, 1(March. 2011), 1-8.

[8] Collins, C., Hasan, S. and Ukkusuri, S. V. 2013. A novel transit rider satisfaction metric: Rider sentiments measured from online social media data. *Journal of Public Transportation.* 16, 2 (2013), 21-45. DOI= http://dx.doi.org/10.5038/2375-0901.16.2.2

[9] Duwairi, R.M. and Qarbaz,I. 2014. Arabic Sentiment Analysis Using Supervised Classification. *In Proceeding of the International Conference on Future Internet of Things and Cloud (FiCloud)*, (Barcelona, Spain, November 27-29, 2014). IEEE Computer Society, 579-583. DOI= 10.1109/FiCloud.2014.100

[10] Farghaly A. and Shaalan, k. 2009. Arabic natural language processing: Challenges and solutions. *Transactions on Asian Language Information Processing.* 8, 4(December. 2009), 1-22.

[11] Getty, R.L. 1999. Ergonomics and the customer satisfaction model: ergonomics in the language of business. In *Proceedings of the Human Factors and Ergonomics Society Annual Meeting,* (Fort Worth, Texas, 1999). SAGE Publications, 815-819.

[12] Hung, S. Y., Yen, D. C. and Wang, H. Y. 2016. Applying data mining to telecom churn management. *Expert Systems with Applications.* 31,3 (October.2016),515-524.DOI= 10.1016/j.eswa.2005.09.080

[13] Kampakis, S. and Adamides, A. 2014.Using Twitter to predict football outcomes. *ArXiv preprint arXiv:1411.1243*, 2014, Retrieved January 20, 2016 from Cornell University Library : http://arxiv.org/abs/1411.1243

[14] Mahyoub, F. H. H. , Siddiqui, M. A. and Dahab, M. Y. 2014. Building an Arabic sentiment lexicon using semi-supervised learning. *Journal of King Saud University Computer and Information Sciences.* 26, 4(December. 2014),417–424. DOI= 10.1016/j.jksuci.2014.06.003

[15] Marcus, A., Bernstein, M. S., Badar,O., Karger, D. R., Madden, S. and Miller, R. C. 2011. Processing and visualizing the data in tweets. *SIGMOD Record.* 40, 4, December. 2011), 21-27.

[16] Mostafa, M. M. 2013. More than words: Social networks' text mining for consumer brand sentiments.2013. *Expert Systems with Applications*, 40,10 (Lisbon, Portugal, January 25, 2013). Elsevier B.V., 4241-4251.

[17] Mustafa, M., AbdAlla, H. and Suleman, H. 2008. Current approaches in Arabic IR: A survey. In G. Buchanan, M. Masoodian and S. Cunningham, ed., *Digital Libraries: Universal and Ubiquitous Access to Information.* Springer Berlin Heidelberg, Bali, Indonesia, 2008, 406-407.

[18] Pak, A. and Paroubek, P. 2010. Twitter as a Corpus for Sentiment Analysis and Opinion Mining. *In Proceedings of the Seventh conference on International Language Resources and Evaluation (LREC'10)*, European Language Resources Association (ELRA), (Valletta, Malta, 2010), 1320-1326.

[19] Refaee,E., and Riesner,V. 2014. An Arabic Twitter corpus for subjectivity and sentiment analysis. In *Proceedings of Language Resources and Evaluation Conference 2014*, (Reykjavik, Iceland, 2014), 2268 - 2273.

[20] Saif, H. He, Y. and Alani, H. 2012. Semantic sentiment analysis of Twitter. In *Proceedings of the 11th International Conference on the Semantic Web*, (Boston, Massachussetts, United States, 2012), Springer-Verlag Berlin, 508-524.

[21] Salampasis, M., Paltoglou, G. and Giachanou, A.2013. Using social media for continuous monitoring and mining of consumer behaviour. *International Journal of Electronic Business.* 11,1 (2013) 85-96

[22] Sauerwein, E., Bailom, F., Matzler, K. and Hinterhuber, H.H. 1996. The Kano model: How to delight your customers. *In Proceeding of the International Working Seminar on Production Economics,* (Innsbruck, lgls, Austria,1996). Innsbruck, 313-327.

[23] Twitter. Twitter.com, 2016.https://twitter.com/?lang=en. Retrieved January 19, 2016

A New Hierarchical Clustering Algorithm to Identify Non-overlapping Like-minded Communities

Talasila Sai Deepak
Google, Mountain View
t.deepak.iitg@gmail.com

Hindol Adhya
Indian Institute of Technology, Guwahati
hindol.adhya@gmail.com

Shyamal Kejriwal
Indian Institute of Technology, Guwahati
shyamalkejriwal@gmail.com

Bhanuteja Gullapalli
Indian Institute of Technology, Guwahati
bhanutejaiit@gmail.com

Saswata Shannigrahi
Indian Institute of Technology, Guwahati
saswata.sh@iitg.ernet.in

ABSTRACT

In this paper, we present a new algorithm to identify non-overlapping like-minded communities in a social network and compare its performance with Girvan-Newman algorithm, Lovain method and some well-known hierarchical clustering algorithms on Twitter and Filmtipset datasets.

Keywords

Community detection; Modularity; Like-mindedness

1. INTRODUCTION

A social network is denoted by an undirected and unweighted sparse graph $G = (V, E)$ with vertex set $V = \{1, 2, \ldots, |V|\}$ such that $|E| = O(|V|)$. Each vertex $v \in V$ is associated with a behavioral vector X_v of dimension d. For example, the ratings given by a user on a movie rating website (with some default rating being given to those movies he has not rated) can be his behavioral vector, the dimension of which is the number of movies available for rating. A similarity metric $sim(u, v)$ is a distance measure between the vectors X_u and X_v representing the behavior of the vertices $u, v \in V$, respectively. In this paper, we use cosine similarity $\frac{X_u \cdot X_v}{\|X_u\| \|X_v\|}$ as the distance measure. Let $C = \{C_1, C_2, \ldots, C_k\}$ be a partition of V, each representing a set of vertices (community) in a community structure having k non-overlapping communities. The **modularity** [7] $Q(C)$ of the set of communities C is defined as $Q(C) = \sum_{i=1}^{k} (a_i - b_i^2)$, where a_i is the fraction of $|E|$ edges with both its vertices in the same community C_i and b_i is the fraction of $|E|$ edges with at least one vertex in community C_i. The **like-mindedness** [6] $L(C)$ of the set of communities C is defined as the average of all intra-community vertex pair similarities. In other words, $L(C) =$

$\frac{1}{\sum_{u,v \in V: u \leq v} \delta(u,v)} \sum_{u,v \in V: u \leq v} sim(u,v)\delta(u,v)$, where the boolean function $\delta(u, v)$ is 1 if and only if there exists a community $C_i \in C$ such that $u, v \in C_i$.

2. LIKE-MINDEDNESS MAXIMIZATION

In this section, we present a bottom-up hierarchical clustering approach in which one starts with each vertex belonging to V as its own community. In each subsequent step, pairs of communities are merged till there is only one community left. The pair of communities that gives the minimum value of a pre-defined linkage criterion (defined below) is selected for being merged in each step. In this agglomerative approach, we get a hierarchy of communities, often visualized as a dendrogram. We observe from the dendograms of several hierarchical clustering algorithms that an algorithm produces higher like-mindedness if small clusters are merged in the early iterations in order to avoid the creation of large heterogeneous communities. Motivated by this fact, we design this algorithm in which we discourage the merging of two large communities in an iteration. At every iteration, we identify the pair $\{C_i, C_j\}$ of communities that has the highest score $S(C_i, C_j) = \frac{1}{max\{|C_i|, |C_j|\}} + \frac{1}{|C_i||C_j|} \sum_{u \in C_i, v \in C_j} sim(u, v)$. The left term is used to discourage the merging of two large communities, and the right term accounts for the average like-mindedness of the inter-community pairs from $\{C_i, C_j\}$. A high value of the right term ensures that the like-mindedness of the set of communities after merging is high, since $\sum_{u \in C_i, v \in C_j} sim(u, v)$ is the sum of the similarities of $|C_i||C_j|$ pairs of inter-community vertices belonging to C_i and C_j.

3. DATASET & EXPERIMENTAL SETUP

3.1 Filmtipset

Filmtipset is Sweden's largest movie rating website, in which a user has the option to rate a movie on a scale of 1 to 5. Apart from this, there is a social network element of the website where a user can *follow* another user in the network. We have $86,725$ such following relationships between the users. We designate two users $u, v \in V$ as friends if u is following v, and vice-versa.

To use the dataset in our experiments, we apply a couple of filters. The first filter is applied on the number of times a

HT '16 July 10-13, 2016, Halifax, NS, Canada

© 2016 Copyright held by the owner/author(s).

ACM ISBN 978-1-4503-4247-6/16/07.

DOI: http://dx.doi.org/10.1145/2914586.2914613

Table 1: Filmtipset and Twitter datasets

Parameter	Filmtipset Unfiltered Network	Filmtipset Filtered Network 1	Filmtipset Filtered Network 2	Twitter Unfiltered Network	Twitter Filtered Network
Number of nodes	91530	4305	983	40096646	5013
Number of isolated nodes	61211	168	152	17522652	1
Edge count (friendships)	56387	10940	1807	232157703	1636971
Avg. clustering coefficient	0.467	0.434	0.338	11.5799	653.09
Avg. degree	1.232	5.082	3.676		0.2063612
Diameter	20	18	16	18 [5]	4
Avg. path length	7.508	5.796	4.817	4.12 [5]	1.874073
Size of giant component	29.54%	90.77%	72.94%		5012
Homophily ratio		26.44	62.07		1.18

Table 2: Symbols used in Figure 1

Symbol	Full form	Running time
LMM/LMMS	LMM Algorithm using (un)interested vector	$O(|V|^2 \log |V|)$
LMMR	LMM Algorithm using rating vector	$O(|V|^2 \log |V|)$
L	Louvain method [1]	$O(|V| \log |V|)$ (estimated)
ML/MLS	Modified Louvain method using (un)interested vector	$O(|V|^2 \log |V|)$ (estimated)
MLR	Modified Louvain method using rating vector	$O(|V|^2 \log |V|)$ (estimated)
GN	Girvan-Newman algorithm [4]	$O(|V|^3)$
S/SS	Single-linkage Clustering using (un)interested vector [8]	$O(|V|^2)$
A/AS	Average-linkage Clustering using (un)interested vector [2]	$O(|V|^2 \log |V|)$
C/CS	Complete-linkage Clustering using (un)interested vector [3]	$O(|V|^2)$
SR	Single-linkage Clustering using rating vector [8]	$O(|V|^2)$
AR	Average-linkage Clustering using rating vector [2]	$O(|V|^2 \log |V|)$
CR	Complete-linkage Clustering using rating vector [3]	$O(|V|^2)$

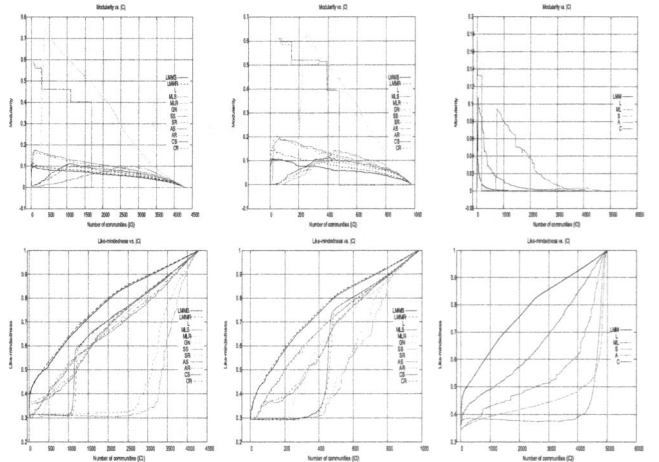

Figure 1: Modularity and like-mindedness scores in Filmtipset Filtered Networks 1 (left) and 2 (middle), and Twitter Filtered Network (right)

movie has been rated. Some movies are *popular* since they are rated by many. We observe that removing the most popular movies from being considered results in a higher ratio of the average similarity (w.r.t. rating vectors defined below) of the pairs of friends to the average similarity of the non-friend pairs. We denote this ratio for G as its *homophily ratio*

$$H(G) = \left(\frac{\sum\limits_{u,v \in V : (u,v) \in E} sim(u,v)}{|E|} \right) \Big/ \left(\frac{\sum\limits_{u,v \in V : (u,v) \notin E} sim(u,v)}{\binom{|V|}{2} - |E|} \right).$$

It can be noted that aiming for too high a homophily ratio reduces the number of movies a lot. Since the number of movies left is used for filtering out inactive users (see below), a high homophily ratio implies a reduction in the number of active users as well. Therefore, we remove movies that are rated at least 50 times in filter 1 since it ensures a large number of movies left after filtering. To see the performance of our algorithm on networks having high homophily ratio, we remove movies that are rated at least 5 times in filter 2.

For each of the movie filters 1 and 2, we define a user filtering criterion as follows. For movie filter 1 (filter 2), we say a user to be *active* if he rates at least 5 movies among the movies left after removing all movies rated more than 50 (5, respectively) times. A user is called *social* if he has at least 5 friends in the network. For each of movie filter 1 and 2, we create an induced subgraph such that each user in this subgraph is active and social. In Table 1, we summarize the properties of these datasets, which we would denote by Filmtipset Filtered Networks 1 and 2. We also note that the degrees of vertices in the Unfiltered Network as well as the Filtered Networks follow a *power law distribution*.

For either of Filmtipset Filtered Network 1 and 2, we consider the movies in an order and each user u is assigned a *rating vector* R_u, each entry of which is either the rating given by him to that particular movie or 0 if he has not rated it. We also create another *(un)interested vector* S_u for each user u, each entry of which is 1 or 0 depending on whether a user has rated that movie or not, respectively. In order to implement the behavioral property based community finding algorithms, either R_u or S_u is used as the behavioral vector X_u of $u \in V$.

3.2 Twitter

Using the publicly available dataset [5] which has about 40 million users including users having more than 10,000 followers designated as *celebrities*, we create a friendship graph

called Twitter Filtered Network of the non-celebrity users having at least 5000 non-celebrity friends. We summarize the dataset in Table 1 and also note that the degrees of vertices in the Filtered Network follow a *power law distribution*.

As before, two users u and v are said to be friends if u is following v, and vice-versa. We create a 0/1 vector F_u (the i-th entry of which corresponds to the i-th celebrity) for each user $u \in V$ and use it as his behavioral vector X_v. The entry in i-th position of F_u for u is 1 or 0 depending on whether u is following the i-th celebrity or not, respectively.

4. RESULTS AND CONCLUSIONS

In Figure 1, the like-mindedness and modularity scores achieved by different algorithms are compared by plotting their values against $|C|$, the number of communities identified. In Table 2, we summarize the running time of the algorithms considered in this paper. The key observation from Figure 1 is that our algorithm Like-mindedness Maximization outperforms all other algorithms (including Modified Louvain method where we add pairs of vertices having higher similarity than the current like-mindedness score as an edge after every iteration of the Louvain Method) on *like-mindedness* metric. Moreover, when the number of identified communities is large, we observe from Figure 1 that our algorithm obtains a community structure with comparable (to other algorithms considered here) modularity. The running time of our algorithm is $O(|V|^2 \log |V|)$, which is much faster than the Girvan-Newman algorithm but slightly slower than other hierarchical clustering algorithms. We also note that the actual ratings (not just the data about whether a user has rated a movie or not) given by Filmtipset users does not give any significant advantage to the performance of the community detection algorithms. This is due to the fact that the similarity matrices of rating and (un)interested vectors of the user pairs are quite similar, e.g., having a cosine similarity of 0.9420 and 0.9062 for Filmtipset Filtered Network 1 and 2, respectively. Another interesting observation is that all the algorithms obtain higher like-mindedness and modularity scores in Filmtipset Filtered Network 2 compared to Network 1, due to it having higher homophily ratio.

5. REFERENCES

[1] V. D. Blondel, J. L. Guillaume, R. Lambiotte and E. Lefebvre. Fast unfolding of communities in large networks. *Journal of Statistical Mechanics: Theory and Experiment*, 10:P10008, 2008.

[2] W. H. Day and H. Edelsbrunner. Efficient Algorithms for Agglomerative Hierarchical Clustering Methods. *Journal of Classification*, Volume 1, pp. 1-24, 1984

[3] D Defays. An Efficient Algorithm for a Complete Linkage Method. *The Computer Journal (British Computer Society)*, 20 (4): 364-366, 1977.

[4] M. Girvan and M.E.J. Newman. Community Structure in Social and Biological Networks. *Proc. National Academy of Sciences*, 99(12): 7821-7826, 2002.

[5] H. Kwak, C. Lee, H. Park and S. Moon. What is Twitter, a Social Network or a News Media? *Proc. 19th international conference on World Wide Web*, 591-600, 2010.

[6] N. Modani, R. Gupta, S. Nagar, S. Shannigrahi, S. Goyal and K. Dey. Like-minded Communities: Bringing the Familiarity and Similarity Together. *World Wide Web*, 17 (5), 899-919, 2014.

[7] M.E.J. Newman and M. Girvan. Finding and Evaluating Community Structure in Networks. *Physical review E*, 69(2): 026113, 2004.

[8] R. Sibson. SLINK: an Optimally Efficient Algorithm for the Single-link Cluster Method. *The Computer Journal (British Computer Society)* 16 (1): 30-34, 1972.

A Comparative Study of Visual Cues for Adaptive Navigation Support

Roya Hosseini
Intelligent Systems Program
University of Pittsburgh
Pittsburgh, PA 15260
roh38@pitt.edu

Peter Brusilovsky
School of Information Sciences
University of Pittsburgh
Pittsburgh, PA 15260
peterb@pitt.edu

ABSTRACT

Past work in the area of adaptive navigation support assumed no difference between different interface implementations of personalization approaches that are conceptually the same. The goal of this paper was to compare the impact of different implementations of the same adaptive navigation support approach on user perception and performance.

Keywords

adaptive navigation support; link annotation; code examples

1. DESIGN CHOICES FOR ANS

Adaptive navigation support (ANS) is a group of technologies that support user navigation in hyperspace by adapting to the goals, preferences, and knowledge of an individual user [1]. Over the years, some efficient ANS approaches were established and evaluated. Many teams suggested different sets of icons to implement conceptually the same personalization approach (such as knowledge-based or prerequisite-based annotations). While each of these efforts was typically evaluated and proven efficient, they implicitly assumed that the choice of icons to implement an adaptation approach does not matter, and that only the approach itself does.

In this paper, we present our attempt to compare different implementations of the same ANS approach in interactive program examples produced by the WebEx system [3]. The original WebEx system has no link annotation, however, more recent versions used simple history-based link annotation: code lines already accessed by the user were annotated with check marks as shown in Figure 1. Our goal was to determine the best knowledge-based annotation approach and to find the best way to combine it with history-based annotation and direct recommendation. We expected that visualizing this information dynamically (i.e., displaying it as a visual cue next to the line) could help users select the most important lines. The design alternatives for icon-based adaptive link annotation in the WebEx examples are as follows.

HT '16 July 10-13, 2016, Halifax, NS, Canada

© 2016 Copyright held by the owner/author(s).

ACM ISBN 978-1-4503-4247-6/16/07.

DOI: http://dx.doi.org/10.1145/2914586.2914615

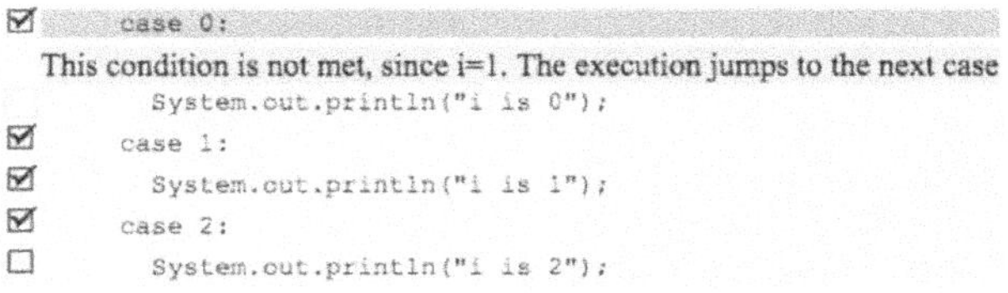

Figure 1: A partial view of an annotated example with a check mark annotation for clicked lines.

Knowledge-based annotation. The first design used a "filling" metaphor displaying icons with different levels of filling to show the knowledge behind each line. This kind of design was explored in the past in [7, 3]. Five discrete filings were defined from 0% to 100%, with 25% increments to represent 0% to 100% knowledge behind the line. This design is referred to as $A1$ (see design $A1$ in the knowledge-based annotation column of Table 1). The second design ($A2$) explored earlier in [6] used different intensities of the green color. As student knowledge increases, the green color of the icons becomes darker (see design $A2$ in the knowledge-based annotation column of Table 1). The third design ($A3$), explored earlier in [5], used a gradient that ranged from orange to green colors for the icons relative to the knowledge of the student. As student knowledge increases, the color of the icon changes from dark orange through yellow into dark green (see design $A3$ in the knowledge-based annotation column of Table 1).

History-based annotation. The first design ($B1$) borrowed the common Web browser design that changes the color of visited links from blue to purple: the icons next to lines that were viewed by the student are filled with a purple color. Since this history-based annotation must be used jointly with knowledge-based annotation, there were three possible combinations: $B1(A1)$, $B1(A2)$, and $B1(A3)$ shown in column $B1$ of Table 1. The second design ($B2$) followed the approach used in the current version of WebEx (Figure 1): a check mark sign over the bullet to indicate visited lines (see three combinations of this design in column $B2$ of Table 1).

Recommendations. Two designs were explored for the recommendation of an example line. The first design ($C1$) simulates the bold font used, for example, in [2], by increasing the width of the icon border to indicate recommended lines. The second design $C2$ used a red star as an indicator of recommendation, just as in [4]. Similar to history-based annotation, the recommendation was used with the knowledge-based annotation designs $A1$–$A3$. Columns $C1$ and $C2$ of Table 1 illustrate how knowledge-based annotations and recommendations were combined.

Table 1: Design alternatives for annotation of links in an annotated example

Knowledge-based annotation	History-based annotation		Recommendation	
	B1	B2	C1	C2
A1				
A2				
A3				

2. THE STUDY

We designed and conducted a user study with 31 students at the University of Pittsburgh to assess design alternatives for the three types of icon-based ANS reviewed above. The designs were shown with the full set of icons for each kind of annotation, as shown in Table 1. The subject was asked to provide her/his opinion about each design alternatives by answering a 5-item questionnaire. After that, the subject performed three tasks (Task 1–Task 3).

Task 1 provided three code examples annotated according to three different knowledge-based ANS alternatives, i.e., A1–A3. The subject was asked to circle the lines that showed *minimum* and *maximum* knowledge in each example and then she/he had to select the design that made finding the lines with *minimum* and *maximum* knowledge easier.

Task 2 provided three annotated code examples and asked the subject to circle already accessed lines. Each example used a combination of knowledge-based annotations A1–A3 and history-based annotations B1–B2, which indicated accessed lines. Odd-numbered subjects received combinations B1A1, B1A3, and B2A2 and even-numbered subjects received combinations B1A2, B2A1, and B2A3. At the end of the task, the subject had to select the design that made finding the accessed lines easier.

Task 3 provided three annotated code examples and asked the subject to circle the recommended lines in each one. Each example used a combination of knowledge-based annotations A1–A3, combined with annotations C1–C2 for showing recommended lines. Odd-numbered subjects received combinations C1A1, C1A3, and C2A2, and even-numbered subjects received C1A2, C2A1, and C2A3. At the end of the task, the subject was asked to select the design that made finding the recommended lines easier.

3. FINDINGS

The alternative designs were evaluated using data collected from both questionnaires and tasks. Analysis of the questionnaire data showed that the annotation approaches that appeared to be interchangeable were actually considerably different from user prospects. The designs that used filled bullets (A1) turned out to be significantly better than the design that used different shades of green (A2) and considerably better than the second-best design (A3) that used a progression of orange to green colors. The design that annotated an example link with a check mark (B2) was significantly better than the design that used the purple color (B1). Similarly, the design that annotated an example link with a red star (C2) received significantly higher preference, as compared to the design that used a thick border for the bullet (C1).

The in-context perceptions of subjects collected during the tasks showed that user preferences changed consider-

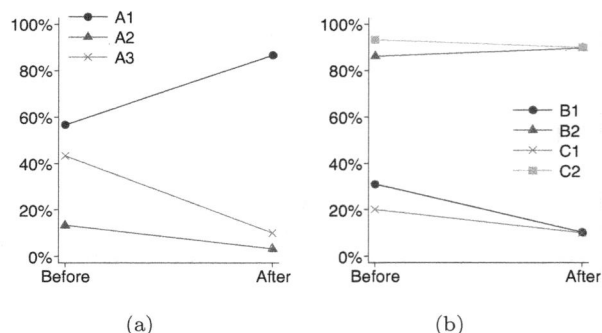

(a)   (b)

Figure 2: Percent of subjects favoring a design before and after performing (a) Task 1, and (b) Task 2 and Task 3.

ably within the task's context. Figure 2a illustrates how the favored design changed after performing Task 1. While an orange-to-green gradient colors were generally considered to be a good idea, this particular color scheme was clearly harder to use in-context for finding lines with the most or the least knowledge, and this resulted in 9 of 11 supporters of design A3 switching fully to A1. Similarly, after performing Task 1, out of 4 subjects who initially favored the design with a different intensity of green, as in (A2), 2 switched to design A1 and 1 switched to design A3.

The favored designs for the history-based annotation and recommendation of links also changed for some subjects after assessing the designs in the context of Tasks 2 and Task 3. Figure 2b combines odd- and even-numbered subjects and shows the change in favored designs for annotating links with browsing history and recommendation. The number of subjects who favored design B2 increased after performing Task 2 while the number of supporters for design B1 decreased. Preference for recommendation designs changed as well. The number of subjects who favored design C1 and C2 decreased with the latter one experiencing less loss, only loosing one of its supporters.

Taken together, these results show that two or more alternatives for the selection of visual cues within the same conceptual ANS approach might differ significantly from the prospect of user perception and task performance. Moreover, user assessment of different ANS design options could considerably change when working with them in both a realistic context and in combinations with other visual cues. However, it was interesting that in all cases, the top designs A1–B2–C2 identified in an out-of-context assessment increased their standing above other designs during in-context evaluation. Our findings stress the need to pay attention to designing visual cues, and not only to the approaches themselves.

4. REFERENCES

[1] P. Brusilovsky. Adaptive navigation support. In *The adaptive web*, pages 263–290. Springer, 2007.

[2] P. Brusilovsky, J. Eklund, and E. Schwarz. Web-based education for all: A tool for developing adaptive courseware. In H. Ashman and P. Thistewaite, editors, *Seventh International World Wide Web Conference*, volume 30, pages 291–300. Elsevier Science B. V., 1998.

[3] P. Brusilovsky and M. V. Yudelson. From webex to navex: Interactive access to annotated program examples. *Proceedings of the IEEE*, 96(6):990–999, 2008.

[4] R. Hosseini, I.-H. Hsiao, J. Guerra, and P. Brusilovsky. What should i do next? adaptive sequencing in the context of open social student modeling. In *10th European Conference on Technology Enhanced Learning (EC-TEL 2015)*, pages 155–168, 2015.

[5] I. H. Hsiao, F. Bakalov, P. Brusilovsky, and B. Koenig-Ries. Progressor: social navigation support through open social student modeling. *New Review of Hypermedia and Multimedia*, 19(2):112–131, 2013.

[6] T. Loboda, J. Guerra, R. Hosseini, and P. Brusilovsky. Mastery grids: An open source social educational progress visualization. In *9th European Conference on Technology Enhanced Learning (EC-TEL 2014)*, volume 8719 of *Lecture Notes in Computer Science*, pages 235–248, 2014.

[7] K. A. Papanikolaou, M. Grigoriadou, H. Kornilakis, and G. D. Magoulas. Personalising the interaction in a web-based educational hypermedia system: the case of inspire. *User Modeling and User Adapted Interaction*, 13(3):213–267, 2003.

E³ : Keyphrase based News Event Exploration Engine

Nikita Jain   Swati Gupta   Dhaval Patel
Department of Computer Science and Enginnering
Indian Institute of Technology Roorkee, India
nk27jain@gmail.com, {sg123.dcs2014, patelfec}@iitr.ac.in

ABSTRACT

This paper presents a novel system E³ for extracting keyphrases from news content for the purpose of offering the news audience a broad overview of news events, with especially high content volume. Given an input query, E³ extracts keyphrases and enrich them by tagging, ranking and finding role for frequently associated keyphrases. Also, E³ finds the novelty and activeness of keyphrases using news publication date, to identify the most interesting and informative keyphrases.

1. INTRODUCTION

News media are publishing ideas, events and opinions in an increasingly wide range of data formats such as news articles, headlines, videos, tweets, hashtags and others. The explosion of Big news data has sparked the text and data mining research communities to focus on developing systems for news data exploration and analysis. Broadly, two types of news data exploration systems are developed till date: *Event centric* (GDELT [1], EventRegistry [2]) and *Content centric* (STICS [3], EMM [4]). In Event centric system, input query maps to real world events, whereas, the content centric system outputs related news articles of a given query.

Although, both types of systems provide up-to-date news information in real time, but they overload the user with the large amounts of results. For instance, given input query "2014 FIFA World Cup", event centric EventRegistry suggested 11,504 news events, and the content centric STICS suggested 1,286,369 news articles having multiple organizations, people and places mentioned. Clearly, there is a need of a system that enables readers to get a broad overview of the news data generated in response of user query.

In this paper, we propose a keyphrase based news exploration engine E³ to summarize high volume news data. In our context, keyphrase is a short and meaningful chunk of text that describes an important news concepts, news entities, etc. For instance, "Bihar election", "Bihar bjp" are examples of keyphrases. Our proposed work is keyphrase centric as recent literature has shown that Keyphrase min-

ing is able to generate a wide range of informational and important phrases from large documents (KEA [5], Microngram [6], ToPMine [7], and SegPhrase [8]). As shown in Figure 1, engine E³ works in two phases: keyphrase extraction followed by keyphrase enrichment. Keyphrase extracation is performed on multi-form news (like article, keywords, and others). As existing keyphrase mining approaches performs poorly on news data, we propose a novel keyphrase extraction technique that leverages linguistic-syntactic feature, and performs very well on short texts like news headlines and video captions. The keyphrase enrichment phase finds important and interesting information related to the keyphrase, such as connected entities, novel (emerging), and active news concepts, and the role played by most frequent entities present in set of keyphrases.

In summary, given an input query q, engine E³ generates a keyphrase template, as shown in Figure 2, where keyphrases are organized into three sections: Type Discovery, Keyphrase Ranking and InfoBox Miner. The keyphrase of type Person, Location and Organization are kept in Type section. The Novel, Active and Frequent keyphrases are annotated in Keyphrase Ranking section. Information like Role played, top most associated Types and Keyphrase for a selected keyphrase is stored in InfoBox section.

2. SYSTEM OVERVIEW

Figure 1 gives an overview of E³ architecture.

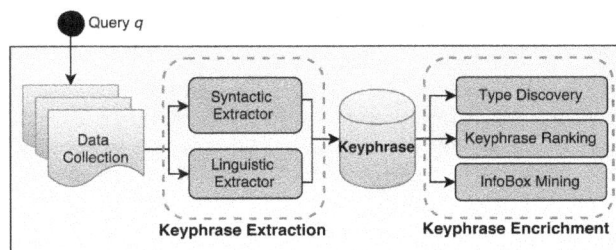

Figure 1: E^3 System Architecture

2.1 Data Collection

For input query q, our data collection module prepares related news data published by news media. The module can either use news search engines like Google News, Yahoo News or online news structured repositories like GDELT [1], EMM [4], iMM [9]. We use our in-house iMM system which periodically extracts news headlines (video title) along with their URL, publication date and meta-keywords. To prepare

HT '16 July 10-13, 2016, Halifax, NS, Canada

© 2016 Copyright held by the owner/author(s).

ACM ISBN 978-1-4503-4247-6/16/07.

DOI: http://dx.doi.org/10.1145/2914586.2914611

Type Discovery

Person	Location	Organization
Narendra Modi	New Delhi	Bihar Assembly
Nitish Kumar	Lok Sabha	Shiv Sena
Jitan Ram	Red Fort	Election Commision
Amit Shah	West Bengal	Lok Janshakti Party
Ram Vilas		Bihar Bjp
Paswan		Rashtriya Janata Dal
Sonia Gandhi		Hindustani Awam
Shahnawaz		Morcha

Keyphrase Ranking — *(Frequency Based) (Top-Bottom; Left-Right)*

Bihar Elections +	Rjd +
Bjp	Nda +
Bihar +	Lalu Prasad +
Nitish Kumar +	Congress
Bihar Polls	Bihar Assembly
Grand Alliance # +	Elections
Narendra Modi +	Election Result # +

 # Emergent   + Active

InfoBox Miner

Entity	Narendra Modi
Role	Prime Minister

Topmost Related Connection

Location:	New Delhi
Organization:	Lok Sabha Polls
Person:	Nitish Kumar
Keyphrase:	Bihar Polls

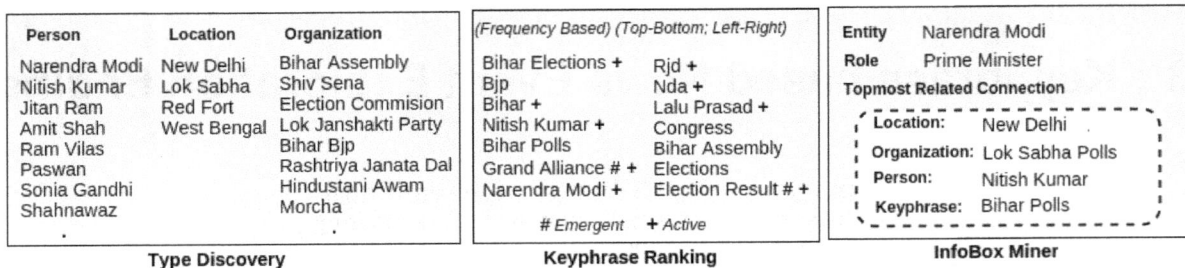

Figure 2: E^3 System Working Example for q: "Bihar Election"

news data related to q, we select URL, if URL's headlines (video title) or URL's meta-keywords contains q.

In summary, for given query q, we prepare a dataset R containing several news records R_q, where each record is described by *Quintuple* {Headline, Keywords, Meta-description, Article, Publication Date}. For "Bihar Election" query, we retrieved 216 records from iMM for further processing.

2.2 Keyphrase Extraction

Next, we extract keyphrases from all the records of news data R. As meta-keywords are small group of meaningful words, a naive solution is to output the meta-keywords as keyphrases. However, not all records in R contain meta-keyword. As a result, meta-keywords are not sufficient enough to describe the news data completely. For example, around 20% news headlines, obtained for "Bihar Election", do not have a meta-keyword. Hence, we require an efficient selection of the relevant phrases.

We observed that news headlines are short in length and contains special tokens such as colon, apostrophe, quotes, hash, dash to emphasize important information. On the other hand, meta-descriptions and news articles are long passage texts and are governed by grammatical rules. Thus, we propose two different keyphrase extractors to handle both kinds of writing styles.

- **Syntactic Extractor** utilises special characters such as colon (:), apostrophe ('), quotes (", '), hash (#), dash (-) for keyphrase extraction. In case of colon (dash), the news headline is tokenized into two parts using colon (dash) and both parts are declared as keyphrases. In case of quotes (hash) the part of text enclosed inside the quotes and hashtag containing the hash is declared as keyphrase respectively.

- **Linguistic Extractor** applies language specific part of speech (POS) tagging on meta-description and article and then annotate collocated nouns, adjectives, noun apostrophe (') connector and numbers present in the input text. These annotated tokens are further used as keyphrases.

At the end, when all the news records in R are processed, we obtain a set of keyphrases R_k, along with the number of times they are generated. For "Bihar Election" query, we obtained around 6000 keyphrases for further processing.

2.3 Keyphrase Enrichment

The size of generated keyphrases R_k may be large and noisy. To resolve this problem, our Keyphrase Enrichment module helps in extracting valuable and actionable information by filtering and ranking the extracted keyphrases. The keyphrases are filtered using news media specific stopwords such as update, video, photo, pti and others. Next, we

apply case normalization and remove duplicate keyphrases. At this point noisy keyphrases are removed. The remaining keyphrases are passed through the Type discovery, Keyphrase ranking and InfoBox mining modules.

- In **Type Discovery** module, NER tagger is used to classify keyphrase into three types: *Person*, *Location* and *Organization*. As existing NER taggers do not perform well on Indian named entities, we use a separate list[1] for Indian named entities, prepared through in-house research work. A keyphrase without any above NER type, are termed as a *News Concept*. For "Bihar Election" query, a sample keyphrases for each type is shown in Figure 2.

- Using **Keyphrase Ranking** module, keyphrases are organized according to the value of frequency, novelty and activeness. The frequency of the keyphrase is already computed during keyphrase extraction process. To compute the value of novelty and activeness, we first extracts the time intervals q_t of an input query q, during which the q was highly popular in news headlines. Next, a keyphrase is *novel* (denoted by # in Figure 2) if its frequency is very high in news headlines only during q_t. Similarly, a keyphrase is *active* (denoted by + in Figure 2) if its frequency is very high around q_t. For instance, "Grand Alliance" and "NDA" are discovered as novel and active keyphrases respectively for "Bihar Election" query.

- **InfoBox Miner** discovers personalized information for selected keyphrase. The InfoBox displays role of keyphrase k that it played with respect to query q. The type-wise top most connections k have, determined with help of co-occurrence value of the keyphrases in R_k. A phrase frequently located near k in the collected news corpus is labeled as the k's role. Generally, keyphrases with type person and organization are preferred for InfoBox mining. Figure 2 shows InfoBox for entity "Narendra Modi" for query "Bihar Election".

3. SUMMARY

The engine is tested for varying the input query ranging from general topics (e.g., Election, ISIS) to specific topics (e.g., Paris Attack, Gravitational Wave) and compared the results[2] with KEA, ToPMine and Micro-ngram. We found that our system outperforms existing approaches in terms of quality and quantity of keyphrases generated. As our engine is online, we can demonstrate the working to the conference participants.

---

[1]https://github.com/NikkiJain09/Transliteration
[2]goo.gl/yoLXTh

4. REFERENCES

[1] K. Leetaru and P. A. Schrodt, *GDELT: Global data on events, location, and tone.* International Studies Association Annual Convention, 2013.

[2] G. Leban, B. Fortuna, J. Brank, and M. Grobelnik, *Event Registry: Learning About World Events from News.* World Wide Web, 2014.

[3] J. Hoffart, D. Milchevski, and G. Weikum, *STICS: Searching with Strings, Things, and Cats.* Special Interest Group on Information Retrieval, 2014.

[4] R. Steinberger, B. Pouliquen, and E. V. der Goot, *An introduction to the Europe Media Monitor family of applications.* Special Interest Group on Information Retrieval, 2009.

[5] O. Medelyan and I. H. Witten, *Thesaurus Based Automatic Keyphrase Indexing.* Joint Conference on Digital Libraries, 2006.

[6] K. Wang, C. Thrasher, E. Viegas, X. Li, and B.-j. P. Hsu, *An Overview of Microsoft Web N-gram Corpus and Applications.* North American Chapter of the Association for Computational Linguistics: Human Language Technologies, Association for Computational Linguistics, 2010.

[7] A. El-Kishky, Y. Song, C. Wang, C. R. Voss, and J. Han, *Scalable Topical Phrase Mining from Text Corpora.* Very Large Data Bases, 2014.

[8] J. Liu, J. Shang, C. Wang, X. Ren, and J. Han, *Mining Quality Phrases from Massive Text Corpora.* Special Interest Group on Management of Data, 2015.

[9] S. Mazumder, B. Bishnoi, and D. Patel, *News Headlines: What They Can Tell Us?* IBM Collaborative Academia Research Exchange, 2014.

Understanding Language Diversity in Local Twitter Communities

Amr Magdy[1], Thanaa M. Ghanem[2], Mashaal Musleh[3], Mohamed F. Mokbel[4]

[1,4]Dept. of Computer Science and Engineering, University of Minnesota, Minneapolis, MN
[2]Dept. of Information and Computer Sciences, Metropolitan State University, Saint Paul, MN
[3]KACST GIS Technology Innovation Center, Umm Al-Qura University, Makkah, KSA
{[1]amr,[4]mokbel}@cs.umn.edu, [2]thanaa.ghanem@metrostate.edu,
[3]mmusleh@gistic.org

ABSTRACT

Twitter is one of the top-growing online communities in the last years. In this poster, we study the language usage and diversity in Twitter local communities. We identify local communities in Twitter on a country-level. For each community, we examine: (1) the language diversity, (2) the language dominance and how it differs from local to global views, (3) demographic representativeness of tweets, and (4) the spatial distribution of different cultural groups within the community. We show fruitful insights about language usage on Twitter which can be exploited in language-based applications on top of tweets, e.g., lingual analysis and disaster management. In addition, we provide an interactive tool to explore the spatial distribution of cultural groups, which provides a low-effort and high-precision localization of different cultural groups.

1. INTRODUCTION

Twitter is one of the most popular social media where people used to post opinions, news items, updates on on-going activities,...etc. Everyday, 500+ million tweets are posted by 320 millions users. With such popularity, many techniques have exploited tweets for language-based analysis. This includes disaster management [3], multi-lingual usage [2], and language identification [4]. In most of these tasks, an implicit assumption has been made that English language is dominating other languages on Twitter to the extent that it could work as a language proxy for other languages [5], so that analyzing English tweets is enough to deduce conclusions about Twitter community. However, some crucial applications, like disaster management, are highly dependent on *local* language usage. For example, during China floods in 2012, propagating information about victims' locations on the Chiense Twitter (Sina Weibo) saved more than

This research is capitally supported by NSF grants IIS-0952977, IIS-1218168, IIS-1525953, CNS-1512877, and the University of Minnesota Doctoral Dissertation Fellowship.

two hundred souls [1]. This imposes an important question weather language usage in popular social media is different on the local and global scales.

In this poster, we conduct a study to analyze and understand different aspects of spatial-language interaction in Twitter data, using a half billion of worldwide geo-tagged tweets. The whole dataset is used as a single global community and we identify country-level local communities based on tweets' locations. Then, we study four aspects of language usage within global and local communities. First, the diversity of language usage within both global and local communities using different measures. Second, the language dominance in the local communities and how this compares to the global Twitter community. This deduces fruitful insights on the overall language usage in Twitter data and clearly shows the prime importance of local languages in Twitter-based applications. Third, the representativeness of Twitter global and local communities for demographics of the real population. This relies on comparing language diversity measures with the data collected by international organizations, e.g., UNESCO. Fourth, the spatial distribution of different languages, and so cultural groups, within the country. This is provided as an interactive web-based tool that provides a low-effort and high-precision localization for different cultural groups inside the country. Such localization is of interest for several users, e.g., administrative authorities to localize Syrian refugees.

2. BACKGROUND AND DEFINITIONS
2.1 Defnitions

Our study mainly work on two concepts:

(1) **Twitter local community** of a certain country is defined by the set of all tweets posted within the spatial extent of this country.

(2) **Cultural group** is defined as the group of tweets that are posted in the same language. Throughout the study, we use Greenberg's language diversity index (LDI) as one of the measures to assess cultural diversity. LDI is used in UNESCO World Report on Cultural Diversity. LDI gives the probability of randomly selecting two persons with different native languages from a certain group of people. The higher LDI value, the higher cultural diversity.

2.2 Datasets

In our study, we use 445+ millions geo-tagged tweets that are collected through Twitter public streaming APIs during the period of October 12, 2013 to March 6, 2014. Each tweet

Table 1: Diversity by LDI

Country	LDI
Macedonia	0.884
AAT	0.865
NA	0.857
Austria, Armenia	0.832
Morocco	0.821

Table 2: Number of countries that encounters % difference in LDI, e.g., 16 countries with difference in LDI values ≤ 5%

% of LDI Difference	Number of Countries
1	4
3	10
5	16
7	22
10	33

is associated with a country using its geo-tag and public geographic datasets[1]. For language data, we use the language attribute, that is attached to tweets, as it comes from Twitter. To enrich our insights from the measured statistics, we compare our statistics with official organizations and major geographical database providers. Specifically, We use ISO 3166 and GeoNames country information datasets for getting country names and statistics on spoken languages. We also use UNESCO World Report on Cultural Diversity for getting UNESCO values of Greenberg's language diversity index (LDI) for different countries.

3. RESULTS AND CONCLUSIONS

In this section, we present our study results and conclusions on Twitter local communities of different countries. In our dataset, we have identified 206 Twitter local communities, each is corresponding to one country. Each community is divided into cultural groups. The dataset contains 55 different languages with average of 18 languages used within a single community and standard deviation of 12. Due to space limitations, we include only the most important results. Our poster presented in the conference would include more results. Below a summary of our results on four aspects of language usage.

Language diversity. In our full results, we use three measures for diversity within the community: (i) total number of languages, (ii) number of languages that cover 80% of tweets, and (iii) LDI as defined above. The last two measures have shown robust and consistent results as both of them consider the distribution of language usage within the community. For example, USA is the most diverse based on the first measure and encounters tweets with 44 different languages. However, 85% of USA tweets are posted in English and only 15% in all other languages, which shows much less diversity than other communities. Table 1[2] shows the most diverse local Twitter communities based on LDI. As shown, Macedonia shows the most diversity followed by Australian Antarctic Territory and Netherlands Antilles. In these three territories, the number of languages that cover 80% of their tweets are nine, seven, and six. This shows much more diversity beyond all other communities, that have 80% of the tweets in one to three languages only.

Language domination. Our analysis shows that tweets of 133 countries (∼65% of the countries) are dominated by the first spoken language in the country while the remaining 73 countries are dominated by a non-first language. This clearly shows that language domination in local Twitter communities is mostly for local language rather than international languages like English. In fact, most of countries that are dominated by English although it is not the first language, which are 41 out of 73, encounter low Twitter activity. This shows that English cannot work as a language

proxy for other languages when the application is concerned with the spatial extent. Our full results shows that the domination of English in Twitter global community is interpreted by the high Twitter activity from USA and UK. In fact, 81.6% of the whole tweets are posted in only seven languages while 48 languages form only 18.4%. This confirms the observation that global language domination exist in Twitter global community which does not contradict with the domination of local languages in local communities.

Demographic representativeness. To assess the validity of using Twitter as a representative for actual population, we consider language diversity based on LDI from tweets compared to real LDI values from UNESCO World Report on Cultural Diversity. Worldwide, for 206 countries and territories, we found a weak Pearson correlation of 0.25 between Twitter and real LDI values. However, we identified 33 countries (∼16% of the countries) that having less than or equal to 10% difference in LDI value between Twitter and the real value. This brings the attention again for focusing on local aspects of Twitter data. Although the global Twitter community does not look representative for the human population, certain local Twitter communities may represent their actual population. Table 2 shows the number of countries that encounters a certain difference in LDI values. For example, there are 16 countries with difference in LDI values less than or equal 5%. Our full results show the countries with the least difference in LDI values, which are the most promising candidates for more investigation on demographic representativeness of their tweets.

Spatial distribution of cultural groups. In our poster, we present a tool that enables visual analysis for language spatial distribution within a certain country. Using this tool, one can visually identify the spread of local cultural groups within the country through a web-based interface. This may be of interest for different users, e.g., local authorities to deal with certain situations like Syrian refugees. Our tool facilitates a low-effort and high-precision localization for different cultural groups around the country.

4. REFERENCES

[1] Sina Weibo, China Twitter, comes to rescue amid flooding in Beijing. http://thenextweb.com/asia/2012/07/23/sina-weibo-chinas-twitter-comes-to-rescue-amid-flooding-in-beijing/.

[2] I. Eleta and J. Golbeck. Multilingual Use of Twitter: Social Networks at the Language Frontier. *Computers in Human Behavior*, 41, 2014.

[3] I. V. et. al. Aid is Out There: Looking for Help from Tweets during a Large Scale Disaster. In *ACL*, 2014.

[4] M. Graham, S. Hale, and D. Gaffney. Where in the World Are You? Geolocation and Language Identification in Twitter. *The Professional Geographer*, 66(4):568–578, 2014.

[5] The Geography of Twitter: Mapping the Global Heartbeat. irevolution.net/2013/06/09/mapping-global-twitter-heartbeat/.

---

[1] https://hiu.state.gov/data/data.aspx

[2] AAT: Australian Antarctic Territory, NA: Netherlands Antilles

The Influence of Features and Demographics on the Perception of Twitter as a Serendipitous Environment

Lori McCay-Peet
Dalhousie University
6100 University Avenue
Halifax, Nova Scotia, Canada
mccay@dal.ca

Anabel Quan-Haase
Western University
1155 Richmond Street
London, Ontario, Canada
aquan@uwo.ca

ABSTRACT

Much research has sought to understand serendipity and how it may be hindered or facilitated in the context of digital environments such as information visualization systems, mobile apps, and social media. Twitter has been described in both the popular media and academic literature as an ideal space for serendipity to occur, though little research has sought to empirically confirm this relationship. The perception of Twitter as a space for serendipitous experiences is fueled by its dynamic qualities, trigger rich interface, and networked nature, which have the potential to prompt unexpected encounters with information and ideas. The present paper examined 184 individuals' use of Twitter features in relation to their perceptions of Twitter as serendipitous and tested for the influence of demographic differences. We found that age and use of Twitter features (checking timeline, tweeting, and searching) were strongly related to perceptions of Twitter as a serendipitous digital environment. Findings have implications for the design of digital environments that endeavor to facilitate serendipity.

CCS Concepts

• **Human-centered computing→ Human-computer interaction→ (HCI) HCI design and evaluation methods.**

Keywords

Serendipity; Twitter; social media; design features; demographics.

1. INTRODUCTION

Serendipity is defined as "an unexpected experience prompted by an individual's valuable interaction with ideas, information, objects, or phenomena" [1]. Dynamic and fast-paced social environments in which people with diverse interests can bump into each other and have casual conversations are often credited with facilitating serendipity ([2], [3]). Knudsen and Lemmergaard [4], in the context of strategic communication in organizational settings, "argue that social media, with its collective affordances of persistence, replicability, scalability and searchability [5] particularly facilitates serendipity, because the complex and multi-way communication challenges control and power over messages and texts" (p. 406).

With recent considerations of changes to Twitter's interface, the potential loss of serendipity has become a particularly hot topic of debate. At the center of the concern is Twitter's plan to change the order in which posts occur on users' timeline— "best posts" rather than the current reverse chronological order of posts. This could

create an "echo chamber," as users would be shown posts they are presumed to like rather than exposing them to a diversity of posts, some located at the periphery of their interests [6].

The present paper seeks to examine how Twitter features impact user perceptions of serendipity. Our main research question is: Do individuals' use of Twitter features share a relationship with their perception of Twitter as a serendipitous digital environment? Because prior research relating to the perception of serendipity [7] was conducted through studies with participant samples that tended to be older than the current sample, this prompted us to also examine potential relationships between demographics and perceptions of serendipity: Do demographic differences influence people's perception of Twitter as a serendipitous digital environment? The motivation for this research comes from a need for a more nuanced understanding of social media that will enable researchers to begin to question design features and their impact on user experience [15].

2. PRIOR RESEARCH

The ability of Twitter to facilitate serendipity has been written about in blogs and the media over the past few years (e.g., [9],[10],[11]). Dubbed "a serendipity engine for the web" ([9], n.p.), Twitter has been credited as a "great tool for serendipity" ([11], n.p.) if used to its best advantage by following diverse and interesting people, participating in conversations on Twitter, setting up searches on topics of interest through platforms such as TweetDeck, asking followers for feedback, and having fun.

Prior research supports the popular notion that social media sites, including Twitter, are digital environments that facilitate serendipity (e.g., [13],[14]). Through interviews with digital humanities scholars on their use of Twitter, Quan-Haase et al. [14] found that Twitter provided a dynamic and diverse environment in which the tweets of others afforded random but meaningful connections, facilitating serendipitous experiences. Characteristics of a digital environment, such as being trigger-rich, enabling connections, and leading to the unexpected, have all been positively related to individuals' perceptions of a serendipitous environment [7]. Dantonio et al. [13] found through interviews with students that they came across academic information serendipitously on Twitter and other social media when they invested time in it—not only absorbing the information contained in these sites, but also creating and sharing content. Research has also examined how Twitter could improve how well it supports serendipity: using natural language processing to extract user interests, Piao and Whittle [12] examined how Twitter could suggest serendipitous connections.

While research suggests that Twitter in general supports serendipity, we have yet to get a clear sense of what is fueling those findings. No research to date, for example, has examined the relationship between serendipity and the use of Twitter features (e.g., tweet, timeline). Moreover, while prior research examined perceptions of serendipity in digital environments among

HT '16, July 10-13, 2016, Halifax, NS, Canada
ACM 978-1-4503-4247-6/16/07.
http://dx.doi.org/10.1145/2914586.2914609

employed individuals and students [7], no research has examined age or other demographic characteristics as factors influencing the perception of serendipity.

3. Methodology

The data were collected as part of a larger study on the uses and gratifications of social media. Only data on Twitter and serendipity are reported here. Data collection took place between November 2014 and January 2016 and participants were recruited in classrooms at a large Canadian university and via social media.

Participants ($N = 185$) were asked to complete a web-based or paper-based survey (for classroom recruitment). The mean age of participants was 25 ($Md = 21$; $SD = 9.0$) Most were female (74.5%) and 147 (79%) were Canadian university students. More than half of the participants (55%) reported using Twitter for at least three years, though they tended to use Twitter less than one hour per day (67%). Participants reported following an average of 278 Twitter accounts ($SD = 334$), being followed by 294 ($SD = 443$), and had posted on average 3,993 tweets ($SD = 7,734$).

The online tool Qualtrics was used to build and host the survey on a secure university server. The survey included a demographics section and Twitter users were asked about their use and perceptions of Twitter as serendipitous. Use questions included: how long they have had an account, how often they use it, number of follows/followers, and tweets. Participants were also asked on a scale ranging from 1 = "never" to 5 = "several times a day" how frequently they check their Twitter timeline, tweet, retweet, use a hashtag (#), mention (@), search, and direct message. McCay-Peet et al.'s [7] previously validated scale was used to measure a user's perception of how frequently serendipity occurs in a specific digital environment. It is comprised of four Likert items ranging from 1 = "never" to 5 = "very frequently". Items include, for example: "Through my use of Twitter, I experience serendipity that has an impact on my everyday life" and "I encounter useful information, ideas, or resources that I am not looking for when I use Twitter."

Of the initial pool of 294 completed surveys, 12 multivariate outliers were removed for a total of 282 observations, of these 184 indicated they had a Twitter account and responded to the Twitter-related questions. Through factor analysis of the four perception of serendipity items using principal components analysis with varimax rotation, a single factor was extracted that explained 77% of the total variance. The reliability of the perception of serendipity scale was very good (Cronbach's $\alpha = .89$). The new scale was computed through the mean of the four perception of serendipity items and used as the dependent variable in hierarchical multiple regression analysis in SPSS. The two demographics variables (age, gender) were entered as control variables while the seven Twitter features use variables (e.g., timeline, tweet, hashtag) served as predictor variables.

4. RESULTS

The mean of the Perception of Serendipity score was 2.6 (SD = .93). Gender and Age were entered in the hierarchical multiple regression as control variables, followed by the Twitter features use as predictor variables (see Table 1). The first model was significant (Adjusted $R^2 = .04$, $F [2,181] = 4.44$, $p < .05$) with Age accounting for a proportion of the variation in the Perception of Serendipity ($\beta = .20$, $p < 0.5$). In the second model, Age together with three Twitter features accounted for a significant portion of the Perception of Serendipity (Adjusted $R^2 = .39$, $F (7,174) = 16.01$, $p < .001$). Age ($\beta = .17$, $p < 0.01$), Timeline ($\beta = .25$, $p < .01$), Tweet ($\beta = .25$, $p < .05$), and Search ($\beta = .22$, $p < .01$), each

contributed significantly to the prediction of the variance if the Perception of Serendipity. In other words, the analysis indicated that the older the users were, the more they checked their timeline, tweeted, and searched in Twitter, the more frequently they perceived they experienced serendipity in Twitter.

Table 1 Summary of Hierarchical Regression Predicting Perception of Serendipity in Twitter ($N = 184$)

Variable	Model 1			Model 2		
	B	*SE B*	*β*	*B*	*SE (B)*	*B*
Age	.02	.01	.20*	.02	.01	.17**
Gender	.10	.16	.05	.07	.13	.03
Timeline				.16	.06	.25**
Tweet				.22	.10	.25*
Retweet				.01	.08	.01
Hashtag				-.03	.08	-.03
Mention				.03	.10	.03
Search				.20	.07	.22**
DM				.00	.10	.00
Adjusted R²		.04			.39	
F for change in *R²*		4.44*			16.01***	

Note. *p < .05. ** p < .01. *** p<.001

5. DISCUSSION AND CONCLUSION

While each Twitter user's experience is unique—each has a different network offering up different opportunities for interaction and information discovery—the current study suggests that patterns may be discerned in relation to perceptions of serendipity through the use of specific features. Results indicate, as Dantonio et al. [13] suggested in their study on social media, that actively engaging on Twitter is an important factor in its perception as a serendipitous environment. Not only checking one's timeline, but also tweeting and searching have an influence on how frequently serendipity is perceived to occur. While this suggests that the availability of these features is important, it also suggests the importance of using these features in order to increase the opportunities for serendipity. Understanding why some people are more likely to experience serendipity in a digital environment like Twitter than others will inform the development of heuristics to design serendipitous digital spaces.

That age surfaced as a factor in the perception of serendipity in this study may suggest two things. First, the meaning of serendipity may differ by age. The term serendipity has evolved since its 18th century inception [16]; findings may reflect an evolution over the past few decades. Second, the use of Twitter by individuals of different ages may be coupled with different motivations for Twitter use and thus different perceptions of its qualities, including serendipitousness. Future research should consider and further explore age and other demographic characteristics as factors in the perception of serendipity.

Social media, predominantly characterized by networked qualities that help link people and information, is well suited to support serendipity. However, as it becomes increasingly apparent to users that changes to the features of their favorite social media platforms change the nature of their experiences within them, perceptions of what these features enable are becoming a focus of interest. It is important to understand how changes affect experiences (positively or negatively) such as serendipity and what variables may be associated with these experiences.

6. ACKNOWLEDGMENTS

The authors would like to thank Kim Martin, Darryl Pieber, and Ellen Whelan for their help with data collection for this research. The project was funded by a SSHRC of Canada Insight Grant given to Dr. Quan-Haase No. R3603A13.

7. REFERENCES

[1] McCay-Peet, L. and Toms, E.G. 2015. Investigating serendipity: How it unfolds and what may influence it. *Journal of the Association for Information Science and Technology, 66*(7), 1463-1476.

[2] Pálsdóttir, Á. 2011. Opportunistic discovery of information by elderly Icelanders and their relatives. *Information Research, 16*(3). Retrieved from http://InformationR.net/ir/16-3/paper485.html

[3] Sun, X., Sharples, S., and Makri, S. 2011. A user-centred mobile diary study approach to understanding serendipity in information research. *Information Research, 16* (3). Retrieved from http://InformationR.net/ir/16-3/paper492.html

[4] Knudsen, G.H. and Lemmergaard, J. 2014. Strategic serendipity: How one organization planned for and took advantage of unexpected communicative opportunities. *Culture and Organization, 20*(5), 392-409.

[5] boyd, D. 2010. Social network sites as networked publics: Affordances, dynamics, and implications." In *A Networked Self: Identity, Community, and Culture on Social Network Sites*, edited by Z. Papacharissi, 39–58. New York: Routledge.

[6] Beres, D. 2016. Twitter's new update could bring you into the echo chamber. *HuffPost Tech.* (February 10). http://www.huffingtonpost.com/entry/twitter-algorithm-update_us_56b8d264e4b08069c7a826d3

[7] McCay-Peet, L., Toms, E.G. and Kelloway, E.K. (2015). Examination of relationships among serendipity, the environment, and individual differences. *Information Processing and Management, 51*, 391-412.

[8] Bowman, M., Debray, S. K., and Peterson, L. L. 1993. Reasoning about naming systems. *ACM Trans. Program. Lang. Syst.* 15, 5 (Nov. 1993), 795-825. DOI= http://doi.acm.org/10.1145/161468.16147.

[9] Brogan, C. 2009. The beauty of collaboration. Retrieved from http://chrisbrogan.com/the-beauty-of-collaboration/

[10] Cohen, A. 2010. Return on serendipity. (March 18). Retrieved from http://adamhcohen.com/return-on-serendipity

[11] InnovationTools.com. 2013. How to increase your odds of serendipity with Twitter. Retrieved from http://www.innovationmanagement.se/imtool-articles/how-to-increase-your-odds-of-serendipity-with-twitter/

[12] Piao, S. and Whittle, J. 2011. A feasibility study on extracting Twitter users' interests using NLP tools for serendipitous connections. In *2011 IEEE Third Int'l Conference on Privacy, Security, Risk and Trust and 2011 IEEE Third Int'l Conference on Social Computing* (pp. 910–915). Boston, MA: IEEE. http://doi.org/10.1109/PASSAT/SocialCom.2011.164

[13] Dantonio, L., Makri, S., and Blandford, A. 2012. Coming across academic social media content serendipitously. *Proceedings of the American Society for Information Science and Technology, 49*(1), 1–10.

[14] Quan-Haase, A., Martin, K., and McCay-Peet, L. (2015). Networks of digital humanities scholars: The informational and social uses and gratifications of Twitter. *Big Data & Society, January-June,* 1-12. Available at http://bds.sagepub.com/content/2/1/2053951715589417

[15] Hogan, B. 2015. Mixing in social media. Social Media + Society, *April-June,* 1-2. http://sms.sagepub.com/content/1/1/2056305115580482.full

[16] Merton, R. K. and Barber, E. 2004. The travels and adventures of serendipity: A study in sociological semantics and the sociology of science. Princeton, NJ: Princeton University Press.

Improving Website Navigation with the Wisdom of Crowds

Naureen Nizam
University of Toronto
Toronto, ON
nnizam@cs.toronto.edu

Carolyn Watters
Dalhousie University
Halifax, NS
carolyn.watters@dal.ca

Anatoliy Gruzd
Ryerson University
Toronto, ON
gruzd@ryerson.ca

ABSTRACT

In this paper, we explore how user-generated content, such as links (web page URLs) shared on social media can be used to recommend relevant and popular web pages to the website visitors. Based on our preliminary findings [8, 9], we have developed a set of guidelines and a prototype called the Social Media Panel (SMP). The SMP displays popular web pages as page thumbnails based on the aggregate information trending on social media sites. We evaluate the SMP via a focus group and a controlled user study, and compare it against conventional website navigation tools (i.e., menus, search, links, and browser tools), for effectiveness, efficiency and user engagement. We found SMP to be effective, efficient and engaging for browsing tasks. Subsequently, ANOVA tests were employed which proved that it took fewer clicks to complete the task using SMP. However, the use of SMP did not prove to make a significant difference in expediting the completion of the task.

Keywords
Human-Computer Interaction; Website Navigation; User Study; Focus Group; Prototyping; Social Media; Mixed-Methods.

1. INTRODUCTION

Websites are an important source of information on the web and they continue to grow[1]. Websites often offer various navigation tools to help users find information, such as menus, search, links, breadcrumbs, tag clouds, etc. and even then navigation within a website remains one of the main causes of user frustration on the web [1, 6] and often lead them to give up before their information need is met [10]. Therefore, the need to have user interfaces that facilitate efficient navigation remains important [3, 4].

The focus of this research is to improve navigation within websites so that users are able to find information effectively and efficiently. Using the notion "wisdom of the crowd", we want to explore if social media data can help solve this problem. Social media sites, such as Twitter, Facebook, and Google+, have become a powerful way for users to create, share and exchange information and ideas allowing the creation and exchange of user-generated content on the web [2, 5].

Companies like Feedly[2] and Buffer[3] are helping users organize, read and share content of their favorite websites in one place. They are relying on user-generated data from social media, however, it requires users to visit their website to access information from a specific website, setup a profile, etc. Whereas, this research is about providing seamless integration of social media data directly onto websites when the user visits that website.

Users frequently share links (web page URLs) on social media sites [2, 7]. Our previous research proved that users share links to web pages on social media during popular events [9]. In addition, it also empowered us to believe that aggregating link sharing information from social media and presenting these web pages in a useful format could potentially help website visitors find information quickly. With this preliminary research at hand, we have designed and developed a prototype, called the Social Media Panel (SMP), which captures aggregates and presents popular links that are shared on social media sites to website visitors in a useful format.

In this paper, we evaluate the SMP by comparing it against the conventional website navigation tools for effectiveness, efficiency and user engagement and for two types of tasks, namely fact-finding and browsing.

2. METHODOLOGY AND USER STUDY

We employed a mixed method to evaluate the SMP prototype, where both qualitative and quantitative approaches were used to collect and analyze the data. First, we conducted two focus group sessions to solicit feedback on the SMP prototype and the concept in general. Participants perceived the SMP to be efficient as it provided quick access to information. The findings from the focus group sessions suggested that sports website would likely benefit from SMP. Based on the findings from the focus group sessions, we refined and configured the SMP prototype for Sochi 2014 Olympics website[4]. We collected over a million (1,596,399) tweets and analyzed all tweets containing links, and selected the top 20 most popular links from the Sochi 2014 website and displayed the web pages as page thumbnails (see Figure 1). We then conducted a controlled user study to evaluate the SMP prototype against conventional website navigation tools and for the two types of tasks, namely fact-finding and browsing.

Each participant completed two fact-finding and two browsing tasks, of equal complexity, either with or without the SMP.

---

[1] http://www.internetlivestats.com/total-number-of-websites/

Permission to make digital or hard copies of part or all of this work for personal or classroom use is granted without fee provided that copies are not made or distributed for profit or commercial advantage and that copies bear this notice and the full citation on the first page. Copyrights for third-party components of this work must be honored. For all other uses, contact the Owner/Author.
Copyright is held by the owner/author(s).
HT '16, July 10-13, 2016, Halifax, NS, Canada
ACM 978-1-4503-4247-6/16/07.
http://dx.doi.org/10.1145/2914586.2914607

[2] www.feedly.com

[3] www.buffer.com

[4] http://www.olympic.org/sochi-2014-winter-olympics

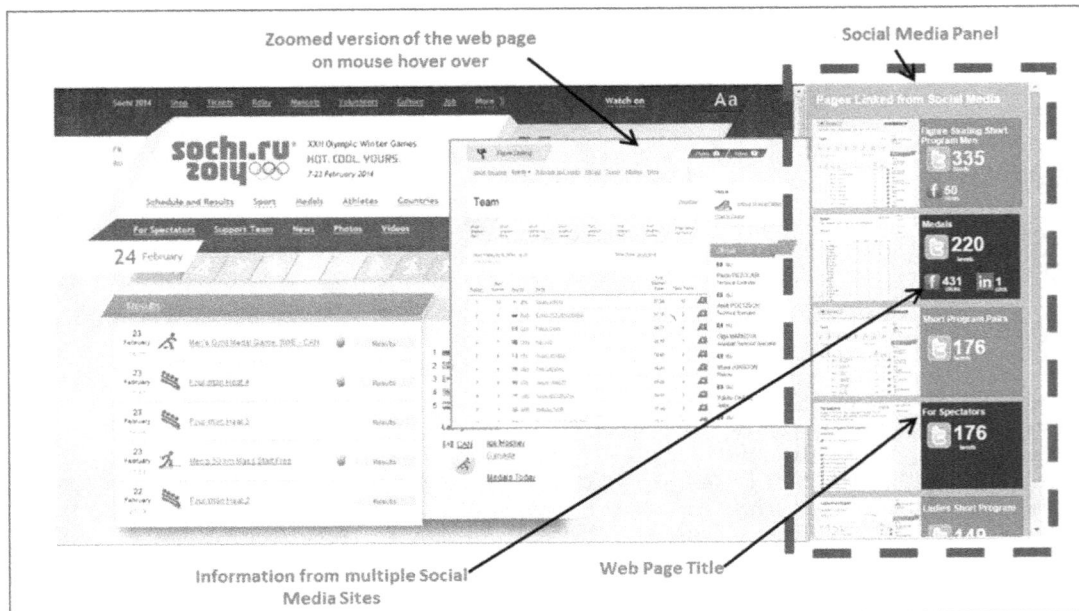

Figure 1. SMP Prototype for the Sochi 2014 website

Participants were asked to complete the task using the SMP if the SMP was presented and were allowed to also use other navigation tools. All four tasks were counterbalanced hence controlling the order effect. A final task (task 5) was given with SMP and participants had the option to use the SMP if desired. After each task, participants were asked to complete a post-task questionnaire. The study concluded with a post-study questionnaire and a semi-structured interview.

3. RESULTS

Thirty-four university students participated in the user study. Participants (53%, 18/34) indicated that they found SMP to be the most useful as it provided them with quick access to information, directed them to a link which was popular, and it was a good starting point. They also indicated that they found it easy to use, effective, efficient and enjoyable; however, it did not help them remember which pages they had visited. In comparison with conventional navigation tools, majority of the participants (more than 50%) found SMP useful over menus, search, links and browser tools for browsing tasks (see Figure 2).

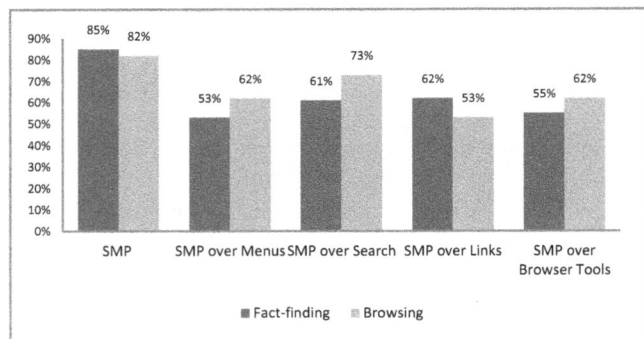

Figure 2. SMP over menus, search, links and browser tools for fact-finding and browsing tasks.

The 2-way ANOVA test for time to complete the tasks proved that there was no statistical significance between the type of task and the presence of SMP in expediting the completion of the task. However, we found a statistical significant difference in the number of clicks used to complete the task (p-value is <0.000). It took more clicks to complete the browsing task than the fact-finding tasks; however, it took fewer clicks to perform the task with SMP than without the SMP.

4. CONCLUSION & FUTURE WORK

In this paper, we have explored how social media data can help improve navigation within websites. To this end, we developed an SMP prototype, which visually displayed popular web pages being shared on social media as page thumbnails. We have evaluated the SMP prototype against conventional website navigation tools (i.e., menus, search, links, and browser tools) via a focus group and a controlled user study. We found SMP to be effective and efficient for browsing tasks and it took fewer clicks when users used SMP to complete both the fact-finding and browsing tasks.

The future work entails: a) implementing the SMP to capture and display information in real-time; b) conducting a user study with different types of tasks and on different types of websites; c) conducting a user study to compare SMP with other similar tools such as Buffer and Feedly; d) customization and personalization of the SMP; and e) exploring the use of SMP on mobile (small screen) devices. For the purpose of this research we focused on the number of times the link was shared and did not weigh in any other factors, such as the credibility of the user who is sharing the link, the origination of the link (i.e., geographic location), the number of comments associated with the link, etc. All these factors may be taken into consideration, assigned a rank, and then displayed on the SMP based on these rankings.

The results presented in this paper are beneficial for those studying navigation tools on websites including website designers and content writers. Furthermore, there may be potential for SMP to assist website visitors to discover and connect with other social media users who are interested in the same topics, leading to the formation of topic driven online communities.

5. REFERENCES

[1] Bessiere, K., Ceaparu, I., Lazar, J., Robinson, J., and Shneiderman, B. 2004. Social and Psychological Influences on Computer User Frustration. In Bucy, E. and Newhagen, J. (eds.) *Media Access: Social and Psychological Dimensions of New Technology Use.* Mahwah, NJ: Lawrence Erlbaum Associates, 169-192.

[2] Boyd, D., Golder, S., and Lotan, G. 2010. Tweet, Tweet, Retweet: Conversational Aspects of Retweeting on Twitter. HICSS-43. IEEE: Kawai, HI, Jan 2010.

[3] Dimitrov, D., Singer, P., Helic, D., Strohmaier, M. 2015. The Role of Structural Information for Designing Navigational User Interfaces. *Proceedings of the 26th ACM Conference on Hypertext & Social Media*, HT 2015: 59-68.

[4] Helic, D., Trattner, C., Strohmaier, M. and Andrews, K. 2011. Are Tag Clouds Useful for Navigation? A Network-Theoretic Analysis, Journal of Social Computing and Cyber-Physical Systems, Volume 1(1), 33-55, 2011

[5] Hughes, A. and Palen, L. 2009. Twitter adoption and use in crisis twitter adoption and use in mass convergence and emergency events. In ISCRAM, 2009.

[6] Lazar, J., Bessiere, K., Ceaparu, I., Robinson, J. and Shneiderman, B. 2003. Help! I'm lost: User frustration in web navigation. IT&Society: A Web Journal Studying How Technology Affects Society, 1(3), 18-26.

[7] Lovejoy, K., Waters, R., and Saxton, G. 2012. Engaging stakeholders through Twitter: How nonprofit organizations are getting more out of 140 characters or less. Public Relations Review, Volume 38, Issue 2, June 2012, Pages 313-318.

[8] Nizam, N., Watters, C., and Gruzd, A. 2012. Website Navigation: An Exploratory Study of Three Navigation Tools for Simple Web Tasks. Proceedings of the 8th International Conference on Web Information Systems and Technologies. April 2012. Porto, Portugal.

[9] Nizam, N., Gruzd, A., and Watters, C. 2014. Link Sharing on Twitter during Popular Events: Implications for Social Navigation on Websites. Proceedings of the 47th 189 Annual Hawaii International Conference on System Sciences, Waikoloa, Hawaii, 6-9 January, 2014, pp. 1745-1754.

[10] Scaria, A., Philip, R., West, R., and Leskovec, J. 2014. The last click: why users give up information network navigation. In *Proceedings of the 7th ACM international conference on Web search and data mining* (WSDM '14). ACM, New York, NY, USA, 213-222.

Author Index